AMERICAN ILIAD

THE 18TH INFANTRY REGIMENT IN WORLD WAR II

ROBERT W. BAUMER
WITH
MARK J. REARDON

THE ABERJONA PRESS
BEDFORD, PENNSYLVANIA

Technical Editor: Keith E. Bonn
Copy Editors: Steven C. Myers and Patricia K. Bonn
Production: Patricia K. Bonn
Maps: Tom Houlihan and Dale Wilson
Printer: Mercersburg Printing

The Aberjona Press is an imprint of Aegis Consulting Group, Inc.,
 Bedford, Pennsylvania 15522
© 2004 Robert W. Baumer
All rights reserved.
Printed in the United States of America
09 08 07 06 05 04 03 02 01 5 4 3 2 1

ISBN: 0-9717650-5-7

On the cover: "The Battle of Crucifix Hill."
© Don Stivers, Stivers Publishing. Used with permission.

*With Appreciation to
The World War II Veterans of the 18th
Infantry Regiment, 1st Infantry Division
and their Fighting Brethren who made the
Supreme Sacrifice*

He stands in an unbroken line of patriots who dared to die
That freedom might live, and grow, and increase its blessings
Freedom lives, and through it he lives—
In a way that humbles the undertakings of most men

CONTENTS

Foreword   vi
Acknowledgments   vii

Organization Day to War, May to December 1941   1

Overseas and the Battle for Oran,
    December 1941 to November 1942   10

The Battle for Longstop Hill, December 1942   44

Sbiba and El Guettar, January to April 1943   72

The Final Push, April to May 1943   107

Sicily, July to October 1943   137

D-Day Normandy, 6 June 1944   174

Northern France, June to September 1944   225

The Westwall, September to November 1944   260

The Hürtgen Forest and the Bulge,
    November 1944 to February 1945   298

The Roer to Surrender, February to May 1945   332

Afterword   360
Honor Roll   363
A Guide to Tactical Unit Symbols   381
Rank Equivalences   382
Notes   383
Index   404
About the Author   415

FOREWORD

The saga of the 1st Division in World War II was that of a division that was consistently given the most difficult assignments which were just as consistently carried out with brilliance and élan.
—Historian Carlo D'Este

This book tells the story of an epic time in American history. Those of us who have been privileged to lead American soldiers in combat have many images deeply engraved in our memories. None are closer to my heart than those of our 18th Infantry soldiers of the 1st Division as they trained in 1941 and 1942, then fought from 1942 to 1945 across North Africa and Sicily, over the beaches and through the hedgerows of Normandy, across France and through the *Westwall*, then into the terrible Hürtgen Forest, and finally across the Rhine to the final days of the war. Some of those images, now sixty or more years distant in time, make me stand a little straighter—proud of the brave men (and, yes, women too, especially the nurses, bless them) whose time with us was too short. Some of those pictures send a shiver down my back, even today. Others bring a smile to my face, because of the camaraderie forged during the war years. All in all, this book is a fitting tribute to those men of our 18th Infantry Regiment who have already found "a soldier's resting place," as well as to those still in our midst who served with us in World War II. It tells our story, and it is an inspiring yet humbling reminder to all of us of freedom's price.

Ben Sternberg
Major General, United States Army Retired

ACKNOWLEDGEMENTS

The writing of *American Iliad* was undertaken on behalf of the 18th Infantry Regiment Association by the authors because the Regiment's history during World War II simply needed to be told. We are indebted to the Association, particularly its president, George T. Gentry, Jr., and to the Honorary Colonel of the 18th Infantry Regiment, Colonel George M. Tronsrue, Jr. US Army (Retired), for their assistance and individual contributions in helping create this book.

Without the recollections, comments and criticisms of the 18th Infantry Regiment World War II veterans still amongst us at the time this effort was undertaken, it is fair to state that this book could not have been written. Despite painful memories of the war, their willingness to relive it by reviewing drafts of this book, providing oral histories to make it more meaningful, and in particular their encouragement to the authors in the process, is gratefully appreciated. Of note, Colonel Robert E. Murphy, US Army (Retired), and Lieutenant Colonel Sam Carter, US Army (Retired), both officers who served with the Regiment whose time and devotion to this process was exceptional, are much appreciated. Despite failing health, Major General Ben Sternberg, US Army (Retired), provided inspirational support to the authors, and to the spirit of the Regiment and its World War II veterans, by offering the prologue for this work just prior to his death on 2 January 2004.

We gratefully take this opportunity to also express our appreciation to the many other veterans who contributed to this book, particularly Lieutenant John P. Downing in his unpublished works *At War with the British*, and *No Promotion*, Lieutenant Franklyn A. Johnson in *One More Hill*, Edward K. Rogers in *Doughboy Chaplain* and Malcolm Marshall and other authors in *Proud Americans of World War II*. Right after the war, many of the officers of the Regiment taught at the Advanced Infantry School at Fort Benning, Georgia. Their monographs contributed materially to this book. Additional contributions from the Cantigny First Division Museum in Wheaton, Illinois, helped the authors, particularly the research efforts and support of Andrew Woods.

The authors would also like to express their gratitude to the technical and developmental editor of *American Iliad*, Lieutenant Colonel Keith E. Bonn, US Army (Retired), as well as copy editors Captain Steve Myers, US Navy (Retired) and Patti Bonn. Patti patiently worked with the authors on production tasks, photo editing, indexing, and the cover design. Carolynn Andrews and Brian R. Sims provided several of the maps. Major Dale Wilson, US Army (Retired), and

Staff Sergeant Tom Houlihan, USMC (Retired), added the finishing touches that contributed even more precision and professional appearance to the maps.

The first undersigned author below also wishes to express his vast appreciation to Lieutenant Colonel Mark J. Reardon. He helped guide this author to relate the accomplishments of the 18th Infantry Regiment in a way where their success in combat was left to speak for itself to you, the reader. As part of the legendary 1st Infantry Division during the war, the record of the Regiment combatants was indeed the single most important contribution to the writing of this book. Lastly, to my wife Shannon, my forever indebtedness to her devotion, help and patience during the many years of research and effort it took to complete *American Iliad*.

Robert W. Baumer	Lieutenant Colonel Mark J. Reardon
Clinton, Connecticut	Woodbridge, Virginia

ORGANIZATION DAY TO WAR

MAY TO DECEMBER 1941

> Those of us to whom the future is entrusted will see that the regiment is always ready, and that we will not fail those who have gone before us.
> —Colonel Ely P. Denson

Spring dawned clearly and crisply over the Fort Devens parade ground just northwest of Boston, Massachusetts, on 3 May 1941. A detail of soldiers was completing the assembly of a reviewing stand and several bleachers in preparation for the 18th Infantry Regiment's Organization Day. This day marked the 80th anniversary of the organization of what had become one of the most prestigious and oldest units in the Regular Army. The barracks were humming with activity as other soldiers made final preparations for the festivities that were scheduled to start with a review at precisely 1000 hours. The enlisted men and noncommissioned officers, some of whom were a bit tired from staying late at a dance the previous night, were all polishing brass, shining their shoes, and pinning insignia on their uniforms. Sergeants were also making last-minute checks to ensure that everyone's personal weapons were immaculate. Indeed, when the Regiment formed smartly on the parade ground that morning, all of its officers and men stood tall in their Class A uniforms with garrison caps.

The Regiment's colors, garlanded with battle streamers awarded for participation in numerous battles and engagements during its long history, snapped sharply in the brisk winds of the day. Colonel Ely P. Denson, now commanding officer of the 18th Infantry Regiment, called his men to attention to begin the ceremonies and then the regimental band, under the direction of Warrant Officer John S. Martin, struck up the Regiment's traditional song, "Happy Heinie." This compilation of two old German songs set to a jazz-march tempo was first adopted by the Regiment in 1906, and ensured that every man would step lively as they passed before assembled dignitaries in the reviewing stands.

By this time the bleachers had been filled with wives, families, and friends of the soldiers, as well as onlookers from other units at Fort Devens. Seated on the hard benches in the reviewing stand were a number of important senior Army officers, to include Lieutenant General Hugh A. Drum, Commanding General of First Army; Major General James A. Woodruff, Commanding General of I Corps; Major General Karl Truesdell, Commanding General of VI Corps; and the Commanding General of the famous 1st Division, Major General Donald C. Cubbison. Retired Brigadier General William H. Bisbee, the oldest living veteran of the 18th Infantry Regiment at a remarkable 101 years of age, sat beside the assembled officers as the guest of honor.

General Bisbee's service dated almost to the beginning of the Regiment's formation, when, by direction of President Abraham Lincoln on 3 May 1861, the infantry arm of the Regular Army was increased by nine regiments, numbering from the 11th to 19th, inclusive. The organization of the 18th Infantry Regiment began in compliance with General Order #16 on 4 May 1861, wherein Henry B. Carrington of Ohio was appointed as the first Colonel of the Regiment. Its new headquarters was in Columbus, Ohio and when recruiting commenced on 1 July that year, Bisbee enlisted as a private and was assigned to Company A. He quickly rose during his first year to the rank of sergeant, then first sergeant, and eventually sergeant major of his battalion. Then in June 1862, Bisbee was commissioned as a second lieutenant, and soon after this he distinguished himself at the Battle of Stones River (Murfreesboro) where he personally rescued his battalion's colors and kept them from falling into enemy hands.[1] Bisbee also participated in the fighting at Chickamauga, Mission Ridge, and Atlanta, all battles whose names were embroidered on the battle streamers that festooned the Regiment's colors on the parade ground this Organization Day.

After the Regiment went west when the Civil War ended, Bisbee was on detached service when a numerically-superior force of Sioux, Arapahoe, and Cheyenne warriors ambushed his Company A near Fort Phil Kearny, Dakota Territory (later in the state of Wyoming) on 21 December 1866. Its commander, Captain William J. Fetterman, and 50 enlisted men from several other companies, as well as 27 soldiers from Troop C, 2nd Cavalry Regiment and two civilians, were all killed during this action. Except for the rout of General George A. Custer's 7th Cavalry Regiment at the Little Big Horn ten years later, this massacre was the US Army's greatest defeat during the Indian Wars.

In September 1866, the 18th Infantry Regiment's 2nd Battalion was redesignated as the 27th Infantry Regiment, and Bisbee went along with his men to the new regiment. After consolidation with the 25th Infantry Regiment in 1869, the 18th Infantry Regiment was deployed to Georgia and South Carolina for duty during the Second Reconstruction, where its men helped suppress the Ku Klux Klan and enforced new federal laws.

During the 1880s and 1890s, the 18th Infantry again returned to the western frontier. During this period, the Regiment's companies were often scattered far and wide at isolated Army posts stretching from Montana to Texas, seldom coming together for training or combat until 1889 when its officers and men were reassembled at Fort Clark, Texas. Nine years later, the United States found itself at war with Spain and the Regiment was transferred to the Presidio of San Francisco for transportation to the Philippine Islands and participation in the Battle of Manila. Although the Spanish-American War ended soon afterwards, the Philippine Insurrection kept the Regiment in "the P.I." until September 1901. Its officers and men then experienced two more tours of duty in the Philippine Islands in the early 1900s, interspersed with assignments in Kansas, Wyoming, and other western posts. By 1914, relations with neighboring Mexico had worsened and the situation along the US-Mexican border quickly grew critical, so the Regiment was deployed to a section of the border near Douglas, Arizona. While the soldiers were growing seasoned and hardened by extremely arduous field duty during this campaign, they came to the attention of then-Brigadier General John J. Pershing. When Pershing put together the American Expeditionary Forces for service in France in 1917, he selected the 18th Infantry as one of the field-hardened regiments to comprise his newly-organized 1st Division.[2]

Organization Day on the parade grounds at Fort Devens in May 1941 was intended to reinforce unit pride in this history of the Regiment. The powerful presence of General Bisbee in the reviewing stand this day indeed served as a vivid symbol of this heritage prior to the Great War, and with many of the older sergeants experienced from combat in France during 1917–18, the current junior enlisted men were provided with a ready source of information about the Regiment's exploits. Stories of the heavy losses amounting to nearly 1,600 officers and men sustained during the fighting at Soissons, then Mont Sec during the St. Mihiel Offensive, and later amidst the tangled debris of the Argonne Forest, were told over and again. Even before these legendary battles, two companies of the Regiment had participated in the attack on Cantigny, the first major offensive carried out by the 1st Division and considered the most significant battle of the Great War for its men. Standing before the red brick buildings by the Fort Devens parade ground for this Organization Day, the officers and men of the Regiment had every reason to proudly wear their distinctive insignia, emblazoned with the regimental motto, *In Omnia Paratus* ("In All Things Prepared").

After the ceremony officially started, Colonel Denson's formal opening remarks were brief, but poignant. To all those present, he said that wartime duty would undoubtedly be thrust upon the Regiment once again, that its record in peace and previous wars was one of which they could indeed all be proud. Then turning to General Bisbee, Denson added, "Those of us to whom the future is entrusted will see that the Regiment is always ready, and that we will not fail those who have gone before us."[3] Denson had good reason to believe war was imminent, for by now most of western Europe had already fallen under the grip of Nazi Germany. The dark shadow of Hitler's empire had changed the fates of millions of people, and Japanese troops had been fighting in China for the past four years.

Colonel Denson knew in his heart that it was only a matter of time before the United States would be drawn into this growing conflict and that the soldiers standing before him would be flung into the crucible of combat.

Like many higher ranking officers at the time, Colonel Denson was not certain that the United States Army, severely cut back after the Great War and further reduced in size during the Depression years, would be able to effectively meet the global threat now being represented by Germany, Fascist Italy, and Imperial Japan, despite the Regiment's proud motto. Malcolm Marshall, in his history of the 32nd Field Artillery Battalion assigned to the 18th Infantry in World War II noted, "The Army was believed to have 120,000 men under arms, scattered around the states and Hawaii. US aircraft numbered in the hundreds and were vastly inferior in quality and replacements. We possessed no armored divisions, nor enough tanks to form one."[4] An officer new to the 1st Division at the time, Gerard Clarke, put the sad readiness of the division this way, "Back in 1940, in our summer training for war, we had broomstick handles for practice because rifles weren't available. To represent cannons, we had logs mounted between two old wooden wagon wheels. Everything was simulated. Our military was really in a hopeless condition to start fighting a war."[5]

Mobilization had nevertheless started, albeit in a modest way, as the new decade began. Recognizing the desperate need to modernize, the United States Army formed two armored divisions in July 1940, less than a month after France fell to German invaders. A number of National Guard divisions were also called up for twelve months service at the time. Limited conscription had been initiated in 1940, and with patriotic young men enlisting in ever-increasing numbers, the 18th Infantry Regiment was continually receiving an influx of recruits to fill up the empty slots in its new table of organization. Despite belated congressional votes authorizing increases in manpower and the purchase of new equipment, like M-1 rifles, for the upcoming fiscal year, in May 1941 the US Army still stood at just eighteenth in size among the world's armies. Not only did the major belligerents, represented by Germany, Italy, Great Britain, and Japan, possess vastly superior military establishments, but neutral and nonaligned countries such as Russia, Portugal, Spain, Sweden, and Switzerland also fielded larger armies than the United States.[6]

Given this appalling situation, the officers and men of the 1st Division recognized the need for hard and realistic training. Immediately following Organization Day, the 18th Infantry departed Fort Devens to participate in a 75-mile motor march through central Massachusetts and southern New Hampshire. Moving in lengthy columns in 13 serials along ten miles of highway, the Regiment participated in a maneuver that was part of an exercise involving the entire 1st Division. In this war game that pitted the mythical states of "Black" and "Blue" against each other, the division had split its forces to provide troops for both sides. Consequently, to oppose the 18th Infantry, elements of the 16th and 26th Infantry Regiments also departed Fort Devens at the same time to occupy assembly areas east of the fort near Hell Pond, in the small town of Harvard, Massachusetts. The

Boston Herald subsequently noted that the maneuver represented, "the largest ever staged in this section of New England and the first extensive action of its kind since the World War."[7]

Early in the morning on 6 May, Colonel Denson began his offensive by directing his regimental Intelligence and Reconnaissance (I&R) Platoon to locate the "enemy" and gain additional information about the terrain on which the Regiment would be fighting. The rest of the 18th Infantry practiced night movement by conducting a road march that started at 2030 hours, then went through nearby Ayer, Groton, and Townsend before the officers and their men occupied a bivouac area in the vicinity of West Groton. In the meantime, the 16th Infantry Regiment shifted its main body closer to the impending scene of battle, advancing through Harvard, Littleton, Chelmsford, and Westford, before finally establishing positions in a wooded area opposite the 18th Infantry in West Groton. In nearby West Princeton, 1st Division medical teams established aid stations and practiced evacuating "casualties" that were expected to come in the upcoming conflict.

On 7 May, wearing black brassards to distinguish them from their opponents, soldiers of the 18th Infantry Regiment began a two-mile advance to converge on their first objective, a piece of high ground named Whittemore Hill. The 16th Infantry quickly engaged one of the 18th Infantry's battalions in close combat, while another warded off a surprise counterattack by the 26th Infantry. As the advance continued through the town of Sherman, many blue-banded troops continued to harass the 18th Infantry, so much so that umpires ruled that their ambushes effectively wiped out a reconnaissance patrol and nearly the entire 1st Battalion as both units were advancing along a road toward Whittemore Hill. Undaunted by this setback, Colonel Denson called for massive artillery support that quickly "obliterated" several companies of the 16th and the 26th Infantry Regiments with simulated indirect fire. Once the mock barrage was completed, he ordered the 2nd and 3rd Battalions to advance cross-country between the towns of Shirley and Lancaster so that they could reach the crest of Whittemore Hill. This sudden and unexpected flanking maneuver persuaded the umpires to declare the 18th Infantry the ultimate victor in these first maneuvers of their kind in over twenty years.

The capture of this hill barely foretold things that were to come, future events of a magnitude that no one within the Regiment could imagine at the time. "Casualty" figures in the practice maneuver were never released, although the Army stated that they were "light, considering the scale of the attack." The *Boston Herald* even reported the next day that an after-action observer in the area had disclosed that the commander of the 26th Infantry Regiment, Colonel Theodore Roosevelt, Jr., son of the former president, "had feinted with a few companies and sent his main force under the cover of trees and bushes into which the men vanished like shadows, up the north and east sides of the hill." The *Herald* noted, "Colonel Roosevelt, his face streaked with sweat and dust, was at the front at all times."[8]

Then-Colonel Roosevelt soon left the 26th Infantry Regiment to serve as Assistant Division Commander for the "Red One," a nickname that by now was synonymous with the 1st Division. In that duty position, Roosevelt constantly interacted with the officers and men of the 18th Infantry Regiment, but it was his conduct during these early practice maneuvers that demonstrated his philosophy of leadership in future combat to them. His military career began in 1917 when Roosevelt volunteered for active duty and was commissioned as a major in the 26th Infantry Regiment, an assignment that began his long association with the 1st Division. During the Great War, he had proven to be a brave commander, often leading attacks at the front rather than commanding from the rear. Reprimanded for taking unnecessary risks at one point, he reportedly had asked, "We're officers aren't we? I always thought an officer's job was to lead his men, not follow them!"[9] By the war's end, Roosevelt was decorated several times and he even held the distinction of being the only reserve officer to command a regiment in the 1st Division.

Once the early May maneuvers ended, the 1st Division began preparing for another precursor to overseas duty, its first formal review since the end of the Great War. Special traffic restrictions were put into effect around Fort Devens on 24 May 1941 to ensure that the 15,000 men of the division and their 2,500 motorized vehicles could stage a smooth pass in review on the main parade ground. More than 100 Great War veterans, as well as their families, were in attendance as honored guests that afternoon. The review started at precisely 1430 hours to commemorate the exact time the 1st Division began its historic attack at Cantigny in 1918, and a half-hour later the parade was in full swing with a conspicuous display of the division's newly issued modern weapons. At 1800 hours, the Great War veterans joined the current officers and men for a special dinner that was followed by a formal meeting of the Society of the First Division, where deeds of courage and sacrifice were recalled and individual exploits told and retold well into the night.

As war clouds loomed large on the horizon in early 1941, the US Army concluded that it would undoubtedly soon have to land large numbers of combat troops on hostile shores. As a result, the 1st Division was ordered to send an infantry battalion to work with the Marine Corps. On 17 June the Regiment's 3rd Battalion departed Fort Devens for Brooklyn and subsequent transport to New River, North Carolina.[10] Once there, the men practiced assault landings over the Fourth of July holiday weekend, then returned to Fort Devens on 8 July. Ten days later, the battalion again left Fort Devens for intensive amphibious training that would last into mid-August. This time, again in conjunction with Marines, the exercises were conducted in Massachusetts's nearby Cape Cod.[11]

At the end of the summer, the entire 1st Division moved down to Fort Bragg, North Carolina for its first show of war readiness, this time against an opposing division-sized force. The large-scale exercises that subsequently took place through the fall of 1941 were known as the "Carolina Maneuvers," and among other purposes, the exercises allowed evaluation of the 1st Division's new "triangular" organization. Prior to 1941, American infantry divisions were still organized as they had been during the Great War, that is, in "square" divisions consisting of two infantry brigades, each with two infantry regiments. In 1936, the Army formed a committee to study possible organizational changes designed to enhance their capabilities. After much deliberation, the group recommended fielding a "triangular" division design similar to those being deployed by some European armies, especially the Germans, thereby placing the United States in step with both its future allies and enemies. From 1941 forward, American infantry divisions would be smaller and more efficiently organized, with three infantry regiments answering directly to the division commander: the brigade level was eliminated altogether, along with one infantry regiment.

Although the details would change over the course of the war, under the triangular organization an infantry regiment consisted of four (later, five) separate companies and three infantry battalions. Command, tactical control, reconnaissance, and administrative capabilities resided in the regimental headquarters company; logistical support was provided by the regimental service company; the main antiarmor capability in the regiment was possessed by the regimental antitank company, with its nine 37mm, and later, 57mm, towed antitank guns; and medical support to the entire regiment was provided by the regimental medical detachment. In 1942, the regiment's indirect-fire capability—restricted until then to that which could be delivered by mortars—was greatly expanded by the addition of a regimental cannon company.

The "triangular" nature of the new organization extended to the three infantry battalions as well. Each one possessed three rifle companies of (at full strength) about 190 men each, as well as a heavy weapons company and a headquarters company. Each was (hypothetically) commanded by a captain, assisted by a first sergeant, who was the senior noncommissioned officer in the company. Each rifle company consisted of three rifle platoons, led by a lieutenant who was assisted by a platoon sergeant. A rifle platoon contained about 40 men and consisted of three twelve-man squads plus a platoon headquarters element. A sergeant led each squad, assisted by a corporal, who together directed two scouts, a three-man BAR team and five riflemen, usually privates or privates first class. Each rifle company's weapons platoon consisted of two .30-caliber Browning air-cooled (light) machine-gun crews and three 60mm mortar crews.

The heavy weapons company provided extra firepower to support the rifle companies. Each included two heavy machine-gun platoons with four .30-caliber water-cooled M1917A1 apiece. There was also a mortar platoon with six 81mm mortars, as well as a headquarters section.

The battalion headquarters company possessed not only administrative, logistical; communications; and command and control elements, but also two very important combat assets. In the battalion headquarters company resided the antitank platoon, with three 37mm (later, 57mm) antitank guns and the ammunition and pioneer (A&P) platoon, which not only handled ammunition storage and resupply, but was tasked with breaching and emplacing minefields and other obstacles as well.

Each company also had its own headquarters section, supervised by the company executive officer (XO), and it contained radiomen, runners, clerks, and supply personnel who conducted the logistical, administrative, and communications activities required to support the company.

Although it would change slightly from time to time over the next few years, the newly-authorized strength of the 18th Infantry Regiment was approximately 3,250 men.

During the tests and other events surrounding reorganization of infantry divisions, the Army realized that it would be even more beneficial to organize each of the three infantry regiments with habitually supporting units, to enhance cohesion and promote unity of command on the battlefield. "Regimental combat teams" (RCTs) were formed in which each infantry regiment could count on the consistent support—and, in some events, even the tactical control—of the same artillery battalion, combat engineer company, and medical company. The former would be trained and, in garrison, administered by the division field artillery brigade, while the latter two could depend on the division's engineer battalion and medical battalion, respectively, for administrative and training support when not in the field.

The artillery battalion assigned to direct support of the 18th Infantry Regiment was the 32nd Field Artillery Battalion, nicknamed "Proud Americans." It consisted of three batteries of 105mm howitzers (with four pieces per battery). Company B, 1st Engineer Combat Battalion, added the capability to build and breach obstacles, improve roads and construct fortifications. Company B, 1st Medical Battalion provided litter bearers, ambulances, and medics to operate a regimental aid station. Together with the 18th Infantry Regiment, these supporting units comprised the 18th Regimental Combat Team.

Beginning on 20 October 1941 at Fort Bragg, the 18th Infantry Regiment took part in a week-long series of larger-scale VI Corps maneuvers designed to test these new formations by focusing on the employment of rifle battalions in the defense, river crossings using assault boats under the cover of darkness, and regimental attacks. On 27 October, VI Corps began simulated combat operations against elements of II Corps, and after another week of maneuvers, both corps then took part in Army-level exercises against its I Corps. At the beginning of the exercise, the 18th Infantry Regiment acted as an advance guard for the 1st Division, which was part of II Corps, with the Regiment's 3rd Battalion operating as the division's spearhead in the attack. During the subsequent maneuvers, when the battalion conducted reconnaissance to avoid surprise by the opposing 1st Armored Division, the 1st Division was able to avoid a massive tank ambush, thereby earning another "victory" in the series.

The 18th Infantry Regiment, now configured as an RCT and referred to as "Combat Team 18" or CT 18, then relocated to a temporary base camp near Ether, North Carolina, on 11 November in anticipation of the larger General Headquarters (GHQ) maneuvers. During the first phase, I, II, and VI Corps, along with two armored divisions, all under the command of Lieutenant General Hugh Drum, attacked IV Corps. This was not the Regiment's finest phase of training, however. Combat Team 18 was "cut to pieces" several times by incessant armored attacks, and three companies of the 3rd Battalion were wiped out, Companies I and L once, and Company K twice. Despite these setbacks, the Regiment was still able to push some 57 miles in a four-day period, and by the end of the first phase, IV Corps was definitely on the run. During the second phase, the 1st Division was not as actively involved, but the Regiment benefited from lessons it learned during successful mass troop movements by motors and its continuing progress in concealed bivouac training.[12]

After the Carolina Maneuvers, CT 18 moved back to Fort Devens by train and truck, arriving on Saturday, 6 December 1941. The soldiers looked forward to some well-deserved leave and a training break over the upcoming holidays. Late in the morning of the next day, however, reports started crackling through radios on the post, much as they did elsewhere across America, announcing the news that the Japanese had attacked Pearl Harbor. Irving Yarock, then a young lieutenant in Company A, was visiting his relatives in nearby Worcester, Massachusetts when the news flashed over his family's kitchen radio. He remembered being nervous, then deciding to return to Fort Devens that night, even though he had leave through the following day. "I was the first officer in the company to arrive," he recalled later. "There was a flood of telegrams and telephone messages from my men who were on leave, asking if they should return immediately. I took it upon myself to tell them to complete their leave, and that if we wanted to cut it short I would notify them. When President Roosevelt declared war the next day [*sic*], that settled that. But I was really impressed when the men all asked if they should cut their leave short. I felt it was an indication of the high morale we had developed in the Regiment."[13]

That night, guards were placed on 24-hour watch around the officer's quarters at Fort Devens. Congress declared war on Japan the following day and on 9 December, Colonel Denson disseminated a series of contingency plans. Machine guns were prepared for rapid movement by truck to various points around the post in case of a surprise air attack. Plans included deployment of rifle battalions into concealed positions in nearby wooded areas as soon as any air raid alert might be given. By this time, many of the officers and men of the Regiment had filtered back from their leaves, and platoons were being ordered to patrol the area around Fort Devens' perimeters looking for saboteurs. Renewed with vigor and seriousness of purpose, Combat Team 18 was now preparing for war and its certain eventual assignment overseas in a combat role.

OVERSEAS AND THE BATTLE FOR ORAN

DECEMBER 1941 TO NOVEMBER 1942

"Keep going, Mac!"

—Lt. Theodore "Toot" Plante, Company B

On the morning of 8 December 1941 when President Franklin Delano Roosevelt addressed the nation at a joint session of the Congress and delivered his famous words about "the day that will live in infamy," the United States was under attack all across the Pacific. The Three-Power Pact (also known as the "Tripartite Pact"), signed in Berlin on 27 September 1940, allied Germany and Italy with Japan and formalized the Rome-Berlin-Tokyo "Axis." This treaty obligated each of the Axis powers to come to the defense of the others in the event of war. Therefore, on 11 December 1941, Germany and Italy declared war on the United States, bringing the country into a worldwide conflict of tremendous scope and ferocity. These events hastened the already progressing preparations of the 18th Infantry Regiment for combat, and its officers and men busied themselves with marksmanship training and the firing of .22-caliber rifles on Fort Devens's 1000-inch range in the days following the announcement of war. Ever more urgent training on automatic weapons was also emphasized, and on 18–19 December, each of the battalions' heavy machine-gun platoons, as well as every rifle company's light machine-gun section, all participated in a firing competition on the nearby Wakefield Range. On 26 December, however, the focus of activity suddenly changed when the Regiment received orders to prepare for division landing maneuvers, their first amphibious exercises as an assembled assault unit, now slated to begin on 3 January 1942.[1]

By now, the War Department staff was deeply involved in talks with their British counterparts to formulate their upcoming offensive strategies for winning the new World War. Two major operational plans were being developed, one codenamed BOLERO that dealt with an invasion of mainland France, and a second known as GYMNAST that called for landings in French North Africa.[2] The 1st Marine Division, formerly a component of the Atlantic Amphibious Force, had by this time been ordered to the Pacific Theater. In light of this, the War Department directed the 1st Division to concentrate on perfecting the skills it needed to storm a defended beach. To practice this, large-scale landing exercises designed to evaluate the readiness of both the Army and Navy components of the new Atlantic Amphibious Force were scheduled to take place at New River, North Carolina, in January 1942. The 1st Division, including the 18th Combat Team, was chosen to conduct a series of contested landings, with the 29th Division acting as the opposing force.

After loading aboard transport ships in the port of New York, the 18th Infantry Regiment steamed south with the rest of the division on 10 January to participate in these landing exercises. While in transit, the location of the practice was changed from New River to Cape Henry, near Virginia Beach, Virginia. Several hours of regimental-level planning then took place the following day and after inter-service conferences aboard ship, the "Blue Force" 18th Infantry Regiment conducted a landing against a beach defended by the "Red Force" 116th Infantry Regiment of the 29th Division on 12 January. After experiencing significant difficulties loading the boats in rough sea conditions, the first wave was launched at 0955 hours while tanks were also lowered into lighters to provide armored support for the assault force. The landing exercise was judged as unsuccessful, however, since the boats touched down on the wrong beach in the midst of very strong enemy defensive positions. The 3rd Battalion was assessed as having suffered 50 percent casualties, but by 1330 hours it was reinstated and the exercise got underway again when the 116th Infantry Regiment set up a new line of defense 1,000 yards inland from the beach at nightfall.

At dawn on 13 January, the 18th Infantry Regiment launched another deliberate attack against the defending 116th. A wide flanking movement by Company L forced this "Red Force" to withdraw from their positions by 1000 hours, and a large number of their troops were captured during the resultant melee. An hour later, division headquarters ordered the Regiment to hold these newly won positions pending a "strategic withdrawal." As the 18th Infantry Regiment started departing shortly after 1500 hours, each battalion was relieved by a contingent from the 5th Marine Regiment, and by 1715 hours, the evacuation was successfully completed.

The following day, Higgins boats (LCVPs, or "Landing Craft, Vehicle, Personnel") were lowered once more into the choppy waters off Cape Henry where 40-knot winds were now creating big seas and whitecaps. The Navy tried to stop the exercises, but the Army insisted they go on. Boats lowered in the first wave of

16th Infantry Regiment soldiers were crushed against the side of the transport and Navy personnel had to pluck the men from the icy Atlantic water. Despite this, yet another craft was dropped in the water and a squad from the 16th soon roared toward shore. As the vessel neared the beach, however, a large following wave swamped it and the Higgins boat flipped over. Miraculously, nobody drowned, but the event prompted the Navy to appeal to higher authorities, who in turn bowed to the realities of the conditions and called off the exercise. The few men who made it to shore never met up with the 29th Division troops defending the beaches until late in the day and as a result, the men in the 18th Infantry never left the ship. Several hours later, all of the 1st Division "combatants" were heading back out to sea and then northward.[3] The Regiment arrived back in New York on 18 January after an uneventful voyage, and its officers and men returned that same night to Fort Devens for more training.

On 13 February, the 1st Division received orders to move to Camp Blanding, Florida, where it continued to conduct landing exercises, marksmanship, and maneuver training.[4] By now, speculation about going overseas had grown and one 18th Infantry Company H soldier's letter home at the time even said, "There are rumors going around that we are leaving for Africa pretty soon."[5]

The incessant tempo of training at Camp Blanding continued through May, then orders came down for the 1st Division to prepare for a move to Fort Benning, Georgia, where it would take part in Air-Ground training under the supervision of Major General Lloyd R. Fredendall's II Corps. The division lost Major General Cubbison at this time, for he had been deemed "too old" at age 60 to command troops in combat overseas, and Brigadier General Theodore Roosevelt temporarily assumed command of the division on 22 May as it departed Camp Blanding.

The soldiers of the 18th Infantry Regiment started their motor trek north toward Fort Benning on a hot, muggy day, and arrived at nightfall two days later. Rather than stay in the permanent barracks on its grounds, however, each of the rifle battalions was allotted a bivouac area off the crowded main post. The 2nd Battalion, for example, was sited in a wooded area near the town of Cusseta. While the amenities were lacking and the mosquitoes were awful, the isolated locations allowed the soldiers of the Regiment to avoid the distractions of the main post. They carried on with their daily training routines instead, including close order drill, repeatedly digging and filling foxholes, road marches, weapons drill, target practice, and running numerous obstacle courses.[6]

It was here at Fort Benning that the soldiers of the Regiment first became acquainted with their new commanding general, the maverick Major General Terry de la Mesa Allen. Born at Fort Douglas, Utah, on 1 April 1888, Allen attended West Point from 1907 to 1911, but he did not accumulate sufficient credits to complete the academic curriculum. He subsequently spent a year at Catholic University of America, where he graduated in 1912 and was commissioned a Second Lieutenant of Cavalry on 30 November. Allen then spent several years in cavalry units before wrangling a transfer in 1917 to the infantry to see combat in France during the Great War. Originally assigned to the Ammunition Train for the 79th Division's 315th Infantry Regiment, Allen was subsequently awarded a front-line command in the 90th Division's 358th Infantry Regiment in August 1918. Although he was seriously wounded in action in September, Allen returned to the 358th the following month, remaining in command of a battalion until the armistice was signed later that year on 11 November.

Following a short stint with the Occupation Force in Germany, Allen then returned to the cavalry in 1920 and continued to serve with troop units for the next twenty years while attending schools such as the Advanced Infantry Officer Course, the Cavalry School, the Command and General Staff College, and the prestigious Army War College. In 1940, he pinned on the single star of a Brigadier General, the first in "his" West Point class-era of graduates to be promoted to this rank. A rapid succession of higher-level command assignments followed, to include command of the 3rd Cavalry Brigade in the 2nd Cavalry Division; Assistant Commander of the 36th Infantry Division; and finally, his appointment as the commanding general of the 1st Division on 29 May 1942.[7]

Shortly after Allen assumed command, the Regiment joined the rest of the 1st Division for a review on the main post parade ground in front of both American and British military dignitaries. No one really knew what the exact purpose of the review was, but with many of the top generals in the new allied armies present, all the officers in the Regiment knew that something big must have been coming. Lieutenant Irving Yarock in Company A remembered, "We marched at route step, fully combat loaded, in front of the stands so the distinguished guests could see what the 1st Division looked like."[8]

The division undoubtedly passed muster, for the 18th Infantry Regiment received new orders on 15 June to prepare for a move to Indiantown Gap Military Reservation in Pennsylvania.[9] Speculation amongst the troops was immediately rampant, for Indiantown Gap was the major staging area for units awaiting shipment overseas. The big day came when the alert was changed to an actual order on 29 June. That evening, the Regiment trucked out in drizzling rain and headed for the nearby railroad yards of Columbus, Georgia. The men then boarded trains for an uneventful all-night trip northward that put them at Indiantown Gap just before sunrise. After unloading, the soldiers boarded yet another convoy of trucks that finally took them to the post's cantonment area.

Within a few short weeks, officers and enlisted men were lining up to have their identification cards and newly-issued dog tags checked. Excess baggage was then shipped home. Olive drab wool uniforms were issued to replace summer khakis, and new helmets (quickly dubbed "Steel Pots") were handed out to replace the flat helmets first issued to American troops during the Great War and worn throughout stateside training to that point. Everyone was given a thorough physical and examined for communicable diseases, then inoculated for smallpox, typhoid, and tetanus. Every soldier was then treated to a particularly short haircut by his company barber to last for the duration of the trip that lay ahead. Soldiers then stenciled their names onto barracks bags before they were carted away by trucks.

During this time, a contingent of 80 newly-commissioned second lieutenants arrived at Indiantown Gap. Every graduate who was single, plus one married graduate from OCS Class 25, had been ordered to the 1st Division to fill its need for officers. Dubbed somewhat derisively as "90-day wonders," OCS Class 25 had graduated on 27 June 1942, after completion of a very rigorous course for officer candidates at the Fort Benning Infantry School. When evenly distributed to the regimental combat teams, it meant that every rifle company in the 18th Infantry Regiment contained graduates of OCS Class 25 in an average of two of its four rifle platoon leader positions. The balance of the company-grade slots were manned by ROTC and Reserve commissioned officers, with a liberal sprinkling of West Point-trained junior officers by this time.[10] A change in command also took place in July. The announcement was made that Colonel Sherburne, who had replaced Colonel Denson as the regimental commander while the Regiment was training at Camp Blanding, was himself being transferred out. The regimental executive officer, Lieutenant Colonel Frank U. Greer, a large, bald-headed man with a no-nonsense personality, assumed command, and with his command came a promotion to colonel.

Like Allen and Roosevelt, Frank Greer had served as a foot soldier in the Great War, but he left the Army soon after the end of the conflict. He subsequently rejoined the Army in 1920 as a captain at the Infantry School at Fort Benning, serving in various troop and staff positions before returning to his hometown of Washington, D.C., where he became the Adjutant for the Military District of Washington. While stationed there, Greer obtained a law degree from George Washington University, then he went on to attend the requisite Army schools, including the War College, before being assigned to the Regiment as its executive officer. When he took command in mid-July, one of Greer's first official announcements to his troops at Indiantown Gap was that the 18th Infantry Regiment was definitely going overseas, and soon.

Many of the officers and men were given a short furlough to visit their families, but they were warned that they had to report back by the end of the month. Then on 31 July 1942, the expected orders arrived for the Regiment to proceed to a port of embarkation on the next day. To preserve operational security, however, their destination was not announced. As had become the custom in their many deployments, the soldiers of the Regiment were roused well before first light the next morning, then loaded up on trucks by flashlight. Convoys of 2½-ton trucks, affectionately dubbed by the soldiers as "deuce and a halves," then moved out to the nearby railroad station where their drivers transferred the men to trains for the short trip to what some from the New York area now knew had to be the Brooklyn Naval Shipyard.

From there, the soldiers boarded ferry boats, then they were shuttled past the charred hull of the French ocean liner *Normandie*. The ship had fallen victim to a careless welder's torch that ignited debris and caused a massive fire which had destroyed the entire vessel weeks before they arrived, but it was widely believed by the men at the time to have been enemy sabotage that caused its demise.

Before long the soldiers found themselves dockside, then marching off the ferry boats in platoon formation right into a huge shed where they were led past loud stevedores loading boxes and crates into the side of another large ship covered with a fresh coat of gray paint. Once known as the "Inevitable Ship" by the owners of the British Cunard Line, but now simply designated as "HMS 250," the vessel selected to transport the entire 1st Division overseas had been considered a noble tribute to the imagination of man when she was first built. With her luxurious furniture removed for new war service duty and placed in storage, however, the vessel was now refitted for what it was to become for many years—an overloaded troop transport rather than a state-of-the-art ocean liner. The hearts of many of the men of the Regiment, though, beat with excitement when they were informed that they were going to sail overseas aboard the *Queen Mary*.

Officers checked names off on their rosters as their men filed up gangplanks onto the ship. Eventually, everyone found their way under, between, and around other soldiers before clambering down into the ship's holds, where many cursed as they tried to find bunks and a place to dump their equipment. Runners weaved their ways through the seething mass of confused humanity to pass orders to each company commander; all the orders seeming to conflict with the last directive they received. Some originated from division level, others from the British naval officers aboard ship, and still more from battalion commanders, but they all had to be sorted through by the Regiment's junior officers, understood, and then passed down . . . or ignored. The men were ordered to sleep fully clothed, no smoking was allowed in quarters or below deck, and fire regulations were explained in detail. Abandon ship and air-raid drills were also practiced over and over again, and the chain of command even conducted weapon inspections.

While the men of the 18th Infantry Regiment were loading aboard the *Queen Mary* on 1 August, their parent unit was officially redesignated; no longer the 1st Division, it became officially known as the 1st Infantry Division, the title by which it would be known for the rest of the war.

By their second day on the ship, everybody had settled in as best they could. General Allen was holding a meeting with his staff officers toward midmorning when the tremor of a vessel coming to life could be felt by many of the men. The *Queen Mary* soon slipped away from Pier 90 and steamed down the Hudson River into New York Harbor, passed the Statue of Liberty, and headed out to sea. Her log entry recorded her departure at 1045 hours on the morning of 2 August 1942. The 18th Infantry Regiment was finally off to its rendezvous with war and destiny.

Two US Navy blimps performed maritime reconnaissance for the *Queen Mary* during her first full day at sea, and both were joined by several American destroyer escorts, which patrolled to the *Queen's* port and starboard. By the time the graceful liner reached her cruising speed of some 35 knots, the destroyer escorts were slamming into waves and quickly losing ground, so the *Queen Mary* sped smoothly ahead towards her destination without them. The huge ship carried over 15,000 soldiers, twice her normal capacity, but the urgent and necessary first crossing of combatants for war took precedent over strict regulations. During the transit, the men were rotated above and below decks for 12 hours at a stretch, "hot bunking" (using the bunk recently vacated by another soldier) and catching what sleep they could during their turns below. Eating became difficult or unpleasant, as most of the enlisted men had to take their meals standing up during the meager 20-minute shifts allowed for this purpose.

By its fifth day at sea, the *Queen Mary* had reached the western approaches to the British Isles, where aircraft again escorted the large ship through the dangerous coastal waters into port. Two tugs eventually pulled alongside and then escorted her nearer to the dock area, which the troops by now had learned was in the port of Gourock, Scotland. The only signs of life the soldiers saw at that early hour were busily darting launches shuttling people between shore and other vessels in the harbor, mostly freighters. The time soon came to disembark; platoons marched up one of Gourock's streets in columns of two, company by company, battalion by battalion, until the officers and men reached the nearby train station. There, the weary soldiers stood at ease awaiting their coach assignments, and within a few short hours, they were all loaded and on their way to an undisclosed destination.

After swaying on railroad tracks all night, the men of the 18th Infantry Regiment arrived at yet another train station the next morning. Platoons soon marched off in columns of twos through a small village, and then continued marching along a winding, tree-lined road that led to another village nearby. The long line of soldiers finally halted in a concrete courtyard surrounded by two-story brick buildings about an hour later. The officers and men of the Regiment had finally arrived at Tidworth Barracks, an old British cavalry garrison on the Salisbury Plain, some 50 miles southwest of London. This was to be their home during their tenure in England.

The Regiment spent several weeks at Tidworth Barracks, with visits to London allowed on the first weekend of their stay. During this time, the men participated in more intensive training, close-order drill, calisthenics, and air-raid practice, and endured frequent equipment inspections. After seemingly endless periods of these small-unit training exercises, Colonel Greer then insisted that each battalion conduct a 24-mile endurance march. In early October the Regiment departed Tidworth altogether for another train trip northward, again to a "secret" destination.

The Regiment spent the first week of the month at a spartan encampment in Scotland featuring muddy ground, deeply rutted dirt trails, and Nissen huts, which were simple corrugated tin structures with cracked damp floors, a single door, and several side windows. The 18th Infantry Regiment had been sent here to pick up where stateside amphibious training had left off, and to increase the pace of this necessary training by practicing landings in the nearby lagoons. The camp never got a name like Tidworth Barracks, Fort Devens, or Camp Blanding, but it was located on the Scottish coast near Rosneath and was maintained by the US Navy. Ironically, the Regiment's British instructors at Rosneath were not Royal Navy sailors, but veterans of the doomed amphibious raid across the English Channel on the French shore at Dieppe, which had taken place shortly after the combat team arrived on British soil. The raid, conducted by the 2nd Canadian Division and a contingent of British commandos—and a 50-man group of American Rangers—was intended to provide an operational foundation for much larger amphibious assaults in the future. The operation failed, with the roughly 6,000 attackers sustaining 907 killed in action, 586 wounded, and 1,946 captured, including three killed and several captured in the Ranger force.

Fortunately, failure in one operation resulted in lessons that could be applied to the next, so following lectures and simulations using scale models to teach the basics to the Regiment's officers, the entire 18th Infantry Regiment moved to a sheltered bay for exercises using actual landing craft. Companies were broken down into 35-man boat groups, the maximum capacity of the LCVPs made available for the practices. The men disembarked from these landing craft right at the water's edge, and then they drilled this repeatedly until the instructors were convinced they had it down well enough to demonstrate that they could make an actual landing under fire from offshore.

Several days later, the combat team found itself at another new encampment that would serve as a base for these continued amphibious exercises. Ironically, this location was formerly a golf course that had been converted into a military bivouac area; it was known as Corkerhill Camp. Scuttlebutt and speculation spread after word was heard that Colonel Greer and a portion of the regimental staff had "disappeared" for what was a supposed secret mission to London. Meantime, tactical training and stationary amphibious exercises continued on the muddy campgrounds, fortunately interrupted by passes for the troops to go into nearby Glasgow at night.

While Colonel Greer was in London, orders arrived directing the 18th Infantry Regiment to return to Rosneath for more amphibious training, this time from the British assault transport *Reina del Pacifico*. To make the exercise more meaningful, the Regiment was pitted against a British commando unit that was to act as an opposing force on shore. These landing maneuvers took place during mid-October on a peninsula near the town of Dunoon on Scotland's west coast. Results were disappointing, however, when organization ashore quickly broke down in the darkness following the landings.

There was a very real purpose for the amphibious landing practices, whether or not perfection was achieved. As a result of several meetings during the summer of 1942, President Roosevelt and Prime Minister Churchill had come to a consensus that an Anglo-American landing in North Africa was to take place before the end of the year. Their decision, which ensured that the 18th Infantry Regiment would soon depart Scotland, represented a convenient political compromise between the two leaders. Roosevelt knew that he had to commit ground forces against the Germans before 1942 ended, both to appease public opinion at home as well as Russian leader Stalin's persistent demands for the opening of a second front. For many reasons, the British had been unwilling to support an American-favored landing proposal in occupied France that year, instead emphasizing their preference to commit Allied troops in North Africa where they could stop *Generalfeldmarschall* Erwin Rommel from gaining an important victory. The operation, therefore, represented a compromise between the political realities of war and military expediency. Renamed TORCH, the invasion of North Africa was now slated to take place in early November.

At Corkerhill Camp, the pace of preparation started to pick up. During the third week of October, while most of the Regiment's officers and men were away on a long road march through the picturesque Scottish countryside, a battalion of Army Rangers showed up at the camp. Therefore, it came as no big surprise when a meeting was called for all personnel shortly after their arrival, particularly since word had spread that Colonel Greer had returned from his secret conference in London. The men soon found themselves in regimental formation by companies in an open field, where they were ordered to attention before their commander. Greer wasted little time jumping up onto a makeshift platform, and after saying how he knew the Regiment would live up to its long-held traditions, he delivered the words everyone had been expecting for weeks. "Men of the 18th," he shouted, "We're goin' a fightin'!"

The next day, the Regiment's vehicles were lined up in the motor pool for waterproofing. Officers and enlisted men anxiously cleaned their weapons, checked gear, and undoubtedly wondered where they were going to be sent to fight. Although the troops would not know their actual destination for another week and a half, orders were received on 24 October 1942 to be ready to move out and board assault transports the following day. That morning, after a thorough cleanup, the men labored through the mud of Corkerhill Camp once more, finally saying goodbye after leaving neat heaps of worn overshoes buckled together in piles at the edge of the grounds. Then, after a quick changeover into clean service shoes and canvas leggings, the men marched to the familiar nearby train station where they boarded up for a short trip to Glasgow. It was the first leg of a long trip that would take the 18th Infantry Regiment into the front lines for the first time in World War II.

Knowing combat was inevitable, on 17 September Colonel Greer had passed some concerns to General Allen in a memorandum that identified the need for a decision regarding the type of weapons that would accompany his assault troops into combat. Reminding his Commanding General that "the Cannon Company has not fired a field piece," Greer recommended that training be scheduled as soon as possible, to include live-fire exercises. He also asked the division commander for "an early decision as to what equipment is to be taken in order that prompt disposal of the excess could be made." Unfortunately, the habits of a waste-not, depression-era economy still governed the disposition of both the division's individual and unit equipment. Reluctant to leave any item behind that might be misplaced, needed for reasons yet unknown, or even stolen, General Allen ordered his commanders to bring virtually everything their units owned when they left Scotland. As a result, the Regiment would soon find itself burdened with an excessive amount of individual gear right after landing on a hostile shore.[11]

When the Regiment finally reached the docks at Glasgow, its men and officers were coincidentally assigned to Transport Division 18 (TRANSDIV 18), which consisted of the assault transports *Reina del Pacifico*, *Ettrick*, and *Tegelberg*. The combat team's equipment was manifested on three freighters, *City of Chattanooga*, *Alicinous*, and *Empire Confidence*. TRANSDIV 18 also included the vessels designated to carry the 1st Ranger Battalion, which was loaded onto three smaller assault ships: *Royal Scotsman*, *Ulster Monarch*, and *Royal Ulsterman*.

Major John L. Powers' 2nd Battalion was assigned to the Dutch manned *Tegelberg*, while Major Richard C. Parker's 1st Battalion loaded onto the *Ettrick*, a British merchant ship refitted for war and manned by a crew of naval ratings. The *Ettrick* was unique in that it was equipped with a specially-rigged cargo net that hung over the hold, jury-rigged in place so that the men could continually rehearse their disembarkation procedures while at sea. The *Reina Del Pacifico* served as the transport for Colonel Greer's headquarters personnel, the Cannon Company, Lieutenant Colonel Courtney P. Brown's 3rd Battalion, and most of the 1st Infantry Division staff. General Allen's support staff was on the *Reina Del Pacifico* because it was fitted out with extra communications gear in case it had to serve as an alternate command ship for the mission.

While most of their passengers were sleeping, the captains of the assault transports weighed anchor on the night of 26 October and headed for a rendezvous point with the main body of the invasion fleet in the Bay of Biscay. The 1st Infantry Division was in a convoy consisting of 61 escorts, 9 assault transports, and 34 merchant ships, all scattered over the waters as far as the eye could see. The convoy initially steamed northwest of Scotland, cleared the Bay of Biscay, then headed into open waters where vessel after vessel started slamming into endless white-capped waves. The weather had turned bad, and barometers aboard the ships started falling almost as rapidly as the stinging rain fell from the lead-gray skies above.

It took three long, miserable days for this weather to break. What made it especially uncomfortable for the troops was that no one but the senior officers amongst them knew where they were heading, and because of this there was no way of knowing when the convoy might reach calmer waters. Many of the men became seasick, even more so when the armada of ships zigzagged in many seemingly pointless directions to mislead German air or water reconnaissance patrols about the intended destination of the flotilla. It was not until five days into the trip that the weather improved and the seas calmed. The daytime sun started to shine ever more brightly and the air turned warmer as the ships began to steady themselves on a more southerly course. Nights brought the glow of a waxing moon, making war seem more like a bad dream than a reality to many of the troops. For some, the rigors of training were easy to forget, as preparation for war now became more of a personal challenge.

Final plans for Operation TORCH called for the deployment of three amphibious convoys, designated as the Western, Center, and Eastern Task Forces, to subdue French Northwest Africa. The Western Naval Task Force would deposit 35,000 troops and 250 tanks under Major General George S. Patton, Jr., at three different points on the Atlantic coast of Morocco, beginning at 0400 hours on 8 November. Patton's ground forces included the 2nd Armored Division, the 3rd Infantry Division, and elements of the 9th Infantry Division, all of which would be transported to Morocco directly from the United States aboard US ships.[12]

The other two convoys would enter the Mediterranean via the Strait of Gibraltar to conduct landings in French Algeria. The Eastern Task Force, consisting of 10,000 American and 23,000 British troops, was ordered to seize Algiers. This landing force, which was commanded by Major General Charles Ryder, consisted of elements of the American 9th and 34th Infantry Divisions as well as the British 78th Division. The Center Task Force, which carried the 37,100 troops of Major General Lloyd R. Fredendall's II Corps, was assigned the principal mission of seizing the city of Oran on the Algerian coast some 200 miles inside the Mediterranean. This landing force would be comprised mainly of the 1st Infantry Division, to include the 18th Infantry Regiment, as well as Combat Command B of the 1st Armored Division.

General Fredendall planned to capture Oran by conducting landings at Arzew, Mersa Bou Zedjar, Les Andalouses, and St. Leu. After the landing phase was completed by infantry troops, a column of 1st Armored Division tanks would conduct a raid inland to capture the main French airfield behind Oran. A battalion of armored infantry from the same division would also enter Oran harbor and prevent the French from sabotaging cargo handling equipment, or from scuttling any ships anchored here that might block the main landings.[13]

As the flotilla carrying the Regiment passed through the Strait of Gibraltar on 6 November, the shroud of secrecy that had been surrounding TORCH was lifted when company officers were finally briefed and issued maps to explain and clearly depict their zone of operations and objectives upon landing. The 18th Infantry Regiment was scheduled to land on Zebra Beach Green with two of its battalions abreast starting at 0100 on 8 November. Major Parker's 1st Battalion, landing on the left, was to move inland to seize St. Cloud, some eight and a half miles southwest of Arzew, using the Arzew-Oran highway. St. Cloud defenses were largely unknown at the time, but it was nevertheless the Regiment's intermediate objective before continuing on to Oran, the division's principal objective. Lieutenant Colonel Brown's 3rd Battalion, in conjunction with the 1st Ranger Battalion, was to secure Arzew and silence its coastal defenses. Major Powers' 2nd Battalion would remain in regimental reserve, while the Cannon and Anti-Tank Companies landed soon after daylight to support the advance of the Regiment's two assault battalions.

Supporting fire would also be provided by Lieutenant Colonel Percy W. Thompson's 32nd Field Artillery Battalion (Hereafter, field artillery battalions will be identified using US Army nomenclature, that is, "32nd FA"), which would put two howitzers from Battery C ashore one hour after the landings began, followed by the remaining 12 105mm howitzers three hours later. The firing batteries were initially ordered to take up positions that would allow them to support the 1st Battalion's advance toward St. Cloud.[14]

As soon as the officers of the Regiment were dismissed from their briefing, they headed to their cabins to more closely read their orders, to study their maps, and eventually brief their men. There was a lot to absorb. This would be their first time in combat, and they wanted to be prepared. Each of the battalion commanders also began to study the plans to identify specific tasks for their companies. Brown's 3rd Battalion, for example, was designated to land at 0120 hours on Zebra Green Beach (West) in a zone that stretched for approximately 2,000 yards. Tasked with securing Arzew, this battalion planned to launch its assault on the military installations near the outskirts of the port. Company K, commanded by Captain Clifford B. Raymer, was given the principal mission of capturing Fort de Sou before moving on to seize the seaplane base, while Captain Henry R. Sawyer's Company I was tasked with attacking the barracks just west of the center of town. Once these positions were secured, the battalion would then assist the Rangers in taking both Fort du Nord and Fort de la Pointe. Captain Donald H. Fogg's Company L was initially assigned to be in reserve, with orders to be prepared to assist either Company I or K, or the 1st Ranger Battalion in accomplishing their missions as needed. The SP 105mm assault guns of the Regiment's Cannon Company, Battery C of the 32nd FA, and the 81mm mortars of Company M, commanded by Captain Francis J. Rosinski, would also provide fire support as needed if the French chose to resist.[15]

Unknown at the time, Lieutenant Colonel Brown's 3rd Battalion had been assigned the most difficult objective in the initial assault. It was later learned that the French *1st Battalion, 2nd Zouave Regiment*, as well as one company of the French *3rd Battalion, 2nd Algerian Tirailleurs*, garrisoned the town of Arzew. Additionally, three coastal artillery batteries equipped with a total of four 105mm and four 75mm guns defended the seaward approaches to the town. American intelligence officers had estimated that there were 1,200 French-led defenders in the immediate area, but they were uncertain about their will to fight.

A portion of Major Parker's 1st Battalion would also land at 0120 hours on adjacent Zebra Green Beach (East),[16] with his remaining elements slated to come ashore three hours later. After assembling the rifle companies, the battalion would then march inland to a point where they could interdict the main road leading to Oran. This force would then have to secure several small villages as they moved forward, most notably the town of St. Cloud, which lay squarely astride of the Regiment's avenue of advance. St. Cloud possessed significant tactical value: an improved road and a railway line leading to Oran intersected there. Military intelligence had indicated that there was no permanent garrison in St. Cloud. They did report, however, that a battery of four 75mm guns belonging to the French *68th African Field Artillery (Artillerie d'Afrique)* had recently arrived from Sidi Bel Abbes, and could be committed.[17]

According to Colonel Greer's plan, the leading elements of Major Powers' 2nd Battalion would not begin landing until daybreak. Due to this, Powers would not have the benefit of planning for a specifically-assigned mission. Once assembled on the beach, however, the battalion would probably either advance in a column of companies directly behind Major Parker's 1st Battalion toward St. Cloud, or, if the French vigorously defended Arzew, attack to support Lieutenant Colonel Brown's 3rd Battalion.

During the afternoon of 7 November, officers and noncoms conducted last-minute inspections aboard the *Tegelberg, Ettrick,* and *Reina Del Pacifico*. Personal effects bearing anything that would identify the Regiment's soldiers had to be turned in at this time. Lodge cards, driver's licenses, old garrison passes—even personal items like old railroad ticket stubs and dance hall souvenirs from London—were all surrendered. The American flags on the left sleeve of every enlisted man's combat jacket was also checked to be sure that they were securely fastened, and that the requisite white brassards were displayed just above their elbows. Once all of the inspections were complete, every man had a few minutes alone with his thoughts. That night on the promenade deck of the *Tegelberg,* many 18th Infantry Regiment soldiers attended the interdenominational services offered by one of the regimental chaplains, Captain Edward K. Rogers.

Just before midnight, Lieutenant John P. Downing of Company F ate cold cuts and bread washed down with a cup of half milk, half bitter British coffee. He expressed what many on the *Tegelberg* were undoubtedly thinking at the time when he remembered, "As I glanced around the room, it seemed inconceivable to me that anyone here would be dead at this time tomorrow. I had been in the Regiment since May, but I knew all the officers and many of us had become close friends. I couldn't visualize any of us getting killed, but still in combat people do get killed and by the law of averages everyone wouldn't come through. Another question that loomed was how I was going to behave under fire. It's easy enough to assume you'll be as brave as the next man, but you can never know or be certain until you actually undergo the sensation of being fired at. Whatever happened, I'd never in my life forget the date 8 November 1942."[18]

Meantime, battalion ammunition and pioneer (A&P) platoons had begun issuing rifle, machine-gun, and mortar ammunition. Men soon grabbed their M-1 rifles and extra bandoleers of ammunition, checked both of the canteens fastened to their cartridge belts, and waited. Some soldiers checked their compasses and first-aid packs. Others reached for their trench knives, then checked their packs to be sure that they had a pair of dry socks and a change of underwear. Gas masks were fitted, then removed and stowed in their carriers, most of the soldiers praying they would not need them. Finally, cartridge belts were tightened, and helmet chinstraps fastened, some helmets stuffed with packets of toilet paper or cigarettes.

In Company H, the heavy weapons company of the 2nd Battalion, Captain Robert E. Murphy talked quietly to his men, first generally checking to be sure that their equipment loads were secured to avoid galling or chafing, then inspecting the four M1917A1 water-cooled heavy machine guns assigned to each of his two machine-gun platoons. Murphy then went to visit his mortar platoon. Their heavy and ungainly weapons had to be hand-carried ashore, and he checked to be sure they were distributed correctly amongst the crews. Mortar squad leaders would carry the sight for each weapon, its bipod, and baseplate, while the remaining men served as ammunition carriers. Each mortar squad was required to carry an ammunition load weighing 276 pounds.[19] The rounds were distributed to the squad's five ammo bearers, each of whom wore six rounds of HE-light (a lighter high-explosive round, weighing just under seven pounds) stuffed into their vests, which had three pockets in front and three more in back. Heavier explosives (HE-heavy) and smoke shells, weighing 15 and about 11 pounds each, respectively, were too heavy to manpack. Murphy's drivers would transport these on the company's jeeps once they were ashore. With munitions distributed this way, Captain Murphy's mortar platoon would land with 144 rounds, which equated to about three minutes' worth of rapid firing before resupply was brought up by his jeep drivers.

Preparations being made for for battle were similar aboard the *Ettrick*, with one notable difference. The men of the 1st Battalion had been assembled on deck, all somewhat nervous, but also excited about finally learning of their mission. Then the ship's loudspeaker crackled to life with the voice of their battalion commander, Major Parker:

> Attention all personnel. We are about to embark upon the first phase of America's partnership with our English allies as we engage the enemy on the shores of North Africa. You men are the fuel that will ignite the torch of liberty. It will be the honor of the First Division to be the first to halt the tide of Nazism and stamp out the evil it represents. The morning of November 8th 1942 will go down in history as the turning point of the war against Germany. You have all been through a vigorous and extended training period to prepare you for this moment. Those of you who are here today have proven your ability to do what we are asking you to do. I have complete faith in that ability and I am sure that you will defeat the enemy at every turn. Remember the great history and traditions of the Big Red One are also at stake. The world will have its eyes on you. Your company commanders will fill you in with the details. As you go forward into battle, remember the

division motto, "No mission too difficult; No sacrifice too great; Duty first." Good Luck and May God be with you.[20]

Aboard the *Reina Del Pacifico,* General Terry Allen was absorbed in studying his overall battle plan for Oran one more time. Just after passing through the Strait of Gibraltar the day before, Allen had called his staff to the lounge where he stood before a large map marked TOP SECRET. Then, waving a pointer in his hand, he started with,

> We are the Center Landing Force. Oran is our primary objective. Another landing will be in Casablanca; another in Algiers. The 16th and 18th Combat Teams will land to the east of Oran near Arzew. The 26th will land to the west of Oran at Les Andalouses. By D+1, the main body of the division will gain and hold a beachhead line extending from the heights of Djebel Khar, a prominent feature located between Pointe Canastel and St. Cloud, through Fleurus, along the northern end of a salt lake and road junction south of En Nekala, before curving back to the Golfe d'Arzew just east of La Macta. The 26th will capture Djebel Santon and Djebel Murdajadjo, which dominate the western approaches to Oran. The landings near Arzew will also be supported by the 1st Ranger Battalion, which will send parties up Cap Carbon to take one coastal battery and into Arzew Harbor to capture another. All three of the 1st Division's infantry regiments will converge on Oran from several directions to force the surrender of the French garrison.[21]

At the conclusion of this briefing, Allen smiled and simply closed with, "Now you know it!"

General Allen then departed for his stateroom as his staff leaped to attention. The division G-2 (Intelligence Officer), Lieutenant Colonel Robert W. Porter, led the assembled officers into a locked and guarded room below deck right after this where everyone joined to view photographic profiles of the Oran coast; topographic maps showing individual buildings and houses in Arzew and Oran; the French "Oran Division" order of battle; suspected and known locations of their defensive positions' names of French commanding officers; the politics of the area; and even charts indicating the expected weather over the next several days.

General Allen kept to himself whatever misgivings he might have had about the plan. Sitting in his stateroom after the briefing and penning a short note to his wife, he could not help thinking about the operation his division was preparing to undertake. In marked contrast to General Eisenhower at Allied Forces Headquarters (AFHQ), a half-mile inside the Rock of Gibraltar across the Mediterranean, Allen did not believe that the French would give up Arzew and St. Cloud without a fight. According to his G-3 (Operations Officer), Lieutenant Colonel Stanhope P. Mason, "General Allen's planning staff had a more pessimistic view. They thought it more likely the invading forces would be greeted by strong opposition, that to plan otherwise was military folly and could lead to disaster. General Allen kept an open mind, but backed his staff position that lack of preparedness to fight our way into Oran was not what he wanted."22

Allen had reason for his suspicions about French resistance to the planned landings. Although many of its units had aligned themselves with the Free French, some elements of the French Foreign Legion *(Légion Étrangère)* were present in the objective area. They were well regarded as a fighting force. Legion units were comprised of about one-third ethnic Germans and another one-third German sympathizers in their ranks. Many Legion officers, although French, were also loyal to the Vichy French government and were likely to resist any Anglo-American landings, unless ordered not to resist. Many government leaders and leading citizens of French North Africa were known to be anti-Semitic, favoring the Germans over the much-more-disliked British. If they failed to put up a fight, they knew their families in France would bear the brunt of Nazi retaliation.

Shortly after midnight on 8 November 1942, General Allen decided to go on deck to watch the first assault boats depart for shore. Accompanied by an aide and a war correspondent, he quietly paced the deck of the *Reina del Pacifico* as the soldiers of the 1st Ranger Battalion and Companies A, C, I, K, and L of the 18th Infantry Regiment clambered down into their British made Landing Craft Assault (LCA) boats. Casting off from the attack transports shortly before 0100 hours, the LCAs started toward their designated landing area four miles south of Arzew, while the boats carrying most of the Rangers headed toward a beach just north of town. As another smaller Ranger raiding party started into the mouth of the harbor, Allen could discern a single innocent electric light that was burning on the outer end of the main dock, seemingly indicating that his hoped-for surprise had indeed been achieved.

As more landing craft were being loaded, President Roosevelt's steady, patrician voice started delivering a planned message over the airwaves to the French ashore. This same oration was heard through the loudspeakers on the *Reina del Pacifico*. "We come among you to repulse the cruel invaders who would remove forever your rights of self-government," the president began. "We come among you solely to defeat and rout your enemies. Have faith in our words. We do not want to cause you any harm." It made General Allen cringe when he heard it, adding to his already highly anxious mood. He did not need to have his assault landing announced, but he had no choice in the matter because political considerations took precedent over military requirements at that particular moment. Like General Eisenhower, President Roosevelt believed the French would not have the will to fight.

By 0120 hours the Rangers were all ashore, and half of their forces were moving through Arzew itself while the other half were deploying along the narrow beach just north of town. They quickly seized the area dock facilities, Fort de la Pointe and the Ford du Nord, and a prearranged Very light (flares) signal—green and amber—was fired, prompting the *Reina del Pacifico* to signal the other transports to move closer to the beach. Then a white flare soon shot up from shore on Green Beach, signaling that the leading echelon of Lieutenant Colonel Brown's 3rd Battalion was also safely in. Since communication from the *Reina del Pacifico* to the beach was not taking place because of the strictly-imposed radio silence, Colonel Greer was now making plans to move his headquarters element ashore. He knew that a commander's place in combat was with his men, not sitting several miles off the landing beach area on some British transport ship.

By 0430 hours, over 1,120 men of the Regiment had made it in without encountering French opposition. Significant delays were experienced in assembling the rifle companies, however, partly due to the darkness, and also because the men were weighed down with too much gear. As one Operation TORCH participant noted, "Each man was carrying on his back an unduly heavy load. It consisted of a light pack, British gas cape, gas impregnated underwear, wool undershirt, shoe impregnate, Halizone tablets, gas mask, goggles, one D-Ration and 3 C-Rations, two extra units of fire per weapon (additional ammunition), two canteens of water, and hand grenades."[23] Uniforms were also impregnated against chemical attack, making them hot, sticky, and very uncomfortable. Although the Americans had been led to believe that all of this equipment would be necessary, even the lowliest private realized that it was impractical to expect a man to carry such a heavy load into combat. As a result, many men were exhausted after struggling through the heavy surf. As the rifle companies began moving, their routes became littered with vast amounts of gear, creating a scene that had all of the appearances of a supply sergeant's worst nightmare.

Meanwhile, after a brief flurry of fighting, the 1st Ranger Battalion had secured both of the shore batteries it had been ordered to capture, at 0250 and 0505 hours, respectively. Having started out from its assembly area near Zebra Beach shortly before 0430 hours, Lieutenant Colonel Brown's 3rd Battalion was now also approaching Arzew with the aid of the first rays of daylight. The leading elements headed toward the French Army barracks, but as Captain Raymer's Company K drew closer, rifle fire cracked sharply and bullets ricocheted into his ranks. Taking cover, the Americans immediately returned with well-aimed rifle and BAR fire, as well as a barrage delivered by Captain Rosinski's Company M 81mm mortars. The defenders of the barracks quickly lapsed into silence, and then 62 French soldiers marched out moments later with their hands over their heads.

Moving onto their second objective, Brown's men first encountered naval security troops guarding the seaplane base. Alerted by the sounds of the earlier fighting, however, several of their machine-gun crews began spraying bursts of tracer bullets at the American infantry from their positions on the south jetty. The mortars of Company M again answered to silence this opposition, then Raymer's Company K and Captain Fogg's Company L swept forward and overran the naval base, resulting in the capture of a dozen Latécoère 298 seaplanes and 60 more prisoners. Meantime, although plagued by snipers, Captain Sawyer's Company I

Overseas and the Battle for Oran

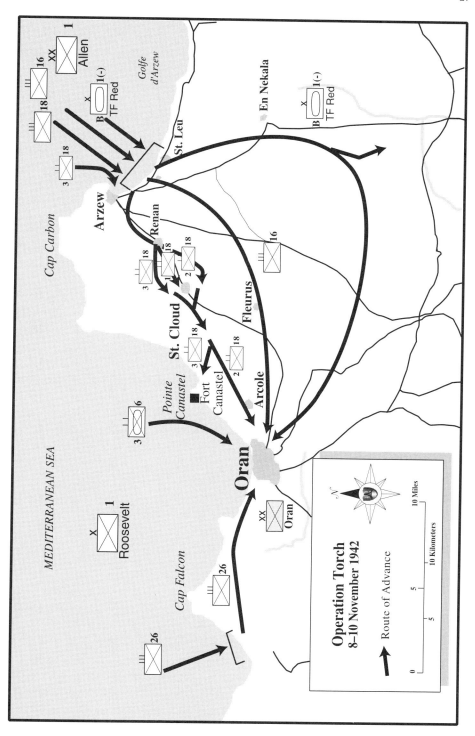

succeeded in cleaning out all remaining French opposition in its designated sector near the south jetty. In the process of securing Arzew, the 3rd Battalion sustained its first battlefield casualties, suffering three killed and seven wounded. The unfortunate killed were two from Captain Sawyer's Company I, Corporal Andrew Colson and Private Clifford B. Moore, and Private Herbert J. Tomlinson in Captain Fogg's Company L.[24]

Like Lieutenant Colonel Brown's men, the 1st Battalion also experienced numerous difficulties after landing at Zebra Green Beach. Captain Renato "Ray" Froncillo, commander of Company C, remembered that "it was a night landing and there was considerable confusion on the beach. Units had become separated and the rifle companies were having difficulties regrouping and starting to move inland. [Major Robert H. York] took charge at that time, calmed people down, and did get the rifle companies moving toward their first objective."[25] Soon after this Captain Froncillo started his unit's advance toward St. Cloud. "We proceeded up to the village, with our 3rd Platoon under the command of Lieutenant Peter Mirakian leading," Company C's Lieutenant Clement Van Wagoner remembered. "My 1st Platoon followed, then when we reached the highway Captain Froncillo ordered us to pass through the 3rd Platoon and take the lead, which we did."[26]

Surrounded by low hills usually covered with vineyards during the growing season, but now cut back and affording little cover, St. Cloud's center was dotted with stone and brick houses, all built at right angles to each other. The local, iron-gated cemetery with its eerie crypts stood on the south side of the town, surrounded by a low wall, and behind the cemetery ran the shallow track bed of the Oran-Arzew railroad. Unfortunately for the men in the 1st Battalion, the French garrison in Oran had been alerted by the abortive attempt at landing a battalion of the 6th Armored Infantry Regiment in Oran harbor, as well as the gun flashes from the earlier firing in Arzew. In accordance with his now quickly organized tactical plans, Major General Robert Marie Jules Camille Boissau, the Commanding General of the Oran Division, sent a platoon of armored cars toward Arzew to investigate the situation. As these armored vehicles departed Oran, General Boissau ordered a larger force, consisting of a battalion of the French *16th Tunisian Tirailleurs* (Infantry), and the *1st Regiment de la Légion Étrangère (French Foreign Legion)*, to assemble and move toward Arzew to counterattack. General Allen's conviction about the French fighting back was certainly materializing as this force departed Oran for the seaport area shortly before daylight.[27]

By mid-morning, the French armored car platoon had encountered the 18th Regiment's 1st Battalion moving toward St. Cloud. Lieutenant Van Wagoner recalled,

> We were hit by French armored cars, all right. They came from the direction of St. Cloud at about the time we were making the change in platoon mission. There was also an ox cart that came up at the same time from the direction of Arzew, however, while the first armored car was coming at us

from the other direction. The ox cart was hauling some five tons of stone, and it was just balanced on two wheels. The driver apparently did not want to get hit by the armored cars, so he pulled off the road and right into the ditch where my platoon was hiding. It went right through us, the hard rubber tires cutting some of my men lengthwise; some crosswise. Captain [Joseph] Hill [Commanding Officer, Company A] came up and took care of the cart, and by this time Major York was on the scene. I directed the medic to stay with the wounded, then we kept going.[28]

When the noisy charcoal burning engines of the French armored cars announced their impending arrival, Company A was actually positioned slightly to the right rear of Company C, and one of Hill's rifle platoons was moving directly along the main thoroughfare. All of the Americans had quickly taken cover along the sides of the road before opening fire. Using rifle grenades and BARs firing armor-piercing ammunition, Captain Froncillo's men disabled four of the five armored cars, killing two French soldiers and also capturing 14 more, both wounded and uninjured, in the process. The 1st Battalion sustained its first casualty of the war when Company A's Staff Sergeant Charles Ertle was killed during this action.[29]

After receiving a report from the one armored car that had escaped this ambush, Major General Boissau had decided to establish a hasty defense in St. Cloud. Though moving warily, the 1st Battalion was not expecting any organized resistance from the village, but when the battalion's main body neared the town just before noon, it was greeted by several salvos of well-aimed 75mm shells from a battery of the French *68th African Field Artillery*. "I had some men in town by this time," Lieutenant Van Wagoner recalled. "Captain Froncillo had been near me, but he got called back to battalion. I was concerned that he might have been in the midst of where the artillery rounds landed. By this time I had lost my first man to the war, Private Frank M. Galan. We did not get any farther into the town, and a little while later a messenger arrived with bad news. Captain Froncillo had indeed been hit. The message was short and it said, 'CO wounded. You are now in command'."[30]

Caught in the surprise, the men of the lead company that had reached St. Cloud in strength, Company A, quickly sought cover. Simultaneously, accompanying forward observers from the 32nd FA registered their own guns on the center of the village, in anticipation of calls for artillery support. When he heard the outbreak of this firing, Lieutenant Irving Yarock, Company A's Executive Officer, was with a platoon of Company C and some stragglers from his own company. Leaving these troops behind, Yarock rushed up to the village in search of the rest of Company A. Upon arriving, he was shocked to discover that Captain Hill was lying in the middle of the cemetery outside the village, near death. To Yarock's further dismay, he then learned that Lieutenant Bradley P. Bacon had been temporarily placed in command after fragments from a "friendly" grenade accidentally wounded another platoon leader while he was attempting to clear out other areas of the cemetery. Immediately after this, Major Parker had ordered Company A to withdraw and Lieutenant Bacon was wounded in the process. In less than an hour, three of Company A's officers had become casualties, and like Lieutenant Van Wagoner, the winded Lieutenant Yarock suddenly found himself in command of a company upon his arrival at St. Cloud.

Company B did not fare much better. Lieutenant Edward McGregor, the company executive officer, was leading the 2nd Platoon because of a shortage of officers. After landing, the platoon had very quietly made its way across the beach in files, eventually reaching the main road that ran up to St. Cloud. McGregor's platoon was in the lead as the company moved forward, and when daylight came they had just passed through St. Leone and were already marching to Renan, one of the smaller villages on the way to St. Cloud. When McGregor and his men reached Renan, a gunner in the surviving French armored car wounded one of them. McGregor immediately moved his men, eventually reaching a crossroads outside of the village, where he ordered them to spread out. Suddenly, there was a series of explosions as French artillery shells hit the entire area.

Some men dove to the ground, but dozens of other soldiers began running to the rear, discarding their packs, gas masks, and other equipment. "It was almost a rout," McGregor remembered. "They were terrified of artillery. I shouted, 'Stop, Stop!' It never occurred to me that in the best-trained division in the US Army this could happen."[31] McGregor quickly organized his men back into platoon formation, however, and the soldiers who had run began to sheepishly gather up their discarded equipment and move back into place.

The artillery fire had been widespread, even hitting the forward elements of the Regiment's Headquarters Company. The regimental S-3, Major Ben Sternberg, who was with Colonel Greer at the time, remembered, "Greer shouted 'Get away from the crossroad! They're zeroing in on us.' It quieted later, and we had organized back into our own platoons by then."[32]

By early afternoon, Company B was also sufficiently reorganized to attempt another assault on St. Cloud. This time, Lieutenant McGregor ordered his platoon to take cover behind the cemetery wall, which was actually some two hundred yards from the village. McGregor then whistled three times, signaling his platoon to follow him and jump the wall for a rapid assault on the outskirts of the village. Only three of his men followed and this did not make him happy at all. Reflecting his anger, McGregor then jumped back behind the wall, assembled his squad leaders, and said, "This is a disgrace. We are going to attack again. Anyone that doesn't go, I'll shoot. The sooner we get into the town, the better it will be. There's cover there."[33] McGregor's subsequent charge may have at first intimidated the French, but their well-aimed rifle fire resulted in the loss of Private Henry Herman from Brooklyn, New York, making him the first casualty of the war in Company B.

By this time, McGregor's company commander, Lieutenant Theodore C. "Toot" Plante, had joined him, and both officers climbed onto a nearby rooftop to try to spot the source of the incoming fire that had killed Private Herman. They did not see much, but McGregor threw a hand grenade at something he thought he saw moving, feeling better knowing that he was at least fighting back. Climbing back down from the rooftop together, Lieutenant Plante then decided to order the company to advance into the town itself, and the men began working their way forward, slowly and very cautiously. McGregor and Plante, both moving in front of the company, then made their way at a dead run to the village's main north-south intersection where they suddenly encountered enemy machine-gun fire. The Company B commander was immediately hit in the head by a burst, of bullets that ripped part of his face away. Lieutenant McGregor instinctively rushed over and dropped beside him to see if he could help, but all "Toot" Plante could say before he died was, "Keep going, Mac."[34]

Company B suffered a number of additional casualties as its men continued to fight their way toward the center of town, but by this time word had already reached Colonel Greer about the unexpectedly vicious resistance at the stronghold. For the regimental commander, this decided the question of where he wanted to commit Major Powers' 2nd Battalion. Before he could issue the necessary orders, Colonel Greer had to check with General Allen to ensure that his intention would be in accord with the division's evolving tactical plan, so he left for Allen's command post. Captain George Morgan, the Intelligence Officer of the 32nd FA, happened upon the hurriedly-organized meeting between Greer and Allen, which was also being attended by the commander of the 32nd FA, Lieutenant Colonel Thompson. The meeting was brief, for General Allen readily agreed that St. Cloud had to be quickly seized. Greer also undoubtedly experienced relief when Thompson informed both Allen and him that his battalion had experienced some difficulties getting their howitzers ashore, but there were now enough guns in position to provide the 18th Infantry Regiment with the artillery support needed for a coordinated attack on St. Cloud.[35]

By then, Colonel Greer had also anticipated using other available elements of his regiment. After being delayed by heavy surf, Captain Frank Colacicco's Cannon Company was finally assembled just off the beach near Arzew. His weaponry consisted of just a pair of self-propelled 105mm howitzers and six M3 half-tracks mounting 75mm howitzers; when his men heard they were going to enter the battle they were somewhat dismayed because the crews had never had the chance to fire their howitzers before. Their half-tracks were still not equipped with any sights for their main armament, but despite these handicaps and Cannon Company's painfully inexperienced gun crews, Colonel Greer nevertheless needed them forward to support the attack on St. Cloud.

Spurred on by Colonel Greer, Major Powers' 2nd Battalion was also now ashore. The battalion was soon moving up to support the 1st Battalion, heading along a narrow-gauge railroad track paralleling the main road toward St. Cloud. By now it was well past noon, and the hot sun was broiling most of the heavily-laden column. Burdened by the same equipment that had slowed others, the men gradually slowed down. Major Powers called for a brief halt in a large field several miles from St. Cloud shortly after this so he could reconnoiter ahead while his men rested.

After waiting for an hour, the battalion received new orders to resume the advance. This time, the rifle company commanders wisely ordered their men to leave their packs behind in company piles. Company E, under the command of Captain Carl O. Randall, now led the 2nd Battalion column with the 2nd Machine-Gun Platoon of Captain Murphy's Company H attached. Captain Charles Penick's Company F trailed behind Randall's unit and Major Powers and his command group fell in behind them. Company G, led by Captain Warren L. Bonnett, followed the command group, then the heavily-weighed-down mortarmen, machine gunners and ammunition bearers of Company H brought up the rear of the column.

Now spurred by an excessive abundance of adrenaline on the part of some of its leaders, the 2nd Battalion began to unravel as it made its way toward St. Cloud. Some rifle squads got out ahead of their companies, and some fell behind. The men of Company E became intermixed with those of Company F, and platoons started breaking down into double files. After nearly two weeks of sedentary conditions en route to the invasion beaches, many of the soldiers were having a difficult time adjusting to a renewal of strenuous activity, as well as the vastly different climate. With every heavy step toward St. Cloud, however, the men heard the sounds of sporadic machine-gun and rifle fire getting closer. Their attention was especially piqued when their ears were filled with the dull crump of exploding French artillery shells.

By this time, Captain Penick had gone forward to reconnoiter the area and this soon prompted Lieutenant John Downing to decide to go up and look for him. Taking a runner with him, the pair moved through a roadside ditch, passing a number of exhausted men before coming upon a dead soldier. "It was an American staff sergeant," Downing recalled later, "He was lying on his back, a hole through his head, his hands stiffly reaching toward his head and a strained expression on his dirty, waxy face. My stomach revolted and my throat constricted. An indescribable feeling of disgust and horror came over me. The idea finally made its impact on me that the maneuvers were over. This was war. No recall bugles would sound later on in the evening. This thing was going to go on for a long time, and the only way out was to be carried out wounded on a stretcher or to lie in a ditch like the sergeant in front of me. I swallowed my rising nausea and moved on."[36]

Downing continued forward until he reached a stretch in the road where he saw a French ambulance flying a Red Cross flag that was careening back to pick up the body of the dead American soldier he had just seen, Company A's Staff Sergeant Ertle. Right behind the ambulance was an officer on a bicycle, peddling down the road as bullets zipped over his head. This unidentified officer waved from a distance, prompting Downing to wave back, awed at the unknown man's seemingly nonchalant bravery. When Downing yelled for him to watch out for snipers, the stranger continued pedaling as if he had not heard or did not care. As he neared, Downing realized that the cyclist was Major Sternberg. With many of the their radios out of action, Sternberg was in a hurry to get back to Colonel Greer's command post with a first-hand report of events at St. Cloud.

The men of the 2nd Battalion's rifle companies were finally getting their wind back as they approached their designated attack positions near the 1st Battalion just outside of St. Cloud. As the long column came abreast of a draw just south of the town, the companies began deploying on line. Captain Penick's Company F and Captain Bonnett's Company G occupied positions alongside the firing line of the badly hit Company A, while Captain Randall's Company E was held in reserve. Captain Murphy then guided his mortar platoon and heavy machine guns past Randall's men before calling his own soldiers to a halt in a nearby vineyard. Expecting to receive additional instructions, Murphy then called his platoon leaders over to join him. He told them what he knew at the time, which wasn't much other than the locations of the 2nd Battalion's rifle companies. After patiently waiting for orders that never arrived, Murphy then took the initiative to deploy the water-cooled .30-calibers of his 1st Machine-Gun Platoon on a ridgeline between the cemetery and the road leading into town. He also directed his 81mm mortar platoon to position its six mortars in a nearby draw and to plot their initial concentrations on the outskirts of St. Cloud. Murphy then found his reconnaissance sergeant, Sergeant Leo Hennessy, and set off up the ridge with him to see for himself what was happening out front.

Near the cemetery, they ran into Major York as he was trying to reorganize the 1st Battalion. As Captain Murphy later recalled, "He told me, Murph, I'm going to make another try at the town. Can you give me any support?" Murphy told him that he had one of his heavy machine-gun platoons and his mortar platoon available, but he would have to check with Major Powers before he could commit them. Murphy then proceeded back down a trail through a vineyard and into the cemetery, where he passed Captain Hill's body. After turning away to examine the town one more time, he then headed back to the 2nd Battalion command post where he found Major Powers, along with his executive officer, Major William B. Chase, behind Companies E and F. Captain Murphy reported where his mortars and machine guns were located, confirming that he would be ready in 15 to 20 minutes to support an attack by their rifle companies. Murphy then informed Powers of Major York's request to support the 1st Battalion's renewed attack. Powers granted permission to provide any requested support, but instructed Murphy to contact him by radio before he began shooting.[37]

Concurrently, Lieutenant Malcolm Marshall, forward observer (FO) for Battery C, 32nd FA, was registering his howitzers on St. Cloud. After his first fire command was relayed to the battery, Marshall observed a burst of dust as the first shell landed two hundred yards beyond the main square. He quickly called in an adjustment, which the gun crews made before answering smartly with another round. This one landed in front of the village, but to the left some one hundred yards. Marshall, who had won the gunnery medal back in the States when he was in Reserve Officers camp, then called back one more time with, "One hundred left; Repeat range."[38] This time the round burst in front of the village precisely where Marshall wanted it to land, and his battery was now ready to support the attack.

Companies F and G moved out toward St. Cloud, just as the 1st Battalion also began its own renewed attack on the village. Captain Murphy's machine guns and mortars coughed into life moments after the first riflemen began edging forward.

Out front, Lieutenant Downing advanced with his platoon across a straight row of low bushes through a nearby vineyard. Downing immediately heard rifle fire halfway across the field, so he ordered his men to dive for the ground before going down himself as bullets hit just to his right. His platoon then began moving forward man by man in short rushes during lulls in the firing, eventually reaching a low stone wall. Downing then dashed forward with some of his men toward a railroad embankment where he came upon a couple of soldiers in a culvert.

"That town is full of troops," one said. "Our company is all shot up. We lost our company commander earlier today. You better watch out. These snipers will get you." Downing asked them what company they were with, and the reply was "Company A, 1st Battalion." Despite the warning, Downing went over the railroad embankment with his men, disregarding the risk that awaited them. By now it was growing darker and the firing from town was becoming more intermittent, with only the occasional "CRUMP" of an exploding French mortar round or grenade. Soon, there was little to no light, and it started raining intermittently. The remainder of Company F had followed Downing's platoon, halting where the cover afforded by the railroad embankment ended. A runner soon came down saying Captain Penick wanted to meet with all of his platoon leaders, so Downing set off, only to learn that the company was going to bed down with the rest of the battalion for the night. His platoon would form a perimeter defense centered on a nearby house located next to a road which crossed over the railroad.[39]

The afternoon's attack crumbled for many reasons. When Captain Colacicco's Cannon Company sent two SP105s forward to assist the assaulting infantry, a French antitank gun knocked one of them out, and the second self-propelled howitzer fired off all of its ammunition before its crew had to head back to Arzew for more shells. As they withdrew, their vehicle was fired upon by nervous American troops who did not immediately recognize it as one of their own. Bullets wounded several of the crew and damaged the recoil mechanism of the howitzer, effectively putting Cannon Company's only remaining SP 105 out of action.[40] "Our own infantry shot it up and ruined the recoil mechanism," Captain Colacicco remembered. "Our guys had not seen, much less operated, a full-track 105 gun before that day. We never got the guns until we boarded ship at Glasgow. The other 105 we lost when its clutch burnt out. It was a fiasco."[41]

The only bright spot in the attack came when the 32nd FA neutralized a French 75mm battery.[42] Despite this success, the combined attack of the 1st and 2nd

Battalions wilted in the face of darkness and heavy fire. Company G was the hardest hit, losing several men killed, including its commanding officer, Captain Bonnett, during the afternoon's fighting.

By evening on their first full day of combat, Major Parker's 1st Battalion was also in shambles. Three officers were dead, including two company commanders. None of his officers had been using radios to transmit orders; directives had to be passed by runners, or even by field grade officers on bicycles, per Major Sternberg's action. As a result, the command and control process was significantly degraded. Before the day was over, Company B lost seven men killed, and another 20 wounded. Company C also met a hail of rifle and machine-gun fire when two of its platoons tried to reenter St. Cloud that afternoon. Two men were killed instantly; another dozen wounded, and two more later died from their wounds. Captain Sam Carter's heavy weapons Company D also lost two men killed, and Carter himself had been pinned down by enemy machine-gun fire and almost killed that afternoon. All told, the battalion suffered 13 killed and 36 wounded on 8 November, their first day in battle.

Even given that they had only received very limited fire support that day, two battalions of the Regiment had nevertheless failed in two attempts to dislodge a French force of roughly equal size in St. Cloud. The defenders knew the ground and were supported by no less than three batteries of 75mm guns and one battery of 155mm pieces, so it was actually fortunate that the afternoon assault did not result in more casualties for the 1st and 2nd Battalions. Major Powers' casualties totaled 12 men, most of them from Company G, which lost five men killed. Captain Murphy's heavy weapons company suffered only one man wounded and another missing. Companies F and E came through the day unscathed.[43]

Lieutenant Colonel Brown's 3rd Battalion, minus a portion of Captain Raymer's Company K that was left behind to secure Arzew, joined with the remainder of the Regiment in the vicinity of St. Cloud that evening. Colonel Greer ordered the battalion to assume positions on the high ground north of the village, designated on Brown's map as Hill 242 (height in meters). The 3rd Battalion's movement subsequently attracted the attention of French artillery observers who began adjusting fire against the newcomers, but as they closed on their objective, cloaked by oncoming darkness, Brown reached the hill and found it to be undefended. Despite the day's setbacks, the Regiment was nevertheless positioned on high ground to the east, south and north of St. Cloud as its first day of combat ended.[44]

In the tiny native schoolhouse in Tourville that was serving as the 1st Infantry Division's command post that night, General Allen and his staff were working by pocket flashlights dimmed with red tissue paper and studying the day's overall movements. Throughout the day, Allen had been constantly pressured by General Fredendall, II Corps commander, to seize Oran as quickly as possible. Glancing at his maps, he could now see that the 16th Infantry Regiment's 1st Battalion was protecting the left flank of the division's advance along the line La Macta-En Nekala. Their 3rd Battalion had met little resistance, and had occupied its intermediate objective, the high ground in the vicinity of Fleurus. St. Cloud, however, remained a problem. The 16th Infantry seemed to be doing well, so General Allen decided to detach a rifle company to assist Colonel Greer in the fight at the village. Additionally, he also ordered a battery of 155mm howitzers from the 5th Field Artillery Battalion to reinforce the fires of the 32nd FA's 105s.[45]

At 2115 hours, General Allen issued Field Order #2 to the commanders of both the 16th and 18th Combat Teams. It stated that the 1st Infantry Division would continue the attack on Oran at 0700 hours the following morning, 9 November, with the 16th Infantry advancing via Fleurus to secure Djebel Khar and the 18th Infantry continuing to attack St. Cloud from its present positions. General Allen assured Colonel Greer that he could count on the additional support of the 1st Ranger Battalion's Company C, K/16th Infantry, and a battery of the 5th FA. Greer, in turn, assembled his battalion commanders and issued corollary orders at 2300 hours, and the directions for these officers were straightforward. (Hereafter, individual companies and battalions from units other than the 18th Infantry Regiment will be identified by the US Army's WWII convention, that is, Company K, 16th Infantry Regiment will be written as "K/16th Infantry," or, if obvious, "K/16th") The 1st Battalion would attack St. Cloud from the east while the 2nd and 3rd Battalions attacked from the south and north respectively. Preparatory fires by the 32nd FA, reinforced by a battery of the 5th FA, would begin at 0645 hours.

As the battalion commanders were planning the attack during the early morning hours, their soldiers were lying on the open ground with little cover, trying to get some sleep. The heat of the day had dissipated into a chilly night, prompting some to start small fires for warmth. A clock in a tower in St. Cloud chimed loudly and incessantly, every quarter hour, further impeding sleep. Later that night, Major York dispatched Lieutenant McGregor on a patrol to find some missing 1st Battalion units, and he departed the company perimeter well before dawn with eight men from his platoon. McGregor became disoriented in the gloomy darkness, however, and he soon discovered that his small group was within 20 yards of the French main line of resistance at the edge of the village. As he later recalled, "The first clue I had that something might be wrong was when I heard some digging. I thought it was our missing battalion men." After shots rang out, he barked out the password challenge "Hi Ho Silver," which was supposed to be returned with "Away!" if the shooters were indeed friendly. But, instead of the hoped-for answer, there were only more shots in response. This time, Lieutenant McGregor yelled in frustration, "Cut it out you damn fools, we're Americans!"[46]

This brought another fusillade, and then a group of French troops jumped out of their defensive positions and forced McGregor and his men to surrender. The French turned out to be very angry, and they subsequently told the American lieutenant in bitter terms that they were attacking a neutral town. McGregor vainly attempted to explain that this was not the case, even saying in broken French *"La France vive encore,"* followed in English by 'We have come to free France!'" But as he later recalled, "It didn't work."⁴⁷ He and his men were now prisoners of the French.

By this time, Lieutenant Downing had awakened to the crow of a rooster in the field in which he was sleeping, and Captain Penick had left to meet the other 2nd Battalion company commanders at Major Powers' command post. It was barely light at the time, and Downing had just finished his first cigarette when Captain Penick returned. The company commander told him to get his men together, that the morning attack had just been confirmed, and that a 15-minute artillery concentration was soon going to awaken St. Cloud.

At 0636 hours, the 32nd FA laid down its ordered barrage, first with smoke, west of the village, followed by three volleys of high explosives. This proved very effective against the defending French artillery, resulting in the neutralization of two batteries of 75mm guns. Although French losses were unknown at the time, observers noted that one battery suffered many casualties amongst its horses.⁴⁸ At 0700 hours, the Regiment renewed its assault against the enemy stronghold, with K/16th attacking in conjunction with Major Powers' 2nd Battalion. Again, however, the stubborn defenders fought off the attackers and only small elements of the assaulting companies got close to St. Cloud before the 1st Battalion joined the fight. Captain Carter was behind a five-foot-high embankment where his mortars were shooting it out with the French artillery that morning, and he remembered, "We were about to fire for more effect, then from a bit forward of us Major York yelled back, 'Captain Carter, cease fire! McGregor is in there where you're shooting.' We then stopped for fear we'd hit our own."⁴⁹

Lieutenant Van Wagoner's platoon from Company C launched an attack that morning, penetrating directly into St Cloud's village square:

> We proceeded down the first street to the north of the main street to get here. By doing this I hoped to avoid the machine-gun fire that had been directed down towards us. At the first crossroad we discovered the town's post office, and we knew the French had this as an observation point. From here they were controlling the main four corners of the town. While we were watching the building and trying to determine the best way to capture it, a round was fired at me and it passed just over my head, through a door, and into the building right behind us.
>
> We eventually moved up to the post office and when I saw someone looking out one of its windows I directed Corporal Yeman to fire a rifle grenade at him. When he did it shattered the glass, so he took aim at another window. This scared the Frenchman, and he and others started to come out of the building with their hands up, like flies. Since others had been controlling the street with machine-gun fire, we lined the prisoners up shoulder to shoulder and used them as a shield so my platoon could move up. This worked for awhile, then they began knocking down their own men to stop us.

I then went around behind the building to look for an open window. I found a small one with a lean-to roof beneath it. I thought I could heave a grenade through it, but I knew if it missed it would roll down the roof and land where I was. I decided to do it anyway, so I pulled the pin and sure enough, it missed the window and hit the wall, then dropped down on the roof. The grenade exploded about the time I hit the ground but I received no wounds and returned back to be with the rest of my men. When I got back more prisoners were coming out of the building, some with their rifles in their hands. This bothered me, so I directed Private Beatty to shoot every one that came out with his weapon in his hands that looked suspicious. I didn't know it, but Corporal Yeman had been down the street trying to subdue a machine gun shooting at us with his rifle grenades by this time. He was hit and then he started back toward us. I yelled to him to get down before he got hit again, but he didn't. Fortunately the machine gun stayed silent, but when he got back to our platoon area we discovered he was shot in the stomach. He applied his own sulfa and then was accompanied to the rear. We were gathering up prisoners when we received word to cease firing and leave town.[50]

Cannon Company also found the second day's fighting in St. Cloud to be difficult. "With three half-tracks, we drove through town and ended up among a French artillery battalion, 75mm guns," Captain Colacicco remembered. "We threw grenades at them, and then I realized we couldn't get out! We had to break out behind them to get back. The connoneers were excited and demoralized, but as we pulled out they fired direct at us. They hit our first half-track, but we got the other two out."[51]

Rather than risk more incidents like this, or being cut off and isolated, the Americans then withdrew to their original lines of departure.

By this time, it was evident that Colonel Greer had grown extremely frustrated by the stubborn resistance being offered by the defending French. He had observed several failed assaults from a forward outpost; reports kept coming back of wounded and killed officers and men; some of his companies were advancing, but their gains had been modest and only measured in yards. As the morning wore on, however, the no-nonsense commander had decided to do something about the situation. Greer returned to his main command post at 1107 hours, and after briefly conferring with Major Sternberg, at 1120 he issued orders for all troops to be withdrawn from the town. After a 30-minute artillery prep, the attack would now be renewed at 1400 hours. The 2nd and 3rd Battalions would assemble and begin moving toward Oran through Arcole, bypassing St. Cloud, with the 1st Battalion following as soon as the stubborn village was finally subdued.

At 1145 hours, however, Colonel Greer received new orders from General Allen which caused a change to his plans. The Regiment was ordered to continue the advance on Oran as quickly as possible, and to link up with the 16th Infantry

Regiment at Djebel Khar. Accordingly, Colonel Greer ordered Lieutenant Colonel Brown to detach Company K to the 1st Battalion to support its new attack on St. Cloud. Greer figured that with five rifle companies and a heavy weapons company at his disposal, Parker's battalion could finally seize the village while the 2nd Battalion prepared for the newly-joined envelopment of Oran in conjunction with Combat Team 16.

At 1350 hours, however, General Allen suddenly arrived at Greer's command post and threw a wrinkle into this plan with orders to cancel the artillery barrage.[52] Apprised earlier of Greer's decision to lay everything at his disposal on the village, Allen was confronted with a dilemma. Although he had initially approved the request, his staff had opposed the artillery concentration on the grounds that getting into Oran was not justified at the cost of the certain loss of life amongst the civilian population in St. Cloud. According to the Division G-3, Lieutenant Colonel Mason, "General Allen did not make a snap judgment. He had the staff G-3 and Chief of Staff principally working feverishly to come up with some alternative solution. He had weighed all the arguments on both sides of the question and had concluded that there would be no artillery concentration on the town."[53]

General Allen's decision had been based on five factors. First, while the size of the military installation in St. Cloud was still not certain, there were nearly 4,000 civilians in the town; second, regardless of Colonel Greer's understandable sentiment, a large artillery attack would make a bad political impression; third, if the town was bombarded and the attack failed, it would be disastrous; fourth, it would take too much ammunition to carry out the attack and; fifth, seizing St. Cloud was unnecessary because Oran—the objective—could be taken without it. To assist Greer in containing St. Cloud, General Allen followed his decision by offering him additional assistance, this time, the attachment of C/1st Ranger Battalion, which was then securing Arzew.

Disappointed, Colonel Greer nevertheless wasted no time in implementing General Allen's directive. Now deprived of artillery support, the planned assault on St. Cloud was simply cancelled and the 1st Battalion was ordered to hold in place. The Ranger company arrived from Arzew at 1600 hours and its commander reported to Major Powers' at his command post. The remaining elements of Captain Raymer's Company K also marched from Arzew to link up with the 1st Battalion, and other orders were changed as well. Lieutenant Colonel Thompson directed A/32nd FA to stay behind to support Major Parker's new containment mission, while his remaining howitzer batteries and the attached battery from the 5th FA began preparing to leapfrog forward to support the 2nd Battalion's advance through Arcole toward Oran. Parker was ordered to contain the French forces until the next morning, at which time it was expected Oran would fall and his 1st Battalion would launch a final attack on St. Cloud without artillery support, instead using his own companies, Raymer's Company K, and the Rangers. At 1640 hours that same afternoon, the 2nd and 3rd Battalions were directed to move out towards Arcole and Djebel Khar in compliance with Greer's new plans.[54]

Both battalions subsequently experienced some difficulty extracting themselves from their attack positions while they were reorienting their line of march toward their new objectives. When Captain Penick ordered his Company F out, the French opened fire and a machine-gun crew had to suppress this so that his platoons could pull out without losing any men. Parts of the company sought shelter and did not budge, however, prompting one sergeant to quickly storm up and down the line yelling for the men to get moving. Now chastened, the soldiers finally charged off into a vineyard, every stride putting them farther from St. Cloud and nearer to the edge of a wooded area where they could find cover from the French small arms fire. As Lieutenant Downing followed them down a path leading to the same area, he came upon a large group of soldiers sitting against the side of a ditch.

The first person he saw was a sergeant; when Downing asked him what company he was with, he was told Company G. When questioned by the lieutenant about where his commanding officer was, the sergeant pointed farther down the ditch. Downing then moved in this direction, passed Major Powers, then Captain Albert W. "Bill" Frink, the 2nd Battalion S-3, where he finally found another officer, Lieutenant George J. Fanning. Fanning greeted him with the news that he had been appointed the new commander of Company G when Captain Bonnett was killed the previous day. Downing then turned back to report to Major Powers, who told him Captain Randall's Company E was already out ahead in another patch of woods. Captain Frink quickly pointed to their exact location, adding that Captain Murphy's Company H was next to them. Now coordinated, the 2nd Battalion was ready to start its advance on Oran, and Lieutenant Colonel Brown also indicated his 3rd Battalion would be ready shortly afterwards. As both battalions began moving out under the cover of imminent darkness, a pelting rain began.

During the night, the advance of the two battalions toward Oran was often subjected to artillery fire and scattered resistance from small groups of enemy riflemen and machine gunners. Under the deepening cover of darkness and windswept rain, the advance nevertheless continued with the motorized elements of the battalions going by way of Fleurus. At 2350 hours, Colonel Greer finally ordered a halt, but the tired men of the Regiment were not destined to get much sleep during the night.

Two hours earlier, a runner had arrived at the 1st Infantry Division schoolhouse command post in Renan with a message from Major General Fredendall, essentially saying that the drive on Oran was going too slowly. Fredendall deemed it imperative that Oran be taken the next day, for in the larger picture that was emerging, General Eisenhower had determined that if Oran and Algiers could be taken quickly, there was a chance to move eastward into Tunisia before the Germans could reinforce the small garrisons they had already established there. While General Allen's plans had already called for attacking Oran in the morning, General Fredendall's message had the effect of driving the scheduled time of the attack forward.

After checking with the 1st Armored Division's Combat Command B (CCB) and division artillery, Allen determined that his infantry units would jump off at 0715, followed by the armored elements of CCB at 0730. Soon after this decision was made, an orderly kneeled down on the dank schoolhouse floor and typed Field Order #3 as General Allen dictated it to him. After reiterating the precise timing of the attacks, Allen closed his hurrying order with, "Nothing in Hell must delay or stop the First Division."

Colonel Greer received General Allen's written order at 0100 hours on 10 November, but deprived of the time necessary to conduct detailed planning, he simply passed on his own very brief order reiterating that the 2nd and 3rd Battalions would continue to move in column formation along the St. Cloud-Oran road toward Oran, and that the attack would now commence at 0715 hours.[55]

As Greer's exhausted officers prepared for the renewed advance, they could not help but ponder their current situation. Most of their men were simply worn down after being awake for nearly two days, and some had even fallen out with permission to catch a little sleep. With cold rain soaking the battlefield, most found sleep fitful, and food had also become a problem by this time. The supply trucks bearing the usual rations had not followed the advance as quickly as the battalions marched forward, so when the men were told of their new orders, most were soaked, shivering, hungry, and generally miserable. Nevertheless, before first light, the companies started making their way along the paved highway toward the town of Arcole, situated just a little over two miles from Oran.

No opposition was encountered until Major Powers' 2nd Battalion reached the outskirts of the village a little over an hour later. The 16th Infantry Regiment had passed through the area unopposed the previous evening, but French troops had filtered back amongst the buildings shortly afterwards. As the leading elements of the battalion drew fire from rifles and machine guns located in Arcole, Colonel Greer ordered Lieutenant Colonel Brown to immediately bypass the area, then he directed Major Powers to conduct a hasty attack against the French village.

The 32nd FA had also displaced forward early that morning, with Batteries B and C occupying firing positions in a defiladed area just west of Arcole. While the 3rd Battalion was able to successfully bypass the French strongpoint as ordered, the extended ranks of these American riflemen soon drew the attention of Fort Canastel's artillery observers, all perched on a high cliff overlooking Oran Harbor. Just five miles west of Arzew, Fort Canastel dominated the area with its 240mm guns, all with 360-degree traverse capability. These guns had pounded the rear positions of the 3rd Battalion companies on the outskirts of Arzew during the previous day. Additionally, at la Briqueterie 2000 yards from Fort Canastel, there was a French antiaircraft battery; its 75mm rapid-fire, high-velocity, flat-trajectory guns were also quite effective against ground targets. Both gun positions were now poised to fire on these troops advancing toward Oran.

As these guns at Fort Canastel began shelling, three forward observers from the 32nd FA requested fires against the French battery. Lieutenant Marshall remembered, "Over the radio they sent back 'Enemy coast defense battery at [grid coordinates] 490-950. Request one round. Will adjust.' While the observers waited, they saw a lone French observer straining forward toward another knoll in front of them, dragging telephone wire and a field phone that kept him connected to his own gun crews. A dozen infantrymen captured him before he had a chance to call back an order."[56]

Meanwhile, Major Powers was starting the attack on Arcole itself by directing the accompanying half-tracks of Cannon Company to lay down a concentration of 75mm fire while his rifle companies were assembling on a sloping hill overlooking the vineyards and truck gardens surrounding the small village. The rifle companies, still under scattered small arms fire from the French, soon began moving down the slope to a wall at the edge of the town. As the 2nd Battalion closed in, the 32nd FA fired two volleys of high-explosive into the village and 200 stunned French soldiers simply surrendered to the advancing Americans.[57] The battalion then quickly reassembled and started hiking through endless vineyards along the main highway. Within an hour the spires that marked Oran began to come into view.

With Arcole reduced, the 32nd FA began to register its guns on Fort Canastel. During the adjustment, the French 240mm guns bracketed Battery B, an ominous accomplishment. Fortunately for the Americans, the crews of the 32nd FA beat them to the punch and damaged all three guns before the giant French weapons could adjust their fire. Two 13mm AA machine guns, two searchlights, and a sound locator were also hit. French casualties at Fort Canastel numbered two killed and 10 wounded during the attack. The French 75mm AA battery at La Briqueterie opened fire on Battery C in reply to the shelling, but after switching their attention to this new threat, the high-explosive shells of the 32nd FA killed another French officer, wounded two enlisted men, and silenced the AA guns.[58]

Then, according to Lieutenant Marshall, "The skirmishing lines of the 18th Infantry, advancing over the rolling bare hills, overran both the Canastel and Briqueterie batteries." By early afternoon, Lieutenant Colonel Brown's 3rd Battalion was in possession of all coastal defenses east of Oran, having taken 500 prisoners in addition to seizing the three 240mm guns at Fort Canastel and every supporting 75mm AA battery.[59] The 2nd Battalion entered Oran just as hostilities were ceasing after some minimal fighting, and the 3rd Battalion joined them shortly afterward. Together, the battalions' soldiers secured key installations, including railyards, warehouses, telephone exchanges, and petroleum storage facilities.

Captain Randall's Company E was the first to push deeply into Oran, followed by Lieutenant Fanning's Company G, which came in on a different street. According to Lieutenant Downing, who followed in right after this with his Company F platoon, "Some civilians came walking toward us and in halting English told Captain Penick that there would be no opposition." Downing also recalled that Penick sensed this might be a trap, so the company deployed into attack formation and headed into an open marketplace. Instead of shots, however, civilians began crowding both sides of the streets, waving and clapping their hands while cheering. As the company reached their assigned square, people continued to mass. Moments later a jeep forced its way down the street with an officer in it, and he started shouting out, "An armistice has been signed. No more fighting!"[60]

Much farther to their east, however, Major Parker's 1st Battalion had started its final attack on St. Cloud at 0815 hours that morning. After heavy fighting, the battalion finally succeeded in seizing three-quarters of the town, but Major Parker lost five men killed and 10 wounded that morning.[61] The Rangers also overran a 75mm battery of the French *68th African Field Artillery* during the mid-morning hours at the cost of one officer and two enlisted men killed. At 1330 hours, a motorcyclist was intercepted bearing instructions from the Commanding General of the Oran Division to the Commandant of French troops at St. Cloud to cease all fire. Moments later, Lieutenant McGregor heard from a French noncommissioned officer that an armistice had been declared, and he and his men who had been captured the day before were freed. The Americans subsequently disarmed 400 French soldiers and gathered up eight heavy machine guns, 20 light machine guns, 15 75mm guns, four 37mm guns, four 60mm mortars, and six half-tracks.[62] With St. Cloud finally in American hands, the first engagement of the Second World War ended for the officers and enlisted men of the 18th Infantry Regiment, and the larger Battle for Oran was over.

Dawn soon came on 11 November 1942. Ironically, it was also Armistice Day, the day marking the end the Great War nearly a quarter of a century earlier. It was, however, the losses in their own ranks that weighed heavily on the officers and men of the 18th Infantry Regiment on this day. "To newly shot over troops with no yardstick of experience by which to measure the severity of an action, these battlefield deaths had a sobering effect," explained the 1st Infantry Division's history.[63]

"We'd indeed experienced death," Cannon Company's Captain Colacicco remembered about the first day of fighting around St. Cloud. "It lowered our morale and made for a tremendous shock, especially as company commanders were killed and two wounded in the leading battalions. But going into combat, knowing death and realizing death is going to happen helps you stabilize yourself; it helps you to function."

"For a while we couldn't function," Colacicco continued. "We were so demoralized! It was like that for everybody when Captain Hill was killed. He was the first officer in the Regiment to die. He was liked, but unfortunately he was killed. Witnessing death is the first shock you have to overcome in war."[64]

THE BATTLE FOR LONGSTOP HILL

DECEMBER 1942

> I know that Colonel Greer would never have approved this "planned disaster" had he really known how the 1st Battalion was going to be used.
> —Captain Sam Carter, Company D

Although the 1st Infantry Division had secured Oran in just three days, the British First Army faced a much more difficult task in its mission to seize the ports of Bizerte and Tunis on the northeastern coast of faraway Tunisia. As part of the Eastern Task Force, the British had driven on Bizerte and immediately run into trouble when their forces encountered German paratroopers stubbornly entrenched in the hills overlooking the main roads leading into the port. These enemy paratroopers were just a small part of a significant Axis force that had recently landed in Tunisia. Hitler had ordered thousands of troops from Germany and Italy deployed to the area to protect the rear of his *Africa Korps,* and to contain the Allied lodgments that had been gained in Algeria and Morocco. In addition to three fresh divisions, the Germans were committing some of their newest weapons to the North African theater of operations as well. New 88mm L/74 antiaircraft guns, *Nebelwerfer* rocket launchers, and menacing Panzer VI "Tiger" tanks joined the thousands of German troops being ferried across the deep turquoise waters of the Mediterranean into the ports of Bizerte and Tunis every day. Hurriedly unloaded by stevedores and cranes, these guns and vehicles were immediately rushed out to bolster German defenses surrounding the port cities. The Italian *1st Infantry Division "Superga,"* initially deployed near Tunis, was quickly shifted to the level and sandy expanses of the desert to the south to protect the Axis left flank from expected Allied envelopments through Sbeitla, Faid, or Sened Station.[1]

On the Allied side, the British First Army consisted of elements of six American divisions and barely a single British division (the 78th) when these forces landed in Algeria and Morocco during Operation TORCH. Although the American divisions (1st, 3rd, 9th, and 34th Infantry, and elements of 1st and 2nd Armored Division) had made it to shore, they were not accompanied by supporting elements needed to sustain the deep drive into Tunisia that the Germans feared. Medical, ordnance, antiaircraft, and Army Air Force service units had necessarily been left behind in England to make more room for assault troops on the scarce transportation assets then available. As a result of this imbalance of forces, the Americans and British were ill-prepared to separately supply the forces needed to mount a creditable assault towards Tunis.[2]

There was also the issue of combat experience. The Americans had not yet fought the Germans in this war, but the British had been fighting Rommel's *Africa Corps* for years. General Eisenhower felt, however, that if the Allies could mass enough strength to attack through the mountains in eastern Algeria toward Bizerte and Tunis before winter, Rommel could conceivably be cut off from supplies and reinforcements. Stranded in the desert, the "Desert Fox's" *Africa Corps* could then be encircled and defeated by the British Eighth Army, which had recently halted the Germans at El Alamein.

As he prepared for his bold attempt to take Tunis and Bizerte, General Eisenhower found himself confronted with a perplexing dilemma. He wanted to send his most experienced troops to the area, but there were very few already battle-hardened British units available to him for this purpose. He could not afford to wait three months for the eventual arrival of the British 46th Division from England, so he had to find other ways to balance the units he did have at his disposal. Otherwise, he faced the grim reality that his scattered armies would be unable to reach Tunisia in time to mount any offensive action before winter impeded offensive operations with heavy rains, miserable cold and knee-deep mud. He did not want to give the Axis time to regroup and use the drier weather to its advantage during the following spring. Then, they would be able to conduct mobile operations when the flatlands were harder. A delay would also afford the Germans time for them to build airfields to help the *Luftwaffe* achieve superiority over the wide-open desert.

Hitler intended from the onset to gain control of the air, and by November of 1942 he had sent two complete *Jagdgeschwader* (fighter wings) of late model Bf-109Gs and a *Gruppe* (a group, usually of about 36 fighters) of the ultra-modern FW-190 fighters into Tunisia. Junkers JU-87 "Stukas" (An abbreviation for "*Sturzkampfflugzeug*," or dive bombers), Junkers JU-88 medium bombers, and several hundred transport planes were also hurriedly transferred from Russia to the desert. Further, Generalfeldmarschall Albert Kesselring, a brilliant *Luftwaffe* officer, had been placed in overall command of this increased German buildup not only in Tunisia, but also throughout the entire Mediterranean.

General Eisenhower had to weigh these factors seriously, and after he deliberated over his scarce options, he selected the less-than-optimal piecemeal build up of the forces he needed to bring a quick end to the war in North Africa.

The port cities of Bizerte and Tunis were separated from each other by coastal flatlands interrupted by lakes and marshes. To their west, hill masses extended from the edge of the cities' harbors into higher ranges. Some of the lush mountain summits were as high as 3,000 feet, and were often shrouded in clouds and mist. Some were also swarming with Germans. Half a dozen rivers meandered west and southwest of the two ports. Given this difficult topography, the Allies would be forced into attacking along the heavily-traveled roads and rail lines that ran beside the rivers and between the mountains. The valley road hubs of Mateur and Djedeida thus became intermediate objectives. Possession of Mateur would open a path to Bizerte, just over 20 miles away, while control of Djedeida would leave a less than 15-mile march to Tunis.

Another 15 miles farther west of Mateur, through steep *wadis* and across cactus-covered rises where Arab plaster-and-thatch huts dotted the hills, the town of Medjez-el-Bab lay in ruins. Once majestic, but now splintered rows of poplar trees lined the main road into the town. There, the village church, the sole place of worship for its Arab Christian and French citizens, was heaped in rubble near the ruins of the once-thriving railway station and a nearby inn. After what had been weeks of fierce fighting to seize the town from German forces, British forces now controlled Medjez, still a key hub of the area's rail and road network. Observation posts, listening posts, and patrols monitored activity to the north and east of the town, occasionally spotting Germans atop a two-mile ridge crowned with seven smaller knobs. The Germans had captured this important, commanding height on 12 December. Local inhabitants knew this hill mass, located seven miles to the northeast of Medjez el Bab, as Djebel el Ahmera. To the British occupation forces in Medjez, however, it had been dubbed "Longstop Hill," for their battles to take the rocky massif had indeed been a "long stop" for them. An entire infantry brigade of the British 78th Division had been shattered during several weeks of see-saw fighting between Medjez el Bab, Longstop Hill, and Tebourba to the northeast.

Although the depleted Allied forces outside Tunis had been augmented by the remainder of the British 6th Armoured Division and a Guards brigade during this period, the British First Army now needed additional infantry to clear the way for an armored thrust on Tunis. To remedy this, Eisenhower agreed in early December to detach a regimental combat team of the 1st Infantry Division to the British until two brigades of their own 46th Infantry Division arrived in February 1943. Responding to General Eisenhower's subsequent order, General Allen had no choice but to select the 18th Infantry Regiment to reinforce the British. While Allen had done this reluctantly and under protest because he did not want his division to be broken up, choosing Colonel Greer's forces was his only option as he had already dispatched elements of the 16th and 26th Infantry Regiments to assist the French XIX Corps. The 18th Regimental Combat Team actually represented the only complete fighting unit remaining within the 1st Infantry Division at the time.

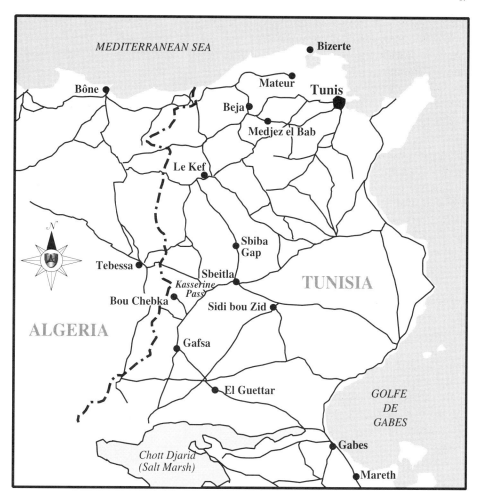

After the fighting ceased in Oran, duty for the men of the 18th Infantry was very uneventful for several weeks. The Central Task Force commander, Major General Fredendall, placed units on alert for movement to the east, but nothing seemed to come of it right away. Some soldiers even remarked that the war had a garrison feeling at the time. There had been seemingly endless outpost duties for weeks, mostly uneventful patrolling at night that never amounted to much. When Thanksgiving Day came, there was a festive dinner and local French citizens had been invited to dine at company tables in an attempt to convince them of the Americans' friendship and intentions to stay the course in North Africa. Predictably, with too much time on their hands and not enough immediate war to fill it, inevitable rumors started spreading from company to company about the

18th's future. Some waxed eloquent about the role its combat veterans could serve back in the States: recruiting duty, with requirements to regale potential recruits with war stories, was one of the scuttlebutt possibilities. Another cast the Regiment's veterans as stateside trainers of newly-formed units, taking advantage of their recent experience to teach the tactics and logistics of amphibious landing operations. The rumors eventually became so bad that General Allen issued a memo telling his men that Oran had just been the beginning of a long series of combat operations, and that orders would soon come down outlining future operations. He then closed with his trademark expression, "Nothing in Hell must delay or stop the First Division."

When British composite ration packs in wooden boxes started arriving shortly after this, it was the first omen 18th Infantry soldiers had that their commanding general was indeed preparing them for something big. This time the rumors were far more accurate. Scuttlebutt reached everywhere that the Division was going to be split up into smaller units to fight beside the French and British, and these rumors began to come true as several of the Division's field artillery battalions left for the Tunisian battlefront in late November. At the time, many of the Regiment's soldiers did not knew where Tunisia was, so officers versed in geography started explaining that this was where the British were being treated roughly by the Italians and Germans, where medium tanks of their own 1st Armored Division were being outgunned, and where *Luftwaffe* dive-bombers were inflicting terrible damage on the American artillery units that had already left to support the British First Army's faltering operations.

By this time Colonel Greer had made changes in command of the 1st and 2nd Battalions. Lieutenant Colonel George Fricke, a West Point graduate and a friend of General Allen's, took command of the 1st Battalion, where Major York remained as his Executive Officer. Majors Powers and Chase were reassigned within the Regiment after Greer made the decision to place his own S-3, Major Sternberg, in command of the 2nd Battalion. Within the 1st Battalion, Major York recommended to Colonel Fricke that Captain Yarock be formally confirmed in command of Company A, and that Captain Archibald C. Cameron assume command of Company B. Captain Herbert A. Scott-Smith, Jr. took command of Company C, and Captain Froncillo went to the battalion staff after he recovered from the wounds he suffered outside of St. Cloud.

As soon as the order arrived to detach the Regiment to the British 78th Division, Colonel Greer ordered his battalion commanders to send runners to their captains so they could tell their men to load up and get ready to move out. They had just three hours to start the move and, other than their weapons, rolls and light packs were the only things the enlisted men could take with them. It was now 15 December, the latest edition of *Stars and Stripes* had said somewhat tongue in cheek that there were just ten shopping days left until Christmas, and cold winter rains had already muddied the landscape.

The Battle for Longstop Hill

The men in Company F had just sat down to have dinner when the order to move out reached them. Both enlisted men and officers hurriedly organized their bedrolls while a noncom from each platoon rushed into the nearby village of Les Trembles to round up any soldiers lingering in town. To hasten the move because it had just started to rain lightly, Captain Penick assigned additional men to KP duty to help the kitchen force close down and load up. A number of deuce-and-a-halves soon roared up and the men jumped aboard and crammed together on the wet truckbeds. Then, in typical Army fashion, they waited. At about the same time the rain became heavier, and as fate would have it, most of the trucks' beds lacked their canvas covers. The company finally started out the next morning for their rendezvous point at l'Arba, where they joined up with the other units of the Regiment that had assembled in a similarly-rushed fashion to get ready for the long motor march eastward.

By 18 December, after crossing a wild spur of the Atlas Mountains where thousand-foot drops plunged off the edge of the narrow roadways, most of the Regiment's truck convoys had made it to the broad plain of Teboursouk. This oasis was usually lush green with fields of crimson poppies, but now it was barren with not much more visible than a cluster of thatch huts surrounding a large administration building. The Regiment bivouacked in a nearby, concealed olive grove to avoid being the target of frequent air strikes in the area. On 21 December, Colonel Greer held a staff conference and reviewed what the 18th Infantry Regiment's role would be in seizing Longstop Hill.[3]

During the briefing, Colonel Greer revealed that Longstop Hill (Djebel el Ahmera) actually had five small knobs, numbered, from west to east. Just about every knob blocked the view of the next until the top of each one was reached. The hill then fell sharply after the easternmost knob, sloping down to a road where there was a railway station called Halte d' el Heri, the first stop out of Medjez.[4] This area was known to contain pockets of enemy soldiers. Farther east, the landscape fell off into a deep gully that gradually rose up to a second peak called Djebel el Rhara, about a kilometer away.

The details of the plan to take these hills seemed reasonable. The 2nd Battalion, The Coldstream Guards, were to attack the easternmost knob at nightfall on 22 December. Colonel Fricke's 1st Battalion would then advance under the cover of darkness and relieve the Coldstreamers "in place" by midnight that same night. Captain Yarock's Company A would do this with Companies B, C, and D in support. To facilitate this maneuver, the 5th Battalion, The Northamptonshire Regiment, was scheduled to mine the Tebourba Gap between the high ground and a lower level on the hill.

The 18th RCT's 2nd and 3rd Battalions were assigned to jump off on Christmas Eve and advance further to the east, bypassing the 1st Battalion as it occupied Longstop Hill. Their mission was to seize el Guessa to the southeast of Longstop, securing the high ground necessary to screen an advance by tanks of the

British 6th Armoured Division. The British armor would then pass between Djebel el Ahmera and Djebel el Guessa before securing Tebourba and pushing farther east. Aided by the British 1st Guards Brigade and 1st Parachute Brigade, the tanks would then continue the thrust toward Tunis, defeating units of the German XC Corps still seeking to bar their entry into the critical Tunisian port city.[5]

With this plan in place, Colonel Greer's Headquarters Company pulled up stakes late on 21 December and set out under pale moonlight that was barely glowing through thickening clouds. A storm was on the way. His party traveled through blacked-out villages until morning, eventually crossing a bridge built by British sappers; it had been partially submerged as camouflage to protect it from *Luftwaffe* aircraft. By afternoon, Colonel Greer and his men arrived near a farm on the edge of the ruined town of Medjez-el-Bab. The engineers who built the bridge were occupying the farmhouse on the property, so Colonel Greer claimed a nearby barn as his new command post for the Battle for Longstop Hill.

In nearby company bivouacs, officers and their men watched across the broad valley at Longstop Hill, fearing many of them might soon face death. Lieutenant Franklyn A. Johnson, newly arrived from the States and now assigned to Cannon Company, was one of these soldiers. He was camped with his men in a position near Medjez and watched guns already firing on both sides of the Medjerda Valley. The surrounding hillsides were illuminated by the exploding shells, and the sounds of the detonations echoed from one side of the valley to the other. The night hung heavy with the anticipation of battle, so he decided to deal with some of his anxiety by visiting his good friend, Lieutenant Paul Carnes, in Company B. Carnes was planning on going into the ministry as soon as the war was over, so Johnson wanted his comfort.

Remembering the evening later, Johnson wrote, "Paul discussed his philosophy about life, but he said he felt pessimistic and foreboding about the coming battle, our first directly against Germans."

"I can't explain it," Carnes had said, "But I have a hunch I won't pull through what's up ahead. I prayed to get here, but now I'm praying for all of us in the coming battle." Johnson left soon afterwards, knowing Carnes had said what was on everybody's mind that night, and he also prayed.[6]

By the time the 18th Infantry Regiment reached Medjez to stage for the main attack on Longstop Hill, the British 78th Division had already been heavily reinforced for the attack toward Tunis. It now controlled two battalions of infantry in the 1st Guards Brigade, three others in the 1st Parachute Brigade and another three in the 11th Brigade. Including the 18th Infantry Regiment, this gave the British 78th Division a total of ten infantry battalions to mount their assault. This meant that nearly 10,000 soldiers were in the leading echelon of the attack, to include those selected for the Longstop Hill battle.

Additionally, there were five battalions of French troops available to assist the British, but they were too poorly armed to be included in this main effort against the Germans. According to British intelligence at the time, there were less than two German companies defending Longstop Hill, with an approximate strength of 300 men. This undoubtedly explained why the Coldstream Guards were so confident of victory when they started their main attack on the night of 22 December.

As so often happens, the intelligence reports proved to be incorrect. Captured documents later showed that when the Coldstreamers first attacked the hill, German troops in place consisted of the reinforced *Combat Engineer Battalion 334* and an infantry company of *Grenadier Regiment 754*, both from the German *334th Infantry Division*.[7] These German troops possessed no fewer than 18 machine guns to assist in their defense. Unbeknownst to the British planners, the defenders could be quickly reinforced by *Combat Group Lang*, consisting of three companies from *1st Battalion, Panzer-Grenadier Regiment 69;* an armored reconnaissance detachment of the *10th Panzer Division;* elements of *Heavy Tank Battalion 501*, a Tiger battalion; a detachment of Semovente self-propelled 75mm guns from the *Superga Division*'s *551st Assault Gun Battalion;* and up to four hastily-thrown-together German "*Marsch Einheiten*" (replacement units) consisting of three infantry and one heavy weapons companies.[8]

British intelligence had significantly underestimated the initial strength and reinforcement potential of the defenders atop Longstop Hill, so the 78th Division plan risked failure from the start. A single battalion of the Coldstream Guards would not be of sufficient strength to overwhelm the defenders within the few short hours allowed in the plan. The British plan was further complicated by the poor timing of the relief of the Coldstream Guards by the 1st Battalion, 18th Infantry Regiment when they did take the hill. The relief in place was slated to be complete just before daylight, which was precisely the time that the Germans were most likely to counterattack, per their tactical doctrine. The Americans would be alone and unsupported on the hill, unfamiliar with the terrain, and unable to dig in before a counterattack materialized.

One other equally important, but unavoidable, issue would also have a significantly negative impact on the pending engagement. As Captain Yarock later pointed out, "You must remember the British were using our infantry battalions as if they were British battalions. A British battalion is self-supporting in the field, but in the American setup infantry battalions are supported by regimental command decisions which provide reinforcement, ammo, and food."[9] This meant that the fundamental execution of battle was much different in practice for British officers than it was for American commanders, and neither army had spent any time at all trying to figure this out, never mind practicing it together, before assaulting Longstop Hill.

There was another ominous factor as well. On 21 December, German artillery observers atop Longstop Hill spotted substantial movements into and around Medjez-el-Bab. Sometime around noon the next day, five hours before the British attack was to begin, German aerial reconnaissance patrols confirmed that there was indeed massed infantry in the area. They also identified a large party of officers and officials around the village, a usual precursor to an impending attack. Thus the element of surprise had been taken away, another inauspicious beginning to any looming battle.

Using pneumatic jackhammers to supplement their usual picks and spades, the Germans put finishing touches on elaborate trench systems that they had constructed on all of the reverse slopes of Longstop Hill. This trench system would afford cover from preparatory fires, but when it halted just prior to the Allied infantry assault, the defenders planned to scurry through connecting trenches on the sides of each hill to cover their flanks, then move forward to envelop their attackers. It was a tactic well known to World War I veterans, and it had not been lost on their successors of 25 years later. Once the attacking Guards or companies of the 1st Battalion came closer to them, German doctrine called for rapid closure, then violent counterattack.

All this was unknown to the Allies before their attack on 22 December as the 2nd Battalion, The Coldstream Guards spent their time making final preparations for battle. Grenades and ammunition were being checked, weapons were cleaned, and some of the British soldiers even managed to get some uneasy sleep. After a hot meal just before dark, the Coldstreamers set out along a railway line for Longstop Hill under a faint and intermittently obscured moon. Before long, they were advancing through thick heather and rosemary nearer to their line of departure at the foot of the hill. Under an umbrella of artillery fire, the assault on Longstop Hill began. A later history described their greeting by the Germans this way:

> Major Chichester came up as planned to advance towards the summit. As the Guardsmen began to struggle up between thick bushes, a succession of flares suddenly lit up the whole landscape and the enemy opened fire. Slow, golden sprays of tracer ammunition soared out from the hillside above, and then came the distinctive rattle of German machine guns. As the Guardsmen drew nearer to the enemy positions, they were met with showers of grenades. Major Chichester was mortally wounded and Company Sergeant Major Callaghan was killed, but after an eternity of climbing the company reached the crest of the hill and took cover amongst the rocks. There the companies did their best to dig with their entrenchment tools in the stony ground, and officers hurriedly organized their defenses while enemy mortar-bombs burst all around.[10]

Sergeant Derek Jackson was with the Coldstream Guards that morning:

> White tapes guided us up the rocky slope onto the hill which was slippery with the rain. Soon the firing became much closer, and I could hear the sound of our artillery exploding over our heads. Looking to both sides of our advance, I could see hundreds of our Brigade going forward, bayonets fixed, with the officers leading, followed by other sections in a huge

The Battle for Longstop Hill

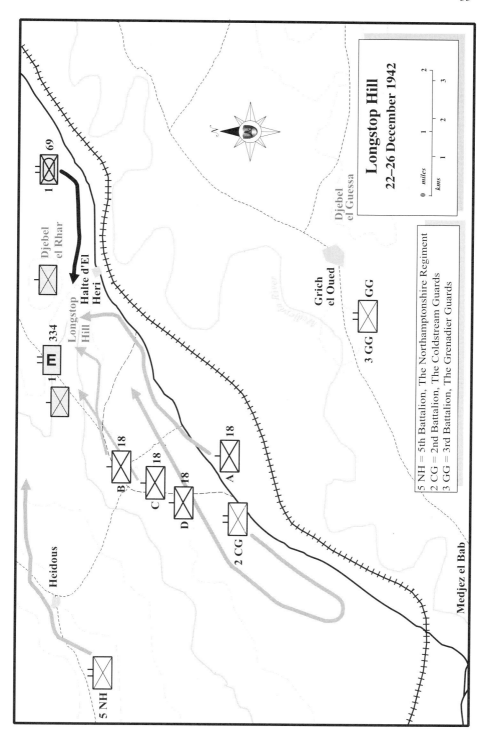

extended line. Behind us came the reserve companies in exactly the same order over ground that was hard and slippery from the rain.

Then we were fired on with rifles and machine guns. The mortaring had stopped but the Germans were now catching us in their well-aimed crossfire. I saw an officer signal me to deploy my section more to the right, so we moved away to a ridge of stones and for a time we were sheltered from the machine-gun fire. But soon, over we went with yells and shouts towards the enemy positions.

When we did I could see grey-clad figures rising from behind rocks and trenches, their arms raised as hand grenades were thrown at us. By now we were about fifty strong on this part of the line facing our enemy. In a few seconds we were amongst the Germans and suddenly it was every man for himself. One cannot describe the moments of hand-to-hand fighting, but the only thing going round in my mind was it was going to be either him or me, and I would sooner it be him, the German. I soon jumped down into a rocky trench and landed on top of a dead enemy soldier who broke my fall. Another man in my section jumped down with me and we took aim on any of the Germans we could see who were not engaged in a fight.

Suddenly, a hand grenade came whistling through the air and landed just in front of our trench, and a Guardsman with me was not quick enough to duck it. He caught a piece of grenade in his throat then dropped to the floor of the trench unconscious. I could do no more so I leaped out of the trench and joined a group of our troops who were consolidating a German position that had been taken. Here I found the rest of my section, or what was left of them.[11]

At the start of the Coldstreamers' assault, The 5th Northhamptons (the unit that Colonel Greer was expecting to lay a minefield) went wide in its own flanking movement toward the high ground to the northeast of Longstop Hill as planned. They quickly got lost, however, and never entered the battle. On the far side of the hill by the railway station, a ten-minute concentration of artillery fire had enabled a British unit to quickly seize the area. Unknown to Colonel Greer, or even the British command, this bombardment blocked the back of Longstop Hill for a few fleeting hours and kept enemy reserves from climbing the hill to reinforce the defenders. Without knowledge of this development, the Allies never exploited its tactical value.

As fate would have it, when British reserves moved up later to reinforce this area after the shelling, they ran into a minefield on the railroad track leading to the station, and two entire sections (squads) were lost. The enemy had wisely used the time to prepare for a counterattack, and when the British finally made it to the area, the Germans attacked with bayonets fixed, lunging into hand-to-hand combat. The area quickly fell back into enemy control, and the fact that neither the British commander nor Colonel Greer knew of this would later prove fatal.

At the moment, though, the Coldstream Guards had control of the first knob on Longstop Hill, primarily because the artillery preparation before their advance had disheartened the Germans. Despite their own preparation, they had exhausted their available ammunition repulsing their attackers, and then fought on as best they could before withdrawing. In a later summation of this action, Oberstleutnant Rudolf Lang, commander of the *1st Battalion, Panzer-Grenadier Regiment 69*, wrote of these attacks:

> Following a brief expenditure of ammunition reminding us of similar cases during the First World War, the attack started on 22 December. In that coverless, hilly terrain, which produces only some miserable and thorny bushes and afforded no chance whatsoever of digging in, the brave German soldier was mercilessly exposed to the hail of shells and to fragmentation of rock. The fireworks claimed their victims.[12]

With the Coldstream Guards in place and the time growing nearer for them to be relieved by the Americans, the British were by now cocksure that they were winning the Battle for Longstop Hill. As time would tell, however, it was not entirely clear who actually controlled the first knob on the hill mass as the 1st Battalion of the 18th Infantry moved into place to relieve the Guards.

On the morning of 22 December, Captain Yarock was briefed that just a single reinforced German company occupied the hill, and it was likely to be attrited by the British attack. Yarock's orders were to get up on the hill as quickly as he could, relieve the British in place, prepare a defensive position, then hold the hill at all costs against an expected German counterattack.

As he prepared to jump off and go up the hill, Captain Yarock counted on the security that was to be provided by the minefield that was to have been laid. Lieutenant Colonel Fricke had told Captain Yarock that Longstop Hill was definitively a British show, that they would eventually take the entire range of knobs that defined the hill mass, and that he was not to start his advance until a planned artillery preparation ahead of his move up the hill had completely ceased. It was also Yarock's understanding that British guides would lead his company into position only when their commanding officer reported that the fighting had stopped on the hill. His Company A would then follow the guides into place and complete its mission of affecting the Coldstreamers' relief.

In the early afternoon, Captain Yarock moved his company to a forward assembly area just outside of Medjez, where he used the time to outline the attack plan to his men. At 1600 hours, he and the battalion's other company commanders were called back to meet again with Lieutenant Colonel Fricke. The original orders were repeated and some administrative problems were resolved. At that time, Fricke assigned an antitank platoon to Company A to afford additional protection for Yarock's flank if German tanks appeared as he went up the first slope on Longstop Hill at 2100, three hours before midnight as still planned.[13]

When Company A crossed the line of departure towards Longstop Hill several hours later, one of Yarock's trucks sustained a flat tire. He used the delay to go back to the 1st Battalion command post to pick up the British guide that would lead him up the hill. After obtaining his guide, the Company A commander then attempted to get to know this man on their return to the company. A corporal in the intelligence section of the Coldstream Guards, the guide told him that holding the hill would likely be an easy job, particularly in light of the casualties that were inflicted on the Germans during the attack; he later added that the artillery barrage scheduled at 2300 hours would also help efforts greatly.

This was Captain Yarock's first omen that things might be going wrong. He had been told that the artillery preparation would come at 2100 hours. The guide was now telling him it would be two hours later when his company would already be on the hill, presumably under "friendly" fire. He challenged the guide on this new revelation, but the guide adamantly insisted that his information was correct.

A few minutes later, Lieutenant Colonel Fricke came up in his jeep to join the forward party and meet with Captain Yarock. Fricke greeted him with the news that the barrage had indeed been rescheduled to 2300 and that Company A's advance was now pushed back to 2400 hours. Right after this, Yarock continued to move his company forward into its attack position and Fricke remained with him. They soon came upon a small British column that Captain Yarock speculated was part of the forward observation detachment for the Guardsmen he would be relieving. His hunch was confirmed when he heard a radio in their truck operating constantly, despite the fact that he had standing orders to maintain strict radio silence. Apparently, the reason they were on the radio was to control the firing of a battery of British 25-pounders. The cover for Company A's advance up the hill had commenced, but when one of their guns fired short, with its projectile landing in the immediate area, Yarock knew something had already gone wrong.

Unlike the British, Captain Yarock had no way to contact his own artillery because the 32nd FA had not yet displaced forward. Worse, by now the British forward observers were no longer close enough for him to tell them to remedy the firing error of their errant gun. He immediately dispersed his company safely to the right side of the road in some scrub brush, away from the shooting. Hearing the roaring of an engine, he then turned to watch in amazement as Lieutenant Colonel Fricke headed off toward the rear in his jeep, shouting as he departed, "Don't let your men run!"[14]

About ten minutes later, sporadic German firing answered the barrage that was being thrown at their forces atop Longstop Hill, and Captain Yarock suddenly found that his company was now the primary target of a well-placed enemy mortar attack. This time, he sent his men past the roadside scrub brush deeper into a nearby field to get away from the harassing rain of enemy fire. After waiting out the first rounds, he ordered his men to follow him forward, staying very close. His guide then led them through pitch-black darkness and pouring rain, until they reached the point where a second guide was to meet them. Again, they waited. The waiting seemed endless, but Captain Yarock's outposts soon made contact with the new guide, who showed up shortly afterward with a second man to help him out.

Soon afterwards, a runner arrived from the rear with an order from Lieutenant Colonel Fricke telling Yarock to go onto the hill at once, and not to wait for any direction from any guides whatsoever. Before he could organize his move, German mortar rounds again began landing in the area, so he stayed where he was until it ceased. Meantime, yet another two guides appeared out of the darkness. These two told Captain Yarock that they knew nothing about where the first two had come from, or who they were, but that they were there to take his company to another position on the hill.

By this time, the mortar barrage was becoming heavier, and was mixed with artillery fire, as well. Captain Yarock was confronted with a tough decision. He had two sets of guides ready to take him up to two presumably different positions on the hill, but he could not know which would take his company to the right place. Just as Yarock was getting ready to give the order to move out with one set of guides, yet another one appeared out of the gloom, this one carrying an air of importance, claiming to be from the British command post. He told Captain Yarock to follow him immediately, not up the hill at all, but to the rear where the British battalion commander was waiting for him.

By now, what patience Captain Yarock had left was giving way to aggravation. He had a mission and he simply wanted to accomplish it. It was approaching 2400 and he was supposed to have started up Longstop Hill an hour ago. Artillery was still pounding away. His commanding officer wanted him forward; the British CO wanted him to the rear.

As fate would have it, his own battalion intelligence officer, Lieutenant John C. Potkay, arrived on the scene. Captain Yarock quickly explained his conflicting orders, but Potkay revealed that he hadn't seen Lieutenant Colonel Fricke or Major York all evening long and didn't know what to tell him. With that, Captain Yarock ordered his company to stay in place, whereupon he accompanied the British runner, with Lieutenant Potkay in tow, through the pouring rain to the British command post to straighten things out. They indeed found the British battalion commander, but it turned out that he had been unable to contact Lieutenant Colonel Fricke, and he simply wanted to afford Yarock the courtesy of giving the order to move up himself. Yarock left even more frustrated, but more determined than ever to carry out his mission and go up the hill.

Captain Yarock was not the kind of leader who would commit his men until he had a solid sense of just what was happening, orders or no orders. In his judgment, things were so fouled up that he needed to take the initiative. When he reached the company, he went up the hill with one of the guides to personally reconnoiter the area ahead. Despite being in the midst of a mortar barrage, Yarock determined that he was close to the command post of the British rifle company he was to relieve and he ordered the guide to take him there. Arriving minutes later, the Coldstream Guards company commander hurriedly explained that he had already captured the hill and simply wanted to be off, right then. Captain Yarock finally understood the tactical situation, and he was certain that the Germans were reorganizing for a counterattack. He was ready to move up his company, but would not do so under a German mortar barrage, and he so informed the British officer. This officer then confessed that he had been unable to get his own battalion commander on the radio for any word affecting the timing of his relief, and that he was acting on his own in requesting that he be relieved immediately. Yarock suddenly realized that this could add to the already existing confusion, but he still was not about to move his men up until the mortar fire had ceased. Yielding to diplomacy, he then suggested to the British officer that the best way for them to straighten things out would be for both of them to go down the hill together and find someone who could. The British company commander agreed, and they departed Longstop Hill together.

When they arrived at the British Command Post, Captain Yarock was surprised to find Lieutenant Colonel Fricke and the British battalion commander heatedly discussing the situation. Apparently, the argument was over the size of the relieving force, with the British commander saying loudly that he was expecting a larger American relief element. The British commander quickly tired of the discussion, and announced in a firm tone that he was going to give his troops the order to pull out. According to Captain Yarock, he barked in frustration, "After that, you Americans can do anything you please, but know that one of your flanks will be open, because I've lost an entire company on the right side of the hill." With that, he turned to his company commander and gave him the order to withdraw.[15]

It was now well past 0300 hours on 23 December, three hours after Company A was scheduled to be on Longstop Hill. The situation remained confused, but the orders were now clear. Lieutenant Colonel Fricke expanded on the attack plan. Captain Yarock would immediately relieve the British company, advancing eastward on the hill after occupying the first knob, then he would seize the second, then the third, and fourth knob, only leaving certain squads behind in each position. Captain Yarock later reported that he questioned the soundness of committing the whole company at once, but that Fricke stood by his order, adding that he would immediately send Captain Cameron's Company B up the hill to seize the three knobs beyond Yarock's objectives. Further, Fricke pointed out that he had Captain Scott-Smith's Company C in reserve, just in case Captain Yarock's Company A or Captain Cameron's Company B ran into any trouble. As Fricke departed, Yarock reminded him that his right flank would be wide open, as the British commander had warned. He also again protested about committing his entire company under the circumstances, but Lieutenant Colonel Fricke said firmly, "I just left Archie [Cameron] and he's going up right beside you." Yarock recalled that "I argued with him [Fricke] again by asking that we wait until daylight, but he wouldn't listen and finally gave me a direct order to go up the hill."[16]

It was shortly after 0400 hours when Captain Yarock and Company A moved out into the dark, rainy night. Lieutenant Ingwald P. Taft, the 1st Platoon leader, advanced directly toward the first knob where he had been ordered to leave a squad and continue the advance toward the second knob. The 2nd Platoon headed for knob three, with one squad diverting to knob four, expecting to make contact with Company B, advancing on the left. No contact with enemy soldiers was reported, which made Captain Yarock uneasy, for his instinct told him it should not have been that simple.

The accuracy of his intuition was confirmed when sporadic small arms fire suddenly began on his right flank, just as he had feared, and just where the British battalion commander said there would likely be a pocket of Germans. To Yarock's utter amazement, however, it was not Germans, but over 100 British soldiers retreating towards him, probably the company that the British commander reported to have been "lost." Wisely suspecting that the Germans would quickly follow, Captain Yarock sent a runner back to find Lieutenant Colonel Fricke and report the situation. He expected this report would cause Captain Scott-Smith's Company C to be dispatched immediately up the hill to cover his open right flank.

A report arrived from Lieutenant Taft shortly afterwards indicating that his platoon had found no enemy troops on the back slope of the first knob, and that he was proceeding toward knob two as ordered. With Germans obviously on his right, Yarock worried that he had not heard anything from his 3rd Platoon, so he immediately sent a runner to ascertain their situation. The runner soon returned and reported that the 3rd Platoon was on knob five, but they knew they were on the wrong knob, and were moving back to their correct objective. The runner also reported that scouts had been to knob six, but that they had not made contact with Company B, leading Captain Yarock to conclude that Captain Cameron's men were not yet on their objective and that his left flank also remained wide open and extremely vulnerable to enemy attack.

Looking past his runner, Captain Yarock then observed a machine gun resting in some solid rocks, not more than a hundred feet to his right. Fortunately, however, these men were wearing British uniforms and helmets. Suspecting that they were simply stragglers who were waiting until Company A relieved them, he then ordered Lieutenant Robert T. Poynter up to within fifteen yards of the position to verify their identity. Poynter quickly returned and confirmed that they were indeed British, and he then moved forward to locate suitable positions to emplace Company A's light machine guns to cover the company's advance. Suddenly, to his left, Captain Yarock spotted another ominous machine-gun emplacement with other men around it. At first they appeared to be moving around nonchalantly, but then they took quick aim at the American officer, and Yarock was trapped. Even though some grenade explosions forced his would-be attackers to seek cover, this respite was too brief. More soldiers, obviously Germans, began to appear in growing numbers and they moved ever closer. Captain Yarock sounded an alert by radio and ordered his men to take cover, but there was no vegetation of any kind and little protection to be found in the slippery rockbed. At that point, all Yarock could do was hope the Germans kept shooting over them until one of his rifle platoons could come to his assistance and close with the enemy from their flank or rear. His SCR-536 radios did not appear to be working at all, however. Only silence greeted his calls for help, and he now knew that he and his men were completely on their own.

The Germans were now closing ranks rapidly, so one of his lieutenants gallantly volunteered to try to make contact with battalion one last time and started out under fire with a runner. Captain Yarock now had about eight men with him, and they were all pinned down. Standing would have meant instant death. Yarock was trying to sort through his options when, to his immediate right, several Germans jumped out of a cave and quickly took aim at him and his men with their machine guns. As he later said, "That was it. They had a drop on us. They gave me the choice of surrendering immediately, or being killed instantly along with my men."

Faced with the most difficult decision a rifle company commander could ever make, Captain Yarock then recalled, "I could see the open country to the rear of the hill, and could only see two tanks, both standing still and not moving at all. I could see the road going into Medjez through the rain and haze, but I couldn't see any reinforcements coming up. I figured that we couldn't have lasted any longer in the best of circumstances, that we hadn't accomplished our mission, but that we couldn't accomplish it by all being killed, so I gave the word to surrender."[17]

Captain Yarock and his men were immediately taken prisoner and moved to the rear at gunpoint, where they were assembled with other men from the company, all with similar stories to tell. The Germans had popped up all around them. From their well-prepared positions, even tunnels where they couldn't be seen at first, the Germans split Company A into small groups, capturing or killing everyone. As it turned out, Yarock was one of the last to be taken. Subsequent after-action reports showed that the company lost its captain, four lieutenants, two staff sergeants, 12 sergeants, 14 corporals, 45 privates first class, and 53 privates during their Longstop Hill debacle. All were at first listed as missing in action, but their statuses were later changed to killed in action or prisoners of war. One sergeant, five privates first class and five privates were wounded in action. Company A lost 142 of its men, about three quarters of its strength.[18]

Private First Class Donald Parker, a Company A clerk, was one of the lucky ones who survived death or captivity that dark and rainy night. He was ready to go with the rest of the company when they started up the hill, but at the last minute Captain Yarock told him to stay at the command post at the foot of the hill in case he had to come up with a message. As Parker remembered, "Yes, I was thankful, but I was concerned about the company. We could hear heavy fighting. As I recall, I even slept some that night. But, few of my closest friends came back. It was a terrible feeling. Someone later suggested that we open Christmas gifts that had come up, but I couldn't even do that. Yet we had little time for grieving. The war went on."[19]

Coldstream Guards Sergeant Derek Jackson came off Longstop Hill when it was handed over to Captain Yarock's Company A, but he remembered a very different mood amongst his troops at the time. "We marched away from the hills towards the Medjez-Tebourba road, whistling 'Pack Up Your Troubles' and other old-time songs, all of us full of the fruits of a victory," he recalled. "We proceeded on our way munching bully and biscuits. The Regiment was in high spirits, and although we had suffered severe casualties we had won a victory, the taking of the legendary Longstop Hill."

Lieutenant Colonel Stewart-Brown, commanding officer of the 2nd Battalion, The Coldstream Guards on Longstop Hill that night, later admitted in his summary of operations that he had estimated the German strength on the hill at "one company, with four to eight medium machine-gun units attached," adding, "this was an underestimate, as was proved later." Although diffident about the outcome of the battle for the Americans, he nevertheless took into consideration factors such as the heavy rain and the differences in command style when explaining the difficulties that affected Company A's relief of his Guards that morning. "It would have been a difficult task to carry on a relief under these conditions, even with another battalion of our own brigade," he wrote in reference to the confusion, concluding, "but with complete strangers of a different nationality, it was near impossible."[20]

In this report, written just days after the battle ended, Stewart-Brown also admitted that when he was asked about the timing of the relief by his own company commander, he told him, "Do it when the situation was clear, and the Americans were satisfied." This was far from what really happened on Longstop Hill that morning. Stewart-Brown also seemed unwilling to take any blame for not holding the hill, for he closed his report with, "There has been much controversy about what happened to the Americans on the hill, and some hard words on both sides. The plain facts are that they did not retain possession of the key points, and did not make a major effort to get them back."

Company D's Captain Carter, however, vigorously defended the disaster that befell his 1st Battalion at Longstop Hill during this first day of battle, declaring the plan was doomed to failure before it was put into effect:

> It was actually pitiful. "I was never briefed to the overall battle plans. There were no maps of the area provided to me for detailed planning. We saw no overall plan as to what part of Longstop Hill we were to take, or just where the British would screen us. Major York was given no plans to work with, but he did his best to give us company commanders some idea as to what we should do. The British 78th Division was simply anxious to get we [sic] Americans to assist them, but when we did there had been little preparation to use us effectively.

We could not study the terrain in advance. It would have been helpful to view the objective, even with binoculars from an outpost with the British explaining to us what the plan was before we attacked. I know that Colonel Greer would never have approved this "planned disaster" had he really known how the 1st Battalion was going to be used. The attack needed a full day of planning to assure success. Neither American nor British artillery were in position to properly support our attack. Fundamentally, we should not have been moved up to relieve the Guards until they had accomplished their basic mission. Lieutenant Colonel Stewart-Brown came, he saw, but he did not conquer Longstop Hill.[21]

Despite the lack of planning for the first attacks on Longstop Hill, Captain Carter's 81mm mortar platoon formed part of a small, yet effective, portion of the Allied fire support assets that were dropping shells on the positions occupied by Oberstleutnant Lang's men later that day. When Captain Yarock's Company A was first assembled for the attack, German mortar shells were also falling around Carter's troops. He then moved his men back to the area of his command post, which was off a road near a *wadi* at the base of Longstop Hill, away from the assembly area for the rifle companies. During this move, he ran into some men in Company B who were still moving up to attack. "I asked them how it was going," Carter remembered. "I was told that they had met some British soldiers and one had yelled 'the Yanks are here' real loud. [*sic*] That was apparently their signal to depart and they disappeared into thin air and there was nothing but Germans in front of Company B after this." Captain Carter did not know it at that moment, but Germans were also patrolling the rocky terrain near where he had set up his command post. "About mid-morning this fully armed German patrol came down the road," Carter recalled. "Leading the patrol was one of my own men, with a dirty face towel at his hips and a pistol in the middle of his back that was being held by a young German officer. My man, a corporal, was fluent in German, and I learned they wanted me to surrender my unit and become prisoners of war. With a fully armed patrol, I guess they thought we would all come out with our hands up. Apparently they were told by their commanders not to come back without any prisoners."

After a brief interlude that convinced Carter that the Germans were indeed not about to depart without Americans, he told his captive corporal in English that he was going to give a section of his machine gunners the order to open fire, and to hit the ground when he gave the order. "Right gun right flank, search left. Left gun left flank, search right. Guns ready. Commence firing!" Carter then barked. The corporal hit the ground and the German officer in command of the patrol was killed instantly. In the ensuing firefight, Carter lost one of his own men, but when the carnage was later cleared, he captured several Germans and turned over handbooks of information taken from the dead patrol leader. "The British had a heyday saying they had captured these documents," he wrote later. "My men did this job." His men then turned their mortars and machine guns onto Longstop Hill.[22]

The Germans considered the fight for the hill mass to be a very critical engagement, as evidenced by what they later wrote about 23 December 1942. Even the German ground commander in Tunis, Generaloberst von Arnim of *Fifth Panzer Army* visited the scene of the action that day. As Oberstleutnant Lang recorded,

> During a somewhat prolonged pause in the fighting at about noon, I was able to describe the progress of the action right on the field of battle to Generaloberst von Arnim, who as commander of *Fifth Panzer Army*, was in command of the Axis forces in Tunisia. He took the opportunity to express Generalfeldmarschall Kesselring's approval, and, disregarding the nearness of the enemy, he decorated some soldiers. Von Arnim's chief of staff, Generalleutnant Ziegler, also paid a visit to the front. However he had little chance to inspect the terrain in the foreground because frequent and sudden concentrations of fire forced us to the ground." Then referring to Captain Carter's Company D barrage at the time, Lang wrote, "The fire increased in intensity and everything indicated that the enemy had reorganized his units, probably brought up additional fresh forces, and was again assembling for an attack.[23]

Despite this fire by Carter's heavy weapons company, Company B was unable to take additional ground on 23 December. Like Yarock, Captain Cameron had carefully reconnoitered the area before committing his men that day, and he found Germans on the third, fourth, and fifth knobs of Longstop Hill.

Lieutenant McGregor was Cameron's XO at the time, and he remembered witnessing the British launch their earlier attacks before Company B was committed to battle. "It was very courageous, but to me it seemed to be foolhardy," he later said. "It reminded me of Bunker Hill because they were going straight ahead, no infiltration. Their men would spread out going up these slopes, but we could see that they were taking casualties—men hit by small arms fire."[24]

Nobody in Company B saw a British guide that day, but Captain Cameron and his men went up the hill anyway, not knowing the fate of Captain Yarock's company. It was later learned that they advanced far to the left of Company A and not abreast, therefore diluting the power of an attack with two companies on-line. Instead, Cameron's platoons moved through positions held by Company C, then in reserve, and renewed the attack against the Germans holding the crest. As McGregor reported, "We didn't know where the Germans were hiding. They were well concealed, well dug in, and somebody said they had smokeless powder, so there was no trace. Our men worked this way and that, trying to get fire on the Germans. One of our sergeants got very mad, so he started charging and some men went with him. The sergeant was hit in the head and killed instantly."

Nevertheless, Company B continually tried to advance, only to find themselves on an open forward slope surrounded by Germans, as Company A had been. McGregor contacted Major York to report their situation, and after some discussion with Captain Cameron on the radio, York thought the company should pull out. Lieutenant McGregor disagreed at the time because he believed that the British were going to commit a substantial force against the defenders to keep the hill. He feared that if his company pulled back, it would leave the British flank wide open. He learned later that a different situation had actually existed, however. "We had no communication with the British whatsoever," he pointed out. "Company A was gone, wiped out, annihilated, captured. Company C on our left had taken casualties, as we had. If we remained on that forward slope, it would have proved to be fatal."

"The Germans ran a reconnaissance force against us, not a real counterattack," McGregor continued. "Bob York asked me to see if I could work my way around the left flank and see if there was anything there. There sure was! I had a few men with me, and boy!—a German machine gun began firing and I couldn't see the damn thing. Bullets were kicking up around me. We were amongst little folds in the ground, but when I put my field glasses on this little elevation, that little gun started hammering and tracers flew over."[25] After McGregor reported what was happening to him, it didn't take much longer before Major York ordered them off the hill.

Lieutenant Van Wagoner's platoon of Company C was to McGregor's left that day. When daylight came, he saw the Germans assembling above his position and he was close enough to hear them talking on a radio. "I then saw a German atop the hill point his weapon skyward and fire what appeared to be a rifle grenade," Van Wagoner remembered. "It was black, about an inch in diameter and some eight inches long. I watched the trajectory before it landed a few yards from me. Then it exploded and killed a man."[26] During one of the few actions in which elements of Anti-Tank Company were actively involved that morning, a lieutenant fired canister rounds back at the Germans on the hill until the enemy platoon moved into a defilade position.[1] ["Canister" rounds were similar to shotgun rounds, filled with steel balls which dispersed over a short range. Fired from the standard 37mm antitank gun, these rounds gave antitank crews a potent anti-personnel capability as well.] The enemy fired back at the antitank gun, and then they turned their weapons on Lieutenant Van Wagoner's platoon, hitting the area between the rest of the company and them.

"I went back to find Captain Scott-Smith and asked him what I should do, and he said we were going to take that stupid hill," Van Wagoner remembered. "I'm not sure that he checked with battalion because we were supposed to stay in reserve. We had no 81mm or field artillery observer with us, and I thought the distance was too great for our own 60mm mortars. I'm not sure where the other platoons were, but when we finally started for the hill we received rifle fire from our front and machine-gun fire from our left that just about destroyed us. Jerry had some sort of rear slope defense that was strange to us. We were pinned down. A BAR man to my left was killed. My platoon sergeant was wounded. I formed what was left of my platoon in a defilade position on the front side of the hill and called for the medic. I soon found my runner and he was dead. I then moved the platoon to our right where we could assume a defensive position and we started firing back. We expended a great deal of ammunition, but then cut back to preserve it by just shooting at targets of opportunity. Towards night all we could do was set up a guard formation."[27]

Colonel Greer had wasted no time in requesting that the British commit their reserves to Longstop Hill. Several times during the day, he went over to Stewart-Brown's command post and raised hell over reinforcements. Stewart-Brown reported that Greer had said, "My men are tired, and they cannot go on without support." Stewart-Brown claimed he had no reserves that he could commit, however, and that he had no other option but to send his troops that had taken the hill the night before back into battle. There were significant delays, though, before this could be accomplished. Greer later wrote in his after-action report that the Guards were in position at 0600 at dawn on 24 December, but they did not commit their forces until much later in the afternoon, almost twelve hours later.[28]

The weather was partially to blame. It had been pouring all day and roads everywhere had become impassable, making frustration rampant. During the day, Colonel Greer tried to employ his Cannon Company and call for tank support in an effort to support the 1st Battalion, but Lieutenant Franklyn Johnson later recalled, "Instead, we spent half the time repeatedly freeing our vehicles from the tenacious mud."[29]

There was yet another incident that spoke more directly about the confusion that day, this one later told to Captain Yarock in a prisoner-of-war camp. "There was a tanker, a brand-new first lieutenant, from the 2nd Armored Division with me," he remembered. "Here he was outside of Medjez in the rain. He kept asking the British for permission to move out before his tanks got stuck in the mud, but they kept telling him he couldn't move out. His tanks eventually got so mired down he couldn't move them at all. They never fired a shot because the British wouldn't listen when he wanted to move his tanks."[30]

The bad weather also exacerbated an already substantially deteriorating situation around Longstop Hill. Colonel Greer's call for reinforcements was justified, for the whole hill mass was now covered with Germans in far greater strength than the British realized. In addition to regaining the crest, the railway station also remained in German hands, thus ensuring that the only hard-surface road leading to Tunis remained under their control. In addition to blocking any Allied armored advance, possession of the road ensured that the Germans could quickly move up their own reinforcements to augment their defenses at Longstop, as well as the second hill mass to the northeast, Djebel el Rhar.

While weather was bogging down everyone on Longstop Hill, a threat to the German defense of Tunis was being posed by the 5th Northamptons. Finally emerging from the hills northeast of Longstop long after they were to have entered the battle, they tentatively began advancing onto more open ground where the German *10th Panzer Division* had quickly rushed troops to meet this unexpected threat. Elements of *Panzer Regiment 7* and an 88mm flak battery of the *10th Panzer Division* were ordered to nearby Tounquar, while another battalion of *Panzer-Grenadier Regiment 69* hurried to the Tebourba Gap. Realizing that this German tank/infantry force would outnumber and outgun them, the 5th Northamptons simply pulled back toward their own lines.

On this same afternoon of 24 December, General Eisenhower met with Lieutenant General Kenneth A. Anderson, Commander of the British First Army, at his command post, some 380 miles from his own Algiers headquarters. Eisenhower realized that his overall offensive was mired down not by just the bad weather, but also by supply problems, lack of effective air support, and vastly superior German strength in the area. Not only had their Tiger tanks proved to be an unpleasant surprise, but their FW-190s had also demonstrated superiority to American and British fighter planes. Making matters worse, the Allies did not have any all-weather facilities to base the planes they did have, for unimproved runways across Tunisia were being turned into quagmires of mud by the unrelenting rain. Only a few paved strips, which were located near Tunis and thus in German hands, could support continuous operations by fighters and attack aircraft. As a result, the *Luftwaffe* had maintained control of the air during the recent fighting. Sobering any hopes for a better turn in the weather, local civilians had also told Anderson that the winter rains lasted at least six weeks. After weighing all of these factors, Eisenhower subsequently called off the ambitious Allied plan forged to quickly reach Tunis and Bizerte.[31]

Later that same afternoon, word of this decision reached the American and British command posts at Longstop Hill. Orders were not issued to cancel the Longstop battles, however, so the British made attempts to contact what they still believed to be the advancing 5th Northhamptons, and turn them back to reinforce Longstop Hill. This failed because thick cloud cover hampered the planes that somehow managed to get into the air to try to find them. Meanwhile, some Arabs had tipped off the Germans about the Northamptons' withdrawal, so Oberstleutnant Lang pulled his units back to reinforce his own depleted forces. Two more companies of *Grenadier Regiment 754* were also quickly dispatched to the hill mass north of Longstop. After a bitter battle with some British troops, the Germans retained this position. Oberstleutnant Lang got the news about this success early that evening, but he had little time to celebrate because by then, the 2nd Battalion, The Coldstream Guards had started their second assault on Longstop Hill.

An angry, rolling barrage of artillery fire flew over the heads of four companies of Coldstreamers moments before they jumped off at 1700, two hours before dark on Christmas Eve. One company passed through Captain Cameron's Company B at the foot of the hill; their mission was to clear the ridge to which the Americans had been clinging. Another company was held in nearby reserve, while a third stayed farther back. The fourth company followed the first up the hill, together storming the lower slopes, despite being greeted with withering machine-gun fire and well-placed mortar rounds. As darkness fell, the Guards retook the ground the 18th Infantry Regiment had tried to hold earlier that day. By Christmas morning, they were able to stare across the gullies into the Madjera Valley from their precariously-held positions.

Meantime, as Christmas dawned, the dirty business of holding this ground was once again about to fall onto the shoulders of the Americans huddled at the foot of Longstop Hill, the proud men of the 18th Infantry Regiment . . . or at least what was left of them after two days of combat. Fortunately, two events brightened an otherwise very tentative beginning to Christmas Day 1942.

First, the rain temporarily stopped. Second, some additional support for the Regiment arrived in the form of a French colonial machine-gun company. Lieutenant McGregor greeted its captain with a spirited *"Bonjour!"* just as a rolling barrage of artillery, mortar, and machine-gun fire landed nearby. Pyrotechnics then shot into the air, followed by another serenade of enemy firepower announcing their renewed defense. The French officer mumbled something to McGregor that he later recalled he could barely hear because the noise was so loud. It might well have been "Merry Christmas."

Oberstleutnant Lang had been buoyed by the knowledge that his right flank was now covered by reinforcements, including units of *Panzer Regiment 7*. Imbued with infectious optimism about his chances to hold Longstop Hill (interchangeably Djebel el Ahmera, or just Ahmera in his report), he later reflected on the German's Christmas morning this way:

> I had made my decision to get us out of a difficult situation by assembling for a counterattack during the Holy Night. The commander who knows his men is entitled to make a demand of this kind on them, even though they had suffered severe casualties, and were tired from extensive fighting during wet and cold days and nights.
>
> While a small group was to force down the enemy by frontal fire from the commanding Ahmera and was to support the advance of the group that was making the main thrust in the east into the eastern flank of the enemy forces, the armored group's mission, carefully timed, was to make a thrust along the valley through the foothills west of Ahmera, to smash the enemy forces on the Ahmera by flanking fire, and to proceed rapidly to the southern spurs of the foothills in order to prevent the enemy forces from getting away. Owing to the lack of older officers, I entrusted the command of the group making the main effort, in which I myself was advancing, to the very competent, high-spirited Oberleutnant Hofmann, holder of the German Cross in Gold. The precise and enthusiastic execution of the commands I personally gave to the individual commanders and leaders resulted in the

success for which we hoped. The enemy forces, fighting stubbornly and obstinately, were caught by the frontal fire as well as that from the tanks into their west flank and were forced to give up. The group making the main effort reached the enemy's east flank unnoticed; the enemy was completely wiped out or captured in close combat action."[32]

Captain Cameron's Company B, with Lieutenant McGregor and the French machine-gun unit in the lead, ran head on into this German attack. As they advanced up the rocky hillside, they were met with machine-gun fire that ripped into their paths while shell fragments blasted all around them. As McGregor remembered, "German soldiers were running and hitting the ground ahead of us to fire a few times, then sprinting to another spot."[33] Effective counterfire also took a toll on the attacking Germans, however, when support from Captain Carter's Company D rained on Lang's riflemen, forcing them back for a time. Forward progress seemed possible for a few fleeting moments, but American hopes were quickly dashed as the German tanks began flanking movements, rapidly closing in on Company B, then all Hell broke loose. "Tanks and infantry hit pretty hard," Captain Carter remembered. "They were simply outgunned and sent reeling."[34]

"I saw some German tanks coming toward us up the valley to our left," McGregor later recalled, "We were up the creek without a paddle! The tanks couldn't climb the *djebel*, but pulled to about 800 yards and began firing directly into our foxholes." Moments later, telephone land lines went dead. Worse, Lieutenant McGregor could not reach battalion headquarters with his radio pack to tell them about the situation.

Despite the deteriorating conditions, the Company B commander was not anxious to pull off the hill. "We'll fight to the last man," McGregor heard Captain Cameron saying. McGregor also remembered thinking at the time, "It would be like Custer's last stand at Little Big Horn in 1876, and I was wondering, 'Why me?'"[35]

By now, Lieutenant McGregor had counted as many as ten German *Panzer IV* tanks with 75mm guns, all taking aim at his men while Lang's panzergrenadiers were moving around Company B's other flank. Things appeared utterly hopeless, but then a faint signal from the 1st Battalion command post down in front of a *wadi* at the base of the hill was heard over the radio and a voice said, "Affect an orderly withdrawal without delay." "So in this semi-orderly fashion, we got out of there," Lieutenant McGregor recalled later, adding that when they got off the hill, "Major York greeted us with open arms." By afternoon, Company B, less a 2nd lieutenant, two sergeants, two corporals, 24 privates first class, and 22 privates, was back in a cactus patch far from Longstop Hill. Before Christmas Day was over, however, the company sustained a total of 51 casualties during the fight to hold the hill mass.[36] One of the lieutenants lost from Company B's roster was Paul Carnes, who had plans to be in the ministry and had had bad omens on the eve of battle about what lay ahead for him. He spent the rest of his war as a prisoner of the Germans.

Lieutenant Colonel Stewart-Brown's report for 25 December 1942 read, "At first light on Christmas Day the Germans counterattacked in force, using heavy concentrations of artillery and mortar fire, as well as infantry. The Coldstreamers, much depleted in numbers and facing great difficulties, were being driven off the hill."

At that point, Brigadier Copland-Griffiths moved the 3rd Battalion, The Grenadier Guards, less two companies, over to help the Coldstreamers and as he also added, "the Americans." Stewart-Brown also directed tanks to move up to support the Allied infantry on Longstop. He was able to find "five medium and five light American tanks," he wrote later. Reflecting the difficulty of getting armor into the battle, but ignoring the fact that any units had been allowed to move before they got bogged down in the mud, he closed this same report with, "The state of the country was not really suitable for their employment."[37]

Colonel Greer's after-action report reflected his anguish over the lack of support he received from the Guards that morning when he noted, "The British [Grenadier Guards] company withdrew around the left flank of the 1st Battalion without notifying the battalion. This left the mortars, which had been supporting the British, exposed and unprotected." The Regiment's S-1 Journal confirmed this, saying the British made "a rapid withdrawal covered by Companies B, C, and D, one hour before the 1st Battalion companies left the hill."[38] The French company that went up the hill with Company B was later sent over to protect Captain Carter's mortar platoon. The French didn't stay long, though. They had machine guns, but no antitank weapons, so they withdrew shortly after they arrived when several German armored cars appeared, again exposing the entire battalion's flank.

Lieutenant Van Wagoner's platoon of Company C was still alone on Christmas Day. Van Wagoner had replaced his dead sergeant with another by this time, but this man had already been wounded. The new sergeant refused to be evacuated and instead asked that ammunition be supplied to him so he could continue the fight. Van Wagoner remembered, "I took a dim view of this, but we stayed in position and used our mortars until we ran out of ammunition. Then a group of the Guards showed up. They said they wanted to help, and then they had their tea. They finally attacked the same position we had been attacking, but they took casualties and were not able to dislodge the Jerries."

Lieutenant Van Wagoner soon received word to withdraw. "I wanted to carry my wounded sergeant down with me, but I decided I didn't have enough strength," he wrote later. "I could hardly move from the prone position. We came off the hill carrying only our weapons and ammo belts. When we were going back I ran into Lieutenant Colonel Fricke behind a large boulder. He was shaving without soap, and he told me he wanted to look presentable when he reported to Colonel Greer. He said that a Jerry had wasted a lot of ammo shooting at him."[39]

The Christmas Day fighting on Longstop Hill, which began at 0600 hours, was over by 0900. The Germans retook the crest that morning, and they were destined to hold it for months. Thereafter, they referred to Longstop as *Wiehnachts Hölle*, or "Christmas Hell." It had indeed been a "long stop" for the British and the 18th Infantry Regiment. Total casualties in the 1st Battalion, first counted by Major York and Captain Carter at 352 not accounted for, were later confirmed as nine officers and 347 men killed, captured or missing—almost half the battalion's strength. The 2nd Battalion, The Coldstream Guards lost 178 officers and men. The original defenders of Longstop, as well as *Kampfgruppe Lang*, probably lost about 200–300 men during the fighting, but this was never documented.

The British War Diaries later stated that Lieutenant Colonel George Fricke had been pinned down by German machine gunners for three hours while Company A was isolated on top of Longstop Hill on 23 December, a fact that helped explain why Company A Captain Yarock had been unable to reach him at crucial times that morning. The British also maintained that they had offered to keep the Coldstream Guards company on the hill, but that Fricke had granted their request to leave. The Regiment's S-1 Journal also recorded that Colonel Greer had no knowledge about the fate of Company A until late in the afternoon of 23 December. Fricke either didn't know what had happened to his company at the time, or he had simply been unable to report it.[40]

The final British entry in Stewart-Brown's "Summary of Operations" about Longstop Hill evidenced a willingness to put aside the ill will and rancor that resulted from the disastrous battles, this first combined effort of American and British forces during the war. He magnanimously offered, "There have been some recriminations and back biting with the Americans, but all of it is over for now, and I hope dead forever." It might have been just as well had Stewart-Brown left it at that, but he also added in closing, "I have nothing whatsoever to say against the Americans myself, except that they were unfitted and unprepared for the task that they were asked to perform, which would in fact have been difficult for any battalion."[41]

Not unexpectedly, the staff officers back at the 1st Infantry Division command post had a very dreary Christmas Day. They got together, sang a few songs, and even set up a buffet table near a small tree they had decorated. One of General Allen's aides remembered, "We had a pretty good time together, but it didn't last long. We thought of the boys up at the front, so we made the big party short." The man with the least Christmas spirit was General Allen. He had grown increasingly distraught as reports came back to his post from Longstop Hill, more anguished than ever that the 18th Infantry Regiment was no longer under his direct command. A staff officer tried to explain some of Allen's frustrations in a letter he wrote at the time to the general's wife when he said, "You see, the division is partly separated. He loves the 1st Division and wants to get us together again."[42]

Captain Carter was still at the front that Christmas morning. His heavy weapons company had fired some interdiction missions at the start of the battle, but they then had to run for their lives when the German tanks started firing back. Carter got his men out first, and then he was almost hit by machine-gun fire as he made his way to safety. That night, he and Major York were going over the company casualty reports again. Rations had not been issued all day, so both were very hungry. "I had a can of meat and beans in my pack," Carter remembered nearly 60 years later. "So Major York and I shared that for our Christmas dinner, the most unforgettable Christmas of my life. But, at least we came out alive."[43]

The sad saga of the Battle for Longstop Hill constituted many firsts for the 18th Infantry Regiment. Not only was it the first time its officers and men fought against the Germans in World War II, but it was also the first time they were under British command in the war. It was one of the worst chapters in the Regiment's long, distinguished history. Moreover, the cost in men during the three days of combat was the largest of any battles for the 1st Battalion in all of its Tunisian engagements. Yet this Christmas 1942 battle hardened the soldiers of the Regiment, and formed the basis for revenge and important victories in the weeks to come.

SBIBA AND EL GUETTAR

JANUARY TO APRIL 1943

> The prisoners knew the 10th Panzers were beaten by us at El Guettar. It was astounding to them. It was the first time in the history of World War II that American troops had beaten a panzer division.
> —Lieutenant Herbert A. Smith, Company M

On 30 December 1942, the 18th Infantry Regiment was attached to the British 6th Armoured Division. This division had been given the unusual role of assuming a static defensive position south of Medjez el Bab after the Longstop Hill battles. Lacking sufficient infantry to hold the sector it was assigned, its commanding general asked for additional foot soldiers to augment the single brigade of infantry organic to his unit. In response, the British First Army selected the 18th RCT for this assignment. Both Britons and Americans, however, had mixed reactions to these new orders.

Colonel Greer was anxious to quickly set aside any differences that might remain following the disastrous Christmas battles at Longstop Hill, so he decided to get to know the British 6th Armoured's Commanding General, Major General Charles A. Keightley. The British general seemed to be of like mind. After visiting the Regiment's command post on the afternoon of New Year's Eve, Keightley wrote Greer a letter that same night indicating he was very impressed with the bearing and spirit of the 18th Infantry Regiment staff officers he had met, and he evidenced his immediate intentions to honor requests Colonel Greer had made that day. Recognizing the poor performance of the American 37mm antitank gun, what American soldiers had dubbed a "pea-shooter," the British general promised to send British 6-pounder antitank guns* and antitank mines to shield the 18th RCT from attack by German tanks in its newly-assigned positions. Keightley was

---

*The 6-pounders were essentially identical to the 57mm antitank guns with which the Regiment would later be equipped. They were far more effective than the 37mm pieces with which the Regiment was deployed to Africa.

also cognizant of the logistical difficulties imposed on the 18th Infantry Regiment while under British command. In the closing paragraph of his letter to Greer, Keightley pledged to quickly address any shortcomings affecting the Regiment, promising that he would "do all in my power to get them put right."[1]

Now that General Eisenhower had abandoned all hopes of quickly taking Tunis, seizing the city was destined to be a more prolonged struggle necessitating a substantially revised plan. Since the rainy weather would not permit resumption of any large-scale offensive for at least two months, resupply became the immediate Allied priority. The British First Army required a significant infusion of new equipment and personnel to replace the losses it had suffered, and the French XIX Corps, equipped with obsolete tanks and guns, had to be provided with modern armor, artillery, antitank guns, and radios. Within the First Army area of operations, units assigned to seize Tunis in December were repositioned on terrain better suited to defense. Simultaneously, limited objective attacks were being planned to secure key terrain and to keep the Germans off balance. For the 18th Infantry Regiment, this new phase in the Tunisian campaign would permit Colonel Greer to rebuild the confidence of his troops and to amend the Regiment's training program to take advantage of the costly lessons learned in combat thus far in the war.

During a lull in the weather on 28 December, Lieutenant Colonel Fricke's battered 1st Battalion had withdrawn to a drier area in a cactus patch next to Teboursouk, a ramshackle Arab town perched on a knoll a few miles southwest of Medjez. Company A was quickly reconstituted and Lieutenant McGregor was appointed company commander. To redistribute combat strength evenly throughout the Regiment, the 2nd and 3rd Battalions transferred men to the 1st Battalion to make up for the losses the 1st Battalion had suffered at Longstop Hill.

When the new year dawned, Colonel Greer received orders to send one of his battalions southeast of Medjez to relieve a battalion of British infantry that had been patrolling in this area since the end of the Longstop Hill fighting. Greer selected Major Sternberg's 2nd Battalion for this assignment, and his companies were soon facing east, looking across a broad opening into the Medjerda River Valley. During the first week of January, rifle platoons occupied trenches and foxholes dug into a horseshoe-shaped group of hills overlooking a prominent crossroads named Peter's Corners. There was a crescent-shaped rise to the battalion's immediate front dubbed "Banana Ridge." It was eventually occupied by the companies of the 1st Battalion, and beyond it stood a lone, whitewashed villa. Company A established defensive positions in a quarry on a small nearby hill, quickly dubbed "Fort McGregor" by the men. Five miles southeastward, across the open area outside of patrolling range that became known as "No Man's Land," was the town of Goubellat. Here, German tanks were rumored to be poised for probing attacks into the 1st and 2nd Battalion's new positions.

During the same time period, Lieutenant Colonel Brown's 3rd Battalion relieved several companies of the 1st Guards Brigade on what had become known as "Grenadier Hill." The Guards' brigade commander decided that it would be wisest to hold a narrower perimeter between the railway station astride Longstop

Hill and a group of knolls to the southeast. These hills had been occupied by the British since mid-December, and by the time the 3rd Battalion took up positions to relieve the Guards, shallow connected trench systems like those dug in by the Germans atop Longstop Hill had been expanded for nearly 2,000 yards across the rocky knolls of Grenadier Hill. The vantage points on the summit of each hill were circled with more trenches, and observers were able to keep the intervening gullies under observation until there was time to block them. The intent was to use the antitank mines and wire that Major General Keightley had promised to Colonel Greer in his New Year's Eve letter.

Anxious to learn more about the German positions to their front, the British 6th Armoured Division sent out 45 Valentine and Crusader tanks in two sorties as a cautious reconnaissance in force on the day after the new year of 1943. One was made through the 3rd Battalion position on Grenadier Hill, then eastward on the Medjez-Tunis Road. The other sortie probed southward toward Goubellat and suspected German positions in front of Major Sternberg's 2nd Battalion sector. Dubbed the "Bubble and Squeak" raid, these moves were actually intended to serve the much-needed purpose of gaining information about the suitability of the muddy Tunisian terrain for bearing the weight of any tanks. Lieutenant John Downing was the Regiment's liaison officer with British 6th Armoured headquarters at the time. "The information was negative and quite a few tanks were lost in the operation," he later wrote. "They bellied down in the mud in front of the lines. The crews escaped back to our infantry foxholes, but those tanks not smashed by German artillery fire were blown up that night by the Royal Engineer demolition crews to prevent their use by German patrols as ambush points."[2]

By early January, Colonel Greer had assumed command of an impressive mix of Allied units. In addition to his own troops, the 32nd FA Battalion, and a company apiece of the 1st Engineer Combat Battalion and the 1st Medical Battalion, CT 18 now included a tank company detached from the 1st Armored Regiment and a company from the 601st Tank Destroyer Battalion. During the month, the following British units also came temporarily under Greer's command: a squadron (company) of the 16th/5th The Queen's Royal Lancers; a squadron of the 2nd Lothian and Border Horse; the 17th/21st Lancers, which had seen much combat as part of "Blade Force" outside Tunis in November; 5th Battalion, The Northamptonshire Regiment; 2nd Battalion, The Parachute Regiment; and No. 6 Commando.[3] Colonel Greer truly was in command of an international force—no wonder some officers of the British 6th Armoured Division unofficially dubbed the 18th Infantry's commanding officer the "uncrowned king of Medjez-el-Bab."[4]

The Regiment spent the month of January in their defensive positions around Medjez. Aggressive patrols—usually groups of 7 to 12 men under the command of an officer—were sent out most days and, eventually, also at the night. These night patrols would often cross the stony plateaus in front of the Regiment's positions to investigate a suspicious cactus grove, a prominent outcrop of rock, buildings, or any points at which suspicious sounds may have been heard. Reconnaissance patrols usually moved in ever-widening sweeps, risky maneuvers that often lasted all night. As one officer remembered after weeks of this duty, "Patrolling undoubtedly had a prosaic sound when it was heard on the radio during news bulletins back home, but it was generally the most unpleasant and dangerous work the front line infantry had to do."[5]

The British 78th Division assumed responsibility for the Medjez-el-Bab sector from the British 6th Armoured Division in early February. By this time, Combat Team 18 had spent nearly a month and a half in contact with the enemy conducting these dangerous patrolling assignments. The time spent in this defensive sector proved to be invaluable later. The Regiment's soldiers repeatedly demonstrated their proficiency in patrolling; emplacing and recovering booby traps and mines; manning observation and listening posts; and rendering accurate reports. Colonel Greer's Summary of Operations also revealed that a high state of coordination had been attained between his infantry units and their supporting artillery. Considering the dangers of the mission, casualties during the period had been relatively modest, with ten men killed, 42 wounded, and four missing. Undoubtedly, the many successes experienced during patrolling missions dispelled a great deal of concern regarding German tactical superiority. The men of the 18th Infantry indeed respected their opponents, but they also now knew they could be beaten.

On 13 February, CT 18's 48th day in the Medjez defensive sector, Colonel Greer was apprised that the British 78th Division's 11th Infantry Brigade would take over the Regiment's sector that night. Sternberg's 2nd Battalion, however, would remain in place until the following night before moving to Beja where it would then come under the control of the British 46th Infantry Division.[6] It was not long before the 1st and 3rd Battalions started moving across stretches of rain-slicked roadway as they exited Medjez through Testour, then made their way back to Teboursouk where hundreds of pup tents were pitched in a nearby olive grove. With time on their hands, many of the soldiers used the period to become reacquainted with friends from other companies, to finally clean up in collapsible canvas baths, and to eventually discover more of Teboursouk. Far above the village, stately columns and temples from the ancient days of the Roman Empire still towered and became prime attractions.

In early February while the 18th Infantry was still in the Medjez defensive sector, Generalfeldmarschall Erwin Rommel's *Africa Corps* withdrew from Libya and occupied pre-war French fortifications known as the "Mareth Line" along the Libyan-Tunisian border. Consisting of pillboxes, antitank ditches, and other prepared defenses, the Mareth Line had been constructed between the wars to discourage Italian colonial aggression. Although the Germans entered this area as a defeated force, Arnim's *Fifth Panzer Army* and Rommel's *Africa Corps* were now fighting back to back where they could switch units between their two armies to quickly mass against either the Americans in southwestern Tunisia or the British Eighth Army advancing from Libya. The Germans also enjoyed much shorter lines of communication to their port facilities in Tunisia, but the British First and Eighth Armies, separated by Rommel and Arnim, could not mutually support each other because they had to move their supplies over much greater distances.

After examining this situation, Rommel determined that the greatest danger to the Axis bridgehead in Tunisia lay in a possible attack by II Corps, originating from Gafsa toward the coastal city of Gabes. Gabes was some 70 miles to the southeast of Gafsa, and a II Corps offensive in this direction would effectively split the two German armies. To prevent this, Rommel proposed an attack to break up the concentration of American forces then at nearby Sbeitla and Sidi Bou Zid. With these towns under German control, Rommel figured that the American troops in Gafsa would have to withdraw or face encirclement. Accordingly, Rommel's *21st Panzer Division* and elements of Arnim's *10th Panzer Division* were ordered to attack the Americans via Faid Pass with the mission of destroying the American forces in that area. At the same time, *Combat Group DAK (Deutsches Afrika Korps)*, a combat group consisting of the Italian *131st Armored Division "Centauro"* and a regimental-sized element of the *Africa Corps*, would force the Americans out of Gafsa. Being somewhat cautious, however, Rommel preferred to wait until the attacks were concluded before assigning any further objectives to his troops, so the timing of the offensive was set for mid-February.[7] On 14 February, the *21st Panzer Division*, reinforced by elements of the *10th Panzer Division*, attacked Combat Command A (CCA) of the 1st Armored Division at Sidi Bou Zid. The defending Americans were positioned on high ground located northeast and southwest of the town where the CCA commander, Brigadier General Raymond MacQuillan, hoped to stop a German attack before it broke out into the open area west of Faid Pass. The German attackers were screened, however, by a sudden sandstorm that let them exit the western end of the pass before the Americans could react. Rommel quickly exploited this. After bypassing dug-in American infantry defending Djebel Lessouda and Gare Hadid, his tanks defeated a number of piecemeal counterattacks conducted by a battalion of the 1st Armored Division. Fewer than six German tanks were lost while knocking out 54 Shermans.[8]

The American artillery and antitank units defending Sidi Bou Zid fared no better. As the German armor continued its sweep around Djebel Lessouda, they overran a platoon of Company A, 701st Tank Destroyer (TD) Battalion. The remainder of this force, along with a company of the 1st Armored Regiment, then moved out of Sidi Bou Zid to meet other German tanks that were flanking Djebel Lessouda. As 30 Panzer IVs emerged from a cactus patch, the TD gunners opened fire at 200 yards, but the Germans moved to their left and immediately overran their positions. Three of the tank destroyer battalion's half-track-mounted 75mm guns and two 37mm SPs burned and exploded soon after being hit by enemy tank fire, and one company hastily withdrew and assembled south of the Sidi Bou Zid-Maknassy road.[9] Meanwhile, all three batteries of the 2nd Battalion, 17th Field Artillery Regiment, positioned well forward to take advantage of the relatively poor range of their obsolescent French-designed, First-World-War-era 155mm howitzers, were also wiped out by German tanks. Dug in forward of the defending infantry as well, all six self-propelled 105mm howitzers of the 91st Armored Field Artillery Battalion's Battery B were quickly overrun, while its two other firing batteries lost four SP 105mm howitzers.[10] As a result of these aggressive

German attacks, by the end of the day, two battalions of the 168th Infantry Regiment of the 34th Division found themselves completely isolated atop the high ground to the northeast and southeast of Sidi Bou Zid.

Pausing for 24 hours to adjust their plans and bring up supplies, the German panzer divisions then fended off a counterattack by a single battalion of American tanks on 15 February. Of 54 Sherman tanks of the 2nd Battalion, 1st Armored Regiment, only two or three vehicles escaped destruction. The Germans then captured 1,600 men of the 168th Infantry Regiment as they tried to escape the following night from Djebel Lessouda and Gare Hadid. As the American defenses dissolved, Combat Command B, 1st Armored Division was hurriedly transferred from Ousseltia Valley, where it had been supporting the French XIX Corps. It then joined remnants of CCA at Sbeitla, the next town on the designated list of German objectives. By retaining Sbeitla, the Americans hoped to protect the critical nearby airfield at Thelepte and prevent the Germans from moving west and northwest through the Kasserine and Sbiba Passes. If the Germans seized these two pass entrances, they could move north toward the massive American supply base at Tebessa; its loss would cripple II Corps while providing the Germans with enough fuel to continue their attack into the rear of the British First Army.

Dug in around the oasis town of Sbeitla, the 1st Armored Division managed to hold off the attacking Germans throughout 16 February, but defenses in the area began to disintegrate that night and the town was evacuated by noon the next day. In response to the tremendous reverses suffered by the Americans at Sidi Bou Zid and Sbeitla, the British 6th Armoured Division was ordered to move the 26th Armoured Brigade and 1st Guards Brigade to Sbiba Gap. At the same time, the full 18th RCT was slated to move to Sbiba where it would revert to the control of the British 6th Armoured Division.[11] Thus ended the 18th Infantry Regiment's rest period of three days and two nights at Teboursouk.

At 1000 hours on 17 February, Major General Keightley left his division headquarters to reconnoiter the terrain in Sbiba. At 1500 hours he met with the commanders of the British 26th Armoured Brigade, the 1st Guards Brigade, and Colonel Greer at Kat Bou Meftaht to discuss his concept for the upcoming defense. By this time, the 18th Infantry Regiment was loaded onto trucks and already underway for their lengthy journey to a new battle

The Regiment's convoy neared Sbiba under the glow of an eerie, nearly full moon that night, and by sunrise the following morning Allied troops were disposed across a new front. The 1st Guards Brigade had taken up positions astride the Sbeitla-Sbiba road and to its west, and, along with the British 26th Armoured Brigade, the 18th Infantry Regiment was positioned slightly behind and to the east side of the road in support. All three of Greer's battalions were then positioned on a line extending generally across the mouth of the valley facing south along this new front. To his right stood a 500-foot hill mass, and to Colonel Greer's immediate left a low, sloping hill of about a hundred feet. The valley straight ahead was a mile wide with the hard surface highway of the Sbiba-Sbeitla Road running right down the middle. Scanning this terrain, Colonel Greer quickly determined that preventing the Germans from seizing the road junction behind his main line of defense was going to be difficult. Later responding to a staff officer's questions about the likely need for additional support in the face of the threat before the Regiment, Greer reportedly bellowed "Don't call me for help. I haven't any. If they attack us in force, we cannot hold. But by God we will. We must!"[12]

What Colonel Greer did not realize at that moment was that Rommel planned to attack both Kasserine and Sbiba, but not until his seizure of Sbeitla was completed. On 18 February, German aerial reconnaissance reports to Rommel indicated that the main body of the 1st Armored Division was already falling back to Tebessa, while leaving behind a strong rear guard at the mountain exits to its southeast (Kasserine) and east (Sbiba). On the basis of these reports, Rommel quickly sent a message to *Fifth Panzer Army* informing Arnim of his intention to conduct "an immediate thrust of comparatively strong forces from the southwest on Tebessa and the area to the north," which would offer a "unique situation to change the situation decisively in Tunisia." Rommel recognized an opportunity to exploit this unexpected rout and do even greater damage to the Allies, perhaps causing them to pull out of Tunisia altogether, prolonging the German presence in North Africa. Rommel planned for the attack to be carried out by three panzer divisions, which together would penetrate in the deep flank and rear of the British forces facing the north Tunisian front, likely causing the entire sector to collapse. Prerequisite to the execution of this operation, however, was the assurance of plentiful supplies provided by Arnim's *Fifth Panzer Army* quartermasters.[13]

A difference of opinion between Rommel and Arnim threatened to derail this daring and bold plan of attack. Consequently, Rommel requested a conference at 0945 hours on 19 February with both Arnim and Generalfeldmarschall Kesselring, who would decide the ultimate German strategy. While Arnim supported the general concept of the plan being proposed by Rommel, he differed on several key points. Arnim argued that the port of Bône should be the main objective of this plan with the town of Le Kef, not Tebessa, as the intermediate goal. Kesselring could not ignore his recommendations. Although he did not agree with every aspect of Arnim's plan, he had to nevertheless admit that the concept proposed by the commander of the *5th Panzer Army* offered many advantages and the prospect for success. Therefore, Kesselring compromised and modified Rommel's battle plan, not to Arnim's complete satisfaction and much to Rommel's consternation.

This new plan allowed Rommel to recall the *10th Panzer Division*, which was in the process of being transferred back to Arnim for the purpose of seizing Pinchon. In the meantime, Rommel could also use his *21st Panzer Division* and *Combat Group Africa Corps* to proceed from Sbeitla and probe both Sbiba Gap and Kasserine Pass to angle north toward Le Kef. The *21st Panzer Division* and *Combat Group DAK* were both veteran units and among the most experienced desert fighters in North Africa; this gave Rommel every confidence in their success against the Allied forces. While the Germans were planning how they could exploit the unanticipated success of Rommel's offensive against Sidi Bou Zid and Sbeitla, the Allies were continuing to array troops to halt them. Task Force Stark—

the 19th Engineer Combat Regiment; the 1st Battalion, 26th Infantry; and the 33rd Field Artillery Battalion—was quickly dispatched to defend Kasserine Pass while the British 6th Armoured Division—to include the 1st British Guards Brigade and the 18th Infantry Regiment—was digging in at Sbiba. Many British officers and enlisted men continued to harbor significant reservations regarding the battle-worthiness of American troops. After all, some asked, hadn't the British 6th Armoured Division and 1st Guards Brigade been put into the line in response to the debacle at Sidi Bou Zid? One British soldier noted that "American Sherman tanks, guns, and trucks were retreating down the road in great numbers. Apart from our 25-pounder guns, their equipment was far superior to ours and we were going to restore the position with inferior equipment. Being highly trained and under expert leadership, the outcome was never in doubt. Some of the American troops were on the sides of the tracks, tents pitched, without any effort to camouflage, brewing up and dining as if they were only [on] a maneuver in Britain, and one could only think these green troops were going to learn the hard way."[14] Tainted by such performance, the author of the Grenadier Guards' postwar history cynically observed that the danger along their new line at Sbiba lay in the more open ground to their left, referring to the sector defended by the 18th Infantry Regiment where, according to the Guards' report, "a hard blow could break the crust of the American defenses and hem the Grenadiers in against the hills."[15]

To help defend in this area, two regiments of the US 34th Infantry Division hastily arrived at Sbiba and established defensive positions on the left flank of the 18th Infantry Regiment. The newcomers had a particularly difficult time reaching this position, since all hills in North Africa tended to look alike in darkness, and a driving rain was falling at the time. From west to east, two battalions of the 1st Guards Brigade, three battalions of the 18th RCT, two battalions of the 133rd Infantry, and two battalions of the 135th Infantry now occupied the defenses at Sbiba. No fewer than four battalions of American and British artillery were also now available for support during the coming battles. On the other side, hemmed in by minefields to their front and impassable ridges on either flank, the German attackers were being denied any opportunity to easily bypass the defenders. Instead, they would have to conduct a frontal assault against entrenched Allied infantry sitting atop high ground protected by minefields.

The first Germans finally appeared south of Sbiba at 1330 hours on 18 February. Two Panzer IIIs, accompanied by limited infantry, first moved onto the nearby Meftah ridge from the direction of Sbeitla, staying out of 6-pounder antitank gun range. From this safe distance, they reconnoitered the Allied defensive position before pulling back when darkness fell. Combat at Sbiba began when British reconnaissance elements spotted a German column, led by a captured American Sherman tank, moving north from Sbeitla at 1000 hours the following morning. Then two panzers, accompanied by infantry, stopped at the minefield in front of Meftah Ridge and began clearing a lane. British and American artillery immediately opened fire, forcing the Germans to withdraw, but not before they had removed enough mines to make a lane suitable for the passage of their tanks. At

1145 hours, German tanks moved beyond the gap that had been opened in the first minefield, and made their way to the main minefield protecting the dug-in Allied infantry. Almost immediately, four battalions of artillery engaged the Germans as the tanks' crews vainly sought to find a gap in the second belt of mines.[16]

The 1st Guards Brigade estimated that the Germans eventually employed 30 to 40 tanks in the initial assault, including six Tigers. They continually probed the formidable Allied defensive line looking for a weak point to exploit. It appeared that their intent was not to attempt to force a passage after encountering opposition, but to leave behind a covering force of tanks and infantry at the furthest point of advance, while swinging the remainder in a northeasterly direction. Not surprisingly, the Germans soon formed a semi-circle of small groups of tanks facing the entire Allied defensive line.[17]

The Germans suffered heavily while continuing to attempt to find a gap in the British and American minefields. Just after midday, artillery supporting the 1st Guards Brigade knocked out four German tanks; a fifth was destroyed by an obsolete 2-pounder (40mm) antitank gun that had been manhandled forward of the main defensive line by troops from the 2nd Battalion, The Coldstream Guards. At 1400 hours, a number of German tanks gathered in front of Captain Raymer's Company K, with a dozen others situated opposite the boundary separating the 18th Infantry Regiment's 2nd and 3rd Battalion positions. The Germans began advancing, only to halt abruptly when mines suddenly halted two of their tanks. As other tanks attempted to bypass the wrecks, supporting artillery started to shell them with what was later described as three week's supply of ammo.

The Germans did not find any weaknesses in Lieutenant Colonel Sternberg's 2nd Battalion's lines that day. Captain Murphy of Company H remembered, "Our defense at Sbiba was as near to textbook as I ever remembered seeing during the war. We had two rifle companies on the main line of resistance (MLR) with a heavy machine-gun platoon supporting each with interlocking final protective lines (FPL) that extended clear across the battalion front. When we laid each gun on the FPL, they were able to fire at the maximum range at which the trajectory of a bullet would not rise higher than a standing man's head. We were not lucky enough to have that kind of ground often!"

"Company H's observation post was just behind the right platoon of Company F, the company on the left of the main line," Murphy continued. "Their right flank was anchored on a small knoll just west of the Sbeitla-Sbiba road, to include the road itself, while Company G controlled the remainder of the MLR. Company E was in reserve, dug in astride the road about a hundred yards back. My company's 81mm mortar platoon was in position and registered to cover both line companies, the minefields, and the barbed-wire concertina that had been in place to protect the main line of resistance. A battery of British 17-pounders [76mm antitank guns] covered the road in the valley that separated us from the Guards Brigade, and they provided our 2nd Battalion's tank defense, to include destroying one of the Panzer IVs supporting the German grenadiers in their failed attack against us. No others crossed our final protective line alive that day."[18]

By late afternoon the tanks confronting the 18th Infantry Regiment had pulled back. Three tanks were left in front of the 1st Battalion and four had been knocked out in front of the 2nd Battalion. Shortly before dark, those German tanks still capable of moving withdrew a short distance behind a ridge facing the Allied defensive positions.

At 1850 hours Colonel Greer ordered patrols out to finish off the remaining disabled enemy armored vehicles. Using bazookas, Lieutenant Gordon A. Jeffrey's Company G patrols succeeded in destroying one of these vehicles, while Captain Russell G. Spinney's Company F set three others on fire as the enemy hurriedly moved a fourth tank back to safety. The Germans were later able to recover three of their knocked-out tanks in front of the 1st Battalion,[19] and one battalion of German panzergrenadiers succeeded in establishing positions on Meftah Ridge in front of the 18th RCT that afternoon. Later that evening, four British tanks were destroyed by long-range antitank fire when the 16/5th Lancers attempted to conduct a reconnaissance in the vicinity of Meftah Ridge.[20]

At 0830 hours on the morning of 20 February, the Germans launched another combined tank and infantry attack against the 1st Guards Brigade. Again, they ran into mines and artillery fire. After four tanks were disabled, the remainder veered back in front of the 18th Infantry's 1st Battalion, where they were slowed considerably by indirect fire. The British lost four men killed and one wounded during this attack, and by early afternoon the Germans were again forced to withdraw. At 1700 hours, however, the 1st Battalion reported another company of enemy infantry approaching their positions. Once again, artillery, infantry mortars, and heavy machine guns fired on the advancing grenadiers, forcing their withdrawal. The attackers suffered 100 casualties this time, as well as the complete loss of eight tanks and damage to no fewer than 30 other armored vehicles.[21]

Colonel Greer ordered patrols out to obtain more information about the enemy unit, but the identity of the attacking German formation remained somewhat of a mystery. Papers taken from a knocked-out Panzer III identified it as belonging to *Panzer Regiment 8, 15th Panzer Division*, another *DAK* unit, and four German engineers taken prisoner by the 2nd Battalion, The Coldstream Guards claimed they were attached to *Panzer Regiment 5, 21st Panzer Division*. Other captured documents taken from the bodies of soldiers of *Panzer-Grenadier Regiment 104* finally confirmed the presence of most of the *21st Panzer Division*.[22]

Very little movement could be seen within German lines the next morning, 21 February. A few parties of dismounted panzergrenadiers surreptitiously probed the Allied defenses, but no German tanks appeared in support of this reconnaissance effort. At 1000 hours, surprising reports were received that indicated the withdrawal of considerable amounts of tanks and infantry, and by mid-afternoon it appeared that the remaining German forces south of Sbiba consisted of only ten tanks and a battalion of infantry on both sides of the Meftah Ridge. Major General Keightley decided that in view of the thinning out of the enemy positions and the arrival of some 20 Churchills of the Royal Armored Corps (RAC), a reconnaissance in force would be carried out that was intended to discover the strength of the enemy positions remaining, seize the Meftah Ridge, and hopefully pin the Germans in place where they would be vulnerable to envelopment.

The plan called for two troops (platoons) of Churchills to go down the Sbiba-Sbeitla road, supported by a company of the Grenadier Guards on the right flank and strong fighting patrols from the 18th Infantry Regiment on the left. Carried atop the Churchills, a platoon of infantry from the Coldstream Guards left at 1727 hours with the reconnaissance in force, but the British infantry came under machine-gun fire and quickly abandoned their exposed perches before reaching Meftah Ridge. The Churchills still continued on through a smoke screen laid down by supporting artillery before running into intense fire from German anti-tank guns. One Churchill caught fire at the eastern edge of the ridge and two more were knocked out before reaching the summit. The five remaining tanks inflicted a number of casualties before pulling back, including one German tank that was destroyed by a direct hit from an American artillery round. The Churchill crews lost eight men during the fight, the majority of whom were wounded in action.[23]

While the Germans were being rebuffed at Sbiba, *Combat Group DAK*, reinforced by the *10th Panzer Division*, was nevertheless finally smashing through the defenders at Kasserine Pass. Rommel's forces were now in a position to advance on Thala, northwest of Kasserine in the direction of Le Kef, and on Djebel el Hamra, west of Kasserine in the direction of Tebessa. Waiting at el Hamra were elements of the 1st Infantry Division and CCB, 1st Armored Division, while the British 26th Armoured Brigade, which had been removed from the defense of Sbiba for just such an eventuality, was deployed in the vicinity of Thala. Given Rommel's new threat here, even more strength was now needed.

Accordingly, on the morning of 22 February, the 18th Infantry was ordered to plan a withdrawal from Sbiba. That very night, the Regiment was to establish another defensive position near Rohia, 12 miles to the Regiment's rear, but closer to the British 26th Armoured Brigade at Thala. The intent of the maneuver was to allow the Regiment to trap Rommel's advancing armor at Thala, cut off the rear approach to Sbiba, and secure the approach to Le Kef from that direction. As darkness approached that night and as his men were preparing to depart, Colonel Greer ordered a covering barrage by the 32nd FA so the Germans would not suspect the Regiment was leaving Sbiba.

When the Regiment arrived in Rohia the next day, everyone had reason for grumbling. Once again, it seemed as if the neighboring British infantry had been assigned positions atop nearby hills while the Americans were left exposed on the valley floor in wide-open positions. Colonel Greer put his best face on this and ordered each battalion to dig in, even though the ground was full of gravel and foxholes and trenches were very difficult to excavate. In further preparation for the expected fight, Greer also insisted that his supporting engineers string barbed wire and lay minefields similar to those that had worked so well at Sbiba.

No Germans appeared at Rohia the next day. It was later learned that after the fierce two-day clash with the 26th Armoured Brigade, 1st Infantry Division elements and Combat Command B of the 1st Armored Division, Rommel had simply retired from Thala, Sbiba, and the Kasserine Pass, leaving Rohia unchallenged. As the history of the 3rd Battalion, The Grenadier Guards later recorded, "The news of his withdrawal was so astonishing that many could scarcely credit it, until we began to move in complete security towards the widening "V" of the Kasserine Pass."[24] Denied Le Kef, Rommel had quickly realized his bold, but modified battle plan could not succeed. Nevertheless, he felt he had accomplished his original objective by buying time for German forces to defend against the British Eighth Army without having to worry about being attacked from the rear by the American II Corps.

Immediately after the Germans completed this withdrawal, Colonel Greer received orders to move the 18th Infantry Regiment back to Sbiba, where the battalions set up camps beside a beautiful, rocky stream. From 26 February to 6 March, time was spent strengthening the Regiment's positions in this area.[25] Patrols were even sent out as far south as Sbeitla, but no contact was made with the enemy. Then, heartening information arrived on 8 March in the form of new movement orders directing the 18th RCT to proceed to Bou Chebka, where it would rejoin the 1st Infantry Division. Colonel Greer and his men were finally trucked out of Sbiba on the night of 9 March and the Regiment started settling into a heavily-forested area outside of Bou Chebka the next morning. A number of replacements soon appeared, many "volunteers" from the 15th and 30th Infantry Regiments of the 3rd Infantry Division in Morocco.[26] To General Terry Allen's joy, his orphaned 18th Infantry Regiment was now reunited with the 1st Infantry Division where it could again fight under his command.

While the 18th Infantry Regiment had been absent from the "Red One" for more than three months and this had been difficult for General Allen, the time spent with the British had served to help mold the Regiment's officers and enlisted men into a more potent fighting unit. Colonel Greer's forces had come a long way since Longstop Hill, and the unfortunate criticism of the 18th Infantry Regiment at that time had given way to compliments from British commanders under whom the combat team served at Medjez and Sbiba. The Regiment's command was gaining confidence, even suggesting a more tactically aggressive attitude. Greer's executive officer, Lieutenant Colonel John Williamson, noted in his diary on 28 February, "Do we have a tendency to overestimate the German and think that just because we hold off his attacks we are doing good work? Hindsight seems to show that we missed a wonderful opportunity to counterattack at Sbiba and destroy a hell of a lot of their tanks and infantry after dark on the first day he put in his tank attack."[27] One incident during this period illustrated the mutual respect that had evolved between the American and British combat troops.

At Sbiba, the 18th Infantry Regiment had lost 10 men killed and eight seriously wounded. Private First Class Robert E. Kassel, a young medic from New York state, was one of those killed while attempting to move a wounded soldier to safety. He was buried beside six other Americans and three British soldiers who had fallen nearby. Each grave was marked with the names of the dead and their next of kin, including their hometown. Edwin C. Blount, a gunner in the British 2nd

Field Regiment, Royal Artillery, was a Londoner who had been a journalist before the war. For reasons unknown, Blount decided to locate Private Kassel's home address so he could send his family a letter. "It may serve a measure of comfort to you to know that your son was given a considerate burial," Blount's letter began. "The view here is grand—a wide area of grassland surrounded on all sides by a range of mountains, splendid in their rugged grandeur. Overhead, the lark trills out a paean of praise to the fallen and nature has worked a carpet of wild flowers at their feet." It was then signed, "Respectfully and sympathetically, E. Blount."[28]

In addition to sorely-needed replacements, the stay at Bou Chebka brought an important change in the Regiment's command structure. Lieutenant Colonel Fricke left the 1st Battalion for reassignment to the Zone of the Interior (the continental United States); he assumed command of a regiment in another division. Majors Powers and Chase had departed the Regiment altogether, with Powers eventually assuming command of a different battalion in Italy and Chase transferring to the Ordnance Corps. Colonel Greer then recognized an officer who had impressed him with his leadership by example. Greer named Major York, whom he had recommended for promotion to lieutenant colonel, to command the 1st Battalion. Captain Robert F. Stockton was assigned as his Executive Officer.[29]

The 18th Infantry Regiment received a visit from its new Corps Commander in early March. Major General George S. Patton, Jr. had been chosen by Eisenhower to replace Fredendall after the latter evidenced ineffective leadership during the battle for the Kasserine Pass. The new II Corps commander was intent on making his own style of command felt immediately. Hell-bent on restoring confidence among his troops, Patton used a variety of techniques to convince the soldiers that they could win in future battles. His first priority was to restore discipline. Among other things, Patton ordered that both officers' and enlisted men's uniform regulations be strictly enforced, and that offenders be punished with fines; to set the tone, Patton personally administered many of them.

Pfc. Louis Newman remembered one such instance. It happened to be very hot one afternoon when Patton rode up in his scout car in full battle dress, escorted by his usual complement of motorcycles. Upon arrival, Patton discovered that neither Newman nor any of the men he was with in Cannon Company were wearing their required ties, helmets or leggings. Evincing a sentiment that was soon to be shared by many in the 18th Infantry Regiment, Newman remembered, "Patton was 100 yards past us when he came back and fined us. That did not endear him to Cannon Company at all."[30] Officers in the Regiment were not spared immediate notice of Patton's directives either. As his biographer Carlo D'Este noted, "One of Patton's first orders was that all officers would wear their insignia of rank on their helmets, even though it would make them better targets. Patton had said, 'That's part of your job of being an officer.' Patton also told his lieutenants and captains that they were expendable and that they must personally lead their men into battle and take the same risks as their lowest-ranking soldier."[31]

On 2 March, ahead of his arrival at II Corps, First Army Headquarters had apprised Patton of his new command's upcoming mission. The Americans were now to conduct an attack against the Axis supply dump at Gafsa, taken by Italian forces during Rommel's Kasserine offensives. This operation was designed to draw off reserves from the enemy forces facing the British Eighth Army at the Mareth Line; to regain firm control of forward airfields; to lend assistance to the British Eighth Army; and to establish a forward logistics base from which mobile forces of the Eighth Army could draw supplies once the Mareth Line was broken. The American forward logistics base was to be established at Gafsa, which would be seized from the Italians no later than 15 March. II Corps was also authorized to probe toward Maknassay to threaten the enemy's lines of communication along the coast. More than 7,000 Italian troops of the *Centauro Division* were thought to be defending in and around Gafsa by this time, and from Sened to Maknassy, about 800 mixed German and Italian troops were also thought to be holding various passes along the Eastern Dorsale mountain range.

Major General Fredendall, in charge of the original planning effort before being replaced by Patton on 6 March, had sardonically christened the attack "Operation WOP." The 1st Infantry Division would attack Gafsa, with the 1st Armored Division protecting the northeastern flank of the advance while troops from the French Southeast Algerian Command would guard the southern flank of II Corps. General Harold R. Alexander and the Chief of Staff of Eighteenth Army Group, General McCreery, approved the tentative plans for this offensive on 8 March at a commander's conference, but the start date was changed to 17 March to align II Corps operations with the projected start of the Eighth Army's attack on the Mareth Line.[32] Gafsa was located in south-central Tunisia, a few short miles west of an important road junction. The junction's right branch began the main 80-mile highway southeast to Gabes, a seashore town in Tunisia on the western side of the great gulf that forms the Libyan coast. Continuing past Gabes, this highway passes to the rear of the Mareth Line, so it was essential for the Germans to be denied this critical route. The left fork out of the nearby Arab village of El Guettar—dubbed the "Gumtree Road" and called "the key to the coast road" by Colonel Greer—branched off to the northeast and passed directly north of Djebel el Ank, a precipitous hill mass that anchored the enemy's defensive position to the east. Tebessa was 84 miles northwest of Gafsa, while Sbeitla was almost as far to the north. Faid Pass was located 72 miles to the northeast and Maknassy some 55 miles to the east-northeast. Gafsa lay perched on the outer ring of this large circle with its line of communications and therefore it was extremely vulnerable.

For the attack on Gafsa, the 1st Ranger Battalion, the 601st Tank Destroyer Battalion, and several additional battalions of field artillery would reinforce General Allen's reunited 1st Infantry Division. Elements of Major General Orlando Ward's 1st Armored Division were also slated to protect the 1st Infantry Division from German counterattacks originating from either Sidi Bou Zid or Maknassy. Allen's plan called for a 30-minute aerial bombardment of Gafsa, followed by an assault by both the 16th and 18th Infantry Regiments and a reinforced battalion of the 26th RCT. The 18th Infantry Regiment would make a 45-mile motor march to an assembly area protected by the 601st TD Battalion the night before the attack. Once the assault force was assembled, the troops would proceed dismounted to a line of departure just west of Gafsa, attacking at dawn the next morning after bombers struck the Italian defenders.

The air strike that was to precede the attack was delayed due to fog, but the 2nd and 3rd Battalions finally jumped off at 1000 hours after the strike was complete. To the attackers' disappointment, Gafsa's defenders had already abandoned the oasis. The garrison of what was later estimated to be just 1,200 Axis soldiers had simply slipped some 15 miles southeastward toward El Guettar. General Allen declared the oasis secure by 1340 hours that afternoon. Allen had already anticipated moving further east to pursue these Italian troops, so he quickly dispatched reconnaissance patrols 20 miles to the north and northeast, where the 1st Infantry Division soon linked up with elements of the division's 81st Reconnaissance Battalion. Additionally, General Allen ordered the 1st Ranger Battalion to move out that night to find the Italian troops who had withdrawn from Gafsa. Accordingly, Lieutenant Colonel William Darby prepared to move his rangers toward El Guettar to make contact with the enemy, to determine their strength and positions, and to secure a foothold for the 1st Infantry Division to exploit when and if so ordered by II Corps. Moving out later that same evening, the Rangers soon found El Guettar undefended, and after leaving behind a portion of his battalion to occupy the town, Darby ordered the remainder of his men to fan out in an effort to locate the Italians. Not surprisingly, they quickly sighted defenses of the *Centauro Division* astride the Gafsa-Gabes road at Djebel El Ank pass.[33]

With Gafsa and El Guettar now in American hands, an officer from II Corps arrived at the 1st Infantry Division command post in Gafsa at 1630 hours on 20 March. He delivered Patton's anticipated alert message for the division to be prepared to attack to the east. It read, "Dear General Allen, Please make all necessary plans, including areas for the emplacement of your artillery, for an attack along the axis Gafsa-Gabes. . . . If this attack comes off, you may be called upon to put it into effect tomorrow."[34] Allen convened a meeting of his key commanders and staff at 1800 hours to discuss the newly-arrived order. A tentative plan was developed for an attack commencing at 0600 hours the next day.

Intelligence reports subsequently indicated that the Italians were defending positions located on many of the steep *djebels* on both flanks at Djebel el Ank pass. Entrenched in the sides of these hill masses, with skillfully sited weapons, the Italians' positions extended for eight miles, stretching from the knife-like Djebel el Ank in the north to the sheer cliffs of Djebel Berda, just south of the Gafsa-Gabes highway. It was the 1st Infantry Division's mission to break through and seize both controlling heights before continuing on toward Gabes, and it was the 18th Infantry's primary mission to gain control of the main El Guettar valley after first driving the enemy out of the hills. To accomplish this, the Regiment was required to first take Hill 336, an extension of Djebel el Ank known as the El Keddab ridge where the Italians occupied well-constructed positions.

At dusk on 20 March, the battalion commanders of the 18th Infantry were summoned to Regimental Headquarters to receive the operation order for the

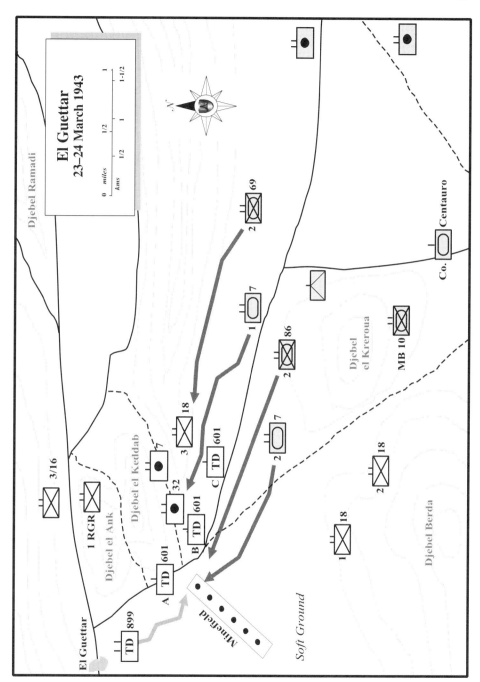

upcoming attack. While the battalion commanders were at the regimental CP, their men were preparing their equipment and being issued rations and ammunition. It was dark when York, Sternberg, and Brown returned to their respective command posts east of Gafsa, but since the skies were clear and the moon would be out at about 2200, everybody knew there would be sufficient light to advance past El Guettar and into the valley. The battalion commanders delivered their own orders to their respective company commanders, and briefings continued through the night; the attackers got what little sleep they could.

Colonel Greer's continuing mission was to attack southeast along the Gafsa-Gabes highway to secure the strongly-held Djebel Berda, located approximately nine miles to the southeast of El Guettar. At the same time, he was also to seize Djebel Mcheltat, a horseshoe-shaped hill mass along the highway eight miles to the east, which formed the backbone of the enemy's main defensive position in the valley. To assure the quick capture of these widely-dispersed objectives, Greer planned three concurrent attacks, each involving calculated risks. The 1st Battalion attack on El Keddab Ridge initially called for a motor move to El Guettar, something Lieutenant Colonel York disliked for fear the noise would draw Italian artillery fire. Since other units were also going to use motor transportation, however, he decided to embrace the concept because it would save three miles of marching and his men would be that much fresher the next morning.

"We had definitely and most assuredly drawn the route most dreaded, the open plain, with nothing but a prayer between us and bullets if we were spotted," Company D's Captain Carter remembered. "But after the men awoke when the trucks arrived, a perfectly haloed moon was up, giving us just enough light to move around and load up."[35] In the haze, towering Djebel Berda could be seen to the southeast, but El Keddab Ridge was hidden beyond the dim moonlight illuminating El Guettar.

The roadway was heavy with traffic that night, as artillery was also displaced to support the attack. At 0330 hours the truck drivers finally stopped and let the men off near a large dirt wall just outside of the village. Captain Carter remembered, "There were a few dogs and Arabs moving around in the shadows and doorways watching us, but so far the enemy hadn't sensed our move."

Lieutenant Colonel York then ordered his battalion to move out toward El Keddab Ridge in a column of companies. Moving across open terrain, they took up extended intervals, with thirty to fifty yards between each company, and five to ten yards between the men. York felt it was imperative that he deployed this formation in the event his men were shelled as they crossed the open valley, but his fears were soon laid to rest when his soldiers reached the foot of the ridge without sustaining any enemy artillery fire. "I will always consider that we were awfully lucky to get across that plain under the cover of darkness and end up just where we had planned to end up, that is encircling the enemy's position and being able to hit them by surprise," York later recalled.[36]

Others fortunately fared as well as York's men, and all of the Regiment's units were in position at 0505 hours on 21 March. As the sky grew light at about 0530, a volley of machine-gun fire suddenly broke the anxious silence before the scheduled offensive was to start at 0600. This ceased after a single burst and word passed quickly through the columns saying that the fire had been laid on by one of the 1st Battalion's own patrols, not the enemy. Lieutenant Colonel Darby had previously told York that his men had discovered that the Italians expected patrols at this hour; to make it appear as if nothing out of the ordinary was going on, York had ordered a patrol forward to achieve this deception.

Shortly afterward, a patrol from Captain Scott-Smith's Company C, the leading element in the 1st Battalion, was challenged by enemy sentries as they approached the rear of the Italian positions. Fortunately, one of the patrol's soldiers within earshot of the enemy was of Italian descent, so he simply answered back with his name, whispering "It's Corrigoni!" and nothing happened. Then moments later, but still several minutes ahead of H-hour, a nervous group of soldiers suddenly fired their self-propelled guns into the enemy's right flank. Hearing this, Captain Scott-Smith quickly realized that he had no choice but to make a fast assault before the Italians could get organized, so his men began scrambling toward their positions, yelling at the top of their lungs and firing. Lieutenant Colonel York, reacting as quickly, then ordered Captain Cameron's Company B to support Scott-Smith, but it turned out to be unnecessary because the Italians were overwhelmed by Company C's surprise assault. Approximately 175 Italians were captured and another 30 killed or wounded.

The 32nd FA was also surprised by the rapid collapse of the Italian position. As their artillery began firing on El Keddab Ridge, the first salvos landed atop Company C's new positions. Confusion reigned and the Americans and their new prisoners had to scramble to take cover from the incoming "friendly" fire. "Our artillery liaison officer contacted *their* artillery and told them it was *our* men on the hill and to cease fire," Captain Carter later remembered with frustration. "But when another salvo landed on the hill, again we contacted them and told them to hold their fire. Again, another salvo came in. This time Lieutenant Colonel York radioed back, telling them it was our men on the hill." York later recalled that the artillery's response indicated to him that their observers were sure they had seen enemy on the hill, but he remembered replying angrily that it was his men, not the enemy that they were actually firing upon. At that point, Captain Carter remembered, "The artillery very reluctantly ceased their fire."[37]

As York's men were securing El Keddab Ridge, Lieutenant Colonel Brown's 3rd Battalion was crossing an open plain to move farther east. Two of his rifle companies were advancing abreast, deployed in squad columns, with his heavy weapons company following and one rifle company in reserve. Lieutenant Colonel Sternberg's 2nd Battalion was also committed north of the 3rd Battalion. This coordinated maneuver around El Keddab Ridge resulted in a rapid double envelopment of the Italian defenses, completely befuddling the already demoralized opposing commander. The only serious challenge occurred when some enemy artillery and mortar fire fell upon Lieutenant Colonel Brown's 3rd Battalion, forcing many of his men to take cover where they could, and also slightly wounding Brown himself.

Despite the confusion and resistance, all three battalions reached their initial objectives by mid-morning, successfully ending the first phase of the operation in the El Guettar valley. As Company M Executive Officer, Lieutenant Herbert A. Smith wrote later, "It was extremely fortunate for us that the enemy had been surprised. The organization of their position was quite extensive. Minefields had been laid and barbed-wire entanglements and obstacles were erected. Gun positions had been dug in and elaborate foxholes with connecting trenches constructed. It is certain that the position would have offered stiff resistance if it had been defended by a determined enemy."[38] Dugouts and emplacements may have honeycombed the area, but most of the Italians were asleep, blankets were lying about, and their breakfast was still warm when they were attacked. Thereafter, many in the 18th Infantry Regiment irreverently dubbed El Keddab Ridge, "Wop Hill."*

At 1130 hours that same morning, Colonel Greer convened another meeting of his battalion commanders to issue new orders. The 18th RCT would now resume the attack at noon to seize the high ground six miles to the east of Djebel el Ank, with Lieutenant Colonel Sternberg's 2nd Battalion attacking on the left and Brown's 3rd Battalion on the right. A battalion of the 16th Infantry Regiment arrived to relieve the 3rd Battalion, which subsequently moved as planned from its position near El Keddab Ridge to seize the dominating high ground north of the Gafsa-Gabes Road on Djebel Mcheltat. For this, each rifle company advanced with two platoons abreast, squads in column, with the heavy weapons company following. The men then crossed extremely rough terrain, dotted with steep, rocky hills and deep *wadis*, which slowed the battalion's movement. The heavy weapons company was especially affected, as its soldiers were carrying their mortars and machine guns rather than using their vehicles.

Twilight was setting in as Brown's men finally halted behind a rocky formation at the base of the *djebel*. Captain Sawyer's Company I was on the right flank at the western end of this horseshoe-shaped area; Captain Raymer's Company K held the center, and Captain Fogg's Company L was on the left flank (east end), with the heavy weapons (Company M, commanded by Captain Rosinski), in position to the rear near Brown's new command post. The 3rd Battalion was ordered to stay in their new positions and protect the guns of Battery B, 32nd Field Artillery, which had also displaced forward to continuing offensive operations

Late that afternoon, Colonel Greer visited York's forward command post to view the 1st Battalion's positions for himself. Feeling invigorated by his earlier success in taking El Keddab Ridge and having Lieutenant Colonel Brown's 3rd Battalion at Djebel Mcheltat, Greer wanted York to continue the attack across the south side of the valley over to the ominous hills of Djebel Berda. Colonel Greer issued the order, but within minutes enemy artillery fire began falling so rapidly that York later recalled it seemed more like continuous machine-gun fire than high-explosive shelling. Worse, it came in very close to Colonel Greer's position,

---

*This reference is included as a historical fact, not with any intention of a slur against Italian-Americans.

immediately convincing him that it was too dangerous to move out in daylight. Greer then rescinded his order, instead directing York to have his men dig in, hold their positions, and await further orders.

It was also dangerous near Company D's forward command post that same afternoon. Soon after El Keddab Ridge fell, Captain Carter had visitors at his vantage point overlooking the Gafsa-Gabes Road—visitors with lots of stars on their uniforms, including II Corps Commander, Major General George Patton, and General Terry Allen. As Patton biographer Carlo D'Este later wrote of the encounter, "On March 21, he [Patton] barely escaped death when a hill at the front was hit with a salvo of 150mm German shells, almost on the spot where he had been sitting, moments after he departed."[39] Captain Carter remembered the incident a little differently, however. Carter had given both Allen and Patton a briefing when they arrived, first explaining the situation to his immediate front. Mindful of Greer's earlier shelling experience at York's command post, he was certain that the Italians already had enough time to site their guns on Company D's positions, so he warned Patton and Allen to that effect. Carter remembered, "As soon as I said this, 'Wheeeeeee, boom, boom, boom, boom;' a battery salvo hit the road to our immediate left rear."[40] Since Carter had just dug himself a foxhole behind a two-foot bank of dirt, he immediately dove for it. According to his account, "Everyone else made for the hole. Never before had the CO of Company D had so many stars trying to get to the bottom of his foxhole." Captain Carter then heard Patton say, "Terry, it's too damn hot. Let's get the hell out of here."[41]

By now the developing American offensive had drawn the attention of Italian artillery observers, and Colonel Greer's regimental forward CP was hit before dark by artillery shells, wounding his radio operator and damaging his jeep. German *Stuka* dive-bombers launched two bombing strikes nearby, subsequently killing two men and wounding an officer. Another jeep was also demolished by a direct hit, as were two howitzers of the 32nd FA. With the element of surprise disappearing even as his 2nd Battalion reached its objective at 1845 hours, Sternberg also reported that there were 15 Italian tanks just to the east of the high ground forward of his positions. He further reported that his men would not be able to advance until tank-destroyer and artillery fire were brought to bear against the Italian vehicles. As night fell, there was some good news, as the last of the Italian prisoners taken that day were processed through the POW enclosure. Tallies showed that the Regiment captured 17 officers and 398 enlisted men, primarily from the *Centauro Armored Regiment* and the *2nd Bersaglieri Regiment*.[42]

At 0945 hours the next morning, Brigadier General Roosevelt visited Colonel Greer's command post, reviewed the overall situation with him, and then decided that the 18th Infantry's advance should be renewed toward the southern side of the valley. The Regiment could then establish positions at the base of Djebel Berda by nightfall. At about noon, Lieutenant Colonel York received this order, another move he anxiously remembered later. "I knew that if the enemy spotted us moving across the desert, they would cut us to ribbons before we could reach the high ground to the other side, and frankly at the time I did not know how in the world they could not help but see us. I would have much preferred this movement at night, but since we can't always choose our assignments, we had to move out."[43]

Fearful of the possible outcome of this daylight advance over featureless terrain, York first ordered a patrol from Captain McGregor's Company A across the valley to reconnoiter the area. When the patrol arrived on higher ground at the base of Djebel Berda without drawing any fire, this indicated to York that the valley was clear, so he ordered his companies to move out with rifle platoons in extended platoon formation, widely separated in case of attack. Remarkably, like his advance to El Keddab Ridge, his good fortunes held. "An act of God, I feel, gave us a route that had just enough defilade to prevent enemy observation," York wrote later. "Although the ground looked absolutely flat from Wop Hill, there was just enough of this defilade to get across without being detected." When the 1st Battalion arrived at its objective, however, it was a different story. By then Italian forward observers had spotted them and they were quick to respond with artillery and mortar fire, the likes of which York remembered "resounded off the hillsides and down through the valley making noises I shall never forget."[44]

York had good reason to remember the incident, for the Italian shelling quickly inflicted several casualties. Shortly after the first salvos came in, a messenger reached Captain Carter with bad news; his executive officer, Lieutenant Stewart W. Grimmer, had been killed by a shell fragment in the skull, and his mortar platoon leader, Lieutenant Paul J. Emerson, was seriously wounded. Dejected at the loss of these key officers, Carter nevertheless sent the runner back with a message for First Sergeant Sam Vartoni to take over as his Executive Officer, and for Sergeant Odel G. Benedict to assume command of the mortar platoon.

By this time, Company A was also under scathing machine-gun fire, so Lieutenant Colonel York quickly ordered Carter's Company D to silence the culprits. Sergeant Benedict was just getting into a position when he received Carter's command to open fire, and he decided to avenge the death of Lieutenant Grimmer by personally aligning a 60mm mortar on the machine-gun nest firing into Company A's positions. The first round was a direct hit, followed by a second explosion that ended the threat. "The second round was fired for good measure," Carter later mentioned. "The enemy machine gun was never heard from again."[45]

Meantime, a 1st Battalion patrol located terrain that permitted York to sideslip his units to the west where they were shielded from fire by the terrain. He was pleasantly surprised to find that this new location was in a protective crescent backed by a thousand-foot sheer wall. With his rear protected, York later recalled with more relief, "It seemed as if this terrain would just swallow our battalion. I recalled uttering the statement, 'All this and heaven, too.'" Adding to York's continued good fortune, his wire team then succeeded in laying a line back to the regimental command post. York used it to report to Colonel Greer and asked him what he wanted him to do. Greer replied that he was anxious to continue the attack, but York advised that he wanted to stand fast until the patrols he had just sent out returned. Only then could he determine the best direction for his battalion's continued attack. Greer acceded to the request, but urged York to renew his assault as soon as possible.

Worried that the 1st Battalion would not be able to reduce the Italians without some assistance, Greer also ordered the 2nd Battalion, still located east of El Keddab Ridge on the northeastern end of the valley, to take up positions on the immediate right of York's companies. By 0430 hours on 23 March, Sternberg's companies had also safely crossed the open plain in the valley east of El Guettar. After being greeted by a patrol sent out by York to guide his good friend and fellow West Pointer to the correct hilltop, the 2nd Battalion established itself on the precipitous hills of Djebel Berda due east of the 1st Battalion. Lieutenant Jeffrey's Company G deployed on the high ground just west of a *wadi* near Djebel Kerousa, a long spur extending northeastward. Captain Spinney's Company F occupied positions overlooking the Gafsa-Gabes road, and Captain Randall's Company E assumed a defense on the east slope of the hill mass. When Captain Murphy's Company H arrived in the valley, he turned the company over to his executive officer, Lieutenant James A. Lucas, and then directed him to proceed to an assembly area while he went over to Company F's position to survey the situation.

After conferring with Captain Spinney, Murphy recommended to Sternberg that a platoon of his heavy machine guns and a section of his mortars be placed in direct support of Spinney's men. Sternberg quickly approved the plan and Murphy ordered Lucas to bring up his 1st Platoon and the mortars.

During this move, York also determined that it was time to coordinate artillery fire to support the expected morning attack by the 1st and 2nd Battalions. By now, the 32nd FA had completed displacing forward to positions southwest of Brown's 3rd Battalion on the other side of the valley, and two companies of the 601st Tank Destroyer Battalion had also moved forward, occupying hull-down firing positions between the Gafsa-Gabes road and the howitzers of the field artillery. A 32nd FA forward observer section soon trekked south in the darkness across the valley to join the 1st Battalion at 0300 hours, so York now had his artillery observer in place. At that time, things were quiet and everyone tried to rest.

An hour and a half later, the quiet night was interrupted by the sounds of many engines. Lieutenant Colonel Sternberg heard these threatening rumbles just as he was settling his 2nd Battalion into position to the east of the 1st Battalion. He was undoubtedly grateful, as it was just an hour earlier that his battalion had been in the valley from whence the ominous sounds were coming. Now, his rifle companies were in position and prepared, and Murphy's heavy weapons were in place to render support. His men were on line with all three of Lieutenant Colonel York's rifle companies, and Lieutenant Jeffrey's Company G was in contact with Captain McGregor's Company A. Whatever the sounds were, Sternberg was ready.

Lieutenant Colonel York, who had been unable to sleep, also heard the suspicious sounds of these noisy engines at about the same time that morning. Growing concerned that both his and Sternberg's battalion could easily be isolated from the rest of the 18th Infantry Regiment across the valley, York decided to immediately report these rumblings to Colonel Greer's command post. He then directed Captain McGregor's Company A to advance slightly toward the valley floor where they could gain better firing positions against whatever force was now moving along the Gafsa-Gabes road. He also ordered Captain Cameron's Company B to now take up positions in the hills above Company A to augment McGregor's defense.

At 0445 hours, men in a 601st Tank Destroyer Battalion reconnaissance outpost on the north side of the valley captured a motorcyclist from the *10th Panzer Division*. He was evidently the point man for an advance guard moving northwest on the road from Gabes. Unknown immediately to York or Sternberg, this German division had just completed a forced march from the vicinity of Gabes. Its tanks and infantry had arrived in the valley occupied by the 18th RCT at 0430 hours. The information gained from the motorcyclist revealed to the tank destroyers' Commanding Officer, Lieutenant Colonel Hershel D. Baker, the size of the force he was about to confront. He also realized just how precarious his positions actually were. Baker's half-track mounted 75mm guns had been sited to safeguard against any attempt by the *Centauro Division* to infiltrate small groups of tanks and infantry amongst the forward-deployed batteries of the 32nd FA. With the *10th Panzer Division* now being nearby with anywhere from 80 to 100 tanks, however, his crews would be in for a vicious fight against a competent enemy who outnumbered his tank destroyers almost three to one.[46]

Shortly after capturing the motorcyclist, the 601st TD outpost reported the German tanks approaching from the southeast. Even though it was still dark, a late moon aided visibility and the men in the outpost were able to discern 16 tanks moving along the Gafsa-Gabes road, with two companies of infantry accompanying them. The men at the outpost decided to wait until the Germans were within 200 yards of their position before opening fire. Their machine gun and 37mm canister fire cut down a number of the grenadiers, but they did not inflict any apparent damage to the tanks. The outpost party then withdrew to new positions after two of their own half-tracks were hit during this pre-dawn engagement.

Early-morning light was also just starting to fill the other side of the valley, but not strongly enough to reveal an immediate view of what was about to greet the 1st and 2nd Battalions at the base of Djebel Berda. As the minutes passed, the motor sounds Sternberg and York had been hearing for some time now grew even louder. Then red, white, and blue tracers shot into the sky, emerging atop the ever-increasing roars that lay mysteriously underneath the still fog-blanketed valley. Moments later more green, purple, yellow, and orange tracers shot up into the air, followed by the deeply rumbling echoes of the firing of large-caliber guns.

Reflecting on the moments when the fog lifted that morning, Lieutenant Colonel York wrote years later, "Seldom in the life of any soldier will he have the opportunity to witness what we saw at that time. Tanks, armored vehicles, artillery, everything, just as far as the eye could see, and we had a ringside seat on the edge of this tremendous arena. The hugeness, clockwork and precision of the *10th Panzer* attack made me temporarily forget our own precarious position. Although we were stunned by such force for a short time, we soon realized that if the panzers we saw flanking El Keddab Ridge on the other side of the valley succeeded, we would be cut off from every Allied unit except the French forces south of us behind Djebel Berda." By now, the panzergrenadiers York was observing were moving up into de-trucking locations in front of their tanks nearer to the 3rd Battalion positions in front of Djebel Mcheltat.[47]

At 0500 hours, Lieutenant Colonel Brown's men began hearing the loud sounds of these tanks closing to their right front. Minutes later, the same tracers that the battalion commanders had witnessed across the valley were also seen by forward observers of Captain Raymer's Company K, then the dim shapes of the approaching tanks and vehicles started to suddenly appear in front of them. At about the same time, Colonel Greer telephoned Brown wanting to know what the noise and firing he was also hearing was all about, and Brown told him that it sounded as if a whole panzer division was moving up the valley. It was now light enough to see out on the plain for about 900 yards and as the enemy moved closer, Company M Executive Officer Smith. remembered, "We watched this show, the sheer magnitude and precision of *the 10th Panzers,* in awe."[48]

Just after 0515 the Germans launched their full attack. Led by what was estimated to be 75 tanks of *Panzer Regiment 7,* all either Mark IIs, Mark IIIs or Mark IVs, supported by infantry from *2nd Battalion, Panzer-Grenadier Regiment 86* and *2nd Battalion, Panzer-Grenadier Regiment 69,* the assault moved steadily towards the horseshoe occupied by the 3rd Battalion at the foot of Djebel Mcheltat. German half-tracks loaded with troops fell in behind the first wave of the advancing infantry, all of whom were proceeding on foot through the valley in a deployed formation. As morning light continued to filter onto the battleground, heavy concentrations of enemy mortar started falling into Brown's positions, immediately followed by ever-increasing numbers of rapidly approaching half-tracks and tanks. As Captain Raymer, commanding Company K square in the center of the attack, remembered, "Jerry's artillery then opened up and it was plenty vicious."[49]

The first Germans to reach his company were an Oberleutnant, followed by his scout. Raymer's 1st Platoon leader, Lieutenant Astor A. Morris, quickly killed his opposite number with a Thompson submachine gun while Staff Sergeant Jackson Hawkins cut down the scout. Nevertheless, *t*he German half-tracks kept closing, sometimes crushing Raymer's men right in their foxholes. The 3rd Battalion was being hit hard across Brown's frontline, especially Company K, which was already suffering very heavy casualties. Brown recognized the desperate situation immediately and ordered the mortars in Captain Rosinski's Company M to start pouring what would soon be 500 pounds of bore-reddening fire at the Germans. Adding to the strike, Lieutenant Morris first pulled his platoon back to the reverse slope of the hill and briefly waited. When he got a signal from his forward outpost a few minutes later, he ordered his men to start hurling grenades over the ridge onto the advancing panzergrenadiers. Brown's front was about 500 yards wide and when the enemy's armor pulled to within 50 yards of this expanse, his infantry greeted them with everything they could muster. As Lieutenant William A. Russell, leading Captain Raymer's 3rd Platoon, said later about these moments,

"You could look in the air and see between 30 and 40 grenades all at the same time."[50]

Evincing the effect of Company K's withering return fire that morning, Ernst Brietenberger, a German machine gunner then attacking Raymer's positions with *Panzer-Grenadier Regiment 69* recalled, "Our group of thirty men manned six machine guns, and we made contact with [the] 18th Infantry about an hour after dawn. Behind us on the plain our tanks, Mark IIIs and Mark IVs in our area, were spread out, but of course they could not get up the steep slopes we were on.... Very soon we were completely stopped. The heavy machine guns did not bother us but we began to take losses from sniper fire.... We could see no gun flashes or even smoke from guns.... We made no progress all day, just lay there. The ground was too hard to dig in."[51]

From dawn onward, the main thrust by the attacking tanks steadily bored into Lieutenant Colonel Brown's ranks while the panzer crews also exchanged continuous fire with the 601st TD Battalion, the 32nd FA's howitzers and the 1st Infantry Division's 155mm guns. Captain Raymer's bazooka teams destroyed several half-tracks and light tanks through the morning, effectively stopping the attack in front of his Company K. A number of German tanks had worked their way to the west, bypassing the tank destroyers and 32nd FA before they were caught between an area of soft sand and American minefields. They simply halted and turned around, towing several disabled vehicles back as they retreated. This seesaw action lasted until the oppressive heat of mid-morning simply wore down everyone on the battlefield. At that point the ammunition-depleted German armored vehicles started retiring farther out of range, leaving only a few tanks as a security force in the rolling ground north of the Gafsa-Gabes road. Eight German tanks had been hit, four of which were recovered at the time and towed to the rear.

As this main German thrust was attacking Brown's 3rd Battalion in an effort to push further west, other German units were assaulting the 601st TD and 32nd FA positions on his left flank. Lieutenant Colonel Baker's Companies B and C, which were arrayed to the front of the howitzers of the 32nd FA, had been involved in intense action since daybreak. The tank destroyer companies had each positioned themselves with two platoons abreast and one in reserve, leaving their SP 75mm guns in defilade among the ridges and small rolling hills. When their forward observers warned of the approaching groups of five or six enemy tanks, the tank destroyers moved up to the top of the ridge and fired, then backed down until another target came along. The German tanks came in so swiftly, however, that most of the tank destroyers were forced to stand and fire back as rapidly as possible. This exposed them to return fire from the German tanks, as well as the extensive German artillery fire. The 3rd Platoon of Company B had been the first to open fire, and this drew the attention of the advancing enemy; the Germans promptly turned their vehicles in their direction and opened fire. This presented other tank destroyer crews with flank shots against the more-vulnerable and less-well-armored sides of the German vehicles. Although the Germans were able to eventually force the 3rd Platoon to withdraw later that morning, the attackers also lost a number of tanks to Baker's opposing TDs.[52]

In an attempt to keep the German tanks at bay, the 32nd FA fired mission upon mission throughout the morning. Major Harry Critz, the battalion XO, had displaced the batteries well forward of El Keddab Ridge just after midnight to support what he thought would be the Regiment's renewed advance at dawn. Critz had not deployed his units with defense against a direct assault in mind. Instead, each battery had been positioned in its own *wadi* at the foot of the ridges beneath El Keddab Ridge, with their guns laid to the east and southeast toward the Gafsa-Gabes Road and into the valley. Battery C was nearest the road; Battery B was in the middle and Battery A was located on the immediate right flank of the 3rd Battalion near Captain Sawyer's Company I. Unfortunately, by positioning his howitzers well forward in anticipation of going on the offensive, Major Critz had unknowingly placed them squarely astride the chosen German avenue of their surprise attack.

Lieutenant Frank Silva, XO of the 32nd FA's Battery B, was adjusting fire on several German tanks approaching the 3rd Battalion's positions that morning. Silva had the exact range, but he wasn't getting any hits, so he radioed back to his battalion fire direction center for help. They replied by telling Silva to have his battery stop firing because the muzzle blast was giving away their location. By then, the Germans were closing in, and with his howitzers in defilade positions in the *wadi*, Silva's crews were protected from the flat trajectory of the enemy tank fire, but not from German artillery behind them that began bracketing his battery. As Silva later recalled, "It was impossible to manhandle the guns to positions to cover our flanks in those moments. We were ordered to destroy [spike] our guns, so we put thermite grenades down the tubes, hoping the molten metal would fuse the breechblock to the breech so the block couldn't be opened. Two section chiefs even poured gasoline on their guns and set them on fire."[53] Before long, several gun positions were completely overrun. The 3rd Battalion was so heavily engaged in its own desperate struggles that Brown simply could not spare anyone else to assist the stricken artillery. Consequently, most of the battery commanders had no choice but to spike their guns and tell their men to run for cover.

With the tank destroyers suffering heavy losses and the 32nd FA temporarily silenced, Colonel Greer made it clear to Lieutenant Colonel Brown that his 3rd Battalion had no choice but to hold their precarious position in the horseshoe at all costs. As Brown hastily prepared for this all-around defense, his company commanders reported substantial reductions in their ammunition supplies due to the morning fighting. In response, he ordered all 19 jeeps in his heavy weapons company to run the gauntlet back to the regimental ammunition supply point. Brown recognized the danger, since the ammo dump was located near Colonel Greer's forward command post nearer to El Guettar, but it was absolutely necessary to take this risk if the battalion was to have any chance in the renewed German attack that was sure to come. The 19 jeep drivers set off on their risky mission at noon and only 13 returned by mid-afternoon, all loaded with the critically needed mortar rounds, grenades, and bullets. Three jeeps were knocked out by German artillery, and *Stuka* dive-bombers destroyed three more. Later, the drivers who made the dangerous trip received the Silver Star for their exceptional bravery.

With the initial German assault temporarily stalled, the 2nd Battalion, 16th Infantry was directed to reclaim the howitzers of the 32nd FA, and by 1230 hours, six 105mm howitzers were back in action due to the their efforts. Their crews immediately began firing missions, this time in support of Sternberg's companies.[54] Across the valley, York and Sternberg's battalions had not been subject to the full brunt of the German attack, but Captain Spinney's Company F had already reported 13 German tanks in front of his position, four of which were subsequently knocked out by the 32nd FA's renewed artillery fire.

The leaders of the 1st Infantry Division made other much-needed adjustments. Reserves from II Corps arrived on the north side of the valley, including a company of new M-10 tank destroyers of the 899th Tank Destroyer Battalion. A battalion of the 9th Infantry Division's 39th Infantry Regiment was attached to the 16th Infantry Regiment and the 7th FA Battalion also came in to reinforce the hard-hit 32nd FA. General Allen ordered the newly-arrived tank destroyers forward, then engineers mined the Gafsa-Gabes road behind them, sealing the exit from the valley by 1340 hours.[55] Meanwhile, II Corps signal intelligence had broken the German tactical codes and they had reported to General Allen's G-3 that their radio intercepts revealed that an all-out German assault would be renewed at 1600 hours using two panzergrenadier battalions, an additional two panzer battalions, and two battalions of field artillery.[56] Allen quickly notified Colonel Greer of this, and he passed the warning to his subordinates. As Lieutenant Colonel Brown confidently remembered at the time, "We were prepared for them."

Lieutenant Colonel York had spent the morning at the base of Djebel Berda not just in awe of the attack, but frustrated that he could do little about it from the other side of the valley. When he received notice from Greer about the timing of the second attack, however, he was confident that the 1st Infantry Division engineers' good work would play an important role in the outcome of the battle. The day before the German attack began, the engineers had laid over 3,200 mines near the Gafsa-Gabes road before taking their place in the line between the tank destroyers and the field artillery that afternoon. "That was the weak zone of our defense," the 1st Engineer Battalion's Lieutenant Colonel Henry C. Rowland remembered later. "It was all broad terrain, good inviting land to the panzer tanks. But, our mine fields were ready for Jerry in [these] channels."[57]

Meantime, II Corps' signalmen intercepted a second German message, this one revealing that the attack was going to be delayed until 1645 hours to allow enough time for a heavy air strike ahead of their ground advance. As General Allen later revealed, "This was too good to keep, so [I] directed the Signal Company to broadcast a message over the German battle net at 1615 hours." Taunting his enemy, Allen's message audaciously read, "What the hell are you waiting for? We have been ready since 4:00 PM. Signed First Division."[58]

At precisely 1645 hours, first the drone of aircraft engines, then the screeching whistles of *Stukas,* and finally the loud echoes of explosions were heard throughout the El Guettar valley as bombs dropped on American artillery and infantry. These relentless air attacks kept coming for ten long minutes. An American lieutenant wrote, "The big black bombs looked as if they were coming straight towards us, but all we could do was turn to face the dirt and claw with our fingertips to hang on. The explosions blew us what seemed to be two feet into the air."[59] Other explosions raged angrily from both sides of the valley, the German field artillery aiming at positions to the 3rd Battalion's rear; the 1st Infantry Division's antiaircraft guns blazing at the incoming *Stukas* and Bf-109s. Almost as quickly as the attack began, the planes disappeared and both sides slackened their fire. As Company M's Lieutenant Smith recalled, "Then the battlefield was ominously silent."[60] Moments later, enemy tanks and personnel carriers again crossed the valley under a curtain of renewed artillery fire, their infantry creeping steadily forward, out in front of the panzers towards the 3rd Battalion positions. Before long, Company K was again under attack. "At about 1730 hours we saw ten half-tracks and three light tanks moving against our 1st Platoon," Captain Raymer remembered. "They were running their half-tracks over our entire position and shooting down into our foxholes." Many in this platoon were captured; others hid in a cave after the attack, the only ones to get away. Soon afterwards, a similar fate befell Raymer's 2nd Platoon, led by Lieutenant Francis H. Tripp, and after very close hand-to-hand fighting, all but eight of his men were killed or captured. Tripp was one of those captured and eventually sent to a POW camp in Germany.

The remaining men of Company K were not about to surrender. By now Raymer's soldiers were weary and outnumbered, yet they were still unwilling to give an inch of ground. Behind them, the Company M mortars coughed loudly, again and again, as they lobbed their rounds into the oncoming German infantry. Rifle grenades, .30-caliber armor-piercing ammunition, and rocket launchers were fired by one of the Cannon Company platoons, quickly disabling two attacking half-tracks. Four of Raymer's soldiers even volunteered to plug a gap in the company's center sector, which had been badly weakened by attrition. Two of these men were killed, but the others held the attackers at bay. Another man crawled behind an enemy machine-gun position, and then blew it to bits with grenades. Later, one of the mortar section leaders found some of the enemy hiding in a *wadi,* and he immediately directed fire that destroyed them.

"It was the sweetest running thing I'd ever seen," Captain Raymer said later. "Morale was almost feverish. The boys had only one thing in mind—to keep the enemy away."[61] Through a continued display of exceptional courage and skill, they succeeded. The soldiers of Company K held their position after losing 9 men killed, 21 wounded and 32 missing—over 60 percent casualties sustained in the process of halting the attack. The total number of Germans killed or wounded by Company K was difficult to count, but Lieutenant Gilbert E. Guth who led the weapons platoon found 50 dead Germans in front of his position the next day. Staff Sergeant Walter Ehlers, also of Company K, said approximately 200 dead

German soldiers were found in front of the company that day, even though the enemy had removed some of their fallen early in the morning.

Captain Edward Kuehn, the 3rd Battalion intelligence officer, walked amongst the dead Germans that morning on the right side of the previous day's combat zone. He remembered, "I saw a young, impeccably-uniformed German officer who was killed, still frozen on his knees with his PK pistol in his right hand and I wondered who the damn fool was who ordered the frontal attack on our company."[62] Cannon Company's Pfc. Louis Newman, fined by Patton back at Bou Chebka, had been crouched in a foxhole most of the afternoon of the attack, but the next morning he, too, went forward to see the carnage in front of Company K. "I looked down from the hill I was on, and below me were light tanks lined up about ten feet apart," he remembered. "They were burned out wrecks, and there were bodies hanging on the tracks, some wedged in the tracks, but all dead."[63]

Soon afterwards, Company K was cited for its outstanding performance of duty on 23 March 1943, the first 18th Infantry Regiment combat team element to receive a Distinguished Unit Citation during WWII. Although Captain Kuehn later assumed command of Company K and retained a life-long pride in the company's battle record, he shared the opinion of many that the entire battalion should have been recognized for its conduct of the defense in the same way as the company. Captain Raymer received a Distinguished Service Cross for his heroic leadership of Company K.[64] The 32nd Field Artillery Battalion was also awarded a Presidential Unit Citation for its outstanding performance of duty in continuing its support to the 18th Infantry Regiment "without interruption," despite the terrible attacks sustained by its batteries all day.

General Allen's decision to use the M-10s of the 899th Tank Battalion on the afternoon of 23 March also proved quite fortuitous. When the enemy attack started, the 899th's Company C was in position, waiting for the enemy armor to come into range. At the same time, DIVARTY (Division Artillery) commenced missions using variable time fuses on its high-explosive shells; this rained fragments on the panzergrenadiers, totally disrupting the German attack. Two Mark IVs ventured out during this melee, only to be wiped out by the three-inch guns of Company C's M-10s, and another TD platoon hit a half-track and an artillery piece. By the time the action ended, the battalion claimed the destruction of ten Mark IVs and two antitank guns, with another three Mark IVs damaged. Rather than exploit the maneuverability of its TDs and the rolling terrain to the fullest, Company C had instead dueled directly with the German armor for over six straight hours that morning. By doing so, it forced many of the enemy tanks into the minefields, resulting in chaos, loss of maneuverability, and more tanks killed.[65]

Later that afternoon, two battalions of German infantry had also formed up 4,000 yards to the front of the remaining elements of the 601st TD Battalion l (?). Their tanks waited behind them, as if to follow the infantry, but instead the German tanks merely milled around, creating dust and confusion. The German grenadiers attacked at 1640 hours in extended formation, generally astride the Gafsa-Gabes Road. They were so tired from lack of sleep and unremitting combat operations that they walked barely upright and moved in slowly, not making any attempt at concealment or maneuver. "We then cut down on them at fifteen hundred yards," Lieutenant Colonel Baker wrote later. "It was like mowing hay. Our tank destroyers fired rapidly, employing all arms, but the heavy-caliber high-explosive shells were the most effective. One gun sergeant bracketed rapidly and fired as fast as he could, making 5-mil deflection changes. He dropped high-explosive shells at 7-yard intervals across the German lines."[66] [This meant that the range at that point was only about 1,400 yards. *Ed.*] Baker's TD Battalion had lost 29 SP 75mm guns during the engagement that morning; there were only two operational half-tracks left in the 601st when the second German assault began. Nevertheless, the surviving vehicles pumped out rounds at a tremendous rate. Altogether that day, the 601st expended 2,740 rounds of 75mm and 49,000 rounds of machine-gun ammunition, and traded their 29 thinly-armored, open-topped half-tracks with WWI-vintage 75mm guns for 30 German tanks.[67]

From the southern side of the valley, Lieutenant Colonel York had a clear view of the afternoon's attack. He later wrote that the absence of any air support "was the only thing that caused our picture to be incomplete." "In my opinion," he noted, "This could have done a world of good." York also gave credit to the RCT's engineers, saying, "I attribute our success in repelling the attack chiefly to the minefield in front of Wop Hill which we could cover with small arms fire, artillery, mortars, and other direct-fire weapons by our stouthearted doughboys."[68]

Avoiding the soft sand of the Gafsa-Gabes road by attacking along its northern edge, the German main effort had penetrated beyond the 3rd Battalion positions, effectively isolating the 1st and 2nd Battalions. As a result, they might have been able to overrun the rest of DIVARTY, had they not been stopped. Lieutenant Colonels York and Sternberg were wise enough to know that they were still at risk of counterattack as darkness fell and the moon rose over many still-smoking enemy tanks, and that the battle for El Guettar was only temporarily over.[69]

Just before midnight, 3rd Battalion soldiers withdrew from their isolated positions in the horseshoe ridge at Mcheltat. Brown's exhausted forces filed away silently, most hearing just the shuffling of worn service shoes that night. Spirits had been buoyed, though, by the sight of once-haughty Germans openly weeping as they were led to POW cages. As Company M's Lieutenant Smith poignantly recalled, the German prisoners "knew the *10th Panzers* were beaten. It was astounding to them since it was the first time in the history of World War II that American troops had beaten a panzer division. It must be remembered that the [soldiers] of this unit belonged to the famed *Africa Corps* and were imbued with their own invincibility and superiority. They considered their defeat a disgrace."[70]

The *10th Panzer Division* had suffered more than 300 casualties on 23 March. Only 32 tanks (6 Panzer IIs, 17 Panzer IIIs, and 9 Panzer IVs) out of almost 80 that began in the battle remained operational. A total of 45 tanks and two self-propelled guns were knocked out during the fighting, and several lost from other causes. That evening, however, the Germans recovered 36 of their disabled tanks (5 Panzer IIs, 18 Panzer IIIs, and 15 Panzer IVs), and many of these would be returned to action eventually. In addition to its sorely-depleted tank regiment, one of the two *10th Panzer Division* panzergrenadier battalions was considered to have sustained moderate casualties, while the other was characterized as "very exhausted." Consequently, a *Marsch Abteilung* (replacement unit) was assigned to the *10th Panzer Division* to replace its depleted infantry component. Additionally, the division was also forced to commit its engineer battalion as infantry.[71] Plagued by heavy tank casualties, the *10th Panzer Division* had to abandon its major offensive against El Guettar, attacking only when a suitable opportunity presented itself.

General Allen granted an interview to several war correspondents late in the day near his CP outside of El Guettar. He was very proud of his men. "I think the division has done well today," he told them. "Everybody deserves credit. The artillery deserves credit, and so do the engineers, the tank destroyers, and the Ranger battalion." At one point, Allen was asked how many tanks he had in battle, to which he gave an answer that would have made more captured Germans cry had they heard it. Smiling, he replied, truthfully, "None!" When asked if he had known all along that the *10th Panzers* were in the area, General Allen remarked, "No, but I knew something was fishy, and we were ready for anything, weren't we? We won this battle when we got on those hills and only the infantry could have done it."[72]

Victory not withstanding that day, both sides had made a number of tactical errors on 23 March. Allen positioned the TDs of the 601st directly in front of his artillery, thus ensuring that the lightly-armored American half-tracked mounted guns would be forced to engage the attacking tanks from their most heavily-protected (frontal) aspect. As a result, the 601st suffered significant losses, perhaps unnecessarily.[73] The attacking Germans, confidently expecting the Americans to fold under their assault, launched their initial assaults relying primarily on their armor for success. Lacking effective support from engineers, infantry, and artillery, the panzers were defeated. The late afternoon assault also lacked combined arms coherence, primarily employing dismounted infantry. The German commander could not have been thinking clearly if he expected foot soldiers to succeed where 80 tanks had failed.

Ironically, the first major victory won by American forces in Tunisia had used a tactical plan drawn up by the disgraced Major General Fredendall before his relief. That plan had been executed by an American infantry division—the Big Red One—that had not fought as a team since it landed in Oran almost five months earlier.

During the next day, 24 March, the 1st Infantry Division remained in defensive positions awaiting another attack. The *10th Panzer Division* did not have the strength to launch major offensive operations, however, the Germans planned a limited-objective drive designed to gain control of the high ground along the southeastern edge of the valley, in particular Hill 772 atop Djebel Berda. This assault was aimed at Lieutenant Colonel Sternberg's 2nd Battalion, still positioned at the foot of the *djebel* along the low hills fronting the floor of the valley. Major Heinrich Drewes' *Motorcycle Battalion 10 (Kradschützen Bataillon 10)*, known as "K-10," conducted this attack. Originally organized as a motorcycle battalion,

K-10 now consisted of two motorcycle companies; one company equipped with half-tracks; a heavy weapons company equipped with two infantry gun platoons and an antitank platoon; and a fifth company with armored cars. For the assault on Djebel Berda, two combat engineer platoons were also attached to Major Drewes's forces.[74]

At dusk on 24 March, Sternberg's men first heard the high pitched whine of numerous BMW R75 motorcycles coming toward them. Dismounting just before commencing their assault, the brunt of the K-10 attack fell on Company G. Being the most exposed on the high ground that jutted out into the valley and a ripe target for the Germans, Lieutenant Jeffrey's men had been under fire most of the day, with none of the Regiment's supporting artillery or tank destroyers available to cover their front. The men of Company G found themselves even more vulnerable, as the supporting tanks and self-propelled guns of the enemy laid fire directly into their foxholes. Eventually, Jeffrey's men broke, their fighting ability crushed by this overwhelming enemy force, and better than two-thirds of his officers and men were killed, captured, or wounded. Pfc. Henry Bowles, whose twin brother, Thomas, was a mortarman in Company G, remembered, "They were under continuous fire that night. Two other men and I were hurriedly working our way over to their front, but when we got there we only saw Germans. Luckily, I found my brother. He and 32 others got out before their position was overrun. Thomas had run out of ammunition, and he told me his lieutenant thought they were going to have to surrender, but somehow they jumped off a cliff and escaped. Everyone else was gone."[75] In addition to many prisoners, the Germans captured several machine guns, six mortars, two antitank guns, and five jeeps. Drewes was later awarded the Knight's Cross of the Iron Cross for this attack and his subsequent defense of this captured ground against the U.S. 9th Infantry Division days later.

Recognizing the peril to his battalion that night, Lieutenant Colonel Sternberg quickly shortened his lines by pulling back Company F. This essentially refused the battalion's flank and prevented the Germans from launching an attack from that quarter. Spinney's men soon linked up with Lieutenant Colonel York's Companies A and C at a new line of resistance on the perimeter of a bowl-shaped depression several hundred yards to the rear. Sternberg then directed Captain Randall to move Company E onto the highest ridge overlooking the bowl to prevent German infiltration behind this new defensive line.

By now it was well past midnight, and both battalion commanders were facing the grim realization that they were closer than ever to the trap both had feared for two days. Sternberg's dilemma manifested itself in yet another scare before dawn. At about 0300 hours, he saw what he believed to be a battalion-sized enemy force working around to the rear of Company E. At the time, Sternberg was with both Lieutenant Colonel York and Lieutenant Colonel Darby, who had moved his 1st Ranger Battalion to the south side of the valley. York wasn't convinced that the Germans could have positioned themselves behind Randall's men that quickly, but both Sternberg and Darby were certain something was there, so they contacted the regimental CP to ask for guidance. Before the regimental commander responded, however, daylight broke and the enemy force in front of the 2nd Battalion had disappeared.

When Captain Carter of Company D witnessed first light that morning, he also saw troops on high ground opposite his battalion. The Germans were using the increasing visibility to register their mortars on his company, but Carter had beaten them to the punch. Anticipating his vulnerability, he had his 81mm mortar platoon register on this hilly point the day before, and he was now about to start his enemy's day by delivering everything his soldiers could fire at them. His mortar squads set up in the open, using the hill for an aiming point, and then let go. The range was some 2,450 yards—well within the weapon's 3,290 yard range with light high-explosive rounds—and as Carter later remembered, "We made short order of the enemy. They scampered down the back side of the hill with our shells dropping all around them until they were out of sight and out of range."[76] Later referring to Captain Carter's work that morning, Lieutenant Colonel York wrote, "Believe me, it was a God-send."[77] Lieutenant Colonel Sternberg then ordered Company E to secure the hill the Germans had abandoned, but their movement was quickly spotted. After taking heavy small arms fire from panzergrenadiers on the side of the hill, Sternberg ordered Randall to stand fast.

Given the resulting stalemate, Greer finally ordered York and Sternberg to withdraw from their exposed position during the afternoon of 25 March. The 1st Battalion commander was somewhat reluctant to leave his position, however. "I thought the ground we were on was tactically important enough to hold if any unit planned to operate over that sector," York wrote later. "Further, I told Colonel Greer that we could hold it."[78] "It was impossible for the enemy to get tanks and self-propelled guns into the hills without extensive labor and time," agreed Captain Carter. "We also asked for reinforcements so we would have enough troops to cover to the east and north. With the aid of another regiment, we could have taken all of Djebel Berda and opened the road to Gabes, giving the armor an opportunity to drive a salient through to the sea, splitting the enemy forces."[79]

The directive had come down from II Corps, however, so York and Sternberg complied. By 2314 hours, the 1st and 2nd Battalions were reported clear of Djebel Berda and were marching to an assembly area by El Keddab Ridge to board trucks back to El Guettar. York's reservations about departing the near solid rock hill mass had merit. On 28 March, the 9th Infantry Division's 47th Infantry Regiment relieved the 1st Ranger Battalion in positions east of Djebel Berda. Over a seven-day period, this regiment and other elements of the same division sustained over 1,800 casualties, to include 430 killed in action, and nearly 900 seriously wounded. Others fell victim to exhaustion, injury, disease, or were captured. On the night of 6–7 April, the 9th Infantry Division finally reached the positions on Djebel Berda that Regiment had so reluctantly relinquished.

The 1st Infantry Division continued to operate northeast of El Guettar for the next two weeks. On 28 March, the 18th Infantry, minus the still regrouping 3rd Battalion in division reserve, was ordered to defend the pass at Djebel Ank in conjunction with a general division advance. The next morning, however, Lieutenant

Colonel Brown's men were committed to battle in concert with a battalion of the 26th Infantry Regiment at Djebel Takadelt. By 1015 hours, they overran the Germans on this objective, after which elements of the 18th Infantry Regiment seized another hill, finally permitting observation of the entire Gabes-Gafsa Valley eastward. "We could look up the valley for miles," Lieutenant Colonel Williamson remembered in his diary, "We took 75 or 100 prisoners of *Panzer-Grenadier Regiment 69*—our Longstop friends. Lots of dead Germans. Our losses very light, mostly from artillery fire."[80]

On 1 April, General Allen's 55th birthday, the 18th Infantry Regiment's sector was reorganized, gaps were filled, and positions fortified. By this time, the battle had evolved into more frequent instances of enemy bombing and strafing raids, with only an occasional Allied fighter defending the air over the ground for which Colonel Greer's forces were still fighting. The absence of air support during the entire engagement found criticism in nearly every report written after the battles ended. Company M's Lieutenant Smith wrote, "If the air corps had given the 1st Division effective close air support, in all probability the *10th Panzer Division* would have been completely wiped out. Every man in the 3rd Battalion realized the value of air support, and wondered about its glaring absence."[81]

To speed up the attack, a task force of the 1st Armored Division made several attempts to break through the valley along the Gafsa-Gabes Road during the first week of April. General Allen judged this effort "ineffectual." German resistance began to crumble, mainly because infantry units of the 9th and 34th Infantry Divisions joined the Big Red One in prying the enemy out of the crevasses and precipitous *djebels* in the remainder of the El Guettar valley. During 6 April, all 1st Infantry Division units reached their final objectives. It was apparent the next day that the Germans had pulled back to save their strength. As General Allen later wrote, "The El Guettar offensive paid dividends. It resulted in drawing off powerful German reserves from the front of the Eighth Army, and thereby greatly helped the Allied main effort. For the 1st Infantry Division, the Battle of El Guettar had a special significance. During the critical early days of the engagement, the 'Fighting First'—alone and unassisted—had stood toe to toe with the *10th Panzer Division* and slugged it out to a well-earned decision. Thereafter, the division had a battle confidence and a belief in itself second to none."[82]

For the 18th Infantry Regiment, credit was placed where it was due, largely on DIVARTY's support on 23 March, especially by the hard-pressed batteries of the 32nd FA. The direct fires of the 601st Tank Destroyer Battalion were also instrumental in the Regiment's success. The valor of the 3rd Battalion's heavy weapons company drivers who "ran the gauntlet of direct tank and artillery fire," also earned accolades, as without whose resupply efforts, the battalion would have run short of ammunition that day. Williamson also noted in his diary that Cannon Company had been particularly effective on 25 March while the 1st and 2nd Battalions were defending Djebel Berda.

The benefits from lessons learned while under British command also played a very positive role during the El Guettar engagement. Prior experience in patrolling, establishing observation posts, efficiently delivering supplies to the front, as well as maintaining communications with subordinate commanders all figured prominently in the outcome. Most importantly, the success of the Regiment's night moves reinforced its importance, particularly for achieving surprise. Reflecting on the battle in the El Guettar valley, General Omar Bradley later pointed out the importance of the Regiment's contributions when he wrote, "It was the first indisputable defeat we inflicted on the German army in the war."[83]

The Regiment's casualty list at El Guettar included 48 killed, 115 missing, and 193 wounded. Casualties were heaviest in the 3rd Battalion at Djebel Mcheltat and in the 2nd Battalion at the base of Djebel Berda when the *10th Panzer Division*'s motorcycle battalion attacked Companies F and G. Well-liked Captain John F. Zimmerman, commander of the 1st Battalion's Headquarters Company, was killed when his jeep ran over a mine. Elements of Company H also suffered a number of casualties. "I lost too many in my company at El Guettar," wrote the CO, Captain Murphy. "Over half of the 1st Machine Gun Platoon and several in the section of the 81mm Mortar Platoon that were in support of Company F . . . all were killed, wounded, or taken prisoner."[84]

Commenting on the fighting at El Guettar, Major General Patton later wrote a letter of commendation to Terry Allen, in which he said, "For 22 days of relentless battle, you have never faltered. Over country whose rugged difficulty beggars description and against a veteran enemy cunningly disposed, you have pressed on. Undeterred by cold, by lack of sleep, and by your continued losses, you have conquered. Your valorous exploits have brought undying fame to the soldiers of the United States."[85]

THE FINAL PUSH

APRIL TO MAY 1943

> It has been a slugging match and one or the other has to break before too long. You may be assured it will not be the 1st Division.
> —General Terry Allen in a letter to his wife

Allied fortunes in Tunisia had changed dramatically even before the fighting at El Guetter concluded. A week prior to the *10th Panzer Division*'s counterattack, the British XXX Corps had passed through the Matmata hills near the seaward flank of the Mediterranean and launched its first attack against the Mareth Line. The Mareth Line stretched 25 miles northeast from the vicinity of Cheguimi in the Matmata hills toward Wadi Zigzaou. After a four-day pause to reorganize, the British attacked this line of fortifications for a second time on the night of 20/21 March. Assault troops from the British 50th (Northumbrian) Division managed to gain a bridgehead across Wadi Zigzaou late that night, but only four supporting tanks succeeded in crossing the flooded depression before daylight brought a halt to bridging operations. A follow-on attack the next night gained more ground when 42 additional tanks of the 50th Royal Tank Regiment (a unit the size of an American tank battalion) crossed the *wadi*, but the *15th Panzer Division* quickly launched a fierce counterattack that drove the British back.

His XXX Corps having now twice failed to breach the Mareth Line, Montgomery was then prompted to switch his main effort to the New Zealand Corps. This corps had conducted a series of attacks to the south of Wadi Zigzaou in support of the British 50th (Northumbrian) Division. By the night of 21/22 March, the 6th New Zealand Brigade had succeeded in carving out a small foothold in the enemy main line of resistance. Exploiting this minor gain, the 4th Indian Division cleared the road through the Ksar el Hallouf Pass and turned northwest toward Cheguimi. Montgomery subsequently ordered X Corps to pass through the New Zealanders in a maneuver designed to finally outflank the southern end of the Mareth Line. After a lengthy aerial bombardment on the afternoon of 26 March, the New Zealanders, supported by the British 8th Armoured Brigade, then launched an attack that rapidly overran the opposing *Italian First Army*.

Nearby, the British 1st Armoured Division of X Corps passed through the leading elements of the New Zealanders and advanced four miles before darkness brought a halt to their progress that night. When the moon rose, the British tanks resumed their attack and quickly drove straight past the German panzers that were assembling for a counterattack against the New Zealanders; the British tankers found themselves within 15 miles of Gabes by dawn the next morning. The bulk of the *21st Panzer Division*, which was cut off and nearly surrounded by this time, escaped only after bitter fighting. At the same time, the *Italian First Army* was able to pull back in fairly good order by committing the German *15th Panzer Division* and *164th Light Division* in a counterattack against the British armor.[1] Axis troops, however, had suffered over 7,000 casualties and lost a great deal of equipment by this time.

After being forced out of the Mareth Line, the *Italian First Army* withdrew to the north of Gabes. The new Italo-German defensive position was anchored on Wadi Akarit, a steep-sided obstacle that had been artificially extended by an antitank ditch to cover the whole of the gap between the sea and Chott el Fedjadj. To its north, Wadi Akarit was dominated by two mountains, Djebel Fatnassa on the west and Djebel er Roumana on the east, both extending almost to the sea. The road from Gabes to Gafsa ran around the eastern end of Djebel Fatnassa in a defile between the mountains and the salt marsh, and the road to Sfax meandered along the coast around the eastern end of Djebel er Roumana. In a natural sense, this defensive line was much stronger than the Mareth positions, and the line of defensive established by the Axis forces took full advantage of this over the course of its 12–15 miles. Italian and German forces deployed there included the Italian XX Corps (*Giovanni Fascisti* and *Trieste* Divisions), and the mixed XXI Corps (*Pistoia, Spezia*, and German *164th Light Divisions*).

General Sir Harold Alexander, now commanding the newly-formed Eighteenth Army Group (consisting of the First and Eighth Armies), had ordered Major General Patton's II Corps to continue to apply pressure eastward from El Guettar in an effort to assist Montgomery's planned assault on Wadi Akarit, which crossed the Gabes-Sfax road a few miles north of Gabes. While the 1st Infantry Division was working along the mountains north of the Gafsa-Gabes road and the 9th Infantry Division was doing the same to the south in early April, General Messe of the *Italian First Army* was so alarmed that he reinforced the depleted *10th Panzer Division* with elements of the *21st Panzer Division*. With his counterattack force now slowly dissipating in its effort to stave off the American advance, Messe started to have doubts about his ability to hold Wadi Akarit. On 5 April, he began sending troops back to Enfidaville, 50 miles south of Tunis, to prepare a secondary defensive line.

Messe was right to have been so cautious, as the subsequent battle of Wadi Akarit lasted only a day. The British XXX Corps attacked at 0400 hours on 6 April, supported by 450 artillery pieces. The attackers gained complete surprise as they moved forward in the predawn darkness, and by 0845 the 4th Indian Division

The Final Push

reported that it had advanced 6,000 yards, triggering commitment of X Corps. Even as defeat loomed on the horizon for the Axis, the *15th Panzer* and *90th Light Divisions* launched a counterattack that stabilized the situation. That night, Messe's entire *Italian First Army* successfully withdrew to Enfidaville and the *10th and 21st Panzer Divisions* rejoined the main body of the Italo-German forces. At 1600 hours on 7 April, an American patrol met a patrol from the 4th Indian Division and the two British armies, First and Eighth, had finally made the linkup so sought by General Alexander after a long and arduous campaign in North Africa.

With the Axis forces now slowly being squeezed into a pocket around Tunis, General Alexander issued new orders to Anderson and Montgomery. He informed the Eighth Army commander that Anderson's First Army would make the main effort in the final offensive in Tunisia with the V and IX Corps commencing their attack on 22 April. The V Corps would attack to the northeast along the Medjez-Massicault axis, with IX Corps heading north of Sebkret el Kourzia on a parallel axis. Montgomery's Eighth Army would conduct a secondary attack along the coast beginning on 19/20 April, employing the British 50th (Northumbrian) Division. The 2nd New Zealand Division would also attack just west of Enfidaville and the 4th Indian Division west of Takrouna.

The American II Corps, now under the command of Major General Bradley, would advance toward Bizerte on 23 April. To accomplish this, the four American divisions comprising II Corps would have to be transferred from the extreme southern end of the First Army zone to the opposite (northern) end, crossing over their existing supply routes and lines of communications to get to their new front. The II Corps plan was to attack with the French *Corps Franc d'Afrique* and the 9th Infantry Division in the north, and with the 34th and 1st Infantry Divisions in the south. General Allen's forces would clear the hills north of the Tine River while the attached 6th Armored Infantry Regiment of the 1st Armored Division would attack the hills on the southern rim of the valley. A regiment of the 34th Infantry Division was to cover the 1st Infantry Division's flank north of the Beja-Mateur road while other units of the 1st Armored Division would constitute the II Corps reserve.

The southern portion of the corps zone, where the main effort was being made, was initially organized to accommodate two divisions moving abreast, with the 34th Infantry Division on the left (north) flank and the 1st Infantry Division on the right flank. The combined frontage of the two divisions was approximately 13 miles, and there were only two natural avenues of approach, the Djoumine and Tine River valleys, both of which led to the initial Corps objective at Mateur. The Tine River valley seemed particularly appealing for the 1st Armored Division's expected advance because it was flat and wide, but it was also heavily mined and flanked by ridges and hills on both sides with little or no concealment other than an occasional wheat field. While the valley broadened at places to about two to three miles, it was still too narrow to permit easy passage as long as the Germans held the surrounding hills. To canalize the attacker into the least-desirable terrain along this front, the Germans had mined the narrow valley and blocked the approaches with accurate machine-gun, mortar, and artillery fire directed from observation posts sited on these flanking hills. American planners dubbed the Tine River valley the "Mousetrap" because it was obvious that infantry had to clear the hills before mobile armored units could use the valley floor.[2]

Despite these tremendous natural advantages offered to the defending Germans, II Corps unhesitatingly accepted the difficult assignment since the American high command was determined to overcome whatever opposition they might encounter in hopes of finally silencing British criticism of the US Army's battlefield performance to date. Warning orders began filtering down through corps to division and then to individual regiments over the next few days. The 18th Infantry Regiment had relocated from El Guettar to Gafsa by this time, and hundreds of tents had taken over the oasis in battalion squares separated by high mud walls. Each of the companies had set up in its own square, and their command posts were usually placed in a clump of palms where there was shade from the hot spring sun. Well-deserved rest was the first order of business for those who had survived the battles at El Guettar. The troops found a natural Roman bath near Gafsa, and hundreds of soldiers soon left to line up for much needed showers in its surprisingly warm waters. Colonel Greer even found a way to relax, as he was known to send out calls for volunteers to play poker at a table set up near his command post.

This all changed on 14 April when Colonel Greer received the order alerting the Regiment to be prepared to move north. The 18th RCT departed Gafsa three days later, leaving at dawn for a day of travel in spring sunshine through Clairefontaine, Souk Ahras, Beja, and Qued Zarga. By just before midnight, the men found themselves in the vicinity of Roum os Souk, about ten miles north of well-remembered Longstop Hill.

The next day Colonel Greer was directed to relieve the 12th Infantry Brigade of the British 4th Division; this was completed successfully at 0400 hours on 20 April. A battalion of the 6th Armored Infantry Regiment in turn relieved the 18th Infantry Regiment's 1st Battalion soon afterwards, and Lieutenant Colonel York's men went into reserve at Djebel Roch Chocki. The 2nd Battalion relieved the 6th Battalion, The Black Watch (Royal Highland Regiment) that same night, in an area largely devoid of cover and concealment. These newly-occupied positions could easily be observed by enemy troops situated on the high ground on the flanks, as well as from ominous Djebel Rmel, Hill 350, to Lieutenant Colonel Sternberg's immediate front. This hill was to be the 2nd Battalion's initial objective in the II Corps drive to open the Tine River valley.

Lieutenant Colonel Brown's 3rd Battalion arrived at Oued Zargar on the 2nd Battalion's left two days ahead of the Regiment's main body, at approximately 2300 hours on 18 April. There was little enemy activity at the time, but sporadic shelling caused some casualties. Brown then decided to send patrols out to probe his opposition, while also making sure that contact patrols were established laterally between his units. No contact was made with the enemy, except for one patrol that was fired on by a single enemy machine-gun crew. As night fell, Brown's companies established defensive positions in the shadow of Djebel el Beida, shown on his map as Hill 407; it was his battalion's first objective for the upcoming offensive. Over the next several days, the officers and men of the 18th Infantry Regiment prepared for battle while the remaining elements of II Corps moved north from Gafsa.

General Allen's plan called for an attack at 0300 hours on 23 April, Good Friday, with three regiments advancing abreast. The 26th Infantry Regiment was slated to be on the left (north) flank, with one battalion in the zone of the 34th Infantry Division protecting the northern flank of the entire division. The 16th Infantry Regiment was in the center, and the 18th Infantry Regiment was on the right. According to General Allen's plan of operations, the 6th Armored Infantry Regiment was to clear the hills south of the Tine River while maintaining contact with the British V Corps. General Allen also allocated one field artillery battalion from DIVARTY as well as one battalion from the 13th FA Brigade to provide fire support for each of the attacking infantry regiments. The 155m howitzers of the 5th FA Battalion were also directed to provide general support to the division effort. Allen's front extended six miles from the hills south of Sidi Nsir to the entrance of the Tine River valley. In turn, each regiment had to cover a two-mile front with the attack generally east along the line from Hill 575 (Kef el Goraa) to Djebel Badjar (Hill 278).

The 18th Infantry Regiment would now confront the most battle-hardened Germans in North Africa. These forces, both in front of the Regiment and the 1st Infantry Division, included the *334th Infantry Division*, commanded by Generalmajor Fritz Krause, and elements of Generalmajor Hasso von Manteuffel's *Division Manteuffel*, an *ad hoc* unit created from various independent regiments hurriedly sent to Tunisia in November 1942.[3] Manteuffel had returned to Germany on sick leave, so his division was currently under the command of Generalleutnant Karl Bülowius. The core of the *Division Manteuffel* was built around *Regiment Barenthin*, a unit made up of *Luftwaffe* volunteers from German glider and parachute schools.[4] Commanded by Major Hans Baier, this regiment consisted of three battalions whose rifle companies still averaged 180 men each, despite the effects of the fighting during the previous six months. As General Bradley later wrote, "In espirit, intelligence, and tenacity, it [the *Barenthin Regiment*] surpassed every other Axis unit on our front." The 1st Infantry Division G-3, Colonel Mason, added to this when he noted, "The elite *Barenthin Regiment* [was] well-led, experienced, and tenacious. It seemed that no matter how many of them we killed or captured, replacements kept them at fighting strength. When the German forces finally surrendered, this regiment marched into the POW enclosure in formation and in step, the only German unit to do so according to the reports I saw."[5]

On 23 April, it was with some reservations that Lieutenant Colonel Brown briefed his officers on the mission assigned to the 3rd Battalion. Djebel el Beida, Hill 407, was an objective that did not look like the other rocky, rolling hills nearby. Rather, it gently sloped upwards some 1,300 feet over sparse grass to its highest point, which was topped by a cluster of what looked to be deserted Arab thatch and stone huts.

The prospect of attacking across this open terrain, despite the seemingly tranquil appearance of Hill 407, troubled Brown. When he called his unit commanders together to receive the operation order on the night before the attack, he was clearly unenthusiastic. "Colonel Brown reluctantly outlined the plan," one of his officers remembered. "He was hesitant because he was afraid that the fight would be expensive in casualties, and we were suddenly sorry for him. He was always sensitive, always a brave soldier, yet sparing of his men's lives. He predicts our attack will be successful, but not easy. Then, as if to emphasize the point, rain began to sodden the battlefield."[6]

As the 18th Infantry Regiment prepared for the upcoming attack, survivors of the abortive December 1942 assault on Longstop Hill might have been heartened to hear that the British had finally launched a brigade-sized attack against the foreboding heights that had cost the 1st Battalion so many casualties. At 2245 hours on 22 April, the 6th Battalion, The Queen's Own Royal West Kent Regiment and The 5th Battalion, The Buffs (Royal East Kent Regiment) crossed their start line, meeting little opposition. By 0530 hours, the British had seized most of their initial objectives, but heavy machine-gun fire then prevented the Royal West Kents from making much progress along high ground to the southeast of Longstop Hill. It was not until 0800 hours on 23 April that they were able to secure their initial objective, but delays of the previous day had made it impossible for the 8th Battalion, The Argyll and Sutherland Highlanders to capture the main hills during the darkness.

By then the commander of the British 138th Infantry Brigade had decided that his plan had been too ambitious. He ordered the Argylls to secure the western slopes of Longstop Hill, supported by the 1st Battalion, The East Surrey Regiment, and the Churchill tanks of the North Irish Horse.

The assault started at 1330 hours and succeeded—but at tremendous cost. For three more days, the opponents jockeyed for position until the British launched a final assault that overcame the German *Mountain Infantry Regiment 756*. It is indeed ironic that the British 78th Division—the same command that had sent the 18th Infantry Regiment's 1st Battalion to take Longstop virtually unaided—was forced to employ four infantry battalions and a complete tank battalion backed by their entire divisional artillery, to finally seize Longstop Hill.

Unaffected by the bitter fighting at Longstop Hill, the 1st Infantry Division's attack jumped off several miles to the north and by dawn on 23 April, the 1st Battalion, 26th Infantry Regiment had seized Hill 565 against light opposition before attacking Hill 575.

The Final Push

The Germans occupied Hill 575 in strength, having prepared strong, well-camouflaged positions where many rocky declivities of the terrain provided overhead cover.

When the 26th Infantry Regiment continued their attack, they had to cross barren, round-topped hills populated with occasional patches of short wheat that provided the only sparse concealment. As the advance progressed, the 26th's 1st Battalion was met by heavy artillery, mortar, and automatic-weapons fire that forced its officers and men to halt 300 yards short of their objective. The 2nd Battalion, 26th Infantry, was then employed in an attempt to outflank the Germans. It also was subjected to very severe fire, and both units were forced to pull back to Hill 565 to reorganize and prepare to continue the attack.[7]

After advancing against virtually no opposition, the 16th Infantry Regiment seized Hills 415 and 374. Its attack then continued against the enemy on Hill 400; it was finally taken after severe fighting that saw the objective change hands three times during the day.

In the Regiment's zone of attack, the 3rd Battalion jumped off at precisely at 0300 hours on 23 April when a patrol from Company L made its way in the dark toward the base of Hill 407. Discovering an enemy trench, Fogg's men quickly overcame German resistance there and captured six while the remainder of the company moved forward to join them and go up the hill. Moments later, the 3rd Battalion companies began a coordinated assault with Company L on Hill 407, advancing directly up its western face toward the summit, with Captain Rosinski's Company M providing support.

A platoon of Company L quickly succeeded in reaching the crest without being fired upon, but as these men began consolidating their position, hidden German machine guns suddenly opened fire. At 0530 hours, Brown reported to Colonel Greer that he already could hear the machine-gun and mortar fire coming from the top of the hill. A little over a half-hour later he reported that the situation had worsened and that the enemy was launching strong counterattacks.

Lieutenant Franklyn Johnson, who was closer to the action than Brown, described what had happened. "We watched the soldiers of Company L struggle to the summit until they were silhouetted against the sunrise," he wrote later. "And then, too quickly, it happened. After the Arab huts spit their machine-gun fire, mortar rounds crashed down, and bayonets slashed. The enemy caught the platoon in that moment of disorganization when an objective is reached—that minute or two when control over squads and teams is weakest."[8]

The innocent-looking thatched huts had concealed German infantry, and the opening blasts of fire that Johnson described were soon followed by a counterattack that tore gaping holes in the ranks of the entire company. Within minutes, Captain Fogg was killed by machine-gun fire, and nearly 50 of his men were also cut down. Soon afterward, Fogg's Executive Officer, Lieutenant William H. Cross, took a direct hit from a mortar shell that ripped him apart before he could reorganize the company. Chaos reigned for the next hour followed by more casualties as the now nearly-decimated company sought to escape relentless German fire pouring down on top of Hill 407.

The stubborn defenders, however, did not focus exclusively on Company L. While German infantry engaged Fogg's men, their artillery observers in the huts were hurriedly calling for fire on Captain Sawyer's Company I and Captain Raymer's Company K as those units scrambled toward 407's bloody crest.

Shrill whistles preceded the incoming shells as artillery fire started hitting the exposed American troops, Rocks, dirt, and bodies began flying as German shells blanketed both rifle companies. Captain Kuehn was one of those caught in the midst of the barrage. As the 3rd Battalion S-2, he was serving as another set of eyes for Lieutenant Colonel Brown, and his experience was much like that of the many struggling soldiers that morning.

"We were in a fight for our lives," Kuehn remembered later. "I already heard that Captain Fogg had been killed and that Lieutenant Cross was also dead. I was in a pocket in a ravine with four other GIs about thirty feet away to my right. Two badly-wounded Germans were on my left, both on their stomachs. A sergeant from Company M was directly in front of me, his mortar tube aimed right up at the Jerries on the hill. Moments later, a shell exploded and killed the GIs and finished off the two Germans.

The sergeant was also hit; I saw that his helmet was half off, and by the time I got to him his face had already turned partly greenish-white. I tried to give him water, first by putting my arm around his back to pull him towards me, but his helmet fell completely off, then the next thing I realized was that the back of his head had been blown off. He died in my arms."[9]

Reacting to the unfolding devastation, at mid-morning Colonel Greer ordered tanks forward to support the faltering 3rd Battalion. By now, some men in Company L had managed to pull back to safety at the base of Hill 407, but the equivalent of two full rifle platoons had been left behind on the crest.

When the supporting tanks arrived, they were hastily directed up a dirt road to an assembly area where Lieutenant Colonel Brown intended to immediately employ them in a coordinated attack in conjunction with Company K against the huts atop the hill. The attack jumped off on time, but Raymer's riflemen and accompanying tanks soon were halted by a deluge of artillery fire and a minefield between Hill 407 and nearby Hill 350. They ended Brown's hope for a quick reversal of his battalion's fortunes.

The Germans soon received a tremendous pounding from American artillery as more FA units joined the battle. The 5th and 32nd Field Artillery Battalions had been answering calls for fire support all morning as Brown's battalion fought to extricate itself from the trap it had entered. High explosive and smoke pummeled the German defenders, knocking out several machine-gun nests and mortar emplacements.

The 18th Infantry's Cannon Company was also redeployed to provide Brown with immediately responsive fire support but the movement of its guns quickly attracted German shell and sniper fire that killed its commander, Captain Denman Fowler, as he was trying to establish a forward outpost.

"I saw Captain Fowler get into his jeep with his driver," Pfc. Louis Newman remembered about that horrible day. "He had his radioman and his wire man with him when they departed. But not too long afterwards they all came back, hysterical, yelling the captain had been killed. Apparently he had left the jeep to look for the best position to move the company up to and he was crossing a large flat stone area where a German lay hidden in a rock formation. After he killed our captain, he disappeared."[10]

Lieutenant Maurice G. Fornier then took over the company and ordered high-explosive air bursts to be used to take out the Germans on Hill 407. Much of Cannon Company's fire was directed at a red-topped house on the top of the hill, where there was a heavy concentration of machine guns and mortars. Fornier ordered rounds on the house through the morning, knocking out two of the enemy guns.

At 1200 hours, however, the 3rd Battalion was still pinned down, and what remained of Brown's rifle companies continued to sustain heavy casualties. Attempts to evacuate the wounded or move up ammo and supplies had also been thwarted despite gallant attempts by Company M mortarmen to create a smoke-screen that would effectively conceal efforts by ammunition trucks and ambulances to reach the forward companies.

Even worse, by now most of the American units had been bracketed by additional enemy artillery. As the day pressed on, the news only got worse. By mid-afternoon, Hill 407 was littered with the blood-soaked bodies of Americans and Germans all across its landscape.

Lieutenant Edward Hendrickson was a forward observer for the 32nd FA and manned his battery's observation post from a prominent position affording a clear view of the hill. His memories reflect both his despair with the situation and his personal efforts in trying to alter the evolving disaster. "I could see the 3rd Battalion's advance, and the German soldiers all day," he wrote later. "I could see bayonet charges back and forth; attacks and counterattacks. It was severe. I'd lay down a smoke shell to get range and direction, then bring in the adjusting battery, which were four of our battery's guns [firing] for effect, backed by eight other guns in the battalion."

"One time that day we were firing four artillery battalions at once to help our men out up there." Evidencing his desperate attempts to reverse the deteriorating circumstances facing the men on the hill, Hendrickson also remembered, "It was the most constructive thing I did in my life with the artillery."[11]

Others also echoed their despair. Lieutenant Franklyn Johnson's 3rd Battalion Anti-Tank Platoon sat in defilade on a roadway near the base of Hill 407, and he had had repeated requests all morning to bring up food and ammo. An imaginative plan was finally devised in which he was to move his vehicles into the open in an attempt to draw fire from the huts on the hill, and once the German positions were revealed, Company M's 81mm mortar platoon would engage the enemy troops.

As Johnson remembered, "My trucks, seemingly larger and juicer targets than usual, crept forward only a few hundred yards before the machine-gun nests, looking right down our throats, set up murderous crossfire that caught the mortar platoon, driving them back and leaving several bodies in the tall grass."

An artillery shell then ripped into the road, barring any further vehicular movement by Johnson's vehicles. "We first heard a shrill whistle, then a roaring crescendo as we hit the dirt," he recalled in remembering that moment. "Tons of soil and rocks erupted like a mushroom and a crater formed as the lane disappeared. Even the adjacent brook changed direction. We surmised that the 'thing' that hit was fired from a coastal defensive position turned inland toward us, probably directed by observers in the Arab huts atop the hill."[12]

Lieutenant Robert Ritchie, a 32nd FA Battalion liaison officer also with the 3rd Battalion, witnessed Lieutenant Colonel Brown's continued frustration as events worsened. He was with Brown at his forward command post for most of the time.

"For the Germans it was like a shooting gallery," he later remembered. "Their mortars, shellfire, and machine guns were knocking down men everywhere around the hill. Colonel Brown kept getting messages from Regiment at the rear to attack, but he'd say, 'Hell, I haven't anything to attack with!'"[13]

One of many wounded during the battle for Hill 407 was Lieutenant Alvin L. Newman. He would later say that he was actually one of the more fortunate officers in the 3rd Battalion at the time. His diary entry of 23 April 1943 recounted, "A mortar shell exploded ten yards away from me at about 1430 hours that afternoon. . . . It got me bad in my left hip and left side. After the first shock, I didn't feel the pain. . . . I was more afraid that I'd be left for *Jerry*, but I was finally evacuated just past midnight after lying wounded for ten hours on the battlefield. . . . It was pretty bad."[14] Newman had shrapnel removed from his lung and stomach the next day, then he and others who were lucky enough to survive Hill 407 were evacuated by ambulance to Bône.

At 1720 hours, Colonel Greer finally determined that the 3rd Battalion was no longer combat effective. Arranging its release from Division reserve, he ordered Lieutenant Colonel York's 1st Battalion to move up and relieve Brown's men that night. When York's advance party arrived, Brown went over his current disposition with them and made arrangements for the relief in place to be completed in drizzling rain.

Later, when casualty counts started coming to his command post, he learned that 23 April had cost his battalion 17 men killed, 25 seriously wounded, with another 48 suffering lesser wounds. The following day, another 48 were still listed as missing in action.

When he learned that most of the missing soldiers were also dead, Brown was reported to have wept.[15]

THE FINAL PUSH

Good Friday initially unfolded in much the same manner for Lieutenant Colonel Sternberg's 2nd Battalion, but it ended differently.

Like the 1st Battalion's attack, the 2nd Battalion was slated to begin its assault at 0300 hours as part of the 1st Infantry Division's attack. Their objective, Djebel Rmel (Hill 350), was the highest in a chain of elevations that guarded the neck of the Tine Valley.

In preparation for his attack, Sternberg sent patrols forward to reconnoiter several pieces of critical terrain to his front, including Hill 303, situated immediately to the northeast of Hill 350.

Shortly afterwards, patrols radioed back that a second German force was on Hill 303; and that the enemy had also heavily fortified the reverse slope of Hill 350.

In the no-man's land to the immediate front of the 2nd Battalion there was a knoll incongruously called Pimple Hill. It was about 20 meters higher in elevation than Djebel Rmel. Just to the west of Pimple Hill, there was a large cultivated tract of land and several buildings identified as "Windmill Farm."

Even though Sternberg now knew that Hill 350 was strongly outposted on its reverse slopes, he had little or no information about the probable German dispositions atop Pimple Hill. Windmill Farm, however, had been previously reported as occupied in force only at night.[16]

By this time, Sternberg had developed an initial concept of operations calling for a preliminary bombardment on Hill 350 from 0300 to 0400 hours. After the artillery lifted, Captain Randall's Company E was to bypass Pimple Hill to the northeast and then attack Hill 350. Lieutenant Jeffrey's Company G would move at H-10 minutes via Pimple Hill to Windmill Farm, eliminate the enemy there, and then assist Company E in the general attack on Hill 350.

Sternberg directed Captain Murphy's Company H to trail behind Jeffrey's Company G, and as soon as Pimple Hill was secured, the heavy weapons commander would emplace his heavy machine-gun platoons and 81mm mortars in position on the hill's excellent terrain. This would provide a base of fire for the assault on Hill 350. Captain Spinney's Company F was to remain in battalion reserve.

After he re-examined this plan, however, Sternberg decided to send out a reinforced platoon from Company G to capture Pimple Hill early in the operation, permitting Murphy to position his supporting weapons much earlier than originally envisioned.

With his heavy weapons company in place before the two rifle companies moved out, Captain Murphy could then provide fire support for the assault on Windmill Farm as well as the attack on Hill 350.

Accordingly, at 0230 hours, the 2nd Battalion's attack on Djebel Rmel began with a rapid advance by a platoon of Company G and they quickly seized Pimple Hill.

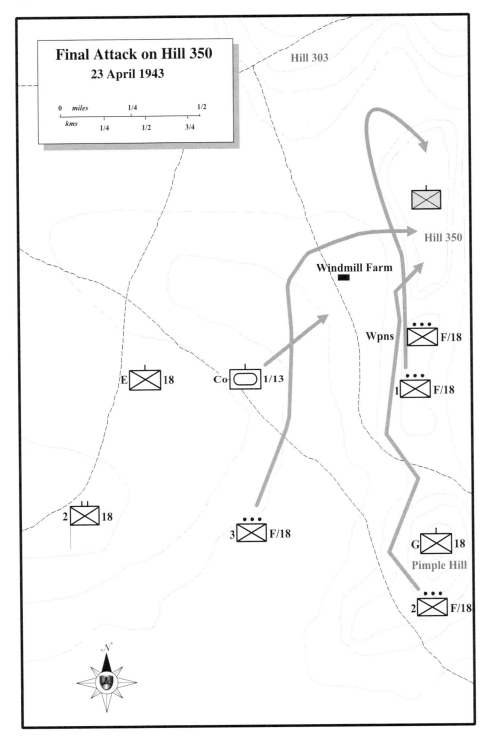

After Company H moved forward as planned, Captain Murphy hurriedly placed his 1st Machine Gun Platoon's .30-caliber water-cooled M1917A1s on the high ground just south of the hill, slightly in defilade, where the crews might deliver fire on the eastern half of the reverse slope of Hill 350.

To be certain that he would be able to rain fire on the crest of Djebel Rmel, terrain on its reverse slope, and also to the northeast, Murphy positioned his 2nd Machine Gun Platoon on the reverse slope of Pimple Hill.

Rounding out his hastily-prepared positions, he then situated the three sections of his mortar platoon behind the machine gunners on high ground overlooking Hill 350. The artillery barrage against Djebel Rmel began as scheduled at 0300 hours, and then Lieutenant Jeffrey's men (minus one platoon) moved forward to reduce the German outpost at Windmill Farm. The farm proved to be more than just an outpost and, much like it had been on Hill 407 for Captain Fogg's Company L, Jeffrey's men were counterattacked from both flanks and driven back with heavy casualties.

Meanwhile, Company E had approached the German reverse slope defenses on Hill 350 undetected by the enemy. A rapid assault succeeded in routing the defenders and they quickly took 35 prisoners from *Marsch Battalion T-3*. Consistent with German tactical doctrine, however, Randall's men had little time to consolidate: supported by artillery and mortar fire, a German infantry company counterattacked the flank of Company E's new position and his men sustained over 40 percent casualties in short order, including Captain Randall who was shot in the thigh. Hill 350 then fell back into enemy hands.

"Randall was missing until later in the day," Lieutenant Colonel Williamson remembered. "It was only then that a few of the survivors of Company E could carry their wounded commander from the battlefield."[17]

Despite this unexpected setback, Lieutenant Colonel Sternberg wasted no time planning a renewed attack. He decided that his assault would be supported by an even more powerful artillery preparation, and his liaison officer responded by coordinating use of no less than three field artillery battalions to deliver a barrage against the Germans from 1115 to 1200 hours. Sternberg also requested and received a company of light tanks from the 1st Battalion, 13th Armored Regiment to support this assault in which Captain Spinney's Company F would follow the same route that Captain Randall's men had taken during their earlier drive on the hill. Germans holding Windmill Farm would be neutralized by six of the tanks pressed into service while the remainder of the tank company (about ten Stuarts with 37mm main guns and machine guns) would follow behind Spinney's men in their own drive on the hill.

The preparatory barrage began at exactly 1115 hours after forward observers of the 32nd FA marked targets with smoke shells. Moments later, 36 105-mm howitzers covered the hill with an inferno of ground-shifting blasts while Captain Murphy's Company H delivered 92,000 rounds of machine-gun fire and 1,200 rounds of 81mm mortar to augment the smothering artillery strike.

Fixing bayonets as they charged past Pimple Hill, Captain Spinney led his men in a spectacular assault against the Germans defending the crest of Hill 350. After fierce hand-to-hand fighting, they seized the hill and took 20 prisoners.

Severely weakened by Company F's assault and the lethal combination of fires delivered by the supporting artillery, mortars, and machine guns, the Germans were unable to muster sufficient force to deliver a counterattack. Instead they began a general withdrawal, abandoning Djebel Rmel, Hill 303, and the adjacent Hill 305.

Even though the 2nd Battalion had prevailed, the cost of victory had been high: 43 men were dead, 160 were wounded, and 20 were listed as missing in action. The 1st Battalion, 13th Armored Regiment reported that they lost 13 light and 5 medium tanks that day. Defending Germans lost more than 40 killed; 60 were captured by the Americans, and an unknown number of wounded were left behind.

Captain Spinney, although wounded, was the only officer left with his company when Hill 350 finally fell.[18]

The fight for Hill 350 later was remembered as one of the classic infantry battalion attacks of World War II, but Lieutenant John Downing, assigned at the time as a liaison officer between division headquarters and the 18th Infantry Regiment, shed more immediate light on the operations. On 23 April, he was ordered to escort Major General Harold R. Bull, a Special Observer from Allied Force Headquarters based in Algiers, to the regimental forward command post where he could join Colonel Greer to witness Sternberg's second attack on Hill 350.

Downing noted, "General Bull said Company F's charge on Hill 350 was one of the bravest things he had ever seen."[19]

Colonel Greer also praised Captain Spinney for his actions that day and later in the war wrote a letter to his mother. "There is one thing I shall always remember about your son," Greer began. "It was during the Battle for Mateur when he led a counterattack on Hill 350. A major general, another officer, and myself watched the attack. We agreed that it was the finest action we had seen in this war—or in the last one All of his officers were wounded, but he carried on and took the hill."[20]

This success, as noted earlier, had not come without significant cost. Indeed, the entire 1st Infantry Division experienced the sad aftermath of bitter fighting on Hill 350. When Lieutenant Downing went back to division headquarters after delivering Major General Bull to Greer's observation post he noted, "The whole atmosphere at the command post was gloomy."

A few minutes later he found out why. "Bob West, the Warrant Officer Assistant Adjutant, called me aside and showed me the casualties," Downing recalled when he looked at the lengthy list of killed, wounded, and missing.

In addition to the officers and enlisted men that he knew personally from his service with the 2nd Battalion, one of his favorites, the very popular World War I veteran Company F 1st Sergeant Herbert W. (Herbie) Merrill, was also a casualty. "He had been hit in the head with a mortar fragment," Downing remembered.

"He had been practically scalped. The wound also paralyzed him from the waist down. He was all through with the war, but he had gone out with a wisecrack. 'As long as they keep hitting me in the head, they can't hurt me', he had told the surgeon. His humor did not change the fact that he was very seriously hurt."[21]

Merrill, along with Platoon Sergeant Ben Worsham and Sergeants Harold B. Hyatt, Cleveland Rhinehart, and George Mauorga, were later recognized in after action reports as having performed their duties in an "outstanding" manner during the assault on Hill 350.

On 24 April, the day before Easter Sunday, Chaplain Edward Rogers spent the morning and afternoon gingerly picking his way along the mine-infested slopes of Hill 350 and Hill 407 to help with the removal of the dead and wounded. Undoubtedly reflecting the entire Regiment's mood, he later remembered his sad duty, "In some cases the men had lain on the battlefield all the day before, to avoid drawing enemy fire. Some were badly knocked about and others were just severely shaken from battle. We were able to get a few dead off the field, but not the majority of them. We tried to get other bodies off that night, but it was very black and the terrain was not familiar. We gave up until morning—Easter Morning. All that day I worked with a detail collecting the dead. I hope I never spend another Easter like that one."[22]

The 2nd Battalion medics had barely finished evacuating their wounded and dead from Hill 350 before Lieutenant Colonel Sternberg received orders to move further east along the Tine Valley. Although his battalion was designated as regimental reserve after the fight for the hill mass, Sternberg was expected to occupy defensive positions on Djebel Zerais and Hill 346 to the north of Hill 350. Sternberg, who along with both Lieutenant Colonels York and Brown would receive the Distinguished Service Cross for their actions at El Guettar, later learned that his 2nd Battalion had been awarded a Presidential Unit Citation for its 23 April assault on Hill 350. The accompanying citation read in part,

> The 2nd Battalion was the only one in its entire sector to take its objective on that day. The conspicuous aggressiveness, valor, extraordinary heroism, and profound devotion to duty displayed by this battalion insured the successful occupation of this vital terrain feature. The eminently significant accomplishment of this gallant and cohesive fighting force was instrumental in breaching the defensive system in this sector, thus enabling the entire II Corps to advance uninterruptedly until the capitulation of the Axis forces in Tunisia.[23]

As medics and chaplains were completing their search of the dark slopes of Hill 350, the 1st Battalion was completing its relief of Brown's battered 3rd Battalion.

Lieutenant Colonel York wasted little time in issuing orders for a renewed attack against Hill 407, commencing at 0300 hours on 24 April. Following a 30-minute artillery preparation, the 1st Battalion jumped off in columns of companies and by 0435 Captain Cameron's Company B reported that his men had secured the crest of Hill 407 after overcoming minor machine-gun and mortar fire. York then directed Captain Scott-Smith's Company C to take up positions on the right flank of Cameron's company, and to send a patrol out to investigate Hill 346. cautioning both to be prepared to repel any counterattack. The patrol reported one battery of 88mm guns, two tanks, one self-propelled gun and numerous infantry in a draw about 500 yards to the east, but the Germans started retreating after several rounds of artillery were fired.

As soon as he heard that this German force had withdrawn, Colonel Greer ordered York to continue advancing to the east to reestablish contact with the *334th Infantry Division*. York ordered Company C to send a patrol to investigate Hill 323, to the northeast, and they found it unoccupied.

York subsequently ordered his company commanders to continue the attack in echelon, with Company C leading. Captain McGregor's Company A would be offset to the left rear, prepared to support Scott-Smith's men and their attached heavy machine gunners if they made contact with the enemy. Captain Cameron's Company B would add depth to the attack, following Company A. Captain Carter was also ordered to deploy his remaining machine guns and Company D's mortar platoon on Hill 323 where they could best support the advance of the rifle companies.

After a brief artillery preparation, the 1st Battalion seized the next hill, Hill 340, without meeting opposition, suggesting that the Germans were conducting an overall withdrawal. Continuing his advance in an effort to discover how far the enemy forces had pulled back, York ordered Company A to send out a patrol to a hill mass farther east, Hill 347; Captain McGregor reported that the patrol had not found any additional Germans, and when the other rifle companies sent out their own patrols, they also discovered no resistance. As night fell the 1st Battalion established defensive positions around the hill with Company C on the right and one platoon of Captain Cameron's Company B on on the left. Another of his platoons defended the gap 1,000 yards west of Hill 347 while Company A was placed in battalion reserve and held as a counterattacking force.

Despite the fact that all three of his rifle companies had been reduced to platoon strength, Lieutenant Colonel Brown's 3rd Battalion followed the 1st Battalion's advance. At 1600 hours on 25 April, his remaining men started moving past Hill 407 toward El Guessa, where they also assumed a defensive posture. Four hours later, Colonel Greer ordered Brown to send out a patrol to link up with Company A at Hill 347. Accordingly, just after midnight, a platoon from Company I set off on this mission and soon contacted one of McGregor's outposts without meeting any German opposition. At mid-morning the next day Lieutenant Colonel Brown moved his battalion command post forward to El Guessa where his men consolidated their positions abreast of the 1st Battalion. Severely-reduced Company L took up a reserve position on the south side of Hill 347 in a ridge next to Captain McGregor's Company A. By this time, Lieutenant Colonel

Sternberg had also consolidated the 2nd Battalion on Djebel Zerais and Hill 346 to the north of Hill 350 in Regimental reserve.

By the foggy morning of 26 April, the 1st Infantry Division completed the initial phase of the offensive to open up the Tine Valley. Further advances would have created a dangerous salient: the remainder of the Division had also moved up considerably farther than Major General Charles W. Ryder's 34th Infantry Division, then located three miles to the northwest.

With its neighbor located in this position to their left rear, the northern flank of the 1st Infantry Division was seriously exposed to counterattacks by enemy units in the 34th Infantry Division's zone. Thus, the Commanding General of II Corps ordered the Division to hold in place, consolidate its positions, and prepare for an eventual coordinated attack in conjunction with Ryder's division.

"We were holding until other units could catch up with us," Lieutenant Colonel Williamson noted in his diary that day. "[The] problem was to keep us from being sent out on a limb where we would be chewed up by artillery fire."[24] The new II Corps scheme of maneuver now required the 34th Infantry Division to capture Djebel Tahant, Hill 609, which was the key fortress in the area. The 1st Infantry Division was to eventually take Djebel el Anz and Djebel Badjar, the remaining commanding heights that both protected Mateur and dominated the Tine Valley approach.

By 0845 hours on 27 April, the 26th Infantry Regiment had moved up and occupied Djebel Berakine without opposition. The activity of the 18th Infantry Regiment was limited to patrolling as far forward as Djebel Badjar during the day where several prisoners from the *6th Company, Grenadier Infantry Regiment 755, 334th Infantry Division* that occupied the hill were taken.

While the overall action in the zone of the 1st Infantry Division was generally quiet that day, the 34th Infantry Division advanced against the lesser heights guarding approaches to ominous Hill 609 and met very strong opposition.

Meanwhile, the 26th Infantry Regiment continued its advance to seize Djebel el Anz, while the 18th Infantry Regiment eventually moved up along Djebel Sidi Meftah to Hill 281. Colonel Greer then ordered his battalions to consolidated in their positions to wait until the 26th secured its objective.[25]

On the morning of 28 April, the 16th Infantry Regiment attacked to the north to secure terrain protecting the approaches to Hill 609. By 0700 hours, the 1st Battalion was on Hill 476 and its 3rd Battalion was on Hill 531. Further advance was impossible because of enemy mortar, artillery and machine-gun fire from Hills 523 and 609.

The 26th Infantry Regiment attacked Djebel el Anz with its 1st Battalion and succeeded in establishing a foothold on the hill by mid-morning in the face of fierce resistance from the *5th* and *7th Companies, Grenadier Regiment 755*. As soon as the hill was taken, the *7th Company* launched a strong counterattack, but it was repulsed after the Germans suffered considerable losses from devastating fire delivered by DIVARTY.

The *7th Company* launched another counterattack during mid-afternoon, but this, too, was smashed by artillery fire directed into its midst with the assistance of 18th Infantry Regiment observers on Djebel Sidi Meftah. At dusk still another counterattack struck Djebel el Anz, only to be repulsed once again.

The Regiment advanced no further, but patrols reached Hill 216, where they were halted by enemy artillery fire.

By the end of the day on 28 April, the 16th Infantry Regiment was pinned down by enemy fire from Hills 523 and 609, the 26th Infantry Regiment was holding its positions on Djebel el Anz, and the 18th Infantry Regiment was still located on Djebel Sidi Meftah to the west of its final objective at Djebel Badjar.

The situation remained essentially the same the next day. While the 16th Infantry Regiment continued to hammer away at Hill 523, it became very apparent that the Germans considered that terrain feature to be a critical component of their defensive system shielding Hill 609 and they defended it furiously.

Despite strong artillery support, assaults by the 16th Infantry Regiment were beaten back through mid-afternoon and its battalions were forced to wait until dark before attempting another attack. For the remainder of the night, DIVARTY continued to pound the hill, as well as targets in the 26th Infantry Regiment's zone, while the enemy counterattacked Djebel el Anz twice. Each attempt failed in the face of accurate and responsive American artillery fire.

To further strengthen the position, the 26th Infantry's 3rd Battalion moved up behind its 1st Battalion, but both battalions' attempts to move forward from Djebel el Anz were met with heavy fire from Hills 523 and 545 to the northwest.[26]

In preparation for the 18th Infantry Regiment's attack on Djebel Badjar, Colonel Greer ordered the 1st Battalion to secure positions opposite Djebel el Anz the same day. York responded by deploying Captain McGregor's Company A to the southwest of Djebel Badjar while Captain Scott-Smith's Company C occupied positions to the northwest of the hill. York augmented Company A with one section of 81mm mortars, a section of 37mm antitank guns, and a section of heavy machine guns. The following day the 16th Infantry Regiment experienced some of the most severe fighting of the campaign. After trying for nearly two days to capture Hill 523, the 16th Infantry Regiment's 2nd Battalion was reinforced by Lieutenant Colonel Charles Denholm's 1st Battalion. His battalion launched an attack during the night of 29/30 April and secured the hillcrest by first light.

Almost immediately after Denholm began to consolidate his gains, however, his battalion was wracked by artillery fire and counterattacked by German infantry. When another rifle company came forward to reinforce Denholm's beleaguered battalion, the leading squad was mowed down by machine-gun fire at the southern edge of a wheat field at the foot of Hill 523, effectively stopping any support from that quarter.

A company of M-4 medium tanks from the 1st Armored Division was sent forward to silence German machine guns, but five of the American tanks were knocked out. The remainder stayed in position for the entire day, engaging any target that became visible, but with little effect.

Despite desperate attempts to retain Hill 523, by early afternoon on 30 April the Germans succeeded in overrunning Denholm's 1st Battalion and retaking their previous positions. The battalion lost approximately 100 killed, 150 wounded, and 150 captured that day, including Denholm himself.[27]

Fortunately for II Corps, the assault against Hill 609 on 30 April met with greater success. Supported by medium tanks from the 13th Armored Regiment, the 34th Infantry Division's 133rd Infantry Regiment battered its way up the northwest slopes of Hill 609 and reached its commanding heights by midmorning. By that night, the attackers finally reduced the extensive web of German strongpoints protecting the hill mass.

For the next several days fighting was not as fierce, but the enemy still maintained positions on and around Djebel Badjar in front of the 18th Infantry Regiment. Wherever II Corps attacked, the Germans put up stubborn resistance, punctuated by frequent counterattacks to recover lost ground. By this time, however, the American advance had gained and retained two pieces of key terrain, Djebel el Anz and Hill 609.

The Germans' failure to recapture this high ground placed them in a precarious position because pushing further to the east meant fighting over relatively level and open terrain. To avoid defeat, they chose to conduct a general withdrawal on the night of 1/2 May and this allowed the 1st Battalion to occupy Djebel Badjar without a fight on the morning of 3 May. With this achievement the heights at the exit to the Tine Valley were finally secure—but at significant cost to Colonel Greer. Regimental casualties in this phase of the final push for victory in Tunisia totaled four officers killed and another eight seriously wounded. Over 80 enlisted men were also killed, 230 wounded, and 40 others were listed as missing in action.[28]

On the morning that the Tine Valley exit was finally opened, General Bradley decided to commit Major General Ernest Harmon's 1st Armored Division to initiate a bold sweep along the upper Tine Valley to seize Mateur and pursue the retreating Germans. Harmon's tanks began advancing at daylight, and his 81st Reconnaissance Battalion entered the city at 1100 hours. The cavalrymen took a few prisoners as their vehicles fanned out amongst the buildings, but most of the enemy troops were able to escape, demolishing the bridges on the eastern outskirts of the city as they fled.

The next day, Harmon issued orders for the 1st Armored Division to begin reconnoitering to the east, and by this time the 1st, 9th, and 34th Infantry Divisions also were advancing eastward to regain contact with German forces defending the ridges between Bizerte and Mateur.

The Axis forces were now stretched to a breaking point. The time had arrived for a definitive assault on the German position in Tunisia. General Alexander wanted to achieve a sudden and impressive victory, not just for the morale-boosting and psychological advantages it would yield, but also because he had become concerned that a deliberate enemy evacuation of Tunisia could result in a reinforcement of Sicily.

To assemble a powerful striking force capable of knifing straight through to Tunis and thwart any buildup in Sicily, Alexander ordered Montgomery to reinforce the British First Army with the best units he could spare. Accordingly, Montgomery sent the British 7th Armoured Division, the 4th Indian Division, and the 201st Guards Brigade to reinforce Anderson's IX Corps to spoil any evacuation plans the Germans and Italians might have.

The British First Army's IX Corps began its attack on the morning of 6 May. Supported by 400 artillery pieces, the attackers quickly advanced over 6,000 yards, reaching St. Cyprien, approximately 12 miles from Tunis. The British V Corps, with the 46th Division deployed north of the Medjerda River and the British 1st and 78th Divisions to the south, then moved to hold the corridor open and prepare to support the IX Corps' continued drive. General Bradley's II Corps, meanwhile, was continuing its own successful advance toward Bizerte.[29]

By now the Axis forces on the tip of Tunisia were reeling under massive Allied air and artillery strikes. Signs of the enemy's collapse were visible everywhere. General Bradley had also ordered General Harmon's 1st Armored Division to boldly thrust further east to drive toward the naval arsenal at Ferryville on the inner shore of Lake Bizerte.

By this time, the 34th Infantry Division had also swung sharply to the east and was driving directly for Chouigui Pass, permitting General Allen's 1st Infantry Division to subsequently shift ten miles to the northeast into an area west of the Tine River and the Chouigui Road. The Division's mission was now to cross the Tine in the area opposite Djebel Douimiss and contain or destroy all enemy forces in the area.[30]

Allen's plan was to attack with two regiments abreast, the 18th Infantry on the left (northern) flank and the 26th Infantry attacking to the south. Allen assigned the task of capturing Djebel Douimiss to the 26th Infantry Regiment, and when Colonel Greer received his orders, he learned that the 18th Infantry Regiment was to attack at 0300 hours on 6 May to seize Hills 232 and 334, both north of Djebel Douimiss. The Regiment's attack would be supported by one company of medium tanks (Company H, 1st Armored Regiment), which would cross the Tine River after the engineers completed the necessary bridges.

What Greer could not foresee when he received this mission was that his 18th Infantry Regiment would soon become involved in a controversy that would forever affect General Allen's relationship with the II Corps Commander, General Bradley.

At 1100 hours on 5 May, Lieutenant Colonel York received a warning order to prepare the 1st Battalion for an attack to seize Hill 121. The hill was located to the south of the 3rd Battalion's assigned objective at Hill 232. Once Hill 121 was secured, the evolving plan called for York's companies to support Lieutenant Colonel Brown's attack on Hill 232.[31]

Shortly after York received his new orders, he conducted a three-hour reconnaissance of the terrain in front of his battalion with his S-3, Captain Froncillo, but all did not go well. Captain Froncillo was struck by German shell fragments and he lost a foot.

After dragging his wounded operations officer back to safety, York reported to Colonel Greer at 1500 hours and was apprised that plans had been finalized for the impending attack. The 1st Battalion was to cross the line of departure at 0300 hours the next morning, 6 May. York's plan of attack, devised as a result of the ill-starred reconnaissance, now called for Company A, augmented by one section of heavy machine guns, to seize Hill 121, thereby supporting the 3rd Battalion attack to seize Hill 232. Company C was to seize Hill 202, located just to the south of Hill 121 to protect the 1st Battalion's right flank, while Company B was held in reserve.

The 1st Battalion's attack jumped off as scheduled. Company A quickly seized Hill 121 and took 17 prisoners from *Regiment Barenthin*.[32] McGregor then led his men up the southern slope of Hill 232, but heavy resistance prevented the company from making any further advance and he was unable to establish contact at the time with the 3rd Battalion.

As the morning dawned, Company A began to receive direct fire from 88mm guns and heavy machine guns, and by 0800 hours both of the company's light machine guns had been knocked out. McGregor was forced to order his men to fall back to a defiladed position south of Hill 232 where the company remained pinned down by heavy machine-gun and artillery fire and out of communication for the rest of the day.

Company C occupied Hill 202 during the morning, but Scott-Smith's men were also pinned down by machine-gun and artillery fire. Reacting to these developments, at noon York ordered Captain Cameron's Company B to occupy the reverse slope of Hill 121, the initial location of Company A.

That afternoon, *Regiment Barenthin* launched a powerful counterattack that penetrated between the positions of Companies B and C, but the assault was repulsed. The Germans lost 35 men as prisoners of the defenders, seven of whom later died of wounds. A total of 25 Germans were killed outright during the costly counterattack. Lieutenant Van Wagoner of Company C remembered:

> The Jerries wanted to use up all of their ammo before giving up, but things were not going well for them. I was on Hill 202 observing for our mortars that afternoon, and the Jerries had me pinned down with their machine-gun fire.
>
> Sometime during this I looked down the hill toward the main company position and saw that our 1st and 2nd Platoons were surrounded. I hollered out to Captain Scott-Smith, who was fairly close on another knoll and told him to take a look at the situation. It did not take him long to make an estimate of things and do something about it. He used his radio and called Lieutenant Mirakian, who was in reserve about a hundred yards back, and told him "The Jerries have our platoons surrounded, so I want you to surround them." Pete did, and he became the hero of the day.[33]

Company C's Lieutenant Peter Mirakian and his platoon sergeant, Staff Sergeant Carl Webb, later were noted in the 1st Battalion after-action report as having "won the admiration of all for their gallant deeds" in wiping out this *Regiment Barenthin* force during the counterattack.[34]

As had happened so often in Tunisia, the 3rd Battalion again found itself in a serious predicament almost as soon as the early morning assault on Hill 232 began.

After a 45-minute artillery preparation, Company I, in the lead and supported by a platoon of the battalion's .30-caliber heavy machine guns and its 81mm mortars, crossed the line of departure at 0345 hours. Company K followed while Company L remained in reserve in a riverbed with the forward command post group. While the two advancing companies met little initial opposition, shortly after first light both suddenly were engulfed by machine-gun fire from both flanks, as well as mortar fire from a ridge northeast of Hill 232. The attacking American troops, caught by surprise in the open along the crest of a ridge, suffered heavy casualties. Only 30 men were able to infiltrate back to their line of departure with Company M's Captain Rosinski when he came off the hill just after 0745 hours.

By 0845 hours, any thoughts of continuing the assault were forgotten, and Brown had no choice but to focus on reorganizing remnants of his once-again shattered battalion in a dry riverbed northwest of Hill 232, where they remained for the rest of the day.[35]

Supporting tanks from Company H of the 1st Armored Regiment had advanced just to the rear of the Brown's infantry soon after the attack started, but they encountered a minefield that quickly knocked out three 3rd Platoon Shermans. After engineers found a route through the minefield, the force renewed its advance, crossed an open valley and headed toward a deep *wadi* in front of Hill 232. As the engineers constructed a temporary bridge over the *wadi*, it collapsed after the four leading tanks had crossed. The rest of the tanks were exposed to heavy shelling from enemy 88mm guns on nearby Hill 334 as their crews waited for the bridge to be repaired. As a result, they could not stop the destruction that befell Companies I and K.

Meanwhile, another tank platoon started out at 0730 and made its way toward the hill from a different direction to take up positions to support the 2nd Battalion. The tank company commander was unable to do so, however, and the tanks spent the rest of the day shooting at targets of opportunity. As darkness approached, the platoon's four Shermans returned to the *wadi* where they waited for the engineers to repair the bridge before rejoining their company. They eventually pulled back with the remainder of Company H's tanks to an assembly area two miles to the rear to await further orders.[36]

Things had not progressed better for Lieutenant Colonel Sternberg's 2nd Battalion that morning. His rifle companies were committed to a supporting attack against the northern slope of Hill 232 to assist the 3rd Battalion. Captain

Spinney's Company F led this strike at 0400 from the low ground to the right flank of the hill, followed by Company E while Company G was held in reserve.

Sternberg deployed Company H in a *wadi* to the southeast of the hill to support the rifle companies with their 81mm mortars and heavy machine guns. Company F's thrust initially appeared to be going well as Captain Spinney's men climbed Hill 232 and reached the crest just after 0600, but the leading platoon unexpectedly encountered mines and booby traps. Company E suffered an equally bad ordeal: its soldiers were repulsed by enemy fire before they could even reach the hill. Spinney's men were only able to hold their tenuous position until 1300 hours when enemy heavy fire from the high ground to the south of Hill 232 finally drove them back. Fortunately, casualties were fairly light, but the Germans nevertheless captured a few of Captain Spinney's soldiers.[37]

Due to the precarious position of all three attacking battalions, Colonel Greer issued orders to withdraw at nightfall and occupy a defensive position near their original line of departure. At 2030 hours, all three battalions began the withdrawal and the move was completed at midnight.

Later, Colonel Greer learned that when Captain McGregor was advancing through a gully earlier in the day, he and several of his men lost contact with the rest of Company A and were surrounded by Germans. For the second time in North Africa, in much the same manner as he was forced into at St. Cloud, McGregor had no choice but to surrender himself and his men.

Greer also learned that Captain Raymer, who had led Company K so gallantly at El Guettar, had been killed, along with two of his platoon leaders. When Lieutenant Colonel Brown heard this, he awarded command of Company K to Captain Kuehn, his S-2. According to the S-1 journal, the Regiment lost 10 killed, 79 wounded, and 193 missing in action that bloody day.[38]

Regimental XO Williamson noted in his diary, "All officers except one in I and K Companies were missing or captured."[39] The next day, what was left of the *Regiment Barenthin* withdrew to the east of Hill 232 while all three of Greer's battalions were shelled with artillery. A few days later, they, too, joined the rest of the *Africa Corps* in prisoner-of-war cages when the Tunisian front finally collapsed.

The failed attack against Hill 232 was an ignominious end to a series of successful, albeit costly, engagements for the 18th Infantry Regiment in the final push in Tunisia. General Bradley later maintained that General Allen had made a mistake in even ordering the Regiment to attack Hill 232 on 6 May. He went as far to accuse Allen of being foolish, adding that the attack was "undertaken without authorization."

"From that point forward," he wrote in his memoirs, "Terry was a marked man in my book. Had we not be en on the threshold of our first important US victory in Africa, I would have relieved him and Teddy Roosevelt on the spot."[40]

Colonel Mason, General Allen's G-3 at the time, remembered the circumstances that influenced Bradley to say this a little differently, however, he wrote later in reference to the day before the 6 May offensive:

Orders were issued by division to the 18th Infantry to make [the] night attack, but by late afternoon Colonel Greer was proposing to division that the attack be cancelled. General Allen wavered in the decision, but was obviously inclined to execute the attack as planned. This uncertainty continued into the evening.

The Assistant Commanding General [General Roosevelt] was also recommending cancellation, but G-2 reinforced General Allen's inclination to make the attack. General Bradley and his operations staff knew full well there was some question at division as to the final decision.

Furthermore, he [General Bradley] had ample information on which to base a decision had he wanted to cancel the attack.

At about 2300 hours, both [the Chief of Staff] and I felt that General Allen had accepted the no attack solution, that if left unmolested the *Barenthin Regiment* would follow its pattern by making a late night feint (which they did) and then make a clean withdrawal. Yet, sometime after 2300 hours and before midnight General Allen ordered the attack executed. He subsequently told me he talked to General Bradley, who presumably had given his approval, though probably with reluctance. This is conjecture; we will never know for sure. The 18th Infantry attack did indeed fail, and having beaten off the attack, the *Barenthin Regiment* reverted to pattern. When the sun rose the day afterwards on the battle area, there were no Germans to be seen. They had withdrawn 15 miles.

Colonel Mason closed his defense of his commanding general on this controversial matter involving the 18th Infantry Regiment by asserting,

> General Bradley unfairly accused General Allen in this instance of making an "unauthorized attack." Unwise and unnecessary, perhaps, in which case the II Corps commander should also share the blame. Or, if General Bradley ordered Allen to cancel the attack, the proper terminology is "direct disobedience of orders." Since that accusation was never made it would seem that the attack was not, as quoted, "completely unauthorized."[41]

Terry Allen was known to be an aggressive commander, who was viewed by many corps-level commanders he served under as a maverick.

One of the most attack-minded general officers of World War II and keenly aware that taking and holding ground costs lives, there was not a man in the 18th Infantry Regiment, however, who would say Allen ever wasted one soldier's life.

Hill 232 may have marked a watershed moment in his otherwise illustrious military career, but General Bradley's judgment about Hill 232 notwithstanding, Allen's performance in the war would later have the Eighteenth Army Group Commander in North Africa, General Sir Harold Alexander, refer to Terry Allen as "the finest division commander I saw in two world wars."[42]

On 7 May, the 34th Infantry Division broke through the Chouigui Pass to make contact with the northern flank of General Anderson's British First Army. With this, the final mission of II Corps in the Tunisian campaign was completed. By mid-afternoon, the 11th Hussars reached the outskirts of Tunis, and at 1530 hours the 47th Regimental Combat Team of the 9th Infantry Division entered Bizerte.

The nearly simultaneous fall of Tunis and Bizerte clearly came to the Germans, both in Africa and Berlin, as a profound shock. It was not until the evening of 8 May that the German High Command issued a statement saying that Africa would now be abandoned and the "31,000 Germans and 30,000 Italians" remaining would be withdrawn by sea.

Alexander commented in a report to Eisenhower that night that the Allied navies and air forces would have to interfere with the Axis evacuation plans, which largely depended on the ability of the German and Italians to hold their escape route at Cape Bon.

The Allies had no intention of permitting their opponents a moment's respite. As soon as the situation in Tunis was under control, the British IX Corps split its forces and proceeded to mop up on the left and right.

On the left, the British 7th Armoured Division was directed northwards up the Bizerte road toward Protville. Simultaneously, the US 1st Armored Division moved towards the area north of the Protville marshes from Mateur. The doomed enemy troops trapped in this pocket consisted of *Division Manteuffel*, the *15th Panzer Division*, and the *334th Infantry Division*.[43]

Total defeat now certain, a delegation of German officers arrived at Allied Headquarters south of Ferryville at 0926 hours on 9 May. Their mission was to surrender remnants of the once proud *Fifth Panzer Army*. At 1140 the same morning, Generalmajor Fritz Krause, the commander of the *334th Infantry Division*, reported to the command post of the 1st Armored Division southeast of Bizerte to request an armistice, but an unconditional surrender was instead reached along the entire II Corps front 20 minutes later. On 11 May, General der Panzertruppen Gustav von Värst, commander of the *Fifth Panzer Army*, directed the last remnants of the *Hermann Göring Division* at Djebel Achkel to comply with these terms. Three days later, Generaloberst Hans Jürgen von Arnim, commander of *Army Group Africa*, was captured at Ste. Marie du Zit. General Messe surrendered unconditionally to General Montgomery's Eighth Army on 13 May.

When the British mopped up the Cape Bon Peninsula, they liberated the 18th Infantry's soldiers captured on Hill 232. Later, a stirring report filtered through the ranks of the Regiment when it was learned that one of their officers had received the surrender of a German general, Generalleutnant Willibald Borowitz The commander of the *15th Panzer Division*, Borowitz ordered a cease-fire in his sector and then turned himself in to one of his former prisoners of war, Company A's commander, Captain McGregor.

In all, 157,000 Germans and 86,700 Italians marched into captivity as the final push in North Africa came to an end.[44]

Word of the German collapse had started down through the ranks within the Regiment two days after the bloodbath on Hill 232, "so suddenly that it was startling to everyone," Lieutenant John Downing remembered. An advance detail of the 3rd Division had arrived from Morocco a few days earlier and Colonel Greer, then still at his tent command post west of the Tine River, received word that the 3rd Infantry Division would relieve the entire 1st Infantry Division on 9 May.

"There was a strong unofficial sentiment that divisions that had fought in Tunisia would be returned to the States to impart combat information to the divisions preparing for overseas duty," Downing pointed out at the time, but this was simply not to be.[45] The 184-day Tunisian campaign was now history, but even as the last of the defeated Axis troops were being rounded up, the 18th Infantry Regiment was alerted to be ready to redeploy to Algeria to prepare for the invasion of Sicily.

The Regiment fought during the long and bitter struggle for North Africa in the best traditions of a maturing United States Army of World War II. Ironically, the 18th Infantry Regiment had already spent more days in combat than their brethren before them did in all of World War I, and the end to the ongoing conflict was clearly not in sight. The Regiment's officers and men, having benefited significantly from hard lessons they could only learn in battle, had developed into a cohesive, well-led combat unit. They had come a long way from the beaches at Arzew where they first landed on a strange and hostile shore laden with so much equipment they didn't need. The unorganized rush to St. Cloud, where so many had seen their first dead buddies on the surrounding roadways and in the village streets was a distant memory now, but those comrades who gave their lives in that dusty town would stay in the minds of the surviving veterans forever.

The loss of nearly half a battalion on Longstop Hill during their first Christmas away from home would also never be forgotten, nor would their prayers cease for their fellow soldiers and officers who were captured on its rocky massif and now lingered in far-off prisoner of war camps. Yet defeat had not been permanently etched in their minds, for a miserable and rainy Tunisian winter had given the 18th Infantry Regiment time to regain its confidence and to then demonstrate its prowess at Sbiba.

Then came El Guettar, the first indisputable, decisive defeat inflicted by American troops on German armored forces, where the Regiment faced some of Germany's best and decisively defeated them. The bittersweet final push evinced the sustained determination of battle-hardened troops who fought tenaciously from hill to hill, particularly on Hills 350 and 407 until the campaign's end.

Throughout the fighting in North Africa, officers led from the front and frequently gave their lives doing so. This demonstrated leadership qualities that had earned utmost respect: it showed to those they commanded that an officer would not ask a soldier to undertake a mission they would not lead themselves.

It was not coincidental, therefore, that planners for the invasion of Sicily were counting on the 1st Infantry Division and the 18th Regimental Combat Team to be in the vanguard of the upcoming battle. After only two days of rest, final orders came down for the Regiment to depart Tunisia on 11 May and head back to Algeria.

The men of the combat team started out on a motor convoy westward destined to take them back to an area they had been in before. Many of the tired combatants were unhappy to not have more time to unwind, particularly when the veteran campaigners soon found themselves passing through so many familiar towns. They spent their first night outside of Guelma and reached the staging area of Chardinaora the next day. At Guelma, most of the rifle and heavy weapons companies boarded trains for the final leg westward. Others were transported in trucks through Il Arba—where Colonel Greer had once established his regimental command post, before continuing on past Blida, Affreville and Orleansville. Finally, expectation of much desired rest and relaxation grew as the men saw the familiar spires that marked Oran, but this hope soon dimmed as they pulled into a drab-tented bivouac southeast of the city near Mangin.

War always has had its injustices, but yet another cruel irony was soon destined to fall on the Regiment. Captain Carter had traveled to Oran by train with his 1st Battalion from Guelma, and his recollections explain why many soldiers felt the way they did when they arrived at this new encampment:

> As the train pulled into Oran we passed large pyramidal tents to either side of the tracks. Inside we could see rows of cots, all nicely made up with sheets, pillow cases, and blankets. We imagined that this was where we were going to be put up. But when we got to the station, no one was there to greet us: no one at all. The train waited for about a half hour, then it started to back up past those nice tents where we thought we'd be let off, but the train kept going backwards until we were near an open field. From there we marched into the saucer-shaped depression near Mangin that was to be our new bivouac area.
>
> We pitched our tents and set up our kitchens, then settled in as best we could. There were 55-gallon drums filled with 100-octane fuel stored on the grounds, and we were told we could wash our uniforms in these drums, and then set them out to dry. We learned we were not going to be issued new uniforms to replace our woolen olive drabs, even though we had been living in them for six months. Most of us had only had two baths during the entire Tunisian campaign, the last one in the warm waters of the Roman baths at Gafsa a month ago. We were not too happy. We had no bathing facilities in Mangin.[46]

Some stunning examples of insensitive leadership by senior officers contributed to the unhappiness of the soldiers of the 18th Infantry Regiment. For example, although General Allen had been using every means at his disposal to procure new lightweight khaki uniforms for his men, his efforts were continually frustrated. By now the weather was hot, and Allen knew that his men were bound for Sicily. With the bitter Tunisian winter and unseasonably chilly spring a fading memory, there simply would be no further need for wool uniforms.

After repeated attempts to obtain new khakis through normal channels met with failure, Allen made a personal appeal for assistance to Lieutenant General Patton. It had long been decided that Patton, as commanding general of the new Seventh Army, would lead the Americans being committed to the invasion of Sicily, and the 1st Infantry Division had been selected to spearhead the landings.

Allen broached the subject about new uniforms just as the two generals were to sit down to dinner one night and received an answer that reveals a side of Patton that is only hinted at in movies and biographies. Colonel Mason, who witnessed the conversation remembered,

> General Patton listened with increasing impatience during the two or so minutes it took General Allen to make the request, then his attitude changed abruptly.
>
> He told General Allen that he wouldn't need khaki uniforms because most of his division was going to get killed trying to invade Sicily, that he didn't think the 1st Division had enough guts to fight its way inland against the better-quality German troops we would be meeting, but that if General Allen could get a foothold on Sicily and still had as much as a third of his division left, he would then see to it that Allen's troops got khaki uniforms.
>
> This reaction was a trademark Patton slur of the 1st Division. And it provoked the customary Allen reaction. While Patton was still raging, he turned his head sideways to me and said, "Let's go." With that, and no amenities whatsoever, General Allen walked away with me in tow.[47]

It was not the first time, nor would it be the last that Allen stood up for his men while they were bivouacked in Mangin. Orders had also been handed down forbidding 1st Infantry Division soldiers to patronize Oran's bars and restaurants; infuriatingly, it was because they did not possess the proper uniforms. Allen issued passes to go into town anyway, despite the "Off Limits" signs at its bistros.

An example indicates the degree of resentful sentiments within the Division's ranks. The new Company K commander, Captain Kuehn, remembered this years later when he wrote,

> One night two jeep-loads of officers went into Oran for a little R&R. Lieutenant Colonel Bob York, together with Captain Brad Bacon, myself, and Lieutenants Moore and Frank Leaman were all involved.
>
> When we got to Oran everything was off-limits, except to the Mediterranean Base Section [MBS] personnel. Military police were posted in front of all the bars, but we still went into the only decent one there—the Golden Rooster. We brushed past the MPs over their protest and went inside where

we saw six smartly-dressed officers around a circular table drinking beer. We asked the bartender to pour us our own beers, but he said he could not serve us any beer.

Colonel York said to give us some wine, but he said no to that, too. That did it. Bob York jumped over the bar and started handing out bottles of beer to all of us. I jumped over the bar to help out. The occupation officers yelled for the MPs, who soon started blowing their whistles at us. But we were already in a beautiful fight, and I can still remember the feeling I had when I landed a punch to some fat major's belly. Then we ran outside, got back in our jeeps and headed back to Oran, singing and drinking our beer all the way home.

We had taken Oran before, and we lost good men doing it. Rear guard troops were not going to keep us from taking it this time, either. The MBS even filed a complaint with General Patton, and they demanded that Terry Allen discipline us."[48]

Although Kuehn did not know it at the time, Allen never did, instead telling Patton, "The troops have been in the line for six goddamn months. Let them celebrate getting back alive. It will stop soon!"

The celebrations died out a couple of days later. No one realized, however, just how far Allen had been willing to show his more rebellious side in support of the 18th Infantry Regiment's stay in Oran.

Years later, at an officer's reunion dinner after the war, then-Major General Mason caught everyone's attention during the opening remarks of his speech that night when he said, "I'll not go into all the background of General Allen helping the 18th Infantry in Algiers in front of the Alletti Hotel by beating up on some rear area MPs when we went back to Oran from Tunisia. . . ."[49]

His talk then continued by describing some profound moments while the Division fought in Sicily, but his attention-getter that night embodied one of the reasons why Allen was forever endeared to the men who fought under him. While Allen served as their commanding general, his loyalty was always to his men; that is why he could get so much out of them. This quality never failed the 18th Infantry Regiment, from the lowest private to its commanding officer. This was particularly illustrated by his support of Colonel Greer.

A letter the general wrote home to his wife on 4 April while the Regiment was still engaged at El Guettar demonstrated his confidence in Greer, even then. In it he told her, "Frank U. Greer, who commands the 18th Infantry, has proven to be outstanding as a combat leader. He has been recommended for a promotion to brigadier general and has also been recommended for the Distinguished Service Cross. So, my judgment on him has now more than vindicated him."[50] Allen had battled with his superiors in the wake of the criticism Colonel Greer had received from British sources about his failure to hold Longstop Hill, criticism that Allen had vehemently refuted in his own report about that bitter engagement.

Colonel Greer indeed received the promotion Allen recommended, and in a memorable speech to his troops at Mangin on 23 May he bid farewell to the men he had brought overseas and molded into a great fighting team. The men of the 18th Infantry Regiment were then introduced to their new commanding officer, Colonel George A. Smith, Jr., who had come from Allied Forces Headquarters in Algiers. General Allen then addressed the entire Regiment, but he did not mention a word about the incidents that raised the hackles of the brass in Oran.

"We loved Terry Allen even more after this frank talk to us at Mangin," Lieutenant Johnson remembered. "He praised the men in the ranks and said we, not him or any other officer, deserved the main credit for the accomplishments of the Division that were now being highly praised back in stateside newspapers. He gave us this credo, 'Do your job. We don't want heroes—dead heroes. We're not out for the glory. We're here to do a dirty, stinking job'." [51]

There were many heroes in the 18th Infantry Regiment during its battles in North Africa, and one not even in their own uniform had especially endeared himself to the officers and men.

He was a war correspondent, one of the few who dared to be with them right in the front lines. One officer remembered pulling him into a foxhole during a battle near Hill 407, where he was subsequently seen feverishly pounding away on his typewriter. Perhaps it was this article that he had started, a column that appeared in newspapers back home a few weeks later, written by Ernie Pyle.

> I only know what we see from our worm's-eye view, and our segment of the picture consists only of tired and dirty soldiers who are alive and don't want to die . . . shocked silent men wandering back down a hill from battle . . . chow lines and atabrine tablets and foxholes and burning tanks . . . jeeps and patrol dumps and smelly bedding rolls and C rations . . . cactus patches and blown bridges and dead mules . . . hospital tents and shirt collars greasy black from months of wearings . . . and graves, and graves and graves.
>
> That is our war, and we will carry it with us as far as we go from one battleground to another until it is all over, leaving some of us behind on every beach, in every field. We are just beginning with the ones who lie in back of us here in Tunisia. I don't know whether it was their good fortune or their misfortune to get out of it so early in the game. I guess it doesn't make any difference, once a man is gone. They died and others lived and nobody knows why it's so. They died and thereby the rest of us can go on. When we leave here for the next shore, there is nothing we can do for the ones beneath the wooden crosses, except to pause and murmur, "Thanks, pal."

SICILY

JULY TO OCTOBER 1943

When we land we will meet German and Italian soldiers whom it is our honor and privilege to attack and destroy.

—General George S. Patton

The decision to invade Sicily originated at the Casablanca Conference back in January 1943 during meetings between President Roosevelt and British Prime Minister Churchill. Detailed planning then progressed on 12 February when copies of the basic concept were provided to General Eisenhower's AFHQ in Algiers, but with his staff caught up in the battles at Sbiba and the Kasserine Valley, the plan lay virtually dormant for several weeks. By the time senior Allied commanders met in Cairo on 6 April to discuss the draft concept in more detail, the planners had actually studied eight variations of the basic concept, with several factors governing the draft finally submitted to General Eisenhower for his approval. Adequate beaches, ports, and airfields in the northwestern and southeastern corners of the island initially led the planners to propose landings in both areas. General Patton's Seventh Army would land near Palermo and make a quick dash for Messina. Simultaneously, the British Eighth Army would land near Syracuse on the opposite side of the island and eventually push Sicily's defenders back to this same port city. At the eleventh hour, General Montgomery insisted that Patton's Seventh Army land at Gela on the southeastern shores of the island, thus placing his forces in a position to protect the left flank of the Eighth Army as it drove north. Even though there were serious misgivings by a number of senior Allied leaders about this late change, both Eisenhower and Alexander adopted Montgomery's new plan for the invasion on 2 May.

Despite the stormy relationship General Terry Allen had with the new Seventh Army commander, the performance of the 1st Infantry Division in North Africa ensured it would be given an important mission in the upcoming invasion of Sicily. Mindful of the Big Red One's proven fighting ability, General Patton had expressed reluctance during the planning meetings to go ashore solely with the green 36th or 45th Infantry Divisions first assigned to him. He believed that of the three assault beaches that his Seventh Army was now required to seize, the most difficult assignment he faced would be seizing the fishing village of Gela and its surrounding beach areas. "I want those 1st Division sons a bitches," Patton said to General Eisenhower during one of the planning meetings back on 23 April. "I won't go on without them!"¹ Therefore it was no coincidence that the 18th Infantry Regiment found itself conducting rigorous amphibious training exercises near Arzew in preparation for the invasion.

Sicily is a rugged, mountainous island offering tremendous advantages to its defenders. Jaggedly triangular in shape, the island's 10,000 square miles of rough surface begins with low hills beyond its beaches in the south and west, then becomes very mountainous progressing inland to the north and east. Ultimately, the high ground culminates at the island's most prominent feature, the 10,000 foot-high volcanic Monte Etna. The port of Messina in the island's northeastern corner was the primary site of communication between Sicily and the Italian mainland; thus it became the key strategic objective for the campaign. Throughout the island the better and more important roads lay near the coastline. The majority of the island's 30 major airfields were located near Palermo in the west, and close to the island's larger southeastern population centers of Catania, Augusta, and Syracuse, with several smaller fields behind the southern shore villages of Biscari and Gela. The airfields were major considerations in the minds of the invasion planners because both the air and naval commanders wanted them captured as early as possible to help protect the invasion fleet from expected aerial attacks.

By the time the plans were finalized, Operation HUSKY (the codename for the invasion) evolved into the largest and most complex amphibious operation undertaken by the Allied armies of World War II. Often overshadowed by the Normandy landings, HUSKY was actually the largest amphibious operation of the war in terms of the geographical extent of the landing areas and the number of divisions put ashore on the first day. The final plan drawn up in early May called for over seven divisions to land along a 100-mile front in southeastern Sicily, while two airborne divisions were landed behind enemy lines. To the east, General Montgomery's Eighth Army planned to land four divisions, an independent brigade, and a commando force along a 40-mile front stretching from the Pachino Peninsula, north along the Gulf of Noto, to a point just south of the port of Syracuse. A glider landing would assist the amphibious troops in capturing Syracuse. In turn, Patton's Seventh Army would land three infantry divisions over an even wider front in the Gulf of Gela while paratroopers from the 505th Parachute Infantry Regimental Combat Team and a battalion of the 504th Parachute Infantry Regiment would support the assault.

General Bradley's II Corps was to conduct landings over a 50-mile front, with Major General Troy A. Middleton's 45th Infantry Division landing in the "Cent" area to the east. The "Thunderbirds" would land on five beaches extending from Scoglitti halfway back to Gela. In the center, the 1st Infantry Division was now slated to come ashore in the "Dime" area, with the 16th and 26th Infantry Regiments on five beaches to the east of Gela. The 1st and 4th Ranger Battalions would land at the fishing village itself with the mission of diverting the Italian defenders from Allen's assault on the nearby beaches. The 3rd Infantry Division and the 3rd Ranger Battalion, under control of the Seventh Army, would be put ashore in the "Joss" Area on four beaches straddling the port of Licata. The 2nd Armored Division, with Colonel Smith's 18th Regimental Combat Team attached, would form the floating reserve, designated for the invasion as "Kool Force."

Responsibility for Sicily's coastal defense lay mainly with the *Italian Sixth Army* under 66-year-old General d'Armata Alfredo Guzzoni. Numbering 300,000-365,000 men, the *Sixth Army* may have appeared extremely formidable to General Patton, but many of its units, including some regular divisions, were ill equipped, poorly trained, and not highly motivated. Some battalions were responsible for defending up to 25 miles of coastline, an impossible task, and the only places that were actually prepared for defense were the naval fortifications protecting Messina, Syracuse, and Trapani. Units stationed here were suffering from poor logistical support, inadequate communications, lack of armament, weakly enforced doctrine, and relaxed training. The *206th Coastal Division*, which occupied most of the sector between Gela and Syracuse, was not highly regarded. Historian Carlo D'Este, in his book about the Sicilian invasion entitled *Bitter Victory*, noted "discipline and training were almost non-existent [in the 206th Coastal Division]. Some company commanders were accustomed to take leave without bothering to place an officer in charge. Sundays and Feast days were taken off by officers to be with their families."[2] Even the 206th's own commanding general recorded, "During surprise visits guards were found asleep at their posts. A mortar unit had never had any practical training. Officers acted more like strutting Roman gigolos in sunglasses. Wherever I go, I see company commanders behaving like cinema actors and leaving their men to engage in some childish occupation."[3]

Generalfeldmarschall Albert Kesselring, the Supreme Commander-South, did not see any real need to correct these flagrant deficiencies because he did not believe Sicily was going to be attacked that summer. In April, he sent an appreciation of the situation to the Supreme Headquarters of the Armed Forces (*Oberkommando der Wehrmacht*, or "*OKW*") in Berlin actually downgrading Sicily as a probable target. He stated, "the enemy would gain more from an operation against Sardinia and Corsica if the Allied objective is the speedy capture of Rome."[4] But General Guzzoni, commanding *Sixth Army*, ironically differed and he had lobbied Kesselring to deploy German armored units to southeastern Sicily to act as a mobile reserve in the event an attack did materialize. At the time Guzzoni's own countrymen in the *Comando Supremo* (Italian Supreme Command) were unenthusiastic about allowing additional German units into their country, but he had correctly predicted where the Allies would land. In mid-May 1943, German forces in Sicily consisted solely of *Division Kommando Oberst*

Baade, which was originally formed to control the flow of replacement units and reinforcements into Tunisia. When it appeared that the North African campaign was irrevocably lost, however, Oberst Ernst-Günther Baade stopped sending units to Tunisia and used them instead to form *Panzer-Grenadier Regiment Palermo* (consisting of four battalions).⁵ By 9 June, when Baade was replaced by Generalmajor Eberhard Rodt, this regimental group had been expanded into *Division Sizilien* (later redesignated the *15th Panzer-Grenadier Division)*, which consisted of three panzergrenadier regiments (named after their commanders, *Ens, Koerner,* and *Fullriede*), an artillery regiment, and supporting troops.

By this time, Kesselring had met with representatives of *Comando Supremo* and convinced them to permit a second German division to deploy to Sicily. When Tunisia fell, the *Hermann Göring Division* lost four infantry battalions, two flak battalions, a tank battalion, and most of its reconnaissance, engineers, signal, and medical elements. The surviving remnants of the division, under the command of Generalmajor Paul Conrath, were subsequently sent to Sicily to reconstitute as a panzer division. When the invasion began, their assembly area was situated at Caltagirone, approximately 25 miles inland from Gela.

Conrath was known to be an aggressive commander. Despite the fact that his division had suffered tremendous losses in Tunisia, when Kesselring asked him if he understood the importance of rapidly launching a counterattack against an Allied landing force on Sicily's southern shores, he had boasted, "If you mean go for them, Field Marshal, then I'm your man."⁶

While the Germans continued to gather troops for their mobile counterattack force in Sicily, the 18th Infantry Regiment was bivouacked in Assembly Area "Kentucky" located near the ancient city of Carthage in Tunisia. Conditioning marches were conducted for six straight days in the surrounding area in late June, with afternoons given to the men to go swimming to escape the African summer heat. Unit training continued right up to 4 July, to include last-minute preparations and test firing every weapon in the Regiment. Despite the high temperatures and the necessity for all personnel to be restricted to the staging area on America's Independence Day, spirits were generally high. Officers noted in their company morning reports that their men showed every sign of being ready to go.

On 5 July, battalion commanders marched their units to the dock area beside the picturesque village of LaGoulette where they were loaded onto LCIs (Landing Craft Infantry). This was the first time LCIs were being used in combat. These vessels were 155 feet long, carried about 200 troops, and disembarked the men off gangways that lowered to either side of the bow when they came ashore. Each infantry battalion occupied six LCIs. The 32nd FA's howitzer batteries and Cannon Company were loaded on four LCTs (Landing Craft Tank), while the combat team's supplies, vehicles, new 57mm antitank guns, ambulances, and additional personnel were loaded on the transports *Robert Rowan, Lawton Evans,* and *Joseph Pulitzer*. Colonel Smith's Headquarters Company sailed aboard the *USS Orizaba*, originally commissioned for the Navy in 1918.

General Sir Harold Alexander, commanding both the British and American armies in the invasion, witnessed the loading of the 1st Battalion that hot July morning. To the pride of his men, Lieutenant Colonel York demonstrated both the Browning light machine gun and an automatic rifle for Alexander before he left their company.

At 1930 hours, Kool Force weighed anchor, sailed out of the Gulf of Tunis, and headed for a rendezvous with the rest of the invasion fleet at the nearby port of Sousse, arriving the morning of 8 July. The men went ashore to stretch their legs and the British fed them a hot meal at noon. In late afternoon, everyone re-embarked for the first leg of their journey into the Mediterranean. By dusk, hundreds of other supply and support craft had joined the convoy and were trailing in the wake of the regimental combat team, backlit by the westering sun as Kool Force headed for Sicily.

On 9 July the reddish morning sky slowly turned leaden gray. By afternoon, idyllic weather that marked the start to the invasion fleet's voyage deteriorated. Before long, winds rose to 40 knots and whitecaps crowned the churning Mediterranean. Forward progress was quickly slowed to less than three knots that afternoon as the roiling seas broke over the decks of the LCIs and LCTs. In confusing darkness after nightfall, five LCIs became separated from the main body of Kool Force.

Even the large transports *Rowan*, *Evans*, and *Pulitzer*, rolled and plunged in the troughs of crashing waves, and maneuvering became increasingly difficult. Captain Robert Ritchie of the 32nd FA remembered, "I was with our 3rd Battalion infantrymen and my artillery liaison party crowded aboard an LCI. That was the roughest damn patch of water I ever did see. We were in a column of boats and the waves were so big, you'd see bows then sterns of the ships lifted completely out of the sea."[7] Ritchie's party included Lieutenant Colonel Brown, Captain Rosinski, Captain Kuehn, seven other officers and 201 enlisted men—many green with seasickness—praying that the "Mussolini Wind" would die.

Despite the heavy seas, Kool Force maintained radio silence as it passed its marshalling area five miles west of Gozo Island and was traversing the Sicilian Narrows by 2300 hours that night. As the invasion convoy neared its destination, wind and sea began to abate, and by midnight the sky was clear and a low-arched moon shone upon the transports. The seas had flattened into broad swells and convoy vessels operated under manageable conditions. H-hour, 10 July 1943, neared.

The Italian defenders in the *206th Coastal Division* spent most of 9 July relaxing, thinking no invasion fleet would be foolish enough to be approaching their coastline in the face of a massive storm at sea. Nothing had moved at the Ponte Olivio Airdrome behind Gela Beach that day. All the planes were tied down and reconnaissance missions had been called off because of the weather. Yet, under the cover of one of the worst storms to ravage the Mediterranean in recent memory, Kool Force had advanced to within a thousand yards of Sicily's southern shores.

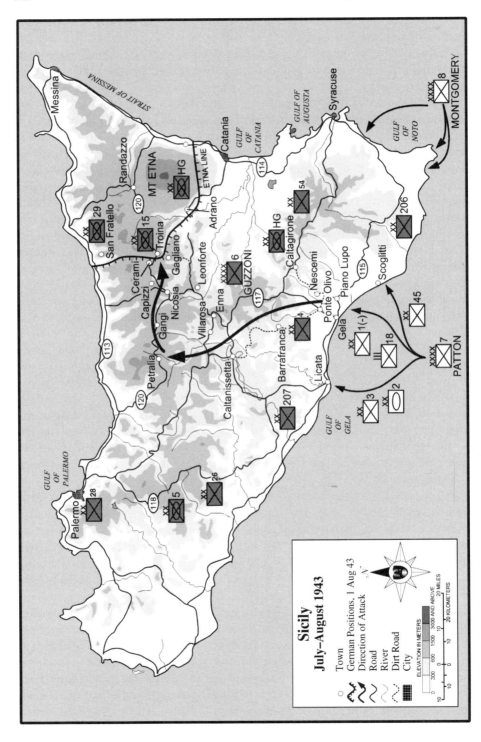

The flotilla then circled just off Gela, where every man and officer awaited their orders to the beach as the invasion commenced.

"During that first night on shipboard, we watched the Italian coastal searchlights flash on, search for our fleet, even put their cruel light on one ship, then switch off," Lieutenant Malcolm Marshall remembered. "It was hard to believe their big guns did not fire."[8]

The Allied assault on Sicily started at 0200 when Rangers under the command of Lieutenant Colonel William O. Darby conducted a diversionary attack on the village of Gela. Then, at 0245 hours a terrific naval gunfire barrage announced the invasion's start. The big guns aboard US Navy battlewagons spat out huge arcs of solid flame towards the Gela shore; their enormous high-explosive shells, each weighing as much as a small automobile, saturated the area beyond the landing beaches with great bursts of red-orange blazes and horrendous destruction. That firepower soon reduced the shore plains around the saucer-shaped Bay of Gela.

The 1st Infantry Division's landings three miles east of the fishing village were successful, but not without incident. The 16th and 26th Regimental Combat Teams went ashore mostly unopposed, and by mid-morning the Rangers had secured Gela, while the 26th RCT was advancing northward toward the Ponte Olivio airdrome.

Colonel George Taylor's 16th Infantry, which had landed to the right of the 26th Infantry, began moving toward Niscemi, approximately ten miles inland. Most of DIVARTY was ashore by 1800 hours, but much material and many vehicles were destroyed during the day by no less than nine *Luftwaffe* attacks.

In the Gulf of Gela, the destroyer USS *Maddox* was sunk after a direct hit by a bomb dropped by a *Stuka* and the minesweeper USS *Sentinel* was badly damaged by other air strikes in the early morning hours.

When the noises of the invasion were heard at the headquarters of *Panzer Division Hermann Göring*, Generalmajor Conrath immediately began planning for a counterattack. His plan was to send two battle groups—one infantry-heavy; the other tank-heavy—against the invaders. After receiving permission to launch his assault, at 0400 hours Conrath's forces began moving from Caltagirone toward Gela. Conrath seriously underestimated the time it would take to move to Gela over hills and rocky terrain between Caltagirone and the beach area., however, and that delay proved costly.

Conrath's men soon found themselves stymied by retreating Italians, American paratroopers, and steep twisting roads. It forced him to postpone his counterattack until 1400 hours—nearly 12 hours after the American landing commenced.

Conversely, the Italians had been quicker than expected in organizing and launching a counterattack against the American beachhead. Two columns of motorized infantry, accompanied by 30 obsolete Renault R-35 tanks belonging to *Mobile Gruppo E* of the Italian *4th Infantry Division "Livorno,"* left Niscemi and headed for Gela before Conrath started his first attack. One column advanced to Piano Lupo, quickly evicted recently-arrived American paratroopers from high ground they had taken, and then attacked Gela from the northeast. The second column advanced along Highway 117, past Ponte Olivio airfield, and then hit Gela from the north.

The Italian column heading for Piano Lupo, however, was surprised by an ambush by the 1st Battalion, 505th Parachute Infantry. While the Americans were able to initially inflict severe casualties on the truck-mounted component of the Italian infantry, the superior firepower of *Mobile Gruppo E* forced the paratroopers to withdraw.

When the 2nd Battalion, 16th Infantry, arrived to engage in the now-raging battle, they found a desperate fight taking place. They also became engaged and were pushed back by 20 Italian tanks before American warships in the Gulf of Gela finally took the enemy armor under fire and broke up the enemy attack.

After losing two Renaults to naval gunfire, *Mobile Gruppo E* pulled back into the hills to the northeast.

Darby's Rangers soundly defeated the second Italian column that had departed from Niscemi when that enemy force attacked the town of Gela. The Italians were on the run by mid-afternoon.

A similar fate befell the Germans. When Conrath's *Panzer Division Herman Göring* finally appeared on the battlefield at 1400 hours, a column of his armor struck the 2nd Battalion, 16th Infantry, but was also soon turned back by determined naval gunfire. Conrath's other column, *Combat Group Schmalz*, attacked the 1st Battalion, 180th Infantry Regiment of the 45th Infantry Division near Biscari, but assisted by a battery of 105mm howitzers from the 171st FA Battalion, the Thunderbirds succeeded in blunting the Germans' initial thrust.

Combat Group Schmalz quickly regrouped and launched a second assault, but when it moved toward the beach, the 180th Infantry's 3rd Battalion suddenly appeared in their path. Unexpectedly confronted with an obstinate American column that was occupying good ground by this time, Conrath's forces had no choice but to withdraw, leaving the combat debut of the *Panzer Division Herman Göring* less than impressive.

While Conrath was fuming at his failure to take back Gela or any other ground that afternoon, Colonel Smith and his S-3, Major Colacicco, were making their way ashore from the *Orizaba* to find an area for the 18th Infantry's regimental command post on the beachhead east of Gela. General Patton had been considering a second airborne drop for the night of 10 July to get more American troops ashore. Given the unstable situation at the beach lodgment, however, he decided to release the 18th Infantry Regiment from its attachment to the 2nd Armored Division. That would allow Smith's forces to come ashore after dark to be in position against the Axis counterattacks that were expected on the following morning.

While enemy aircraft were bombing Allied ships in the Gulf of Gela, at 1530 hours Colonel Smith radioed instructions for the combat team to start landing that night on Beach 67 Red, in zones marked as "Yellow" and "Blue" beaches. Those strips of sandy shore were a few miles east of Gela near the location of the morning's 16th Infantry landing. A significant portion of this beach area was not suitable for LCIs to come ashore in large numbers, and the beachmaster had made alternative arrangements for LCVPs to pick up the troops and bring them in.

Despite this, there were unexpected difficulties. As the combat team started landing that night, many of the LCVPs could not clear a submerged sand bar that ran parallel to the landing zone. Some soldiers found themselves swimming ashore, resulting in confusion and danger.

A few LCVP coxswains transporting the 2nd Battalion were not able to beach their craft at all, forcing the riflemen to leap into waist-high water 75 feet from the water's edge. Captain Ritchie, landing after midnight, had the same experience as others. "When our boat bumped shore, I went down the ramp fairly heavily laden with pack and all," he remembered. "When I stepped off the ramp I was right on the bottom. I walked a little bit and the water was over my head. I just kept right on walking! We had some people drown, but I just managed to keep on walking right out of it. If I'd panicked as some of them did, I'd probably be dead today."[9]

Four men did drown during the 1st Battalion's landing, while others struggled to get in safely. Chaplain Edward Rogers, who landed with his party, wrote, "We came into the beach at about midnight. . . . It was treacherous. We stepped off our craft and were soon in water over our heads." Chaplain Rogers was one of the more fortunate. A walking stick he had cut from an olive tree in Tunisia saved him from drowning. "I held it out," he remembered, "and someone nearer to shore pulled me out of the hole I had walked into."[10]

Rogers then extended his trusty "campaign stick," as he called it, to others and his party soon found themselves on shore—soaked and with no blankets.

Lieutenant Downing, now assigned to Headquarters Company, the 2nd Battalion, made it to shore much later, but he landed safely because his life vest inflated just as he hit the water. When he got to the beach, he found a discarded blanket and wrapped it around his dripping body.

"A few light tanks ground ashore near me at the time," he explained later. "They halted close to where I was and the drivers started gunning the motors. A loud backfire reported, and I thought we would wake up every German from here to Berlin. I walked up behind the exhaust and the heat started to dry my trousers. Then dawn began to break."[11]

By 0600 hours, the 18th RCT infantry companies were all ashore. The 32nd FA, now under the command of Lieutenant Colonel Edward S. Bechtold, followed shortly after daybreak. A battalion of the 2nd Armored Division's 41st Armored Infantry Regiment also landed, as did ten medium tanks of Company I, 67th Armored Regiment. The Shermans promptly got stuck in soft sand, and despite every effort to extricate them, the tanks remained unavailable to support the establishment of the beach lodgment. Some trucks also landed but other vehicles, including most of the Regiment's jeeps, still were offshore on transports.

Reflecting frustrations felt at this early hour of the morning trying to get supporting armor and vehicles ashore, the US Army's official historian later noted,

"The chief result of Patton's decision to land the floating reserve was that four additional infantry battalions equipped with just hand-carried weapons were now ashore."[12]

Things started to change quickly at about 0700 hours. Colonel Smith got word that German tanks were suddenly assembling for another counterattack before the 16th Infantry Regiment's positions. A few minutes later, Brigadier General Roosevelt contacted him and told him that Conrath's forces had penetrated the 26th Infantry's lines. A group of 20 Mark IV tanks was moving down the main road leading toward Gela, and before long, Smith heard that the panzers had approached within 2,000 yards of the town.[13]

At 1030 hours, an enemy fighter-bomber hit an LST loaded with elements of the 33rd FA Battalion and a section of antiaircraft guns. The vessel exploded with a tremendous roar, scattering vehicle parts, ammunition, and bodies in all directions. It was fortuitous that the combat team already was ashore by this time because at 1000 hours, enemy shelling grew in intensity and beachmasters quickly were forced to temporarily close all landing beaches except Green 2.

Several hundred yards inland, Colonel George Taylor's 16th Infantry Regiment was now facing 30 tanks from Conrath's *2nd Battalion, Panzer Regiment Hermann Göring*. When two of Taylor's battalion commanders were seriously wounded and evacuated, he had no choice but to hold his men together while waiting for his Cannon Company to come forward to support the infantry. He ordered, "Everybody stays put where he is. Under no circumstances will anyone be pulled back!"[14] By noon Taylor reported that tanks were overrunning one of his battalions and that 10 panzers were in front of another. There were as many as 30 more Mark IIIs and IVs now ringing his forces. Conrath's tanks were overwhelming this time, forcing the main body of the 2nd Battalion, 16th Infantry to withdraw into rough terrain where the panzers could not follow them. Some American units stood their ground bravely and exacted a toll on Conrath's panzergrenadiers.

General Conrath's armor eventually penetrated the center of the 1st Infantry Division's defenses, however, and bore down on the 18th Infantry Regiment's new positions near the beach.

Lieutenant Franklyn Johnson was near Colonel Smith's regimental command post at the time, and his excitement reflected the feelings of other hastily-assembled men nearby, "At 1230 hours, 12 German Mark IVs started approaching us, firing every few hundred feet," he remembered. "Gradually they veered to our left, Green Beach. By 1300 hours there were 22 panzers only a thousand yards away, and by 1330 the number had grown to 50 and we were witnessing the greatest attack by German armor since El Guettar."[15]

Like Taylor's infantry, there was little Colonel Smith's men could do to ward off this frightening attack with just the small arms they carried ashore. By now, positions held by Lieutenant Colonel Brown's 3rd Battalion were being penetrated by the *Hermann Göring* elements en route to the beach, as well as enemy tanks that had broken through the 16th Infantry's lines. These were now shelling Lieutenant Colonel Sternberg's 2nd Battalion.

The soldiers manning the Company A command post also reported an estimated 30 enemy tanks coming down at the 1st Battalion perimeter from the north.[16] York's men did not have a single antitank gun, but his men clung to their foxholes, determined to resist with their grenades, mortars, and small arms.

Supporting fire was not long in coming from the batteries of the 32nd Field Artillery that had made it to shore. Just off Gela Beach at the right edge of the Gela Plain were a series of sand dunes and gulches. The coastal road ran southeasterly about a thousand yards inland and cut the Gela Plain. It then bent sharply to the northeast where there were more sand dunes and a 200-foot high plateau where the howitzers of Lieutenant Colonel Bechtold's 32nd FA were now being drawn into place. It was here that Lieutenant Marshall's battery set up to fire, and he remembered what happened when they did, "With tubes leveled, we fired directly at the oncoming tanks. It was no easy thing to stand behind guns with a small quarter-inch steel gun shield, and shoot it out against oncoming mobile tanks with several inches of armor that deflects all machine-gun bullets and many antitank hits. But with artillery fire, mortars fired by our infantry on the flanks, and fire from a couple of our Shermans that got ashore, the lead panzers were knocked out."[17]

Captain Charles Cooke had managed to get his jeep ashore earlier that morning and he had used its mobility to find a suitable position for his Battery B howitzers to engage the approaching German armored vehicles.

Cooke sent his guide back to the beach to bring up the guns and he then set out with his driver to find an alternate firing position on the right flank of the 18th Infantry Regiment's sector.

Along the way they picked up a paratrooper who was lost, and right after he hopped into the jeep they rounded a curve where a German machine gunner opened up, killing them all. Despite their commander's demise, the men of Battery B occupied the position he originally selected, and they soon began firing at Conrath's tanks to avenge his death.[18]

At about the same time in the 1st Battalion sector, American artillery, SP guns, and a couple of tanks turned on the approaching panzers and, according to later reports, proceeded to "exterminate the enemy." The panzers were moving across a level plain with no cover, while the American guns were positioned in a wooded area.

"It was a beautiful exhibition of direct fire," the 1st Battalion Adjutant, Captain John B. Kemp, wrote later. "Several of the enemy tanks were destroyed. Battalion losses were one man killed and several wounded."[19]

The 2nd Battalion also assisted the field artillery by moving their guns to a position that enabled them to fire on the approaching tanks.

"It was direct firing with sighting through the gun barrels," an officer remembered. "Each time a 105 went off they would roll backward down a small grade, for the firing was such that the gun trails could not settle into the ground. Our infantry lads were right there and after each shot helped roll the guns back to the crest for the next shot."

"At times, through the dust and murk, there would be a flash and a column of black smoke. That meant a Jerry tank was finished."[20] Battalion reports later stated that after a German tank commander was killed, the rest of the tanks seemed lost.

Due in good part to the efforts of Bechtold's 32nd FA batteries and the Regiment's infantrymen, none of Conrath's tanks ever reached the landing beaches. Regimental after-action reports also credited Battery C, 33rd FA, in position near the 1st Battalion, with assisting in the repulse of the German assault.

Joined with the 16th Infantry Regiment's Cannon Company and a platoon of four medium tanks of the 2nd Armored Division, the 18th Regimental Combat Team played an important role in halting the German counterattack. At least 30 German tanks were counted during the attacks, but prisoners later stated that there had been 50 in the battle.

In total, 17 enemy tanks were confirmed as knocked out by the 1st Infantry Division.[21] Those that were not recovered by the Germans were destroyed later that night by 3rd Battalion demolition teams.

Naval gunfire had also played an important role in smashing the German counterattacks that afternoon, particularly the supporting fire provided by the cruisers *Savannah* and *Boise*. In addition to the fires of the 32nd and 33rd FA battalions, other DIVARTY units also performed in an exemplary fashion in support of the Regiment during the day, the fire personally directed by the DIVARTY commander, Brigadier General Clifton Andrus. Captured enemy officers later indicated that they had not expected to find any artillery ashore in strength and that they had been told the troops which had landed could easily be swept back into the sea.

General Andrus later added, "[Our] methods of coordinating the naval and organic artillery support produced the most effective and rapid fire that the 1st Division received in any of its three assaults on hostile shores during the war. It was the opinion of those who participated that it was more effective than the method which was later adopted for the invasion of Normandy."[22]

Praise was widespread, much of it crediting Colonel Smith for outstanding leadership in his first combat engagement. Even General Bradley, not one to easily heap praises on the 1st Infantry Division, later said, "On every hand heroism was commonplace," and adding, "Only the perverse Big Red One with its no less perverse commander was both hard and experienced enough to take that assault in stride."[23]

An otherwise proud day for the 18th RCT was marred by one incident in the Gulf of Gela. An attack by 20 German JU-88 medium bombers laid a carpet of incendiaries across the harbor late in the afternoon, and one bomb fell squarely onto the Liberty Ship *Robert Rowan*. Fire soon swept to ship's ammunition and gasoline stores, and huge columns of black smoke were visible for miles.

Following abandon ship orders, Captain William K. "Soup" Campbell and his men of Service Company jumped overboard, and were later rescued when a cruiser approached and lowered a rope gang-net. The *Robert Rowan* had about one-third of the combat team's transports in its cargo; the 2nd Battalion was particularly hard hit, as over 60 of its jeeps and trucks burned and went to the bottom of the Gulf of Gela.[24]

Casualties had been light, considering the intense combat that day. Six 18th Infantry Regiment soldiers were killed in action; one officer was wounded, as were 21 enlisted men. This was in sharp contrast to the 16th Infantry Regiment, which suffered almost 100 killed and several hundred wounded.

With the opposing sides fighting at close quarters, the supporting naval gunfire was often silenced out of fear that the shells would hit friendly troops. Even this did not prevent problems, however. "One five-inch shell hit our forward battalion communications section," Company K's Captain Kuehn remembered, "It made a big hole and you couldn't find a fingernail anywhere because we scratched for cover wherever we could find it. I was close when it hit and covered with dirt. I only had a nosebleed, but I was deaf with a concussion for days."[25]

Although the 1st Infantry Division had primarily fought a defensive battle on 11 July, all three regiments would go on the offensive that night. Word filtered down after dark that General Allen had told his staff, "We're going to sock the hell out of the damn Heinies before they can hit us again."[26] The immediate mission of the 1st Infantry Division was now to straighten out a salient that had been pushed into its lines by Conrath's counterattack. Three American columns set out from Gela to achieve this.

By first light, Rangers succeeded in capturing the commanding high ground of Monte Lapa and Monte Zai on the Gela-Butera road. The 26th Infantry Regiment, reinforced by Sternberg's 2nd Battalion, started out to secure Monte della Guardia and the Ponte Olivo airfield. A third column, consisting of the 16th Infantry Regiment, was to seize the town of Niscemi.

The 2nd Battalion departed at 2100 hours on an eight-mile march northward to join the 26th Infantry Regiment. Except for resistance at a small roadblock—which was quickly overrun—the move was uncontested When the 26th Infantry Regiment neared Il Casteluccio, a tall hill crowned by the ruins of a medieval castle, its lead companies were taken under fire by artillery of the Italian *4th Infantry Division "Livorno."* Rough terrain and incoming shells quickly disorganized the attacking American formation, necessitating a temporary halt until dawn, but at daybreak a battalion of the 26th Infantry Regiment surged up the slopes of Il Casteluccio while another secured Monte della Guardia. The 2nd Battalion initially was pinned down by the same Italian artillery fire and was then attacked by Italian tanks. Just after daybreak, however, two platoons of Company H, 67th Armored Regiment entered the battle and 900 Italians soon surrendered.

The Regiment's 1st and 3rd Battalions had also been active while Sternberg's men went up to Ponte Olivio to assist the 26th Infantry in the capture of the airfield.

The 1st Battalion, supported by a platoon of medium tanks, had to fight off a column of German tanks moving in from the northwest along Highway 115.

York's men had deployed on the division's left flank shortly after midnight with the mission of screening the 16th Infantry Regiment's attack against Niscemi. Artillery fire from the 7th FA and supporting Shermans destroyed two German tanks while the 1st Battalion was making this move. In the meantime, Brown's 3rd Battalion, initially in reserve, moved up to support the 1st Battalion.

The Germans launched several fierce counterattacks against the 16th Infantry Regiment through the morning, inflicting heavy casualties. This temporarily prevented the 1st Infantry Division from seizing Niscemi. In the melee, the Germans and Italians suffered heavy losses as the morning wore on, including four Tiger tanks; 29 Panzer IIIs and IVs; 10 Renault tanks; and two batteries of 149mm howitzers.[27]

That night, the 1st Infantry Division learned that the Chief of *Carabineri* (Police) in Niscemi had received orders from the *Italian Sixth Army* ordering the immediate evacuation and destruction of supplies in the area. At the same time, the Italian commander had directed all German and Italian troops to withdraw to Caltagirone. Some local farmers also informed General Allen's intelligence section that a German colonel told them "naval gunfire necessitated a withdrawal, but that if the Allies pursued too far inland they would be engaged by superior German forces and destroyed."[28] The enemy indeed withdrew in the face of a renewed advance by the 1st Infantry Division the following morning, offering little resistance as they scurried inland, and the threat of more Germans was not about to stop General Allen.

The decision to pull back stemmed from Hitler's belief that the fall of Sicily was inevitable. This was a vast departure from the "fight to the last man" approach he had ordered during the final phase of the fighting in North Africa, but by this time the British had seized the port of Syracuse on the far southeastern corner of the island. Italian units were in disarray, and some had simply abandoned their positions and retreated in chaos as the Allied forces advanced. Others had fought and been destroyed. The *Livorno Division*, for example, had already been decimated in a series of futile counterattacks against the American beachhead at Gela. Elements of the *206th Coastal Division* had surrendered in droves, to include the division commander and his staff.

The Germans now planned to resist the Allied advance by establishing positions along the Etna defensive line, a series of strong points that stretched from Catania on the east coast, and then ringed the southern base of Monte Etna before jutting northward to San Fratello. Final evacuation of the island was planned in phases, with each strategic withdrawal matched by a retreat to ever-shortening defensive lines. In Hitler's grand scheme, Axis troops would then be evacuated in stages and ferried across the Strait of Messina to Italy to fight another day.

There were just four narrow roads that intersected the Etna Line, and only two ran all the way to Messina. Possession of these arteries was vital, and their control became the focal point of the continuing campaign.

Elements of Montgomery's Eighth Army were first to move along the Adrano-Randazzo road toward Monte Etna, while other British forces drove toward Messina along the eastern coastal road, Route 114. Alexander then assigned the only two northern roads that would pinch Messina to the US Seventh Army. The first, Route 120, ran along the interior of Sicily from Nicosia, through Troina, to Randazzo. The second hugged the northern shore all the way from Palermo to Messina. There was one main artery, Route 117, which led northward to Route 120. This road ran directly from the Ponte Olivio airdrome behind Gela, through the city of Enna, then to Nicosia where it intersected with Route 120. The 1st Infantry Division's new mission, now that the landing fields near the beachhead were secure, was to seize the road junction at Nicosia, straddling Route 117 as it went north.

Before moving further inland, a number of changes took place within the regimental chain of command. During the afternoon of 15 July, Lieutenant Colonel Brown received orders to report to Colonel Smith's command post, where the newly-arrived 2nd Battalion S-3, Captain Frink, joined him. Lieutenant John Downing coincidentally reported to the command post at the same time, and he witnessed what happened during the meeting.

"I heard [Brown and Frink] being told by Colonel Smith that they were being returned immediately to the States for assignment to a new division where they could utilize their combat experience in training a new unit," he remembered.

Then he added, "Captain Frink was happy, but in a subdued way. We all envied their going home but we were glad to see them get a break. They were both excellent officers, and the choice was a fair one."[29]

Lieutenant Colonel Brown had been with the 18th Infantry Regiment since 1941 when he commanded Company B. Captain Frink had also served in the Regiment for a long time, having commanded Company H in the States before moving up and relinquishing command to Captain Murphy at Indiantown Gap.

Captain Frink may have been subdued that day because the 2nd Battalion S-2, Lieutenant Dick Koehler, had been killed when a mine exploded under his jeep.

Lieutenant Colonel Joseph W. Sisson, Jr., who had been with Regimental headquarters before departing for England, was appointed as the new 3rd Battalion commander. Captain Jack A. Requarth became his Executive Officer, and the commanding officer of Company I, Captain Sawyer, became the new battalion Operations Officer.

By this time, the 2nd Battalion had departed Ponte Olivo to penetrate inland. Lieutenant Colonel York's 1st Battalion, meanwhile, had moved to an assembly area just west of Niscemi, arriving at 1700 hours on 15 July; his companies then proceeded a few miles north to a position supporting the 3rd Battalion.

Although the Germans were withdrawing, they left behind rearguards consisting of self-propelled guns and infantry to harass the advancing Americans. Several Germans opened fire with SPs and machine guns against a limited attack launched by Company L, now commanded by Captain Frank N. Fitch. This fire brought the highest losses since the landings began, inflicting 25 casualties, including two dead.

"Company L was to my right, and my Company K was on their left at the time," Captain Kuehn remembered. "Fitch's men were ordered to make a frontal assault, but they were stopped and took the casualties. I heard that my jeep driver from North Africa when I was a battalion S-2 had been killed during this action. Then a few minutes later, Lieutenant Colonel Williamson came forward to my command outpost, and I asked him who the damn fool was that had ordered that attack."[30]

Williamson, the Regiment's Executive Officer, had been forward with the 3rd Battalion before Lieutenant Colonel Sisson arrived to take formal command. He told Kuehn that he had ordered the attack, and then added, "Now I want your company to go get whoever shot up Company L." Captain Kuehn was reluctant to commit his entire company, and caught up in his anger and thirst for revenge he instead told a shocked Williamson, "The hell I will. I'll go out myself."

Kuehn eventually took some volunteers with him in what never developed as a company-sized attack, but he worked himself around the enemy machine gunner who had killed his driver. After spotting him napping in the hot sun, he accosted the young German soldier and captured him.

Kuehn then marched his captive back to the company perimeter and sent him over to his own executive officer with orders to get him to the Regimental Intelligence Officer for interrogation.

That same day, 15 July, brought significant advances all along the divisional front. Lieutenant Colonel Sternberg's men seized the road junction that controlled access to Monte Bobbonia and Monte la Serra north of Ponte Olivo without incident, while the 1st Battalion proceeded northwest to a defensive position on Monte la Solfara to the 2nd Battalion's left. General Roosevelt visited Sternberg at Monte la Serra that afternoon, and had just left when Lieutenant Richard Lindo, Sternberg's artillery liaison officer, discovered an assembly area of Italian trucks and personnel in a wooded area to the east.

The 32nd FA then poured several hundred rounds of high explosive on the Italians, and shortly thereafter Lieutenant Colonel Sternberg ordered Company E to attack the enemy position. Approximately 250 Italians soon surrendered, abandoning 30 of their trucks and 11 100mm guns.[31]

By this time, Patton determined that the first phase of the Allied plan calling for the establishment of a secure beachhead across the II Corps front had been completed. The need for Palermo as a base of supply—a factor that had figured so prominently in the formulation of the original plan—now came into consideration.

General Alexander issued orders to Patton turning the direction of the Seventh Army's advance to the northwest on 15 July. At the same time, the order enlarged Montgomery's Eighth Army area of operations, to include the road network connecting Leonforte to Enna in central Sicily before it went up to the southern slopes of Monte Etna near Canicatti. This gave Montgomery room for a second axis of advance in addition to the main coastal roads leading to Catani and Gerbini. The Eighth Army was mounting the main effort toward Messina at the time, with the US Seventh Army still conducting supporting operations, guarding the British flank against enemy efforts from the west.

The Seventh Army order of battle remained largely unchanged with these new orders, except that the 45th Infantry Division was cut off in its sector by units of the British Eighth Army, thus necessitating that the division be shifted to the left flank of II Corps. With the 1st Infantry Division now on the right and the 45th on the left, Seventh Army began its drive to cut the Enna-Alia road, the Nicosia-Arda road, the coast road, and its new mission to attack Palermo.

On 16 July, General Bradley's II Corps commenced operations in pursuit of these missions. The 1st Infantry Division made contact with the enemy at first light just south of Barrafranca, key terrain because its occupiers could overlook Route 117. It was fiercely defended by elements of the *15th Panzer-Grenadier Division*'s *Panzer-Grenadier Regiment 1*, reinforced by a company of tanks from *Panzer Battalion 215*, and a battalion of rocket launchers (*Nebelwerfers*, which were multi-barrelled rocket launchers firing either 150mm or 210mm rockets) from *Nebelwerfer Regiment 71*.[32] The 26th Infantry Regiment soon succeeded in driving the Germans from their positions just north of the Barrafranca-Mazzarino road, but the Germans launched a counterattack, sending in a company of tanks and a company of panzergrenadiers.

The panzers succeeded in forcing the 3rd Battalion, 26th Infantry Regiment to pull back, but the 70th Light Tank Battalion and fire from 1st Infantry Division DIVARTY destroyed eight Panzer IVs. This eventually drove the Germans off. Fighting continued late into the afternoon, ceasing only when the Americans finally occupied Barrafranca just before 1700 hours.

The 2nd Battalion went forward to assist the 26th Infantry Regiment during the afternoon, but fighting had died down before Sternberg's companies arrived. Sternberg then went forward to reconnoiter the area and found the Barrafranca-Mazzarino road heaped with dozens of enemy dead, abandoned trucks, guns, and other equipment, to include a number of smoking tanks. During the evening, Sternberg moved once again to an assembly area six miles north of Pietraperzia with orders to assist the 16th Infantry Regiment in an attack on nearby Monte Copovarso. At the last minute plans changed, and his battalion was instead placed in reserve. The 1st Battalion joined the 2nd, and soon afterwards the entire combat team went into Division reserve and moved to a bivouac area just outside of Villapriolo.

Their respite did not last for long. On 19 July, the 18th Infantry Regiment moved by truck to Villarosa to secure several key avenues of approach leading into the 1st Infantry Division's sector. The 1st Battalion initially made contact with the enemy about two miles west of the stronghold, and then after detrucking, quickly reduced enemy forces encountered there. The battalion then occupied positions north and south of the town.

When the 3rd Battalion moved forward to support York's companies, they ran into heavy mortar, machine-gun, and artillery fire. Company K's Captain Kuehn was again engaged during the combat, and this time the battles had an even more profound impact.

> I was called to go to battalion headquarters after Brigadier General Roosevelt ordered Lieutenant Colonel Sisson to make a reconnaissance in force that day. He had just finished giving the order to Company L, but when I arrived he wanted me to take it. He knew I knew what was out there because Company K had been farthest forward.
>
> I told Colonel Sisson that a daylight attack would be suicide but he said, "I know, Ed, but those are the orders and I want you to do it. Take whoever you want." So I took a heavy weapons section from Fritz Rosinski's Company M, two rifle platoons from Company L and a forward observer from the 32nd FA. I soon gave the order, which was to include an initial barrage from the artillery and random shelling from the mortars. I knew the Jerries had their tanks with 88s located on the road opposite the two hills by us, but we didn't know where their mortars were located.
>
> My advance platoon, commanded by Lieutenant William Schoenleber, jumped off on time, but the heavy tanks and enemy mortars bombarded us. I'll never forget that when our own young artillery observer finally reached me, he said, "You doughboys sure earn your pay."
>
> I told him to get me some fire on the tanks, so he took off and got his bearings. It was his first day in combat, and he must have exposed himself because he got killed. Moments later, a heavy mortar shell came over into the ravine I was in with my radioman and I was hit with fragments in the foot, neck, and shoulder. I told the radioman to have my exec come forward to take over, and to report my being wounded to battalion. At that time we were ordered to stop the advance and dig in for the night.[33]

Kuehn's wounds were much more serious than he described. It was nearly midnight before aid reached him, and an ambulance took the badly-wounded officer to an evacuation hospital the next morning.

Kuehn then learned that Lieutenant Schoenleber had also been hit, and that 18 others became casualties that day. One of his sergeants, Thomas Brown, came to see him in the hospital two days later. Kuehn first told him to tell his men he would be back in a couple of weeks, but even then Sergeant Brown knew that Captain Kuehn's war was over.

"You're the finest officer I ever served under," he told him in despair before leaving. Kuehn later said, "That meant more to me than being given the Medal of Honor."[34]

On 17 July, General Alexander reacted to changing circumstances in the Eighth Army sector and modified his original directive by ordering the Seventh Army to "drive rapidly to the northwest and north, capture Palermo, and split the enemy's forces." By this time, General Montgomery's progress on the heated Catanian Plain had been virtually stopped by two regiments of the *1st Parachute Division*, supported by the *Hermann Göring Division*'s *Combat Group Schmalz* and elements of the *15th Panzer-Grenadier Division* that had also been moved into position to defend the area. To bring maximum weight against the German forces, General Alexander decided that the goal of operations now would be to have the Seventh Army brought into line with the Eighth Army for a breakthrough to Messina. Patton was to exploit the demoralization of the Italian Army by continuing his advance on Palermo, but on reaching the north coast, his Seventh Army would immediately send strong reconnaissance elements east toward Messina into what had previously been the Eighth Army's zone of operations. Patton was also permitted by Alexander to send in stronger forces if the situation allowed.[35]

For the next week, the 18th Infantry Regiment trailed behind the leap-frogging assault regiments of the 1st Infantry Division, alternately supporting the 16th Infantry or 26th Infantry Regiment by conducting flanking movements to unhinge the enemy defenders holding up the lead elements of the attack toward Nicosia and Highway 120. On 20 July, the 1st Infantry Division contacted the 1st Canadian Infantry Division at Enna before continuing on to Villapriola, eight miles to the northwest. By the next day, it was apparent that the enemy was pulling out his troops in the path of General Allen's advance. This enabled him to extend the Division's front through Alimena toward the coast road north of Castelbuono in spite of demolitions and other delaying activity on the part of the Germans and the Italian *28th Infantry Division "Aosta."*[36]

The 18th Infantry Regiment was committed to clear up a situation north of Bompietro on 22 July. After withstanding a short artillery barrage, the 2nd Battalion passed through the village to take up positions protecting the Division's left flank. This move had been difficult for Captain Penick's Company E. As soon as his men detrucked, one shell landed in the midst of one of his rifle platoons, killing 12 men and wounding 11 others.[37]

After the 3rd Infantry Division captured Palermo the same day, General Patton became obsessed with beating Montgomery to Messina, not just for his own personal triumph, but also for what he perceived to be the prestige of the United States Army. Carlo D'Este, his biographer, described Patton's thoughts at the time when he wrote, "Once his [Patton's] forces got rolling and began to gobble up chunks of Sicilian terrain, he knew it would henceforth become impossible for Alexander again to relegate American troops to a secondary role."[38] Patton had determined that the capture of Messina would now require Seventh Army to seize control of both the coastal highway from Palermo to Messina, as well as Route 120, the interior mountain road running through central Sicily near which the 18th Infantry Regiment was bivouacked.

Patton flew to Syracuse the next day to meet with Montgomery to discuss his new orders, and the Seventh Army's continuing operations.

D'Este noted, "To [his] utter incredulity Montgomery not only agreed with [this] concept, but actually suggested that Seventh Army capture Messina."[39] Montgomery was still suffering setbacks on the Catanian Plains at the time, but he had also committed one of his corps to make a "left hook" around Monte Etna. Without continued pressure against the northern end of the Etna Line by the 1st Infantry Division, the British troops moving around Monte Etna would be extremely vulnerable to counterattack from the northwest. Thus, the Big Red One found itself in a dual-purpose role by late July.

The 1st Infantry Division would now attack and seize the hilltop town of Troina and the crossroads there to protect Patton's right flank as the Seventh Army moved toward Messina, while it also protected the left flank of Montgomery's Eighth Army now facing the Etna Line.

During the last week of July, German forces in Sicily continued to fall back using delaying tactics to dig in along the Etna Line through Troina. This line was anchored in the north at St. Stefano, and in the south against the slopes of Monte Etna.

The 18th Infantry Regiment seized Petralia at 0900 on 23 July and immediately turned east on Highway 120. The II Corps, on the right flank of the Seventh Army, followed and began to wheel to the east in the vicinity of Nicosia initially to face the German line west of Troina.

The Germans, however, were prepared to dispute this latest II Corps maneuver. The *15th Panzer-Grenadier Division* and Italian *"Aosta" Division* had already established strong blocking positions east of Nicosia along Highway 120, and the advancing 26th Infantry Regiment gained contact with the defenders on the morning of 24 July. This ignited a three-day seesaw fight with both sides reinforced, and a stalemate seemed certain to be in the offing.

During the evening of 25 July, the 18th RCT received orders to move to an assembly area closer to Gangi, six miles east of Petralia, to support the Nicosia attacks. The move was complete by 2300 hours. Early the next morning, General Allen ordered Colonel Smith to move toward Nicosia, a shift of another 15 miles to the east. Major General Bradley had also released two battalions of the 16th Infantry Regiment from Corps reserve. With the 26th Infantry Regiment stalled along Highway 120 west of Nicosia, Allen decided to send the 16th Infantry south of the highway and around massive Hill 962 to first secure the town of Sperlinga. The 18th Infantry Regiment was to swing north of the 26th Infantry, take the high ground on the top of Sperlinga, and then cut Highway 117 where it ran just west of Nicosia.

As the 16th and 18th Infantry Regiments slowly made their way across the tortuous hills surrounding Nicosia, General Allen hatched an imaginative plan to send the 70th Light Tank Battalion, reinforced by a platoon of medium tanks from Company A of the 753rd Tank Battalion, in a night attack designed to pave the way for a double envelopment of the town. The mission of the 70th Tank Battalion would be first to disrupt enemy defenses west of Nicosia, then withdraw as the 26th Infantry Regiment moved through to finish off what remained of the Germans defenses located along Highway 120.

When Company B, 70th Tank Battalion left Gangi late in the afternoon of 27 July accompanied by the heavier Shermans of the 753rd, one tank commander remembered, "We were told to go in, shoot everything, and come back out. It was quite dark, and we had no lights on. So we went in, everything ablaze. We were shooting; the Germans were shooting; we could see their guns flashing."[40]

General Allen's novel application of tanks that night inflicted heavy losses on the enemy and it also distracted him from the flanking movements being conducted to the north and south of Nicosia by both the 16th and 18th Infantry Regiments. The assault, however, was not without cost. Three light tanks were knocked out and seven men were killed or wounded. Nonetheless, Allied patrols entered Sperlinga at 0630 hours and within two hours they were probing the outskirts of Nicosia itself, forcing the Germans to pull out during the night of 27/28 July to avoid encirclement.

The threat of being flanked on both sides of the town demoralized the enemy troops, which included the *Combat Group Fullriede* of the *15th Panzer-Grenadier Division,* elements of *Nebelwerfer Regiment 71*, and a depleted force of the Italian *"Aosta" Division.* Before many of these forces fell back to Troina, however, over 700 Italians and 51 Germans surrendered.

Over the next two days, the 18th RCT continued its attack in the hills on the 1st Infantry Division's northern flank to maintain contact with the retreating enemy. The division's pursuit of the *15th Panzer-Grenadier Division* toward Troina temporarily stalled on the morning of 29 July when heavy rain and stubborn enemy resistance stopped the 16th Infantry Regiment four miles short of Nicosia, but by that afternoon forward elements of the Division were dug in atop a range of hills overlooking Cerami.

Lieutenant Colonel York's 1st Battalion had moved eastward along Highway 120 to Mistretta by this time, taking 100 prisoners in the process. The 3rd Battalion, assisted by the French 4th Tabor of Goums, also succeeded in driving the enemy from nearby Capizzi, but during the fighting Captain Rosinski was shot through the arm and had to be evacuated.

It subsequently took until daylight on 31 July for the Goums to finally clear the town. "All our troops were pretty well worn out from constant moving," Lieutenant Colonel Williamson remembered.[41]

By this time, the Big Red One had completed shifting its axis of advance eastward along Highway 120 and Allen's forces were now advancing against lighter resistance astride this Troina-Nicosia road. Troina itself was situated atop a high, dominating ridge, and the village was home to almost 12,000 Sicilians. Highway 120 did not pass directly through Troina; rather it ran up to the base of the town from the west, and then went north through a pass to the east toward the neighboring town of Randazzo. Troina's dominance of Highway 120, however, made it key terrain for any occupier.

By now General Allen had learned that the Division would soon be relieved by the 9th Infantry Division at Troina, and so he decided to employ Colonel Harry "Paddy" Flint's newly-arrived 39th Infantry Regiment in the assault to ensure that at least one regiment of the 9th Division possessed some knowledge of the sector's ground before it was turned over.

The 39th Infantry Regiment's attack started off auspiciously enough when it occupied Cerami without a fight, but as Flint's advance continued his men encountered well-placed machine guns and accurate mortar fire that forced him to deploy the soldiers to take the next range of hills beyond the town. Artillery support provided by the 1st Infantry Division subsequently succeeded in knocking out two *Nebelwerfers* and inflicting a number of casualties on the defending Germans, but the 39th Infantry Regiment had to halt for the night for reorganizations before launching another attack on Troina in the morning.[42]

As Flint moved from the high ground toward his objective the next day, his 3rd Battalion was counterattacked by panzergrenadiers liberally supported by their own artillery. The 1st Battalion, 39th Infantry Regiment suffered a number of casualties when it was strafed by German fighters. The 4th Tabor of Goums moved forward in support, but they, too, were quickly pinned down by artillery fire. The 1st Infantry Division G-2 had simply not known that Troina was now defended by virtually the entire *15th Panzer-Grenadier Division*, or that the *1st* and *2nd Battalions* of its *Panzer-Grenadier Regiment 3* were positioned north of Highway 120. Adding to the enemy defense of Troina, the *3rd Battalion, Panzer-Grenadier Regiment 3* was also now dug in as a reserve slightly to the west, and two battalions of *Panzer-Grenadier Regiment 1* were dug in atop a two-kilometer-long ridgeline south of the stronghold.[43]

Enemy observers who could call on the entire artillery pieces of the *15th Panzer-Grenadier Division,* as well as *Nebelwerfer Brigade 71,* now had excellent observation of all routes leading to the town. Unknown to General Allen, any daylight attack by the Americans was now doomed to failure unless these German guns could be neutralized.

Allen was now faced with a decision whether to commit more 1st Infantry Division strength. He had received word that the rest of Major General Manton Eddy's 9th Division would be arriving as soon as it moved up from Palermo by truck. He felt it was his moral obligation to capture Troina first, thereby allowing a tight sector to be turned over to Eddy's men, and except for an unsuccessful attack by the 26th Infantry, 2 August thus became a day of preparation for this new offensive.

His subsequent Field Order #20 that night called for the capture of Troina, cutting the Agira-Adrano road south of the town, and development of the situation toward Cesaro and Adrano. Flint's 39th Infantry was to continue its frontal drive along Highway 120, while the 16th Infantry Regiment advanced and ultimately cut the roadway above Troina. The 4th Tabor of Goums was to protect the left flank of the division while the 26th Infantry enveloped Troina from the southwest and cut the Troina-Adrano road. Colonel Smith's 18th Infantry was alerted for a movement by truck around to the south flank via Gagliano. The role of the Regiment was now to back up the 16th Infantry's assault in the next attack, slated to begin at 0300 hours on 3 August.[44]

In preparation for the main drive on Troina, the 2nd Battalion of the 26th Infantry moved out shortly after midnight, leading the 18th Infantry in its swing toward the southern corner of the German defensive line. By dawn the next morning, the 2nd and 3rd Battalions of the 16th Infantry Regiment were halfway up the slopes of the ridge held by *Panzer-Grenadier Regiment 1*, but as daylight wore on, increasingly accurate German machine-gun and mortar fire pinned these forces down and by noon it was apparent that the attack was going nowhere. At that point, General Allen decided to reinforce the 16th Infantry Regiment with the 2nd Battalion, 18th Infantry Regiment.

In concert with a battalion from the 16th Infantry, Sternberg's 2nd Battalion would now push beyond its originally-assigned objective and secure the high ground one-half mile south of Troina at Monte Bianco, thus taking the pressure off the main body of Colonel Taylor's infantry that was pinned down by German fire. The 32nd FA and the 62nd Armored Field Artillery (AFA) Battalions were also alerted to support this attack.

Knowing that his unit now had the mission of making this wide flanking movement against Troina by way of Gagliano, at 1500 hours on 3 August Sternberg, his S-3 Captain Randall, Lieutenant Colonel Williamson, and the battalion's company commanders all went ahead with the reconnaissance officers of the 62nd AFA Battalion to examine the terrain leading to Monte Bianco. After they established a command post in a gully one mile southeast of Gagliano, Williamson remembered, "The country from our side is much lower than the heights held by the enemy and will be tough to take."[45]

Sternberg's Executive Officer, Captain Elisha Peckham, brought the battalion forward on trucks that night, arriving at the assembly area on the south side of Gagliano at 1930 hours.

At 2200 hours, the 2nd Battalion commenced its approach march. Captain Murphy's Company H hand-carried their 81mm mortars and heavy machine guns because it was impossible to find a motor route in the darkness that night. The battalion closed into its assembly area at 0400 hours on 4 August without encountering enemy opposition, and when daylight arrived, Sternberg was surprised to discover that his companies were now situated on a very small hill, hardly large enough for a platoon and dominated by high ground to its south and east. Amazingly, the ground he had occupied overlooked not only Monte Bianco, but also the whole left flank of the enemy position around Troina.

The Germans soon discovered the 2nd Battalion's presence and began harassing them with combat patrols from nearby Monte Pellegrino. The ensuing series

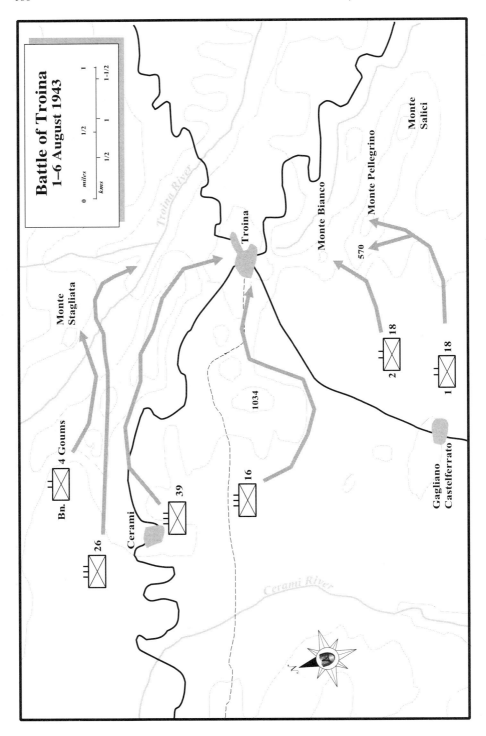

of small, sharp actions prevented the the battalion from continuing its advance and because additional difficulties were experienced by company commanders in locating their exact positions on maps, Sternberg was denied permission to call for artillery fire that day. This chain of events prohibited him from taking full advantage of the excellent observation he had of enemy defenses, and he reluctantly had to hold fast that night. Nevertheless, General Allen later wrote, "This operation by the 2nd Battalion, in aggressively extending the attack on the south flank, contributed greatly to the quick success of the division in the final attack."[46]

Unbeknownst to Lieutenant Colonel Sternberg, another battalion from the 18th RCT was in the fight even as his 2nd Battalion made its way to Monte Bianco. During the day, General Allen ordered Colonel Smith to send York's 1st Battalion to reinforce his positions. Smith had also been afforded operational control of the 1st Battalion, 16th Infantry.

The 1st Infantry Division now had four infantry regiments poised to make a coordinated attack against Troina (its organic three, plus the 39th Infantry Regiment), and Allen hoped to encircle it with the 18th Infantry Regiment in the south and the 26th Infantry Regiment in the north, while the 16th and 39th Infantry Regiments fixed the attention of the defenders by conducting a frontal assault.

The attack began in the late afternoon of 4 August with a massive aerial and artillery bombardment that left the defenders stunned and demoralized. While eight artillery battalions rained fire on the landscape of Troina, two flights of A-36 dive-bombers dropped 500-pound bombs on the town. (A-36s were North American P-51 fighters modified for the dive-bombing role.)

Despite the shattering preparatory effort, the Americans were only able to make slight gains before the Germans responded with their own artillery fire and infantry counterattacks.

The 18th Infantry Regiment made progress when the 1st Battalion maneuvered into a position from whence it could roll up the Gagliano salient and then launch an attack against the southern face of Troina itself.

Company A, now commanded by Lieutenant Bacon, led the assault, first meeting stiff resistance. Captain Cameron's Company B was committed that afternoon, and one of his platoons drove a company-sized enemy force from the northern fringe of Monte Pellegrino, capturing nine of the enemy.

Realizing the importance of the positions held by the 2nd Battalion, General Allen and Colonel Smith visited Sternberg's command post that afternoon. After their personal reconnaissance of the terrain, Sternberg was given permission to use the supporting artillery denied him the day before.[47]

Freed from this restriction, Sternberg's artillery liaison party now had a field day knocking out enemy batteries and shelling hostile defensive positions, all of which were in view from the 2nd Battalion command post. Lieutenant Colonel Bechtold's 32nd FA, which was reinforced by the 1st Battalion, 77th FA Regiment, expended 705 rounds in the course of 41 fire missions that afternoon.

As a result of this shelling, observers assessed that 18 German trucks were destroyed or damaged beyond repair; 11 enemy guns and howitzers were destroyed or neutralized; and one *Nebelwerfer* was demolished. Numerous casualties were also inflicted upon the German infantry, but the actual number was difficult to determine.[48]

Company F had secured the crest of nearby Hill 570, but a German counterattack forced it to withdraw. Throughout the day, both Companies E and G had engaged enemy patrols trying to infiltrate into the 2nd Battalion's flank and rear from Monte Pellegrino, but because of the excellent work of Captain Murphy's Company H heavy machine gunners and mortarmen, this proved costly to the Germans.[49]

That evening, the 1st Battalion finally worked into position on the right of the 2nd Battalion, permitting Lieutenant Colonel Sternberg to deploy his rifle companies in a further drive toward Troina itself. Lieutenant Jeffrey sent a platoon out first and his men seized and held a small hill on the southern approaches to the town.

Fierce hand-to-hand combat ensued as the rifle platoon and the Germans battled for control of the hill, with the opposing sides barely more than 50 yards apart for the remainder of the day. During the same afternoon, the 3rd Battalion moved through Gagliano to a point just east of that town. During early evening, Sisson's men moved forward three miles and deployed to the rear of the 2nd Battalion, assuring depth in the Regiment's new positions.

The men of the 1st Battalion resumed their assault on Monte Pellegrino on the morning of 5 August. A rifle platoon from Company B worked its way to within 200 yards of the hilltop; the platoon was soon astride its crest. During the advance, the Captain Carter's Company D mortarmen maintained pressure on the enemy and in the early afternoon, Lieutenant Bacon's Company A brought a rifle squad up to the summit of Pellegrino where a well-prepared enemy observation post was found abandoned.

Soon afterwards all of Bacon's men occupied the right half of Monte Pellegrino and were overlooking Troina, where they opened fire on enemy forces that were pulling back in the face of the assault being made by the 16th and 39th Infantry Regiments. By 2000 hours, York's men had secured all of Monte Pellegrino, thereby unhinging the entire southern anchor of the German defenses around Troina.

As the 1st Battalion consolidated atop the mountain, the 2nd Battalion successfully linked up with the 16th Infantry Regiment's 1st Battalion on their left. At dusk, Captain Penick sent a platoon to relieve Lieutenant Jeffrey's on Monte Bianco, and this difficult move was completed at 2200 hours, despite numerous casualties. The 3rd Battalion had also been ordered to move forward on Troina, but as Sisson's men advanced, it seemed certain that the enemy was preparing to pull out altogether. There were many guns and vehicles abandoned along their path, most of which appeared to have been knocked out by the artillery and dive-bombing attacks earlier that day.

By the morning of 6 August, it was clear that the enemy had almost completely withdrawn from Troina for all that was left behind were a few rear-guard elements. General Allen ordered Colonel Taylor's 16th Infantry Regiment to scale the steep slopes up to the hilltop town and by noon his men were roaming its rubble-strewn streets.

With the seizure of Troina, the German defensive line facing the Seventh Army's advance on Messina had been broken at its strongest point. The *15th Panzer-Grenadier Division* sustained over 1,600 casualties in the process, many at the hands of the 18th RCT.

"The continuing progress of the 18th Infantry Regiment in this attack proved to be the decisive factor," General Allen wrote later in reference to the team effort of Colonel Smith's men during the fighting.

Then putting credit where it was due, Allen continued with, "The enemy's loss of the commanding high ground on the deep south flank had a telling effect. The 1st Battalion, Lieutenant Colonel Bob York commanding, completely demoralized the enemy defenses. [His] operation contributed greatly to the success of the 1st Division...."[50]

While the 18th RCT was recovering from the fighting at Troina over the next few days, *Time* magazine's 9 August 1943 edition featured a handsome picture of General Allen, with an inscription saying:

> Major General Terry Allen of the 1st Division
> The infantry, the infantry, with dirt behind their ears.

Inside, the article began with:

Last week somewhere along the German's [sic] last line in Sicily, General Allen and his men were very busy. Also on the line were at least four other US Divisions. All of them fought well. Yet, upon Terry Allen and his 1st Infantry Division, as upon no other commander or unit in Sicily, there has fallen a special mark on war and history; a mark reserved for front-line fighting men, and esteemed by them. It was the mark of the greatest division in being and of a great division commander in the making. These inseparable reputations—the reputation of the division and that of its commander—are the first of their kind to be publicly recognized in the US Army of World War II. To all soldiers there is food for thought, and to many there is satisfaction in the fact that the joint reputation was won by a division of infantrymen, the men who fight on foot and who, up to now, have finally had to win the battles and the wars.

In another of the ironies of war, this article appeared at almost the same time that General Allen and Brigadier General Roosevelt were relieved of their commands in the 1st Infantry Division. Allen first heard about it on 5 August, at the height of the Troina battles when the order inadvertently reached his headquarters in Cerami via routine mail delivery. Although sensitive and supposed to be delivered personally by General Bradley, some bungler had instead placed the order in a mail pouch from II Corps headquarters.

When an aide at the 1st Infantry Division Command Post opened the piece of mail, he rushed the order over to Colonel Mason, Allen's Chief of Staff, who then turned to the G-2, Colonel Porter, for advice. Both were personally astounded by what they had read, and they hurriedly discussed whether they should inform General Allen of the order's contents. Deferring to the fact that others undoubtedly knew, they felt it best to let him see what had just been received.

Allen was briefing his subordinates on the next attack. He read the order, then turned to Porter and whispered, "Bob, what do I do with this?"

Tears welled in Allen's eyes, but he continued to give instructions to his staff. Then he called Bradley but the II Corps Commander said, "Carry on, we'll sort this out later."[51]

Not long afterwards, the phone rang. It was General Patton. Bradley must have called him to let him know Terry Allen had the news. Patton then asked him if the order for his relief had arrived, to which Allen simply replied, "Yes."

Patton then shot back, "Well, you're not relieved. I say you're not relieved until you've taken Troina and the 1st Division has completed its job in Sicily!" Later, George Patton came down to Allen's command post to console him.[52]

That night, General Allen penned a letter to his wife, the contents of which evinced both his shock and resigned acceptance of what had just happened.

August 5, 1943
My dear Mary Fran,

    I just received orders today, which came as a great surprise and the actual meaning of which I do not exactly know. Ted and I both have been relieved from the Division and have been directed to report to the American Commander in Chief (Eisenhower) at Algiers for future assignments.

    George Patton came around to see me today and said that he understood that I was being relieved from the 1st Division. He also said that before doing so I would be temporarily attached to American Headquarters in Algiers and there would be held at British Headquarters in order to confer with them about the combat methods and tactics of the 1st Division during eight months of campaigning and particularly its actions with the Navy during the Sicilian Invasion. All of this, of course, was merely Patton's supposition and I really don't know what my exact status will be until I have reported to Eisenhower.

    Ted R. does not know what his next assignment will be. Personally, I did not expect to be promoted to be a Corps Commander. The accomplishments of the 1st Division would have been equally as good under almost anyone else.

Frankly, my dear, the conceptions that most people have of actual combat are all wet. There is very little thrill to it. It's a dirty lousy job that must be accomplished as quickly as possible, with the maximum damage to the enemy and the least damage to our own soldiers. By now, you will surely understand how impossible it was for me to leave or to seek an assignment which would have evaded the responsibilities thrust upon me.

Actually, relief from the Division here will not be effective until the results after these actions I am involved in have ceased. That is, we must finish the actual battles we are now engaged in until the Division has been withdrawn from the front lines and we can turn it over to my successor. Clarence Huebner will succeed me.

It will be a wrench to leave the "Fighting First." We have survived some hard times together and the whole gang has loyally stood by me. Our doughboys have been wandering around steadily for 27 days and at least 14 nights. Their tenacity and loyalty in the face of terrific hardships are really fantastic.
All my love,
Terry

General Bradley accepted full responsibility for making the decision to relieve Allen and Roosevelt. He had made up his mind to do so early in the Sicilian campaign, but apparently was waiting for the right moment. Several events precipitated Bradley's decision to issue the order when he did, not least of which was his determination to pull the 1st Infantry Division out of the line once Troina was taken.

There were other factors that explained why Allen's and Roosevelt's relief took place, as Bradley's opinion of both officers had been crystallized by several events. He looked at divisional command with detached feelings about the individual commanders' reputations and was still simmering about the 18th Infantry Regiment's losses in its ill-advised attack on Hill 232 during the final push in North Africa. Additionally, Bradley had been embarrassed when word was leaked to Eisenhower of the indiscipline exhibited by the members of the 1st Infantry Division in Oran, after the completion of the Tunisian campaign.

In his post-war memoir, *A Soldier's Story,* Bradley attempted to persuade his readers that the decision was a logical and passionless one. He noted:

In time of war the only value that can be affixed to any unit is the tactical value of that unit in winning the war. Even the lives of those men assigned to it become nothing more than tools to be used in the accomplishment of that mission. War has neither time nor heart to concern itself with the individual and the dignity of man. Men must be subordinated to the effort that comes with fighting a war, and as a consequence men must die so that objectives might be taken. For a commander the agony of war is not in its dangers, deprivations, or fear of defeat but in the knowledge that with each new day men's lives must be spent to pay the costs of that day's objectives.[53]

Unfortunately, it seems that Bradley had also developed the opinion that the 1st Infantry Division was suffering from Allen's and Roosevelt's style of command.

He felt the Big Red One, despite its accomplishments, had become an organization that manifested its own self-image through its charismatic leaders and he held Terry Allen responsible for not reducing the Division's pride to be a more Bradley-like team player.

General Bradley went so far as to say, "The Division thought itself exempted from the need for discipline by virtue of its months in the line, and it believed itself to be the only division carrying its fair share of the war."[54]

Bradley, however, undoubtedly did not make the decision to relieve Terry Allen and Teddy Roosevelt independently. He needed Patton's approval, at least tacitly.

Patton was an astute politician and well aware of the changing favors of the Army's senior leadership at the time. He knew Terry Allen had fallen into disfavor with Eisenhower and was not going to object to Bradley's reasoning and go against Eisenhower merely because of his friendship and loyalty to Allen. In retrospect, Patton and Allen's friendship while assigned to the Cavalry School at Fort Riley was often a stormy one, as both were strong-willed individuals who argued constantly over professional issues.

Thus, while it might have been a difficult decision to make, Patton was not indebted to Allen to the point that he would go against Eisenhower. Bradley later wrote, "The decision was mine and mine alone. George [Patton] did nothing more than concur in the recommendation."[55] There is ample evidence that bears this out; and there was no animosity between George Patton and Terry Allen after he was relieved. In fact, General Allen accepted his fate like a good soldier, as did Teddy Roosevelt.

To the soldier on the line, however, the departure of Generals Allen and Roosevelt brought an end to a deep emotional bond that had been formed between the senior leadership and soldiers of the 1st Infantry Division. As always, confusion accompanied change, for the men held varying opinions about why Allen and Roosevelt were called away. Many heard Allen was being sent home because he was suffering from "war weariness." Some were convinced Allen, Patton, and Bradley simply did not see eye to eye. Others believed the changes were all about the fact that the soldiers themselves were difficult to control and that Bradley had a particularly hard time with this. In a way, they were all right.

One view of the command change was pragmatic and it revealed the obvious to some 18th Infantry Regiment soldiers. "Most of us were of the opinion that this change was a bad omen," Lieutenant Downing wrote. "General Allen had commanded the division through Africa and Sicily, and the old rumors were being revived that we might be sent back to the States after the campaign. However, if a new general took command, we could be sure that we would continue on somewhere in combat. A new general would not be appointed to lead troops back to the States."[56]

Lieutenant Franklyn Johnson made another insightful observation when he got the news while walking back down the slopes of Monte Pellegrino. "No one announced the reason," he noted, "but we angrily recalled the clashes between Allen and Patton over the spirited high-jinks of our units in Oran after the Tunisian campaign. Tough old Terry Allen was strict on discipline, but he would go to bat for any man of his, colonel or private."[57]

Whatever the general feelings were at the time, the dismissal of Allen and Roosevelt was summed up most succinctly by General Bradley when he said, "To save Allen both from himself and from his brilliant record and to save the division from the heady effects of too much success, I decided to separate them." Bradley saw Allen and Roosevelt as too tightly regarded as one to leave Roosevelt with the Division. He felt General Clarence Huebner should be left to pick his own Assistant Division Commander.

According to Bradley, therefore, "Roosevelt had to go with Allen for he, too, had sinned by loving the division too much."[58]

The incoming commanding general, Major General Clarence R. Huebner, entered the Army as an enlisted man in 1910. After he completed basic training, he was assigned to the 18th Infantry Regiment. He learned how to soldier while serving as a company clerk, mess sergeant, and supply sergeant. He was one of the Regiment's most efficient soldiers, its best rifle shot, and the most neatly dressed. His devotion to duty soon attracted the attention of his officers, and he passed the tests to be commissioned in 1916. He then went to the School of the Line in Fort Leavenworth, Kansas, just before the United States entered the First World War. A month later, he was on his way to France, in command of a rifle company in the 1st Infantry Division.

In France, Huebner had a few months to train his company of raw recruits before they entered combat. In March 1918, his company found itself in the Beaumont sector north of Toul, where Huebner was wounded and initially reported as killed. A month later, he returned to head his company, and when his battalion commander was killed in an ensuing battle, he took command of the unit, earning the Distinguished Service Cross (DSC) in the process.

In June 1918, he was promoted to major, wounded again, and awarded an Oak Leaf Cluster to his DSC. Returning to command in time for battles near Saizerais, the St. Mihiel attack, and the Meuse-Argonne Offensive, he was promoted to lieutenant colonel in October 1918 and assumed command of the 28th Infantry Regiment.[59] After a year of occupation duty in Germany, Huebner then returned to the United States, where he reverted to his permanent grade of captain and spent the better part of the next 20 years in regimental duties.

When the Second World War started, Huebner was a brigadier general serving as the Army Field Forces' Director of Training. He remained in that position until

March 1943, when he was reassigned to North Africa as the Theater G3. After barely a month in that position, however, he was reassigned as the Deputy Chief of Staff for the combined Eighteenth Army Group Headquarters, under the command of General Sir Harold Alexander. It was a critical time: American forces had just been defeated in the Kasserine Pass battles, and Alexander missed few opportunities to disparage the fighting ability of American troops in Tunisia.

Alexander was loath to give the Americans any significant responsibility, which quickly began to cause problems as the US Army strove to find a way to redeem the reputation of its leaders, soldiers, and weapons in the wake of defeat. At Eisenhower's direction, Huebner joined Alexander's staff to erode further favoritism based on nationality and to lobby for a genuinely allied approach to future battles. In fact, Huebner rankled Alexander so much with his crisp, abrasive style that he was fired from the Eighteenth Army Group staff while the 1st Infantry Division was fighting in Nicosia. Among other things, Huebner had openly called Montgomery "a really obnoxious bastard." His mouth probably got him in trouble with the British, whom he genuinely disliked, but he was Bradley's kind of commander. A no-nonsense officer, Huebner was a stern disciplinarian and an excellent trainer. His effect on the 18th RCT would be felt immediately.[60]

"I carried instructions from the new commanding general to Colonel Smith," Lieutenant Downing remembered of that time. "Since the Regiment was in a rest area by now, I was returned to my unit. The men were to utilize this rest period in zeroing in their weapons and taking conditioning hikes.

"I communicated the instructions as directed, and like good loyal officers, the regimental staff received them without comment." This response was not duplicated throughout the ranks, however. "The reactions of the company grade officers were violent and blasphemous," Downing added later. "After hiking and fighting for 30 days, the idea of resting by firing weapons and taking hikes seemed a little grotesque."[61]

Lieutenant Franklyn Johnson's antitank platoon bivouacked in an orchard overlooking Monte Pellegrino after the Regiment was pulled out of combat. When he received his orders to clean up his guns and zero them, he was shocked to discover that only two of his 57mm guns would fire. "It made our hair stand on end," he recalled. "Brand new in Africa, they were test-fired with excellent results, but for some reason the new commanding general had ordered new firing pins inserted. We never had the opportunity to use all the guns during the fighting, so we had no way of knowing that all the pins but one in my platoon were short."[62]

Perhaps General Huebner's orders were already being seen by Johnson as beneficial, but when he went to the firing range the next day, Huebner appeared in person. It was embarrassing for Johnson, as he did not even see the general coming. His platoon had been resting on the grass when Huebner came up behind him, and then snapped, "Get up, Lieutenant!"

"I called the men to attention," Johnson wrote later. "General Huebner reprimanded me for allowing my men to relax and for not spending the time between firing in close-order drill. He then ordered the men to fall in at left dress instead of the ordinary right dress. A new replacement happened to be the man on our front squad's left end, and with the command, 'Dress left, dress,' instead of holding fast so that all the men could line up even with him, the new man stepped to his left and the whole platoon started side-stepping down the hill. To the general this gross error was infuriating, but to me it was hilarious and I could not hold back a smile."

General Huebner made a grim effort to control himself, and then demanded to see if Johnson's men could salute. As Johnson pointed out, "Having done no saluting while campaigning, the platoon was extremely ragged." After Huebner witnessed this he barked, "Terrible!" and then shouted, "Johnson, how long will it take you to teach these men how to salute?" Johnson thought about the work he still had to do that day with firing practice, and then answered, "Twenty-four hours, Sir." General Huebner was not amused. Instead, he shot back with, "I'll give you three minutes."[63] Moments later he turned and left with his staff. The next day, regiment-wide training schedules called for intensive close-order and saluting practice.

General Huebner also made a profound impression on his own headquarters staff. Colonel Mason remembered that the mood at the command post when Huebner arrived was formal. "Those of us who had been plebes at West Point acted like plebes again, saluting, 'Yes, Sir,' 'No, Sir,' 'No excuse, Sir,'" he remembered years later,

> This went on day after day. We were addressed by title, and we responded in kind, formal and military, and secretly mad as hell at this new CG.
>
> Gradually, very gradually, my dull brain began to analyze what was going on, though. Orders were being obeyed, not questioned. All ranks were saluting, like soldiers. When we were chewed out, we ended up mad as hell but not humiliated. I began to realize that the CG knew where his units were, what they were supposed to be doing and how well or poorly they were doing it. Then, one by one, the old man got us in his pocket. One big question often bandied about was: JUST WHEN did the 1st Division fully and without reservation accept General Huebner as the Division Commander with no backward look to Terry Allen or Ted Roosevelt? In Sicily he assembled all the officers and noncommissioned officers and made a short talk to them. His talk was simple, straight from the heart, utterly sincere, and was on the heritage of the 1st Division—its World War I accomplishments, covering his own involvement; what it had accomplished so far in World War II; and what still had to be done. He knew we were spearheading the Normandy Invasion, but the rest of the division did not know. I felt the reaction of that assemblage and it was, in my opinion, the turning point. From then on, I am sure that he had the hearts, minds and loyalty of the 1st Division.[64]

While the 18th RCT was in their final days of fighting at Troina, Major General Lucian Truscott's 3rd Infantry Division was battling stiff German opposition at San Fratello, the northern boundary of the Etna Line. Here, the *29th Panzer-Grenadier Division* had been brought over from the Italian mainland to secure the northern flank of the Etna Line and had entrenched itself on a ridge overlooking the north coastal highway. The "Rock of the Marne" Division made several vain attempts to crack the San Fratello position beginning on 3 August, but they failed to gain much ground. The strength of the enemy defensive position then prompted him to try and outflank it by an amphibious assault behind the Germans' lines. On the night of 7/8 August, a force landed on the coast, achieved complete surprise, and quickly blocked the coastal highway, but the Germans had coincidentally chosen that night to withdraw from San Fratello to join many of their troops who had already retired toward Messina.

At Patton's insistence, Truscott launched a second bid to trap the *29th Panzer-Grenadier Division* on 11 August with another amphibious operation, this time at Brolo. On this occasion, the withdrawing Germans turned on the landing force, which consisted of a reinforced infantry battalion, destroying all of the supporting American tanks. Matters were not helped any when "friendly" A-36s knocked out all four of the self-propelled howitzers that had accompanied Truscott's landing force. A number of Americans were killed, wounded, and captured as the numerically-superior German force then made its way unhindered toward Messina.[65]

By now, time was running out for the Allies to trap the Germans before they were evacuated to mainland Italy through the Straits of Messina. On 11 August, the day Patton launched the Brolo operation, the Germans also accelerated their evacuation efforts. General der Panzertruppen Hans Valentin Hube, commanding *XIV Panzer Corps*, had ordered the implementation of Operation Lehrgang ("Curriculum"), the five-night plan to ferry German troops across the straits, beginning that night. On the morning of 17 August, elements of the 3rd Infantry Division entered Messina just hours after the last Axis troops had boarded ships for Italy.

Anxious to avoid the tremendous losses that befell their forces in Tunisia, the Germans had succeeded by this time in evacuating 39,951 troops, 9,789 vehicles, 51 tanks, 163 guns, and significant quantities of fuel and ammunition. When the Italian evacuation of Sicily ended on 16 August, they had also removed an estimated 59,000 troops, 3,000 sailors, 227 vehicles, and 41 artillery pieces. Shortly after General Patton personally accepted Messina's surrender that morning, a column of British vehicles wound its way into the *piazza* in the center of town. The British commander, Brigadier J. C. Currie, offered his hand to the Seventh Army Commander and simply told him, "It was a jolly good race. I congratulate you."[66]

By this time, the 18th Regimental Combat Team had occupied an assembly area near Randazzo after a motor march from Troina made difficult by poor road conditions, blown out bridges, and extensive mine fields. The latter were particularly difficult for the engineers to detect due to the presence of magnetic lava formations around Monte Etna. Randazzo had been leveled by American artillery: its streets were choked with debris and bulldozers had to clear a narrow path so the combat team could pass through. As the 3rd Infantry Division was securing Messina, Colonel Smith tentatively probed for routes northward in case the Regiment was called upon to support operations in the final days of the Sicilian campaign. His regimental Intelligence and Reconnaissance (I&R) Platoon explored one unimproved road as a possible route for a march northward, only to discover that after 15 miles of travel, the route simply disappeared.

The 18th Infantry Regiment was never called on to participate in the final phase of the Sicilian campaign. By 17 August, its men were bivouacked in the vicinity of Mojo, a small village east of Randazzo where trucks were assembled to take the men to Licata on Sicily's southern shore near Gela. After traveling back through many of the towns for which the Regiment had battled during its combat days in Sicily, the motor convoy reached Licata on 20 August. The next several days were spent on setting up camps, refitting, and resting.

Training was resumed on 25 August including close-order drill, conditioning marches, patrolling, and marksmanship practice. As had become his custom, General Huebner made several appearances with his staff to watch over the men's progress. In this way, he ensured that they were indeed learning how to behave like a disciplined unit again.

"Our emphasis was on marksmanship, training lieutenants, and watching out for the general," Lieutenant Colonel Williamson remembered.[67]

Several promotions were announced, the most notable of which was a change of command in the 2nd Battalion. Lieutenant Colonel Sternberg went to Regiment to become Colonel Smith's Executive Officer, ending his long association with the 2nd Battalion since being assigned as the Commanding Officer of Company E in 1941. Lieutenant Colonel Williamson, a West Pointer like Sternberg, assumed command of the battalion.

The men of the 18th Infantry Regiment were warned soon afterward to polish their boots in preparation for an appearance by General Patton on 27 August.

The Seventh Army Commander's visit unfortunately came on the heels of a show put on a few days earlier by an entertainment troupe led by Bob Hope. It included the popular stateside singer Frances Langford who, to the delight of the men, appeared on stage clad in a white brassiere. The announced visit of General Patton had prompted one GI understandably to remark, "Who the hell wanted to see him after that Langford?"[68]

Unknown to just about all of the combat team's officers and men at the time, Patton had been ordered by General Eisenhower to apologize to units whose soldiers he had slapped in evacuation hospitals earlier that month. Apologizing was an activity to which General Patton was unaccustomed, but his attempt to do so was remembered by the men of the 18th Infantry Regiment as they sat in a natural bowl with thousands of other 1st Infantry Division soldiers that day.

"General Patton gruffly poured out an amazing message," Lieutenant Johnson recalled.

He remembered Patton started with, "First, I thought I'd stand up here and let you soldiers see if I'm as big a son of a bitch as you think I am." Like so many that day, Johnson did not understand what Patton was referring to at that moment, though he guessed that it was a sly reference to the reliefs of Generals Allen and Roosevelt.

Even Patton's biographer, Carlo D'Este, commented on how his message was confused and not well-received, saying "Patton's speech to the 18,000 men of the Big Red One was greeted with stony silence, although one eye witness recalls hearing a few scattered boos."[69]

Most 18th Infantry Regiment soldiers remained slightly mystified as Patton hastily concluded his speech a few minutes later by thanking the Division for its part in the Sicilian campaign. One officer, Captain Carter, spoke openly about Patton many years later to help explain the reception his "apology" received that day:

> He sure had an amazing legend in World War II, but Patton was disliked by many of us in the 18th Infantry," he reflected. "It started back in North Africa at El Guettar when a lieutenant who had made three separate attacks on a hill, and who should have been decorated, was instead fined by Patton for not having his leggings tucked in and his tie straight. Word of this spread throughout the 1st Division by that night, and we had no use for him after this.[70]

One factor weighing more heavily on the Regiment's ranks than Patton was the number of malaria, jaundice, and dysentery cases that appeared during their hot weeks on Sicily. The causes varied, but the monotonous canned food diet, a lack of fresh meat and vegetables, and the lethargic effects of atabrine tablets (Atabrine was then the state-of-the-art prophylactic against malaria) that had to be taken daily all contributed. Open latrines, the multitude of flies, and the effects of the glaring hot summer sun were also factors that kept the battalion doctors very busy.

By this time, disease was cutting so deeply into the Regiment's strength; it prompted one officer to say, "We were beginning to feel that if we didn't get out of this disease-ridden country, we would all rot away."[71]

After spending a brief period in Mazzarino guarding an airfield and then another month of intense training (to include a day where General Huebner ordered officers to demonstrate their ability to fire their own weapons), the Regiment was finally alerted on 13 October to move to the port of Augusta on Sicily's eastern shore. In pouring rain, the men boarded the familiar *Reina del Pacifico* on 18 October and departed into the Mediterranean.

After a brief stopover in Algiers, the 1st Infantry Division convoy headed through the Strait of Gibraltar where rumors soon spread about the Division's destination. When the weather started turning cooler and the sea began changing color from blue to green on the open Atlantic, few guessed that the convoy was headed back to the States.

Several days later, when skies began filling with fog and after duty officers started exchanging the multitude of currencies the men had accumulated in Sicily and North Africa for British pounds sterling, the guessing was over.

At long last the *Reina del Pacifico* pulled into the docks at Liverpool where the men anxiously crowded the rails to get a glimpse of "civilization." Except for MPs and a few civilian workmen, the docks were bare and quiet.

The arrival of the 18th Regimental Combat Team in England was secret; their presence was to be kept silent so German spies would not know that the battle-hardened men of the Big Red One were there to train for their upcoming role in spearheading the invasion of France.

An obligation of operations security carried down to every man in the 18th Regimental Combat Team. During the voyage, orders had been issued to remove all traces of their association with the 1st Infantry Division. Big Red One patches were ripped off uniform shirts, jackets, and overcoats. Helmets were painted over to conceal any link to the veteran fighting team. Ribbons denoting combat time were also removed. All personnel were firmly cautioned not to mention anything about having come from the Mediterranean. Instead, if asked, the soldiers were to say that they had just arrived fresh from training in the States.

D-DAY NORMANDY

6 JUNE 1944

At 1130 hours, the Germans, in the last organized defense at the St. Laurent draw [E-1], surrendered to the 2nd Battalion of the 18th Infantry. Thus in a little over an hour, concerted bold action had brought the most substantial improvement on the beach since the start of the landings.
—Gordon Harrison, *Cross-Channel Attack,*
Army Official History

After advance details met the Regiment's companies at the disembarkation ramps in Liverpool, the men marched out of the dockyards in columns of twos toward the nearby rail station at Dorset. The veteran combatants were quickly packed into compartments in a long line of trains, and they were soon rolling through the countryside toward England's southwestern shores. Two days later, the men arrived at the Dorchester Station, where a billeting party of the 3rd Armored Division first provided mess support. Trucks then brought the men southward over narrow, winding roads to their new billets, arriving on 8 November—the first anniversary of the landings in North Africa.

The 1st Battalion initially moved into a modern camp near the picturesque crossroads at Piddlehinton, and then subsequently occupied barracks at Chickerell Camp, just outside of Weymouth.

The 2nd Battalion and Cannon Company were quartered in a collection of Nissen huts near the villages of Broadmayne and West Knighton, where they were later joined by officers and staff of the 32nd FA.

The 3rd Battalion and Service Company settled into encampments near the county town of Dorchester itself, while Anti-Tank Company moved to the rural setting around Winterborne St. Martin.

Colonel Smith and his staff, along with Regimental Headquarters Company personnel, took over Ilsington House, located three miles west of Dorchester in Puddleton. The first few days were spent organizing camps, then formal training began. At first, it was limited to a couple of hours a day, but this soon changed to a full eight-hour schedule where units were scattered across the hills and ravines of the countryside, all focused on reviewing valuable battlefield lessons learned thus far. Officer's schools were held at night, while daytime training gradually increased in scope, to include assaulting and demolishing concrete defensive pillboxes like those the Germans were known to have in the Atlantic Wall across the English Channel. River crossing exercises were held, rifle marksmanship was honed, and 16-mile roadmarches—completed in less than four hours—kept the men in top shape. At the same time, elements of the Regiment provided assistance to units of the British Home Guard, both in training and in protecting vital installations around the causeway leading to the lighthouse at Portland Bill, as well as in the large harbor of Weymouth itself.

As November ended, Colonel Smith recognized that his men needed rest and relaxation. He announced that ten percent of a company at a time would receive one-week to ten-day passes, issued in rotation. Many soldiers traveled to London or even as far away as Edinburgh, Scotland, to go sightseeing or to reacquaint with people they met during their stay in England and Scotland in 1942.

When Christmas came a short month later, the Regiment celebrated it in a far more traditional manner than had been possible in the previous year on cold, dark, and rainy Longstop Hill. Mail sacks arrived with packages from home and the Army provided a turkey dinner with many of the conventional "trimmings." As one lieutenant remembered, "No effort was spared by the US Army from Supreme Headquarters down to company headquarters to make the celebration as homelike as possible."[1]

The year 1944 brought a resumption of training as the Division geared up for the inevitable cross-channel invasion. In abandoned and bomb-shattered sections of Weymouth, the Regiment's rifle companies practiced street fighting in rubble-strewn alleys that led from one ruined house to another. Machine gunners and riflemen used live ammunition during these exercises, and they were made even more realistic by mortar-emplaced smoke screens. In Cannon Company, Anti-Tank and in FA support units, road convoy procedures were practiced, aircraft and armor identification was reviewed, and range firing exercises were held with individual and crew-served weapons. Radio codes and artillery "call for fire" procedures were also studied intently. Replacements began to arrive, bringing companies up to full strength again. As a matter of planning for the upcoming invasion, each rifle company slated to take part in the initial assault would eventually receive 50 extra soldiers as immediate replacements for what everyone believed would be an extremely costly landing operation.

On 16 January, the 1st Infantry Division received a visitor whose rank and importance reinforced already widely held convictions that the Big Red One would find itself in the lead when the invasion of Europe came. The newly-appointed Commanding General of the Twenty-First Army Group, Lieutenant General Montgomery, arrived in Dorchester where he delivered a rousing address, following it with a spirited letter to General Huebner. In the letter he said, "The

Division has already won reknown in battle in Africa and Sicily. I have absolute confidence that it will do even better in future engagements with the enemy."[2] Before January 1944 ended, it was announced that Montgomery would be the Ground Component Commander for the upcoming invasion, subordinate only to General Eisenhower.

After more training during cold, rainy February and into March, the 18th Regimental Combat Team was put on short notice alert on 23 March for movement to marshaling areas in Weymouth for the commencement of the largest amphibious operation in military history. In early April, the Regiment participated in a brief exercise to practice river crossings at nearby Blanford, and later that month the entire chain of command, from General Eisenhower on down, came to inspect the Division and emphasize the importance of using valuable time left before the invasion to train even harder.

"Operation FABIUS," a practice exercise and full dress rehearsal for D-day, took place at Slapton Sands along the Devonshire coast on 28 April. Many problems were worked out during the exercise, and the next morning brought orders to move by motors and trains back to Weymouth. By this time, General Huebner and his staff had refined the Division's role in the invasion based on plans developed by Major General Leonard Gerow's V Corps. The V Corps' mission on D-day was to secure a bridgehead on the Normandy coast between Port-en-Bessin and the Vire River, and then push southward toward Caumont, some 25 miles inland, where its forces would link up with the British Second Army.

V Corps would arrive in Normandy in three echelons. The initial assault force, designated as "Force O," consisted of the Big Red One's 16th Infantry, reinforced by the 116th Regimental Combat Team of the 29th Infantry Division, as well as artillery, armor, and engineer units and the Provisional Ranger Force consisting of the 2nd and 5th Ranger Battalions. The 115th Infantry Regiment of the 29th Infantry Division and Colonel George A. Smith's 18th Regimental Combat Team would reinforce the assault echelon three hours after the initial landings. Two regiments of the 1st and 29th Infantry Divisions (26th and 175th, respectively) also were prepared to land on D-day, depending on the tactical situation.

As what was to be an unusually warm and sunny May began, every man in the 18th Infantry Regiment could sense that the invasion was growing closer and many wanted to know their roles in the vast undertaking. General Eisenhower paid another visit to each of the Regiment's battalions early in the month, heightening the anticipation, and he spoke individually to some of the officers and men. General Bradley and his staff visited the combat team a few days later. This time the Regiment was lined up in battalion formations for an inspection, followed by an assembly of individual officers in line by rank. When Bradley decided to speak, he stood by a jeep and called everyone to group closely around him. Lieutenant John Downing remembered the general's talk that day, later writing:

> His speech was personal, logical, and inspirational in its simplicity. He used no fiery rhetoric, but told us that although we would have an unpleasant

job, we would be supported by every resource the Allies had. He said this would be no sideshow invasion like Africa or Sicily; that this was to be an all-out effort. The invasion would not fail because too much was at stake. Divisions would pour in behind us at a rate we could not dream of. On D-day plus 30, over 40 divisions would be ashore. General Bradley stated figures to prove that the number of people that could be killed in battle was small compared to the number of people that would be engaged. He even said, "I wouldn't miss this show for anything in the world. Some of you will be killed, but a person who lives through this invasion will be proud for the rest of his life for having been a part of it."[3]

After Bradley's visit, the activity preparing for invasion picked up at a feverish pace. Blouses (the jackets of dress uniforms), garrison caps, and neckties were turned in. Officers' trunks were sent off to be stored indefinitely. A new type of gas mask with a snout canister was issued, along with cans of anti-gas shoe daubing. Gas-proof underwear, socks, shirts, trousers, and leggings were handed out, all treated with special chemicals. Even eye ointment and plastic eye-shields, designed to protect a man's face from mustard gas, were distributed.

Sailing lists were sent down from the personnel office, resulting in men shuffling to new camp areas to join others in planned landing groups. Soldiers were issued sleeveless canvas assault jackets made with front and rear pockets and other features designed to allow them to replace the packs used in previous combat. All men received a fuse, lighter, and a small, quarter-pound block of TNT or nitro starch powerful enough to blow a crater in the ground that could be converted into a foxhole.

Maps of France printed on pieces of linen the size of a handkerchief were distributed to officers and NCOs of the first three grades, along with small compasses and magnetized pencil clips that could be used as compasses. Battalion surgeons instructed men in the use of the first-aid kit that they had all been issued. Sulfa tablets in waterproof paper packets were handed out; these early antibiotics were to be consumed immediately after being wounded to prevent infection. Camouflage nets were stretched over all helmets, and 1 x 3-inch vertical white bars were stenciled on the backs of each officer's, while horizontal bars were added to the backs of each NCO's (In the confusion that was expected on the assault beaches, these markings would help soldiers understand whom to follow.) The planned combat load, combined with weapons, ammunition belt, bayonets, entrenching tools, canteens, rations—even candy, cigarettes, and toilet paper—was heavy, but necessary.

After the officers were hurriedly assembled and marched out in columns of twos to a former staff officers' quarters one late-May morning, the enormity of their role in the upcoming invasion was about to sink in. Assembled in a dining room behind closed doors, the officers were first given an introductory speech by Colonel Smith and then briefed on the upcoming mission by Major Frank Colacicco and Major Henry V. Middleworth.

The field order issued to Regimental Headquarters on 10 May was a huge Top Secret portfolio detailing over 100 pages of instructions, information on the enemy, and the specific missions for each unit.

Using a series of wall maps covered with annotated overlays, Major Colacicco described the sequence of actions that would take place on D-day. Here the officers learned for the first time that they would be landing on the coast of France east of the Cotentin Peninsula at a place called Omaha Beach, a 7,900-yard long curve of Normandy shoreline situated between the Carentan Estuary and the port of Arromanches.

Omaha Beach actually stretched along a shore that curved slightly inward. The beach itself sloped very gently toward the high-water mark during a rising tide, making a stretch of sand averaging about 300 yards in depth from the water's edge at low tide to the full-tide line. It was at this high-water mark where the tidal flat terminated in a bank of washed-up stone and coarse shingle and then suddenly sloped up steeply to a height of some six feet to either side of the Regiment's landing area near the E-1 exit draw. Above this naturally-formed seawall and before the bluffs lay a beach flat, a marshy area some fifty yards deep that had been heavily mined by the Germans. The bluffs that formed beyond this marsh were over 150 feet in height, partly covered with low scrub and brush, and completely dominated the landing beaches.

The Combat Team 18 was to land squarely in the center of Omaha Beach on a section named *Easy Red* at H hour plus 3 hours and 15 minutes (H+3:15), just over three hours after the first wave went ashore. The Regiment's advance inland would depend on the 16th Infantry Regiment's success in opening the E-1 draw.

The keystone of the beach defense in the 1st Infantry Division zone was the village of Colleville-sur-Mer, situated just to the east at the head of the Ruquet River Valley. The small valley of this river led inland, the E-1 draw itself forming curves slightly away from neighboring St. Laurent. A tiny stream bisected this heavily-wooded area. Engineers accompanying the first wave were to ensure that supporting armor, jeeps, trucks, artillery, and half-tracks of follow-on echelons could quickly get off the beaches.

The road running through E-1 was normally not used by vehicular traffic. Indeed, it mainly served as a way for local villagers to get down to and back up from the beach, mostly on foot or horse-drawn cart. To make it passable for vehicles and tanks, it had to be bulldozed—a job that was expected to be finished by the time the 18th RCT landed.

Moving inland, Colonel Smith's men were then to secure the east-west roads to the west of the city of Bayeux that connected the port of Cherbourg with the city of Caen. British troops from their 50th (Northumbrian) Division would take Bayeux itself, while the 18th Infantry Regiment secured their flank. Colonel Smith was also ordered to seize high ground north of Trévières where slopes there and at Mont Cauvin afforded good observation into the adjacent Ruquet valley. By securing these objectives on D-day, the 18th Regimental Combat Team would

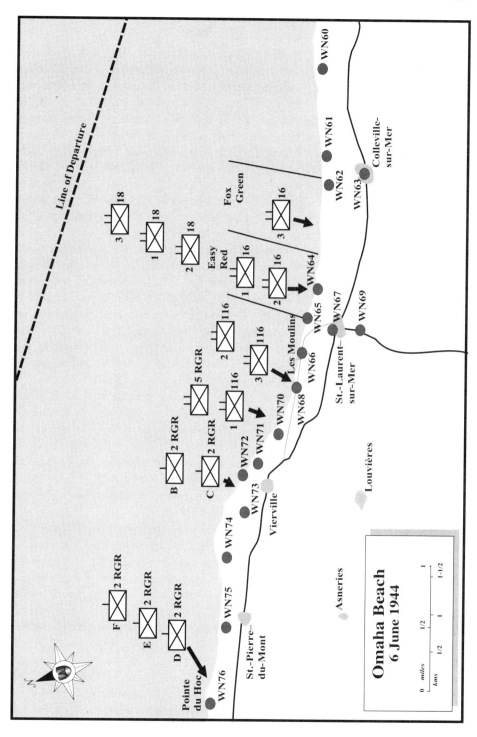

help establish a solid defensive perimeter along the entire V Corps front in preparation for German counterattacks.

Once the assembled officers had become familiar with this overall mission, Major Middleworth revealed that Lieutenant Colonel Williamson's 2nd Battalion had been chosen to lead the Regiment's first wave during the landings. Williamson's men would be supported by the attached 2nd Platoon of the Regimental Anti-Tank Company, the 2nd Platoon of Cannon Company, and the 1st Engineer Combat Battalion (minus Company B). The battalion was to secure the high ground in the area of the E-1 exit before continuing inland to block the main east-west route leading to Bayeux. Once this was accomplished, the battalion would establish a defense position near the village of Mosles, approximately five miles to the southeast. Williamson was also informed that his unit would become his responsible for assisting any elements of the 16th Infantry that might have failed to seize their objectives before his 2nd Battalion landed.

Lieutenant Colonel Sisson's 3rd Battalion companies would arrive on the beach approximately 20 minutes after the 2nd Battalion. With his organic rifle companies, the 3rd Platoon of Anti-Tank Company, the 3rd Platoon of Cannon Company, and Company B of the 1st Engineers, the 3rd Battalion's mission was to reconnoiter the high ground to the southeast of Mandeville. Mandeville lay between Mosles and Trévières; the latter village was designated as the 3rd Battalion's final objective on D-day. Lieutenant Colonel York's 1st Battalion was scheduled to land at the same time as the 3rd to work its way inland along the right flank of the combat team, angling toward the Forêt de Cerisy.

Captain Robert L. Weir's Cannon Company, minus attachments, would land behind the infantry battalions at 1030 hours, move off the beach, and establish firing positions to support the advance of the combat team to its final objectives. The 32nd FA would hit the beach about a half-hour later, move up the bluffs through the E-1 exit, and then go inland to a position where its batteries could furnish defensive fire support for the Regiment's rifle companies. Service Company would land at the same time, establishing supply and ammunition dumps as directed by the G-4, 1st Infantry Division.

With the maps, charts, and sketches of Omaha Beach, there were also recent photographs of the steep and bare cliffs facing the combat team's sector at Easy Red. As Lieutenant Franklyn Johnson in Anti-Tank pointed out, "The diagrams clearly showed us what units would proceed shoreward in what order. The pictures of known and suspected underwater and beach obstacles that would aid an eighteen-foot tide to hamper us, intricate machine-gun positions, artillery emplacements, ammo dumps, O.P.s [observation posts], and bristling concrete pillboxes—graphically portrayed the deadly impediments we faced before Normandy might become a beachhead."[4]

Colonel Smith provided a short, inspirational address at the close of his officer's briefing. After it, the men who would lead the 18th Regimental Combat Team into battle on D-day marched back to their battalion areas with maps under their arms and called their units together.

Some felt the situation did not look too promising. Others reasoned that the Regiment's task was not as tough as that assigned to the 16th Infantry, and that going in behind them gave them a better chance of getting through the landings alive. Still, they had to brief their men. It was the last week in May, and all of the Regiment's units had been sealed off in their various camps around Weymouth. The delivery of the secret plans to every participant was about to happen.

Enemy defenses at Omaha Beach that concerned Lieutenant Johnson and others recently had been augmented by troops from the German *352nd Infantry Division*, a unit that had only been in existence since December 1943. It was originally comprised of the remnants of three infantry regiments that had previously fought in Russia. One was manned with veterans from Stalingrad and two others were made up of units from the Kursk Offensive of the previous summer. Still other enemy soldiers came from hospitals where they had recovered from wounds received in Italy and North Africa, and very many more of its members were conscripts with no battle experience. The principal goal of the *352nd*'s new commanding general, *Generalleutnant* Dietrich Kraiss, was to impart proficiency in collective skills through intensive training at squad, platoon, company, battalion, and regimental levels within his ranks.

Beginning in early May, the *352nd* had moved from its garrison locations in the vicinity of St. Lô-la Haye du Puits to conduct a series of coastal defense exercises.[5] Kraiss's three infantry regiments (*Grenadier Regiments 914, 915,* and *916*) rotated through periods of manning fortifications during the first two weeks of May, each alternately acting as a divisional counterattack force, followed at mid-month by a stint as the German *LXXXIV Corps* tactical reserve.[6] Since the *352nd Infantry Division* was not responsible for manning a portion of the coastal defenses, Kraiss was instructed to take over the western half of the sector originally assigned to *Generalleutnant* Wilhelm Richter's *716th Infantry Division*. The *716th* had been responsible for defending the sector from Cabourg, northeast of Caen, to the Carentan Estuary at the southeastern base of the Cotentin peninsula.

During late May, the *352nd Infantry Division* was made responsible for the portion of Richter's sector running from the Carentan Estuary to Port-en-Bessin, a small fishing village just west of Arromanches. Richter's *Infantry Regiment 726* remained in place during this period to permit the *352nd* to rotate its regiments through training, rather than being exclusively tasked with manning the coastal defenses. The sole exception to this was the transfer of *2nd Battalion, Infantry Regiment 726* to the east where it remained as the *716th Division's* tactical reserve.

Unfortunately for the Allies, since the move of the *352nd Infantry Division* was primarily for training purposes, neither ULTRA decrypts of German operational radio traffic nor the French resistance reflected this.

Elements of the *352nd* that were conducting coastal defense training in late May were also rotating through the sector vacated by 2nd *Battalion, Infantry Regiment 726,* almost exactly in the middle of Omaha Beach where American forces were going to come ashore on D-day. Elements of *Grenadier Regiment 915* also manned this sector for two weeks before being assigned as the *LXXXIV Corps* tactical reserve southeast of Bayeux. On 4 June, two days before the invasion, troops from Hauptmann Griesel's *2nd Battalion, Grenadier Regiment 916* assumed responsibility for the sector, and took over a portion of the beach defenses that consisted of six strong points (*"Widerstandsneste"*) numbered WN 65–70. Those all eventually were manned by soldiers from Leutnant Heller's *6th Company* and Leutnant Berthy's *7th Company*, augmented by heavy weapons crews from *8th Company*. Each of the defending German companies also retained a small reserve for use in local counterattacks, while Leutnant Hahn's *5th Company* was designated as a tactical reserve.

To the east of *2nd Battalion, Grenadier Regiment 916* laid six strong points (WN 59–64) manned by Leutnant Bauch's *3rd Company, Infantry Regiment 726*.[7] Then directly to the west of *2nd Battalion, Grenadier Regiment 916*, there were four more strong points (WN 71-74) covering Vierville sur Mer manned by Leutnant Sonneborn's *11th Company, Infantry Regiment 726*.[8] Thus, on D-day the attacking Americans would face four reinforced German companies boasting approximately 60 machine guns, almost two dozen mortars, and 18 antitank guns ranging in caliber from 50mm to 88mm. The defenders were also supported by no less than four battalions of artillery, three from the *352nd Infantry Division* and one from *Artillery Regiment 716*, numbering 48 tubes, as well as several Army coastal batteries. This artillery fire, all pre-plotted, was destined to rain down on the landing Americans throughout D-day.

The Germans also reinforced their positions by emplacing numerous obstacles along beach landing areas in their zones of defense. Long stakes carved from tree trunks cut from the nearby Forêt de Cerisy were drawn by horse wagons to the beachhead, topped with mines, and then placed in the sands at the water's edge; these were to destroy landing craft. Concrete walls were constructed to stop Allied tanks and other vehicles from advancing beyond the beaches. Barbed-wire fences, tanglefoot obstacles, and concertina-wire barriers were set up just above the beach shingle to provide a second barrier at Easy Red. Thousands of mines were emplaced in the bluffs adjacent to the beach exits.

There was only one fault with the German anti-landing defenses. They were designed to stop a landing at high tide, when the attacking infantry would have the least amount of open beach to cross. Unknown to the Germans, their invaders would come ashore at low tide, when all of the obstacles they had laid into the shoreline would be exposed—and easier to avoid.

Allied invasion planners knew nothing about these German dispositions on Sunday, 4 June when the men of Combat Team 18 had their last hot meal before loading up to cross the English Channel. Trucks, escorted by military police, arrived at dusk to move the anxious invaders to Weymouth harbor. At the outskirts of town, officers and men jumped off their trucks and formed in columns of twos to march down a concrete stairway onto a sandy beach.

Minutes later, the columns were at the port facilities. The men went into large tents where their canteen cups were filled with coffee, doughnuts were passed around, packs of cigarettes were handed out, and books were given to everyone to help pass the time as the landing craft crossed the Channel. The men then marched back onto the beach, past seaside hotels and pubs, to the docks.

After climbing down several gangways, they boarded vessels and selected bunks. Unknown to the soldiers, however, D-day had been postponed that day because of the windswept rain and terrible weather on the English Channel.

During the next morning, short periods of calisthenics were held dockside and religious services were conducted. Weymouth Harbor stirred with activity all day, as General Eisenhower had determined that a break in the weather allowed D-day to now be set for the next day, Tuesday, 6 June. At sunset, naval personnel started heaving lines as hundreds of craft moved away from the docks, and then steamed off to form a single file and make their way into the English Channel.

Lieutenant Downing remembered what undoubtedly were the thoughts of many at the time, later noting, "As we embarked on this campaign we knew there would be no end to it until the war itself ended. But after two years overseas, the end of the war seemed as distant, hazy, and incomprehensible as Judgment Day."[9]

Combat Team 18's transports now making their way into the English Channel were a small part of the massive Allied fleet destined for a rendezvous point south of the Isle of Wight, dubbed "Piccadilly Circus."

Under Colonel Smith's command were 3,659 soldiers with 222 vehicles loaded aboard ten LCIs and three Attack Transports (APA), the largest of which was the *Anne Arundel* carrying his regimental staff. The 32nd FA, with 525 men, 86 vehicles (including one liaison plane), and 12 105mm howitzers, aboard another APA, was combat loaded onto seven separate LCTs. The 1st Engineer Combat Battalion, comprised of 303 men and 16 vehicles was aboard three other LCTs, while Cannon Company with its men and vehicles was aboard another two. The 5th FA Battalion's 542 men, 83 vehicles, and 12 155mm howitzers was also crossing with the combat team, as were 407 men and 97 vehicles of the 745th Tank Battalion. Combined with antitank units, a detachment of Division Signal Company personnel, a prisoner-of-war interrogation team of four civil affairs liaisons, a language interpretation team, three war correspondents, two photographers, four surgical teams, and other units making the move, CT 18 totaled 8,510 personnel and 786 vehicles and artillery pieces as it made the crossing to Normandy.[10]

The lead wave of the Regiment, Lieutenant Colonel Williamson's 2nd Battalion, was organized into assault teams carried on combat loaded LCVPs. These boat teams, six per company, were loaded by mixing rifle and weapons platoons that could land on the beach and fight independently. This thirty-man per LCVP mixture maximized the number of men aboard each landing craft while compensating for the possibility that one or more boats of the 18 battalion LCVPs could be sunk. Each assault boat team was organized with a five-man rifle section, a four-man BAR section, a four-man bazooka section, a four-man 60mm mortar section, a four-man wire cutting team, a two-man flamethrower section, and a four-man demolition squad. The rifle teams would be the first to disembark when the LCVP ramp went down, led by the boat team leader and followed by an officer with his M-1 carbine, grenades, and a SCR-536 radio.

If all went according to plan, the wire-cutting team would move out past the riflemen once they got ashore, using their wire cutters and Bangalore torpedoes to open gaps in the barbed-wire defenses. The two-man bazooka teams would then fan out to either side of any pillbox in front of them and fire rockets into openings created by the wire team, while being covered by the BAR section. The 60mm mortar section would also provide support fire and smoke while the demolition team and flamethrowers assaulted any enemy pillbox blocking the way.

Captain Murphy's Company H, the heavy weapons company of the leading 2nd Battalion, was cross-loaded in several LCVPs, two of the larger Landing Craft Mechanized (LCMs), and the LCI carrying Lieutenant Colonel Williamson's headquarters elements. This load was necessary because Company H was split up into seven-man heavy machine-gun squads and eight-man 81mm mortar squads, and then distributed evenly among rifle companies to support the landings. Once ashore, the heavy machine guns would lay in either to the flank of an attack line and fire on a pillbox to keep it contained, or suppress enemy rifle fire coming in from an outlying pit while the Allied riflemen attacked.

Murphy's 81mm mortar sections would fire at enemy support positions that ringed a pillbox, using either HE (high-explosive) or smoke rounds. Demolition teams with pole charges then would be able to clear the way for the riflemen to clean out an enemy bunker.[11] Captain Murphy did not have the direct ability to coordinate his company's work until after the assault landings were completed.

By the time the convoy passed "Piccadilly Circus," it was past midnight and land was long out of sight. Ships appeared as indistinct shapes on a horizon lit dimly by a full moon that occasionally broke through thick cloud cover. Winds were brisk, coming in from the northwest at more than 15 knots; they caused the LCIs and LCTs to roll in short-troughed waves as they clumsily turned southward toward Omaha Beach.

Below, soldiers were playing cards, reading, writing letters, or just lying in their bunks, thinking or praying. The men-of-war slated to deliver fire on enemy beach targets sailed past the combat team's transports toward designated positions at Fire Support Areas KANSAS, OREGON, and OHIO. Landings were to be aided by two battleships (USS *Arkansas* and *Texas*), three cruisers (British *HMS Glasgow*, and French *FFS Montcalm* and *FFS Georges Leygues*), and 12 destroyers.

H-hour (0630) was based on a variety of factors, the most important of which was that it allowed for at least 50 minutes of daylight prior to the landings to facilitate naval and aerial bombardments.

At H-40 minutes, Allied naval vessels initiated saturating fire on enemy shore batteries and beach defenses. Unfortunately, most major combatants did not fire at the strongpoints overlooking the landing beaches, but instead engaged emplaced German heavy guns capable of returning significant fire against the invasion fleet. USS *Texas*, for example, for a time focused exclusively on the German 155mm battery at the Pointe du Hoc, while USS *Arkansas* engaged German gun emplacements near Port-en-Bessin, before she switched to targets near les Moulins.[12]

At H-20 minutes, 474 B-24 heavy bombers of the Eighth Air Force dropped tons of 100-pound bombs on the landing beaches. The previous night it was agreed that because cloud cover might force the bombardiers to make a "blind drop" using radar, aircrews would delay the release of the bombs for several seconds to ensure they did not hit the first waves of forces now approaching Omaha Beach. As a result, only two percent of the bombs were estimated to have landed near their targets.

As the first wave moved in closer to the beach, Navy destroyers closed to within 1,000–2,000 yards of the shore. At H-1 minute, nine LCTs (R) launched their rockets at selected strong points lying behind the bluffs overlooking the landing area. Many rockets fell on, near, or over their targets, starting fires and raising a huge dust cloud. Many rocket craft skippers deliberately aimed 'long' to avoid hitting LCTs carrying medium tanks, which by that point were only 300 yards from the shoreline and slightly ahead of the infantry.[13]

At H-hour, the first of the surviving duplex-drive (amphibious, or DD) tanks crawled ashore—many had been swamped making their way to the beach. The invasion of France had begun.

H-hour saw two radio teams of the Regimental I&R Platoon landing on Omaha Beach with the assault units of the 2nd Battalion, 16th Infantry. They received heavy enemy fire. One team, under the command of Lieutenant Howard P. MacConchie, suffered a direct hit on its LCVP while it was still a hundred yards offshore, destroying all equipment and leaving the survivors to swim to the beach.[14] The second team, commanded by Lieutenant Cecil Fitzpatrick, beached in the face of extremely heavy fire, and his men were forced to wade ashore through neck-deep water. Private Carlton W. Barrett, exhibiting extreme courage under intense barrages of small arms and mortar fire, repeatedly returned to the surf to assist his comrades, saving several from drowning, and then carrying some to an evacuation boat lying nearby. In addition to his assigned mission as a guide, Private Barrett spent the next hour carrying messages the length of the fire-swept beach and assisting many wounded men. He demonstrated high courage and leadership constantly, as well as exhibiting coolness and bravery while repeatedly risking his own life. Noting that his "inestimable effect on his comrades was in keeping with the highest traditions of the US Army," Private Barrett was awarded the Medal of Honor for his heroism in these early troubled hours on D-day—the first received by an 18th Infantry Regiment soldier in the war.

Sixteen obstacle-breaching teams had landed with the leading wave, each consisting of 28 Army engineers and a Naval Combat Demolition Squad composed of an officer and 12 enlisted men—seven from the Navy and five from the Army. Each team was to blow a gap 50 yards wide in the beach obstacles; the naval units working seaward and the Army units clearing inshore.

Eight support teams, four from the 146th Engineer Combat Battalion and four from the 299th, as well as two command boats, were to follow no later than H+8 minutes. Each support team included an M4 tank dozer and a crew that was to be landed from an LCT.

The gap teams were unable to accomplish their mission for three reasons—bad weather and high waves at the water's edge; heavy enemy machine-gun and mortar fire, causing 41 percent casualties; and the fact that defensive obstacles were far more numerous than anticipated.[15] As a result, landing craft began to stack up because their coxswains could not locate the gaps they anticipated. Some intrepid LCVP and LCM coxswains were able to slowly thread their way through the deadly obstacles, but a carefully-planned schedule of landings began to go awry.

Easy Red Beach, which fronted the E-1 Draw, had not been reduced as planned. The 2nd Battalion, 16th Infantry was supposed to land here with its Companies E and F abreast, Company F on the left, Company G in reserve, and Company H in support. Due to wind, wave, and cross-current conditions at the time, two companies landed far to the east of the draw, near the 3rd Battalion, 16th Infantry's landing zone. Only two boat sections actually landed in the correct location. The invaders were immediately subjected to withering machine-gun and antitank fire as they waded ashore, enemy firepower that was far worse than expected. Three German strongpoints in this zone (WN 66–68) were supposed to have been bombed, shelled, and wiped out by the Air Force, Navy, and rocket craft, but they were active. Worse, there were no DD tanks to cover the advance of the assault troops and no bomb craters on the beach for the men to find refuge. In the first half hour of the landings, just 100 men made it to shore safely in the Easy Red sector. This early misfortune left the E-1 exit devoid of assault troops in sufficient strength to reduce the German defenses in the draw, and this was destined to change the mission of the 18th Infantry's 2nd Battalion when they landed later that morning.[16]

Adding to the confusion, Company E, 116th Infantry arrived on schedule, but landed 1,000 yards to the left of its intended area among troops of the 2nd Battalion, 16th Infantry. Four DD Shermans also made it ashore, but a 88mm antitank gun in WN 73 firing down the beach quickly silenced three of them. Two of Company E's LCVPs were hit by artillery, killing three and wounding several other men in its 2nd and 3rd Sections. The 5th and 6th Sections each suffered 10 to 15 casualties on the exposed sands, including their company commander, Captain Lawrence Madill.

The first fleeting break came when a sergeant knocked out a pillbox with a bazooka, opening a gap in the German defenses. Approximately 55 men wound their way through a hole in a barbed-wire fence, but after they reached an antitank ditch they were pinned down by machine-gun fire.[17]

Company G of the 16th Infantry Regiment, under the command of Captain Joseph T. Dawson, reached its line of departure 2,000 yards off the beach at 0635 hours. Intense enemy fire was falling, and as the men got halfway to shore, this German fire began to land in and around their LCVPs. Landing craft coxswains experienced great difficulty maintaining formation, and one of the vessels capsized about 200 yards from the beach.

The remainder of the boats almost succeeded in reaching shore before lowering their debarkation ramps, and most of Captain Dawson's company was able to hit the beach. Very heavy artillery, mortar, machine-gun, and rifle fire was falling by this time, and the combined effects inflicted many casualties as Dawson's men crossed an open-beach expanse before the sea wall. A large number of men from the first wave were already behind this earthen mound, crowding together in the only area of safety; they left Dawson's men unable to advance onto the steep bluffs beyond.[18]

The heavy weapons company of the 16th Infantry's 2nd Battalion was scheduled to land at 0710 hours, but it had to contact a Navy control boat and time was lost. Instead, the company landed at 0727 hours, encountering heavy machine-gun and mortar fire that inflicted a number of casualties. The tide was rising by this time and many wounded men drowned as water rushed over them.

Much equipment was lost, to include all of the combat team's radios. One of the company's heavy machine guns was set up, however, and it began engaging a pillbox and several open emplacements situated on the left flank. By this time Dawson's Company G had reorganized, placing several light machine guns and 60mm mortars in positions where they could rake the tops of the coastal bluff.

Other men moved forward and infiltrated through a narrow gap in the minefields between the earthen mound and the base of the bluffs. A section from Company E under the command of Lieutenant John M. Spalding and two other sections from Company E, 116th Infantry were pinned down at the base of the cliff. Those soldiers were told to move inland and to the right, where the remainder of their companies was located. Spalding and the men from the 116th then moved out, as did the 5th Section of Captain Dawson's Company G, all advancing toward the crest of the bluff. Two machine-gun nests were destroyed and the 5th Section took one prisoner while the remainder of Company G surmounted the bluffs and moved several hundred yards inland.

At 0735 hours, the 5th Engineer Special Brigade landed on schedule with the mission of taking over responsibility for clearing beach obstacles and transit areas. Like the waves before them, they were pinned down by German crossfire, preventing the engineers from developing and expanding a beach roadway system and from opening the E-1 exit. Instead, the Brigade became disorganized and was unable to regroup when its commander, his S-3, and S-2 were killed or wounded.

At 0815, Colonel George A. Taylor, commanding officer of the 16th Infantry Regiment, finally began to gain some semblance of control over his scattered, damaged unit. Nearly an hour earlier, his regimental executive officer and 35 men from his headquarters company had been lost to machine-gun and mortar fire while crossing the dangerously exposed tidal flats near the beach.

Taylor's fearless command style was now starting to pay dividends. After rallying his men with his famous words—"Two kinds of people are staying on this beach: the dead and those who are going to die. Now let's get the hell out of here"—small groups were placed under the command of noncommissioned officers and advanced through concertina-wire gaps. Meanwhile, Colonel Taylor hurriedly established his command post just below the crest of the bluff while his staff continued to urge more troops to move inland.

The 1st Battalion, 16th Infantry Regiment also met strong resistance when it began landing on Easy Red at H+70 minutes. Led by Companies A and C, then followed by a second wave consisting of the battalion Headquarters Company, Company B, and elements of the 1st Engineer Combat Battalion, it moved ashore. A third wave, made up of the battalion's heavy weapons company and some miscellaneous elements landed 20 minutes after the leading rifle companies.[19]

Company A lost its commander and 45 others in the perilous minutes it took to cross the beach, but survivors kept pushing toward high ground. Reaching the bluffs, the company encountered numerous machine-gun nests, which its men engaged in a prolonged firefight that lasted until nightfall.

Company C, which landed midway between Fox Green (an adjacent landing area) and Easy Red, also encountered severe artillery fire that sank one LCVP and forced coxswains to drop their ramps in almost seven feet of water.

After suffering casualties from enemy fire and drowning, German fire pinned the company to the beach until it eventually cleared a path through a minefield, allowing the men to find safety and reorganize.[20]

Company D, 16th Infantry Regiment landed as scheduled on Easy Red, then quickly moved off the beach to take up positions against the same low shingle mound that had provided shelter for others from enemy machine-gun fire. The mortar sections and 2nd Machine Gun Platoon went into position along the beach and opened fire on German positions approximately 75 yards away. Company B landed on Easy Red amid concentrated enemy fire; the LCVP carrying the company headquarters personnel received two artillery direct hits and sank as it was landing. Nevertheless, the company quickly moved up to the wire where section leaders reorganized the men.

Using five gaps in the wire that had been opened by Company A, many of these men pushed on through a minefield in front of the wire. The 3rd and 5th sections attempted to infiltrate over the bluffs, but the men were pinned down by machine-gun and mortar fire in a second minefield. The two sections withdrew, moved left, and eventually reached the top of a ridge 400 yards to the left of the E-1 exit.

Across Omaha Beach, by now everything was behind schedule. All the main exits remained closed. Mislandings and high casualties had nullified the planned employment of coordinated and concentrated unit assaults. Determined actions had allowed small units to begin moving off the beach, but without the use of the E-1 exit, heavier equipment, all of the tanks, and other necessary vehicles needed to support the troops would remain confined to a narrow strip of sand.

Aboard General Bradley's command ship, the cruiser USS *Augusta*, there was very little good news. Bradley later wrote, "As the morning lengthened, my worries deepened over the alarming and fragmentary reports we picked up on the Navy net. From [these] messages we could piece together only an incoherent account of sinkings, swampings, heavy enemy fire, and chaos on the beaches. By 0830 hours, the two assault regiments on Omaha had expected to break through the water's edge defenses and force their way inland, yet V Corps had not yet [even] confirmed news of the landing."[21]

At 0855 hours, Colonel Smith received his first message from the I&R Platoon on the beach, and it also indicated that things were going badly. The message reported that enemy machine guns and mortars were holding up the general advance. Then at 0910 hours, word came to Smith from Brigadier General Wyman to have his 2nd Battalion land immediately to assist Combat Team 16 in overcoming opposition on the beach.[22]

The situation was not good, even for Williamson's forces offshore. Landing craft carrying his men were fighting extremely rough seas as they circled, waiting for scheduled landing times. Many soldiers were seasick, and one boat had swamped, forcing its soldiers and crew to transfer to the naval boat group commander's craft.

Confusion reigned, as LCVPs continued to wait without heading to the beach. Lieutenant Colonel Williamson found a Navy officer who told him that the USN boat group commander for the 2nd Battalion's landing force was missing—that he was now in command—but did not know where to land. Williamson's orders were clear, however. Instructions had been received to land on the right side of Easy Red at the mouth of the Ruquet River. He passed this information to the naval commander, but the minutes continued to tick by and the plunging, near-floundering LCVPs failed to head to shore.

The original group commander finally was found, and a frustrated Williamson was told that no channels had yet been marked, and for that reason it was not safe to go in. With his unit desperately needed ashore, the no-nonsense 2nd Battalion commander simply would not stand for this rationale and angrily ordered the naval officer to send the boats in, regardless of whether the channels were marked.

The lead LCVPs, carrying Company F (now under the command of Captain Orin Rosenberg), part of the battalion command group (including Lieutenant Colonel Williamson), and Captain Penick's Company E finally began lining themselves up for the pounding trip to the beach. Nearby was another group of LCVPs, to include one loaded with Company H; Captain Murphy and a section of his mortars that were attached to Rosenberg's riflemen; a platoon from Captain Jeffrey's Company G; and a signal party comprised mainly of radiomen from Headquarters' Company. Captain Murphy remembered at the time, "I looked over the bow of our LCVP, and the first wave of 16th Infantry was just small dots in the distance. I then turned towards the helmsman and he suddenly said, 'Here we go, sir!'"[23]

By this time, Lieutenant Spalding's Company E platoon and Captain Dawson's Company G had started making their way up the bluffs. Spalding and his assault section of 22 riflemen had been the first over the top at 0900 hours, and at that time they were spread out over an area from 100 to 500 yards. "We were in hedgerows and orchard country," Spalding recalled. "We found a construction shack near the strongpoint overlooking E-1. Sergeant Kenneth Petersen fired his bazooka into the tool shed, but no one came out. We were about to go on when I spied a piece of stove pipe about 70 yards away sticking out of the ground."

Spalding then spread his men out in a semi-circular defensive position, and when they came under small arms fire, he and another sergeant went forward to investigate the source. "We discovered an underground dugout," Lieutenant Spalding recalled. "There was an 81mm mortar, a position for a 75mm antitank gun and construction for a pillbox. All this overlooked E-1. The dugout was of cement, had radios, excellent sleeping facilities, dogs. We started to drop a grenade in the ventilator, but [the sergeant] fired three shots down the stack instead."

Moments later, several Germans surrendered and Spalding's men began frisking the prisoners for hidden weapons.[24] Then, looking out into the Channel, Spalding remembered he could make out the indistinct shapes of yet another wave of landing craft preparing to head for the beach. It was the first wave of the 2nd Battalion, 18th Infantry.

As those LCVPs were completing their final stationkeeping orbits and approaching shore, low cloud cover and limited visibility that had hung over the morning of D-day was giving way to intermittent clearing. As the sun rose higher, the mist that had hung over Omaha Beach was also starting to burn off.

The helmsman on Captain Murphy's LCVP had just completed one last circle, and was now maneuvering to head ashore. It was approximately 1045 hours, nearly two hours after the 18th Infantry Regiment had been ordered to land. Captain Murphy's craft was now in the middle of the amphibious grouping, with other LCVPs spaced approximately 15 yards apart. As soon as they were in line abreast about 2,000 yards from the beach, helmsmen exchanged signals and the LCVPs headed in.

"The roar of the guns of a battleship I saw on the way in was terrific and encouraging," Murphy remembered later. "But the sea was rough where we were, we were taking on water over the bow and the sides of the LCVP, and everyone was soaked and miserable. We could still see shell bursts along the bluffs, but the engines were noisy enough so that much of what was going on around us was muffled. As we got in closer, however, I moved to the side of the LCVP to look out at the beach and what I saw gave me a chill. There were a lot of soldiers hugging the seawall and a great deal of equipment that was not moving."

Moments later, Captain Murphy forgot these thoughts when his landing craft went through a whistling fusillade of shells followed by a hail of gunfire that pinged from the bow to the stern of his LCVP. Everyone instinctively hit the deck, except the coxswain, who dared not. When Murphy looked around at the boats near him a few seconds later, he saw that the LCVP on the outside to his right was in trouble, limping along. He waved to the landing craft; someone waved back, and then the determined captain turned towards his coxswain and simply yelled, "Keep going! Get me into shore."[25]

Minutes later Murphy's LCVP came to a sudden stop and he and his men were thrown against the forward ramp before it could be lowered. The heavy weapons company commander charged off the end of the ramp the minute it dropped and instantly was in water up to his knees. As he was gaining his footing, one of his machine gunners waded past him but sank into the water up to his waist, quickly raising his weapon over his head. He then took another step and all Murphy could see was his machine gun aimed skyward as he sunk into a sandy depression. His worst fears materialized, but moments later his 2nd Platoon commander, Lieutenant Carl L. Hester, ran down the other side of the ramp and went to his right where he found shallow water.

It was now 1105 hours. Captain Murphy charged ashore, and then dove into the sand next to Lieutenant Hester. Quickly realizing the disarray and danger of their open position, he ordered Hester to move the men up to a seawall while he tried to find Lieutenant Colonel Williamson.

Disregarding his own safety, Murphy raced down the chaotic beach and ran into a command section of the 115th Infantry Regiment, part of a group of men from five LCIs that had mislanded on top of the 2nd Battalion a few minutes earlier.[26] They told him that they thought Williamson might be farther down the beach, so Murphy took off to his left toward a bunker where he saw some Germans surrendering. By this time, Williamson had made numerous trips across the beach to start organizing his battalion, even leading a daring assault on one enemy strongpoint that eventually cleared the way for the lead companies to advance.

Technical Sergeant James E. Knight originally landed with a special demolition team of the 299th Engineer Combat Battalion. Just before Captain Murphy rushed to shore, Knight was on a dune near the E-1 Exit where he later remembered, "The situation looked hopeless, but all of a sudden a destroyer loomed out amongst the dozens of landing craft and amphibious vehicles. She was headed straight toward me. Even though she wasn't listing or smoking, my first thought was that she had either struck a mine or taken a torpedo and was damaged badly enough that she was being beached. But, the destroyer started to turn to the right and before she completed the turn to be parallel to the beach, all her guns opened fire. At the same time I saw smoke leave the gun barrels, and shells landed a few yards above my rock cover."[27]

Owen F. Keeler was the gunnery officer in *USS Frankford*, the destroyer approaching Omaha Beach at that moment. This was the warship that had given Captain Murphy so much encouragement when he was coming to shore. *Frankford* was the coordinating ship for naval forces at the start of the landings, commanded by Lieutenant Commander James L. Semmes. Most of the other destroyers in the screen had been released early on to augment gunfire support at the beachhead. About mid-morning, however, they had expended their bombardment ammunition allowance and returned to the screen.

Frankford had been ordered back a short time later to provide support wherever it was needed on Omaha Beach. The actual order came by way of tactical voice radio from Rear Admiral Carleton F. Bryant at 0950 hours when he said, "Get on them, men. Get on them. We must knock out those guns. They are raising hell with the men on the beach, and we can't have any more of that. We must stop it!"[28]

Lieutenant Commander Semmes decided he would take *Frankford* in for a closer look. He remembered, "In clear daylight I could see that things were going very poorly on Omaha Beach. All the soldiers on the beach were huddling low behind stone walls and no movement up the hill and off the sand could be seen."

Semmes ordered his communications officer to make contact with spotters ashore so he could line up the *Frankford's* firing positions at the strongpoints around the E-1 exit. Semmes, knowing he was on a rising tide, was not about to give up. "With a sick feeling in my stomach that we were facing a total fiasco, I left the assigned sea area and moved in as close to the shore as I could without bumping the bottom," he recalled. "This gave us closer distance to improve vision for picking up enemy movement and strong points. My gunnery officer (Lieutenant Keeler) in the gun director found pillboxes, machine-gun nests, and other targets of opportunity."[29]

Keeler recalled later, "The tide was in our favor at that moment. Navigating by fathometer and seaman's eye, he [Semmes] took us in close enough to put our optical rangefinder, ranging on the bluff above the beach, against the stops. We were 300–400 yards away. The camouflage on the beach was still good. We could not spot a target—and frankly we did not know how far our troops had advanced. Then one of our light tanks that was sitting at the water's edge with a broken track fired at something on the hill. We immediately followed up with a five-inch salvo. The tank gunner flipped open his hatch, looked around at us, waved, dropped back in the tank and fired at another target. For the next few minutes he was our fire-control party. Our rangefinder optics could examine the spots where his shells hit. By this time, we knew none of our troops were on the hill, so we used the rangefinder to pick out targets, including apparently at least one artillery emplacement. We did have the satisfaction of seeing our soldiers take some prisoners out of one of those bunkers. When we had expended our limit, we returned to our screen station, but not before seeing our troops moving up the hill toward the crest."

The *USS Frankford's* Deck Log later showed that she had first fired at 1021 hours at a pillbox in the River Ruquet valley, and the "target was destroyed." At 1036 hours the log entry read, "Troops on Easy Red were being held up by battery located on ridge by River Ruquet. After close observation the exact location of the battery was noted at 1032 hours. At 1036 commenced firing on the battery using direct fire, range about 400 yards. On the fifth salvo a direct hit was obtained, a large cloud of green smoke was noted and the battery ceased firing. Our troops then advanced and a number of German troops were seen to surrender." Minutes later, the *USS Frankford* was nearly bumping the bottom, her port side to shore and again firing. "Two machine-gun nests were spotted covering the road leading from the Ruquet River valley to St. Laurent. Commence firing. Ceased fire at 1057 hours, having effectively stopped all machine-gun fire from the nests." Somehow, right in the middle of this at 1050 hours, the *Frankford* had also pulled five wounded American soldiers from the water.[30]

Just after 1115 hours, Lieutenant Spalding saw other infantry across the E-1 exit for the first time—men of the advancing 2nd Battalion, 18th Infantry Regiment who were now starting off the beach. "We set off our last yellow smoke grenades to let the Navy know that we were Americans, since their time fire was getting pretty close," Lieutenant Spalding wrote later.

Spalding learned from a captain in his own regiment that his Company E's objective was changed; that there would be no patrols into Trévières. "We never crossed the E-1 draw. Instead we went along the trail towards Colleville-sur-Mer," he noted. The change in mission had been brought about when the 2nd Battalion was ordered by General Wyman to assume the post-landing responsibilities of the battered 2nd Battalion, 16th Infantry. Unknown to Williamson at that moment, however, was the fact that Spalding's forces had made his battalion's work a bit easier.[31]

By 1120 hours, Company E had worked its way up the right side of the E-1 exit and Captain Rosenberg's Company F had moved up on the left where 20 stunned Germans surrendered to his men. The US Army official history later noted, "At 1130 hours, the Germans, in the last organized defense at the St. Laurent-sur-Mer draw [E-1], surrendered to the 2nd Battalion of the 18th Infantry. Thus in a little over an hour, concerted bold action had brought the most substantial improvement on the beach since the start of the landings."[32] Within a half-hour, engineers were clearing mines in the draw and other units were working bulldozers up the slope to push through the exit past blockhouse fortifications at the edge of the roadway hit by the *USS Frankford*. An abandoned German antitank gun located there was no longer pouring deadly fire onto the beach.

The command group of the Regimental Cannon Company had arrived on Easy Red at 1100 hours on the heels of Lieutenant Colonel Williamson's companies. It was a grueling ordeal from the start when the men responsible for transportation and heavy equipment came under severe artillery fire while trying to negotiate sunken entanglements and mines at the water's edge. Upon landing, the group reorganized beside a wrecked M3 half-track, but then quickly moved to take shelter a few yards above the high-water mark. Advancing towards the bluff, the men then attempted to move along an as-yet-unswept mine path. That trial-and-error attempt was aborted when the Cannon Company commander, Captain Weir, was seriously wounded, and fragments from a mortar round wounded his radio operator moments later. When another man ran to inform the company executive officer of the casualties, he, too, was hit.

A landing attempt by Cannon Company's 3rd Platoon proved unsuccessful when its LCT was ordered back after coming under heavy fire. A second attempt a half hour later resulted in chaos when the naval commanders ordered the platoon's vehicles into the water too far from the beach. The first two half-tracks immediately sank when they went down the ramp.

One jeep floated off to the right and never made it in. A 6 x 6 supply truck flooded and stalled. The landing craft's commander decided to pulled back again, and when he finally came in for a third time he ordered two vehicles into the water despite a depth reading "as shown on the measuring rods was greater than the length of the exhaust extensions of the vehicles."[33] Both were flooded by water pouring down through their elevated exhaust pipes 150 yards from shore.

Two enlisted soldiers then swam to the beach through the heavy surf to try to locate a vehicle with a winch. Luckily, they found a half-track that was so equipped. They ran the cable to the water, somehow swam back out and attached it to one of the submerged vehicles, but when the winch reeled in, its cable snapped.

Medics and mechanics were desperately needed on the beach, and so instead of waiting, two other men on the LCT brought a mechanic and a medic ashore on their shoulders because neither could swim.

After a sergeant repaired the cable, another gallant try was made to pull the vehicles to shore. This time, it succeeded.

Pfc. Paul Hurst was one of the men who swam from shore with the cable that day. He also brought the medic in. His bravery saved lives and also contributed to getting many other men to the beach. "When the ramp went down our half-track and 105 mm cannon were the last to go and we traveled only far enough to run into a crater and flood out," Hurst wrote years later. "After attaching the cable and drawing it up tight, it was used by many soldiers to make their way ashore through the remaining deep water. Finally, we winched our unit to shore."[34]

The 1st Platoon of Cannon Company also received orders to "hit the beach and hit it hard." Luck was with them as their landing craft commander was able to get his vessel to within 25 yards of the beach after he wormed his way through underwater obstacles—just moments after being told to wait so that an LCT carrying badly needed bulldozers could go in first. As the Cannon Company after-action report read, "All vehicles then landed in water so shallow that hardly the fenders of our half-tracks got wet." To the credit of Lieutenants Michael Miller and Robert L. Bullard III, whose grandfather had commanded the 1st Division in World War I, all of the 1st Platoon's half-tracks were moved into position and their fire support was available to the infantry battalions by nightfall.[35]

By 1300 hours, Lieutenant Colonel York's 1st Battalion was approaching shore in LCVPs through the few narrow gaps opened by the engineers. The landing had been delayed because of the mix-up between the 115th Infantry Regiment and the 2nd Battalion, as well as the fact that most of the 1st Battalion men had to be transferred into LCVPs because it was felt that their LCIs were too vulnerable to artillery fire. While substantial damage had already been inflicted on the defenders of the E-1 exit, the 1st Battalion still came under artillery and machine-gun fire when they landed a few hundred yards east of the Ruquet River, wading ashore in waist-deep water. York's men then threaded their way up a steep incline littered with mines and booby traps until they reached an assembly area about 500 yards inland.

"Since the last enemy troops had been reduced at the E-1 Draw by our 2nd Battalion men, we could move off the beach," Company D's Pfc. Raymond Klawitzer remembered. "We quickly got up the slope because it was lined with toilet paper and we stayed within the boundaries the engineers had cleared. But a lieutenant from the mortar section stepped outside the line and was killed."[36] Company D Captain Carter gave credit to the efforts of the *USS Frankford*, saying she was one of the principal reasons the 1st Battalion got off the beach with a minimum of casualties. "To this day," he said nearly 60 years later, "I thank the Lord for that destroyer."[37]

Chaplain Edward Rogers landed with the 1st Battalion that afternoon. Recipient of several citations for bravery during World War II, including two Silver Stars and the Bronze Star, he was no stranger to the perils of frontline fighting men.

When his LCVP came to shore, shells from behind the beachhead were bursting in the water around him. His landing craft almost hit a mine as it approached the beach before it backed off under a hail of bullets, and then finally turned back and came in again. "Then we got on the beach, and that was a relief," Rogers remembered. "I can't say that the beach looked very encouraging at that moment. Beached craft and floundering equipment could be seen about. There appeared to be considerable chaos. There were many men sitting in foxholes, or digging them. But we had a battalion intact and that was worth a lot just then." Chaplain Rogers then went up the slope in a single file through a minefield with a five-man detail. It was their job to collect the dead and get litters to the wounded.

"I hadn't gone far until a soldier from amongst those who previously landed on the beach asked if we had a litter to bring a wounded man out of a swamp between the beach and the slope," Chaplain Rogers remembered. "Four of us took the litter into the swamp and found a patient chap lying there in mud and water. After lifting him out, we took him to the water's edge where he could be lifted back to England, and then we went back to get another."[38]

The men Chaplain Rogers had been helping were not of his own 1st Battalion; they were with the 115th Infantry Regiment. At this point, he had no more litters for his men because he had provided the two he had to aid the wounded men of that unit. "Our place was with the long line of men winding their way up the slope," he wrote later. "It is not good to get separated from one's unit at such a time." Rogers then started up the hill where he recalled, "Dead and wounded were not hard to see."

Moments later he was in a swamp in water up to his shoulders. After he got through he gave aid to a soldier who had his leg blown off by a mine. "It was a strange sight watching men go up that slope," he remembered. "Every now and then there would be a puff of smoke and a man would topple over—another mine victim. One officer sitting on the path when the column stopped rolled over to let someone go by. It cost him his life."

Once Chaplain Rogers reached the top of the slopes, there were fewer mines, but enemy using automatic weapons were everywhere. "It seemed to be the policy of the Germans to retreat slowly, leaving machine-gun nests and snipers as a rear guard," he recalled. "They didn't waste their artillery on us to any extent when we were off the beach. The concentration there was a great target for them, so they threw all they had down that way."[39]

Company C, under the command of Captain Scott-Smith, found itself in trouble when the men reached the top of the hill. Two platoons of German infantry had entrenched themselves in the center of the area the 1st Battalion was now crossing, and it took over an hour of sharp fighting before six of the enemy were killed and ten were captured. Captain Cameron's Company B also encountered resistance while moving along Company C's left flank when they came upon a detachment of Germans attempting to withdraw from a knocked-out emplacement, but two squads quickly worked down a ravine, killed eight, and wounded many others before the Germans succeeded in breaking contact.[40]

The almost bloodless success of the 1st Battalion in reaching the top of the bluffs overlooking Easy Red beach was in large part attributable to the previous combat experience of its officers and men. Every company commander and many of their platoon leaders had fought through North Africa and Sicily. Staff Sergeant Christopher Cornazzani, assigned to the Headquarters Company of the 1st Battalion, spoke for many that day when he said of the battalion commander, "I just followed Lieutenant Colonel York's footsteps. Everyone watched him; he never showed any fear and was like a rock. He made you feel that everything was what was expected, so everything was normal."[41]

The Regiment's 3rd Battalion, under the command of Lieutenant Colonel Sisson, began landing at 1340 hours. Despite the fact that they were landing seven hours after the first wave had gone ashore, the battalion was subjected to steady three- and six-round volleys of artillery fire. As with the other 18th Infantry landing teams, the omnipresent obstacles along the beach caused significant delay. The LCI carrying Captain Frank N. Fitch's Company L and a contingent from the 3rd Battalion Headquarters Company struck two mines approximately 150 yards from shore. Major Frank Colacicco, the Regimental S-3 who was working towards shore at that moment remembered, "The bow hit a mine, and as she started to sink the stern hit another mine."[42]

The only casualties during this incident were men well forward near the LCI's bow. Given the distance the survivors had to wade to reach shore, many ran into trouble upon debarking.

An alert Navy crew rigged lifelines to an object on the beach, but the heavily-loaded infantrymen had to struggle through the deep water with one hand on the rope and the other carrying weapons. Numerous casualties resulted as the battalion continued landing under such circumstances, particularly when artillery and mortar barrages hit the men struggling to shore. Later reports said that of the 96 casualties incurred by the 3rd Battalion on D-day, over 80 were inflicted in getting off their landing craft to the water's edge and the beach.[43]

Private Howard J. Johnson was one of those in Company L trying to reach shore that afternoon. He had already seen one of his buddies lose his arm in the blast when his LCI hit mines, then he remembered, "As we got closer we could see Germans running around the top of the cliff, as well as enemy shells hitting the water and sending up great spouts of water into the air. Now and then we'd see a direct artillery hit on one of our boats and we knew that men were dying." Johnson later recalled, "Being stationary targets was nerve wracking. We felt so helpless." Fortunately, help was on the way, however, and Johnson noted, "We shall always be grateful to one of the sailors who tied a rope around his waist and dove overboard. Swimming through heavy water, he got to shore and tied the rope to a log sticking out of the water. Another sailor then swam in and thus provided us with two ropes to the beach. The Germans were throwing everything they had at us, yet most of us got onto the sandy beach where we found it difficult to move because of the intense firepower. We could see sand exploding all around us from the bullets and shells."[44]

When he made it to shore during the 3rd Battalion landings, Major Colacicco ran down the beach where he met a forward observer from the 32nd FA who told him that Brigadier General Wyman wanted him. "Just about then, a shell came in beside us," Colacicco remembered. "The blast of pebbles knocked me down, but I finally got up and found General Wyman under a wrecked half-track. He told me to take over [the mission of] the 1st Battalion of our 16th Infantry . . . so I went back and got my men."[45]

One of the men near Major Colacicco when he landed was Company K's Staff Sergeant Walter Ehlers, who was now getting ready to lead his squad off the beach. Although his men were taking direct fire from bunkers on the bluffs overlooking the water's edge, Ehlers knew their only chance for survival was to stay together and move up to high ground.

Prior to the invasion Captain William Russell, his company commander, had called Ehlers and his older brother, Roland, in to meet with him. Russell told them that they would be separated on D-day and placed in different units. Both had been in Company K since North Africa, and the older Ehlers was a squad leader. Captain Russell told them there was only a 50 percent chance that they would survive the invasion, and that the older brother would be transferred over to Company L so both would not be in the same unit. Although Staff Sergeant Walter Ehlers did not know it as he was leading his men up the bluffs, his brother, Roland, had been killed instantly several hundred yards down the beach when a mortar round struck the ramp of his landing craft.[46]

As soon as they hit the beach, the 3rd Battalion was ordered through a marked minefield where combat engineers had by now cleared a narrow lane. "We crawled single file only a short distance into the minefield and halted," Company L's Pfc. Johnson wrote years later about those moments coming off the beach. "The taped path led through the sand to a 20-foot cliff. We just laid there while the enemy fire took a heavy toll. Someone finally said there was just one German sniper holding us up. Every time one of our men stuck his head over the top, the sniper would fire. He'd already killed and wounded some of our men. Captain Fitch got frustrated and excited about the delay and the number of casualties we were taking. I saw him jump up from behind my position and run outside the taped area. A mine blew off his foot, and he fell back in the sand. Seconds later, we saw him disappear in a cloud of smoke when a shell hit him. We turned our heads away. We didn't want to see any more."

Two or three Company L riflemen nearer to the top of the cliff eventually outflanked the sniper and captured him. Pfc. Johnson recalled later that someone lying in the minefield said they should have killed the SOB, not captured him. "As they brought the sniper through us, he kept pointing and saying '*Minen*,' smiling all the while," Johnson wrote later. "We wanted to get a hold of him we were so mad. The sniper had run out of ammo and then surrendered, after killing as many of us as he could. His smile at us set us off."[47]

By this time Major Colacicco had started up the bluffs with some men from the 3rd Battalion to move farther inland. After going up the one-man wide trail, he reached the top where he found Lieutenant Colonel Sisson. "We were told to keep advancing until we heard firing, and then stop," he said later. "We did so on a small road where we later spent the night."[48]

The regimental Anti-Tank Company, under the command of Captain George R. Jones, Jr., experienced problems similar to those of Cannon Company when they landed on Omaha Beach. Lieutenant Franklyn Johnson was commanding the 3rd Platoon, and his men were assigned to Sisson's 3rd Battalion during the landings. From the start, things did not go well. Two of Johnson's best men were killed on the beach and all of his equipment, with the exception of one 57mm gun and a one-and-a-half-ton truck, was lost in the sea.[49]

After helping Captain Jones get the company organized, Lieutenant Johnson then started through a minefield, later remembering, "[It] was marked by a handkerchief or a sheet of toilet paper and we had to keep a strict trail. Other objects lay beside the path. Several moaning and bloody men were awaiting litters; others' faces were covered with blankets."[50]

Lieutenant Johnson moved on through a scrubby area of brush near some smashed German pillboxes, eventually passing concrete mixers that had been used to build the defenses. He saw discarded tools and "dead Germans all over the place." He soon found Major Colacicco, and after briefing him Johnson remembered, "He was very alarmed to learn that the 3rd Platoon's equipment was still out on the water somewhere, and he told me that he had no G-2 on the antitank situation ahead." Both men had been on Sicily, and they were very concerned that enemy tanks might counterattack that night.

Captain Marshall was the artillery liaison officer supporting the 3rd Battalion on D-day. He had landed with Lieutenant Colonel Sisson, the battalion S-3 Captain Sawyer and Lieutenant Morris, the S-2. As always, he carefully chronicled his experiences, noting that at 1330 hours, "Many beach obstacles still intact . . . only sizeable gap in obstacles in our area was filled by two stranded LCIs . . . occasional mines going off as ships struck barriers. One medium tank was burning fiercely 400 yards down the beach . . . several drowned jeeps were in the water . . . enemy shelling of beach spasmodic by one or two batteries of guns . . . shells landing exactly on water's edge and on boats—either observed fire or adjusted after landing began."

The LCI carrying Captain Marshall went in beside an LCT stranded on a sandbar. The vessel was loaded with two half-tracks and a wrecked jeep. Then Marshall remembered he "crossed sand, shale, and then stopped to unpack [his] radio . . . medics were busy digging in on the beach . . . nobody seemed to be doing anything else . . . shelling started up again on our left not too close." He then crossed a 50-foot marshy area where the 3rd Battalion companies were starting up the bluff. At the time his observations were, "Whole hillside anti-personnel mine uncleared . . . saw no members of beach parties doing any mine clearing, collecting wounded, rescuing vehicles, or anything else . . . when men started passing others they stepped on mines. . . . I waved to liaison party to cross the marsh and wait. They did so."

When Captain Marshall started up the bluff, the soldier ahead of him stepped on a mine, and another man next to him was hit in the eye with a fragment. Marshall climbed the hill by stepping over men who had halted and were waiting for the whole line to move. When he reached the top he first found himself in an open field with no one in sight, but soon spotted five men from an unknown unit in a bomb crater, and then after crossing two fields he found the 3rd Battalion command group, including Lieutenant Colonel Sisson. Sisson had just given the command for two of his rifle companies to begin moving in line abreast toward their pre-designated assembly area.

At this point, Marshall was sent back to the beach to bring up his party. Before he returned to the crest of the bluff, a shell landed in the field he was crossing. Fortunately, it bounded down the face of the bluff before it exploded.

When Captain Marshall reached the edge of the cliffs, he discovered why the men in the bomb crater were not moving. "The CP group of the unknown outfit were the only ones within hearing and they did not pass the word to move out to the 3rd Battalion men, and no one moved," he wrote. "I was afraid Lieutenant Colonel Sisson would move out immediately, so I went back up to join him knowing the party would follow sooner or later." He then sent an officer back to stay at the top of the bluff and to keep his men coming up.[51]

The landings on D-day were no less costly to the remaining elements of the Regiment. Many jeep drivers of Service Company labored exhaustedly as they gunned their vehicles off the ramps of their landing crafts when they came ashore, only to find themselves submerged in the surf or brought to a halt because of the underwater obstacles. Extensive waterproofing of all regimental transportation assets and the experience acquired during Sicily landings resulted in surprisingly few losses. Every organic support unit of the 18th Infantry Regiment continued to function, despite the artillery and mortar barrages in the landing area. Logistical sustainment for the Regiment, under the direction of Major Frank Dupree, Jr., provided the infantry battalions with ammunition, water, rations, and the other necessities of combat during the day.

It was the progress of the 2nd Battalion that continued to make D-day history.

When orders were received from Brigadier General Wyman to take over the mission of the 16th Infantry's 2nd Battalion, Lieutenant Colonel Williamson slipped his forces to the left a few hundred yards before starting inland through the minefields. The narrow paths they crossed were jammed with troops from the 16th Infantry, a number of whom had had their legs or feet blown off.

Captain Rosenberg's Company F was in the lead and was the first to contact the rear elements of Lieutenant Spalding's men atop the bluff before they continued moving toward Colleville-sur-Mer. Williamson's command group was trailed by Company G, then Company H's mortars and machine gunners followed. At 1300 hours, Company E was still held up to the right of the mouth of the Ruquet River valley, but Captain Penick's men continued to work feverishly to clean out German nests of resistance.

"It was actually well after noon when Company E reached the top of the bluff, then deployed and attacked due south to cut off the St. Laurent-Colleville Road," Captain Murphy remembered. "They forced this flank and formed the wedge that allowed many others to get off the beach."[52] During Murphy's climb up the bluff, his men were under sporadic rifle and automatic weapons fire. By this time he had positioned himself with the battalion command group and had retrieved his 81mm mortar section that landed with Rosenberg's Company F. Together with the section commander, Lieutenant Francis O'Grady, the units continued moving inland.

As they were heading down the road towards Colleville-sur-Mer, Murphy heard an artillery shell coming in and yelled a warning. He and the lieutenant both dove at once—the heavy weapons commander into a ditch on one side of the road, O'Grady to the other. As Captain Murphy remembered, "The shell hit very close and only showered me with dirt, yet when I looked to the other side of the road my worse fears were confirmed. The shell had landed right where O'Grady was. When I ran over the first thing he said was, 'How bad am I hit, Captain?' I told him I didn't think it looked too bad, and then I turned and called for a medic. When aid arrived I told him I had to go and that I'd see him when he got back from England."[53]

As the rifle companies and the heavy weapons company of the 2nd Battalion were approaching the lateral road connecting St. Laurent with Colleville-sur-Mer, the 2nd Battalion Headquarters Company was struggling to get off their LCI and onto the beach. It was well past 1400 hours by this time and the LCI was still cruising back and forth along the shore waiting to land. Nearby, an LCT had been hit by a shell, and was low in the water. Its crew was jettisoning bedrolls, cases of rations, ammunition, and gasoline cans to try to keep the landing craft afloat, but its stern was rapidly dropping below the waterline. Lieutenant John Downing, now the Headquarters Company Executive Officer, recalled at that time, "Being aboard ship began to irritate everyone's nerves. We wanted to land and get it over with. We were all conscious that the thin-skinned landing craft was highly vulnerable to any kind of fire. We wanted to get ashore and get close to the ground where we would have a chance. Cruising up and down off the beach like a duck in a shooting gallery was highly nerve-racking for ground soldiers."[54]

Minutes later, orders finally came to get ready to land. The men were called up from below and lined up at the bottom of the companionway stairs, all combat loaded and ready. They came up the ladders and filed out on deck, then crouched behind the bulkheads on each side of the prow near the exit ramps. The LCI then turned into shore, picking up speed, but it eventually grounded with a jolt 50 yards short of the beach. The impact threw everyone off balance. The craft's ramps on either side dropped and teams started down, in single file.

German machine-gun and rifle fire quickly opened up and bullets soon zipped and cracked, some hitting the side of the landing craft.

Riflemen cried out, some in water over their heads, many with their weapons lost in the confusion.

Some men were able to climb on a wrecked craft grounded nearer to shore just as more bullets sprayed around them, but others were already beyond help. One man was dragged back onto the lowered LCI ramp, but his face had a greenish, deathly hue. Major Elisha Peckham, the 2nd Battalion Executive Officer, yelled from the bridge, telling everyone to stay where they were. The LCI then pulled back from the beach, and Downing remembered, "The men in the water screamed at us as they saw us pull away."[55]

Unknown to all but the Navy crew, a valve had blown off a fuel tank in the LCI's engine compartment and gasoline fumes were filling the hold. The few men who remained below came rushing on deck as the LCI pulled away out of firing range, turning this time toward the right flank of the landing zone. Again it went to shore, this time hitting the beach edge after just missing a *Teller* mine. But as soon as the ramps went down, the Germans spotted the movement. Smoke and sand rose in front of the men, blurring their vision, and shells fragments hit the starboard side of the LCI. Major Peckham again yelled for everyone to stand fast, and the LCI pulled back once more.

By this time, LCVPs had pulled up alongside the LCI, and a Navy lieutenant came off the bridge to help Downing into the first boat while he stayed to supervise cross-loading the other soldiers from the LCI. Waves were four or more feet high at the time, and the loading was harrowing. As men stepped down the rope netting to jump in, the LCVPs would dip into the trough of a wave, leaving the men hanging on the netting or grasping one of the LCI's stanchions.

When the waves lifted the LCVPs closer, many soldiers simply jumped, often losing their balance. The smaller landing craft eventually steadied as more men jumped aboard, however, and then they moved furiously toward the smoke-filled shore where most ran into sandbars before they reached the beach. Engines roared as coxswain tried to power forward, only to give up as officers ordered them to just drop their ramps and let the men off. Some of the lucky troopers had lifebelts that inflated as they sank in water up to their chests. A hail of bullets greeted others before they could pull their vests' safety rings. Nearby, another LCVP tried to come in, but it was on fire.

As they reached shore, the men rushed to the base of the bluffs and beyond the heavy enemy guns. To their front was an open gravelly stretch where a bulldozer had been working to clear the E-1 exit. While shells crashed into a hill on their left, riflemen first made for safety behind the bulldozer, but then they moved forward across a flat, grassy expanse toward a path already marked with the white tape that had led others off the beach. More confusion greeted them, this time as troops mixed at the head of the draw where it led away from the beach. There was another path, just to the left of the draw, and men started organizing in single file, even as exploding mines sent some reeling.

Ahead was a swamp about ten yards across; the lead soldiers started wading across it. Others followed, afraid to spread out for fear of stepping onto more mines, but the men who got across the swamp quickly yelled for others to follow.

As Lieutenant Downing advanced, he came upon a soldier who was lying on his stomach, his face swathed with bloody bandages. This soldier warned him about mines being all around him, just as a sharp explosion rocked the path. Downing went down, as did a private right behind him. He was a new replacement and his face quickly turned white. Meantime, others were passing, and another shell slammed into the hillside. More men hit the ground.

Downing looked back down the path to see Major Peckham struggling up the hill unconcernedly. He kept coming, passing Downing, and then a shell came in that landed down the hill, followed by yet another that hit near the head of the column.

Downing moved forward, only to find that medics were treating the 2nd Battalion executive officer and another officer. The latter officer had been hit in the leg. Peckham's helmet had saved him from being killed. A piece of flying metal had cut open his scalp, but Peckham's helmet kept it from penetrating his skull. Another shell fragment was buried in his neck. Before he was evacuated Peckham told Downing to take over and to try to contact the rest of the 2nd Battalion.

Lieutenant Downing then found a radioman down the hill, but his radio would not work. "The situation was now all messed up," Downing remembered. "I had no idea where I was or where the battalion was." Still, he turned to move up the hill again. When he got there he found the Headquarters Company Commander, Captain Spinney. Spinney already had decided to reconnoiter forward to see if he could find the rest of the battalion; Downing joined him and they made for an open field while taking enemy fire. During their advance they passed a man sheltered with canvas, which they recognized as the 2nd Battalion S-4, Lieutenant Pavlak. Fortunately, he was not dead.[56]

Avoiding possible minefields, both men eventually came upon a shallow ditch where Lieutenant O'Grady was now with another man. O'Grady was weak, yet he managed to report that they were waiting until dark when it would be safer to go down the hill with a medic. Downing and Spinney then left to move over to the edge of a hedgerow where they found a Company F sergeant and a few of his men with their backs to a dirt embankment.

The party then combined before making for a corner of another hedgerow, where they came upon a group of officers and two observers from the 32nd FA Battalion. Convinced that Lieutenant Colonel Williamson had to be close by, Captain Spinney left to go back down to the beach to find Colonel Smith and his Regimental Headquarters staff, not knowing that they had already established their first command post on French soil in a German pillbox on the beach. Lieutenant Downing continued until he finally found Lieutenant Colonel Williamson's command group sheltering near a road intersection.[57]

By this time, the main body of 2nd Battalion had worked its way close to the lateral road where it met the western edge of Colleville-sur-Mer. The Americans had made good progress moving along sunken roads that bordered many hedgerows. The Germans, who controlled many openings along the hedgerows and zeroed in with rifles and machine guns, had by this time succeeded in inflicting several casualties. A crew of Captain Murphy's Company H mortars was trying to blast them out of their hidden positions. Passing by the body of a soldier sprawled face down on the ground and bloody from a grenade explosion, then another dead soldier lying against the edge of the hedgerow, Lieutenant Downing then joined up with Captain Spinney. Spinney had found a working radio and was in communication with Lieutenant Colonel Williamson. Major Middleworth and Captain Robert W. Green from the regimental staff separately also had linked up with Spinney.

Middleworth radioed their location to Lieutenant Colonel Sternberg who was manning the command post on the beach. At about the same time, Lieutenant Colonel Williamson called for Downing to come to his new location near some houses on the outskirts of Colleville-sur-Mer.

When Downing found Williamson, he was sitting on the edge of a slit trench with his S-3, Captain Randall. Downing radioed Captain Spinney to say he had made it safely to the assembly area, found his way to a nearby ditch, had a cigarette, and fell asleep.

By this time, Captain Penick had moved Company E almost to the road that ran from St. Laurent to Colleville-sur-Mer. During the movement inland, Penick's company, with the assistance of Company E, 16th Infantry, had eliminated several German positions between the two villages. After Company F, led by a platoon commanded by Lieutenant David Bramlett, succeeded in driving back other German units opposing progress toward the same lateral road, the 2nd Battalion consolidated its positions to the southeast of Colleville-sur-Mer, the original objective of the 16th Infantry Regiment.

At 1800 hours, Colonel Smith received a change of orders from Division that prohibited his men from advancing south of the lateral road connecting St.

Laurent and Colleville. Instead, the battalion was to secure the gap between the 18th Infantry Regiment and elements of the 116th Infantry Regiment making their way toward St. Laurent. The 1st Infantry Division command post did not know it when the order was issued, but the 2nd Battalion had already accomplished that mission and was starting to dig in.[58]

As the 2nd Battalion Record of Events later noted, "In our position we found no enemy in front of us, but a large number of enemy behind us between our location and Colleville-sur-Mer. We had constant small brushes with enemy troops manning defensive positions or trying to escape. Just before dark, Company F was [deployed] north of Company G, which formed a three-sided box around the enemy troops in and south of Colleville-sur-Mer. Small arms fire [was] kept up through the night as the enemy attempted to escape."[59] The Army Historical Record of D-day later stated, "The main damage to German forces in Colleville-sur-Mer was inflicted by the 2nd Battalion of the 18th Infantry, posted south and southeast on the escape route from the village."[60]

At 2100 hours adjustments were made in the supporting armor. With the 2nd Battalion farthest forward, Colonel Smith diverted three tanks that were ashore from the 3rd Battalion over to support the 2nd Battalion south of Colleville-sur-Mer.[61]

During that night, enemy artillery essentially ceased, primarily because the Germans' ammunition resources almost were depleted.

Fortunately for the Americans, the *352nd Infantry Division*'s artillery battalions had not displaced forward with their larger loads. That fact only permitted them to engage targets for a single day before running out of high-explosive shells.

Unhindered by indirect fire, the rifle companies of the 2nd Battalion were able to clean out a number of pockets of resistance that night, taking over 160 prisoners and killing about 50 Germans before 0900 hours on 7 June.

By the end of D-day, the 1st Infantry Division had scratched out a toehold on the continent of Europe.

The 2nd Battalion, 18th Infantry made the deepest penetration into the beachhead, farther south than any other American unit that landed in Normandy. By doing so, Williamson's men had pushed through the "beachhead maintenance line," an area controlled by German artillery that had been raising hell on Omaha Beach all day.

"[Their position] was indeed thin," British historian Chester Wilmot noted. "But it was held by men who had been ashore before in North Africa and Sicily and could not be dismayed even by the most desperate situation. Had this sector of Omaha Beach been assigned to troops less experienced, less resolute, or less ably commanded, the assault might never have penetrated the beaches."[62]

The cost to the 18th Infantry Regiment for taking the beachhead was stated in the last S-1 Journal entry at 2140 hours on D-day. One officer and 11 enlisted men were killed, 12 officers and 136 enlisted men had been wounded, 45 were missing, with most of the killed and wounded lost on the beach and in the minefields bordering the blood-soaked paths to the top of the bluffs.[63]

The remainder of the 1st Infantry Division (16th and 26th Infantry Regiments) suffered 719 casualties on D-day. The 116th Infantry Regiment suffered 328 killed, 281 wounded, and 134 missing, while supporting V Corps troops lost 85 killed, 265 wounded, and 91 missing.[64]

That night the 18th Regimental Combat Team was charged with the mission of expanding the beachhead at all costs. Pressing forward in the coming days and nights and inflicting heavy casualties on the enemy, in eight more days the Combat Team would be 23 miles inland, near Caumont, further into France than any other American unit in the lodgment area on D-day.

Two weeks following the invasion, Colonel Smith wrote a letter to his wife in which he revealed unabashed pride in his men. After he explained that he had spent the night of D-day in "a German dugout that was 20 feet under the ground and smelled to high heaven," he wrote about his men, "Since then we have pushed steadily into Normandy. These lads of mine are fighting fools. They have marched, fought, and dug trenches day after day without a complaint and with a wonderful spirit. Who says this modern generation is soft? Hitler has no more claim that he has all the supermen."[65]

On 17 June, General Huebner approved a Presidential Unit Citation for the 18th Infantry Regiment based on its D-day achievements. He followed with a personal comment, "The courage, devotion to duty, and determination of the personnel of this unit are a credit to the Army of the United States."

Part of the citation read, "The individual calmness, endurance, superior efficiency, and devotion to duty exhibited by the men of this Regiment was a direct contribution to the successful establishment of a firm beachhead on the ramparts of 'Fortress Europe' and will without doubt result in a successful conclusion to the war in Europe."[66]

The flat reach of earth above the bluffs crossed by the 2nd Battalion is now the location of the permanent Normandy American Cemetery and Memorial.

Weary soldiers of the Regiment who slept on the night of D-day did so only with great difficulty. As the rattles of enemy burp guns were followed by the return of mortars near the hedgerows astride Colleville-sur-Mer, the guns of the 5th FA were firing inland while the 32nd FA was still working its way off the beach. One ammunition bearer in Company H's 81mm Mortar Platoon trying to nod off to sleep on the ground south of Colleville gave up and instead, hurriedly wrote a note to his mother telling her about his day. He closed by saying he wondered what everyone back home was doing.

In the United States, most Americans only learned that D-day had been raging in France during the routine of starting their morning. Virtually no one knew what units had landed or if their cherished sons, boyfriends, or husbands had survived. They would not know if any of them had been killed or wounded until telegrams started to arrive, weeks later.

Church bells tolled across the land, school bells rang in every town. Factories repeatedly sounded their whistles, and solemn foghorns blasted away in seaside harbors all over the country on D-day in the USA.

Before sunrise, lines formed in front of St. Patrick's Cathedral on Fifth Avenue in New York City. At 7:30 AM Eastern War Time at Independence Hall in Philadelphia, the Liberty Bell pealed for the first time in over 100 years, ringing to a nationwide radio audience.

Early morning editions of local papers hit the streets with large, often half-page banner headlines announcing the invasion. Many printed the text of General Eisenhower's Order of the Day, including several statements made through Berlin about the landings that suggested there was "a terrific bombardment" and "GIs were engaged by German shock troops." *The New York Daily News* dropped its editorial page and, instead, printed *The Lord's Prayer* on the morning of 6 June 1944.

In Normandy that night the moon was full, the air was cold and the sounds of war were still all around the exhausted Company H ammunition bearer as D-day ended. He was freezing, too proud to admit it, and homesick. Suddenly he watched a flare go up 100 feet from him, undoubtedly sent aloft by hopeful Germans trying to tell their few remaining artillery units where they could find American infantry targets.

Thousands of miles across the sea, back home, another flare was burning in New York Harbor. On Liberty Island, a woman was holding up a dimly lit torch that was normally a beacon for ships and airplanes. She is a symbol of Freedom. She is the Statue of Liberty, a gift originally from the country being freed that night by thousands of young soldiers who sailed by her on their way to war.

On D-day, in New York Harbor, one half hour after sunset, the 96,000 watts of floodlight that had made her so visible before war's blackout conditions shone upon her again. Then her torch started blinking in a sequence of three short flashes and one long flash, repeatedly for 15 long minutes.

Lady Liberty majestically proclaimed to the world "V for Victory" and, at the close of a day, the mayor of her city called it "the most exciting moment of our lives," while every American remembered it as a time their country was never stronger, more right, or more determined.

If she could have spoken, she might have whispered the immortal words of Pericles—to her homeland's liberators who lay scattered and dead across a fragile beachhead far across the sundering sea.

Heroes have the whole earth for their tomb.
And in lands far from their own
Where the column with its epitaph declares it,
There is enshrined in every breast a record unwritten
With no tablet to preserve it except that of the heart.

COMMANDING OFFICERS

Colonel Ely P. Denson
(*HQ, 1st Battalion, 18th Infantry*)

Brigadier General Frank U. Greer
(*Greer Family, Frank U. Greer IV*)

Colonel George A. Smith, Jr.
(*Family of George A. Smith, Jr.*)

Colonel John Williamson
(*HQ, 1st Battalion, 18th Infantry*)

OTHER COMMANDERS

Lieutenant Colonel Henry G. Learnard (Foreground) and Major Robert E. Murphy (*Robert E. Murphy*)

Major Sam Carter (*Norma Carter*)

Lieutenant Colonel Robert H. York (*Joel Kiekbusch*)

(L–R) Lieutenant Colonel Courtney P. Brown, Jr., Captain Bradley Bacon, Captain Edward Kuehn, unknown Arab, Lieutenant Colonel Joseph Sisson (*Edward Kuehn*)

(L–R) Major General Clarence Huebner, Major General Terry Allen, Lieutenant Colonel Harold "Paddy" Flint (39th Infantry), Lieutenant Colonel Robert H. York, Lieutenant Colonel John Corley (26th Infantry), Lieutenant Colonel Ben Sternberg (*CMH*)

(L–R) Lieutenant Colonel Ben Sternberg, Major William K. "Soup" Campbell, Major Edward McGregor (lighting cigarette), Colonel John Williamson (*Tess McGregor*)

Major Robert E. Murphy (*Robert E. Murphy*)

(L–R) Major General Louis Koeltz, Commanding General of the French XIX Corps; Major General Terry Allen; Brigadier General Theodore Roosevelt (*CMH*)

(L–R foreground Major General Terry Allen decorates Lieutenant Colonel Ben Sternberg (*Cantigny First Division Museum*)

TRAINING

Company A in garrison caps, overcoats, and cartridge belts in formation during a winter drizzle at Fort Devens, 1942 (*CMH*)

As their officer and noncommissioned officer leaders look on, gunners and assistant gunners for a full platoon's worth of M1917A1 heavy machine guns from Company D prepare to open fire on a landscape target during practice on MacArthur Range at Fort Devens, 1942 (*CMH*)

Prime Movers of the 32nd Field Artillery Battalion tow the unit's 105mm howitzers over the long winding hills of Virginia enroute to Camp Blanding, Florida, 1942. (*CMH*)

1st Sergeant Jacob Halpern, Company B, 1942. "One of the old-time pre-war Regulars." Note the pre-war/early war 1st Sargeant's insignia with only two rockers. (*CMH*)

Troops boarding a landing craft during amphibious training Scotland 1942. (*CMH*)

NORTH AFRICA

Graves of the combat dead, Arzew, Algeria. (*Edward Kuehn*)

General Terry Allen and Colonel Frank U. Greer outside St. Cloud, Algeria, November, 1942. (*CMH*)

Front (L–R): Captain Russell Spinney, Lieutenant Waldemar Hobratsck; Back (L–R): Lieutenant Orin Rosenberg, Lieutenant James Lucas, Captain Robert E. Murphy.

French prisoners taken after the fight for St. Cloud. (*CMH*)

Longstop Hill. (*Patton Museum*)

Company D at El Guettar just prior to German attacks. (*NA*)

Captured German outpost after the Battle for Hill 350, Tunisia, April 1943. (*Robert E. Murphy*)

SICILY

General view of D-day—Gela Beach, Sicily. (*CMH*)

Lieutenant Colonel William O. Darby, US Army Rangers. (*CMH*)

Concentration of LCI invasion craft loading in preparation for departure from Tunisian port for Sicily. (*CMH*)

M-7 105 mm self-propelled howitzer advancing while Sicilian civilians cheer them on. (*CMH*)

NORMANDY

Half-tracks on maneuver. (*CMH*)

Troops boarding landing craft in England. (*CMH*)

First Wave—H-hour D-day in Normandy. (*NA*)

Boarding the landing craft for the trip across the Channel. (*NA*)

Follow-up wave at Easy Red. (*US Army Signal Corps*)

Higgins boat on fire.
(*US Coast Guard*)

D+1—Troops of Company F, 16th Infantry Regiment on D-day. (*US Coast Guard*)

American soldiers killed by machine-gun fire in the Normandy hedgerows. (*NA*)

EUROPE

Sherman tanks of the 3rd Armored Division pursue retreating Germans near Mons, Belgium, September 1944. (*NA*)

1st Battalion, 18th Infantry Regiment in ruined Heistern, November 1944. (*NA*)

M-10 tank destroyers navigate a muddy trail in the Hürtgen Forest, Autumn 1944.
(*NA*)

Soldiers from Company M, 18th Infantry Regiment searching for German paratroopers outside Eupen
(*NA*)

American infantry advancing across open snow-covered Belgian countryside, January 1945 (*NA*)

Locals welcome 18th Infantry Regiment soldiers in German village (*Joel Kiekbush*)

Private Nicholas Schaeffer of the S-2 section, 18th Infantry Regiment interrogates prisoners taken in the Harz Mountains (*NA*)

The 18th Infantry Regiment command group after D-day (*Family of Colonel Smith*)

NORTHERN FRANCE

JUNE TO SEPTEMBER 1944

We couldn't see the sun because the sky was full of shells,
And after that trip across the beach, brother bring on hell!
—1st Division Verse

During the night of D-day, V Corps took control of the troops that had landed on Omaha Beach, permitting General Huebner to return his full attention to the 1st Infantry Division.

Adjustments were made immediately: the 16th Infantry Regiment needed time to reconstitute its battered battalions. Accordingly, Captain Dawson's and Lieutenant Spalding's depleted Companies G and E were attached to the 1st Battalion, 26th Infantry to mop up around Colleville-sur-Mer. When that task was complete, the combined force was ordered to sidestep to the east and to take high ground west and southwest of Port-en-Bessin, including Mont Cauvin, before linking up with the British XXX Corps. Meanwhile, the 3rd Battalion, 26th Infantry Regiment, which had moved south of St. Laurent-sur-Mer to take up a position on the right of Lieutenant Colonel Sisson's battalion, was attached to the 18th Infantry Regiment.

At 0730 hours 7 June, Major General Huebner directed regimental commanders to launch a coordinated attack to seize the 1st Infantry Division's original D-day objectives. The 18th Infantry Regiment was to secure the high ground just north of Trévières and the Mandeville-Mosles area south of the Aure River. Colonel Smith then made plans to attack and take Mandeville with the 1st and 2nd Battalions moving abreast, while the 3rd Battalion followed the 1st.[1] The time for the attack was set at 1100 hours.

Captain Scott-Smith's Company C was selected to lead the 1st Battalion's advance, despite the fact that the previous night had been a harrowing one. Many of the company's riflemen had been fighting unassisted in a maze of hedgerows.

A few soldiers crawled into the center of the large earthen mounds to attack Germans who had been sniping at the Americans.

During the vicious firefight, the soldiers killed five Germans, and took two others prisoner. Company C's exhausted soldiers were now given the burden of leading the attack southward in the center of the new zone, while Company A, commanded by Captain Bacon, and Captain Cameron's Company B spread out on their flanks with Captain Carter's Company D in close support. The 1st Battalion then pressed forward under heavy enemy fire through two miles of Normandy hedgerow terrain.

By evening, York's men were in a favorable position on the high ground overlooking the Aure River near Engranville.

Naval fire control parties and 32nd FA observers, anticipating an 18th Infantry Regiment attack on Mosles during D-day, had already established a forward observation post at le Chateau Rouge. That happened before the 2nd Battalion, with a platoon of tanks from the 745th Tank Battalion and two platoons of 57mm antitank guns in support, crossed their line of departure south of Colleville at 1100 hours to set off toward the Aure River. The bulk of the battalion advanced in a column of companies in the center of the attack direction, with Captain Jeffrey's Company G in the lead, trailed by Company H and their battalion Headquarters Company. Company F advanced along a small dirt trail 600 yards to the right of the line, while Company E started down another dusty, sunken lane bordering high hedgerows, passing French farmyards and small groups of scattered houses.

At about 1300, enemy machine-gun and mortar fire suddenly opened up from across the Aure River, directed at Captain Jeffrey's men just as his lead platoon was approaching a strip of woods near Houtteville. The small village was located opposite Mosles, connected by a causeway.

Jeffrey's men quickly deployed and engaged the enemy while Company F rushed a platoon across the causeway. In response enemy troops, consisting of elements of the 2nd *Battalion, Grenadier Regiment 916*, greeted Rosenberg's platoon with heavy small arms and machine-gun fire.

Lieutenant Colonel Williamson immediately ordered five tanks of the 745th Tank Battalion, as well as an additional tank from the 743rd Tank Battalion, to cross the river to join in the skirmish. When these Shermans crossed over, they immediately drew concentrated fire, but their advance enabled the rest of Captain Rosenberg's men to move safely over the causeway, behind the last tank. After Captain Jeffrey's men followed and fanned out to the right just after crossing the bridge, a heated engagement ensued. Leaving behind small pockets of the enemy posted near the Houtteville side of the bridge (to be mopped up by Company E), Captain Murphy led Company H over the bridge, enabling his heavy machine guns and 81mm mortars to join the battle.

Mosles was taken after several hours of sharp fighting, but the skirmishes resulted in the deaths or injury of several infantrymen and tankers. The Germans suffered more substantially before retreating further southward, losing over 45 dead with several captured. When the 2nd Battalion established a defensive line astride the Bayeux-St. Lô Road to the south of Mosles by last light, Lieutenant Colonel Williamson set up his command post in a dugout near a lone house in an apple orchard.

Before the 3rd Battalion moved out on its mission on 7 June, a sniper wounded Company I's commanding officer, Captain Hershel T. Coffman; Lieutenant Robert E. Hess assumed command. Even though the battalion had now lost two of its three rifle company commanders within a 48-hour period, Lieutenant Colonel Sisson's men pushed off at 1215 hours that afternoon, advancing along several hedgerow-bordered trails toward the village of Surrain.

By 1530 hours, it was obvious that the Germans had evacuated the town. Instead of gunfire, Sisson's men were greeted by the town's inhabitants bearing wine, flowers, and fruit. After passing through the well-wishers, the battalion continued to advance toward Mandeville, which sat astride the main Bayeux-Isigny road.

After crossing the road, the battalion came under heavy fire. Losing four killed and 24 wounded, the battalion established defensive positions in a cup-shaped hollow southeast of Mandeville.

In exchange for his losses that day, Sisson captured a dozen prisoners from *Construction Engineer Battalion 17* and *Grenadier Regiment 916*, including a German noncommissioned officer who had a complete map of the defensive positions of the *352nd Infantry Division*. Later that evening, Colonel Smith reported to division headquarters that the original D-day objectives had been reached along the Regiment's entire front. He then moved his command post from Omaha Beach to Surrain at 1930 hours.[2]

The coming of darkness did not result in a cessation of fighting in the 3rd Battalion's sector. At 0200 hours on 8 June, a large German patrol breached the battalion's defensive perimeter, getting as far as the rear command post and unit motor park before encountering resistance. In a savage point-blank firefight, the battalion suffered numerous casualties while capturing 16 Germans and killing or wounding at least 10. The 3rd Battalion operations journal curiously noted, "The Germans, with very few exceptions, were all very young and from their actions seemed to be half insane or doped."[3]

Captain Marshall was forward in Mandeville as an observer for the 32nd Field Artillery that night, and he, Lieutenant Colonel Sisson and the battalion S-3, Captain Sawyer, reconnoitered the area, looking for suitable company positions. At about 2100 they returned to the battalion command post in an orchard near the village.

As they were coming down a dirt road, a soldier with the group suddenly fired two shots at what he thought to be a German. Sisson first challenged the GI when he did this, telling him he thought it was a Frenchman. When the soldier persisted and said he saw a German with his own eyes, he was right; to Sisson's good fortune, the German turned and ran when his weapon jammed. After that harrowing experience, Sisson joined his staff in the orchard entrance, where they tried to get some sleep.

At about 0200, Captain Marshall was awakened by machine-gun fire and moments later he was accosted by four Germans and captured. Immediately ordered to move toward the orchard entrance, he heard more shots from the direction where the battalion vehicles were parked, near a farmhouse close to the town. Marshall used the confusion to feign being hit, first moaning and staggering, and then falling into some bushes.

Major Colacicco had been on his way over to meet Marshall. He, too, was captured after the Germans ambushed and killed a soldier guarding a Sherman tank at the roadway to the orchard.

In the ensuing melee, a group of drunken young Germans began screaming and charging the battalion area, smashing radios and telephone equipment, nearly killing Lieutenant Colonel Sisson in the process. It was only the swift action of an alert officer who pushed Sisson down that saved him. Captain Sawyer barely got a call out to Colonel Smith to report an attack, force size unknown. He was unable to pinpoint the assault's direction.

When the chaos finally settled down, five Americans lay dead. The event had quite an impact in the rear area, where the news caused concern at corps level that a large-scale enemy counterattack had started.

Major Colacicco and Captain Marshall escaped wounds, and Colacicco even turned the tables on his captors and later captured them. He explained, "We were lucky. Very lucky. The interrelation between the various supporting elements hurt us. We had a tank battalion, supposedly friendly, actually with us, and I think that was what started our problem. These assigned tanks were stationed inside the narrow streets in Mandeville. The tankers, rather than keeping men on watch, buttoned up their tanks and then didn't tell us."[4]

It had been a close call. Thinking enemy tanks might be attacking two of the battalion's companies bivouacked at the edge of the orchard, Colacicco had been rushing to find Marshall so they could call for artillery and naval support fire. Captain Sawyer had been confused about the probable location from which the Germans were coming, first telling Regiment it might be Trévières, but then being cut off before he could clarify.

"This is not the way a war should go," Lieutenant Franklyn Johnson remembered. "We had heard that the Nazis frequently got a group of soldiers drunk, usually boys fifteen to nineteen years old, then sent them out as suicide squads to do as much damage as they could before being cut down."[5]

During the morning of 8 June, the main effort in the 1st Infantry Division zone shifted to the extreme left flank where the 26th Infantry Regiment was still trying to secure original D-day objectives near Tour-en-Bessin. It would not prove to be a day of rest for the 18th Infantry Regiment, as 1st Infantry Division headquarters telephoned Colonel Smith at 0645 hours to stress the need for the combat team to maintain contact with the enemy. Moments later, all battalions were ordered to

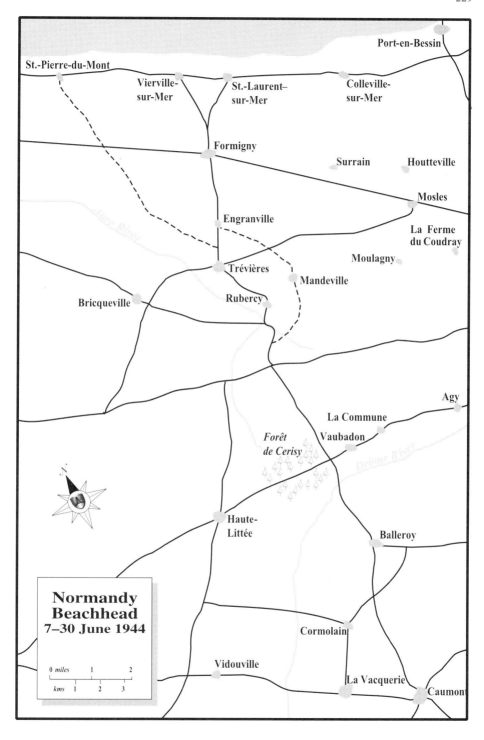

conduct extensive patrols. Sisson's men patrolled westward to Trévières while the 1st Battalion focused on Engranville to the south. The 2nd Battalion drew the lot of sending men as far as possible in all directions from Mosles.

The Commanding General of V Corps was determined to keep pressure on the retreating Germans. At 1545 that afternoon, General Huebner and General Wyman visited Colonel Smith's command post in Surrain with new orders. Shortly afterward, Wyman arrived at Lieutenant Colonel Williamson's position to explain the necessity for him to secure a ridge just south of Mosles near Moulagny so the 1st and 3rd Battalions could jump off from the new line the next day. Movement started well before dark. Company E was in the lead, accompanied by a platoon of tanks.

The company worked toward the designated ridge with little trouble until a firefight broke out as they neared a German strongpoint 500 meters southwest of Moulagny. Soldiers filing up behind Penick's men heard the sounds of his rifles and BARs, as well as the noise of of German burp guns and panzerfausts. The .50-caliber machine guns on the Sherman tanks quickly joined in the fight, but by the time Captain Murphy's crews emplaced their water-cooled .30-calibers and 81mm mortars on either side of the road, the fighting had quieted down. The enemy, however, was reported to be just 300 yards ahead when darkness fell, and the Americans dug in for the night with all three rifle companies on the line.[6]

The 1st Battalion, solidly entrenched on high ground facing the Aure River and the fortified city of Trévières, spent most of 8 June consolidating its positions; patrolling its front and flanks; and assisting troops from the 2nd Infantry Division who advanced slowly to their right rear. The battalion's immediate right flank, however, was exposed for most of the day, permitting German units to fire into its lines and stubbornly contest the advance of adjacent American units. Company B conducted a limited-objective attack in nearby Formigny late in the evening. In in a brisk but bitter struggle, they cleared the town of German troops. Ten enemy were killed, 15 were captured, and a quantity of vehicles and supplies were seized. After midnight, the company withdrew from the town, leaving a platoon behind. During the night, Germans facing the nearby 2nd Infantry Division discovered that their supplies had been lost and withdrew to the southwest. The pressure on the flank of the 1st Battalion was relieved, and the 9th Infantry Regiment of the 2nd Division was able to move on line just after midnight.[7]

The 3rd Battalion saw little action on 8 June. Instead, Sisson's officers concentrated on turning over their area to a battalion of the 9th Infantry Regiment. Subsequently, the 3rd Battalion was to move southeastward the next morning to a 2nd Battalion assembly area at Moulagny. Verbal orders at 2000 hours called not only for Sisson's men to be relieved, but also for York's 1st Battalion to give up its sector to another 9th Infantry battalion, so they could vacate high ground overlooking Trévières and move to the new assembly area.

By this time, the enemy had reorganized, and division intelligence had been able to identify remnants of two battalions of *Grenadier Regiment 916* in the woods south of Mosles. Elements of *Grenadier Regiment 915* had also sidestepped east from Formigny after Company B cleared the town and established defensive positions behind York's 1st Battalion. Division also opined that *Mobile Battalion 517*, believed to be located in Gottun, was capable of a counterattack into the flank of Smith's south-moving battalions.

As a result, General Huebner decided to assign the 18th Infantry to a much narrower sector for the next day's attack—to reduce the number of enemy troops they might encounter. Introducing the 2nd Infantry Division into the line had allowed narrowing this sector.

Fighting among the ancient farm fields, each surrounded by high, thick earthen berms topped by hedges (called '*le bocage*') had proven unexpectedly difficult. The men who fought there often called this phase of the fighting in "The Battle of the Hedgerows."

"The hedgerows actually compartmentalized the battlefield," historian Martin Blumenson explained. "The hedgerow is a fence, half earth, half hedge. The wall at the base is a dirt parapet that varies in thickness from one to four or more feet and in height from three to twelve feet. Growing out of the wall is a hedge of hawthorn, brambles, vines, and trees, in thickness from one to three feet, in height from three to fifteen feet. Delimiting each field, they break the terrain into numerous walled enclosures. Since the fields are tiny, about 200 by 400 yards in size, the hedgerows are innumerable and because the fields are irregular in shape, the hedgerows follow no logical pattern."[8]

The morning of 9 June brought a weather change. Drizzling rain began at daybreak; the air grew chilly and damp.

The 3rd Battalion had departed Mandeville late the night before and made its way along a desolate road, past the tiny village of La Cour, and bypassed a stand of donut-shaped woods near Beaumont before bedding down near a large barn on the Bayeux-St. Lô Road.

The 1st Battalion had also moved from their positions south of Engranville. By 1100 hours, Lieutenant Colonel York's companies were assembled 1,500 yards south of Mosles and prepared for the afternoon attack. At 1300 hours, the two battalions passed through the 2nd Battalion's positions, and the 2nd Battalion reverted to regimental reserve. By now, Colonel Smith had moved his command post to Mosles and a battery of self-propelled 105mm howitzers of the 62nd Armored FA Battalion had reinforced the 32nd Field Artillery. The Regiment's line was now at its 7 June (D+1) objective, some five miles south of the landing beaches and centered on Ferme (farm) Blay, three kilometers south-southeast of Mosles.

At 1400 hours, the leading elements of the Regiment crossed the line of departure at Moulagny with the 1st Battalion on the left and the 3rd on the right. At first things progressed well for Lieutenant Colonel York's men; however, the 3rd Battalion ran into stiff resistance when the head of Sisson's advancing column met enemy machine-gun, mortar, and small arms fire from the hedgerows. Colonel

Smith was anxious for Sisson to continue pressing forward, and so after directing him to bypass this enemy strongpoint, he ordered Lieutenant Colonel Williamson to move two companies forward to deal with the isolated German position. Company F jumped off first, followed by Company G, while Captain Murphy ordered Lieutenant Waldemar J. Hobtratschk to commence supporting fires with his 81mm mortar platoon.

In the ensuing fight, over 20 Germans from *Füsilier Battalion 352* were killed or wounded and others were taken prisoner.* Several American riflemen also lost their lives and seven soldiers were wounded. During the engagement, two enemy shells had landed near the Company E CP, where several men were hit.[9]

During the fighting, German shells also caught Company H's mortar section on the move and Captain Murphy lost several men, including Pfc. Robert A. Baummer. The soldier was one of two left besides Murphy on the original company "Gangplank Roster" written aboard the *Queen Mary* in August 1942 before the untested unit headed off to war.

As Company H mortar platoon ammunition carrier Pfc. Paul E. Stegall recalled years later, "We were moving from one hedgerow into another that day. We were going by a wagon trail—that's the way the farmers would get from one hedgerow to the next. We didn't think the Germans would pick us up, but they must have seen us coming, because they let go with shells and rifle fire that was unbelievable. My best friend, Pfc. Baummer, took a direct hit from a shell. He never knew what hit him. It happened so fast. But when it was over, there were bodies everywhere. So many were lying there, heads were gone, as were legs and arms. It was just awful. I had his blood and flesh all over my uniform. I was lucky. I only got hit by splinters from the shell that killed him, as well as some shrapnel. Others got it, too. Private Ralph J. Spinosi was killed. All they found was his field jacket. It had 'Smiling Jack from South Philly' written on the back. That's how they identified his remains. Corporal Eugene Sproull died, too. Four others were badly wounded, including Private William Uhouse who had all his flesh stripped from the outside of his thigh on his right leg. I'll never forget that day for as long as I live."[10]

Company C had reverted to a much-deserved support role when the 1st Battalion jumped off and two platoons each of Companies A and B attacked abreast at 1715 hours that afternoon. The two Company B platoons were about a thousand yards south of Coudray Farm, advancing at bayonet point through a mass of hedgerows and woods, when a cleverly camouflaged, determined enemy force attacked them. Undaunted, Cameron's men fought viciously in close combat with their enemy, and by sheer tenacity and drive, they rolled over the enemy positions. Company B's lead platoon also ran into an equally difficult situation, and Captain Cameron's men fought their way through four separate hedgerows

---

*At this stage in the war, each German infantry division was organized with a *Füsilier* battalion that performed special missions—reconnaissance, raids, or other tasks requiring a higher level of proficiency and physical fitness among its soldiers. As such, they were relatively elite units.

finally managing to reach the Regiment's intermediate objective along the Trévières-Bayeux road.

The 1st Battalion had destroyed a company of *Replacement and Training ("Feldersatz") Battalion 352* that afternoon, killing or wounding several dozen enemy soldiers and capturing 30 others. The crust of the German resistance was now broken on the left flank, but the advance of the battalion did not stop here. Under orders "that you sacrifice everything to reach the next phase line [railroad] before darkness," Captain Scott-Smith's Company C picked up the advance by swinging wide around the battalion's eastern flank, then leading the pursuit of the enemy's collapsing forces. The Tortonne River was crossed, the Bayeux-le Molay road secured, and the important Paris-Cherbourg railway (the phase line) was cut in their remaining drive further south that day.[11]

All of the rifle companies in the 3rd Battalion, aided by two platoons from Company B, 745th Tank Battalion, were active in the afternoon's push. During this fighting and other engagements the next day, two soldiers were recognized for singularly conspicuous gallantry.

On 9 June, Staff Sergeant Walter Ehlers heard for the first time that his brother, Roland, had been killed in action on D-day. He and his brother had been very close and his death made Ehlers not only very sad, but also incredibly angry. As his Company L commander Captain George K. Folk said later, "After this he tried to win the war all by himself."[12]

As Staff Sergeant Ehlers explained years later, "I was leading my squad that night and they were following me. I started up a hedgerow, and I just automatically knocked the Germans in there out. I didn't wait for the squad to come up. I then went to another hedgerow where I ran into a machine-gun nest, and knocked it out. My squad was still following me. The same thing happened at an enemy mortar position, but by this time I had the squad fix bayonets and the Germans started fleeing. The bayonets scared them to death. They didn't surrender, so they all got shot. Then the squad came up and they shot the ones I didn't kill."[13]

Led by stalwart noncommissioned officers such as Ehlers, it is no wonder that the 3rd Battalion pressed onward until it reached the Regiment's final objective at 2330 hours, bringing operations for 9 June to a close.[14]

The 18th Infantry Regiment resumed its advance at 0630 hours on 10 June with York's and Sisson's men again attacking abreast. The 1st Battalion encountered slight opposition at la Catherine in the early going, but this was soon cleared up after first light. Nearby Tronquay was bypassed and the village of la Commune on the Bayeux-St. Lo road was secured. Twenty German prisoners were rounded up as York's men began organizing a defensive position. A temporary order to halt had been given while Regiment made adjustments and the 2nd Battalion quickly moved up behind York's companies to establish their own positions near Tronquay.[15]

Lieutenant Colonel Sisson's 3rd Battalion, advancing toward the village of Vaubadon on the main Bayeux-St. Lô highway, made contact with an ominous group of enemy soldiers at 0900 hours. The leading companies ambushed a reconnaissance party of the *17th SS-Panzer-Grenadier Division "Götz von Berlichingen,"* killing several Germans and capturing 10 others.[16] The battalion's advance then continued until Lieutenant Hess's Company I and Captain Folk's Company L were pinned down by fire from a German strongpoint hidden in the northeast corner of the Forêt de Cerisy.

Despite supporting fire from the crews manning the Sherman tanks of Company B, 745th Tank Battalion, Lieutenant Colonel Sisson was forced to order Hess to withdraw 500 yards to the east to allow Folk's men to launch a flanking attack against the enemy position. An additional platoon of tanks soon arrived to further support the assault because Sisson estimated that the opposing force consisted of at least a full company of infantry supported by mortars and machine guns. By 1830 hours, the German pocket was finally vanquished, with 50 enemy troops killed or wounded in the process and another 30 taken prisoner.

The bitter fighting that afternoon was again remembered by Staff Sergeant Ehlers, who explained, "We were in an unintended position at this time. I was deploying my men on another hedgerow that happened to have Germans on each side of us, and another in front of us—on three sides. Captain Folk asked us to withdraw, but I knew that we would be picked off if we withdrew one by one, so I stood and fired in a semi-circle with my M-1, trying to keep the Germans pinned down while the squad pulled out. When I turned and saw some Germans putting in a machine gun at the corner of the hedgerow to my right, I picked them off, but got hit in the back. It spun me around, and I saw a German soldier behind me in the hedgerow, so I shot him. After I got up, I saw my BAR man was wounded, so I pulled him off the battlefield and then went back and got the BAR because it was the only automatic weapon we had in the squad."[17]

Staff Sergeant Walter D. Ehlers was recognized for his heroic actions. His Medal of Honor citation expanded on his extraordinary bravery at the time, stating [his] "intrepid leadership, indomitable courage, and fearless aggressiveness in the face of overwhelming enemy forces served as an inspiration to others."[18]

Not far from where Ehlers was fighting, Company K Staff Sergeant Arthur F. DeFranzo was leading his squad when one of his scouts advanced across an open field and was hit by enemy fire.* DeFranzo raced into the field, and although he was wounded at the time, brought his scout back to safety.

Refusing aid, Sergeant DeFranzo continued to lead the advance toward the enemy. In the face of two separate machine gunners that were constantly firing on him, DeFranzo kept charging forward, firing uninterruptedly, and silencing each emplacement. Again wounded during this thrust, he nevertheless pressed on until he was within 100 yards of the next enemy position, waving his men forward.

By the time his men reached him, Staff Sergeant DeFranzo was down with another severe wound, but he courageously picked himself up and ran forward,

---

*In 1944, each US Army rifle squad had two men assigned as scouts.

leading his men until he was hit yet again. As he started to fall, his last act was to throw several grenades at the remaining enemy position in front of him, completely destroying its gun. For his singular actions in stalling an attack that would have delayed Company K's assault that day, Staff Sergeant Arthur F. DeFranzo was also awarded the Medal of Honor, posthumously.[19]

Soon after DeFranzo had subdued opposition to his company's front, the 3rd Battalion reached Vaubadon where it began establishing defensive positions. It lost 4 killed, 15 wounded, and 3 men missing in the day's combat.[20]

This village was perched atop a cliff overlooking the Drôme River and a chateau was built into its high stream bank. Vaubadon had been a German corps headquarters a few days earlier; now abandoned, however, it was available to Lieutenant Colonel Sisson for his command post. Having posting two 57mm guns from the battalion Anti-Tank Platoon on the road fronting the chateau's large lawn, Sisson's headquarters party then settled in for the evening while his men in their bivouacs were reunited with their clothing, blankets, and bags that had finally come up from the beach. Across the deep river valley from the chateau was Balleroy, the 3rd Battalion's next objective.

On 11 June, the 2nd and 3rd Battalions continued carrying the battle to the enemy, while 1st Battalion went into regimental reserve. Lieutenant Hess's Company I was first sent forward on the right flank to make contact with the 2nd Infantry Division before the rest of the 3rd Battalion advanced on Balleroy. The 2nd Battalion was ordered to send a reinforced company to occupy the Bois de Baugy at the edge of Forêt de Cerisy before the rest of the battalion occupied this area. Williamson selected Company E for this mission. Given the urgency about the move expressed by the Regimental Commander, Company H's jeeps were unloaded and Penick's men used them as personnel carriers. The convoy pulled out onto the road to Bois de Baugy at 1515 hours. The riflemen motored swiftly to the objective, meeting only limited resistance before they reached the woods just before dark.

The rest of the battalion started out along the same roadway late in the afternoon, but to everyone's surprise no enemy was encountered. "We drove along the highway as if we were joy-riding back in the States," Lieutenant Downing remembered of that afternoon.[21]

Balleroy initially proved to be a tough nut to crack for Company I when it attacked early in the afternoon, but the Germans withdrew and Company K occupied the town by 1500 hours.

The rest of the 3rd Battalion quickly moved across the Drôme River and then joined in Balleroy's occupation by early evening.

"The population of Balleroy was joyous of their liberation," Lieutenant Franklyn Johnson recalled of that day. "They tossed roses at us and waved homemade US flags."

Sisson's men had little time for celebration, however, because they were ordered to take up positions to the west of Balleroy for the night. Johnson noted, "This was one of the strangest spots my guns were ever emplaced. For a thousand yards on either side of the road great double lines of aged firs crisscrossed straight and regular in breathtaking beauty. The rows created verdant tunnels above intersecting dirt lanes, and square fields of grain extended between the rows. My guess was that it was once the site of a royal hunting lodge, a country place of nobility."[22]

By now, V Corps had finally gained the ground essential to secure the beachhead taken on D-day. The advance, led by the 18th Infantry Regiment, had carried over twelve miles inland. The right flank of V Corps now rested securely on the Vire-Elle river line and Major General Gerow was ready to link up with VII Corps to the west.

The principal objective in the next phase was to secure the left flank of V Corps by seizing the crossroads town of Caumont. Gerow assigned that mission to Major General Huebner, who in turn directed the 26th Infantry Regiment to take Caumont, with the 18th Infantry Regiment seizing the high ground west of the town. The 16th Infantry Regiment, still reorganizing from its losses on D-day, remained in reserve. To the west of the 1st Infantry Division, the 2nd and 29th Infantry Divisions were ordered to seize objectives south of the Forêt de Cerisy and the Elle River. The 2nd Armored Division, as corps reserve, would be held in readiness while the infantry divisions continued their move southward.

V Corps' upcoming attack was closely tied to the plans of the adjacent British XXX Corps that day. In hard fighting seven kilometers east of the Bois de Baugy on 11 June, the British 50th (Northumbrian) Division failed to dislodge elements of *Panzer Lehr Division* from their positions between Lingevres and Tilly-sur-Seulles. The British offensive was to be renewed the next day, with the aim of outflanking the entire German defense in the Caen area. That would be accomplished by sending a brigade of the 7th Armoured Division on a daring raid to seize the crossroads at Villiers Bocage, 25 kilometers southwest of Tilly-sur-Seulles and 10 kilometers east of Caumont. The American V Corps' adjoining advance would aid the 7th Armoured Division by threatening enemy efforts to prevent the British from securing the roads at Villiers Bocage.

In preparation for the assault, Lieutenant Colonel Williamson joined with Sisson and York and met with Colonel Smith just before midnight on June 11/12. After Smith briefed them on the Regiment's continuing mission, each of the battalion commanders met with their company commanders to designate specific units tasks and by 0300 hours the attack plan had been disseminated within the 18th Infantry Regiment.

The 1st Battalion was assigned to the right on the LD; the 2nd Battalion would attack abreast with them, while the 3rd Battalion remained in reserve.

When the leading battalions attacked as scheduled at 0600, they were hit by enemy artillery, but the rifle companies nevertheless continued moving through the shelling all morning until they reached the first phase line.

The 1st Battalion was still advancing through small arms fire at noontime when they received more artillery fire, and at 1300 hours the situation appeared to be changing for the worse when reports arrived, saying that four German tanks faced the battalion's front. York quickly sent a patrol out to investigate, but when no enemy attack followed, he ordered his men to continue moving south.

At a little after 1400 hours his men captured seven German paratroopers, prompting York to request permission to keep moving toward le Bisson. By then, Regimental signal crews had laid sufficient telephone wire to permit Colonel Smith to talk with all three of his battalion commanders, and they had all agreed that only light screening forces were offering opposition to the Regiment's assignment.

With evidence thus mounting that the Germans were preparing for a general withdrawal, Colonel Smith gave York permission to continue his advance, and by dark, two rifle companies from the 1st Battalion had moved over two and a half miles more and taken up positions near la Vacquerie, le Haye, and le Bisson.

With these three villages in his possession, York ordered his companies to establish roadblocks along the main St. Lô-Caen highway, and a hundred mines were brought up to place hasty minefields in front of the roadblocks. While reconnoitering the newly-won ground the next day, York captured two enemy scout cars and personally captured a number of Germans.

Maintaining its position on the flank of the 1st Battalion, the 2nd Battalion reached Cormolain (two kilometers northwest of Caumont) at noon on 12 June. After securing the town, Lieutenant Colonel Williamson ordered his companies to advance to the high ground just west of Caumont and by 1730 hours all of the 2nd Battalion companies occupied positions near Villeneuve. With the 2nd Battalion now blocking the two main highways leading west, any Germans seeking to withdraw from Caumont toward St. Lô would only be able to do so after trying to fight their way through Williamson's men.

Williamson established his command post in a farmhouse on a broad field. At dusk, faint columns of smoke could be seen near Caumont, but it was nearly midnight before reports arrived that the 26th Regimental Combat Team was on the outskirts of that town.

The 3rd Battalion, 18th Infantry Regiment finally left its reserve position late that same morning, and after passing through drab, unoccupied Cormolain in mid-afternoon, they bypassed Breziers in the gathering darkness. The battalion established defensive positions near a network of gravel roads, orchards, and fields just to the west of the 1st Battalion. After ordering a platoon from Company L to cover a slight gap along the battalion boundary, Sisson set up his command post overlooking a stream in a shallow valley on the Regiment's extreme right flank.

By evening, the entire combat team had completed its four-mile advance to the Caumont-St. Lô highway. There, verbal orders to halt were received from Division, as the Regiment's steady progress placed it two miles farther south than elements of the 2nd Infantry Division on their right.

Later that evening, patrols from the 26th Infantry, probing toward the center of Caumont, found that it was held only by a small reconnaissance unit of the *2nd*

Panzer Division. Shortly after midnight, an attempt was made to capture the town, but the enemy reconnaissance unit had been reinforced by engineers and more troops from its parent unit. Although the Americans were unable to seize the town that night, Caumont fell to the 26th Infantry Regiment the next day.

The British Second Army almost immediately tried to take advantage of the success of the 1st Infantry Division's move to Caumont by launching an attack to outflank the western end of the German line stretching east to Caen. They sent a brigade-size armored column to capture the key crossroads at Villers-Bocage, seeking to be in a position to threaten the rear of the German forces defending Tilly-sur-Seulles. Protected to the west by 1st Infantry Division units at Caumont, by late afternoon on 13 June the British 22nd Armoured Brigade first succeeded in entering Villers-Bocage virtually unopposed. Elements of *SS-Heavy Tank Battalion 101* immediately launched a counterattack, destroying a number of tanks of the 4th County of London Yeomanry.

With the situation in Villers-Bocage rapidly becoming unstable, the British 7th Armoured Division withdrew to defensive positions two miles northeast of Caumont. As a result, both Tilly-sur-Seulles and Villers-Bocage remained in German hands, where for the next several weeks these towns anchored the western end of a defensive line across the Caen-Orne Valley sector.

A week after landing, the 18th Infantry Regiment was now 23 miles inland. British misfortune at Villers-Bocage and difficult resistance encountered by the 2nd Infantry Division resulted in the 18th and 26th Regimental Combat Teams being in an exposed salient centered on Caumont. Fortunately for the 1st Infantry Division, the German *Seventh Army* was too occupied defending Caen and St. Lô to launch a full-scale counterattack against the newly-won Allied positions. Conversely, the US First Army was focused on Cherbourg, which meant that the Division would not be called upon to conduct significant offensive operations for the next six weeks. As Captain Marshall of the 32nd FA sagely noted, "We were simply ordered to dig in until the 2nd [Infantry] Division on our right and the British Second Army on our left could catch up."[23]

All was not entirely quiet during this period. The Regimental S-1 Journal for the last two weeks of June noted that plenty of activity took place in the Caumont sector. Patrols were dispatched daily by both sides and numerous skirmishes resulted.[24] During this period, artillery and mortar fire were often used to saturate enemy positions, and interdictory fires were also used each night to stifle German replacements and supplies. Enemy strength opposing the 18th Infantry Regiment at the time was estimated at between 1,000 and 1,500 troops.[25]

All routes of approach into the 1st Infantry Division's main line of resistance were heavily protected, and many units were ordered to remain on alert throughout the short late spring nights, with the men sleeping during some of the much longer daylight hours.*

---

*Northern France experiences about 17 hours of daylight each day during this time of year.

On 19 June, Colonel Smith decided to reconnoiter the enemy's rear areas by sending out three small patrols. When reports of increased German activity came in, Smith ordered the 1st Battalion's outpost line extended 1,000 yards south to la Haye, and west to le Bisson.

Bitter engagements followed, particularly near la Haye, where the Germans repeatedly attacked two positions held by a platoon of Company B, led by Lieutenant Bobbie E. Brown, and a platoon from Company A, under Lieutenant Jesse R. Miller, respectively. During one fight the next day, Brown's platoon launched a preemptive assault against a like-sized enemy force, killing or capturing 20 Germans.

Due to generally poor ground-level observation in the Norman hedgerow terrain, a church steeple in la Vacquerie served as a forward observation post for the 1st Battalion. On 23 June, the Germans avenged the loss of a tank to bazooka crews from the 1st Battalion by shooting the spire off the church.[26] Fortunately, the 1st Battalion commander was not in the steeple at the time.

Although 3rd Battalion remained in reserve during most of June, its soldiers dutifully shouldered their fair share of the burden by sending patrols across the Drôme River to their front and to the village of Bréziers on their right flank.

On 25 June, a cleverly-disguised enemy force allegedly wearing captured American helmets and uniforms that resembled GI field uniforms took Company K under fire near Vidouville, and both sides sustained casualties. Two days later, the enemy repeated the same ruse, this time wearing field jackets and helmets taken from Company K prisoners. When a patrol from Company I encountered the Germans, they hesitated to engage what appeared to be a group of fellow Americans and instead sustained several casualties when the Germans opened fire first.[27]

On 26 June, the 3rd Battalion commander ordered Lieutenant Franklyn Johnson to conduct a patrol toward a suspected enemy pocket near Vidouville. Sisson had heard that there was an enemy tank in that location and directed Johnson to knock it out. Johnson departed shortly afterwards with a green lieutenant and a bazooka team. They approached to within a couple of hedgerows of the panzer's suspected position, but were ambushed.

As Johnson turned toward the new officer, he was hit in the back and fell, bleeding profusely. His patrol departed to get aid, leaving him alone. Long before they could return, however, the Germans found Johnson and carried him back to their lines.

The following day, Lieutenant Johnson was operated on by the Germans in the field and then transported to a hospital in Rennes that was manned by captured Allied doctors under German supervision.[28]

Colonel Smith ended the Regimental journal for June 1944 by noting, "[The Regiment] inflicted severe casualties on the enemy. Thrusts into our positions were successfully repulsed with no loss of ground. The Regiment, at present, is intact and awaiting any future missions it might be called upon to undertake."[29]

June had been an historic month in the 18th Infantry Regiment's already long World War II combat record, starting with its key role on D-day. It had also been a costly month. While only one officer had been killed in action—Captain Fitch on Omaha Beach—77 enlisted men had been killed since the landings. Also, 18 officers and 406 enlisted men had been wounded in action and evacuated. A total of 85 soldiers were listed as missing in action, to include Lieutenant Johnson, who recovered from his wounds and was liberated a month later before being sent back to the States for additional medical treatment. On the bright side, the Regiment had captured two German officers and 320 enlisted men.[30]

As the month of July began, Colonel Smith was pleased with the combat performance of his men, particularly noting the increased proficiency they showed in patrolling. "All in all," he wrote, "Our situation had afforded an excellent training period from which a wealth of knowledge was being obtained in the art of land warfare. Although constantly subjected to heavy mortar and artillery fire, the state of morale was extremely high."[31]

Major General Gerow visited the 18th Infantry Regiment on 8 July. Following an inspection of all of the Regiment's defensive positions, he reported that he was quite satisfied with them and the manner with which the entire combat team had performed since coming ashore.

Four days later, Colonel Smith announced a number of changes to the Regiment's command structure. Major Elisha Peckham, who had returned to the 2nd Battalion after treatment for the wounds he suffered on D-day that night, was promoted to command of the 3rd Battalion. Captain Carter left Company D, which he had commanded since the landings in Arzew in North Africa, to become the 3rd Battalion's Executive Officer. Major Frank Colacicco became the new 2nd Battalion Executive Officer, and Captain Murphy relinquished command of Company H for a well-deserved promotion to become the battalion's Operations Officer (S-3). Lieutenant Colonel John Williamson retained his command of the 2nd Battalion.

To their bittersweet surprise, officers and men of the 1st Battalion saw Lieutenant Colonel York depart to assume command of the 83rd Infantry Division's 331st Infantry Regiment, newly arrived in Normandy. His departure ended his longtime association with the 18th Infantry Regiment.

York's transfer ended a loyal and emotional bond that had been formed by his competent and committed style of command. Reports indicated "there were few dry eyes upon his departure, but the soldiers who served under him were nevertheless pleased that his efforts had been rewarded. The name and spirit of YORK will always live among the ranks of the 1st Battalion and the 'old timers' of tomorrow will swap many yarns of his famous exploits on the battlefield."[32] It would have been difficult for any man to assume command of the 1st Battalion under these circumstances, but Lieutenant Colonel Sisson was transferred from the 3rd Battalion to fill the vacuum left by York's departure. This certainly eased the transition for Colonel Smith, for he knew that Sisson was equally respected, well known, and a much better choice than any replacement from outside the Regiment.

On 14 July, which marked the 18th Infantry Regiment's thirty-ninth day of continuous operations since landing on Omaha Beach, the newly-arrived 5th Infantry Division's 10th Infantry Regiment relieved Colonel Smith's men in their positions on the Caumont line. The relief took place one platoon at a time, so that it didn't leave the entire regimental position unprepared to repel an attack. When a new platoon from the 10th Infantry Regiment arrived at a designated rendezvous point, they were guided to a position being held by the line companies where the outgoing lieutenant briefed the incoming officer on the position and overall situation. Vehicular transportation was arranged for the departing units, and by the following morning all of the outgoing companies were resting at Bricqueville-sur-Mer on the coast.

Among apple orchards overlooking the sea, the men wrote letters home, cleaned up, washed their clothes, and generally enjoyed the rare freedom of not being under enemy attack. The 9th Infantry Division—fellow veterans of the North African and Sicilian campaigns—sent a large stock of *Wehrmacht* liquor and French wines to the Regiment while they were in Bricqueville, sharing their celebration of the recent seizure of Cherbourg. A truckload of the captured booty also arrived at Colonel Smith's headquarters at about the same time the July official liquor ration arrived from First Army, sending morale sky high. As one lieutenant noted somewhat tongue in cheek, however, "This set up was too good to last."[33]

The overall progress of the Allied forces after the initial landings in France had been slow largely because of the difficult hedgerow terrain throughout Normandy. Casualties were high and daily advances had been measured in yards. The use of armor for dashes around and behind the German lines was generally unsuccessful due to enemy's many prepared defenses. By 18 July, however, the First Army had seized Cherbourg, captured the vital road junction of St. Lô, and cleared the Normandy Peninsula generally to a line north of the St. Lô-Lessay road. The XIX Corps, employing the 9th and 30th Infantry Divisions, also had secured ground along this road, thus allowing the First Army to mount the breakthrough operation codenamed COBRA.

The First Army plan for Operation COBRA, the breakout from Normandy, called for Major General J. Lawton "Lightning Joe" Collins' VII Corps to make the main effort in the center, between St. Lô and le Mesnil-Vigot. At the same time, the mission of VIII Corps on the right, as well as XIX and V Corps on the left, was to conduct supporting attacks and maintain strong pressure on the enemy while preventing the Germans from withdrawing or reinforcing units facing VII Corps.

To carry out its mission, VII Corps was arrayed in two echelons. A breakthrough force composed of the 9th, 4th (less Combat Team 22), and 30th Infantry Divisions formed the first echelon. These divisions, arrayed respectively from west to east, occupied a five-mile section of front opposite the *Panzer Lehr Division*.

Coiled behind this force in concealed assembly areas was the exploitation echelon composed of the 1st Infantry Division [with Combat Command B (CCB), 3rd Armored attached], the rest of the 3rd Armored Division, and the 2nd Armored Division (with Combat Team 22 attached).

The VII Corps plan called for a three-stage operation: Phase I consisted of a 1,850-plane saturation bombardment of the designated breakthrough "strip," measured as some 7,000 yards wide and 2,500 yards in depth. Following the aerial bombardment, Phase II called for the first echelon of three infantry divisions to open a gap in the German main defensive line, hold the gap open, and clear routes of advance for forces behind them. Phase III of COBRA would take place when the gap in the enemy main defensive line was secured and routes leading to the south were cleared and blocked. At that time the exploitation force would quickly advance to the south until it reached Marigny. It would then shift its avenue of advance to the west, securing a blocking position along the coast north of Coutances. The intended result of this bold maneuver was to encircle all enemy units facing VIII Corps while unhinging the westernmost end of the weakened German defensive line in Normandy. When the German forces at Coutances were shattered, VIII Corps would then have an open road to Brittany, free of Normandy's surly, claustrophobic hedgerow bonds and through the crossroads of Avranches to the south.[34]

"To make certain the blitz would get off to a fast start," General Bradley recalled in planning the outbreak, "I called on the Big Red One to pace it."[35] In turn, General Huebner decided to lead the attack with the 18th Regimental Combat Team in concert with Combat Command B, 3rd Armored Division.

During the night of 20/21 July, the Combat Team 18 moved to a new assembly area near St. Jean de Daye, where the men spent the time preparing, loading, and reconnoitering from the assembly area to the breakthrough gap in the 9th Infantry Division's zone of operations. Commanders at levels down to company were then taken to mosquito-infested forward observation posts to observe the area that they would be attacking.

The 1st Infantry Division planned to pass through the 9th Infantry Division along two roads that the latter unit was to make passable. General Huebner envisioned a strike in depth spearheaded by CCB, with the main body of the Division configured in columns of combat teams trailing each other closely. The specific order of march would be: CCB, 4th Cavalry Reconnaissance Squadron, Combat Team 18, Combat Team 16, then Combat Team 26 (minus its 2nd Battalion).

CCB's mission was to move rapidly to seize, organize for defense, and hold successively-designated objectives until relieved by elements of Combat Team 18. These objectives included the high ground near Camprond (four miles northeast of Coutances), the high ground near Monthuchon (two miles north of Coutances), and Coutances itself. After these objectives had been secured, CCB was to be prepared to move to the north along the Coutances-Periers road and destroy enemy forces in its zone of action.

Northern France

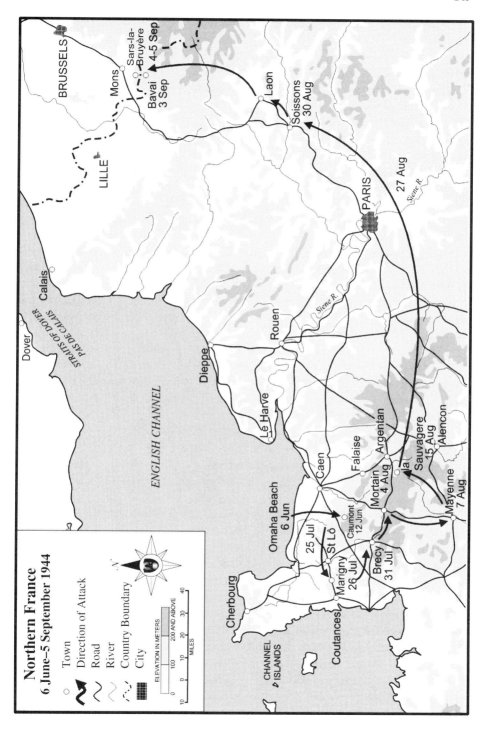

Combat Team 18 would follow CCB to Camprond where it would relieve elements of the 3rd Armored Division with a reinforced battalion that would hold in place until it was relieved by Combat Team 16. Colonel Smith's remaining two battalions would continue rapidly behind CCB to the next objective (Monthuchon), relieve Combat Command elements occupying that area, organize the ground for all-around defense, and prevent encircled enemy forces north of Coutances from breaking out to the south.

The artillery elements of Combat Teams 16 and 26 were to support the initial advance of Combat Team 18 from forward positions in the area vacated by the 9th Infantry Division. In addition, two corps artillery battalions of 155mm howitzers had been designated to reinforce the fires of the 1st Infantry Division. In anticipation of enemy resistance at Marigny (four miles east of Camprond), an aerial bombardment was planned. Four fighter-bombers would then circle the leading elements of CCB to provide "armored column cover" for the advancing tankers.

The date for COBRA at first had been set for 21 July. It was successively postponed to 22, 24, and 25 July, however, because weather was unsuitable for the aerial bombardment to precede the ground attack. H-hour for the breakthrough was finally confirmed for 1100 hours on 25 July when fair weather with little or no fog was predicted for that day and the next, as well as the subsequent period of 27 to 31 July.

During the delay, General Huebner devoted his efforts to prepare the 1st Infantry Division for the upcoming operation while Colonel Smith refined his own tactical plans. Lieutenant Colonel Sisson's 1st Battalion was chosen to lead the Regiment's advance, augmented by a battalion of tanks from Combat Command B of the 3rd Armored. That armored unit had just fitted all tanks with a modification known as the "Culin Device"—a set of steel prongs welded to the front hull of the tank which protruded forward like multiple tusks. This field-expedient modification allowed tanks literally to bull through the Norman hedgerows, rather than expose their thinly-protected undersides when crossing the tree-crowned earthen banks.

In addition to the battalion from the 3rd Armored Division, the CT 18 would include many of its habitually supporting attachments, to include the 32nd FA Battalion; Company B, 634th Tank Destroyer Battalion; and Company B, 745th Tank Battalion. Lieutenant Colonel Peckham's 3rd Battalion was to follow closely behind the 1st Battalion, while the 2nd Battalion initially remained in reserve.

The dawn skies on 25 July were indeed sunny and clear as forecasted, allaying any concerns that COBRA would be cancelled again. The 18th Combat Team completed its approach march to a forward assembly area near the villages of la Pilerie, la Cullourie, and Sadot early that morning without incident, and all units positioned themselves just north of the St. Lô-Periers road. Lieutenant John Downing, standing on a slight knoll overlooking la Cillourie remembered, "At mid-morning we heard the dull, persistent roar of plane motors and saw the large armada of bombers come over high in the sky. They traveled slowly and inexorably with an appearance of devastating power toward their objective. We all stood motionless in a farmyard watching them. Black puffs of antiaircraft fire dotted the sky around them. Far in the distance they started dropping their bombs. We could see a slight haze rising from the impact area. We could hear the faint rumble of explosions. Although we could not see any of the destruction they were causing, the quantity of planes was an awe-inspiring sight."[36]

Captain Carter, with the 3rd Battalion command group, was equally impressed. "The area we were assembled in was rather low and saturated with water," he recalled years later. "When the bombing started, the ground began to shake like jelly. When standing, your trouser legs jumped up and down. When you sat, your body shook. Planes were coming from the north as far as you could see. They kept coming and dropping bombs and we kept shaking. We thought the Army Air Corps was never going to finish the bombing."[37] To Chaplain Edward Rogers, who was in the 1st Battalion bivouac at the time, it looked the same. "Wave after wave passed over us," he remembered. "That parade of death through the sky lasted an hour and a half. With field glasses we could see the bombs leave planes as they followed the smoke markers of the leading planes."

Even General Huebner, a wounded combat veteran of World War I and thus intimately familiar with front-line duty, said the bombing was one of the most terrifying things he had ever seen.[38]

What was not apparent to Huebner was that the air attack was dealing death and destruction indiscriminately, on friend and foe alike. Errant bombs hit the 30th Infantry Division area, as well as 9th Infantry Division troops and supporting corps elements. Despite the losses, all of the assault battalions eventually moved out with the exception of the 3rd Battalion, 47th Infantry Regiment. Disorganized by losses to its command group, this battalion's mission was taken over by the 1st Battalion, 39th Infantry Regiment, while the bulk of the 9th Infantry Division not hit in the bombing runs moved ahead against moderate resistance. The advance of the nearby 4th and 30th Infantry Divisions was held up by heavy fire from automatic weapons and artillery reported to be 105mm and 150mm, or typical German division artillery. By late afternoon, however, elements of the 9th Infantry Division were within reach of the village of Montreuil and they had also gained the area north of Hebecrevon by 2100 hours.

The 30th Infantry Division avoided the heavy German artillery by maneuvering right into the zone of the 9th Infantry Division, a move that enabled two battalions of the 119th Infantry Regiment to advance rapidly to their objective. After first flanking to the west and advancing along a creek north of Hebecrevon, the 30th Division's 120th Infantry Regiment then stopped and was unable to make additional progress.

By the end of the day, the 4th Infantry Division's 8th Infantry Regiment had gained the most ground (three and one half kilometers), while some units of the 9th Infantry Division advanced as far as the 30th Infantry Division, generally pushing its line forward some two kilometers. Although the enemy was being forced back all along the line, his front was still firm and there was no indication of withdrawal.[39]

At VII Corps headquarters, Major General Collins was now faced with the difficult decision of whether to commit his exploitation force as scheduled. If a penetration were achieved, he did not want to give the Germans time to recover and establish positions to block 1st Infantry Division's advance through Marigny. He considered that if the German main line of resistance remained unbroken by nightfall, premature commitment of the Division and attached CCB would create additional congestion and confusion, leaving VII Corps ripe for a counterattack. Absent any apparent coordination in the German defenses as the day wore on, however, Collins decided an aggressive tack was worth the gamble. On the afternoon of 25 July, he directed his exploitation element to attack the following morning.

At 0700 hours on 26 July, Combat Command B, followed by Combat Team 18, crossed their line of departure and headed south toward Marigny. Not long afterward, CCB was fired upon from an enemy hedgerow strongpoint just north of Montreuil, a mere 1,200 yards south of the start line. However, CCB and CT 18 were only held up until pinpoint bombing and strafing missions neutralized the strongpoint. They bypassed another pocket of resistance in this vicinity and left Williamson's 2nd Battalion to subdue it so that the advance of the main column would not be delayed.[40]

The 1st Battalion was advancing cross-country just to the west and parallel to the road-bound column of CCB when the first heavy firefight broke out. Company A, now under the command of Captain Scott-Smith, was moving ahead of Company B, now commanded by Lieutenant Bobbie Brown. The former commander of that company, Captain Cameron, was now leading the battalion heavy weapons company, which he had taken over when Captain Carter became the 3rd Battalion executive officer. Cameron's Company D, which was trailing behind the leading rifle companies, was followed by the 3rd Battalion headquarters personnel. Portending difficulty, after moving just 600 yards against scattered resistance, Company A ran into heavy artillery, mortar, machine-gun, and small arms fire.

According to the Regimental Operations Officer (S-3), Major Middleworth, "[This] pocket of resistance occurred because the 47th Infantry had not cleaned it out."[41] Company A suffered several casualties in the melee, but soon inflicted heavy losses on the enemy, killing a number, and capturing 14. Reacting to the developing situation, Brown's Company B was employed on the right of Scott-Smith's men as the fighting grew even fiercer, but the two companies continued advancing slowly through the afternoon, abreast of each other. Company B eventually killed 12 Germans while capturing 36 others over the next several hours.

To make matters even more difficult that day, the 1st Battalion could not make effective use of their supporting tanks because the bomb-blasted terrain rendered armor nearly ineffectual. Both Companies A and B were being blasted by German indirect fires by early afternoon, and every other hedgerow was found to contain a stubborn pocket of resistance. Major Middleworth recorded that the 1st Battalion also received scattered fire from enemy 105mm artillery, indicating it came from south of the St. Lô-Periers. He noted that "it was the heaviest the Regiment had experienced in France."

Ground observation was limited all day from the smoke caused by the bombings and other debris, thus restricting Captain Cameron's mortars from contributing to the fires of the 32nd FA Battalion. As one participant noted, "It was strictly a doughboy's show for the entire day with bullet, bayonet, grenade, and bazookas paving the way for the continued division advance."[42]

As a result, 1st Battalion casualties were heavy, with two having a profound effect on its commanding officers. Captain Marshall, who had earlier served as artillery liaison with Lieutenant Colonel Sisson in the 3rd Battalion, explained the circumstances of the battalion commander's near-death experience late that afternoon:

> I had been very worried about our infantry colonel's disregard for his own safety. As the German screening forces allowed us to more rapidly advance, Lieutenant Colonel Sisson would put two companies abreast with some 180 men each and spread out, then keep one company and the heavy weapons company to the rear. As the two companies abreast fanned out across the fields, they tended to lose contact with each other, especially if a firefight broke out at one corner. Meanwhile, the colonel, his staff, my radio section, and I would follow up the middle. First the colonel would hear by radio of a hold up on the right, and we'd dash off that way, then on the left, and we'd trot back. It was apparent our zigzags as staff were taking us through fields and orchards never covered by rifle-toting doughfeet. In my mind, at any wall we might stumble across a German machine-gun team, and we'd all be killed.[43]

Marshall's concerns proved to be correct. Lieutenant Colonel Sisson and his staff had stopped at the open corner of a field to consult their maps that afternoon. A German soldier was in a nearby hedgerow and he fired a burst of 9mm rounds from his MP 40 machine pistol (submachinegun), wounding Sisson and killing Captain Cameron as he tried to pull Sisson away from the incoming fire.

Walter Smith of the 32nd Field Artillery was near Lieutenant Colonel Sisson when this incident happened. Smith was returning through an open field and had just taken cover next to two other soldiers when the fire erupted. "I just got between them when this guy opens up with his burp gun," he recalled. "I think he hit Lieutenant Colonel Sisson four times, and one shot went right through Captain Cameron's temple. The shooting stopped and we were putting first aid packs on the colonel. He leaned toward me and said quietly, 'How's Cameron?' I had to tell him he got it through the head." Sisson was hurriedly evacuated and Lieutenant Colonel Henry G. Learnard took command.[44]

CCB had been making slow progress down the roadway because of the many bomb craters it encountered on the afternoon of 26 July. By 1440 hours, its tanks finally arrived at a point one kilometer north of Marigny, where they veered west, bypassing the town as they headed for Camprond. Combat Team 18 had received an incorrect report that CCB had captured Marigny, but as Major Middleworth noted later, "Unknown to the 1st Battalion, there were numerous enemy both in the town itself and on the high ground to the south of the town." When Learnard's men bumped into the unexpected resistance, they sideslipped to the east around Marigny and later arrived at the tiny village of St. Benoir. Major Middleworth later noted, "I thought the battalion was on its objective, while it was [now] actually in an area assigned to the 4th Division."[45]

The error was discovered by early evening, and Colonel Smith ordered the 1st Battalion to move to the high ground near Cametours, 2,000 yards to the northeast. As the men tried to bypass Marigny, however, they ran into German forces that had taken up positions in the hillsides, and they had to cut to the north to bypass the enemy pocket.

Fighting continued after nightfall and it wasn't until midnight that Cametours was finally secured. Peckham's 3rd Battalion, which had trailed behind CCB all afternoon, also discovered the "hard way" that enemy forces occupied Marigny. One platoon from Company K probed the town at midnight and they soon found themselves ambushed and then trapped, only finally to succeed in untangling and returning to battalion bivouac before first light.

As 26 July wound down, evidence of tough enemy opposition mounted. Colonel Smith now realized that the Germans in Marigny would have to be overcome or forced to withdraw before the 1st Infantry Division continued its advance toward Coutances. Accordingly, he planned to conduct a coordinated attack the following morning using the 1st and 3rd Battalions. The 1st Battalion was still some distance east of Marigny by day's end, so the brunt of the initial assault would fall solely upon Peckham.

At 0300 hours on 27 July after getting this assignment, he called his company commanders to his command post. Peckham explained that Hess's Company I was to spearhead the drive by moving down a trail paralleling the road between Marigny and the village of la Bosnardière, where he would attack the Germans from the northeast of town. Captain Folk's Company L would then advance along the high ground east of Marigny until reaching a position where his men could support the attack. Once the town was secured, Company I would clear the high ground south of town that permitted German observation of a road leading to Camprond. The main assault would begin at 0700 hours following a brief artillery preparation.

Captain Hess was provided with maps, aerial photographs of the area, and other information about the town before he attacked. The aerial photographs revealed that the entire area was made up of small fields and orchards, bordered by hedgerows, that provided excellent enemy cover and concealment. The French civilians near the town helped identify enemy observation posts, and they also provided Hess with information about the terrain and an estimate of the enemy force defending Marigny. He learned that the forces he faced were combined elements of the *5th Parachute Division* and *Grenadier Regiment 942, 353rd Infantry Division*, numbering about 400 men. Both German units were reported to be well dug in on the outskirts of the town, and defended several key central buildings.

Hess's company was at full strength at the time, his men's morale was high, and they were well supplied. Company I also was augmented by a platoon of tanks from Company B, 745th Tank Battalion; the 81mm Mortar Platoon and a heavy machine-gun platoon from Company M; 32nd Field Artillery forward observers; combat engineers; and a platoon of 57mm antitank guns.

Hess's 1st Platoon, under the command of Lieutenant John C. Conway, had the toughest mission. They had been designated to go into Marigny ahead of the rest of the company, search the town for snipers, and then to occupy the town square.

Thirty minutes before H-hour, that is, at first light, the 32nd FA began to shell Marigny and the surrounding high ground. Hess' men then jumped off in platoon formation moving along both sides of the trail they would use to go past the line of departure, with tanks rumbling down the middle, followed by Company M's heavy machine guns. Conway's platoon quickly reached the northeastern edge of town, then advanced to the center of Marigny, encountering only moderate resistance. They captured an 88mm gun, complete with crew, leading Conway to believe the Germans were not going to put up much resistance before surrendering. Another of his rifle platoons located only six Germans as they swept through the southern part of town.

By 0745 hours, Marigny was in American hands without much of a fight. Hess then sent his 3rd Platoon to occupy high ground south of the town that looked back on Marigny along the Camprond road . . . where the fate of Company I was about to change.

The lead squad, led by Staff Sergeant Jack Carter, first crossed a stream just south of the village without incident. The German defenders allowed the platoon's accompanying lead tank to approach within 75 yards of hidden defensive positions before engaging it with a panzerfaust. Fortunately, the Sherman was not hit and it crew hurriedly pulled it back as nearby riflemen sought cover.

At the same time, a second squad deployed left and took cover in a small ditch; then a third squad moved to the right rear where every man was pinned down by fierce enemy fire. It took three hours before the 3rd Platoon could work its way back to the stream.

Hearing the commotion, Hess ordered Lieutenant Conway and his men to assist the 3rd Platoon. He rushed his men in columns of squads toward the stream where they also came under heavy enemy fire. Unable to advance without incurring unacceptable casualties, Conway then sent a rifle squad to the right in an attempt to outflank the most dangerous German machine-gun positions, which appeared to be located in a sunken trail in a hedgerow. He also sent a squad to the left, but those men were immediately pinned down. With the movement of their supporting tanks limited by a single narrow trail covered by panzerfausts, none of Company I's platoons could make any headway against the German position.

At noontime, Peckham directed Company L to launch an attack against the high ground in support of Captain Hess's men. Folk's riflemen, however, were stopped when they reached a point just to the left of Hess's scattered positions at the foot of the enemy-occupied hill. Captain Russell's Company K had been in reserve all morning, but Peckham now had no choice but to order it to move to the southern outskirts of Marigny and take up additional defensive positions near Company I's pinned-down men.

With CCB continuing on to Camprond, Colonel Smith now realized that he could not commit his entire Regiment behind the tankers because of the developing fight. Accordingly, he ordered the 2nd Battalion, which had already started out for Camprond earlier that morning, to bypass it to the west. Company F, leading the column, was already receiving "overs" (bullets which missed their intended targets and continued on a ballistic trajectory) from the fight the 3rd Battalion was experiencing on the hillside south of Marigny. To avoid casualties and becoming involved in this fight, Company F's CO first led his men through fields to the north of the village, and then he swung southwesterly through rough brush to work his way back onto the roadway.

At noontime on that intermittently rainy day, Lieutenant Colonel Williamson received a message from Regiment instructing him to proceed with all haste to his objective. Colonel Smith, now realizing that the fighting at Marigny had seriously delayed the 1st Infantry Division's overall timetable, knew that he must secure Camprond to close the jaws of the retreating German units now south of Periers.

Williamson was told to ignore security to his flanks and rear, in part because elements of the 16th Infantry Regiment were coming up behind the 18th and would offer protection. With Company F still off the improved roadway to avoid stray fire south of Marigny, Williamson pushed Company E, now commanded by Captain Carmel DeCampo, out onto the main road leading to Camprond. This would allow the 2nd Battalion to use the shortest and quickest route to their objective—regardless of the danger. In a later interview with Williamson and battalion S-3, Captain Murphy, it was noted "So rapid was [DeCampo's] advance that a number of Germans, attempting to cross the road and withdraw to the south, were captured as they fled."[46]

As the 2nd Battalion approached to within a half-mile of Camprond, several flights of P-47s and P-51s strafed the German units attempting to contest Williamson's final approach to the town and eliminated them. By this time, several American tanks were exchanging shots with a last group of enemy panzers in front of DeCampo's men.

These Americans also were receiving scattered automatic weapons fire from the vicinity of nearby la Chapelle. Williamson then ordered DeCampo to veer northward to avoid this fire, and just as his lead platoon turned off the road, a pair of

German officers decided to shoot it out with the squad on point. In a brief exchange, one German officer was wounded in the arm before they both surrendered.

Next encountering small arms and machine-pistol fire from a hastily organized group of Germans about a thousand yards outside the village, Lieutenant Colonel Williamson sent two medium tanks forward, followed by a platoon from Company E, to make a frontal rush on the enemy. Assisted by flanking fire from engineers from CCB, the attack succeeded in scattering the Germans and finally cleared the high ground north of Camprond. Williamson then made contact with a company of American medium tanks, an armored infantry company, and another platoon of engineers.

As afternoon fell into darkness and pouring rain, no further opposition was met until elements of the 2nd Battalion circled south to reduce remaining entrenched snipers, machine gunners, and a few German tanks.

The 2nd Battalion and its attachments completed the encirclement of Camprond by 2300 hours and substantial enemy stores and equipment were captured in some barns and houses in the town. Interestingly, Major Middleworth later pointed out, "It was believed this area had been a command post of the *352nd Division*, as the troops captured around the town were to a large extent [members of a] divisional staff."[47] He also told an interviewer who later asked him to recollect 27 July, "The prettiest maneuver of that day was the move of the 2nd Battalion to Camprond."

Casualties during this march were relatively light. One soldier was killed and 16 others were wounded, while five more Americans were carried as missing in action. Lieutenant John Downing, another long-time veteran of the Regiment who fought all through North Africa and Sicily, was among the wounded when he was hit by artillery fragments; he was later evacuated to England.

In sharp contrast to the almost bloodless seizure of Camprond, enemy fire on the 3rd Battalion south of Marigny became even more intense after noontime that day. An 81mm mortar section from Company M came forward to assist the pinned-down rifle companies shortly after 1400 hours, but no artillery support could be mustered because forward observers were not yet in position to adjust fire on the Germans. Throughout the afternoon, both Hess's and Folk's companies were pinned under scathing enemy fire from the hilltop. Later reports recorded, "This fire was the heaviest [the battalion] had experienced since landing in France. Despite the scale of the attack, however, the defending troops were still not visible to the American soldier. This enemy fire was primarily aimed fire, and the troops were forced to crawl everywhere."[48] Then, at about 1800 hours, more misery rained down when the Germans suddenly opened up with even deadlier and more accurate artillery fire. One soldier remembered, "It was accurate for sure. They had observation on us and were looking right down our throats."[49]

The shelling continued into the night. The only relief to the men was an order from Lieutenant Colonel Peckham to have Captain Russell's men withdraw and attack to the west of Marigny. They would assist in securing a line of departure for 16th Infantry Regiment columns trailing behind the 2nd Battalion.

When German fire mysteriously tapered off just after midnight, Lieutenant Colonel Peckham sent patrols out to determine if the enemy was starting to pull back. By 0100 hours, a patrol reported that the Germans had begun to abandon their hilltop positions, leaving behind ammunition, scattered equipment, and a multitude of empty emplacements.

As those forces were pulling back, several German JU-88s suddenly screamed down on the hilltop, sending the men on the ground diving for cover. "The sky then lit with their large amber flares," Captain Carter remembered later. "To us these flares seemed to burn forever." Nearby, an artilleryman also recalled this moment when he said, "The sky was really lit up, bright as anything with chandelier flares. Then the bombs started down."[50]

Remembering this bombing years later, Captain Malcolm Marshall wrote:

Who in the 32nd Field Artillery battalion could ever forget that night when the German night bombers caught us on the road? Our vehicles were jammed up waiting for our infantry to move when that uneven throb in the sky signaled the unsynchronized motors of those JU-88s. Their chandelier flares cast a garish half daylight on us, while some of our own distant 90mm antiaircraft guns banged shells across the clouds, but to no avail. When the rising wail of the bombs began, explosions ripped along the road we were on. Men jumped from trucks and crawled to any ditch or hole they could find to escape the steel fragments. When it was over, delayed fuse butterfly bombs continued to explode, and medics rushed everywhere trying to locate and patch up the wounded.[51]

Captain Carter, who, under machine-gun fire at the time, had heard from Colonel Smith that he had been promoted to major, had a very close call in that night's bombing attack.

When the bombing started, we looked for places that would provide us with some protection. There was a large farm on the right side of the road we were on that had a dry cement dipping vat. Lots of men got to it. There was also a large hedgerow about eight feet high that was thick enough for me to jump into. Soon a JU-88 flying low east to west dropped three screaming bombs. The Germans put whistles on the fins to scare people before they crashed. The first bomb hit the opposite side of the hedgerow, there was a large explosion, and I was really shaken up. When I got over the shock and opened my eyes, I thought I was blind. But my arms and legs moved and I soon smelled the strong cordite odor of the explosives. After my men came over to dust me off, I went around the hedgerow to see where the bomb hit. There was a hole big enough to bury a three-quarter ton truck. I learned moments later that my radio operator, Sergeant Easter, had been killed when the bomb landed on our side of the hedgerow. His body was lying on the outer edge of the crater. He was a fine soldier, an excellent radio operator, and a great loss to our unit.⁵²

In much the same manner as the American saturation bombing went awry on 25 July, the *Luftwaffe* rained as many bombs on their own men as they dropped on the Americans. When the JU-88s initially appeared, it seemed as if their pilots were mistaken about the positions of their own men on the ground. As a result of this highly-probable poor air-ground cooperation, the pilots assumed that the Americans already occupied the high ground south of Marigny. They had not. The Germans subsequently suffered a number of casualties from the attack of their own bombers and their forces left on the hill were completely disorganized by the mistaken attack.

After the bombing stopped, Lieutenant Conway encountered no resistance when he was able to take a patrol of tanks down the road south of Marigny to the main road between St. Gilles and Coutances. Captured prisoners subsequently stated that there had been a general withdrawal of the German forces starting right after 0200 hours that night, just as their own planes hit them.⁵³

When Major Carter returned to his jeep after the bombing ceased, he found Lieutenant Colonel Peckham excitedly radioing his units to find out how they had fared when the bombers screamed in. When he reached Captain Folk, Peckham was informed that Company L had had no immediate cover and German bombs had taken a large toll. *Luftwaffe* pilots had dropped anti-personnel bombs on Folk's unit, grouped no more than five yards apart at the time. "The company suffered 18 killed and about 50 others were wounded when this happened," Major Carter remembered. "Lieutenant Colonel Peckham asked Captain Folk if he wanted the next company in the line to take his place, but he said, 'No sir. The company is already reorganized and on the move.'" Major Carter also wrote some fifty years later, "There was not a better infantry company commander in World War II than Captain George Folk."⁵⁴

The battles at Marigny had proven extremely costly to the 3rd Battalion. German defense had proven to be far better organized than any that had been encountered while the Regiment was in the Caumont sector. "The battalion was tired," another report revealed. "It had marched to 0400 [hours] on [27 July] and fought all day." Company I suffered 41 casualties alone that day; Company K lost 14 men.

If the number of enemy bodies found on the German held hilltop was any indicator, their casualties also were heavy. In a later interview, Major Middleworth noted several reasons why casualties had been so severe, explaining "The 1st Battalion could not be ordered to fire long-range weapons [in support of the 3rd Battalion] on the hilltop resistance south of Marigny because of the uncertainty as to where they were. Radio communications were bad." He also pointed out that

Cannon Company had never been able to fire a shot due to the poor opportunities for observation.[55]

On 28 July the rest of Combat Team 18 was directed to move by truck to Camprond to relieve elements of CCB. General Huebner ordered Colonel Smith to organize a 360-degree defense while also sending patrols north to contact VIII Corps.[56] Smith finally withdrew the 3rd Battalion from Marigny, and then Peckham proceeded intact to Camprond, closing on the position at 2210 hours.

While combat teams of the 1st Infantry Division were battling their way westward against enemy pockets bypassed by CCB, elements of the 3rd Armored Division made contact with the 4th Armored Division of VIII Corps at Monthuchon. The 4th Armored had pushed south along the coast and entered Coutances at noon that day, completing the giant encirclement. Unfortunately for the Americans, however, most of the German units north of Coutances had already withdrawn to the southwest. Enemy troops screening their retreat put up fierce resistance, most of it encountered by Combat Team 16 near la Chapelle.

As a result, CCB was directed by General Huebner to turn back to Camprond to assist the Division in overcoming the enemy resistance in the west.

Huebner later realized that 28 July was actually the turning point of Operation COBRA. At the close of operations, reports at First Army headquarters indicated that the enemy between the Vire River and the west coast of Normandy had become completely disorganized and incapable of any continued coordinated action. Isolated pockets were putting up fierce resistance like that encountered by the 16th Infantry Regiment, but the Germans were estimated to be incapable of offering any concerted action resembling a cohesive defensive operation. Their losses had been tremendous. Roads in the southwestern part of the area around Coutances and points further south were clogged with fleeing German columns.

The original mission of VII Corps, pushing through Coutances to the coast to complete the encirclement of enemy forces to the north became unnecessary when VIII Corps seized Coutances. Consequently, VII Corps was given a new twofold mission that called for the rapid elimination of the remaining pockets of resistance in the area and pushing the Germans even farther to the south.

On 29 July, the 1st Infantry Division continued slugging toward Courcy, while Combat Team 18 remained in position on the high ground surrounding Camprond to continue blocking off the enemy forces trapped north of Coutances. On 30 and 31 July, Combat Team 18 moved by truck and on foot to a Division assembly area near St. Denis-le-Gast. Later reports, reflecting the optimism of the officers and men, read, "The 18th Regimental Combat Team was now fighting a war of lightning advance and quick maneuver against a retreating enemy who had been dealt a deadly blow. What might have appeared as a stalemate in Normandy had been in reality a period of planning and preparation.

The Regiment was now out of the Normandy bocage and in rolling, gentle country where armor could function as intended, and we were supported by tankmen and a superb air force. The Germans had been so badly beaten in the last week of July that no front line could be distinguished in the American sector. Morale was excellent and spirits high. It was the determination of all to lick the enemy in Berlin."

In a terse statement in the 2nd Battalion record, Captain Randall also reflected the pride felt by every man in the Regiment when he wrote, "The breakthrough has been completed, and now we are in pursuit of a fleeing enemy. The tanks and the air have done a wonderful job. It looks as though the American Army is coming into its own."[57]

At 1000 hours on 31 July, the 1st Infantry Division moved out once again, this time with the initial mission of seizing the high ground south of the Sienne River in the vicinity of Brécy. The ultimate objective, however, was the commanding ground near Mortain and the security of the right (southern) flank of VII Corps.

For this operation the Division had CCA, 3rd Armored Division attached. Under the command of Brigadier General Maurice Rose, CCA was organized into three battalion-sized task forces designated as "X," "Y," and "Z." It was to move south in three separate columns and spearhead the advance. The 1st Infantry Division would follow in two columns, Combat Team 18 on the right and Combat Team 26 on the left, while Combat Team 16 would remain in division reserve. The 18th Infantry Regiment's advance was to be led by Lieutenant Colonel Williamson's motorized 2nd Battalion, followed on foot by the 3rd and 1st Battalions.

Except for the crossing of the Sienne River where Task Force "X" received heavy enemy fire from the opposite bank, the move to Brécy was accomplished with relatively little interference. The progress of Williamson's column was slowed only by skirmishes with small enemy reconnaissance units that were brushed aside.

After advancing twelve and a half miles, trucks picked up the tired men of the 3rd and 1st Battalions and carried them the rest of the way to Brécy, which they reached by nightfall.

During the night of 1 August, orders were received to secure commanding high ground south of the town, and at 0530 hours on 2 August Learnard's 1st Battalion quickly moved out. They reached their objective at 0700 hours, and a reconnaissance in force was sent to the east where an enemy company holding a crossroads defensive position was encountered and a brisk firefight ensued. Many Germans were killed or captured with only light casualties suffered by the Americans. Afterwards the 3rd Battalion moved southeast to Hill 242 without contacting the enemy and Peckham consolidated defensive positions.

At noon on 2 August, elements of CCA crossed the Regimental front and continued pursuit to the east, with Combat Team 18 following. German troops manning isolated strongpoints offered considerable resistance, but the tanks quickly neutralized them. The march then continued to the high ground east of and overlooking the town of Mortain where the 3rd Battalion was sent to retake the village of Juvigny-le-Tertre (eight kilometers northwest of Mortain). It was occupied by elements of the *116th Panzer Division*. After a brisk firefight, the village was retaken before dusk.

During the advance from Brécy to Mortain, the 18th Regimental Combat Team had moved through some of the richest orchards and dairy land in France, passing through thronged village streets where the local populace often was attired in holiday clothes to greet and cheer their liberators. Reflecting the upbeat mood at the time, Colonel Smith wrote, "We were well on our way towards completing the encirclement of the German *Seventh Army*, which we were slowly annihilating in our lightning moves. Allied spearheads pointed well towards Paris, and we were to be an intricate part of this gigantic operation."[58]

Mortain, a small, ancient town whose buildings combined both old Norman and Renaissance architecture, sat astride the roads leading out of Avranches toward Brittany and southeastern France.

On 3 August, General Huebner designated the 18th Infantry Regiment to seize a commanding height known as Hill 314, which was just to the east of Mortain. In turn, Smith chose Lieutenant Colonel Learnard's men for the assignment, with Captain Russell's Company K attached. "Mortain was a mysterious spot, quiet but full of tension," one officer remembered. "We held our position at the edge of a plateau, facing east. Below the ridge ran a deep gulch, perhaps 700 feet, very steep, and beyond the gulch a sharp knoll rose back up to the plateau level, and beyond that lay a large valley of rolling hills."[59] Suspicious noises were heard throughout this area and artillery observers spotted enemy tanks. After Company K tangled with *Füsilier Battalion 275* in a sharp fight, the 1st Battalion quickly took the hill.

Some of Learnard's men then moved down and occupied Mortain itself, while the 2nd Battalion moved onto a hill (285) two kilometers to the northwest. The 3rd Battalion, positioned on the extreme southern flank of the 1st Infantry Division zone, began placing roadblocks along the network of highways and trails to the southwest of Mortain.

Company C shifted north to secure the crossroads of l'Abbaye Blanche as the remainder of the 1st Battalion, along with Company K, dug in atop Hill 314.[60] By nightfall, the Regiment had established roadblocks on all major routes leading into and out of the area. The following day, Learnard's men were hit by a German attack, but after suffering heavy casualties from well-aimed American artillery fire, the enemy withdrew to the east, leaving the 18th Infantry Regiment in undisputed possession of Mortain.

That night shells began to rain down on the town and it quickly became apparent that the Germans had not abandoned thoughts of retaking Mortain. Flares lit up the sky, but bombs did not fall. A reconnaissance patrol was engaged just outside of town. Evidencing a continued commitment to retake Mortain, at about 1900 hours the following night the *Luftwaffe* attacked again, this time bombing the town for over an hour.

"Three-story buildings just crumbled and fanned out in a circle from a great crater in the ground, " Chaplain Rogers remembered about that night. "Time and again concussions beat savagely against our heads. It was a bad hour. When the planes departed we went out to find debris everywhere. Fires were burning briskly in all directions and there was little hope in bringing them under control. Our men dynamited walls and blocked the path of some fires; others just burned all that night and the next day. They were still crackling away when I left the place early the next evening."[61]

Some civilians were killed in the attack, along with several of Learnard's men. Company B's Supply NCO, Staff Sergeant Walter J. Michalewski died, one of the last few remaining "originals" in the company. Outside of town, the Regiment's supply lines were hit and several soldiers in Service Company were killed.

The 18th RCT, however, was not going to fight for Mortain. At 1200 hours on 6 August, the 30th Infantry Division's 120th Infantry Regiment relieved Colonel Smith's forces to allow the Regiment to take part in the encirclement of the Germans in what came to be known as the Falaise-Argentan Pocket.

The 2nd Battalion, 120th Infantry Regiment took over the positions from Learnard's men on Hill 314, while the 1st Battalion of their regiment assumed responsibility for defensive positions held by Williamson's companies on Hill 285 northwest of town. As the 1st and 2nd Battalions were conducting their relief in place, the 3rd Battalion, 120th Infantry Regiment quickly took over firing positions and foxholes occupied by Peckham's men to the south of Mortain.

Of note, now the 18th's former 3rd Battalion Commanding Officer in North Africa, Lieutenant Colonel Courtney P. Brown, was in command of the 30th Division's 3rd Battalion, 119th Infantry Regiment, just north of Mortain. Brown's battalion had relieved elements of the 16th Infantry Regiment before the 1st Infantry Division continued south to Mayenne. He soon would find himself involved in fighting as desperate as any he had previously experienced in Tunisia during a fierce German counterattack on Mortain.

After a bitter five-day struggle, the 30th Infantry Division, reinforced by CCB, 3rd Armored Division, finally succeeded in defeating that last desperate enemy counteroffensive in Normandy.

In the larger picture at this time, General Patton's newly-activated Third Army was barreling deep into France at le Mans. The opportunity to trap the German *Seventh Army* seemed increasingly possible.

On 8 August, having conferred with General Eisenhower, Lieutenant General Bradley telephoned General Montgomery to reveal his plan to do this, and Montgomery adopted the bold strategy. If the Canadians moved southward to Falaise and Patton's forces rolled north to Alencon and then to Argentan, there would be just a 15-mile gap separating Canadian and US forces. By closing this gap, the jaws could be shut around 21 German divisions west of Falaise and Argentan.

During the week that fierce fighting was raging at Mortain, Combat Team 18 consolidated strong defensive positions on high ground surrounding the town of Ambrières-le-Grand, approximately 18 miles to the southeast. Then came a time of relative inactivity, except for patrolling and the inevitable skirmishes.

The 1st Infantry Division shifted back onto the offensive on the morning of 13 August.[62] General Huebner had been ordered to move the Division northward to the gap by way of Couterne, Bagnoles, and la Ferte-Mace. In accordance with the new directive, the 18th Infantry Regiment pushed reconnaissance toward La Chapelle-Moche. The 1st Battalion attacked the town on 14 August and seized it the next day. The Regiment then continued pushing northward toward Coulanche, reaching that new position overlooking a key valley in the rear of the *Seventh Army*.

After a swift enveloping move forced the Germans to withdraw, the Regiment relocated along a dominant ridge in the vicinity of la Sauvagère on 15 August, placing Colonel Smith's men just ten miles south of Falaise on the southern perimeter of the Argentan-Falaise Gap. Meanwhile, the Canadian First Army moved to within four miles of Falaise from the north, securing the city on 16 August as Patton's Third Army made its way eastward toward Dreux, Chartres, and Orléans.

The Germans fought desperately for several days, but after nearly 80,000 enemy soldiers were penned into an enclosure resembling an elongated horseshoe, Hitler finally gave permission to withdraw across the Seine River on 16 August, in hopes of salvaging as many troops and headquarters cadres as possible. Over the next five days, cloaked in rain and frequent heavy mist, what remained of the Germans' *Army Group B* slipped eastward, leaving behind thousands of destroyed weapons and vehicles, the bloated bodies of many horses, and almost 10,000 German dead. Another 42,000 German soldiers were captured by Allied forces.

At this point in the campaign, the overall plan was assessed to be about ten days ahead of schedule. That prompted Eisenhower to consider an immediate thrust to the German border. Patton crossed the Seine on the night of 19 August, and given the German force pell-mell retreat to the homeland, Eisenhower decided to forego halting at that river barrier.

As the month of August ended, elements of the British Second Army pushed across the 1st Infantry Division front, and in doing so pinched the 18th Infantry out of its zone.

While the liberation of Paris was receiving headlines back home, further movement eastward was certain to come for the officers and men of the Regiment, but a definitive date had not been set. Combat Team 18's sector near la Sauvagère reverted to a rest area for the troops, and between overhauling and replacing equipment the men busied themselves with taking showers, swimming in nearby lakes, and watching movies.

On 24 August, the 18th Infantry Regiment left Normandy and motored to an assembly area 110 miles to the east, in the vicinity of les Châtelets, a small town 20 miles west of the city of Chartres.

It was now clear that the 1st Infantry Division would skirt Paris altogether, and the next day it moved another 60 miles to the east.

Over the five days that followed, the Regiment covered many historic miles, this time generally northeastward, crossing the Seine on 27 August. This passage brought an end to the "free" ride, and the soldiers dismounted their trucks for a difficult 25-mile foot march in high summer heat before other transportation brought them to the historic Marne River.

The Regiment reached Soissons on 30 August. Many of the men were honored with the solemn opportunity to visit the cemetery where so many who had given their lives during the Great War were buried. That night, the Regimental CP was established on high ground a thousand yards from the site their predecessors had occupied in the First World War, the conflict fought—at least by the Americans—to end all wars.

Colonel Smith wrote at the time, "The last week of August had carried the Regiment 300 miles across Northern France. Practically no contact had been made with the enemy, which was utter proof of the destruction and defeat suffered by the great German Army of the West. Evidence of this was seen along the routes of advance in columns upon columns of destroyed enemy vehicles and equipment."

The war was far from over, even though the Regiment did not fire a single shot at Soissons. "France had been liberated," Colonel Smith noted cautiously in ending his August report, "But Germany lay just ahead."[63]

THE WESTWALL

SEPTEMBER TO NOVEMBER 1944

> We won for ourselves a fame that will go down in the annals of the glorious history of the "Fighting First."
>
> —Colonel George A. Smith, Jr.

While the rapid Allied pursuit of the German army across France was breathtakingly dramatic, it had placed a serious strain on pre-invasion logistics calculations. The US Army was not able to repair bomb-damaged French railways and pipelines fast enough to support the lightning advance, The only alternative course of action was to seize additional seaports along the French and Belgian Atlantic coast.

Montgomery's Twenty-First Army Group shifted northward toward Antwerp and the Scheldt Estuary, while Eisenhower directed Bradley to split his Twelfth Army Group to maintain contact with the British. Under this revised Allied plan, Lieutenant General Courtney Hodges' First Army would pass north of the Ardennes Forest in Belgium, while Patton's Third Army continued eastward to Lorraine.

By the end of August, Hodges' First Army advanced with three corps abreast— XIX on the left, V Corps in the center, and VII Corps on the right. As the operation unfolded, however, many disorganized German units were identified in front of XIX and V Corps. These were the remnants of the *Seventh* and *Fifteenth Armies* retreating toward Germany with the hope of escaping encirclement and destruction. On 1 September, Hodges ordered General Collins' VII Corps to wheel north toward the crossroads town of Mons, Belgium, in an attempt to trap the Germans herded eastward by the other two corps.

Departing Soissons that day, the 18th Infantry Regiment moved by truck with the 1st Battalion acting as advance guard. Lieutenant Colonel Learnard continually found his companies encountering groups of retreating Germans. Firefights broke out whenever the opposing columns unexpectedly collided, often at a small village or crossroads, but the Germans quickly capitulated because they were usually outnumbered and outgunned. Even though the retreating enemy armies still possessed an estimated 120,000 men, those forces were making little or no attempt to retain decisive terrain in the hopes of delaying the American advance. Instead, it was clear the officers of the combat team that the *Wehrmacht* seemed to be under orders to break contact and retreat so they could live to fight another day.

The 3rd Armored Division captured the city of Mons at 1900 hours on 2 September, placing VII Corps squarely in the path of the retreating Germans, as Hodges intended. With the area now opened for a continued drive toward the German border, orders came down that afternoon for Colonel Smith to prepare for a move east of Mons in anticipation of future operations; his Regiment's mission was to secure crossings over the Meuse River between Namur and Givet. The 18th Infantry Regiment's mission was to support the 1st Infantry Division's seizure of crossing locations over the Meuse by first securing Bavai, a tiny hill town a few miles from the Belgian border.

The Germans moved toward Mons in the early hours of 3 September, as Collins expected. As fighting broke out between them and the 3rd Armored Division, Learnard's 1st Battalion entered Bavai at 1000 hours. It happened that a large convoy of Germans was also entering the town at the same time, and they were immediately engaged by the Americans. Before long, over 200 enemy prisoners were rounded up while others, less fortunate, lay dead beside a building in the town square.

When a German antiaircraft unit was encountered on the far side of Bavai early in the afternoon, the 1st Battalion's battalion's advance guard launched a hastily-organized attack, taking another 400 prisoners. Late in the day, the Americans routed a third enemy column seeking to enter the village from a wooded area to the southwest.

"September 3 was a slam-bam free-for-all that will make it a day forever remembered by the battalion," Learnard's after-action report later read. "Enemy were popping up everywhere—woods, streets, alleyways, vacant lots—but they were dealt a swift and deadly blow."[i] He had personally assisted in the day's actions when a single shot he fired from a .30-caliber machine gun on his jeep stopped an enemy truck, jamming one of the escape roads north out of town and bringing a column of other retreating German trucks and tanks to a halt.

The 3rd Battalion also moved into Bavai late that afternoon and Peckham's companies joined Learnard's in consolidating their newly-won positions. The US Army Air Forces struck an enemy column moving away from the town to the northeast during the day, so Peckham placed forces on the exit roads at the town's edge to bar any enemy infiltration during the night. Concurrently, the 2nd Battalion moved into an assembly area on the southeast edge of the Forêt de Mormal, and later sent a platoon of infantry and two tanks to assist the 32nd FA when its batteries were surrounded northeast of town after darkness fell. Swift action here soon netted another 165 prisoners.

Intelligence reports located elements of five additional enemy divisions in the forested areas around Bavai—the *6th Parachute, 18th Luftwaffe Field Division,* and the *47th, 275th, and 348th Infantry Divisions.*

By early morning on 4 September, the 1st and 3rd Battalions were manning a series of blocking positions around Bavai to prevent enemy infiltration, but at noontime, Division G-2 alerted Colonel Smith that German units had been spotted approaching from the northeast. At 1530 hours, based on this information and his fear that the enemy strength may have been underestimated by division intelligence, Smith ordered the 2nd Battalion, augmented by the 2nd Platoon, Company B, 745th Tank Battalion, to move several miles northeast of Bavai to probe enemy forces in the area.

After carefully studying the overall situation, a cautious Williamson then ordered Captain Jeffrey to have Company G proceed as advance guard towards Sars-la-Bruyère, first sending out flank patrols to be sure the route was clear for safe passage of the remaining companies. Based his own intelligence reports, Williamson had decided that the greatest enemy threat upon reaching Sars-la-Bruyère would be from the north and west, so Jeffrey's men were to take the sectors of the town's outskirts extending from the Dour road to the Mons road farther to the northeast. Captain DeCampo's Company E was to assume positions extending southwest from Sars-la-Bruyère to cover the railroad line entering the town from the south. Cannon Company, now led by Captain Penick, was to go into positions on the east edge of town and outpost the area while the battalion Ranger Platoon remained at the battalion command post as a reserve force.* Company F, now under the command of Captain Alfred E. Koenig, had displaced on the road leading from the west into Bavai out of the Forêt de Mormal so his men could probe for other suspicious activities.

After the heat of the early September day started dissipating, Jeffrey's advance guard reached its line of departure for the march to Sars-la-Bruyère. Major Colacicco, now the 2nd Battalion Executive Officer, led the main body forward until the head of the column met up with Jeffrey's platoons. At the time Colonel Smith was looking for Williamson to tell him he had received a report from locals that a German regiment was bivouacked nearby. Smith discounted the veracity of this report, but Captain Jeffrey and Lieutenant Colonel Williamson were warned of a possible nearby larger enemy force.[2]

Jeffrey's men had six and a half miles of forested area to reconnoiter en route to Sars-la-Bruyère. Patrols were sent to each flank with orders to probe the forested areas to depths of 300 to 400 yards on either side of the roadway to be sure they

---

*The battalion "Ranger Platoon" was an ad hoc outfit consisting of carefully selected men tasked with the conduct of special missions, such as ambushes, raids, and other particularly demanding tasks. It was not unusual for such organizations to be raised in American infantry divisions during this period; they had various names, including "ranger" or "raider" units. They were not associated with either of the Ranger Battalions in the ETO at that time.

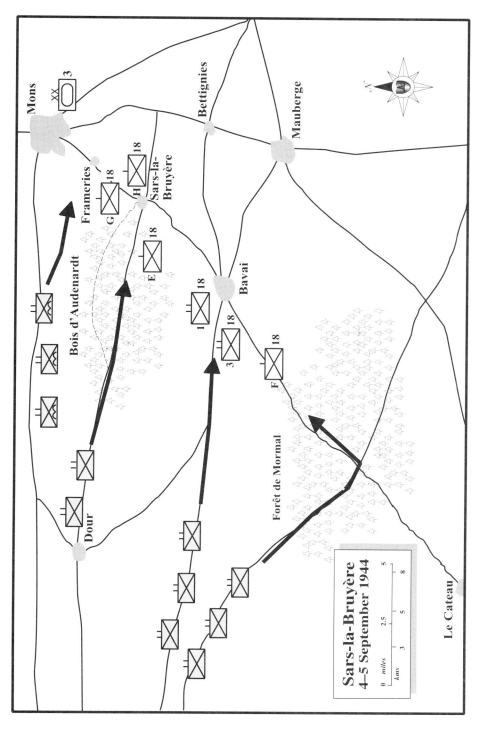

were free of Germans. The roadway was jammed with dead horses, vehicles, and men of an enemy column that had been strafed earlier in the day, and it was nearly 2000 hours before the leading platoon reached the Bois d'Autenardt, still just south of Sars-la-Bruyère. The battalion moved nearer to the village, arriving an hour later without incident.

Roadblocks were immediately established, with Company H, now commanded by Captain Carlton Crouthamel, emplacing a machine-gun platoon to cover Company E's sector on the west road to Dour, where it bisected the Bavai road. Crouthamel's 81mm mortar platoon was split, with sections going to each of the rifle company areas. They were capable of massing fire into either sector if an attack materialized. The supporting tank platoon occupied positions in the center of town, aiming their 75mm main guns at the road leading east, as well as the Bavai Road and the main paved intersection that led to Dour.

By this time, the 2nd Battalion's staff had occupied a large building resembling a castle near the center of town—a setting replete with a walled-in courtyard, high walls, and a moat. Radio communication to Regiment was sporadic; the Communications Platoon was instructed to lay landlines to all company positions and the tank platoon. By 2200 hours, all of the roads were blocked, an aid station had been set up in the courtyard, communications were working, shifts had been organized for the night at the castle command post, and the men dug in for what sleep they could get.

The calm of the night was broken by a call from Captain DeCampo a half-hour later when he reported to battalion S-3 Captain Murphy that one of his listening posts had picked up the sounds of a column with horse-drawn vehicles several hundred yards out on the Bavai Road. The report was received with skepticism, as this area had been reported clear just two hours earlier; when Williamson heard it reported, he ordered clarification.

By the time Murphy got there, DeCampo's men had reported that a column of enemy infantry was on the same road the battalion had used to get to Sars-la-Bruyère earlier that night. "I had ordered my first lieutenant to pull a minefield over the roadway by this time," Captain DeCampo remembered, "He had almost been yelling about the German troops marching right into our sector."[3]

Murphy quickly suggested to DeCampo that he hold his fire until the enemy column got closer, and then he called Captain Crouthamel and had him shift his mortars to cover the roadway. Murphy then called Williamson to report what he had done, and the battalion commander told him to come back to the command post while he notified Cannon Company, the tank commander, and Captain Jeffrey about the new situation. At the battalion command post everyone remained calm, as it was difficult to conceive at the time that there was anything on the Bavai Road but a small force of stragglers looking for someone to whom they could surrender.

Thirty minutes later sounds of a terrific fusillade of small arms fire were heard from the direction of Company E's platoon-sized roadblock, followed by the unmistakable "ripping" of German machine guns and machine pistols. "We came to in a snap," Captain Murphy wrote later in describing the changed mood at the command post. "It suddenly became apparent that this group of Germans was not of the same category as those the battalion had been encountering for the past several weeks."[4] It turned out that DeCampo's initial fire had caught the head of the enemy unit as it moved in column along the road, but the Germans quickly reacted by sending a company-sized force to both of his flanks as they developed their hasty attack. German indirect fire was soon added to the equation when two enemy guns started firing down the Bavai Road.

"Their 75mm cannon shells hit my command post," Captain DeCampo remembered. "The first shell killed two of my runners, and also wounded my executive officer and my first sergeant. I had to call battalion and tell them we were abandoning this command post for a new line at the edge of an orchard. I tore out the phone and picked up the runner's M-1, then a hand grenade exploded in the next room."[5] Williamson reacted by contacting his artillery liaison officer to see if a forward observer was with DeCampo's men, but the answer came back negative. Murphy then hurriedly telephoned Captain Penick to see if Cannon Company was able to fire any missions. Penick replied that his howitzers were actually already firing but that his shells were landing well behind the enemy's assaulting columns.

By now DeCampo's men were being attacked across their entire front, communication with his 2nd Platoon had been lost, and his left flank was being enveloped. "Cooks and administrative personnel were even on the line," he remembered as his other flank was assailed. "About 20 Schmeisser pistols [submachineguns] were firing at every angle. At first some of the men didn't see the sparks of these guns, and just maybe four or five riflemen responded. In time, fewer of our guns were braving the hail of bullets. I had the ammo corporal ripping open boxes of ammo, and I would take loads of bandoleers to each man, two apiece. At midnight I notified headquarters that we were outnumbered at least thirty to one, and that I could not keep the enemy from making an end run on my right side."[6]

In response to this report, Williamson directed Lieutenant Parker of the battalion Ranger Platoon to send a patrol to the west of his command post to determine the size of the attacking force. Crouthamel's Company H was ordered to concentrate its fire to DeCampo's front, and then as if on cue for his machine gunners and mortars, the moon came up. The entire landscape then transformed from poorly-lit dimness to a brighter, natural light that provided both sides with a nearly panoramic view of the entire area. Lieutenant Parker reported that he could make out a large enemy force moving south and east toward Sars-la-Bruyère. Immediately Williamson directed the Ranger Platoon to extend the left flank of the battalion so they could block any enemy movement from the southeast.

By now casualties were coming into the aid station in the castle courtyard and the battalion surgeon was tending to over 30 wounded, with more reported inbound. As Captain Murphy remembered when he heard this report, "This was the first indication things might not be going in our favor at all."[7]

It was reported that a section of Company H's 1st Machine Gun Platoon had also been overrun and that a jeep loaded with ammunition exploded when friendly forces mistakenly pulled a daisy chain of mines underneath its wheels, killing the driver. The transportation officer appeared at the battalion command post, wounded in the arm, explaining that his motor pool had been overrun, all of the field kitchens had been captured, and that trucks loaded with extra ammunition had been seized.

Williamson directed Captain Murphy to run out to Company G's position with orders to have Captain Jeffrey organize a platoon counterattack in an attempt to restore DeCampo's positions on the Bavai Road. At the same time, the battalion commander ordered two tank sections attached to Jeffrey's platoon for this attack.

Anticipating that trouble to the battalion's front would become even more dangerous, Williamson had ordered one of his officers to go to nearby La Bouveries where the 33rd FA Battalion was located. Although their batteries technically were supporting the 26th Infantry Regiment, Williamson was hopeful he could obtain their support. The artillery liaison officer complied, and agreed to support Jeffrey's counterattack platoon, whose men now were deployed by squads on either side of the Bavai Road and ready.

Tanks were also in place, prepared to head down the center of the road with their guns firing, while Company G squads followed behind. It was now nearing 0115 hours. The artillery forward observer in Sars-la-Bruyère had found a building tall enough for him to see his targets, and he proceeded to register the 33rd FA's guns "as much by sound as by sight."[8]

"Company G's platoon moved out accompanied by the tanks right on time," Captain Murphy recalled later. "But they had hardly started when it became apparent that the Germans wanted no part of this new force, and they soon began to withdraw after firing a few rounds. Then as they fell back, they were caught by a combination of well-placed artillery fire by the 33rd Field Artillery batteries and small arms from the elements that remained of Company E."

Indeed, by 0200 Jeffrey had restored the position and tied in with the left platoon of DeCampo's men, who had stood their ground. Crouthamel had also responded by organizing his 1st Platoon and remaining two of Company H's lost guns.

Two hours later, at about 0400, the Germans launched a second company-sized attack just south of the Bavai Road, supported by artillery. This time Crouthamel's mortars poured down on them and the Germans were hit on both flanks by terrific fire from Captain Jeffrey's squads, ending this second attack at sunrise.

"It was about 0610, and we were even asked if we could be of any assistance," Captain DeCampo recalled. "A lieutenant and an observer came down from battalion. I felt the enemy had holed up behind some buildings ahead of us about 300 yards. I asked for smoke shell to determine the range, then the mortars fired. They were right on target. I ordered 24 rounds of high explosives in. Unknown to us, the Germans had set up their aid station in the rear of these buildings. Before the last 81mm shell landed we heard screaming and yelling, '*Kamerad, Kamerad.* SURRENDER!' We stopped firing."[9]

After surrender negotiations were finalized between Captain Murphy and the badly wounded German regimental surgeon, Murphy organized 493 prisoners to be led back into Sars-la-Bruyère. "Everyone left in my outfit kept their guns ready," DeCampo recalled. "But [the Germans] were formed in column of four abreast, without helmets and only their mess gear."

In all, 845 enemy were wounded or captured; 92 dead were later counted; six horse-drawn 105 mm howitzers were captured; 200 horses and more than 100 wagons loaded with ammunition were taken; and supplies and equipment were confiscated. The 2nd Battalion lost 15 men killed and 58 wounded.

Later that morning, as the battlefield was being cleared, Major Carter met Captain Murphy on the Bavai Road and the two made their way around a hedge-bordered lake to look at a machine gunner's position from the night before.

Scattered on the ground were piles of brass shell casings from what Carter believed had to be at least two full belts of ammo. "I stared around, trying to imagine what happened," Carter recalled later. "Then I turned to Captain Murphy and suddenly realizing what probably did happen, I said whoever did this should be written up for a citation."[10]

Major Colacicco later told Carter about what had actually happened. "The Company H commander had posted a two-man machine-gun team in a position alongside the road we had come along [to Sars-la-Bruyère]. In the darkness, the machine-gun crew saw a silent, single file of men coming up the road towards them. Beyond, they heard horses' hooves and the rattle of equipment, then all hell broke loose."

Pfc. Gino J. Merli, the machine gunner, maintained his position when the Germans attacked. He first covered the withdrawal of Company E's 1st Platoon by helping break the force of the enemy's initial assault, but Merli's assistant gunner was shot through the head and eight other Americans in a nearby position were soon forced to surrender.

To avoid capture, Pfc. Merli overturned his machine gun and feigned death, first slumping over his dead assistant's body then taking jabs from enemy gun butts and bayonets when the Germans walked over his foxhole.

As soon as the enemy passed by him, Merli resumed fire against the German troops. "Throughout the night, Merli stayed at his weapon," Captain Murphy added later. "Our negotiating party, who accepted the German surrender that morning, found Pfc. Merli still manning his position. On the battlefield lay 52 enemy dead, 19 of whom were directly in front of his gun."[11]

Captain Murphy indeed wrote Pfc. Merli up for a citation, adding "[his] gallantry and courage, and the losses and confusion that he caused the enemy contributed materially to our victory." Major Colacicco noted, "We then put him in for the Medal of Honor, and he got it." Years later, Merli reflected on that incredible night and modestly wrote in a letter to Major Carter, "I had a choice. I could have done nothing instead of what I did. Maybe I was motivated by my dead buddies or by my hatred of war. I just know that I had a decision to make and I made it."[12]

The Sars-la-Bruyère engagement was long remembered. Important lessons were learned, one on how complacency had no merit when the enemy was thought to be on the run. Captain Murphy later wrote, "Although morale was very high at the time, many of the old timers who had been through North Africa and Sicily were beginning to incline toward over-cautiousness, especially when they compared the German forces confronting them now with the last days of the African campaign. Many believed the war was in the closing stages and certainly were not in favor of becoming a casualty this late in the game."

"The mission of the battalion to secure and defend the crossroads near Sars-la-Bruyère appeared to be a little ambitious," Murphy continued critically. "We were an understrength battalion, less one rifle company that was five miles from us. Indeed, Company F could have been relieved by one of the six rifle companies near Bavai without weakening the area. The entire plan was impregnated by an underestimation of the enemy's capabilities, but allowing the enemy to initially approach very close to the battalion position before opening fire probably saved the day."[13]

Although the German attack was well coordinated with three battalions against the understrength 2nd Battalion, the enemy had made no apparent attempt to reinforce their early penetration into Company E's position. "Considering the facility with which they mounted their attack it is hard to conceive why this was not done," Murphy observed with relief. "But their action in this respect saved the battalion from complete defeat, and instead gave us a victory."[14]

In all, over 17,000 Germans were killed or captured by the 1st Infantry Division in a series of engagements around Mons. A historic day for the Regiment was marked on 6 September as the men moved out eastward, toward the German border. "This advance was unopposed," Colonel Smith wrote in his September report. "We received a rousing reception from thousands of civilians who lined the streets of Charleroi, where we bivouacked that night."[15]

These were indeed happy days for the men of the 18th Regimental Combat Team. The Ninth Air Force had laid bombs in advance of their motor march, and the remnants of the enemy presence were strewn in rubble along the way farther east. Little opposition was encountered in what reports indicated was a very pleasant 60-mile approach to the German frontier. On 10 September, the combat team moved across the Meuse River toward Herve, one of the last large Belgian towns before the border. Once again the Regiment drew closer to the fleeing Germans and encountered rear guards. Colonel Smith reacted by setting up strong defensive positions around Herve, sending Lieutenant Colonel Peckham's 3rd Battalion to occupy fixed Belgian fortifications in nearby Battice. Again, the enemy withdrew eastward.

The Regiment remained in these positions until 11 September when it advanced seven miles toward Aubel. High ground near Obsinnich was taken on the next day. Two days later, the Regiment encamped north of Gremmenich in the Aachen State Forest, overlooking the city of Aachen on the fortified frontier of Germany itself.

The 3rd Battalion seized new positions at the junction of the Belgium-Holland-Germany border and for several days had outposts in all three countries. Resistance was more evident.

When Lieutenant Colonel Learnard's 1st Battalion moved into the Aachen State Forest, lead scouts had no sooner set foot on German soil when a vicious firefight ensued. Pillboxes and trenches held by the enemy were quickly overrun and then used to provide cover from cold, rainy continental weather.[16] The latter half of September 1944 then marked a period of relatively static warfare.

The Americans, although triumphant, now found themselves badly overextended. First Army had reached the German border on a front of 80 miles, and the VII Corps front included 25 of them.

The doctrinal frontage for a corps in such a situations was five to ten miles, but First Army possessed no reserves. Such extended frontages had been advantageous during the pursuit, but the Allies were about to learn that the pursuit was over.

In sharp contrast, the Germans were well into the process of reconstituting forces retreating from France. Determined to defend their homeland, the Germans enjoyed the advantage of a fortified line—known to their forces as the *Westwall* and to the Allies as the Siegfried Line.

In contrast, the Allied efforts at the time suffered tremendously from logistical shortfalls. Gasoline had to be brought up from Normandy by truck, an operation that often consumed as much gasoline as it delivered. Supply lines were so strained that on the day VII Corps crossed into Germany, Hodges' First Army was forced to begin feeding its troops captured rations.

While the 1st Infantry Division was establishing attack positions inside the German border, another 18th Infantry Regiment soldier earned the Medal of Honor on 24 September. Captain Hess's Company I was defending Stolberg, a small mining town located just south of Aachen. Staff Sergeant Joseph E. Schaefer was in charge of a squad from the 2nd Platoon that had the mission of holding an important intersection. Attacked by two German infantry companies that day, one of the platoon's nearby rifle squads was forced back and another captured, leaving only Schaefer's men to defend the position.

Fearing that the Germans would make a two-pronged assault against his now-exposed flank, Schaefer shifted his men to a defensive position in a house a short distance from the vital intersection. He then stationed himself at the top of a stairwell near the front door of the house as Germans appeared.

"The flashless powder in the staff sergeant's M-1 did not reveal his location here," Major Carter wrote in describing what greeted these Germans a few seconds later. "He quickly broke the first wave of infantry thrown toward the house. The Germans soon attacked again, this time with flamethrowers and grenades, but they were turned back when Sergeant Schaefer killed and wounded several of them. When they regrouped for a third and final time, one enemy force drove at the house, while a second group advanced stealthily along a hedge bordering the roadway in front of the home expecting to follow their first group into the front door. Recognizing the threat, Sergeant Schaefer fired rapidly at the enemy coming at him, killing or wounding all six, and then with no cover whatsoever he dashed up to the hedges and killed five more, wounded two others, and took 10 prisoners."[17]

By this time, Captain Hess' men had launched a counterattack to regain control of the intersection. Sergeant Schaefer assisted one of the other rifle squads to regain the position they had lost earlier, then "crawling and running in the face of heavy fire, he overtook the enemy and liberated the Americans captured earlier in the battle," according to Major Carter when he wrote up the Medal of Honor citation. "In all, single-handedly and armed only with his rifle, Sergeant Schaefer killed between 15 to 20 Germans, and wounded just as many. His courage was responsible for stopping the enemy breakthrough that day."[18]

The house from which Schaefer had moved was also occupied by a 57mm AT gun crew commanded by Sergeant Frank Gaysek. "I could see about 20 sets of feet moving along the hedge towards the house," Gaysek recalled. "We needed a higher position, so we ran to a third-floor attic with two dormers. I fired 20 clips of ammunition, then I saw six more Germans crawling toward the farmhouse with their arms halfway in the air. We took five prisoners. We could see several more in a foxhole about 500 yards away. After another barrage, some got up and started running."

Later, Sergeant Gaysek was guarding prisoners when machine-gun and cannon fire started hitting the house. There were breaks in the communication wires, though, so an American Sherman had started errantly shelling the house, its crew thinking it was occupied by Germans. Gaysel got everybody out as the building was engulfed with flames and took them into a pillbox across the road, later receiving a Silver Star for his valorous leadership.[19]

To the north of Stolberg, Aachen was situated in the middle of a wide valley running generally from east to west at the junction of the borders of Germany, Belgium, and Holland. The core of the ancient city itself was filled with crooked streets, stone-and-brick buildings, and since it was located on the border, several belts of steel-reinforced concrete fortifications added to its protection.

Historic Aachen was the capital city of Charlemagne's European empire in the early Middle Ages, his final resting place, and the coronation site for the Holy Roman Empire from 813 to 1531. As the first German city threatened with capture by Allied troops, Aachen was a symbol far beyond its actual strategic value. Hitler, who could not afford the propaganda defeat when the first German city fell to the Americans, ordered Aachen to be defended to the last. Allied planners, faced with a prime opportunity to demonstrate to the world that the demise of the Third Reich was inevitable, were just as eager to secure Aachen.

Captain Robert Botsford of the 1st Infantry Division G-2 section put the situation in perspective when he wrote, "During the month of October, the eyes of all

The Westwall

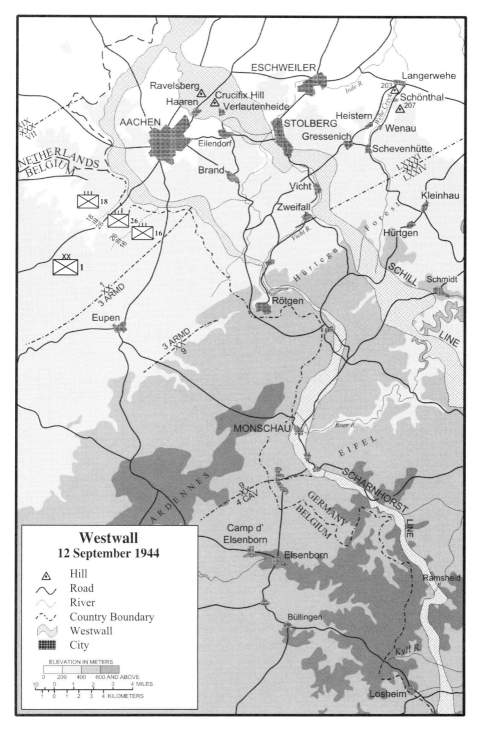

Germany were on Aachen. The enemy had to solve a problem that was far more important than a purely local operation. On the political side, the enemy had to decide whether to minimize the importance of Aachen and prepare the homefront for the possibility of its loss, or to face the fact that it was the ancient imperial German city, the testing ground for the *Wehrmacht*'s determination not to yield a foot—or at least a conspicuous foot—of sacred German soil. Aachen was a critical point in the Siegfried Line. Although the line had already been pierced, it was still the German High Command's plan to hold the line, or what was left of it."[20]

By 1 October, the 1st Infantry Division was holding an extended ten-mile defensive line south of Aachen from Stolberg westward to Vaelsquartier with all three of its three regiments on the line. The 18th Infantry was on the left immediately east of Aachen, the 26th Infantry in the center, with the 16th Combat Team on the right. According to operations reports of the 18th Infantry, "Opposing this lineup was the *246th Volks-Grenadier Division* and attached units, disposed as follows: In the southwest and central outskirts of Aachen, *Grenadier Regiment 404*; from southeast Aachen to Haaren, *Grenadier Regiment 352*; from Verlautenheide to Stolberg *Replacement Battalion 453*. Static defense troops in Aachen proper comprised the *Luftwaffe Fortress Battalion XIX* and the *Fortress Machine-Gun Battalion 34*."[21]

Captain Edward McGregor, now the 1st Battalion S-3, noted cautiously:

The *246th Division* had been activated only two months previously. It included a conglomeration of naval personnel, physical misfits, deferred defense workers, and new recruits. The static defense units were a little better. Owing to the poor quality of the personnel and the limited training they had experienced, the combat efficiency and morale of these units were quite low. However, they were defending well-prepared fortifications and many of their leaders were skilled *Wehrmacht* officers. These defenses were being constantly improved and being backed up with more and more artillery as each day went by.[22]

By this time most of Aachen's pre-war population had fled, and the Americans estimated that not over 15,000 to 20,000 civilians remained in the city. Defending forces in Aachen were estimated to be 3,000 to 4,000 strong. Foremost of the hill bastions around Aachen was Crucifix Hill, which dominated the approaches to the city. Nearly 800 feet in height, Crucifix Hill had been a battlefield during the religious wars that swept Europe some 500 years earlier, and during the Napoleonic era stones had been cut to build a huge, 60-foot high crucifix to mark the many lives lost on the hill, giving it its name. It was considered impregnable by the Germans; a massive pillbox system had been built up around its base as well as on adjacent hillsides, leading to the bald hilltop and the crucifix.

The Ravelsberg, a wooded hill also about 800 feet high, stood 1,500 yards to the northwest of Crucifix Hill. An important east-northwest road ran between the Ravelsberg and Crucifix Hill and was the main route of supply to the soon-to-be-besieged Aachen garrison.

The Ravelsberg was important for several reasons. If the enemy held it, the garrison of Aachen would continue to enjoy a secure line of communication. Excellent observation from the Ravelsberg enabled the enemy accurately to direct artillery into the flank and rear of positions held by the 16th Infantry Regiment to the south. As long as the defenders retained control of the Ravelsberg, they would be able to prevent any major attack on the city during daylight. Controlling the Ravelsberg was thus essential for the seizure of Aachen. Crucifix Hill had to be taken before the Ravelsberg could fall.

The 1st Infantry Division plan called for a two-phase attack. The first phase would focus on surrounding the city, which would entail the capture of Würselen to the north by the 30th Infantry Division and the seizure of the Ravelsberg by the 18th Infantry Regiment. When that was accomplished, a 24-hour surrender ultimatum would be delivered to the commander of the garrison, Oberst Gerhard Wilck.

If he failed to agree unconditionally, the second phase would commence. The 26th Infantry Regiment would launch an attack against the center of the city with the objective of destroying the German garrison. Medium bombers of the Ninth Air Force, as well as the massed fires of VII Corps artillery, would support the assault.

Colonel Smith's plan called for the 2nd Battalion to attack at night through positions held by the 16th Infantry Regiment to seize the village of Verlautenheide to the east of the base of Crucifix Hill. The 2nd Battalion would then establish blocking positions to the north and farther east to blunt any potential German counterattack.

Once this was accomplished, the 1st Battalion would move up to Verlautenheide before swinging west to seize Crucifix Hill and cut the Aachen-Haaren Road. The 3rd Battalion would launch a supporting attack from nearby Eilendorf to seize Hill 192 northwest of Haaren, diverting attention from the Regiment's main effort at Crucifix Hill.

Company B, 745th Tank Battalion, with 15 Sherman tanks, would be attached to the Regiment, along with a platoon of four tank destroyers from the 643rd Tank Destroyer Battalion. Company B, 1st Engineer Combat Battalion would furnish support as well. Company A, 87th Chemical Mortar Battalion would be in direct support with its 4.2-inch (107mm) heavy mortars, and other indirect fires for the attack would be provided by Cannon Company and the 105mm howitzers of the 32nd Field Artillery. Reinforcing fires were to be provided by the other battalions of DIVARTY and the 155 mm SP guns of Battery A, 957th FA Battalion of VII Corps.

Due to the relatively poor and unstable weather conditions, a date had not yet been set for the start. The mood of the officers and men of Combat Team 18 seemed pensive, and this was reflected by Captain McGregor when he wrote:

> The men of the 1st Division faced the Aachen offensive with mixed feelings. In as much as the Division had achieved a series of outstanding successes along the historic path from Normandy to Aachen and the gates of Germany, they were battle veterans with a sense of destiny—a feeling that they were always selected for important tasks because they had always accomplished their mission. They knew that Aachen was heavily prized by both friend and foe. If captured, it would be the first German city to fall into Allied hands, and Hitler himself had ordered that it be defended to the last man. Thus, espirit de corps was excellent.
>
> On the other hand, there were causes for personal misgivings concerning the forthcoming operation. The rapid dash across France and Belgium and the apparent destruction of the German Army in the west had raised the hopes of final victory and a sudden end to the war. These hopes had been shattered by the abrupt increase of resistance on German soil. The Siegfried defenses, although manned by troops with low morale and poor combat efficiency, were proving difficult to reduce and it was apparent the enemy intended to defend his homeland by waging a fierce war of attrition against the invader. Casualties were mounting, and morale, while good on the whole, was a factor that varied with the comparative success or failure of each day's operation."[23]

Preparations made by the 1st Battalion staff in planning the attack on Crucifix Hill reflected the wisdom gained over nearly two years of battle experience. While enlisted men got some rest after being relieved on 2 October by the 237th Engineer Combat Battalion, Captain McGregor joined Captain Murphy and Captain Henry Sawyer at the regimental command post where the S-3s coordinated their respective battalions' actions. Afterward, McGregor returned to his battalion command post where he discussed the regimental plan with Lieutenant Colonel Learnard and the artillery liaison officer. The trio huddled together to study maps, aerial photographs, and overlays of German defensive positions on Crucifix Hill and in the surrounding area. Before bedding down that night, the officers made plans for a detailed reconnaissance the following day.

Lieutenant Colonel Learnard already had some second thoughts about the regimental plan and he voiced his objections directly to Colonel Smith as his men slept that night. The supporting VII Corps SP 155mm gun battery had been placed in defilade south of Eilendorf, some 3,300 yards from Crucifix Hill. Although the commander of the 957th FA expressed confidence that his guns would destroy many of the pillboxes during a nighttime preparatory barrage against Crucifix Hill, Learnard asserted that the 155s should instead be employed in direct fire during daylight hours. Colonel Smith thought otherwise, advising that if the guns were employed closer to the front they would be vulnerable. Learnard remained concerned, but he had no choice but to accept Smith's refusal to change the regimental fire support plan that night.

The next morning Captain McGregor and his operations sergeant joined with Learnard and the Company D commander, Captain Robert E. Bowers, to visually reconnoiter Verlautenheide and Crucifix Hill.

Verlautenheide, which was connected by a good road with Eilendorf, stood on the crest of a bare ridge. It ran approximately 1,000 yards to the west, rising gradually until it reached Crucifix Hill.

Haaren, a small village just outside of Aachen, was located at the southwestern corner of this ridge, at the base of Crucifix Hill.

Now, for the first time, the observation party saw many large pillboxes that studded the crest and southern slopes of the hill; the firing ports in each overlooked the intended assault path. No mines were visible, but the Americans did notice that belts of barbed-wire entanglements protected communications trenches running from pillbox to pillbox.

Since patrols had not been able to infiltrate past the German outposts protecting the valley between Eilendorf and Crucifix Hill, little information was known about the enemy's dispositions. Intelligence reports indicated that *Replacement Battalion 453* occupied Verlautenheide itself and that a reinforced company of *Grenadier Regiment 352* was manning the pillboxes on Crucifix Hill.

The reconnaissance party also saw that the enemy's observation and fields of fire were excellent, and that there would be little cover or concealment when the assault began. Moreover, an approach route from Verlautenheide to Crucifix Hill also had no cover and the best approach to the hill appeared to be a road that curved out of the northeast end of Eilendorf. It offered some protection from direct fire for about half the distance to the hill.

When McGregor and Learnard returned to the battalion command post they arranged all pertinent maps, photographs, and overlays to facilitate discussion of their attack plans with every key officer.

Recognizing that Crucifix Hill would have to be taken with a deliberate and aggressive assault, a training program reorganized rifle platoons into assault teams. The 1st Battalion's Ranger Platoon set up a training area as served as instructors. Dummy pillboxes were constructed by the Ammunition and Pioneer (A&P) Platoon; necessary weapons and demolitions were issued; and the men were soon armed with pole charges, satchel charges, bangalore torpedoes, and flame throwers for several practice attacks against the hastily-simulated German pillbox fortifications.

The next day, 4 October, saw further preparation—this time in the form of another reconnaissance of Crucifix Hill with all rifle company commanders, Lieutenant Colonel Learnard, McGregor, the battalion S-2, and communications officers. As commanders responsible for executing the attack were briefed on the overall regimental plan, terrain features were pointed out, and the best route of approach to Crucifix Hill was agreed upon. Noting that the rifle companies would move by truck to the village of Brand before making a foot march to a forward assembly area in Eilendorf, Lieutenant Colonel Learnard issued his operation order and directed each company commander to continue reconnoitering the objective area the next day. They would take with them all of their officers and noncoms, to include squad leaders.

After viewing the landscape the next morning, one sergeant evidenced the value of Learnard's thoroughness in preparing them for the attack when he wrote:

> Every bit of enemy activity was noted and recorded; every pillbox closely watched; every likely approach studied; every last discernable fold in the ground was tucked away in our memories. Not deeming it sufficient to permit each man to rely on the evidence of his own eyes, we later critiqued the operation until we were certain that we were getting the best and fullest and most reliable information possible. The importance of the mission was drilled into us. No stone was left unturned to insure that this operation would be a complete success with the fewest possible casualties.[24]

A pilot from the Ninth Air Force reported to Learnard the next morning. His role as air liaison officer was to direct fighter-bombers during the attack.

McGregor returned to Eilendorf with the air liaison officer, and platoon leaders from the supporting tank company, tank destroyers, and the regimental antitank company. As the time for the attack now neared, McGregor made plans to return in the morning for a final observation, this time with the company commander who would lead the assault on Crucifix Hill.

Captain Bobbie Brown, now commander of Company C, was selected for this task. At 41 years of age, he was older than most captains in the Regiment, but this had not deterred his selection as a rifle company commander. He was a "Mustang," an enlisted man who received a battlefield commission. His previous battalion commander, Lieutenant Colonel York, later recalled that decision, which was made prior to Normandy:

> I had to choose between a group of very fine young officers with college educations, some at West Point. These officers were very capable men who had been with me through North Africa and Sicily. I finally made one of the toughest personal decisions of my life. I decided to give the company to Bobbie in spite of his limitations. Bobbie hadn't completed one year of formal schooling, but the report noted that he had all the characteristics of an outstanding officer. He had an intense desire to kill Germans and was shrewd in figuring out ways to do it. He was an expert at ambushing, patrolling, and scouting techniques. He had a sense of timing that was

unusual. He was a scrapper, and when it came to soldiering he was right there. He was absolutely fearless. [25]

On 7 October McGregor and Captain Brown made one final reconnaissance of Crucifix Hill, and Brown later remembered that the reconnaissance took most of the day. He noticed that ditches and mines were the first barriers his company would have to cross, that the ditches were some twelve feet wide and about 75 yards in front of the "dragon's teeth" (concrete antitank obstacles) that formed a 50-foot-deep belt at intervals along the base of the hill. Behind them, ditches and barriers gave way to a series of 50 pillboxes and emplacements. Pillboxes were about 90 feet in circumference and covered, except for their turrets, with brush and long grass. Captain Brown was unable to see beyond the crest of Crucifix Hill, however, which meant that he had little or no information about the hill's reverse slope.

The weather during this entire period was harsh. Rain fell often and visibility during daylight was limited by low clouds and ground fog. The ground was damp and cold, making life uncomfortable. Tracked vehicles were limited to the road; otherwise they risked bogging down.

While artillery and fighter-bombers had been busily hitting targets of opportunity when weather permitted, current conditions made McGregor fear that there would be restrictions on fire support when the attack began. All of these factors weighed heavily on him that night when he returned from reconnoitering Crucifix Hill with Captain Brown, only to learn that the warning order had already come down from Regiment. The attack was on for the next morning, 8 October.

During this period, the 3rd Battalion was occupying positions at Eilendorf, under the nose of the enemy atop Crucifix Hill. The battalion, which was temporarily attached to the 16th Infantry Regiment, suffered constant shelling and mortar fire. Despite the deadly interruptions, the combat team's soldiers continued refining their own plans for the supporting attack against Hill 192.

At the same time, 2nd Battalion patrols conducted daylight reconnaissance, using the 3rd Battalion perimeter as their departure point. Patrols had not been able to determine the enemy strength at Verlautenheide, which concerned Williamson because he feared the enemy might be capable of bringing up reinforcements undetected from east of the ridgeline. He knew his rifle companies would be attacking down another ridge to get to Verlautenheide, and that this area was constantly subjected to small arms, artillery, and mortar fire. The 2nd Battalion would have to storm huge concrete pillboxes that guarded the approaches to the ridge while simultaneously assaulting a fortified town. Once Verlautenheide fell, moreover, Williamson and his men would have to hold the town while being subjected to fire both from the front and from the direction of Aachen to the rear.

At 2215 hours, the 2nd Battalion moved to Brand, where men detrucked before continuing on foot to a forward assembly area, arriving an hour before midnight. The battle for Crucifix Hill began at 0300 hours when artillery fire crashed into Verlautenheide and the ridge itself. An hour later, Williamson's men jumped off with Company E, now being commanded by Captain Hershel T. Coffman, on the left flank and Company F assaulting to the right, while Company G initially remained in reserve. Company H mortars remained behind the line of departure to support the attack, while a platoon of heavy machine gunners each accompanied the assaulting rifle companies. Surprisingly, there was little activity in response to the American advance until a sergeant in Company F yelled too loudly at a straggling soldier. The startled defenders then quickly filled the night sky with parachute flares.

Fortunately, a low-hanging blanket of fog prevented the Germans from seeing the Americans well, and this cover permitted the rifle companies to keep moving with a minimum casualties. Visibility started improving at 0700 hours, just as the lead elements of Company E entered Verlautenheide.

The Germans then unleashed a scathing artillery and mortar attack in reaction, but they were too late to prevent the Americans from gaining a foothold in the village. Company G hurriedly moved up from reserve and its men soon were involved in house-to-house fighting—fighting that was destined to continue for several hours.

Artillery, panzerfausts, mines, and poor road conditions took a devastating toll on the Shermans of Company B, 745th Tank Battalion as they tried to support the attack. One tank got stuck in the mud before leaving Eilendorf and another was knocked out by artillery fire near the railway overpass north of town. A third Sherman hit a mine, blocking the road to Verlautenheide, halting the advance. A panzerfaust fired from a house along the same road knocked out one of the stalled tanks. This left one operational Sherman, which pulled off the road into an orchard and waited until mines on the roadway were cleared, four hours later.

A similar fate crippled the second platoon of tanks. One Sherman fell out with mechanical problems just outside of Eilendorf, while another was put out of action by a mine. The three remaining tanks then waited for an hour just south of Verlautenheide as mines were cleared. Tank commander Sergeant Earl R. Jacobsen remembered the event vividly, later writing, "We experienced the worst artillery fire I have ever seen. The tanks had scarcely an opportunity to return fire. They couldn't move."[26]

Despite this, by 1200 hours the 2nd Battalion reported Verlautenheide in its hands; the town was finally cleared of enemy stragglers by 1600 hours. Coffman's men had also reduced a number of pillboxes behind the town by this time, after coming at them from the rear with satchel and pole charges. The enemy had suffered heavy casualties, and 61 were captured. Williamson lost 5 men killed, 74 wounded, and 9 missing. Incoming enemy artillery was so heavy during the day that it was impossible to evacuate the wounded until nightfall.

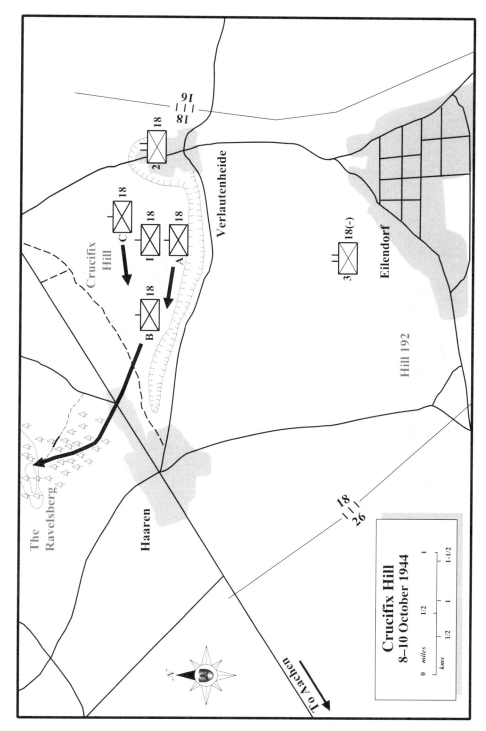

Earlier that morning, Colonel Smith ordered Learnard to launch his attack on Crucifix Hill. Learnard had protested, requesting that the operation be delayed until Verlautenheide was cleared, but Smith insisted that the attack start. Given the uncertainty of the situation, Learnard then decided to lead the attack personally. His command group took off across the open stretch toward Verlautenheide, running a gauntlet of artillery fire before safely reaching the village. Several homes were found to be still sheltering Germans, but they were soon cleared out and the battalion staff settled into their new forward command post in a cellar.

Learnard called Colonel Smith to report the situation, and he then arranged for smoke shells to be fired on either side of the approach to Verlautenheide while his rifle companies advanced. Ominously, the telephone line to the Regimental CP went out after that report.

Major Robert E. Green, the 1st Battalion Executive Officer, had moved the rifle companies to an assembly area near his command post south of Verlautenheide. At 1000 hours Learnard radioed Green and told him to start infiltrating forward to the line of departure, one company at a time. Artillery smoke shells were laid as requested, but the smoke quickly dissipated in the strong wind.

When Green started out on the expanse of the bare approach to Verlautenheide, the 1st Battalion's rifle companies sustained heavy casualties from the almost constant enemy artillery fire. "Casualties were high in all companies," one officer wrote. "This was despite our extreme caution; despite the use we made of all possible cover and concealment; despite the perfect dispersion. In spots where Jerry could not directly observe us, he had previously registered his supporting fires. We had to move in single file. It was a slow, tortuous move."[27]

Company A, now commanded by Captain Scott-Smith, was hit the hardest and he lost almost an entire platoon. It was necessary for his company to reorganize, as the evolving plan called for his men to protect the rear and flank of Company C when it assaulted Crucifix Hill. By now Brown's rifle platoons were busily huddling over their situation maps in the cellars of the houses in Verlautenheide and hurriedly studying the pillbox locations on Crucifix Hill one last time. The company Executive Officer, Lieutenant Clement Van Wagoner, had the company well organized, allowing Brown to make last-minute adjustments as needed. "I had my artillery and 81mm mortar observers get on a housetop where they could observe the objective area," Brown wrote later. "I had also placed the heavy machine guns on other housetops so they could have a good field of fire. I then put out a covering force and had all the platoon leaders join their platoons to await my return from my ground reconnaissance."[28]

Captain Brown took his radio and headed off westward to observe the situation on Crucifix Hill, but when he got about 400 yards away from Verlautenheide, rifles and machine guns opened fire and the enemy began dropping mortar rounds near him. "I hit the ground and crawled in the direction of the small arms fire and again several bursts from machine guns came in my direction," Brown recalled. "I then withdrew to a small cemetery where I had my covering force. One of them opened fire, and three enemy put their hands up and surrendered. I took the prisoners back to my command post, where I discovered the Ranger Platoon also had 22 others in a cellar."

Brown then assembled his platoon leaders and gave them the final attack plan. The 1st Platoon would move along the trail leading up the right side of Crucifix Hill, reducing each pillbox they encountered along the way. The 2nd Platoon would attack on the left slope of the hill with the same mission. The attached battalion Ranger Platoon would act primarily as security against a German counterattack on the company's left flank, so they were assigned only one pillbox to capture. the company's 60mm mortars would go into position west of Verlautenheide, then move forward with the attached heavy machine guns from Company D. The 81mm mortar and artillery observers were to follow the two assault platoons. All three rifle platoons had a radio, and Brown carried an extra set (belonging to the Ranger Platoon) so he would have two ways to communicate with his executive officer, Lieutenant Van Wagoner. "I then checked to see that everyone knew the signals to lift fires, or to call for fire. Final watches were set, and the time was 1140 hours," Brown recalled later. "All of the platoon leaders were then directed to return to their men and give them these instructions."[29]

"Half in jest, but with butterflies in our stomachs, we christened the coming operation either 'Operation Massacre' or 'Operation Decimation,' one of Brown's officers wrote. "It was thoroughly obvious to us that the job ahead was to be a rough one."[30] Captain Brown by then had returned to the battalion command post with Lieutenant Van Wagoner and his communications sergeant to find that there was a final message from Regiment. The message read, "You will neutralize and destroy all enemy activity on Crucifix Hill. You will then organize and prepare a permanent defense on the hill and be ready to repulse any and all counterattacks."[31] The time of the attack was set for 1330 hours. Completely satisfied with Brown's preparations when he reviewed them with him, Lieutenant Colonel Learnard only wished him good luck. Brown then returned to his command post in a nearby cellar to inform his men of the time of the attack.

Brown was relying heavily on air support to cover his advance to Crucifix Hill, but when the tanks of the 745th were stalled earlier that morning, the air liaison officer who was in a VHF-radio equipped Sherman never made it forward in time for his assault. Unknown to Captain Brown, he would now only have air support offered by two pre-arranged flights of P-47s when his attack started. By this time, the opening rounds of the scheduled artillery barrage were already falling on Crucifix Hill, and Brown was moving his men up to their attack positions on the line of departure. Company C attacked at exactly 1330. Immediately, things began to go wrong.

An enemy forward observer on the southern slope of Crucifix Hill brought down a tremendous barrage on Brown's men, inflicting numerous casualties before they could get close to their assigned pillboxes. Within minutes, the Ranger Platoon also found itself under heavy fire from two strong points. Through this,

Brown was still able to lead his command group to the base of the hill where he, his radio operator, and his runner quickly jumped over an embankment. A call came in on the SCR-536 radio saying that Lieutenant Joseph W. Cambron, the battalion Ranger Platoon leader, had been wounded, followed moments later by another call indicating that both of his assault platoons were pinned down and could not move. Preparatory fires and air strikes having been ineffectual, his radio operator then yelled, "Jesus, the air force and the artillery didn't do a goddamned thing to those pillboxes, did they. What the hell happens now?" Brown, taking in the totality of the situation, simply responded with, "I guess I'll have to take them myself."[32]

The opened mouth radio operator then uttered an incredulous "Sir?" as if to question Brown's sanity. The determined captain, though, studying a dark pillbox to his front, responded flatly with, "What we'll need is a couple of pole charges. And throw in some satchel charges, too." A nearby sergeant then nodded and said, "Guess the only way to do it is to send up some engineers, eh, Captain?"

Bobbie Brown shot back with, "No, I wouldn't ask a man to commit suicide. I told you I'd do it myself." Lieutenant Charles Marvain, the 2nd Platoon leader, had managed to work his way forward by this time and he quickly threw a satchel charge, which was loaded with 60 quarter-pound blocks of TNT and had a three-second fuse, over a bank to him.

Brown said later:

I picked the charge up and crawled to the pillbox, then I ran up to the aperture. At the time an enemy rifleman opened the door and started out. However, when he saw me, he dashed back inside. I jumped at the door and tried to slam it shut; however the excited German had left his rifle in the doorway. I opened the door at the same time I pulled the fuse on my charge and tossed it inside the bunker, slammed the door, and jumped back over the embankment as the pillbox and its occupants were blown up.[33]

Brown then rushed back to his men and arrived just as another radio report came from the Ranger Platoon saying that Lieutenant Cambron had been hit a second time, but that the platoon had destroyed its assigned pillbox. "But my assault platoons were still pinned down, and we were receiving both artillery and mortar fire," Brown remembered after acknowledging this report. "So my runners and I picked up more pole charges and satchel charges so we could move to another pillbox. Then we fired a yellow smoke grenade on the south side of the pillbox we wanted in order to signal the 155mm in Eilendorf to lift its fire so we could make our assault." Armed with two explosive charges and again alone, Captain Brown took a wide, circuitous path up the 100 feet that brought him behind this pillbox, crawling most of the way. As he worked his way closer, machine-gun fire started spraying the ground nearby, but he stayed on his belly and dragged himself under the trajectory of the enemy's guns.

He could not get close to the rear door this time, and so before the Germans could emerge from the pillbox he braced the pole charge against the front aperture, pulled the fuse, and then dove into a nearby crater. Seconds later the pole charge exploded thunderously, stunning the occupants of the pillbox. Brown took immediate advantage of this and charged the aperture once more, this time lobbing a satchel charge into the opening where it exploded, sending smoke and flames rushing from the pillbox's vents.

This time when he returned to the base of the hill, Captain Brown was told that Lieutenant Cambron of the Ranger Platoon had been hit for a third time and had been killed.[34] Cambron's platoon sergeant, now in charge of the platoon, had also reported that they could not move because of the intense small arms and artillery fire to their front.

By this time, one of the squad leaders from Brown's nearby 2nd Platoon had also been hit, and the remainder of the squad had joined him. The sergeant now in command of the squad reported that he was prepared to launch an immediate assault, prompting Captain Brown to plan yet another coordinated attack against more of the enemy fortifications.

"The squad had a flamethrower, so I assigned them to a third pillbox, and with the help of a good rifleman to keep the aperture closed a fourth pillbox was soon neutralized," Brown remembered. "This relieved the pressure on both assault platoons." During this action, Brown attacked another pillbox by himself, one of the largest on the summit of Crucifix Hill. It had a steel door in the rear that was facing another thick block that Captain Brown determined was most likely the entrance to an underground ammunition bunker. He watched as a German soldier came out of the pillbox, and then made his way down into this bunker. When the German emerged with his arms loaded with shells, Brown sneaked up on him just as he reentered the rear of the massive pillbox. He then cagily waited until the stocky German put down his ammo to close the door before dropping a lit satchel charge inside the box at the man's feet.

Brown then slammed the door in the German's stunned face and ran like hell as a tremendous explosion rocked the summit of Crucifix Hill. This time he was wounded, once on the wrist and once on the chin. As he went back down to find his men Brown remembered, "I saw three pillboxes go out at one time from actions of the assault platoons, so I sent my runner back to give Lieutenant Van Wagoner an oral order to move up all the remaining detachments and the support platoon to one of the destroyed fortifications, then for him to proceed to the battalion command post to let the battalion commander know the situation." Nearby a sergeant exclaimed, "You did it, sir. That finished 'em for good. The hill is ours." Captain Brown's modest reply was simply, "Good, it was the only job they expected us to do."[35]

At 1410 hours, the small command group accompanied Brown toward the fallen crucifix atop the hill, which had been knocked down by the earlier air strike. Lieutenant Snyder of the 1st Platoon had been wounded, but he was still leading his men to check on other pillboxes. Brown soon found Lieutenant Marvain, the 2nd Platoon leader, and they then rushed down off the hill to a small cemetery near a pillbox sited along a trail on the left slope of the hill. It was not manned, but nine enemy lay dead around the bunker.

Brown received a hand signal from Lieutenant Snyder indicating that all the pillboxes had been cleared in his area. Brown's radio operator then contacted battalion and told Lieutenant Colonel Learnard that the hill had been taken. Soon afterward, Captain Brown watched his support platoon move up, and then he told his accompanying artillery observer to bring fire on Germans trying to assemble south of Crucifix Hill for a counterattack.

It was now 1530 hours and the Americans wounded in the assault were being evacuated to the battalion aid station in Verlautenheide. Seventy-six Germans had already been captured and the remainder of what had been the reserve company of *Grenadier Regiment 352* were either dead or wounded.

The rest of the 1st Battalion was not doing as well. Captain Scott-Smith's Company A had still not recovered from the numerous casualties it sustained when his leading platoon moved up from Eilendorf earlier that morning. In all, the company had suffered 20 casualties from enemy mortar and artillery fire; 13 of these were in the 3rd Platoon. A complete reorganization was effected in the cellars of Verlautenheide before the company finally launched an attack at 1410 hours in support of Captain Brown.

Company A's left flank came under fire from several pillboxes on the southwestern slope of the hill, but he continued advancing slowly along a large ditch that led in from Haaren. Three pillboxes and 23 prisoners were eventually taken, but Company A had progressed only 300 yards from its line of departure by the time Crucifix Hill was secured.

Captain McGregor explained the company's continuing plight by noting, "At this point its advance came to an abrupt halt. The assault teams had been driven back from three mutually supporting pillboxes to its front. The company commander, directing the attack from a house in Verlautenheide, then reorganized and attacked again, committing his support platoon this time."[36]

The Germans reacted quickly with machine-gun and rifle fire, forcing Scott-Smith's men to seek cover in the pillboxes they had first taken. At 1500 hours, while Captain Brown was busily preparing for the expected enemy counterattack, Company A reported to Captain McGregor that they were completely stopped.

In the light of Company A's situation, Lieutenant Colonel Learnard began adjusting his original scheme of operations. His first thought was to employ the SP 155mm guns of the 957th FA in Eilendorf to engage the pillboxes holding up Captain Scott-Smith, but without knowing the exact positions of all of Captain Brown's men he was reluctant to do this. At 1505 hours, Captain Miller of Company B reported that his men had finally closed into Verlautenheide despite suffering several casualties as they moved up from Eilendorf, so Learnard decided to order his company to occupy the gap between Crucifix Hill and Verlautenheide.

To accomplish this, Miller's men had to link up with the right flank platoon of Company C as well as the rifle company protecting the 2nd Battalion's left flank.

By now, Captain McGregor had gone forward to find Captain Brown in a tank ditch with his command group. Given Company A's predicament and the fact that enemy troops still held pillboxes to the left rear of Brown's axis of advance, McGregor advised him to establish an all-around defense and to coordinate with Captain Miller when Company B arrived to tie his position in with the 2nd Battalion in Verlautenheide. It was now about 1830 hours, and Captain Brown finally had an aid man tend to his wounds before returning with McGregor to the 1st Battalion command post.

While Learnard was satisfied with the day's progress, he still had to concern himself with the fact that the battalion had not cleared the entire zone of enemy and that an unknown number of Germans remained in several pillboxes situated between Companies A and C. Remembering the tentative mood later that night, Captain McGregor wrote, "The battalion was jutting out to the west like a sore finger with a cancerous growth. The pillboxes were in defilade from the tanks that had moved up to the ridge and into Verlautenheide. Rain was starting to fall again, night was coming, and visibility was limited."

After weighing several options, Learnard decided that Captain Scott-Smith's Company A, despite being pinned down earlier in the day, would renew the attack in the morning.

"Defensive preparations then proceeded rapidly," McGregor recalled after realizing from his communications with Learnard that what the Americans needed was a defense for that night, and not preparations for the morning's offensive. "Close-in barrages and concentrations on both sides of the ridge were planned by our battalion FA liaison officer. The battalion's antitank guns and the attached Regimental Anti-Tank Platoon were then brought up from Verlautenheide, and additional heavy machine guns from Company D were also displaced forward while the 81mm mortar platoon remained in Eilendorf where their fires could be coordinated with the supporting field artillery. Resupply of ammunition was completed by nightfall and the dead and remaining wounded were evacuated to Eilendorf. New field telephone lines were laid, and the circuit leading to the Regimental command post soon came back to life."[37]

Long before the 1st Battalion began organizing for defense that night, the 3rd Battalion had jumped off from Eilendorf in the planned supporting attack to seize Hill 192. Companies I and K led the effort. Although both companies received intense mortar and small arms fire from the high ground south of Aachen, they succeeded in taking their objective in a little less than two hours. Captain Folk's Company L was then ordered to clean out the village of Rothe Erde, located to one flank of the battalion's axis of advance; seesaw fighting ensued for most of the night in a large rubber factory. An American platoon held one half of the building; the Germans controlled the other. That night orders came down from Regiment directing Peckham to seize Haaren on the next day.

With Hill 192 secure and the earlier defensive preparations completed, the 1st Battalion staff planned a follow-on attack against German pillboxes studding the southwestern corner of Crucifix Hill. Acting on orders from General Huebner, Colonel Smith suddenly changed the battalion mission to seize the Ravelsberg, the important prominent wooded feature some 1500 yards to the northwest. Since the hill was located on the far (northern) side of the road connecting Aachen with Haaren, its seizure would completely sever the German main supply route in the sector. Williamson's 2nd Battalion, which had been reporting a heavy buildup to the east, would relieve the 1st Battalion on Crucifix Hill under the new plan. Remembering the reaction in the Verlautenheide cellars that night, Captain McGregor wrote, "This [plan] did not set too well with the battalion commander."[38]

By now the tempo of artillery and mortar fire that was along the Crucifix-Verlautenheide ridge was increasing hourly, evidence of an imminent large-scale German counterattack.

The Ravelsberg had never been mentioned to Learnard in any discussions during the advance planning to take Crucifix Hill, and the information needed to accomplish this task could only be garnered from studying maps. Moreover, no intelligence was available about the Ravelsberg itself, other than the fact that several pillboxes were located on its southern and western slopes. After Learnard discussed these disquieting facts with Colonel Smith, it was agreed that the attack would take place in daylight, after the expected enemy counterattack on Crucifix Hill was repulsed, and only after the pillboxes holding up Company A were reduced.

Learnard then developed a simple plan for the attack. The 1st Battalion would advance in column with Company B passing through Company C, which would retain the Ranger Platoon. Company A would mop up the pillboxes to their front, and then move to Crucifix Hill to await further orders.

German attacks were now growing louder and their shells were falling on Verlautenheide at the rate of one per minute. Shortly after midnight, this cadence increased in tempo as the Germans stepped up artillery fire, prompting Captain McGregor to later recall, "The ridge literally shook with the impact of the crunching shells. In the inky blackness of the rain-swept night, the men of the battalion cursed and dug, prayed and waited. The silence between each succeeding round was deadly, but the weary men strained their ears and other senses for tell-tale signs of an unwelcome visitor."[39]

Shortly after 0400 hours, enemy shelling abruptly ceased. "The enemy then attempted to retake Crucifix Hill by storm," Captain Brown remembered as whooping Germans came charging up the northern and western slopes of the hill. "Three waves of infantrymen and assault engineers came over the slopes. My men held their fire until the Jerries were almost upon us. Then, as the enemy was silhouetted by our artillery flares and illuminating shells, my men opened up with murderous grazing fires that piled the onrushing Germans in front of their foxholes."[40]

During the counterattack, Captain Brown adjusted artillery fire quite close to his own positions, and this resulted in pinning down several of his squads manning captured German fortifications on the western slope of the hill. Brown had also expected that his attached heavy machine guns would slaughter the attackers; he was not disappointed. Their barrels cooled by the clumsy-looking water jackets on their WWI-design weapons, Lieutenant Yarbor's platoon of heavy machine guns continuously blazed away at the Germans. "The enemy then withdrew as suddenly as they had attacked, leaving behind 40 dead within rock-throwing distance," Brown noted after this fire. "Over 100 other dead could be seen out in the path of the artillery and our mortar fires."

Captain McGregor, watching the action from Verlautenheide as artillery shells illuminated the area added, "Crucifix Hill became an erupting volcano. The effect on the Germans was deadly. Their bodies were stacked like cord-wood in front of Company C's positions." "Huns dropped like flies," an officer in one of the nearby pillboxes remembered. "We counted a number of dead Germans not more than 75 yards from our machine-gun positions, and about 50 more in the general area."[41] Prisoners later identified the dead as soldiers of a company of *Combat Engineer Battalion 12* and a company of *Füsilier Regiment 27*, both elements of the *12th Volks-Grenadier Division*.

Later that morning, two self-propelled 155mm guns were emplaced north of Eilendorf to engage the enemy still holding out in front of Company A. After several volleys of high explosive, the defending Germans were killed, neutralized, or forced to retreat. "This completed one of the most difficult and important missions ever assigned to the 1st Battalion," Captain Brown noted in a later report. "We lost one officer in the Ranger Platoon and five of our own enlisted men. Two officers were wounded, as were 33 enlisted men. No one was captured by the enemy." Brown's only criticism was that if Company B had been moved south of Crucifix Hill earlier to take the pillboxes that had been holding up Scott-Smith's men, it would have saved precious time and lives.

"As was expressed by witnesses to the action," Captain McGregor wrote in his account of the Crucifix Hill battle, "the success of Company C in accomplishing an extremely difficult mission was largely due to the effort of one man, Captain Bobbie Brown. His incredible action had inspired the men of his company with an unbounded fighting spirit. For his brave and inspiring deeds, Captain Brown was awarded the Congressional [*sic*] Medal of Honor." Major General Huebner later commented on Bobbie Brown with equal praise, saying, "This man was worth a regiment to me." Lieutenant Colonel Learnard's 1st Battalion was also awarded a Presidential Unit Citation for its outstanding performance at Crucifix Hill.

Williamson's 2nd Battalion was not as fortunate on 9 October. When their artillery pummeled Crucifix Hill at 0400 hours, the Germans also fired an intense bombardment into Verlautenheide, hitting both Company F and the battalion staff. At the same time Captain Brown's company was counterattacked, the enemy deployed a battalion-sized force from the *12th Volks-Grenadier Division* against

Williamson's positions in the village. By 0420 hours, a platoon from Company G was almost overrun. Shortly afterward, Company F reported that the enemy was within 40 yards of Company F's perimeter. A few minutes later, the enemy gained control of the railroad junction just across the road from the battalion CP.

Captain Koenig immediately rushed a squad from Company G and another squad from his own 1st Platoon toward the building housing the command group and joined with the 2nd Battalion's Ranger Platoon in setting up a firing line. Adding to the already precarious situation, the Germans ignited a fire in a barn some 20 feet away from where one of Jeffrey's platoons was sheltering in a potato cellar. The barn was soon engulfed, and were it not for the quick thinking of Technical Sergeant William L. Reed, who fired his Thompson submachine gun into the attackers, the American platoon might have been overcome by smoke. Instead, they all got out.

There was a lull in the action for about 45 minutes until the Germans tried to approach even closer to Williamson's command post. This time they were able to fire antitank rockets at the house, and some of the enemy made it across the street opposite the doorway leading into the battalion headquarters. Fortunately, the firing line built up by Captain Koenig and the Ranger Platoon was able to hold the Germans at bay.

Just before daylight, Williamson requested tank support. At dawn, five Shermans and one tank destroyer rolled into the village, taking up positions just north of his command post. Williamson quickly ordered the tankers "to shoot at everything" across the street, and moments later the Shermans and the TD began spraying the buildings the Germans were hiding in with 75 mm and 76 mm high explosive and machine-gun fire. In the ensuing fight, a platoon from Company E and a squad from Koenig's ranks joined the tanks, finally forcing the Germans to pull back. The regimental report noted, "The line was then restored at 0830 hours." A relieved Williamson quickly ordered a search of every house in Verlautenheide to look for German stragglers.

The 2nd Battalion suffered many wounded during the counterattack, along with three men killed in action and 12 more missing. Evacuation of the wounded had been hindered by the enemy's well-aimed artillery fire during the morning, and it had been necessary to employ half-tracks to dash into Verlautenheide to pick up the more seriously hit. On the plus side, two officers from the *12th Volks-Grenadier Division* were captured along with 75 German enlisted men. It was not possible to calculate the number of enemy casualties.[42]

Enemy artillery and mortars also hit both Companies I and K for about an hour that morning on the ridge at Hill 192. After it was lifted, the enemy was seen infiltrating forward from a number of pillboxes and a draw that flanked the companies' positions. Company M's 81mm mortars and the rifle companies' 60mm mortars fired on them, but the enemy was too close to friendly infantry positions to take a chance on using the less-accurate and more-powerful howitzers of DIVARTY. As the enemy drew even closer, Hess ordered his men to execute their final protective fires, a last-ditch measure designed to place a barrier of bullets and steel fragments between the attackers and the forward trace of defensive positions. This hail of steel killed or wounded a number of Germans at close range.

During this time, Folk's Company L was still fighting in Rothe Erde, but by afternoon the town was completely cleared and he and his men were overlooking the center of Aachen. Later reports indicated that 1,000 rounds of enemy mortar and artillery fire had fallen on the 3rd Battalion that day. Colonel Smith, uncertain of the outcome of the fierce enemy attacks across the Regiment's front, temporarily postponed Peckham's assault on Haaren and Learnard's move to the Ravelsberg at noontime that day.

Learnard's men then spent 9 October cleaning out the remaining enemy-held pillboxes in their sector and preparing for the advance on the Ravelsberg. Numerous additional artillery rounds were fired on enemy foot troops and vehicles moving along the main road between Crucifix Hill and Ravelsberg. A column of panzers was spotted rumbling northward early in the afternoon, and the air liaison called in an air strike after artillery marked the target with red smoke. That action stopped the panzers. Captain McGregor and Captain Miller made a visual reconnaissance of Ravels-B from Crucifix Hill later that day, and what they saw concerned them.

Unlike barren Crucifix Hill, Ravels-B was covered with trees and brush, concealing German defenses. What was worse, the main artery out of Aachen would have to be crossed before reaching the base of the mysterious hill and this move would expose the attacking Americans to intense enemy fire. After taking in the entire scene, both officers agreed that the best approach would be along a ridgeline extending through an orchard to the southern slope of the hill.

By early-afternoon the 2nd Battalion finally had the situation in Verlautenheide under control, and 1st Infantry Division headquarters—anxious to seize Ravels-B so a surrender ultimatum could be delivered to the commandant of Aachen—ordered the 18th RCT to launch its attack as previously ordered. Since General Huebner specifically directed that a major portion of the 1st Battalion remain on Crucifix Hill, Colonel Smith decided to attach Company I to assist in Learnard's assault. He then ordered the 1st Battalion to seize Ravels-B with a force not to exceed two reinforced rifle companies. Given the length of time it was expected to take for Hess' men to redeploy from near Hill 192, however, Learnard feared that his attack would not take place before nightfall.

Given this possibility, Learnard decided to launch an unsupported night attack in column of companies against the Ravelsberg with Miller's Company B in the lead. Sections of heavy machine guns would be attached to both companies, with one section of 81mm mortars assigned to Captain Miller. To maintain secrecy, no communication wires were to be laid, and the companies would maintain strict radio silence until they made contact with the enemy. The plan was issued at 1630 hours, but the attack was not able to jump off until 1830, in exactly the darkness the battalion commander had feared.

In inky blackness, the two rifle companies moved up to their line of departure along an unimproved dirt road on the western slope of Crucifix Hill. Loaded down with their rifles, heavy bandoliers of ammunition, grenades, mortar baseplates and tubes, ammo cases, and light machine guns, the soldiers started out in single file along the crest of the ridge between the two hill masses. Captain McGregor later described that move as "[so difficult] each man could reach out and touch the back of the man in front of him without seeing him. With Captain Miller walking slowly as the first man in the column, he could see practically nothing as he slowly made his way down the western slope of Crucifix Hill. He was relying solely on his compass and his memory of the terrain features. What he would find en route to Ravels-B [the soldiers' name for the Ravelsburg] was anybody's guess."[43]

"The first recognizable terrain feature he encountered was the Aachen-Haaren Road," McGregor later noted. "No sooner had Captain Miller reached this point at 1955 hours than he heard a group of men approaching from the northeast. He then passed the word back along the column to halt and get down, and the strangers proved to be a column of German infantry marching towards Aachen. Lying on the roadside, he could have reached out and grabbed any one individual by the boots, but his instructions were to reach Ravels-B without a fight so he elected to remain silent." Another officer remembered seeing "caisson and wagon wheels, shod in iron, adding to the din up and down the road" as squads waited, kneeling in the dark, unseen by the busy German drivers bringing supplies into Aachen.[44]

After the enemy column moved past, Captain Miller carefully infiltrated his men across the road. More enemy traffic continued to appear, both vehicle and marching troops, however, so it took nearly two hours before the assault companies reached the far side of the roadway.

Forming up once more in single file, the Americans noiselessly made their way across the ridge to the base of the Ravelsberg. Captain Hess joined Miller to advance with him at the head of the column. They avoided several pillboxes but nevertheless passed so closely to them that the enemy could be seen and heard moving about. An officer from Company I noted, "Three enemy could actually be seen sitting on top of one box smoking and talking. Six or eight were spotted moving parallel to the column."[45]

Two long and very anxious hours later, both American infantry companies reached the Ravelsberg without contacting the enemy. It was a moonless, opaque midnight by this time, but the formidable hill appeared to be unoccupied. The Americans organized a hasty perimeter before systematically investigating pillboxes within each company sector. "This careful search was rewarded when, in one pillbox, we found the regimental commander and a reconnaissance party of the unidentified German unit," Captain McGregor wrote later. "They had been asleep and were surprised to find themselves prisoners."

Several more pillboxes were cleared before sunrise and by 0800 hours all German fortifications were emptied of enemy soldiers without a shot. Serendipitously, a detail of four Germans happened into the area with chow for 65 comrades; all were captured. Preferring hot food to their cold rations, the American infantrymen readily partook of German breakfast.

Later that morning, eight Germans hidden in a chateau on the hill unwittingly moved over toward a position where a BAR man fired at them, killing an officer and two enlisted men. Two escaped, but a lieutenant colonel and two sergeants were captured. The sound of that action disclosed the American position atop the Ravelsberg, resulting in a number of skirmishes and eight friendly casualties before the day ended.

Throughout the night, the 1st Battalion command post had been unaware of the seizure of the Ravelsberg. Learnard had last heard from Captain Miller when he made a brief report via radio after crossing the Aachen-Haaren Road. The absence of additional reports left the 1st Battalion commander in a state of unease that was matched only by the anxiety evinced by Colonel Smith, who had made frequent visits to Verlautenheide for situation updates that simply could not be provided.

At first light on 10 October, Captain Brown was ordered to send a patrol to investigate the situation. After making contact with Captain Miller at about 0700 hours, the patrol reported that the Ravelsberg was securely in American hands. "A weary battalion commander uttered a string of unprintable words," Captain McGregor wrote reflecting the upbeat mood in the cellar when they heard the report, adding, "[Lieutenant Colonel Learnard] then joyfully informed an equally weary regimental commander of the success of his men's mission."[46]

At 1100 hours that morning, the village of Haaren fell to Company L, prompting Hess to reposition his company to the northeast, to occupy positions atop the Ravelsberg overlooking the Aachen-Haaren road. At the same time, Hess was also able to successfully tie in with Company C. Company A then shifted its platoons to the western slope of Crucifix Hill on Brown's immediate left, permitting the 18th Infantry Regiment to stand shoulder to shoulder along the northern flank of the 1st Infantry Division salient near Aachen. A platoon from Company B, 1st Engineer Combat Battalion was able to clear the road from Verlautenheide to Haaren by early afternoon, ensuring a clear route of supply to the rifle companies.

The 1st Battalion command post displaced to Haaren on 10 October, where indirect fires to support the defense of the newly-won ground were immediately planned and registered. The 2nd Battalion was ordered to extend its positions northward to take over the ground vacated by Company A. Final preparations were then made to defend the Ravelsberg-Haaren-Crucifix Hill triangle. The staff of the 1st Infantry Division expected the 30th Infantry Division, which had been making steady progress in Würsulen, soon to make contact with Captain Miller's men on the Ravelsberg, blocking enemy infiltration from the north.

Given the success of the 18th Infantry Regiment's mission and the isolation of Aachen, at 1000 hours an ultimatum to surrender was delivered to Oberst Gerhard Wilck, the German garrison commander.

With the main supply road and route of escape out of Aachen interdicted, the 1st Infantry Division could concentrate on the battle for the city. Colonel Smith's forces would continue to guard the ring being drawn even more tightly around the enemy garrison, preventing him from reinforcing the city from the east.

When the surrender ultimatum drew no response, the Americans began a two-day preparatory bombardment of the city. Twelve battalions of artillery fired 4,800 rounds into the bastion on 11 October, and four groups of IX Tactical Air Command added 62 tons of bombs to what once was an ancient, beautiful, historic German city.

Evidence of an enemy counterattack on Ravelsberg was clear; it was first indicated at 1800 hours on 11 October when the 1st Battalion reported German tanks firing to their front. Just 15 minutes later, the Germans launched a counterattack, with the main effort focused on the area between Company B's sector on the Ravelsberg side of the Aachen-Haaren Road and Company C's positions on Crucifix Hill. Miller's platoons, which were now attached to the 3rd Battalion, received heavy artillery fire all afternoon. It increased at a terrific rate in the evening, but the company held their ground through several vicious German infantry onslaughts. When darkness fell, the enemy ceased their frontal attacks, but the artillery did not lift and it was clear they would try to retake this important terrain feature the next day. Observation posts on Crucifix Hill observed vehicular movement to the northeast on the Weiden-Merzbrück Road as more enemy reinforcements were brought up.

Yet another series of significant counterattacks took place on 12 October as the Germans sought to reopen lines of communication with Aachen. Considerable German armored activity along the Aachen-Haaren Road began at sunrise to the east of Companies B and I at the Ravelsberg and increased throughout the day. Colonel Smith hurriedly called for air support toward mid-morning to slow the German movement, and by this time the 1st Infantry Division G-2 was predicting that the *116th Panzer Division* would soon strike in full force.

Given this threat, all units of the 18th Infantry Regiment redoubled their defensive preparations throughout the day. The 1st Battalion started laying minefields using the A&P Platoon and two platoons of supporting engineers. A composite company consisting of the Regiment's Mine Platoon (from the Regimental Anti-Tank Company), the I&R platoon, and a reconnaissance platoon of the 634th TD Battalion, was rushed to reinforce troops defending the Ravelsberg. Meanwhile, the 3rd Battalion took a terrific pounding from enemy artillery and mortars as Company K tried to contact the 30th Infantry Division, which was still moving south from Würsulen.

Colonel Smith was notified the next morning that he could expect to remain in his current positions for some time, so more defensive improvements were initiated. Even more minefields were laid on the Ravelsberg and barbed wire was installed along company perimeters where defensive positions were already sandbagged.

Positions were quickly prepared on the reverse slope of the hill so that the maximum number of men could be pulled back during the day, leaving only nighttime observation posts on the forward slopes. A howitzer platoon from Cannon Company was attached to the 3rd Battalion to increase the number of heavy weapons available to respond to the now-imminent German counterattack.

A platoon from Company K, again attempting to link up with 30th Infantry Division, encountered enemy resistance before moving 100 yards and was forced to return to their lines.

Back in Verlautenheide, enemy activity quietly increased during the night and wagons and tracked vehicles were heard moving in from the east until daylight.

At 0630 hours on 15 October, under the cover of a heavy barrage, at least 10 German tanks and several self-propelled guns moved to within 100 yards of Koenig's Company F perimeter in Verlautenheide.

Koenig quickly called Captain Murphy, and the 2nd Battalion S-3 in turn hurriedly phoned Company E's Captain Coffman to determine the situation in his sector, and to tell him about the mounting attack in front of Company F.

While the call was taking place, an artillery shell hit the battalion command post above the room occupied by Captain Murphy and his staff. A shell fragment pierced Murphy's upper right arm, knocking the phone out of his hand. That injury resulted in his subsequent evacuation to England for a recovery that took two months.[47]

Two enemy self-propelled guns and one panzer quickly succeeded in overrunning another outpost, only to be knocked out by mines and antitank guns as they approached the 2nd Battalion's main line of resistance. Two more German tanks were destroyed as they approached to within 200 yards of the Company E perimeter.

Several more hours of stiff fighting took place, but the 2nd Battalion's preparations eventually paid off, particularly the excellent emplacement of Anti-Tank Company's 57mm guns; they forced the Germans to withdraw at 1000 hours.

While continuing to launch counterattacks against the Americans holding the Ravelsberg, the *116th Panzer Division* was also concentrating on ejecting the 2nd Battalion from Verlautenheide. Strong combat patrols continued to probe the positions throughout the day and into the night. At 0600 hours the next morning, more enemy tanks and infantry were detected as they approached Verlautenheide, this time from the west.

When what seemed to be panzers from a distance drew closer they turned out to be German self-propelled guns. One of the American 57mm antitank guns covering the approach misfired. That allowed the enemy force to penetrate the Company F perimeter before they were stopped. Three enemy guns were knocked out, two by mines and antitank gunfire, and the third by bazookas.

A POW reported that his SP gun platoon had been ordered to proceed into Verlautenheide to meet supporting infantry, but the German foot soldiers turned out to be the dismounted survivors of self-propelled gun crews.

Excitement had barely died down when yet another report came in from Captain Koenig, this time stating that tanks and infantry were hitting his north flank. Four of the German tanks and a platoon of infantry were allowed to move to point-blank range before the Americans opened fire. Captain Koenig's men inflicted heavy losses on the foot soldiers and forced them to retire in haste, but the tanks remained.

Two German tanks made it within 75 yards of Koenig's positions before antitank fire could be employed. A heavy German artillery and mortar barrage was initiated during the first assault against Verlautenheide, and it continued even after the enemy pulled back.

Despite the rain, fog, and oncoming darkness, the enemy was still determined to attack. They launched a coordinated tank-infantry assault against Company G, which by 1830 hours was overrunning its rightmost platoon. When supporting infantry were killed or wounded, however, the German tanks withdrew.

In Aachen, Colonel John F. R. Seitz's 26th Infantry Regiment, aided by the 1106th Engineer Combat Group, fought house to house against what the 1st Infantry Division reports termed "fanatic enemy response." With Germans launching heavy counterattacks against the 18th Infantry Regiment that day, the Division suspended offensive operations within the city until the external situation was brought under control.

During the night of 16 October, the enemy added aerial bombing to their harassing artillery fire when several planes flew over the 1st Battalion before strafing traffic on the Aachen-Haaren Road.

That morning a frantic attempt to break the 3rd Battalion's position on the Ravelsberg materialized as expected; it was made by the *3rd Battalion, Panzer-Grenadier Regiment 8* of the newly-arrived *3rd Panzer-Grenadier Division.*

Battle raged throughout the day. On the night of 16/17 October it was dark on the Ravelsberg with gusting winds and increasing rain. At a roadblock on the east side of the hill, two squads of Company K's 3rd Platoon were returning to their positions when the enemy came in behind them, cutting off one of the squads. The other squad reached the company perimeter, but these men were overrun as the Germans retook four pillboxes.

Two tanks supported the lightning German foray and then started firing directly into the center of Company K's positions, knocking out their light machine gun section. A German POW taken earlier revealed that there were 15 tanks and assault guns that would make a second assault in the morning, showing that the Germans were not about to give up their efforts to retake the Ravelsberg.

Even though his 3rd Battalion was suddenly subjected to murderous fires when this attack came after daylight on 17 October, Lieutenant Colonel Peckham's men refused to yield ground. With artillery, mortars, machine guns, and their own small arms, the battalion threw back the Germans and inflicted staggering losses. Captain Folk's Company L found itself under vicious mortar, tank, and artillery fire, but two enemy tanks were destroyed and the pillboxes reoccupied by the enemy were recaptured. By 1700 hours, the Americans had taken control of a total of nine pillboxes and had cut the last road from Aachen.

The Commanding Officer of the *116th Panzer Division,* Oberst Siegfried von Waldenburg, wrote of the determination and tenacity of the 3rd Battalion that day when he noted that their ". . . defense and counterattacks alternate. It is very, very tough fighting, and the casualties are accordingly high. Contrary to expectations, the American fights well. My own people perform splendidly. They were under uninterrupted fire. But the Americans were succeeding in the encirclement of Aachen; they broke through the *246th Division* . . . even the deployment of the *3rd Panzer-Grenadier Division* would not change anything."[48]

During the morning of 18 October, the Germans launched yet another powerful counterattack against the Regiment's positions on the Ravelsberg, supported by a massive preparatory barrage and no fewer than 22 tanks. An enemy dismounted force, estimated at two platoons of infantry, attacked the 1st Platoon, Company K, but they were eventually forced to withdraw in the face of withering counter fire.

After more armor, mortars, and artillery shelled Russell's 1st Platoon, the *3rd Panzer-Grenadier Division* tried a second time to take three pillboxes on the northern slope of the Ravelsberg, but they were again forced to withdraw.

The enemy repeated this pattern through the day, only to be greeted by determined resistance by the men of Company K. Three pillboxes were finally abandoned, however, to avoid continued heavy losses.

While he was removing wounded from the blood-soaked Ravelsberg that day, Sergeant Max Thompson noticed that a group of Germans were charging forward on Company K's 3rd Platoon to his right. Reacting immediately, Thompson ran to a nearby abandoned machine gun, manned it alone, and fired upon the swarming enemy until a fragment from a tank shell bursting close by destroyed his weapon.

Although he was shaken and dazed, Sergeant Thompson somehow regained his presence of purpose, picked up an automatic rifle, and started firing burst after burst at the Germans who were rushing into the gap in the platoon's line. Before the enemy scattered away from Thompson's fire, his weapon jammed. Throwing it aside, the sergeant took up a rocket gun he found, firing this time on a nearby armored vehicle and setting it ablaze.

"There were so many dead Germans in front of his gun at this time," Major Carter wrote later, "members of Sergeant Thompson's squad told me they could then walk to the tank without putting their feet on the ground."

By this time elements of the 30th Infantry Division had finally reached the Ravelsberg and taken over some of the pillboxes held by Company L on the north side. At dusk on 18 October, Company B reinforced Russell's 1st Platoon, and together they retook the pillboxes lost to the Germans earlier. As the first one fell, 6 enemy were killed and 11 prisoners were taken after a vicious fight. Two hours later the second pillbox in enemy hands was surrounded by two squads and reduced. Artillery was then used to knock down nearby trees so that forward observers could gain better observation of the enemy. Volleys of high explosive hit three enemy Mark IVs and a squad from Company B attacked the third pillbox.

Darkness had completely shrouded the Ravelsberg by this time. Sergeant Max Thompson lay exhausted and badly wounded. Earlier, when his men were faltering in an attempt to take the last enemy pillbox, he had crawled alone on his stomach 20 yards to take it himself. He threw grenades through its apertures as he got closer.

Despite a heavy concentration of fire by enemy forces trying to hold this pillbox, Sergeant Thompson kept up his own shower of grenades until he finally forced the Germans outside. A squad from Company B then attacked with pole charges, bazookas, and rifle grenades and took back the pillbox. The skirmish ended a very bloody day on the Ravelsberg.

"It took three of Sergeant Thompson's men to get him out of the bunker the next morning," Major Carter remembered later. "When they got him back to an aid station where our battalion surgeon, Captain Lawrence Caruso, could work on him, he was completely out of his head. He was apparently stunned right from the time he took the light tank out, and had no idea what he was doing after this. So many times the tide of battles are determined by the actions of one soldier, and Max Thompson was one soldier who did on Ravels-B that day." Later drafting the citation for the Medal of Honor awarded to Sergeant Thompson, Carter said "[His] courageous leadership inspired his men and materially contributed to the clearing of the enemy from the last remaining hold on the hill."[49]

At 1500 hours on 19 October, the enemy mustered every remaining weapon and struck simultaneous blows against two portions of the 3rd Battalion perimeter. The Germans fought stubbornly in a final effort to relieve the pressure on Aachen, and once again penetrated the Company K's lines.

Without hesitation, battalion officers again adjusted artillery fire on their own positions, rather than surrender this key terrain. The barrage inflicted casualties on the Americans, but the enemy suffered far more and was compelled to withdraw, sealing Aachen's fate. Later referring to Captain Russell's bold stance during those three crucial days, reports said, "This was the grandest action of a rifle company to date in the battalion's history."[50] The 3rd Battalion was later awarded a Presidential Unit Citation for its actions from 8 to 19 October 1944.[51]

The battle in Aachen was slowing to a walk as its defenders realized that they were encircled and the noose was drawn. On 21 October, the 26th Infantry's Regiment's 1st Battalion reached the railroad embankment that marked the western edge of central Aachen and attacked into the city center. Just to the north of the inter-regimental boundary, elements of its 3rd Battalion prepared to destroy a bunker—not knowing that one of its inhabitants was Oberst Wilck himself.

When Wilck recognized his predicament, he radioed a message to his command announcing his determination to fight to the end—and then he promptly surrendered.

The 18th Infantry Regiment's casualties during the encirclement and fall of Aachen totaled 782. Of these, 52 were killed in action and 406 were seriously wounded. Another 220 received lesser wounds or were evacuated with battle fatigue, while 112 others were declared missing in action.

During a German counterattack, Captain Bobbie Brown was observing a night attack on one of his positions when a German 120mm mortar round landed next to the bunker he was occupying. While none of the mortar fragments hit him, its concussion ended the combat career of one of the finest officers to ever serve in the 18th Infantry Regiment.

From 19 October 1944 until the end of the month, enemy activity in the Regimental sector was light. Patrol contacts were numerous, but relatively minor. While on reconnaissance with Lieutenant Colonel Learnard, Captain Malcolm Marshall detonated a minefield tripwire and was severely hurt.

November opened with the Regiment in strong defensive positions on the low, rolling ridgeline that formed the eastern perimeter of what once were Aachen's city defenses. Then, on 8 November, the second anniversary of the landings at Arzew in North Africa, the 1st Infantry Division was relieved by the 104th Infantry Division (the "Timberwolves"). The 413th Infantry Regiment took over the 18th Infantry Regiment's sector.

It was a special moment for the Timberwolves' new commander, Major General Terry Allen. In a memorandum dated 14 November 1944, General Allen noted "the distinct pride" his Timberwolves were given in taking over a battlefield from the 1st Infantry Division, ending with "We hope that the fortunes of war will permit us to continue our advance in step with the 'Fighting First'."[52]

THE HÜRTGEN FOREST AND THE BULGE

NOVEMBER 1944 TO FEBRUARY 1945

> We cannot fail but to be impressed by the fighting infantryman, his devotion to duty, courage and resourcefulness as he fought his way during the most arduous of conditions to achieve his mission.
> —Captain Edward M. Solomon

"After the rapid sweep we made across France to the Belgian-German border, and after cracking the German Siegfried Line on both sides of Aachen, breaking through to Düren and the natural barrier of the Roer River looked on a map like a short distance to go," Captain Malcolm Marshall wrote some years later in *Proud Americans*. "But maps did not show the forests except by name, or the deadly ravines and elevated observation posts the Germans held above them. They did not show the fir trees whose branches, down to the ground, hid machine gun nests, dug-outs, self-propelled guns, mortars, artillery, all in mutually supporting and long-ago planned array. Add to that the winter rains, mud and snow, thousands of mines planted for every approach avenue, and you could not think of a deadlier place to attack. I don't think the higher command had much of an idea of what the cost would be, just within four weeks."[1]

The battles for this area, the Hürtgen Forest, actually started in September 1944 while the Regiment was closing in on Aachen. The 50-square-mile forest begins about five miles south and east of Aachen and falls into a triangle pointed by the now-captured ancient city and the towns of Düren and Monschau.

At the time, the Commanding General of VII Corps, Lieutenant General Collins, was eager to smash through the German border defenses barring access to the heartland of the Third Reich, but before he could move east toward its first barrier, the Rhine River, the Corps had to cross the Roer River. In September, Collins's sector was a narrow corridor passing through heavily-urbanized terrain south of Aachen and into the large Hürtgen tract, known as the Stolberg Corridor. This area was cleared en route to crossing the Roer. Since the terrain limited him to employing only two or three regiments at a time, Collins felt that his drive across the Roer would be threatened by enemy counterattacks from within the forest. The First Army commander, Lieutenant General Courtney Hodges, agreed that the Hürtgen posed an unacceptable threat, so he and Collins ordered the forest cleared of German troops.[2]

During the period of 12–20 September, elements of the 3rd Armored Division (Task Force Lovelady) participated in a series of small engagements in the Hürtgen. Unable to achieve any measurable success during this period, the 3rd Armored was then relieved by Major General Louis A. Craig's 9th Infantry Division. Craig attacked with two regiments abreast, moving from the northwest toward the villages of Hürtgen and Germeter, both located several miles north of Schmidt, but his 47th Infantry Regiment's advance was stalemated by *Grenadier Regiment 48* of the *12th Infantry* (later *Volks-Grenadier*) *Division*. His 60th Infantry Regiment was drawn into a fruitless five-day battle with the *89th Infantry Division* for control of the high ground east of Germeter. Craig's commitment of his 39th Infantry Regimental Combat Team also failed to break the deadlock. Major General Norman D. Cota's 28th Infantry Division replaced the 9th Division in late October, but even this fresh American formation also failed to realize any appreciable success and was cut to pieces in the process. Now it was the 1st Infantry Division's turn.

The Division's primary mission was to seize jumping-off points at the northeastern corner of the forest past Langerwehe so that bridgeheads could be secured across the Roer River for VII Corps' continued drive toward the Rhine. To accomplish this, the 26th, 16th, and attached 47th Combat Teams would first advance northeast until they reached the northern edge of the Hürtgen where it overlooked the Cologne Plain. Once this maneuver was completed, Combat Team 18, initially in reserve, was to pass through leading elements to secure Langerwehe, permitting Combat Teams 16 and 26 to continue the attack eastward. Before Langerwehe could be secured, CT 18 had to capture the small villages of Wenau, Heistern, and Schönthal, all situated near a road that ran parallel to the Wehe Creek. In turn, the capture of these intermediate objectives depended on how quickly the Regiment could secure Hills 203 and 207, located to the north and south of Schönthal.

The 18th Infantry's assigned front through the forest was less than two miles, but the upcoming period was to have no equal in intensity, physical hardship, and heavy fighting.

This work began on 9 November, one day after the Regiment was relieved by the 104th Infantry Division. Lieutenant Colonel Learnard's 1st Battalion motored several miles to the east that day into a wooded assembly area near the German town of Zweifall where it reorganized, intensively trained, and planned for the Hürtgen mission. New men were trained in firing bazookas and rifle grenades, while noncoms ensured that weapons were cleaned and test fired.

Living conditions were rugged. The men kept out of the nearly freezing weather by improvising crude huts, while the division's engineers worked constantly on the roads to prevent them from turning into quagmires of mud under the continuous rain and wet snow.

Leading elements of the 2nd Battalion made their way to an assembly area 1,000 yards southwest of Zweifall on 9 November. Reflecting on the conditions, Lieutenant Colonel Williamson's battalion report for the period noted sardonically, "One wet, muddy, equipment-laden soldier looked at the dripping trees and rain-soaked ground and said, 'Huh, and we come as conquerors?' That summarized everyone's feelings about our bivouac area. Everyone felt miserable and became more so when the water level was discovered to be only a foot under the soil and no slit trenches could be dug."[3]

The next day, the 3rd Battalion moved to an assembly area in the Münster Forest near Stolberg. Williamson's men constructed lean-to quarters from logs because foxholes could not be dug in the water-soaked bivouac. Some roads were totally impassable by vehicles; those were built up with logs. Training of newly-arrived reinforcements and officers commenced, and planning for the forthcoming operation occupied much of the battalion command team's time.

The 1st Infantry Division remained in the southwestern fringes of the Hürtgen for a week while its subordinate elements conducted individual and collective training similar to that of the 18th Infantry Regiment. Continued poor weather continued delaying the impending offensive, as skies did not clear before 16 November. Then, however, Allied air forces conducted Operation QUEEN, a preparatory strike.

At 1115 hours that morning, an armada of 1,100 heavy and medium bombers from the 8th Air Force, supported by hundreds of British aircraft, conducted bombing runs against targets in the Division's zone. War correspondent Ivan "Cy" Peterman, who watched the aerial assault from Stolberg Castle, later remembered, "We thought there couldn't be a live Kraut west of the Rhine. But there was."[4]

Just before 1300 hours, the 16th Infantry Regiment jumped off in the center of the division zone from Schevenhütte towards Hamich. To the north, the attached 47th Infantry Regiment began moving toward Nothberg, while the 26th Infantry Regiment advanced from Schevenhütte toward Merode and Jüngersdorf, located two miles to the northeast.

These initial attacks indicated just how difficult it was going to be in the Hürtgen Forest was going to be. Strong enemy resistance met the 16th Infantry's attacks during the cold, snowy morning; by late afternoon, the Regiment had moved just one-half mile to the north, in the face of the well-entrenched *Grenadier Regiment 48* in Hamich. Heavy German heavy artillery and automatic weapons fire continued unabated.

By dusk, the 16th Infantry Regiment finally entered Hamich. When elements advanced through the heavily-wooded area toward nearby Hill 232 the next morning after artillery saturation fire, however, the Germans countered with tanks, self-propelled guns, and heavy artillery of their own. After a desperate fight to retake Hamich, by 1700 hours stubborn German resistance forced the 16th Combat Team to consolidate and the town was lost.

At 0800 17 November, the 3rd Battalion of the 16th Infantry attacked and quickly regained control of a third of the village, but its forces remained for most of the day under heavy artillery fire directed by German observers atop Hill 232. No appreciable gains were made, and it was not until the next afternoon before the 2nd Battalion, 16th Infantry, supported by two platoons of tanks and a platoon of TDs, finally succeeded in capturing the contested hill. The price paid for the Hürtgen ground by the 16th Infantry was starting to mount heavily, with 120 killed and over 491 officers and men medically evacuated.

General Huebner, now concerned about the resistance being encountered, decided to commit the 18th Infantry Regiment, even though the 16th and 26th had not yet reached their initial objectives. At 1400 hours, 19 November, Lieutenant Colonel Peckham's 3rd Battalion moved from their concealed bivouac area and joined the battle for the Hürtgen Forest when Captain Hess's Company I and Captain Russell's Company K set out for Wenau. As both companies advanced slowly abreast through heavily-wooded areas, German artillery rounds detonated in the treetops, raining fragments of steel and wood down on the soldiers.

Despite rising casualties, the battalion pushed on and by nightfall, its men had arrived at the southern outskirts of the town.

Colonel Smith ordered Williamson to move his 2nd Battalion to an assembly area near Schevenhütte where he could also be in position to support an assault toward what was to be a much more difficult approach to the Regiment's objective, Langerwehe. During this move, Williamson personally reconnoitered river crossings for the battalion and with a minimum of causalities maneuvered assault elements across the barren terrain.

The 3rd Battalion began moving again at 0100 hours on 20 November, first bypassing Wenau at daylight, moving toward the village of Heistern. Enemy shelling grew heavier throughout the morning and blown bridges and minefields slowed the battalion's progress.

"Every movement we made brought heavier artillery fire," Major Carter remembered. "Our radios were not working well, so we had to lay wire so Lieutenant Colonel Peckham could stay in touch with the line companies. But we could not depend on wire along the road because every time it was laid artillery would knock it out. Connections seldom lasted over five minutes. It was truly a danger zone."[5]

Supported by a platoon of tanks, Company L managed to reach the northwestern outskirts of Heistern late in the afternoon, and Company K occupied the southern half of the village by nightfall.

Lieutenant Robert E. Weisenberg, new to the company five days earlier, was found on the steps leading into one of the houses with fatal wounds to his head. "He shook hands with everybody when he took command," Private Julian Richett remembered. "An outgoing artillery shell fired over us as he was clasping my hand, and he instinctively pulled me into a hole we had dug that was just big enough to put your head into. He wasn't taking any chances." Richett had been wounded by artillery fragments the day before, and now his new platoon leader, like too many new to the Regiment, was dead.[6]

At 0330 hours on 21 November, the *47th Volks-Grenadier Division* counterattacked Heistern with two infantry companies led by Oberst Josef Kimbacher, commander of *Grenadier Regiment 104*. Division artillery first thwarted the attack. When high-explosive shells started raining down on his companies as they sought cover in the town's buildings, fighting broke out at point-blank range. Intense street fighting seesawed back and forth until dawn the next day.

In the morning Company L launched a limited-objective attack to secure the buildings to the north of Heistern's main street, while Company I fought to hold the southern side of the village seized by Company K on 20 November. The effort met with enough success to clear the way for the commitment of the 1st Battalion, and Lieutenant Colonel Learnard was ordered at noontime to pass through the village and advance northeast to secure Hill 203 north of Schönthal. After Learnard's forces infiltrated Heistern under enemy artillery and mortar fire, his leading company encountered small groups of German infantry in buildings at the northern edge of town, as well as in a nearby wooded area. Captain Miller's Company B reacted quickly, first clearing the buildings and overrunning the enemy position in the woods, but while a few prisoners were taken and some dead were found, the majority of the Germans escaped.

On the morning of 22 November, Companies B and C were ordered to advance to a line running roughly from northwest to southeast at the northern edge of the woods by Heistern. Miller's men moved just 500 yards before being pinned down by small arms fire, while the men of Company C crawled tentatively for an additional 300 yards before encountering the German main line of resistance. The defense was composed of log bunkers protecting infantry with automatic weapons; each provided excellent fields of observation and fire. Company C suffered about 50 casualties, and was forced to withdraw into a ravine 150 yards distant.

According to the 1st Battalion S-3, Captain McGregor, "Some of the men even returned to Heistern to report that the company had been wiped out, but in reality part of the company had withdrawn and taken up positions to repel a counterattack that the Germans had started with the apparent purpose of infiltrating to the rear of Company B, which had been ordered to hold its position because of

The Hürtgen Forest

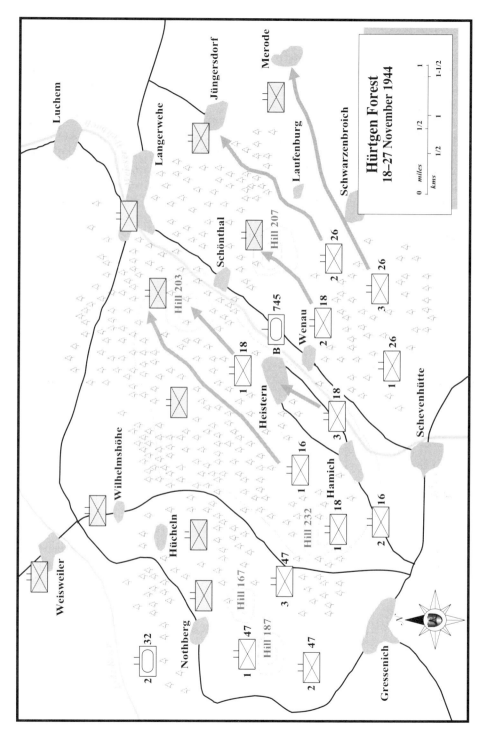

its exposed flank."[7] Later in the day Company A, commanded by the former Company C Executive Officer, the newly-promoted Captain Van Wagoner, was ordered to move up from Heistern to restore the positions that remained defended by Company C. There, they were to tie in with the right flank of Miller's company. After Van Wagoner carefully moved his men forward at 1700 hours, they completed this mission despite heavy enemy mortar and artillery fire. The company ran into more trouble that night, encountering some Germans who engaged them in hand-to-hand combat. Twelve of the enemy died of bayonet wounds.

Williamson's men fared no better during these two days. The 2nd Battalion had been ordered to seize Hill 207, south of Schönthal, in conjunction with the 1st Battalion's attack toward Hill 203. Trouble first began for the battalion at 0230 hours on 21 November when enemy artillery and mortar fire began to fall on Company E. The company nevertheless jumped off to seize Hill 207 at 0815 hours, but more heavy small arms, mortar, and artillery fire immediately forced the men back into their foxholes. At the same time, heavy fire began to fall on both Companies F and G.

By nightfall, the 2nd Battalion could not show a yard gained for the 78 casualties it suffered that day. During the night, Williamson decided to recoup by holding Coffman's men in place while Company G attacked the hill. Moving forward at dawn, his men succeeded in taking the southern slope of Hill 207, but no further progress was made.

Mixed news also arrived at the Regimental command post that day. By early afternoon, Lieutenant Colonel Peckham reported that he had finally gained complete control of Heistern, but it was a victory that came at great cost when a sniper killed one of his best officers, Company K's Captain Russell. Lieutenant Leon Bennett, an artillery observer supporting the 3rd Battalion at the time, remembered, "I was standing at a door facing a street with Captain Russell. We were trying to locate some Germans down the street who would fire in our direction whenever anyone would move. The captain was frustrated and on impulse he waved his map board across the doorway. One shot rang out and the bullet got him. This was one of my saddest days in combat during the war."[8]

"We brought Captain Russell back to an aid station on a litter across the back of a jeep," Major Carter recalled. "The bullet had split his skull. He was alive but in a coma, and there was nothing we could do for him but hold down the pain. He died before he reached the evacuation hospital. We lost one of the great infantry company commanders of World War II."[9] Russell, who had been with the Regiment since North Africa, was posthumously awarded the Distinguished Service Cross for his earlier command on the Ravelsberg.

The 3rd Battalion after-action report later underscored the difficulties all of its men endured on 22 November when it noted, "[We] faced some of the most intense artillery and mortar fire in our two years of battle and the dense woods enabled the enemy to use their artillery to its maximum effect on us that day."[10] In all, the battalion suffered 172 casualties taking the small village, but in return it captured 250 Germans. Many Germans were also killed or wounded, most of the latter being left behind to the mercies of American medics. Badly battered Company K was taken over by Captain Randolph Paulsen, who had previously been Company G's Executive Officer. The company's depleted roster was well remembered by its executive officer, Lieutenant Robert Bullard III, when he wrote in his notebook, "Lieutenant Heinrich was the only officer [platoon leader] left in the company until replacements arrived."[11]

In all, there were nearly 50 new men added to Company K's roster during its reorganization before two fresh lieutenants arrived directly from a basic infantry course in France.

With Heistern now securely in American hands, Williamson received orders from Colonel Smith to launch another assault on Hill 207 on 23 November, which was coincidentally Thanksgiving Day. Without the benefit of an artillery preparation, Company E stormed the hill at 0700 and not only took it, but also continued advancing until heavy casualties finally forced the men to stop 500 yards beyond the hill.

Company G then jumped off, overrunning a second German defensive position on nearby Hill 210 before halting. Eager to exploit the 18th Infantry Regiment's success, General Huebner scheduled an artillery preparation by 21 battalions in support of a renewed attack by the 2nd Battalion. It was scheduled to begin at 1300 hours. Due to the unclear locations of the forward infantry companies, Williamson was told to pull his men back to preclude friendly casualties. His artillery liaison officer, Captain P. K. Smith, remembered, "It was my job to adjust the artillery for this mission, which I did. We had sent out runners to the forward units, telling them to fall back to reserve positions. As the hour approached, all the companies had reported in, except for Company E."

Smith then recommended postponement, but his request was disapproved and he was told he would be relieved if he did not obey. "The shoot took place. It fell right on top of Company E. Later, I sat at the aid station, feeding cigarettes to the wounded and feeling guilty as hell. Jeff (Captain Jeffrey) staggered in and I talked to him. He said that as the rounds started to pour in, five Krauts jumped up about 20 yards away and ran as fast as they could."[12]

The barrage inflicted tremendous friendly casualties, leaving Company E so badly disorganized that Company F was ordered to pass through and continue the attack. Koenig's men were able to advance only 500 yards from the edge of the woods before darkness fell, due to heavy small arms fire to his front. Later it was learned that during the early phase of the attack, some scouts from the 2nd Battalion S-2 Section had been ordered to reconnoiter a draw between Hill 207 and Hill 194 to the east. Moving forward, the scouts were almost completely destroyed by the American artillery fire that mauled Company E.

Heavy enemy fire continued to fall on the 2nd Battalion's positions. Casualties were mounting so quickly that later reports recorded the battalion was being reduced to a mere shadow of its former self. "Lieutenant Colonel Williamson even told our 3rd Battalion commander that it took nearly two days alone to remove the dead and wounded, mostly from Company E," Major Carter remembered.[13]

The 1st Battalion's advance north of the Schevenhütte-Schönthal road to take Hill 203 resumed. On the morning of 23 November, Company B succeeded in gaining another 500 yards, but was eventually stopped by incoming fire that produced more tree burst casualties than any other day the 1st Battalion spent in Hürtgen Forest.

As darkness approached, Captain Miller conducted a platoon reconnaissance in force of German positions on Hill 203, but shortly after the rest of the company moved up, heavy small arms fire, most of which came from two houses located just to the north of the hill, stopped them. The company suffered 22 casualties before pulling back, but when Captain Van Wagoner's Company A was ordered forward to gain contact with the enemy south of Hill 203, he soon reported that the Germans had withdrawn.

On the morning of 24 November, Company F began clearing the main road northeastward to Schönthal. After a brisk firefight, they seized a large country manor. Weakened by ever-growing casualties, the 2nd Battalion reorganized there that evening, but Lieutenant Colonel Williamson noted in his after-action report, "Not much was accomplished other than telling replacements what platoon and squad they were in, and trying to select noncommissioned officers to lead those men that were left. Company E was in the worst condition of all, having more new men than old."[14]

Captain Coffman had been wounded the day before, and Lieutenant Samuel M. Lehman temporarily took command on 24 November, before Lieutenant Jack Streeter assumed responsibility. Company G's Captain Jeffrey had also been evacuated after he went back into the line following the fratricidal artillery strike on 23 November.

Despite the 2nd Battalion's difficulties, Van Wagoner's Company A sprang forward early that morning to clear the woods by Hill 203, while a reorganized Company C moved up and established defensive positions while in battalion reserve. The company had a new commanding officer by this time, Captain Richard Lindo. Lindo had asked Colonel Smith for a company command, and having been a liaison officer serving with infantry companies in the front lines since the Regiment's days in North Africa, Smith was willing to give him this task. "I joined the company when it was down to 48 or 49 men," Lindo remembered when he went into the line on 24 November. "I wanted to meet every man, so I crawled from foxhole to foxhole in the woods. These soaked holes were covered with logs because of the heavy shrapnel that was being deflected from the trees, and at the time we were under a renewed artillery attack. When I was called back to a battalion officer's meeting later, Colonel Learnard said we would be making a divisional attack the next day. They sent me, I think, 30 men as replacements that night. The poor bastards didn't have a chance, because they didn't know who their sergeants were, or who anybody else was."[15]

Reinforced by some scouts from the 1st Battalion S-2 Section, Company B made two unsuccessful attempts to seize Hill 203 that next day. The only gains came during late afternoon, when an enemy strongpoint 150 yards south of the hill was eliminated with the aid of a pair of Sherman tanks.

Describing the task that still awaited, however, the 1st Battalion after-action report noted that day, "The German defenders at Hill 203 were the most stubborn encountered by us on a battlefield. Pounded continually by our mortars and artillery, they preferred to hold and die on the reverse slope in order to delay us the use of the hill as the all-important observation point on the plains of Cologne which lay beyond."[16]

The 1st Battalion again attacked Hill 203 on 25 November, this time with a platoon from Company B and one from Company A. Observers first located a company of Germans protecting an artillery outpost on Hill 184 to the battalion's right front that stood before Hill 203; DIVARTY quickly placed heavy fire on it and caused an apparent displacement of the enemy guns to the rear.

Two tanks from the 1st Platoon of Company B, 745th Tank Battalion were then called upon to reduce a row of houses where fire was holding up Miller's platoon, and the tanks first shelled these buildings with HE and white-phosphorous rounds as they rumbled forward. When the leading tank approached within 100 yards of the first house, a mortar observer spotted an enemy 75mm antitank gun in the woods, and tried to stop the tank from advancing. The tank proceeded to a spot off the road at the edge of the woods, but the antitank gun's crew scored two direct hits, killing one crew member and wounding three others.

Both platoons attacked again at 1600 hours, quickly killing or capturing the defenders in one position near the base of the hill. After leaving a squad from each platoon behind to hold this newly-captured ground, the remainder of the assault force attempted to seize the crest of Hill 203. They were caught, though, in murderous grazing crossfire from enemy machine gunners, panzerfausts, rifle grenades, and rifles when they reached a point 100 yards short of their goal; the men were forced to dig in. Later that night, Lieutenant William E. Tolbert of Company B reached a forester's observation tower atop the hill.

The next day, 26 November, the 1st Battalion was still fighting on the hill and to its flanks, but Lieutenant Colonel Learnard gained a small respite when elements of the 3rd Battalion, 16th Infantry knocked out the well-camouflaged 75mm antitank gun that had created havoc on the previous day. By now, however, both Companies A and B had gained partial observation of the Regiment's final objective, Langerwehe, prompting Colonel Smith to order the 3rd Battalion out of reserve for the attack on the village.

At 1030 hours the next day, the 3rd Battalion advanced toward Langerwehe under a heavy smoke screen laid down by Company A, 87th Chemical Mortar Battalion. The goal of the Battalion's mission was to loosen the German grip on the Regiment's now thoroughly-bloodied sector of the forest. Artillery supplied heavy preparatory and supporting fires, with Army Air Force fighter bombers furnishing close-air support as the 1st and 3rd Battalions made their final push on Langerwehe and Hill 203.

"First, the artillery laid plenty of smoke," Major Carter recalled. "Major Sawyer, our S-3, was in a plane directing other fire to be sure it was properly placed, and the Germans would not know what we were doing. The smoke had to be placed just west of the road and woods into Langerwehe, and it had to be dense for as long as we needed it. There was a field that was open, used for farming. I was sure this area was poorly defended."[17]

The 3rd Battalion attacked, with Company L leading, and pushed into the village. First, its men cleaned out a section south of a railroad line by mid-afternoon.[18] Another smoke screen was laid down and Company I crossed the open ground and attacked the town from the west. "I had just one call," Major Carter recalled. "They had received two random rounds of mortars. No damage. The field had absorbed their effect. Langerwehe was entered with no casualties."[19]

After fighting their way across the railroad tracks toward the main lateral road in the village, however, an enemy antitank gun fired at Hess's men as they started entering the houses on the north side of the roadway. As soon as the gun was located the enemy was cleared by rifle fire and the gun was destroyed. During this time, Captain Paulsen moved Company K to occupy the southern part of town just to the north of the rail line while Captain Folk rushed a platoon across the tracks and assisted Hess's men in clearing buildings in their zone.

"It was chaos at this time," Major Carter said. "The Germans were using every route they could find to abandon the railroad station and the surrounding area." By nightfall the area south of the tracks and the western end of town was firmly in the 3rd Battalion's hands, but small arms fire continued through the night along the northern streets of Langerwehe. "The Germans could now only move east, where they were going to run into our 2nd Battalion," Carter declared.[20]

Williamson had launched his attack that morning in support of the 3rd Battalion. He sent Company G to the northern end of the woods outside of Langerwehe where they ran into the Germans' positions. These locations were methodically reduced; 40 Germans were killed or captured before the company halted at dusk.

Company F, which had advanced in support of Company G, encountered heavy enemy resistance all day. Proven that the Germans were determined to fight on, prisoners taken by Company F disclosed that the *3rd Battalion, Parachute Regiment 5* had relieved the *15th Army Assault Battalion* during the previous night. A platoon of Company E was redeployed to cover a gap that opened between Companies F and G, but when it became clear that little more progress would be made before the next morning, Williamson ordered his men to halt and dig in for the night.

During the night of 27/28 November, the enemy unit facing Company F suddenly withdrew, leaving behind only a few scattered stragglers. The Americans took advantage of the opportunity early on 28 November, and against practically no opposition quickly moved to the edge of the woods facing the northeastern outskirts of Langerwehe. Williamson then directed Company E, with tanks in support, to pass through Company F to continue the assault along the main road leading to the village. Adding to the final reduction of the Langerwehe defenses, Company E made contact in the afternoon with Company L and assisted in clearing out the eastern end of town. Koenig's platoons followed, arriving at dusk where his men established defensive positions for the night. The railroad underpass had been destroyed, however, so no vehicular traffic could get into town. Ammunition and rations had to be hand-carried to the forward companies even though Langerwehe was now securely in the possession of the 18th Infantry Regiment.

As the village was being mopped up, Company C was designated to make the final assault on still unsecured Hill 203. Since the company had lost most of its experienced officers and NCOs in previous fighting, Captain Lindo organized a mixed assault platoon using the few remaining veterans he had at his disposal. The composite unit was then placed under the command of Lieutenant Charles Marvain, leader of the Weapons Platoon.

With just two officers and 27 enlisted men, Marvain assaulted the hill from the west as two medium tanks raked the northern slopes with HE and machine-gun fire. Hill 203 fell in just 15 minutes, but there were only two officers and four enlisted men left when the fighting ended. The 1st Battalion report later noted, "Our objective had finally been taken after several days of costly fighting and now the much-needed observation was made available to the artillery.

That night the 1st Battalion withdrew to Heistern for rest and reorganization. Company C remained in position on Hill 203 to secure the vital artillery observation post until relieved the evening of 28 November. The final days of the month saw the 1st Battalion move to Jüngersdorf to relieve the 3rd Battalion, 26th Infantry."[21]

The Hürtgen battles resulted in one of the worst periods of the war for casualties in the 18th Infantry Regiment, and the time in the forest was remembered by its veteran fighters as being as gruesome as the last two weeks in the hills of North Africa. Battalion reports reflected the losses with descriptions of casualties that "reduced [their ranks] to a mere shadow to their former selves,"[22] and that "men and officers whose gallantry and combat leadership were second to none in the history of American arms"[23] died during the fighting. According to the 1st Infantry Division history, "Seven infantry divisions and one armored combat team tried to break the Hürtgen. All had emerged mauled, reduced, and in low spirits. Only two got all the way through—the 1st Division along the northern edge, and the 78th [Infantry] Division, which eventually seized the dams as the campaign ended. Statistics revealed for every yard gained, the Hürtgen claimed more lives than any other objective the Americans took in Europe."[24]

After losing 1,000 officers and men to shellfire, bullets, exposure, and trench foot, Colonel Smith wrote in his November 1944 After-Action Report:

It was the first time that replacements had to be employed hurriedly to bolster the waning numbers of the line companies. However, the enemy paid even more heavily for his war of attrition in spite of the fact that he fought on ground of his own choosing in well-prepared positions with a maximum of support from artillery and self-propelled guns. Seven hundred and twenty-two prisoners [from the] *3rd Panzer Grenadier Division, 12th Volks-Grenadier Division, 47th Volks-Grenadier Division,* and *3rd Parachute Division* were processed through the regimental prisoner-of-war cage.[25]

While the Germans lost the key towns of Hamich, Heistern, and Langerwehe by the end of November, their weakened situation did not diminish their resolve to continue to fight to the east of the Hürtgen Forest.

The 26th Infantry Regiment approached Merode, which was located just out of the forest where the reconstituted *3rd Parachute Division* opposed its advance on the first day of December 1944.

On 3 December the 16th Infantry Regiment seized Luchem, held by *2nd Battalion, Parachute Regiment 8* just north of Langerwehe. The 18th Infantry had been alerted for an attack eastward toward Düren that day which called for the seizure of the stepping stone villages of Obergeich, Geich, and Echtz, prompting Colonel Smith to order Williamson's 2nd Battalion to establish an outpost line several hundred yards east of Langerwehe. This would provide security for other combat team forces when they jumped off. The Germans eventually withdrew, but maintained surveillance over Williamson's positions for two days. Still evincing their stubbornness, German troops probed the 1st Battalion lines that had moved just north of Jüngersdorf along the Aachen-Cologne Railroad.

After Luchem fell, the Germans looked farther north, toward Lucherberg, which was held by the 104th Infantry Division. An attack failed and did not spread into the 1st Infantry Division lines. Patrolling during the first week of December then revealed that enemy activity had declined substantially, and on 4 December, the 9th Infantry Division received orders calling them to relieve the exhausted 1st Infantry Division. That effectively cancelled the plans for Combat Team 18's further attacks to the east.

Instead, the Regiment moved far to the rear, back to the villages of Plombières, Gemmenich, and Romerdale in Belgium, to rest for what was expected to be an entire month. Welcomed as heroes in Gemmenich where the town square had been renamed "Place de Colonel Peckham," troops were billeted in the warm homes of its grateful residents. Every man in the Regiment was issued new uniforms; company parties were held; some passes were issued for trips to Paris; and USO and motion picture shows provided some distraction from the recent carnage of the Hürtgen Forest. American Red Cross Clubmobiles were also made available to the troops.

The entire area was dotted with small villages, sweeping hills, beautiful orchards, and pastures. The very friendly Belgian people eventually welcomed troops from every unit into their homes.

This serenity belied the violence that lay ahead. Just eight days into the rest period, the 18th Infantry Regiment was instructed to be ready to move southward to Eupen to help stem a massive German offensive in the previously quiet Ardennes sector.

On the foggy morning of 16 December, the Germans launched a well-planned counteroffensive between Monschau and Echternach, Belgium, with the *Fifth Panzer Army,* the *Sixth Panzer Army,* and the *Seventh* Army. The Germans termed this operation WACHT AM RHEIN, while American soldiers later dubbed it "The Battle of the Bulge" after the initial salient those forces made in the Allied lines.

The primary objectives of the massive German assault were the capture of the Belgian capital of Brussels and the important seaport of Antwerp. By seizing the latter city the Germans would split the Allies in two, with the British isolated to the north along the Dutch border and the Americans south, in Belgium. Strategically, the Germans hoped that this physical rift would also bring about a political schism that could lead to the conclusion of a separate armistice in the West, allowing them to continue the struggle with the Soviets.

At 1530 hours on 17 December, under direct orders from V Corps, Colonel Smith's 18th Regimental Combat Team was trucked to Eupen where the men established defensive positions on the eastern outskirts of town. Smith's mission was to organize a defense of an important road center here which controlled traffic to the front from several key American supply dumps. He was also directed to prevent any enemy force from entering Eupen via Monschau and Malmédy. While enemy mechanized units had not been detected in the vicinity of Eupen, a force of 500 German *Fallschirmjäger* (paratroopers) had been dropped into the heavy woods several miles south of the town on the night of 16/17 December.

A small element of these paratroopers was reported to have cut the Eupen-Malmédy Road on 17 December, prompting Colonel Smith to send Company L south the following morning. Captain Folk had been given the mission of clearing out any hostile force interdicting American vehicles attempting to travel along the road. A reinforced platoon of the 16th Infantry Regiment moved north, so the two forces could converge on the paratroopers and capture them. The Americans linked forces late in the afternoon after capturing four Germans, but the majority of the paratroopers moved more deeply into the woods rather than contest the American infantry.

Interrogation revealed that the captured paratroopers were from *Combat Group von der Heydte,* a special unit under the command of the highly experienced and decorated Oberst Friedrich A. *Freiherr* [Baron] von der Heydte.

Before nightfall on 18 December, Colonel Smith deployed Paulsen's Company K south to reinforce Company L, and both rifle units established blocking positions to prevent German paratroopers from moving closer to Eupen.

In the meantime, V Corps Headquarters, which was growing increasingly concerned about a reported German buildup east of Monschau, had alerted Colonel Smith on 18 December to be prepared to send a battalion eastward to reinforce the 9th Infantry Division's 47th Infantry Regiment. The situation changed rapidly as the afternoon wore on. At 1400 hours another alert was issued, this time warning Smith to be prepared to move to the vicinity of Waimes where the enemy was threatening an armored breakthrough. Colonel Smith noted with apparent frustration, "By nightfall we had received so many warning orders owing to the uncertainty of the enemy's next move that we were actually prepared for any task."[26]

It was not until the next morning when the situation became clarified. At 0800 hours, the Regiment received orders to resume its sweep of the woods south of Eupen while CCA, 3rd Armored Division relieved the combat team from V Corps control. That enabled Colonel Smith to bring the entire division to bear in blocking the *12th SS-Panzer Division "Hitlerjugend"* (the "Hitler Youth" SS armored division) for the occupation of Bütgenbach, south of Eupen. Before night fell on 19 December, Company K had captured 12 additional paratroopers prisoner and rescued 23 Americans who had been captured before the Germans withdrawn into the dense forest south of Eupen.

At 0720 hours on 20 December, the Regiment was alerted to move to an assembly area in the vicinity of Sourbrodt (four miles northwest of Bütgenbach), to be employed as Division reserve. Shortly afterward, Colonel Smith was ordered to dispatch the 2nd Battalion to the sector of the Combat Team 26, under whose control it would operate. The Regiment completed its move to Sourbrodt by 1635 hours and, due to very heavy pressure throughout the 26th Infantry Regiment's sector, the 2nd Battalion was immediately committed on a broad frontage

At 0430 hours on 21 December, *SS-Panzer-Grenadier Regiment 25*, reinforced by the *3rd Battalion, SS-Panzer-Grenadier Regiment 26, SS-Panzer Regiment 12*, and *SS-Tank Destroyer Battalion 12*, launched a fierce attack against the American positions on the high ground outside Bütgenbach. Many German tanks rolled through the hail of American artillery fire to assail the flank of the 26th Infantry Regiment's 2nd Battalion; although American antitank guns destroyed several panzers, the 57mm guns protecting the sector were soon knocked out. The German tank crews next began silencing American machine-gun positions to permit their supporting panzergrenadiers to advance.

Having created a gap in the American defensive perimeter, the Germans quickly began moving toward the Dom Bütgenbach, a large country manor south of the town itself. An M-10 TD from the 634th Tank Destroyer Battalion was able to claim seven kills as the German armor drove more deeply into the American lines, but five panzers still broke through and headed for the command post of Lieutenant Colonel Derrill M. Daniel's 2nd Battalion, 26th Infantry Regiment. Two Shermans sitting behind a barn next to the command post knocked out a pair of German tanks before they were destroyed, yet the surviving trio harassed Daniel's command post personnel for several hours until TDs knocked out two of them. The surviving tank made it safely back to German lines, chased by bursting 81mm mortar rounds of the battalion's heavy weapons company.

At 0630 hours the following day, the Germans launched another attack against the 26th Infantry Regiment's sector, this time consisting of elements of both the *12th SS-Panzer Division* and *12th Volks-Grenadier Division*. Four enemy tanks broke through Company G, 18th Infantry Regiment, now commanded by Captain Nelson Park, but three of the panzers were soon stuck in the mud and became stationary targets. At 0955 hours, Learnard's 1st Battalion was alerted to move to the vicinity of the reported breakthrough and to counterattack in a southeasterly direction to restore the position. After several changes in plans, the situation improved significantly when both the commander of the 1st *Battalion, SS-Panzer Regiment 12* and 3rd *Battalion, SS-Panzer-Grenadier Regiment 26* were seriously wounded, taking much of the drive out of the German push. Rather than counterattack, Learnard's companies then moved to Bütgenbach that afternoon to effect a relief of the 1st Battalion, 26th Infantry; this was completed by 1000 hours on 23 December.

Williamson's 2nd Battalion then redeployed southwest of Bütgenbach, as the 18th Infantry Regiment assumed control of the sector south of the town. Colonel Smith moved his command post to Nidrum, a small village north of Bütgenbach, and Lieutenant Colonel Peckham deployed his 3rd Battalion into a reserve position on the northern outskirts of the village the next day.

The Division's plan now called for holding this newly-organized line south of Bütgenbach indefinitely. Colonel Smith took immediate steps to prepare strong defensive positions. Extensive patrolling was to be conducted to the south to guard the northern approaches to the Bütgenbacher Heck, a vast wooded area running parallel to the new front. For several nights afterward, engineers, riflemen, antitank squads, and pioneers toiled ceaselessly to sow minefields, erect roadblocks, prepare dummy gun positions, and string barbed wire. Frequent reconnaissance and combat patrols carried the fight to the enemy's lines in small but bitter actions, prompting Colonel Smith to flatly note, "In reality, the Bütgenbach sector became a deadly training ground for a high percentage of new men."[27]

It was also Germany's weather and downfall that was on Colonel Smith's mind as the month ended. "The temperature dropped; the north wind blew fiercely and snow storms covered our positions with a white blanket," he remembered. "Winter had come to the 18th Infantry on the Western Front. Squad and platoon shelters were constructed underground out of hewn timber and stoves were installed in them. Thus the year 1944 ended with the Regiment dug in on a barren, snow-covered front in eastern Belgium, and what the new year would bring only time would tell."[28]

The new year brought a First Army Letter of Instruction dated 1 January, directing VII Corps to launch an attack on 3 January with the mission of gaining contact with elements of the Third Army in the vicinity of Bastogne.

At 0830 hours that morning, VII Corps counterattacked along a 25-mile front, making gains all along its lines, while the adjacent V Corps conducted a strong demonstration to present the appearance of another general attack. At the same time, XVIII Airborne Corps continued to apply pressure along the left flank of VII Corps, forcing the enemy to begin withdrawing from the northwestern shoulder of the Bulge salient on 9 January.

Phase two of the First Army offensive called for V Corps to seize the defile below Ondenval, located ten miles southwest of Bütgenbach, while securely anchoring its flank south of the village. Once these tasks were completed, V Corps was to secure a line from Mirfeld, the high ground four miles southeast of Möderscheid, to Büllingen, six miles southeast of Bütgenbach. The Commanding General of V Corps ordered the 1st Infantry Division to seize the defile below Ondenval and in turn, Division assigned that mission to the 18th Infantry Regiment. Colonel Smith then directed Learnard's 1st Battalion to secure the defile. The 2nd and 3rd Battalions were to conduct a support attack southward to capture dominating terrain near Schoppen, a small town located to the east of Ondenval.

The Regiment's new area of operations consisted of a series of high ridges cut by deep draws and wooded ravines. The approaches to both Ondenval and Schoppen, however, were completely exposed with fields surrounding the towns, leaving infantrymen exposed to fire as they advanced.

The Bütgenbacher Heck was situated on a ridge with adjoining high ground providing the Germans complete domination over the snow-filled ground between their lines and those of the 2nd and 3rd Battalions south of Bütgenbach. Wind-whipped snow averaged two feet in depth, with drifts as high as five in places; temperatures were well below freezing, even during the day.

Troops from *Parachute Regiment 5* manned the main line of resistance facing the 18th Infantry Regiment, which consisted of a series of log bunkers along the northern edge of a large wooded area directly in front of the 2nd and 3rd Battalions. The German line contained numerous automatic weapon positions, as well as trenches that connected the enemy riflemen to these emplacements, making the olive drab-coated American infantry ripe targets for sharpshooters in a no-mans land of deep, white snow.

Colonel Smith issued his order for the upcoming offensive on 14 January. The 3rd Battalion was to attack at 0600 hours on the next morning and seize Hill 566, located 1,500 yards south of his line of departure, while the 2nd Battalion would remain in its current location to defend the line south of Bütgenbach. Peckham requested permission to launch his attack at 0300 hours, so his men could cross the open ground well before first light, but higher headquarters refused because it might alert the enemy regarding the impending First Army offensive. A compromise was reached, permitting the 3rd Battalion to commence its attack at 0500 hours, still well before first light.

Lieutenant Colonel Peckham's orders called for Captain Hess' Company I, with a platoon of TDs from Company B, 634th TD Battalion, and a section of heavy machine guns from Captain William E. Coshun's Company M, to conduct the main attack against Hill 566. Captain Folk's Company L, with a platoon of tanks attached from Company B, 745th Tank Battalion, was to attack on Hess's left with the objective of securing an area known as the Schleid. Company K, now commanded by Lieutenant Clark Johnson, was to remain on the line of departure as battalion reserve. Coshun's 81mm mortar platoon would support the attack from positions 1,000 yards behind the line of departure, assisted by a platoon of 4.2-inch mortars from Company C, 86th Chemical Mortar Battalion. A platoon of Company B, 1st Engineer Battalion, would clear gaps in friendly minefields along the line of departure before the attack kicked off. To maximize the element of surprise, no preparatory fires were scheduled.

The attack began on an inauspicious note when Company L crossed its line of departure 45 minutes late. When dawn came, Folk's exposed rifle platoons were raked by heavy machine-gun fire while they were moving in waist deep snow in full view. The company quickly began sustaining casualties. By 0630 hours, German artillery and mortar fire also began raining down on his men while the platoon of tanks was having its own difficulties trying to negotiate the gap in the minefields. The first two Shermans failed to weave through the narrows of the gap and were disabled by mines. The third tank made it all of the way through, but was destroyed by enemy fire before it advanced 200 yards. The last tank simply bogged down in the deep snow.

Captain Folk's radio messages to Peckham reflected just how badly the assault began. At 0600 hours his first report simply said, "Two tanks lost." At 0610 hours he radioed that the third tank had been hit, and he reported the fourth tank stopped in the snow at 0630 hours. Then, at 0645 hours Folk's fourth message read, "Two assault platoons decimated. Am committing support platoon."[29] That attempt fared no better, quickly wilting away under blistering machine-gun, mortar, and artillery fire. Peckham immediately asked Colonel Smith for permission to withdraw Company L to the line of departure under a protective cover of HE and smoke fire, and this permission was granted. By 0830 hours, the last of Folk's surviving soldiers had reached friendly lines, but when the roll was taken his executive officer revealed that just one officer and 43 men from the assault platoons had returned. Some of the unaccounted for men remained pinned down in the open, while others who were seriously hit were destined to die in the frigid cold of no-man's land. Tracked carriers ("Weasels") moved some of the wounded out in early afternoon and other exhausted and freezing men returned to the lines later in the day.

Company I had encountered far less trouble when its supporting attack kicked off at 0500 hours. Captain Hess's attached TDs successfully negotiated minefield gaps, while assault platoons advanced some 1,200 yards by 0600 hours without serious resistance. As dawn broke, his men were just 200 yards from the German main line of resistance, which ran parallel to a railroad embankment that cut across the company sector. Daylight brought some fire to Hess's front, as well as flanking fire from the woods adjacent to the rails, but tank destroyers came forward and took the wooded area under direct fire with their 76mm guns while Coshun's mortars fired over the company's front line into the German positions.

Company I's attack was ultimately halted by effective German artillery, mortar, and machine-gun fire. This prompted him to commit his own support platoon to the east of his line of advance, but this was where Company L was then under fire. Although the tank destroyers fired continuously for the next several hours with just a section at a time returning to the rear to replenish ammunition, Company I's repeated attempts to advance were halted. At 1800 hours, Company K was rushed up to attack through Hess's men, but Lieutenant Johnson's attempts to attack south into the German lines were also stopped. Artillery supported the attacking companies through the day, but other than Company K making contact with Company K, 16th Infantry Regiment, neither attacking force could do little more than dig in for the night and protect the day's modest gains.

Armored bulldozers started clearing a road to the new line after dark as the 3rd Battalion S-4 launched a tremendous effort to get hot food forward from the battalion trains to the battered rifle companies. The drivers of the Weasels again did yeoman's work evacuating the wounded as well as bringing up much-needed ammunition and supplies, but the battalion aid station soon reported to Peckham that the day's operations had been almost as costly to Companies I and K as they had been for Company L. Captain Hess lost 50 percent of his leading platoons' strength during the attack while Lieutenant Johnson's men also suffered 15 casualties. One of Hess's men, Sergeant James Brannen, remembered years later just how bad 15 January had been for his 3rd Platoon.

"Our squads were well dispersed with scouts out front," Brannen reflected. "I was immediately behind my two scouts. The Germans let them get within about 100 yards of some planted pine trees and when they cut loose with everything the first machine-gun burst killed both scouts."

Brannen instinctively dove for the ground, knowing his only chance for survival was to lie in the snow and feign death. In a few minutes every soldier in the open field near him was either killed or wounded from the withering German fire. When the gunfire stopped, Sergeant Brannen continued to play possum, and he listened anxiously in the stillness to the occasional moans and cries of his wounded comrades. "I then thought I could hear noises that indicated the Germans were pulling out of the woods in retreat, but I could not be sure," he remembered. "After a time, I began to crawl slowly, inching my way back across the field. I soon came upon my platoon leader, Lieutenant Anthony J. Monz, and he was covered with snow and wounded in the chest, but still alive and calling out for aid. I reassured him he would get it as quickly as possible and then I immediately got up and dashed for the safety of the tree line back near the company command post. I found two or three men, and I sent one for the medics and took the others back to the lieutenant. Together we dragged him through the snow and then off onto a little road in the trees, where an ambulance Jeep arrived to take our lieutenant back to the battalion aid station."[30]

It was later reported to Sergeant Brannen that Lieutenant Monz had died. Many years later, Sergeant Brannen could still vividly remember that 15 January of 1945. "I was the only man in my squad to come out of that fire fight. Sadly, I don't remember any of the other men, since they were replacements and I didn't have them long enough to even learn their names."

Those who did survive the day's attack and who were left in the line on the edge of the forest were miserable that night. As Anti-Tank Company Commander Captain Edward M. Solomon later noted in his operations report for the period, "Water in the five-gallon cans brought up by the Weasels was frozen by the time it reached the troops, as was the water in the men's canteens. "C" rations were also frozen and the issued heat tablets were insufficient to thaw out the contents of the cans. The wool overcoats and gloves the men wore were wet from constant contact with the snow. Overshoes also proved inadequate to protect a man from the wet and cold. Although adequate in defensive stands in sheltered positions, [their issued clothing] proved useless in the attack through the deep snow."[31]

The 3rd Battalion received 150 replacements by late afternoon on 15 January, 100 of whom were sent to Company L, now in battalion reserve. The other 50 were marched through the snow and ice to Captain Hess's Company I. The next day, the 3rd Battalion focused on reorganizing its shattered rifle companies while the 16th Infantry Regiment attacked Faymonville and Schoppen on their right flank.

On the morning of 16 January, the 2nd Infantry Division's 23rd Infantry Regiment, temporarily attached to the 1st Infantry Division, jumped off from Ondenval (which they had captured the day before), with the mission of securing the villages of Iveldingen and Montenau. The 23rd's attack was stopped by heavy small arms and artillery fire from German positions on the high ground immediately south of the Amel River, and only one of its rifle companies managed to reach the river bank. Exposed to direct fire from eight self-propelled guns of *Parachute Tank Destroyer Battalion 3*, the Americans suffered heavy casualties and as their position became untenable, they pulled back to high ground southwest of Ondenval. Learnard's 1st Battalion, which was originally scheduled to attack near Büllingen that afternoon, saw its plans changed as a result of the 23rd's difficulties. New orders were issued at 2200 hours attaching Learnard's men to this unit. The 1st Battalion was then directed to travel by truck to its new area of operations at 0700 hours the next morning for what was soon to be dubbed "Operation YUKON."

While Learnard was busy redeploying his battalion, at 0200 hours on 17 January, Captain Hess's Company I and Lieutenant Johnson's Company K again attacked southward on a 600-yard front along the Bütgenbacher Heck.[32] After advancing 500 yards against moderate resistance, the rifle companies encountered a frozen stream in a gully where the snow was between four and five feet deep. Despite enemy mortar rounds exploding in this gully, the attacking companies continued to move forward in the heavy snow until they reached higher ground, but they were finally held up by fire of all types and daylight found the two companies barely holding on the crest of Hill 566. Casualties for both companies numbered 30 to 35, with one-third of the losses attributable to frostbite. Efforts were made during the day to get the men sorely-needed additional winter clothing, but the attempt was only partially successful until a tank dozer managed to clear a path that allowed some supplies to reach the freezing troops by nightfall.

By this time, the 1st Battalion had completed its move to a position 2,000 yards west of the summit of the Wolfbusch, a mountain about 750-feet high near the 23rd Infantry Regiment's original line of departure. Learnard's orders were to assemble at Ligneuville, and then to attack the enemy entrenched near the base of the Wolfbusch just south of Ondenval on the Amel River. The information on the enemy positions was very sketchy, but it was known that they had a great deal of artillery, mortar support, and self-propelled guns. Given that little was known about their dispositions or strength, Learnard made the bold decision to take his battalion to a new attack position atop the Wolfbusch, where he intended to establish his line of departure for an attack that would quickly take him into the enemy lines from their rear, minimizing his casualties.

A map reconnaissance disclosed that there were no roads leading to the top of the mountain, and that the few trails that wove upwards were not passable except by Weasels. Deep snow covered the spruces on the mountainside and blowing snow reduced visibility almost to zero when Learnard's men moved out that afternoon.

The infantry companies moved without their attached tanks and TDs, which were left behind in Ligneuville. The march up the Wolfbusch was very difficult, but after short breaks every four to five hundred yards and having to backtrack halfway down the hill after guides lost their way to the summit, Learnard's men found a suitable route leading them to the north face of the mountain.

Captain Miller's Company B led the battalion to an attack position about 900 yards south of the enemy's main line of resistance. An outpost was captured without losing the element of surprise. The exhausted Americans then quickly started to dig in for the night, most using logs and branches to cover their foxholes. Before darkness fell, a patrol was sent out to reconnoiter the enemy's positions while Learnard and his company commanders, accompanied by a security detail, conducted their own patrol to develop a plan of attack for the next morning. After discovering a firebreak amongst the thick trees that afforded an opportunity to attack straight downward, Learnard decided that Companies B and C would conduct the assault abreast on either side of this lane while Company A remained in reserve. Captain Bowers' heavy weapons would be divided, with a platoon of heavy machine guns each going to Companies B and C, while his 81mm mortars would fire from their current positions atop the mountain to support the assault.

When the reconnaissance patrol returned after dark Learnard noted that they "had not been detected and the enemy still didn't have any idea that a whole battalion had moved to the high ground just 900 yards to his rear that night."[33]

The 1st Battalion attacked at 0830 hours as planned, into a driving north wind and a blinding snowstorm. The advance was hampered as winds whipped up through the dense trees, and since firebreaks and trails were covered with snow the Americans could not locate them. Consequently it was impossible to find the boundaries between the two companies and direction could only be maintained by using compasses in the face of the fierce storm.

As soon as Captain Lindo's Company C crossed its line of departure, the 1st Platoon encountered a strong enemy patrol. A sharp firefight ensued and eight enemy were killed, 12 were captured, and the remainder were driven off.

This skirmish delayed Lindo's other platoons, but since the artillery preparation for the attack had already started to fall on the German positions, it was necessary for Company B to continue down the fire lane in the bitter cold while Lindo's men stayed echeloned to his left rear. This resulted in both companies having open flanks, but their riflemen nevertheless attacked down the hill.

In some places, a nearly vertical drop forced the men to slide in the snow while grabbing tree branches to slow their descent. Enemy artillery had opened up shortly after Lindo's men were discovered by the enemy patrol, most of the volume coming from the right rear of the battalion line from the vicinity of Montenau.

A few men were killed and wounded from the crashing thunder of tree bursts caused by the enemy artillery, but since the Germans did not know the exact location of Learnard's attack and their observers were also blinded by the snow, most of this fire was ineffective. Cannon Company, however, lost its forward observer at approximately 0900 hours, the well-liked Lieutenant Leonard N. DeNucci, when a shell landed near one of Captain Van Wagoner's platoons near the top of the Wolfbusch.

Since the enemy was now alerted, Learnard ordered his rifle companies to push down the mountain rapidly and close on the Germans before they could reorient their forces to meet his strike from their rear. The two attacking American companies moved in quickly, employing a heavy volume of marching fire, and by 1100 hours the entire German position had been cleared. According to the enemy battalion commander who was captured with his entire staff, every defender from the *3rd Battalion, Parachute Regiment 8* was either killed or captured. Three 88mm antitank guns and a four-gun battery of 105mm howitzers, together with their prime movers and several half-track personnel carriers were also taken. A later battalion report even noted, "The weather had been so severe, the terrain so difficult, the prisoners of war we took expressed surprise that we had been able to attack at all."[34]

With the road leading around the base of the mountain from Ligneuville toward Montenau now cleared, tanks and TDs were brought to a forward assembly area near Ondenval, and two TDs were placed in positions along the road going southward to the small village of Montenau. By this time, Companies B and C had taken up a defensive position on the slopes facing to the south and the east.

Captain Van Wagoner's Company A remained atop the Wolfbusch with the headquarters staff and Company D, less the detached machine gunners.

Early that evening, Learnard received orders to move out the next morning to continue his attack and seize Montenau. He called a meeting of his company commanders and his staff where he then divulged his next imaginative plan. Lindo's Company C, with a section of heavy machine guns from Company D, a platoon of tanks from the 745th Tank Battalion, one platoon of tank destroyers of the 634th Tank Destroyer Battalion, and a platoon of engineers from Company B, 1st Engineer Combat Battalion, were to assault Montenau from the north. The balance of the 1st Battalion was to move down the mountain through a belt of low trees to a position where it could launch its attack against Montenau from the west. Whoever got into position first was to hold up so that both elements could attack simultaneously. Ironically, during the night a violent blizzard with winds of up to 50 mph sprang up, and it was into this bitter storm that the troops moved out at daylight on 19 January.

The 3rd Battalion also jumped off south of Bütgenbach at 0500 hours with all three rifle companies in the attack, but this effort was halted after gaining another 400 yards through deep snow. Defensive positions were then prepared with Company I on the left (northern) flank, Company L in the center, and Company K on the right. Due to poor visibility, the effectiveness of Captain Coshun's 81mm mortar platoon was severely hampered and the 3rd Battalion made no further advance this day. From the 30 to 35 prisoners taken, it was learned that elements of *Grenadier Regiment 1055, 89th Volks-Grenadier Division* were holding the eastern half of the Bütgenbacher Heck. That night, tank dozers and bulldozers cleared the roads to the front line and replacement overcoats, socks, gloves, shoes, and hot meals were brought down from Bütgenbach.

With winds still raging, Learnard's 1st Battalion continued towards Montenau after daylight that morning. Later reports noted, "So great was the force of the wind that trees were blown over in the very path of the marching troops. The snow was over waist deep in some places, and so slippery in others that it was necessary to move on all fours. Visibility was less than 20 feet."[35] Companies A and B, moving down the mountain again with nothing but compasses to maintain direction, finally arrived at their assembly area 1,000 yards due west of Montenau at 1300 hours.

Captain Van Wagoner's men then went forward to occupy an attack position on the edge of the woods about 200 yards from the town. In the meantime, "Task Force Lindo," with its tanks and tank destroyers, started down the road leading to Montenau from the north at 1430 hours. This force met considerable opposition on its way, including dug-in captured Sherman tanks as well as extensive minefields. Additionally, the battalion was receiving heavy friendly fire across its front and Learnard was unable to attack until 1630 hours. It was later pointed out, "It took this long to get the message to the 23rd Infantry command post and get a confirmation that the fire would be lifted."[36]

The Hürtgen Forest

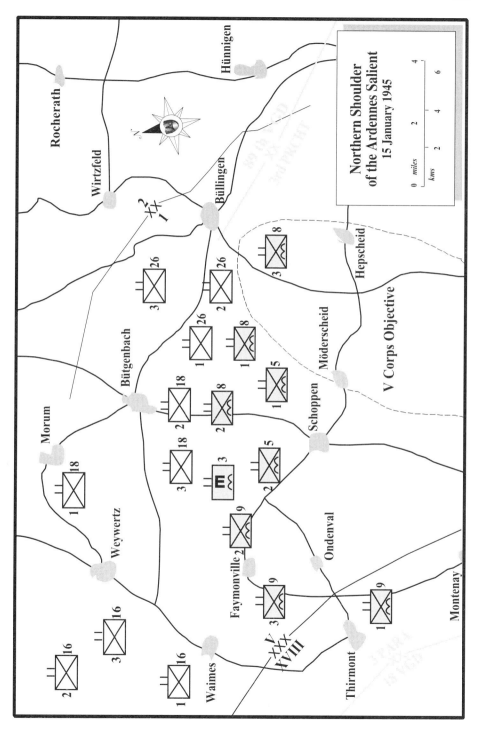

By this time, the enemy was thoroughly aware of Learnard's intentions, and alarmed by the loss of their force at the foot of the Wolfbusch. It appeared as if the Germans were determined to hold on to Montenau. As Company A emerged from the edge of the woods at dusk to cross yards of open ground before they reached the town, Lieutenant John Downing witnessed Task Force Lindo's initial attack and remembered, "A tank began firing on the town. There was the crack of the discharge, the humming of the shell as it traveled through the air, and then the sharp explosion as it landed in the town. Interspersed with the shellfire was the staccato rattle of its .50-caliber machine gun. The tracers flew in a red dotted line from the tank to the town. Some hit stone walls and ricocheted slowly up into the air. Then a tank destroyer began to fire along with the tank. There was a quick flash and explosion from the direction of the tank. Flames shot up and black smoke was outlined against the dark sky. The tank went out of action. We later found out that the TD had accidentally fired a round into the rear of the tank."[37] Downing, an injured veteran of Normandy, had returned to the lines after his hospital stay in England and now was a forward observer for Captain Bowers' mortar platoon.

Fortunately, Captain Van Wagoner's platoons had crossed through the open field relatively unscathed and had started working through the houses on the outskirts of the village. After checking on his attached machine gunners to make certain they could cover his platoons, Van Wagoner then went forward with his command group. One of his support platoons entered Montenau at the same time, just as enemy shells landed in the town's center. Other salvos soon followed, but after this stopped a few minutes later the Americans picked themselves up and began fanning out from house to house, encountering small arms fire and taking casualties. Lieutenant Downing also crossed the open field and made his way into town. He came to a building that looked like the town hall. When he was searching over the area to call back mortar fire direction, he heard moans from inside. "One of the men then told me that shells had landed near the building, killing and wounding some of our CP group," he recalled. "I went into the cellar with the company exec and in the first room were some bunks, formerly occupied by Germans. Our wounded were laid out on these."[38]

Downing also noted that the tankers and tank destroyers of Task Force Lindo were unable to get their vehicles across the Amel River because they feared the bridge was mined. When Lindo's task force approached from the north, they had been met with heavy artillery, self-propelled gun and mortar fire, and the Germans destroyed it. Despite their past 48 hours of grueling fighting in the bitter cold, Captain Lindo's men plunged into the river, waist deep at the ford and full of ice, crossed it, and attacked the part of the town on the east bank.

By this time darkness had set in, reducing the accuracy of the enemy artillery fire. After a number of sharp hand-to-hand skirmishes enemy strong points were seized and the town was secured. Casualties from the attacks were amazingly light, but a large number of the men in Company C who forded the river had to be evacuated due to frozen feet and exposure.

On 20 January, elements of the 7th Armored Division were able to move through Montenau and onto the open plains leading to St. Vith. The 1st Battalion was released from attachment to the 23rd Infantry Regiment, and the men shuffled back to assemble at Ondenval where they were then motored in a wet snowfall to billets in Nidrum. They thawed out, were treated for frostbite and trench foot, and received hot meals and badly needed rest. Later, correspondents who wrote about the 1st Battalion's feats entitled them, "The Battle of Learnard's Gulch."

Not all of the news about the 18th Infantry Regiment would turn out so positive, however. For the next two days, Peckham's 3rd Battalion continued pushing through the Bütgenbacher Heck against a skillfully dug-in enemy. On the night of 20 January tragedy again struck Company L when a 20-man combat patrol was ambushed as it attempted to probe the enemy's defenses; only three men returned safely to the lines. Another attack was launched at 0500 hours on 21 January, but the 3rd Battalion's efforts to advance were again to no avail because the exhausted condition of the assaulting troops precluded any real progress. Colonel Smith then decided to relieve the 3rd Battalion and ordered the 1st Battalion into the forest to take up the fight. The relief in place was conducted during the night of 21/22 January and Peckham's depleted companies, estimated at just 40 percent of their normal strength, returned to Nidrum for reorganization. The enemy had not escaped without casualties: Graves Registration teams counted 100 German dead in the woods where the 3rd Battalion had been fighting.

Learnard's forces, somewhat rested after spending two nights in warm quarters, at 0500 hours on 22 January conducted a limited-objective attack on the north flank of the Bütgenbacher Heck against *Grenadier Regiment 1055*, and by the next morning, his 1st Battalion had succeeded in driving the enemy further back. After being prodded by his superiors, Colonel Smith ordered a coordinated attack by the 1st and 2nd Battalions on 24 January. Learnard's companies were to clear the remainder of the Bütgenbacher Heck, first securing an important enemy road junction deep in the forest, and then seizing the high ground to its east. At the same time Williamson's 2nd Battalion was ordered to capture Möderscheid and the ridge line to its east, about seven miles south of Bütgenbach.

The 2nd Battalion attacked southward in column of companies at 0400 hours on 24 January. By daylight, Williamson's men had overrun an enemy defensive position outside of Morscheck, a small village located 1,000 yards south of Dom Bütgenbach. The battalion continued southwest toward Möderscheid. The column moved through the snow with as much speed as possible until Company E, once again under the command of Captain Coffman, encountered a small enemy outpost about a half-mile north of the village. "Company E sent three scouts out to dispose of this outpost," battalion S-3 Captain Murphy, recently returned from his hospital stay in England, remembered. "They fired three rifle shots, killing one and wounding the other two."³⁹

After this, the 2nd Battalion continued forward, deploying into attack formation along the edge of the woods outside Möderscheid. An enemy self-propelled gun, located in the woods 1,000 yards east of the village, fired on the rear of the battalion column as it neared the town, and this gun managed to get off 100 rounds before it was silenced by American artillery. Two platoons of attached tanks quickly moved up to rendezvous with the assault companies, but the lead tank hit a mine and was temporarily disabled. As a result, the other tank commanders were reluctant to move forward without some additional persuasion, so it was not until 1700 hours when Coffman's rifle platoons were loaded on the tanks for their final assault on Möderscheid.

Infantry squad leaders directed the tanks' fire as they rumbled into position on the outskirts of the town. Using voice, arm, and hand signals, they pointed out targets to the Shermans's crews as they fired their machine guns as well as their 76mm and 75mm cannons, depending on the situation. With its supporting tanks positioned well forward where they might rapidly furnish such responsive fire support, the 2nd Battalion was able to secure a foothold in the village. Möderscheid was secured by 2115 hours. The attackers secured 131 prisoners from *3rd Battalion, Parachute Regiment 5*, and a number of other defenders were killed before German troops withdrew to Hepascheid, three miles to the east.

Lieutenant Colonel Williamson then deployed Companies F and G 800 yards to the east to take advantage of this dominating ground while Coffman's Company E formed a perimeter defense around Möderscheid itself. Weasels again drew up supplies, this time because they were the only vehicles that could travel offroad to the front, since the Germans still had a strongpoint overlooking the Möderscheid-Schoppen Road. "Teamwork was the main factor that brought about the successful completion of the attack with a minimum loss of our lives," a Company E report later noted about the taking of Möderscheid. "The attack was planned using a vast amount of intelligence and patrol work. Aerial photographs were also used in connection with this work, and they proved to be most helpful. It was the thorough knowledge of the enemy's defensive positions that ultimately resulted in this complete surprise."⁴⁰

On 13 January, when Learnard expected to attack in the Bütgenbacher Heck the next day, an 11-man patrol under the command of Lieutenant Walter Burt of Company B left Nidrum to reconnoiter a junction of five roads in the thick woods. This key terrain was located about 1,200 yards to the front of the 1st Battalion's main line of resistance.

The patrol gathered important information. The enemy was occupying defensive positions in force during daylight hours only. Well-beaten paths and trails were discovered around the road network, indicating routes of supply and communication into the junction. There were also numerous dugouts and foxholes in the area.

Learnard's crafty plan for what was blithely dubbed "The Attack on Forty-Second and Broadway," was largely based on Lieutenant Burt's efforts. The loss of this junction would be very costly to the Germans, for it would force them to use rough, secondary routes of supply and communications to continue to retain positions on the north shoulder of the Bulge.[41]

The 1st Battalion, less Lindo's Company C, was to strike at 0530 hours on 25 January in a column of companies, with Company B in the lead, to take the road junction from the south. Company C was to conduct a demonstration using tanks, machine guns, and rifles in front of the German line to the north. To maintain the element of surprise, there would be no artillery preparation. "Colonel Learnard told me, Lindo we've got an easy job for you," he remembered years later in recalling his commanding officer's orders that night. "I want you to make a hell of a lot of noise. Use your tanks, TDs, everything."[42] It was clear that Lindo's job was to make the Germans think the attack was coming to their front, while it would again come from their rear. When Captain Miller briefed his platoon leaders, it was known that the junction was defended by an estimated strength of 200 men from *Grenadier Regiment 1055*.

Precisely at 0530 hours the next morning, Company B left their line of departure just off the Bütgenbach-Büllingen road. At 0630 hours, Miller's 1st Platoon captured a two-man outpost without firing a shot and proceeded south still undetected. By this time, the other platoons of the company were moving toward the roadway about 100 yards apart and on line to the north, silently and still concealed by darkness. The 1st Platoon swung 300 yards further south and bypassed the German main line of resistance, but just as it entered the heart of the enemy defensive position, the Americans received machine-gun fire at a range of 75 yards.

These Americans, many of whose weapons were frozen and would not work, sustained ten casualties in a matter of minutes and were pinned down.

The 2nd and 3rd Platoons of Company B had halted when this firing broke out. Their radio operators were unable to contact Captain Miller, so the leader of the 3rd Platoon took it upon himself to move forward to determine the situation. After making a quick reconnaissance, he ordered his attached heavy machine-gun section to occupy a firing position on the edge of a road behind the enemy position. Covered by its fire, two squads hurriedly moved out, formed a skirmish line, and assaulted the German position from the rear. Assaulting squads first used marching fire to overcome the German defenses and, after closing as rapidly as the thick snow-covered underbrush would permit, overran three machine guns pinning down the 1st Platoon.

By 0910 hours, Company B had seized this piece of key terrain behind the German main line deep in the Bütgenbacher Heck, prompting Captain Van Wagoner's Company A to move up and tie to the left flank. Captain Lindo, having successfully distracted the Germans with his demonstration to their front, was then ordered to push south. "We were very, very undermanned," Lindo remembered. "I hadn't expected this. We'd exposed our position, but we started. Most of my sergeants were acting sergeants. I couldn't get the tanks to go forward because they told me the gears were frozen. So we had to proceed without the tanks."[43]

Even without their armor support, Company C's attack soon forced the remaining Germans to pull back. In a perfectly executed and coordinated maneuver, Company B killed 12 enemy soldiers and captured 50 others while losing one man killed and 14 wounded. Additional friendly casualties would have certainly been suffered, but it was later pointed out, "The initiative and immediate decisive action of the 3rd Platoon leader in sizing up the situation, laying out a plan of action, and putting the plan into action avoided this. Every second's delay would have meant more casualties and more time for the completely surprised enemy to get organized."[44]

With mounting momentum, the 1st and 2nd Battalions again moved out on the attack at 0600 on 25 January. The 2nd Battalion eliminated the enemy force holding the road to Schoppen and then captured a high ridgeline southeast of Möderscheid. From there, the enemy in Heppenbach could be seen preparing defensive positions. Learnard's 1st Battalion, finally attacking through the last 200 yards of the Bütgenbacher Heck, captured the majority of the now-encircled *2nd Battalion, Grenadier Regiment 1055*, and by afternoon, the battalion had reached the ridgeline that delineated their limit of advance for the day.

The next few days were spent organizing defense of the ground gained: a hastily-laid minefield soon protected the Regiment's main line of resistance. Antitank guns were also dug in to support the forward echelons, while TDs and tanks were positioned in depth. With the attack temporarily halted, Colonel Smith ordered supplies brought up. Now that the frozen and slippery roads were safer from enemy artillery strikes, the half-tracks of Cannon and Anti-Tank Companies were able to haul up supplies and rations while mechanics toiled day and night to keep their vehicles running. Colonel Smith moved his command post to Bütgenbach on 26 January, but while replenishment and resupply activities were being carried out, the enemy was devoting time to strengthening his own defenses. On 27 January General Clifton Andrus, commanding the 1st Infantry Division since General Huebner took over V Corps, ordered the attack to continue eastward, and Colonel Smith in turn selected the 1st and 2nd Battalions to seize Hepschied and Heppenbach.

At 0500 hours on 28 January, the 2nd Battalion moved out for Heppenbach with Companies F and G leading the assault. Shortly after they jumped off, two supporting tanks bogged down in the snow, and Williamson had to order the remaining tanks and TDs to bypass them. Abandoning all pretense of cross-country movement, the tanks then followed behind a platoon of Company E and a mine detector team moving along the Heppenbach-Mirfeld road.

When the 2nd and 3rd Platoons of Company G entered the open fields north of Heppenbach, they came under heavy fire from the rear, as well as from the enemy's positions in the village. Williamson discovered that a German combat patrol had overrun one of Company E's outposts, placing them in a position to bring Company F under fire from their rear.

As dawn broke, Company F entered the southern half of Heppenbach against stubborn resistance, but the fighting swung in favor of the attackers as soon as several tanks entered the village. The Shermans quickly began shelling the buildings and forced the first groups of Germans, elements of *Parachute Regiment 5,* to emerge with their hands in the air.

With resistance in the village subdued, Captain Park sent his 1st Platoon to deal with the combat patrol that had overrun the Company E outpost, later identified as an element of *Parachute Regiment 8*. This threat was summarily dealt with and silence descended on Heppenbach. Soon afterward, Williamson redeployed the 2nd Battalion 1,000 yards eastward along the Honsfeld Road to take advantage of high ground in that area. During the afternoon, he observed movement of troops to the south, between Heppenbach and Wereth. With the aid of his fieldglasses alone, Williamson discovered an enemy force, estimated at company-size, organizing a defensive position astride the road about 1,200 yards to the south and east. Captain P. K. Smith, the artillery liaison officer, soon experienced the "artilleryman's dream," and within minutes the 32nd FA was placing battalion concentrations on the surprised enemy. Direct hits were observed and the enemy defensive position was destroyed.[45]

The 1st Battalion also encountered snow and icy roads as it moved along a trail leading to Hepscheid. Led by Company A, which was supported by a mine-detection team, the 1st Battalion column gingerly picked its way toward its objective in the pre-dawn darkness along a snowdrift-covered trail. With the mine clearing team at work, Van Wagoner's men quietly inched forward, followed at a distance by the supporting tanks. When his men and the tanks burst into Hepscheid just before daylight, the remnants of the defending *Grenadier Regiment 1055* quickly surrendered. "They were 40 of the most surprised men in the whole German army," correspondent Iris Carpenter wrote later. "They simply could not believe that anyone would attack in such conditions. One prisoner said, 'We knew Yanks were crazy, but never thought them that crazy'."[46]

That evening, Colonel Smith received orders to continue the attack to seize Honsfeld and Hünningen. He assigned the first mission to the 1st Battalion. Just after dusk, Learnard ordered a strong combat patrol by Company B, with two squads of Anti-Tank Company's Mine Platoon attached, to first clear the road into Honsfeld. The Mine Platoon's squads soon filled nine boxes with explosive devices extracted from the roadbed while a combat patrol captured a seven-man enemy outpost located in a farmhouse outside the village. Under a full moon, the 1st Battalion then attacked at 0100 hours on 29 January with Companies A and C mounted on supporting tanks and half-tracks attached from other units. At 0200 hours, Van Wagoner entered Honsfeld against light resistance, and within 30 minutes, Captain Lindo was also in the town.

Both rifle companies were soon clearing what remained of elements from *Parachute Regiment 5*, and over 100 prisoners were taken before daylight.

The 3rd Battalion moved out at 0700 hours to seize Hünnigen, just a mile to the north of Honsfeld. A task force of dozers, medium tanks, half-tracks, Company L, and an artillery forward observer, all under the command of Captain Wardner, of Company B, 745th Tank Battalion, moved along the Hepscheid-Honsfeld road without encountering resistance.

As the column approached Hünnigen, the leading tanks deployed off the road and began to fire upon likely targets in the center of town while a second element of the American column took up positions on a ridge overlooking the southern half of the village. From this position, a platoon of tanks and a platoon of tank destroyers established a base of fire to support the assault on the town. Captain Folk's men initially met strong resistance, but as the forward observer called in artillery fire while direct tank fire was laid into the enemy positions, the last remnants of the *2nd Battalion, Grenadier Regiment 1056* and *Füsilier Battalion 89* capitulated.

Hünningen was in American hands by 1000 hours, with 100 prisoners rounded up. In the process, Company M, commanded by Captain Harry F. Carey, took heavy casualties. "I was amazed at the high number of casualties, since a weapons company usually suffered less than a rifle company," Lieutenant John Downing, now the company's executive officer wrote. "Captain Carey gave me the list of casualties and told me that just as the machine-gun platoons were about to assemble near the road to follow our rifle companies in the attack, our own artillery laid down a barrage on them. This barrage, which was of course a mistake, had battered up the machine-gun platoon pretty badly. The morale-breaking factor was that the casualties had been caused by American artillery. The unit responsible was a battalion of heavy guns far to the rear, which was supposed to have supported a concurrent attack by the 82nd Airborne Division on our right and which had fired into the wrong area."[47]

The capture of Hünningen and Honsfeld coincided with the German retreat from the last of the ground they had captured during the Battle of the Bulge, but for the 18th Infantry Regiment, victory had again come with enormous cost. Colonel Smith lost approximately 750 men during the counterattacks on the northern shoulder of the Bulge, with the 3rd Battalion sustaining the most during its attempts to gain the Bütgenbacher Heck.

In addition to the killed and seriously wounded, trench foot, frostbite, and exposure took a tremendous toll on the Regiment's ranks. "The seven-day attack through this strongly-defended position under the worst of conditions completely exhausted the assaulting troops," Captain Soloman remembered in concluding a later report. "The fighting efficiency of the individual soldier and leader was sharply decreased as the days wore on. But the enemy's practice of defending the towns from the buildings therein instead of the dominating terrain in the locality portended his defeat. Occupying the buildings for defense restricted his observation, reduced the firepower he could effectively employ against our attacking troops and, lacking mutual support, the defending forces invited defeat."

Underscoring the plight of the men during the period, Soloman also noted, "We cannot fail to be impressed by the fighting infantryman, his devotion to duty, courage, and resourcefulness as he fought his way during the most arduous of fighting conditions to achieve his mission—the destruction of the enemy."[48]

Major Carter, the 3rd Battalion Executive Officer, commemorated the cautious optimism shared by many others in the Regiment at the time when he wrote, "We decided that with the Bulge reduced, Hitler had made his last great attack."[49] There was indeed reason for Major Carter to be hopeful that the end to the war was nearing. "On 1 February 1945 the enemy's position gave him little cause for celebration," the 1st Infantry Division's history noted in agreement. "The great counteroffensive which had looked so promising six weeks before had been reduced from a "Bulge" to a desperate defense of what little ground remained to him west of the Siegfried Line. Moreover, this defense was conducted by Germans with an apprehensive eye over their shoulder."[50]

By this time, the 1st Infantry Division had been reassigned to the XVIII Airborne Corps. This resulted from General Bradley's desire to exploit the weakened condition of defeated *Wehrmacht* units facing the 12th Army Group by quickly resuming the offensive into Germany. Accordingly, Bradley issued orders on 27 January for a multi-corps attack against the *Westwall* on a 25-mile front from Monschau to Lützkampen near the northern tip of Luxembourg where Major General Matthew Ridgway's XVIII Airborne Corps was to make the main effort on the right wing of the First Army. Holding the 7th Armored and 30th Infantry Divisions in reserve, Ridgway planned to send the 1st Infantry Division and the 82nd Airborne Division against the pillboxes of the fortified line between the *Schnee Eifel* and Weiserstein, astride the Losheim Gap.

After receiving these new orders, the 1st Infantry Division encountered tremendous difficulties reorienting its forces from south of Bütgenbach eight miles east to the *Westwall*. Every few hundred yards along the road network leading into their new sector engineers had to clear the debris of rubbled villages. When the leading riflemen of the Division finally reached their assembly areas, only one artillery battalion managed to displace forward to support their attack. Despite these difficulties, General Andrus was determined to strike as scheduled. Accordingly, he gave orders to Colonel Smith to launch a battalion assault designed to carve out a bridgehead for the remainder of the division to again cross into Germany.

The plan called for the capture of Ramscheid, a small village six miles east of Büllingen. Colonel Smith awarded this mission to Lieutenant Colonel Williamson's 2nd Battalion. The attack was to begin at 0400 hours on 2 February, but given that the order was delivered to him very late the night before, last-minute reconnaissance was impossible, and Williamson was limited to holding a brief meeting with his company commanders. A bright moon shone, silhouetting the men against the snow that night, and Koenig's Company F moved out across a clearing with Park's Company G on his left. The leading elements of this attacking force soon cut their way through the wire entanglements that encircled Ramscheid's defenses, winding their way past a line of dragon's teeth concrete antitank obstacles before running into an uncharted minefield. With neither the mine detectors of the engineer company or the battalion pioneer platoon available, one of Koenig's platoons continued to press on, losing men to exploding mines, but this formed the path his soldiers following them needed to get through.

Captain Koenig then rushed his whole company through this gap in a single file. When they reached the other side of the minefield, the attackers found that the enemy was alert and waiting, and a firefight started at the first pillbox, which drove the defending Germans inside. A few of Koenig's men were then left behind to secure the pillbox while the remainder moved forward to attack a second and third pillbox, all soon falling into American hands.

By now daylight was filling the sky and Koenig placed a heavy machine gun at the first pillbox, deploying his two light machine guns to cover the other two pillboxes in case of counterattack.

At the same time, Koenig sent out patrols to investigate and knock out two additional pillboxes within easy small arms range of the trio his company had just captured. When that was accomplished, he rushed his 1st Platoon, commanded by Lieutenant Joseph W. Novoteney, directly into Ramscheid along with some elements of Captain Park's Company G that had made it forward by this time. This mixed force eventually stopped three local counterattacks while the rest of Koenig's men concentrated on securing the remaining pillboxes in his company zone, one by one.

By this time, the patrols from the company had forced a fourth pillbox to surrender after firing white phosphorous grenades into it.

A prisoner then volunteered to try to "talk out" the occupants of the fifth pillbox. His efforts were successful.

The sixth and largest pillbox, which was now known to be the command post for the others, was occupied by Germans who continued to fire on the company, prompting a later report to note, "This box had a turret of steel one foot thick with six portholes and a periscope. Unless this box could be reduced quickly, the position was still in danger because it dominated the entire terrain."

Captain Koenig reacted to this by deciding to send the cooperative prisoner forward to try to talk the occupants into giving up, but they refused, adding that they would shoot any other intermediary who continued to try to negotiate their surrender. Koenig then decided to take a bold gamble. He sent the prisoner back to the observation pillbox, this time with an ultimatum to "surrender within thirty minutes, or be blown sky high by TNT," according to a later report. It was also noted, "What made it a daring gesture was the fact that Koenig had no TNT available to him at the time."[51]

To show that their captain was serious, his men opened fire on the observation periscope atop the pillbox, quickly putting it out of action. Koenig then directed one of his machine-gun teams to open fire with sustained bursts at the muzzle of one of the German machine guns protruding from a firing slit in the pillbox, and after a few lengthy bursts the flash hider and muzzle of the weapon were hit several times. Half an hour went by, but there was no surrender. At this point Koenig ordered his men to simulate planting dynamite charges along the sides of the emplacement. Moments later, the garrison in the pillbox capitulated.

Several Sherman tanks appeared at dusk after the engineers cleared gaps in the minefield, followed by the remainder of Companies G and H, putting Ramscheid securely in American hands.

"The score for the battle was 87 enemy killed, scores of wounded, many prisoners of war, [including] one captain and two lieutenants, nine pillboxes and one town taken," the company report read.[52] Citing the "indomitable spirit and extraordinary heroism" of Captain Koenig and his men on 2 February 1945, Company F was later awarded a Presidential Unit Citation for its bold seizure of Ramscheid.[53]

A well-deserved rest finally came to the 18th Infantry Regiment on 4 February when they were relieved in place by units of the 99th Infantry Division's 393rd Infantry Regiment. They were to be sent back to the deep rear near Nemoir, south of Liége, Belgium.

The first signs of an early spring had emerged. The air had turned moldy, and mud on fire trails and roadways leading to recent battles was almost bottomless from the melting snow cover. Under pine trees dripping water and amid wet clods of falling snow, the men of the Regiment organized for most of the day, gathering their equipment before they eventually mounted transport bound away from the front. The exhausted infantrymen departed in the gathering dusk and fog that afternoon, finally leaving behind the discarded flotsam of war—destroyed equipment, old shoes, scattered telephone wires, broken toboggans, and bloated bodies clad in German field gray and American olive drab—all lost during their battles on the northern shoulder of the Bulge.[54]

THE ROER TO SURRENDER

FEBRUARY TO MAY 1945

> The 1st Division continues to spearhead any advance—anywhere—at any time.
>
> —From *Danger Forward, The Story of the First Division in World War II*

On 8 February 1945, the 1st Infantry Division was still assigned to the XVIII Corps as it took over the northern sector of the front south of the town of Krezau. This new disposition placed the division on the corps' north flank with, the 82nd Airborne Division to the south. The boundary between the two divisions was slightly north of the junction of the Kall River Valley and the Roer River.

When the Americans first reached the Roer River in late December, the river already presented a serious obstacle. With melting snowfall in the Eifel combining with prolonged rains in early February, the Roer rose very rapidly. Although V Corps had captured the Roer dams by 10 February and had driven the defending Germans into nearby forests, the enemy succeeded in dynamiting the floodgates of the two largest dams before they retreated. Millions of cubic feet of water rushed onto the Cologne Plains, sending the Roer three feet above its high water mark and inundating the surrounding countryside.

By that time, the 18th Infantry had moved to Gressenwicht Forest, near Vicht, where its officers and men were waiting for the Roer to abate so the Cologne Plain offensive could be renewed.

For most of February, the troops rested in a wet, thickly-forested area that was houseless, remote, and gloomy. Muddy, slippery roads had to be covered with timber to remain passable, much as in bivouacs prior to bitter fighting in the Hürtgen Forest. Pyramidal tents were used as orderly rooms and kitchens in battalion areas, while line companies cleared brush and fallen timber to build small log cabins to shelter the men.

Despite these conditions, the routine chores that accompanied duty continued. Weapons needed to be cleaned; ammunition basic loads had to be replenished;

and worn clothing and equipment had to be salvaged or replaced. Passes were given to the men, some to Paris, others to Brussels, some to Verviers where a regimental "rest home" was set up, and many even to England. Stoves and oil lamps were confiscated and brought into the makeshift log homes to comfort those left behind, and some of the pyramidal tents were turned into drying rooms to hang musty clothes and tattered uniforms.

This comparative peace and quiet all too quickly came to an end, but not before Colonel Smith was reassigned on 25 February to the position of Assistant Division Commander of General Allen's 104th Infantry Division. With Colonel Smith's departure, Lieutenant Colonel Williamson assumed command of the Regiment and Major Frank Colacicco became the new Commanding Officer of the 2nd Battalion.

After a meeting with his battalion commanders, Williamson issued an alert order the next day for a renewed offensive deep into Germany. The initial phase of 1st Infantry Division operations now required that each regiment clear all enemy territory east of the Roer River up to the western bank of the Rhine, to secure key terrain north of Bonn. All of the towns east of the Roer had been divided into battalion zones, with each battalion in turn specifying blocks that its companies would be responsible for clearing. "The prospect did not look cheering," one officer remembered at the time, "but then no attack order ever tends to raise anyone's morale."[1]

Beneath overcast skies lit by the flashes of a tremendous preparatory bombardment, trucks carrying the 18th Infantry threaded their way through the town of Düren on 26 February. They deposited their sodden human cargo in a wooded assembly area on the west bank of the Roer. Using a pontoon bridge, Lieutenant Colonel Learnard's 1st Battalion and Major Colacicco's 2nd Battalion crossed without incident that night, and then both battalions silently filed forward to relieve the 28th Infantry Regiment of the 8th Infantry Division in and around the town of Stockheim. By the time Lieutenant Colonel Peckham's 3rd Battalion crossed the river the next morning, Learnard's companies had already jumped off for their initial objective two kilometers eastward, Jakobwüllesheim, and had taken it. Patrols then rapidly moved forward to their next target, Kelz, another two and a half kilometers to the east.

The terrain surrounding Kelz was flat, like most of the terrain between the Roer and the Erft Rivers. During the good visibility that characterized opening days of the renewed offensive, German forces easily observed troops advancing toward the towns they were defending. When Learnard's forward patrols determined that they could not get across the open ground fronting Kelz without being subjected to artillery and mortar fire, they returned to the battalion area. Major Carter, now the Regimental S-2, highlighted the obvious solution to the problem by noting, "When there's no concealment or cover, you've got to attack at night."[2]

The attack on Kelz began with an artillery preparation at about 2200 that cool night. There were two roads that ran in a roughly parallel fashion from

Jakobwüllesheim to Kelz. One rifle company, riding on half of the battalion's attached tanks and TDs, attacked down one road while a similar team stabbed down the other. Both forces got across the open approaches without any difficulties. When they entered the town, the firepower of the fast approaching tanks proved overwhelming and Kelz fell quickly. "These tactics, using tank-mounted infantry, then became SOP for all of our attacks," Major Carter said later. "The only hazard proved sometimes to be the loss of the lead vehicle, but usually only one would be lost in this manner. As soon as a minefield was discovered, our supporting engineers would then sweep the road under the concealment of darkness and the over-watching armor."[3]

Once Kelz was secured, the 2nd and 3rd Battalions moved out toward their next objectives. Major Colacicco's companies departed from Frauwüllesheim with the mission of establishing a bridgehead on the far side of the Neffel River four kilometers to the east. When the battalion arrived on the west bank, Colacicco found the bridge still intact and a bridgehead was secured on the opposite shore before daylight on 28 February. Peckham's 3rd Battalion moved through the 1st Battalion positions in Kelz that night, and then his companies entered the narrow, muddy streets of nearby Irresheim and seized the village without a fight. Thereafter the 1st Battalion, with Captain Park's Company G temporarily attached, leapfrogged forward with the mission of securing additional bridgeheads at Norvenich and Hochkirchen, then Darweiler and Pingsheim, each another two to three kilometers to the east.

Toward dusk on 28 February, Darweiler fell without difficulty to Van Wagoner's Company A, but Company C got pinned down north of Pingsheim. The company was advancing from Hochkirchen across open ground toward the objective when they ran into an aggressive and well-equipped German motorized unit. The enemy delivered sharp machine-gun, SP, and mortar fires against the Americans, augmented by four medium artillery pieces located on the northwest side of the town. The Germans illuminated the area by setting fire to rows of haystacks, exposing crouching American infantrymen to even deadlier fire. Company C lost its executive officer, Lieutenant James A. Lucas, every platoon leader except Lieutenant Poovey, and 16 noncommissioned officers.

The town and its garrison of two officers and 140 men capitulated at 0623 the next morning after Captain Miller's Company B swung around the carnage in Company C's sector to deliver an assault against the rear of the enemy position. Captain Lindo, promoted on 24 February to battalion S-3, only could mourn the losses in his former company when he saw casualty reports that morning.

Company G was far more fortunate on the night of 28 February. Its men first skirted a wooded area after they jumped off, and then they dashed across a 400-yard open field fronting the small town of Rath and reduced its garrison, capturing 35 prisoners.

With the axis Rath-Pingsheim-Darweiler secured, the mission of pushing on to the Regiment's intermediate objective—a line running along the Erft Canal and the Roth River—went to Peckham's 3rd Battalion. After passing through the 2nd Battalion shortly before 2400 hours on the night of 1 March, Peckham's men clambered aboard armored vehicles and barreled down the road to Mellerhof. They next steamrolled straight through the village to Gymich. A reconnaissance patrol of the 14th Cavalry Group's 32nd Cavalry Squadron secured the tiny hamlet of Herrig before the 3rd Battalion's arrival, and with that, the battalion's southern flank was protected. The 18th Infantry Regiment then held the Erft-Roth line without incident until relieved by the 14th Cavalry Group during the first week of March.

"Progress at this point in the war was strange," an officer in Company M who reached Gymich remembered. "All the people we met from North Africa to Germany just loved Americans, and yet you had to fight to get into every town. At present the war is strategically over, and even the most stubborn German should have been able to see that the end was just a matter of time. Yet every little village had to be fought for and more people had to be killed needlessly. Nobody was mad at anybody, and still everybody was blowing each other's heads off."[4]

By this time, most German units west of the Rhine had fallen into disarray. In the wake of their retreat eastward, enemy demolition crews had blown many Rhine bridges from Düsseldorf to Koblenz. On 7 March, midway between the two cities, Major General John W. Leonard's 9th Armored Division had secured a tentative footing across an intact railway bridge at Remagen. As a result, the 1st Infantry Division's boundary was altered sharply south to encompass Bonn, which had formerly been in the 9th Infantry Division's zone. The 18th Infantry Regiment was assigned a sector on the extreme right flank of the division's new zone and the Regiment's objective was now the southern half of Bonn, while the 16th Infantry, on the Regiment's left, was to seize the northern half of the city.

The use of artillery during the attack on Bonn was prohibited because of its hospitals and large civilian population. Williamson assembled his men in the vicinity of Buschoven in preparation for the capture of Duisdorf, a beautiful college town that was in the path of the Regiment's advance to Bonn.

In the early morning hours of 8 March, Learnard's 1st Battalion crossed the Regiment's line of departure approximately four kilometers southwest of the outskirts of Bonn and began advancing astride the Buschhoven-Bonn road toward their objective. Although flanked on both sides by high ground, this route was the most suitable road for the employment of armor supporting the advance. The enemy had situated his main line of resistance in Duisdorf, siting a number of SP and 20mm AA guns on the town's high ground. Company B led the advance, and Miller's men soon found themselves in a short, sharp firefight as they approached the enemy main line of resistance. While the defenders were later identified as two reduced training battalions of the *12th Volks-Grenadier Division* with about 250 men each, their plentiful supply of 20mm automatic cannon made it necessary for Miller to lead his men cautiously while keeping an eye out for cover. His company, later supported by Company C, eventually worked its way into the northern half of Duisdorf, and as Company B consolidated their newly-won positions, Company A seized the southern half of the town. Company C then attacked a barracks in the southeastern part of town, clearing it of defenders before finally moving into Lengsdorf, a suburb of Bonn. High ground east of Lengsdorf commanded a view of the entire city, but the Germans continually sprayed it with automatic weapons and high-explosive fire. After a patrol was forced away from an observation post it had established, Company C decided to pull back into Lengsdorf to prepare for a more deliberate advance the next morning.

By this time, the 2nd and 3rd Battalions had penetrated into the outskirts of Bonn and their companies were situated on a line roughly along the main railroad tracks that passed through the center of the city. Bonn itself was completely secured by 9 March, as the main body of the German garrison withdrew without a fight. Several prisoners stated that there had been a plan to counterattack the 18th Infantry Regiment in a double envelopment using 400 infantry and 25 armored vehicles, but a shortage of fuel prevented this. Hundreds of prisoners were later counted from remnants of *Replacement Battalion 365*, to include many misguided *Volkssturm* and regular soldiers dressed in civilian clothes. The Rhine bridge at Bonn had been blown on 8 March and it would now be another week before the 18th Infantry Regiment crossed the river.

While waiting at Bonn, tragic news made its way through the ranks of the Regiment. As the assault battalions of the 104th Infantry Division's 414th Infantry Regiment were crossing the Erft Canal north of the 18th Infantry's positions, a German *Sturmtiger* from *Sturm-Mörser-Kompanie 1002* lobbed a gigantic 380mm mortar round at the house where the command post of the 2nd Battalion, 414th Infantry had been set up. Although it did not explode, the shell killed several men, to include Colonel Smith, Colonel Anthony J. Touart, Commanding Officer of the 414th Infantry Regiment, Lieutenant Colonel Joseph H. Cummins, Commanding Officer of the 2nd Battalion, the battalion's S-3 and one of its captains. Eleven others were wounded, including the Commanding Officer of the regiment's 3rd Battalion.

"It was a queer turn in the fortunes of war," the 18th Infantry Regiment record noted at the time, "that after leading us through four campaigns including the assault on Omaha Beach and the intense Aachen and Hürtgen fighting that Colonel Smith was killed in action during the first week of his new assignment."[5]

Far more heartening news on the First Army front was the seizure of the Ludendorff Bridge at Remagen, 20 miles south of the Regiment's positions. Within the perimeter of the small bridgehead on its east bank, Army engineers had strung several pontoon and treadway bridges to move troops over to protect the area. On 9 March, German artillery scored a direct hit on the Ludendorff Bridge, but before it collapsed into the Rhine a week later, the 18th Infantry Regiment crossed over on 13 March, stepping into the heartland of Germany for the second time in its history (The first time was as part of the Army of Occupation at Koblenz in 1918). In comparison to the Regiment's fight from the

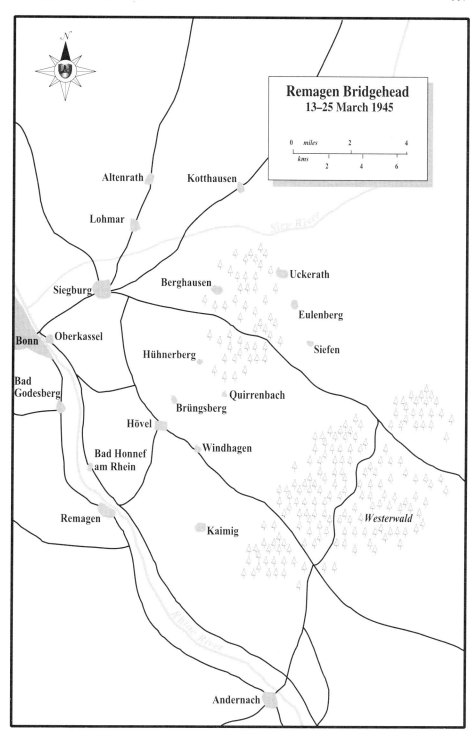

Roer to the Rhine, the fighting to enlarge the bridgehead east of the Rhine was to be decidedly tougher.

On the night of 16 March, Company A moved northeast from Remagen to secure the town of Hühnerberg, as well as a high ridgeline to its east that dominated all points for miles around. Seizing this area was essential to the Regiment's advance. Dubbed the "Gravel Pit Operation" by his men, Captain Van Wagoner's plan was to move out at 2400 hours that night in a column of platoons with a section of heavy machine guns. One rifle platoon would attack up the ridge to the left of a narrow-gauge rail line that ran up to a large gravel pit, with another to its left and a third platoon some 400 yards to the rear. Once the lead rifle platoon was on the objective, the company's 60mm mortars would follow and deploy in a nearby quarry. Extra bandoliers of ammunition were issued, and a medical evacuation station was set up just before the company started at midnight.

The platoons first trekked past their line of departure onto narrow trails in pitch darkness, and then they started into the dense woods. Since visibility was poor, the enemy did not detect them at first, but a German machine gun broke the silence of the night a scant 200 yards into the move. A squad rushed to destroy the weapon, only to return to report that the men had run into an enemy outpost. Captain Van Wagoner investigated the situation and quickly directed his nearby support platoon to attack the outpost.

In the ensuing fight, the main body of the enemy force ran for the woods after about a dozen Germans were shot or captured, several personally by Captain Van Wagoner when he used his sidearm at close range.[6]

With the Germans gone, the Americans continued to move up; they soon approached a wide clearing. A rifle platoon set up a base of fire to cover the opening while another threaded its way along the edge of the clearing that bordered the quarry, a move seeking to reach the high ridge to the front. By this time, the entire company was under heavy enemy artillery and mortar fire, but these rounds fell behind Van Wagoner's swiftly-advancing men. The lead rifle platoon reached the top of a hill, triggering a close-range firefight, but the enemy again soon scattered and trailing platoons quickly started organizing defensive positions atop the ridge. Enemy indirect fire had grown more accurate, and numerous casualties were inflicted on Van Wagoner's men before they could dig in. Small groups of German infantry attempted to infiltrate the company's positions, but were all either killed or captured.

With no evidence of an imminent large-scale counterattack developing, Van Wagoner and his weapons platoon leader joined with a few other men and ventured forward to reconnoiter the immediate area.

They soon found themselves staring into the eyes of eight Germans manning a heavy machine gun. Armed only with pistols, the company commander and his small entourage were at a tremendous disadvantage, but they yelled for the enemy to surrender. To their surprise, the Germans did just that, emerging from behind their gun with hands held high.

The company's attack then closed on the remaining Germans. With the critical ridge atop the quarry in friendly hands, the Gravel Pit Operation was over and Colonel Williamson could now order the remainder of the Regiment forward.

Colacicco's 2nd Battalion took over positions held by the 78th Infantry Division in Brüngsberg, one mile south of Hühnerberg, by noon on 17 March. The rest of the 1st Battalion came up that night. Hill 310 and Quirrenbach, where the valley of the Quirren River separated the towns of Brüngsberg and Quirrenbach, a mile southeast of Hühnerberg, were now the Regiment's next objectives. Given that the 78th Infantry Division had been in Brüngsberg for some time, it was expected that the Germans would not be surprised if they were attacked frontally across this valley. Colonel Williamson, however, had other plans.

His plan called for one company of the 2nd Battalion to fix the defenders from the south, while Learnard's 1st Battalion, with Captain Park's Company G attached, executed a wide envelopment to the left designed to gain the rear of the enemy defenses undetected. Once this was completed, the 1st Battalion would then attack and secure nearby Hill 310, an enemy observation post. To hit the Germans in Quirrenbach from the rear, Park's men would have to maneuver through woods. Since both his and the main body of the attacking force's thrust would both be moving through this wooded terrain, support from the Regiment's attached tanks was going to be limited.

The attack went off as planned and Learnard's men gained the crest of Hill 310 against negligible resistance, ahead of schedule, by early morning on 18 March. Company G, trailing to the rear of the 1st Battalion, turned south and descended through the wooded ground above Quirrenbach while the 2nd Battalion attacked the southern outskirts of the town. The enemy fought tenaciously, but by afternoon they lost the fight and a number of prisoners were taken. "The exception to the attack going according to plan," a later interview with now Regimental S-3 Major McGregor disclosed, "was the result of Captain Jesse Miller's Company B 4th rifle platoon—47 colored volunteers who joined [the assault by] Company G without orders from anyone."[7]

The presence of African-American soldiers assigned to a white infantry regiment was unusual, given that the US Army was not integrated in 1945. Integration came about as a result of a critical problem facing General Eisenhower: namely a tremendous shortage of infantry soldiers following the costly fighting in the Hürtgen Forest and during the Battle of the Bulge. The 1st Infantry Division, for example, was only at 60 percent of its assigned strength. As a result, Eisenhower made the decision to permit African-American soldiers to volunteer for duty as combat infantrymen with the understanding that after the necessary training they would be committed to frontline service.

Some 2,200 volunteers were organized into 53 rifle platoons and then assigned to rifle companies throughout the 12th Army Group. One of these platoons had been previously assigned to Company B on 13 March while the 18th Infantry Regiment was in Bonn.

The 1st Battalion After-Action Report noted at the time, "The Negro platoon assigned to Company B arrived and its men were indoctrinated as to the merits, accomplishments, and expectations of members of the 1st Division in a talk given by the assistant Division Commander, Brigadier General Taylor."[8] A white lieutenant and a sergeant who had combat experience led the volunteer platoon, which was to be used tactically in the same manner as the other platoons. Colonel Williamson later explained to his own staff, "This was an experiment to see if colored troops could be employed efficiently in combat mixed with white soldiers."[9] He emphasized that, contrary to practices on segregated Army installations, colored troops wearing the Red One would receive equal treatment with white troops regarding mess, billets, and recreation. In addition, they would be required to hold up their end in combat without special favor, but also without prejudicial assignments.

Major McGregor, remembering Miller's 4th rifle platoon's first day in battle on 18 March at Quirrenbach noted, "They simply helped Company G in its fight without orders from anyone. They proved to be a very real help to the company, disposing of at least 25 Germans. The battalion commander was much impressed with their initiative and fighting spirit, though their inexperience did result in an unusually high number of casualties. In their first two shows they lost 20 of their 47 men."[10]

Captain Lindo also remembered the time he had an African-American platoon under an earlier experiment during the Battle of the Bulge. "They were all volunteers that had heard of this," he recalled. "All came as buck privates, many having taken reduction in grade to serve under white officers in our outfit. They volunteered for the job to prove themselves, and I could not keep them 'out of trouble'. Whether in reserve or in attacks, they killed Germans."[11]

Based on this earlier experience commanding a 4th Platoon at the Bulge, Captain Lindo later added, "What it proved to me is that the color of your skin or your face didn't mean a damn thing." The fighting at Quirrenbach was noted in the 2nd Battalion report and it reinforced what Lindo believed, recording, "Their actions were comparable to that of the other platoons of the Regiment, and a source of deep pride to its members."[12] This successful employment of African-American platoons by the 18th Infantry was one of the many precursors that eventually led to full integration in the US armed forces.

Unfortunately, the 2nd Battalion lost its commanding officer during this time. Major Colacicco had received an update from his S-3 about the position of two of his companies outside of Quirrenbach on 18 March, but then a call came to the command post saying tanks could be heard and an attack seemed imminent. "I commandeered the first jeep I could," Colacicco remembered. "Then I jumped in and took off for the front lines. From our OP, our men had seen one of our tanks blow up. We didn't know whether it was a German gun or a mine that did it. As we hurried along the road, I saw the smoking, blown-up tank, knew it was a minefield, and shouted at my driver to stop. But it was too late. We were blown up. It broke both my ankles and perforated my eardrums, but the most painful part was that as I was blown out of the jeep my hip hit the machine gun mounted behind the seat and it also ripped up my leg. That was the end of the war for me."[13] Ironically, Major Colacicco later learned that it was his own tanks moving up that his men had heard, and not approaching enemy panzers.

As Colacicco was evacuated, Major Henry V. Middleworth took command of the 2nd Battalion. Middleworth was immediately ordered to seize Eudenbach (one mile northeast of Quirrenbach), but the order did not come down in time to organize an assault before 0900 hours on 18 March. His battalion approached Eudenbach via a wooded, concealed route during the morning, reaching the town's outskirts undetected by 1300 hours; the remainder of the afternoon was spent fighting house to house.

Having secured the village, Middleworth's men had to repulse two German counterattacks later that night. "It was a rough show," Major McGregor recalled, "but they held the town."[14]

On 20 March, Colonel Williamson received orders to attack Uckerath, located on a prominent ridgeline six miles to the northeast of the Regiment's position. The 18th Infantry Regiment, together with the 16th Infantry Regiment on their left, was given the mission of securing the town and a paved road that ran along the crest of the ridge on 25 March. It was one of the opening moves of the VII Corps' assault to break out of the Remagen bridgehead, a drive to be spearheaded by the 3rd Armored Division. The town and ridgeline were subsequently taken in what Major Middleworth's after-action report noted was "one of the last great battles for the 2nd Battalion of World War II."[15]

During planning for this mission, Captain Murphy received a call from the Regimental Executive Officer, Lieutenant Colonel Ben Sternberg. He was ordered to assume duties as the Executive Officer of the 1st Battalion on 21 March.

Company F, now commanded by Lieutenant Stanley V. Summers, jumped off first for Uckerath at 2030 hours on the moonlit night of 22 March, followed by Captain Coffman's Company E and Park's Company G. The enemy had established a series of strongpoints covering the approaches to the town, and stiff opposition was encountered as the 2nd Battalion made its approach march. All of the rifle companies fell far short of their goals by daylight. The enemy had positioned dug-in infantry, a dozen panzers, and numerous SP guns near Uckerath to cover approaches to the town.

The 2nd Battalion was to have advanced over 3,000 yards of open ground and cross a stream before daybreak, but Middleworth instead found his companies slowed by increasingly intense small arms, mortars, artillery, and direct fire from enemy tanks. Company G, quickly deploying to the left after daybreak, crossed the open ground during the day, and by dark it had captured a group of buildings on the northern edge of town. When Company E tried to cross the same area, it was held up by direct fire from several enemy tanks and SP guns at a point about 800 yards from Uckerath's outskirts. At 1800 hours, Major Middleworth redeployed

Lieutenant Summers' Company F abreast of Company E to help, but Summers also became pinned down by merciless enemy fire. After this, Middleworth decided to regroup and launch another coordinated attack.

At 2000 hours, the battalion again tried to approach the town under the cover of dark and smoke. Company G, which was still holding onto its earlier gains, benefitted from the concealment, as did Companies E and F as they assaulted from the west.

Both companies had little difficulty getting into town, mainly due to Park's efforts, but staying there proved not so simple.

The Germans had blocked every roadway into the village to prevent supporting American armor from entering, but their own Mark IV tanks were free to move about. The panzers began to fire at point blank range into each building suspected of harboring the newly-arrived American troops, making reorganization virtually impossible.

Despite the difficulty now confronting Middleworth's men, orders were received that night that Uckerath had to be secured as a jumping-off point for the 3rd Armored Division by the morning of 25 March. Major Middleworth complied with these orders by having his entire unit coordinate a night assault on the center of town at 0430 hours.

As the attack unfolded, it became apparent that the enemy was completely disorganized, and anticipated house-to-house combat turned into a mopping-up operation.

Over 200 prisoners were taken, and two German tanks and one SP gun were destroyed. The 2nd Battalion battalion suffered 76 killed and wounded during the fighting.

When German prisoners were questioned, they revealed that elements of both the *11th Panzer Division* and the *363rd Volks-Grenadier Division* had been in the town. Major Middleworth also discovered from the prisoners that the Germans were forming up for a counterattack when his 2nd Battalion struck first. "Uckerath had been a continuous action," Major McGregor later said in an interview where he asserted that the 2nd Battalion had broken the back of the enemy's resistance. "In fact, the troops had not completed mopping up before the 3rd Armored Division was able to pass through early on the 25th."[16]

Midway between Quirrenbach and Uckerath stood the small town of Eulenberg where Major Carl Randall, who had assumed command of the 3rd Battalion from Lieutenant Colonel Peckham when he left for a 30-day leave, had been in a tough fight for what would normally have been an unimpressive piece of German real estate. Facing several panzers, *Volkssturm* and regular German Army units the day before Uckerath fell, Lieutenant Clark Johnson's Company K succeeded in taking the high ground on the left flank of the battalion's advance, then his men had entered the town itself.

The enemy responded by making no less than 14 company-sized tank-supported counterattacks against Johnson's position that day. During the grueling fights, his 1st Platoon found itself so desperate for ammunition that the men began using captured German weapons. Three panzers had joined the fight during one counterattack that lasted over three hours before it was repulsed. At the conclusion of the engagement, enemy dead were found as close as 50 yards to the front of the Company K command post, but the strong stand by the company, supported on its flanks by the other rifle companies of the 3rd Battalion, ensured Eulenberg remained in American hands.

The 18th Infantry Regiment was now ordered to protect the northern flank of the Division area of operations while rapidly displacing east along the Sieg River. In motor movements reminiscent of the dash across France, for the next few days the Regiment passed through numerous towns that had already been cleared by the 3rd Armored Division.

On 30 March, Company K found itself in another brutal fight in heavily forested Eisern, about two miles south of Siegen, in the Ruhr Pocket. There, two of its men were singled out for the nation's highest award for valor and Lieutenant Johnson earned the Distinguished Service Cross.

While the company was under heavy small arms, machine-gun, and mortar fire during the fighting at Eisern, Company K's 2nd Platoon had been given the mission of outflanking an enemy position while remaining platoons provided a base of fire.

Staff Sergeant George Peterson, a squad leader with the 2nd Platoon, crawled forward to an advantageous position during the start of this attack, and then motioned for the rest of the platoon to follow. A mortar shell fell close by, severely wounding him in both legs, but he refused to be evacuated and instead continued forward to confront two hostile machine guns at close range. Braving a hail of automatic weapons fire, Sergeant Peterson worked his way alone into a shallow draw in front of the enemy strongpoint, where he raised himself to his knees and threw a grenade into the nearest nest, silencing the weapon and killing or wounding its crew. At this point, the second gun was immediately turned on him, but he threw another grenade into that nest and killed all of the Germans who occupied it.

As Peterson continued forward he was spotted by an enemy rifleman and shot in the arm. Somehow he managed to crawl forward another 20 yards until a third machine gun opened fire on him. Peterson again raised himself to his knees and fired a rifle grenade, killing three of this enemy gun crew and causing the lone German survivor to flee.

Sergeant Peterson allowed himself to be treated by the company aid man, but when he observed one of his men seriously wounded by a mortar, he leapt from the hands of the medic and began to crawl forward to assist his comrade. In sacrificing attention to his own wounds, he was struck and fatally wounded by an enemy bullet.[17]

During this same time Lieutenant Walter J. Will displayed similarly conspicuous gallantry. He courageously exposed himself to withering hostile fire to separately rescue two wounded men, and although he was painfully wounded himself when this happened, he made a third trip to carry another soldier to safety from an open area. Ignoring his wound, Lieutenant Will then boldly led the remaining men of his platoon forward until they were pinned down by murderous flanking fire from two enemy machine guns. Will crawled alone to within 30 feet of the first enemy position, killed its crew of four, and silenced the gun itself with a grenade. He then pulled himself through intense enemy fire to within 20 feet of the second position, where he leaped to his feet and made a solo charge, capturing the four-man gun crew and their supporting riflemen. Observing another platoon pinned down by two more German machine guns, he then led one of his squads on a flanking approach, rose to his knees in the face of direct fire, then deliberately lobbed three more grenades at the Germans, silencing one gun and killing its crew. With extraordinary aggressiveness, he ran on again toward the other gun and knocked it out with his last remaining grenade. Lieutenant Will then returned to his platoon and led his men in a fierce charge, forcing the enemy to fall back in confusion, but as in the selfless action of Sergeant Petersen, Lieutenant Will was mortally wounded in this last act of bravery.[18] Both men, having provided inspiration to all of those who witnessed their deeds, were awarded the Medal of Honor posthumously.

Near a crucial point toward the end of the fighting at Eisern, Lieutenant Johnson organized his company against a late German counterattack and crawled through a hail of enemy fire to personally place his five friendly tanks in the most advantageous positions possible.

Johnson signaled the start of the last offensive by firing his carbine as he ran forward; the effort was to prevent a linkup between the enemy in Eisern and approaching reinforcements. After this was successfully accomplished, the lieutenant led one of his platoons in a surprise attack on the German command post, killing many of the defenders and personally accepting the surrender of the commanding officer of the Eisern garrison and his staff.

Given the self-sacrifice and courage exhibited by Lieutenant Will, Sergeant Petersen and Lieutenant Johnson, it is no wonder that Major John H. Lauten, the 1st Infantry Division G-2 wrote, "On April 1 the enemy was in the unbelievable position of not knowing just where he was taking his worst beating. Allied spearheads were biting deep into his bone and muscle all along the front, and his reserves and replacement units had been chewed up and overrun along with his front-line troops. But whether he realized it or not, the enemy was about to meet his worst isolated, single defeat in the encirclement of the Ruhr. His heavy industries and major coalfields, still producing though crippled by the air forces, were about to be surrounded, as well as one entire army group and two others. The circle was not fully welded, and the vast tank and training depots of Paderborn had not yet been taken on 1 April, but the full swing of the wheel was only a matter of time."

"Nor were the enemy's future prospects any better," Major Lauten continued. "He could not write off the Ruhr and fall back to a line of defense to the rear. There was no line to the rear, except possibly the purely geographical barrier of the Weser [River] and further east, and much too close to home, the Elbe. The only possible ace in the hole—the case ace—was the Harz Mountains, an area difficult and forbidding militarily as it was scenic in peacetime. There might be hope to reassemble whatever forces he still had on hand to stage a reverse Bastogne. The mountains would take time to reduce for no other reason than terrain, and when defended by even the low-caliber troops at hand, the area might possibly hold out successfully enough to throttle down our high-geared drive into the vitals of the Reich."[19]

The mission of the 18th Infantry Regiment as of 1 April, Easter Sunday, was to protect the left flank of the 3rd Armored Division as it continued to act as the leading echelon of the VII Corps penetration that flanked the Ruhr. It was awaiting the arrival of the US Ninth Army before advancing to the east to encircle the German forces mentioned by Major Lauten.

With the possibility of an enemy attack in the Division zone that might allow remnants of 19 enemy divisions in the area to escape eastward, on 2 April Colonel Williamson was ordered to use one of his battalions to reinforce the 26th Infantry Regiment. Major Middleworth's 2nd Battalion was detached and together with the 26th Infantry, they seized several objectives in the early days of April 1945, helping to seal off the last possible escape route for the trapped Germans. The 2nd Battalion returned to the control of the 18th Infantry Regiment three days later.

By this time, the 3rd Armored Division had made contact with the 2nd Armored Division of the Ninth Army outside of Lippstadt (the Third Armored Division's Commanding General, Major General Maurice Rose, was killed in action on Easter Sunday). The divisional link-ups closed a pocket encompassing 317,000 men of *Army Groups B* and *H*.

On 5 April, orders were received for the 18th Infantry Regiment to take up positions on the bank of the Weser River, several miles to the east. The Regiment was now charged with gaining a bridgehead near the village of Lauenforde on the opposite bank to facilitate the 3rd Armored Division's renewed advance to the east.

"The Weser was the only continuous line which the enemy might have defended," wrote Major Lauten in explaining the scarce options left to the Germans if they hoped to launch an attack to open a "chink in the encircling ring" in the vicinity of the Lippstadt-Paderborn gap.

"In its better days the enemy would have made it [crossing the Weser] far more difficult and costly than the Roer. Only scratch units, such as *Artillery Observation Battalion 6* and various engineer and replacement units were on hand to oppose the Americans. It was plain, though, that the enemy, despite his sorry collection of troops (an estimate of combat effectiveness that, of course, did not apply to his

Waffen-SS units) was also in the process of organizing some sort of order out of the chaos."[20]

It was in this atmosphere of uncertainty that the 3rd Battalion was alerted on 6 April for its mission to cross the Weser River. On the day before the attack, which was supposed to take place on the 8th, no enemy action or movement had been noticed. It was estimated that the defending forces on the far side of the river in Lauenforde, however, were "at least company strength."[21] Captain Paulsen, now back in the line and commanding Company L, was to lead the initial crossing, and when Company L had secured the village, it was to push east some 3,000 yards.

The battalion plan called for him to hold in place for 36 hours while engineers constructed a bridge. Company K was to cross this bridge and advance through Company L, to take an important road junction on high ground another 2,000 yards eastward.

Company I, now under the command of Lieutenant Clifford Chandler, would move up and seize another road junction on Company K's opposite flank. As soon as this was done, the 3rd Armored Division would start across the newly constructed bridge, move through the bridgehead the 3rd Battalion had established, and continue rolling deeper into Germany.

The enemy had blown a bridge over the Weser on 6 April after their last retreating forces had crossed, requiring combat engineers to rebuild a span capable of supporting tanks. When Paulsen reconnoitered the area on 6 April, he saw that the explosions which reduced the old bridge had also destroyed several structures on the town's waterfront road and that eastern approaches to what had been the bridge were impassable. Given this, he decided to push a patrol across the river to reconnoiter, identify likely defensive positions, and then look for the best avenues of tactical approach. When he returned to his company at Ringelstein, he detailed plans for an attack with his rifle platoon leaders.

The next day, the 3rd Battalion moved in half-tracks to Kneblinghouser where they joined with B and C Batteries of the 32nd FA, and then at 1530 hours all company commanders met at Natingen where Major Randall held a meeting to discuss crossing the river. While the men were being placed in billets and the supply train was being brought up, battalion staff and representatives from Company L hurried some ten miles to make contact with the 3rd Armored Division near Beverungen to co-ordinate the final phase of the operation.

As H-hour approached, Paulsen's men left Kneblinghausen by truck and motored until they reached a point two miles west of Beverungen, where they proceeded by foot through a dark, moonless night to the edge of the Weser. There they boarded engineer assault boats. It was nearing 0200 hours on 8 April 1945.

"The patrol, in all readiness, assembled and received last-minute instructions from their commander before loading into boats," the Company L after-action report noted. "Silence reigned momentarily and they paddled across the river. The night was still and each little noise seemed to magnify itself in the dead silence. The patrol crossed several yards of water when all hell broke loose. Firing seemed to come from all directions, with the automatic fire the most intense."²² The patrol managed to land a few minutes later, but one Company L rifleman was killed and another was seriously wounded as they stood to debark. A hail of fire covered the earth around the men who started up the riverbank, wounding several others. Some of the men had helped the engineers to back off the assault boat to return to the opposite shore, while others started closing upon their attackers.

These men quickly worked their way up to the back yards of houses bordering the river, leaving behind a cleared path for the next group of riflemen the engineers would bring across. In the next half hour of sharp fighting, a machine-gun nest was destroyed and 10 enemy were killed with as many as 30 others wounded.

The after-action report said, "At times the fighting was so close that hand-to-hand combat ensued and some of the enemy tried to slip through and cut us off from the rear. Alert men quickly engaged them with bayonets, or fired on them. Every precaution had been taken to prevent our own men from being mistaken for the enemy. The enemy, two companies strong—one an SS unit—fought bitterly from their prepared positions, giving little ground at first, then forcibly giving way under the tremendous fire from our troops."²³

Bringing up reinforcements was easy. Two boats capsized, and with the springtime river current running strongly, another ended up south of Lauenforde, on the wrong bank. By the time additional rifle platoons assembled within the fragile beachhead, house-to-house searches often resulting in room-to-room fights now were taking place in the little town. Enemy artillery positions were still hurling indirect fire at the Americans, but the first light of day permitted the company to work more carefully through the streets. "Resistance was bitter and the diehard fanatical enemy fought stubbornly using panzerfausts and other antitank weapons," the company report explained. "But our men moved forward, using rifle grenades on locked doors and at snipers while throwing hand grenades into windows."²⁴

The 2nd Platoon of Company L soon neared the far edge of town, where houses thinned out. Patrols were quickly sent 1,000 yards to the east to reconnoiter and, specifically, to check a nearby railway underpass to see if it was passable for armored vehicles. An outpost was set up while more American infantry streamed across the river into the town.

The 1st Platoon moved south through the 3rd Platoon, hitting heavy opposition. At times men moved across rooftops to surprise and trap the Germans.

Several key events occurred during the next few hours. Enemy mortar, artillery, and tank fire continued to saturate the streets, reducing less well-constructed houses to rubble and forcing the Americans quickly to scramble into basements or more stoutly built shelter. Despite this, Paulsen's 2nd and 3rd Platoons made their way into the center of the village, where they set up automatic weapons to prepare for a counterattack. By then, the company's Weapons Platoon had moved across the river and employed its 60 mm mortars to defend the strongpoint in the center of the village. As the afternoon wore on, however, enemy artillery fire continued to harass Paulsen's men while German patrols repeatedly tried to penetrate the defensive perimeter.

The enemy's effort that day climaxed in a platoon-sized counterattack toward dusk that was quickly repulsed. Several other feeble counterattacks were thrown against Company L's newly-won positions during the night and early the following morning, but Paulsen's men were alert and no appreciable ground was lost.

Division engineers attempted to construct a bridge across the Weser on 9 April, but enemy artillery fire was still too heavy to complete this important task. It was nightfall before the job was finished. Company L was isolated for the entire day, so Lieutenant Johnson had been ordered to move Company K across the river to reinforce them at 1600 hours. Company I followed after Company K crossed and its men passed Johnson's flank as they moved through the woods to reach a first road junction 3,000 yards to the east.

By this time, the Germans had fled into nearby woods and hills. Division intelligence later noted, "These SS men withdrew, ordering a dispirited collection of stragglers and replacements to resist to the death, like heroes."[25]

The cost of defending Lauenforde had been heavy for the Germans who lost 150 killed or wounded. The 3rd Battalion's after-action report noted with justification, "Thus the objective, the breaching of the defenses on the eastern bank of the Weser River, the capture of the town of Lauenforde, and the flat level terrain several thousand yards and beyond, was achieved. The 3rd Armored Division was able to cross and sweep through the enemy defenses beyond."[26]

Some 20 miles east of the Weser stood the Harz Mountains, the highest terrain in northern and central Germany. It was here that the Regiment would fight its final battles of World War II. As Major Lauten wrote in his Intelligence Report:

> Apparently the last hope of the enemy was to pull back as many men as possible, as well as the great part of his armor, into the Harz Mountains. This would also give him time to regroup into some kind of integrated unit. That the Harz Mountains were the refuge of more than a single German corps was not immediately apparent as the 1st Infantry Division pushed rapidly to overrun the first line of German outposts positioned in front of the hills and the forest. Later in the fighting, both from the variety of the units encountered of divisional and independent unit status, it became evident that the Harz Mountains were defended by four German corps-sized formations—the *VI* and *IX Corps,* both converted *Wehrkreis* affairs; *LXVI Corps* and the *LXVII Corps*—old line outfits which had moved up from the south.* Not one of these corps was by any means up to the level of a German corps in the *Wehrmacht*'s salad days, but there were certainly enough troops on hand

---

*Wehrkreise were German military districts that were administrative entities used for purposes of recruiting and providing replacements. At the very end of the war, some were used as tactical headquarters, as in this case. *Wehrkreise* were not organized or equipped for such tasks, which they therefore performed in a generally unsatisfactory fashion.

to make the reduction of the Harz Mountains a tough proposition, especially since there was also present a liberal seasoning of SS men from the *Westphalia Brigade* and a core of experienced and high-grade soldiers from such units as the *9th Panzer Division* and the *116th Panzer Division.*

Moreover, the terrain which the enemy could use for his defense was about as forbidding to an attacker as could be found. It was more favorable to the enemy than the Ardennes because the road net was more limited; it was tougher than the Hürtgen Forest because the woods were thicker and the ground was more broken by ravines, hills, and draws. The roads capable of carrying heavy traffic were child's play to block. The number of trees that could be felled across the roads at critical spots was only limited by the amount of explosive on hand and the number of men available to handle saws. The roads that wound around the sides of the hills could be cratered at a moment's notice. The enemy had plenty of men—probably close to 100,000—and he had supporting weapons in strength that gave him equality with our attacking forces, if not superiority except in artillery. True, there was little possibility that the Harz could hold out forever surrounded on all sides, but there was always hope that some sort of delay could be imposed on the Americans which would grant more time to the High Command—time to do what was never clear.[27]

"The Harz Mountains fighting started out on the wrong foot," Major McGregor remembered about the 18th Infantry Regiment's entry into this foray. "Three separate units were all assigned the mission of taking Osterode. The 3rd Battalion was assigned the mission of coming in from the east, while a squadron of cavalry and a task force of the 3rd Armored Division were coming in from the south and southeast. When the 3rd Armored Division's task force observed [other] troops converging on Osterode, they immediately called for air support and the 3rd Battalion's column was dive-bombed. Fortunately they took cover and suffered no casualties."[28]

Osterode, on the southwestern corner of the Harz Mountains, was the division's primary objective on 11 April. When American units converging on the town each identified the presence of the other and finally, as Major McGregor later noted, "established sufficient contact to determine what the mission of all three units was, each did a 'Alphonse and Gaston' act regarding entering Osterode. As it developed, the 3rd Armored cleared the town."* Meanwhile, the 2nd Battalion encountered its own set of difficulties when men were clearing a nearby wooded area the same day.

---

*Alphonse and Gaston were popular comic-strip characters created by Frederick Opper for the *New York Journal.* Their conduct was so excessively polite and unctuous that it often prevented anything at all being done. "After you, Alphonse," Gaston would say, and "No, Gaston, after you," would be Alphonse's reply. With neither willing to proceed before the other, both would be stymied.

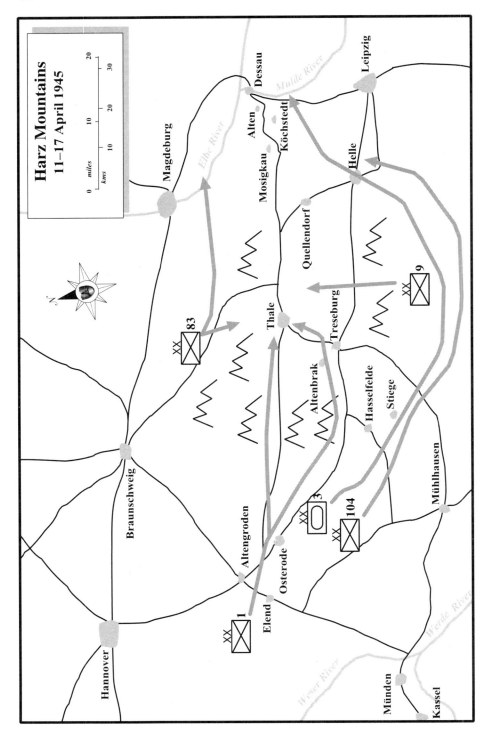

Four of the battalion's attached tanks were knocked out by rapid fire from a camouflaged 88mm gun. Major McGregor added to his explanation about why the Regiment had started out badly in the Harz offensive when he offered, "All of these tanks were picked off from the rear after they passed the gun emplacement because they were traveling too close together."[29]

On 12 April, Learnard's 1st Battalion was attached to the 3rd Armored Division. Its start on the northern border of the 1st Infantry Division zone to clear toward Dessau was equally difficult. The battalion had been organized as part of Task Force Y, which in turn was a part of Combat Command A of the 3rd Armored Division. One battalion from the 9th and 104th Infantry Divisions, respectively, were also assigned to this force.

Learnard commented later,

> When the battalion was attached to the 3rd Armored Division, two battle groups were immediately formed. One battle group consisted of two tank companies and a rifle company; the other included two rifle companies and a tank company. One group was heavy tank (M-26 Pershing) and all the others were M-4s. It was a makeshift arrangement, designed only because it was impossible to split three evenly in half.
>
> Communications did not work very satisfactorily at the time. We had our own communications setup within the battalion, but it [did not work as well] when our rifle companies were out riding the tanks. A rifle company commander had no chance to talk to his rifle platoon leaders, and the company commander had to fight with whichever platoon he happened to be with physically. The 3rd Battalion of the 47th Infantry was working on our left during [most] of the action, but it was very difficult—in fact, ludicrous in detail—to get in touch with their infantry for coordination purposes. First, I had to contact the task force commander, who relayed the message to the combat commander, who in turn notified the division commander, who in turn notified the other combat commander. And then it went to the task force commander who passed it on to the infantry battalion commander, whom I could have whistled at in the first place.
>
> My men rode six per tank generally. Those left over rode two-and-a-half-ton trucks, which were road-bound. Half-tracks would have been better. Two rifle companies were usually mounted on the tanks; the battalion command group and the heavy weapons company used organic transportation, and one rifle company and Headquarters Company rode on trucks. We encountered light opposition during the first few days of the advance, but we got into three big fights before it was over—Köchstedt, Alten, and north of Dessau.[30]

Company C, which had suffered many casualties since the Hürtgen Forest, led the advance on 16 April as the 1st Battalion moved from Quellendorf northeast to attack Köchstedt. About halfway to Köchstedt, a well-camouflaged minefield was encountered. It was cleared within a half hour and the advance continued.

Just as the lead platoon entered the outskirts of town, the tank on which they were mounted was knocked out by a panzerfaust, killing or wounding every infantryman on the tank's deck. At the same time, the enemy opened up with machine guns and small arms from well-prepared positions. Company C's rifleman responded by launching a hasty attack that quickly penetrated into the village. Van Wagoner's Company A deployed on Company C's flank and began clearing the left half of Köchstedt while the enemy, supported by artillery and mortars, fought a stubborn delaying action.

Finally, at 2230 that night Köchstedt was cleared of all enemy troops. A total of 300 prisoners were captured, but losses were unusually heavy to both Van Wagoner's men and Company C. Miller's Company B, in action at the village of Mosigkau (one mile to the northwest of Köchstedt), met more moderate resistance while seizing that town by late afternoon.

"The difficulty with Köchstedt was that it was actually much larger than it appeared on our maps," Lieutenant Colonel Learnard noted later. "Southeast of the Quellendorf-Dessau road were the sumptuous *Luftwaffe* barracks, which did not show up on the maps, but housed some fanatical troops who held the advance up with small arms fire. Moreover, as soon as we thought we had reached the end of the town, here would come a couple of more blocks of houses uncharted by the maps."[31]

The Regiment's mission, less the 1st Battalion, was now to move to the vicinity of Hasselfelde, ten miles southwest of Thale, and take over from the 9th Infantry Division's 60th Infantry Regiment.

The final rout in the Harz Mountains began on 19 April when the 18th Infantry Regiment pushed into rear areas of the last German positions in its zone. Once the Altenbrak-Treseburg crust was broken, Major Randall's 3rd Battalion started northeast through the woods toward Thale.

"The route of advance offered many opportunities for the enemy to conceal himself from our troops mopping up in this area, Company I's Lieutenant Chandler remembered. "As a result there were a large number of ambushes. One of the most serious occurred when the enemy set up a trap for our battalion commander, Major Randall."[32] Randall was seriously wounded that day by machine-gun fire in the same leg that he had been hit in near the end of the North Africa campaign.

Captain Hess, who had commanded Company I from the Normandy beachhead through the Ardennes offensive before becoming Randall's S-3, was seated next to him in their jeep when the firing started. Hess, like too many men this late in the war, was shot in the head and killed.

Captain Park's Company G found itself 4,000 yards northeast of Wenderfürth on 19 April. Wenderfürth lay just northeast of Hasselfelde and west of Thale in the middle of a small valley, surrounded on all sides by high mountains and heavily-wooded terrain. In addition to reducing the town itself, Park also was tasked with clearing the woods between his line of departure and the village. The company pushed off at 0700 hours, clearing the dense woods as they went, and by the time they reached a narrow river about a kilometer south of Wenderfürth Park's men had captured about 20 Germans and had not taken a casualty. Captain Park then decided to reconnoiter with his platoon leaders to decide the best way to cross the river with the least risk to the company. What they saw indicated their continuing mission first appeared daunting, but achievable.

Both sides of the river sloped to its banks over open ground about 100 yards in width, neither side with cover or concealment. Given this, Park decided to send a platoon across the river first to secure a small bridgehead so the rest of the company could cross over safely. At 1300 hours, his 3rd Platoon crossed the river and established outposts, and then radioed back for the rest of the company to follow.

The remaining Company G platoons crossed safely, and then the 3rd Platoon led the way to a high ridge that overlooked Wenderfürth. At this point, 15 Germans were spotted on a high knoll west of the village, and infantry and vehicles were seen in the town. Soon afterward, Park decided to make another reconnaissance, this time to plan the attack on the enemy position.

The plan that quickly evolved called for the 1st Platoon and the attached heavy machine-gun section to establish a base of fire from their present position overlooking the town. Upon Park's order, this force was to hit Wenderfürth itself, then deliver fire onto the high ground opposite the town where he suspected there were targets of opportunity. Volleys to the hill behind the town were to serve at the very least as a diversion, as it was Park's plan to attack the town from the rear with his 3rd Platoon leading, and then follow them with the rest of his company.

Captain Park waited until he could confirm the enemy was digging in on the north side of the town, saw that they were facing him, and then ordered the intiation of the attack. The 3rd Platoon quickly worked its way behind the Germans forces, capturing one soldier without being detected and well before the main body of the enemy even suspected they were being attacked. "Then it was too late," the company report later noted. "The surprise caught them completely off balance. Just before the 3rd Platoon even started shooting, the order was given for the 1st Platoon and the heavy machine guns up on the ridge to open up. Immediately after this, the 3rd Platoon also opened up and managed to get into town and secure it before the enemy could put up any resistance at all."[33]

While there were a few scattered rifle shots during the attack on Wenderfürth, Company G sustained no casualties. Park then ordered his men to dig in, with platoons guarding the high ground northeast and south of the village, while both heavy and light machine-gun sections covered approaches to the north and south. Later counts showed that the company had taken well over 100 prisoners, killed 30, and wounded 20 enemy soldiers. The Germans never counterattacked.

The town of Stiege (two miles southeast of Hasselfelde), and the high ground overlooking the large city of Thale, were occupied by Major Middleworth's 2nd

Battalion and the 3rd Battalion the next day. During the advance to Stiege, Hill 510 had proven to be a tough nut for the 2nd Battalion. "They took it for granted that it was going to be easy, and sent a platoon to make a frontal attack on the hill," Major McGregor stated later. "Somebody who knew his stuff must have given the Germans good instructions on their positions because they commanded all approaches to the hill and were hard to get at. The platoon was soon pinned down by automatic weapons fire from these strongly defended positions, so a full company was dispatched to the scene. It also attempted an unsuccessful frontal assault on the hill, and it wasn't until another company of infantry hooked around from the east side of the hill that they finally succeeded in reducing the resistance."[34]

Despite this problem, a total of 4,300 prisoners were netted along with an enormous amount of enemy equipment when Stiege and Thale fell. By this time, the 26th Infantry Regiment had also cleared east of Elend and the Brockenberg area, the highest point of ground in the Harz Mountains.

The 1st Infantry Division history says "the payoff of the entire operation" came on 20 April. In the center of the division sector, Elbingerode (ten kilometers northwest of Elend) was taken and the *1st Regiment* of *Division "Potsdam"* surrendering *en masse*. Major Lauten, analyzing the enemy catch that day in his periodic intelligence summary dated 1 May, noted, "The move which broke any hope to the enemy of reassembling for a counterattack was the drive into Thale by the 18th US Infantry. Of the 10,000 prisoners taken that day, nearly 8,000 were captured by the 18th Infantry in the Thale-Timmenrode area. It was the biggest prisoner haul in the history of the 1st Infantry Division and outdid any single day's take in the Mons pocket. The PW cage was a tumultuous babble of crowds and confusion. Prisoners came streaming in all day, and all night."[35]

Company I's Lieutenant Chandler remembered this time well when he noted with obvious satisfaction, "There were plenty of [German] brass hidden away in the chateaus and castles here, and they evidently issued strong orders to their personal bodyguards to pick troops to hold at all costs. This phrase 'hold at all costs' had been heard before in the German army, but evidently the stakes for top-ranking personnel were much higher this time. All organized resistance ceased after Altenbrak, and from then on it was merely a problem of rounding up the prisoners and separating them from the gaping civilians. This was sport, and did not entail too much work. As my Company I approached Thale, the prisoners came in uncontrollable droves, happily driving their own cars and horse carts, and decked out in all their braid and insignia."

"There was really only one old boy who caused us any trouble," Chandler remembered. "He was a general in a hut in the middle of the woods who claimed he thought it was cowardly to surrender when he had an Iron Cross with cluster*"

---

*The Knight's Cross, Nazi Germany's highest decoration, was actually the only award that could be modified by a device called "the Oakleaves," so that is probably what this general was wearing. The *Ritterkreuz* looks like a scaled-up version of the Iron Cross, but is worn around the throat, so it is easy to see how Lieutenant Chandler could be mistaken.

and had awarded many of the same medals to his men who had stood bravely and fought without surrendering. Our answer was to line up six tanks pointed directly at his hut, then draw up a platoon of infantry. We had scarcely gotten into place before the general's medical officer came out and announced that the general would now surrender."[36]

One last order awaited the 1st Battalion, 18th Infantry Regiment. Lieutenant Colonel Learnard's men were still attached to the 3rd Armored Division and pockets of enemy to the east of the Thale-Timmerode area remained to be cleaned out. The battalion's final mission was to clear out the area from Thale toward Dessau, reduce a barracks complex to the east, and then finish off the Germans located at the junction of the Mülde and Elbe rivers, a scant 60 miles from Berlin.

While the 2nd and 3rd Battalions were rounding up prisoners around Thale, both Van Wagoner's Company A, and Jessie Miller's Company B had remained in Köchstedt and Mosigkau. At 0330 hours on 21 April both companies hurriedly crossed their lines of departure and moved forward for the attack on Dessau. Just before dawn, Van Wagoner worked his rifle platoons into the southern outskirts of Alten, a suburb of Dessau, while Miller moved in from the north. The attack was a surprise with little resistance encountered and Captain Miller's men finished a lightning sweep through the buildings in his section of town before the sun came up.

"In one small-unit action that morning," Learnard remembered, "Captain Miller burst into a room occupied by three enemy riflemen, sprayed two with his tommy gun, and knocked the other out with a deft upper-cut from the butt of his gun. I always regarded him as the best rifle company commander in the entire division. He was fearless and aggressive. His positive leadership made him the idol of his men ever since he landed with the division in Oran."

Alten was clear by daylight on 21 April, but Captain Miller had a vulnerable, exposed left flank that extended out some 300 yards to a rail line. "Somebody stirred up a hornet's nest here," Learnard later recalled, "then approximately 1,000 infantry began swirling in behind his company. These men appeared to be disorganized as a unit, and were probably school troops or convalescents. They acted like casual recruits, but there were some 33 other men mixed in with the group. Apparently some wanted to fight and others wanted to give up, but it was very difficult to distinguish between the two states of mind from a distance."[37]

In the ensuing confusion, small knots of enemy fought sharply while others quickly laid down their arms.

A little later Captain Miller was cleaning out a house infiltrated by several Germans when shots rang out from a machine pistol, killing him instantly. "He was a fighter from the word go," Learnard remembered. "He was tactically smart . . . carried out every mission and did more than his share himself. He had a great personality and was worshipped by his men."

Following the death of Captain Miller, the command of the company passed to Lieutenant Thomas Yarborough, who was also killed the same afternoon. Van

Wagoner's Company A and Miller's loyal men eventually rounded up 750 prisoners of war, and Dessau and Alten were completely cleaned out the next day.

Even though the war was now just two weeks from ending, enemy forces located to the east of Learnard's 1st Battalion were not ready to give up. "Task Force Y [of the 3rd Armored Division] then tackled the hardest part of our operation," he remembered. "This was a small peninsula of land north of Dessau between the Elbe and the Mülde rivers."[38]

Anticipating that their foe would attempt to cross the Elbe at this strategic point, the Germans had decided to deploy a well-protected defensive position manned by highly-motivated personnel from an officer candidate school to deny the Americans this crossing.

The ground the 1st Battalion was tasked with taking at this river junction did not favor the attacker. It was level and beside a dried up riverbed where the Mülde once reached through a cut to the Elbe, hence the "small peninsula" Learnard referred to. The area was marshy and several small lakes dotted lowlands that lay beneath the river's high water mark, making it difficult tank terrain.

True to their defensive doctrine, the Germans made clever use of wire obstacles. To shield all approaches to the peninsula they stretched barbed wire tightly in front of all defilade spots and made it impossible for an attacker to get within hand grenade-throwing distance.

The low lying and brushy terrain also made it easy for the German machine gunners and riflemen to move around and stay unobserved through small folds in the ground, but the Americans, on more exposed terrain, could be seen readily.

"The 47th [Infantry of the 9th Division] ran into this position eight hours ahead of us," Learnard commented later. "But because of our terrible system of communication we had received no information about this."

Lacking the benefit of the experience gained by the 47th Infantry Regiment, the 1st Battalion discovered the enemy positions only when Captain Van Wagoner sent a reinforced platoon out to mop up the area between the rivers north of Dessau on the night of 22 April. German opposition was later recorded as "so startlingly strong that operations were suspended for the night."[39]

After conducting a personal reconnaissance of this forbidding terrain, Learnard determined that a frontal assault was the only solution. The next morning, 23 April, brought a deliberate attack that began with several field artillery battalions firing concentrations on the enemy position. After the preparatory fire ceased, patrols from Company A tried in vain to find a hole in the enemy wire, even bringing up Bangalore torpedoes to blow the openings when none could be found. Enemy automatic fire was so intense that the mission collapsed, and it was not until a frontal assault was made just after noontime on a position where the wire did not bar entry that any progress was achieved. After counterbattery fire silenced the enemy's mortars, 3rd Armored Division tanks were brought up as far as the soggy ground permitted. They doused the Germans with machine-gun fire.

Bitter fighting seesawed back and forth all afternoon, but the 1st Battalion made little progress, mainly due to the overhead cover the Germans had fashioned atop their dugouts and entrenchments. Much like it had been used in both the Hürtgen Forest and the Bulge, and these features made it difficult for the Americans to locate opposing positions.

The attacking infantry—Companies A and B—finally achieved a breakthrough after two routes capable of supporting tanks were discovered. Several Shermans were brought forward, their drivers slowly negotiating the soft ground, and as they ground their way closer, the Germans started to scatter in retreat.

A total of four 1st Battalion officers and 60 enlisted men were casualties during this last real fight—some killed trying to ford or swim over the Elbe to chase the retreating Germans. In turn, 220 prisoners were taken and 50 other enemy soldiers were killed or wounded, but many had succeeded in escaping by swimming across the river.

As Learnard later discovered while walking through the area, "The enemy position was so thoroughly organized and defended that few casualties to him were suffered in the area itself. I expected to find many German bodies in that hot spot, but there were a great many less than I had hoped to find. But one of the larger problems we were confronting at the time was the high number of officer and NCO casualties suffered by the 1st Battalion overall. We lost 18 officers in the battalion during the time we were attached to the 3rd Armored, and a large percentage were [formerly] noncoms."[40]

On 27 April, the Regiment was on the move again with the 1st Infantry Division and in contact with the enemy once more—this time across the Czechoslovakian frontier after a long move from the Harz area. By now, enemy forces facing the Division consisted of whatever units they could scrape from the bottom of the *Wehrkreis XII* barrels. As Major Lauten noted, "The only enemy unit that had ever been heard of before was the *2nd Panzer Division*, which was in contact to the south of the division zone and reportedly possessed of no more than six tanks. The enemy was not very disposed to fight and he was altogether incapable of attacking."[41]

"On May 1 1945, the Germans were all through," agreed the 1st Infantry Division's own history. "The political leaders and the party boys were still grabbing for straws, but the *Wehrmacht* and the ordinary civilians were through. There was no big picture of the enemy situation, because there was no enemy except in Czechoslovakia, which of course was where the 1st Infantry Division happened to be. The only question at hand was whether the enemy would fall over of his own weight, or whether he would have to be pushed."[42]

In the end, it was decided that the Germans needed a little more convincing. On the morning of 5 May all three regiments of the 1st Infantry Division, operating in conjunction with CCA of the 9th Armored Division, continued the attack into Czechoslovakia. On 6 May, divisional units destroyed some German antitank guns and the 18th Regiment Infantry sustained more casualties, losing eight enlisted men and one officer.

Shortly after the sun came up the next morning, four years from May 1941 when the Regiment stood proudly on the parade grounds at Fort Devens for Organization Day under the threat of looming war, a message was received at Colonel Williamson's command post, as relayed from V Corps stating, "All troops to halt in place and maintain defensive positions. Effective at once. Details to follow."[43] Later that morning the details fell into the hands of Captain Murphy at the 1st Battalion command post in the form of orders. Originating from Colonel Williamson, his instructions first contained the words every man in the Regiment had been anxiously waiting for:

A REPRESENTATIVE OF THE GERMAN HIGH COMMAND SIGNED THE UNCONDITIONAL SURRENDER OF ALL GERMAN LAND, SEA, AND AIR FORCES IN EUROPE TO THE ALLIED EXPEDITIONARY FORCE AND SIMULTANEOUSLY TO THE SOVIET UNION COMMAND AT 0141 HOURS CENTRAL EUROPEAN TIME 7 MAY.

Williamson's final sentence was clear, evidencing urgency. "The above will be read to all men of this Combat Team by organizational commanders, TODAY."[44]

The following morning at 0815 hours, Major General Andrus issued the final order to "CEASE FIRING."[45] For the officers and men of the 18th Infantry Regiment, World War II—their American Iliad—had come to an end after two and a half years of fighting across North Africa and Europe. Just 29 officers made it the whole way from Arzew in North Africa to war's end and stayed in Germany.[46] In any given rifle company, there were few, if any, "originals" who survived the war without becoming a casualty, and unit rosters in Czechoslovakia bore no resemblance to the gangplank rosters of 1942. During its wartime operations, the 18th Infantry Regiment suffered 5,490 casualties, of whom 1,513 were dead.[47]

Those who survived either went home or stayed in Germany for further duties. In 1947, the war dead were either starting to be buried in permanent American cemeteries in Africa or Europe, or their caskets were being shipped home for re-internment on slow transports—unrushed, as the *Queen Mary* had been to bring many of them off to war.

Staff Sergeant Donald Parker shared his thoughts and the emotions of many when he heard the end of the war had come on 8 May 1945. He was on a 30-day leave on his family's farm in western Illinois, and one of the thousands who had sailed by the Statue of Liberty in August 1942 to go overseas to fight. "After the news came I sat down in a stall with my favorite riding horse and bawled," he remembered. "I had lost too many friends, but for what? Just because one man—Hitler—was so greedy and narrow minded? He had created a following that caused the death of millions, and several of those were close friends of mine I could never forget."[48]

Captain Irving Yarock, captured at Longstop Hill in Tunisia during the first battle the Regiment fought directly against Germans two and half years earlier, was liberated by the 14th Armored Division in Moosburg, Germany, at the northern end of the Brenner Pass. He heard that the war had ended while he was waiting for a plane to fly him to Camp Lucky Strike, where he took command of 200 other POWs who had to be processed before their trip back to the States. "After almost three years overseas I was elated," Yarock remembered. "I was going home at last."[49]

Lieutenant John Downing reflected the feelings of many who fought in the Regiment during the war when he later wrote, "When we got home we faced a rebirth into the complexities of civilian living with the immediate necessity of choosing from scratch a job, a home, and a way of life. But we had the personal satisfaction gained from knowing that for a period in our lives we were associated with men who collectively accomplished missions that changed the course of history without haggling over the price. We knew that when and if the occasion should ever rise again that we would not be satisfied with anything less than being called upon to serve once more with the same type of soldiers we fought with in this war."[50]

Another officer later shared what many others who fought in the 18th Infantry Regiment undoubtedly felt during the years after the war ended. "World War II is so impressed in my brain, my heart, my body, and my soul that it will not end until the day I die," retired Lieutenant Colonel Sam Carter wrote on his 90th birthday from his home in Florida.

"Wars that one personally fights never end."[51]

AFTERWORD

Just as in 1918, the 1st Infantry Division was again called upon in 1945 to serve as an occupation force in Germany. Yet while the 18th Infantry Regiment remained in Germany, most of the soldiers who had served in it with such courage and sacrifice from North Africa to Czechoslovakia returned individually to the "ZI" (Zone of the Interior, or the continental United States) for discharge and their return to civilian life.

Those who remained in Europe, however, were the core of a proud unit with more than 140 years of distinguished military history; its valorous accomplishments upheld traditions which continue to be a standard in the active rolls of the United States Army.

After Germany surrendered, the world divided into different armed camps. The 18th Infantry Regiment performed many varied duties in the stabilization and reconstruction of occupied western Germany. With compassion for the suffering German people, it performed with the same esprit and determination that had characterized its combat actions. Ironically, while serving as Honor Guard at the Nürnberg trials, the 18th Infantry Regiment also stood ready to defend the former enemy. The same would be true during the Berlin airlift in 1948–49. Subsequently, the Regiment faced communist armed forces across the East German-Czech border during the Cold War.

Regimental headquarters moved from place to place in the early years of the Occupation, finally settling in Aschaffenburg, Germany. There, under command of Colonel Rinaldo Van Brunt, the 18th Infantry Regiment adopted the nickname, "Vanguards."

By 1955, the Cold War had stabilized. The 1st Infantry Division returned home to Fort Riley, Kansas. Homecoming was not a jubilant celebration, as had occurred in 1919. The Army was changing—and the old regimental system was passing.

Army policy at the time moved the colors, but not the men. Battle-hardened old soldiers wept as their beloved 18th Infantry Regiment returned to the United States while they remained in Germany, now assigned to alien units. At Fort Riley, the history and traditions of the Regiment lived on with the colors and the men who served under them.

The next generation to serve under the colors of the 18th Infantry Regiment soldiered on through the Cold War before fighting in Vietnam, where they added to the honors of the Regiment. Soldiers of those times again were part of the 1st Infantry Division, the first standard infantry division to land in the Republic of

Vietnam. As part of the Division's 2nd Brigade, the soldiers of the Regiment's 1st and 2nd Battalions continued the tradition, "No mission too difficult! No sacrifice too great! Duty First!"

The full story of their courage and sacrifice is yet to be told, but it will include describing the circumstances of two "Valorous Unit Award" citations (1967—"Binh Long Province," and 1968—"Di An District").

After leaving Vietnam in April 1970, a generation of young American enlisted men and their officers served with the Regiment through the tedious, demanding, and potentially explosive remaining years of the Cold War. Just as the Soviet Empire collapsed, however, the Regimental colors were carried to the war to liberate Kuwait from Iraqi conquest. Four battalions of 18th Infantry Regiment soldiers saw combat in the Gulf War of 1991. Although they wore a different shoulder patch, their courage and sacrifice remained true to the 18th Infantry Regiment's traditions. In their time, they also embodied the spirit of the Regiment. Their deeds were in keeping with those of the Regiment's soldiers of earlier days.

In 1996, an Army reorganization returned the 18th Infantry to the 1st Infantry Division, and now 18th Infantry soldiers again wear the Big Red One on the left shoulder of the uniform, as well as the Regimental distinctive insignia on their shoulder loops. Our soldiers today serve in the 1st Battalion, 18th Infantry, with the 2nd Brigade, 1st Infantry Division. Recently stationed in Schweinfurt, Germany, they are *In Omnia Paratus!* ("In All Things Prepared") They saw duty in harm's way in such places as Bosnia, Macedonia, Kosovo, and, as of early 2004, in Iraq. While stationed in Schweinfurt, they were reminded of the Regiment's traditions of service and sacrifice with regular visits by two of its retired senior combat veterans—an Honorary Colonel and an Honorary Sergeant Major of the Regiment. They are supported in substance and in spirit by veterans of the 18th Infantry Regiment Association at home, wherever their duties may take them.

Reflecting on that spirit, we recall that the colors of the 18th Regiment of United States Infantry first waved during the Civil War. Men have fought and died under those colors whenever the country called. Over time, the spirit of the Regiment, indefinable to the literalist, is what has held its soldiers together under some unimaginable stresses, knowing only that they could not forsake each other.

The spirit of the Regiment, to the soldier who has time to think about it, is partly the pride of knowing that good men have gone before him, that good men now serve beside him, and that other good men will follow him as he moves on to the next high ground.

If the World War II soldier of our Regiment had to explain the heart of the matter any more succinctly, he might look back to us and say, borrowing a bit for the 18th Infantry from an unknown author:

"Do not stand at my grave and weep.
I am not here. I do not sleep."

I'm in the wind that lifts the leaves,
Then lets them rest beneath the trees.
I am now moving on, my friends.
Duty first! Follow me!

George T. Gentry, Jr.
President, 18th Infantry Regiment
Association, 2001–2004

George M. Tronsrue, Jr.
Colonel, United States Army, Retired
Honorary Colonel of the Regiment

HONOR ROLL

This is a list of soldiers of the 18th Infantry Regiment and the 32nd Field Artillery Battalion who made the ultimate sacrifice during World War II.

ABATE, GEORGE N.	CPL	ANDLER, DONALD S.	PFC
ABBOTT, DON	PFC	ANDRADE, ARTHUR C.	PFC
ABBOTT, OPIE L.	PVT	ANDREWS, RAYMOND P.	PVT
ABELS, JOSEPH P.	PVT	ANGEL, LEE M.	SGT
ABRAMS, BILLY	PFC	ANNIBALDI, LEVIO J.	SGT
ABRAMS, BERNARD A.	PFC	ARCARO, ANTONIO L.	PFC
ACARDO, CHARLIE	PFC	ARCHILLA, JORGE I.	PFC
ACKERMAN, BEN	PVT	ARNOLD, BRADFORD	PFC
ACKERMAN, WALTER J.	PVT	ARNOLD, JR., CHAUNCEY J.	PVT
ACOSTA, MARTIN U.	PFC	ARRENDONDO, ERNESTO C.	PVT
ACQUILIN, EDWARD V.	PFC	ARTHUR, ONYX B.	PVT
ADAMCZYK, EDWARD W.	PFC	ASARO, TONY	SGT
ADAMS, ALBERT A.	PVT	ASHLEY, VICTOR R.	PFC
ADAMS, EVERTT W.	PFC	AUGUSTIN, JR., CHARLES J.	PVT
ADAMS, HARVEY L.	PVT	AUTOVINO, MATHEW J.	CPL
ADAMS, JAMES W.	SSG	AVERY, JR., GEORGE M.	PVT
ADAMS, PAUL E.	PVT	AYERS, GORDON W.	SGT
ADAMS, VINCENT J.	PVT	BABCOCK, WALTER E.	PVT
ADAMS, VIRGIL L.	PVT	BADDICK, JACOB L.	SSG
AIDALA, SALVATORE A.	PVT	BALL, OLAN L.	PFC
AIPLE, ADOLPH J.	PVT	BAMBAUER, CHARLES P.	PFC
ALBRECHT, RICHARD J.	PVT	BANCROFT, MELVIN F.	PVT
ALEXANDER, JR., NELSON A.	PVT	BANKS, WALTER W.	PVT
ALEXANDROWICZ, LOUIS	PFC	BANKSON, DOYLE G.	SGT
ALEXSON, WALTER A.	PFC	BARENBLITT, ALEXANDER	PVT
ALLEY, NORMAN E.	PVT	BARKSDALE, EDGAR E.	SSG
ALMEIDA, EDWARD L.	PVT	BARNES, JR., JOHN B.	PVT
ALONZO, TEOFILO	PFC	BARNETT, LEE A.	PVT
ALVANOS, ANTHONY	SSG	BARON, JOHN C.	PVT
AMATO, FRANCISCO J.	PVT	BARTH, KENNETH O.	SGT
AMBROSE, AMOS H.	PVT	BARTO, JOHN	PVT
AMENT, JULIAN L.	CPL	BARTOLOTTA, RICHARD J.	PFC
ANDERSON, CARL N.	PFC	BARTON, MARION K.	PVT
ANDERSON, CHARLEY F.	PVT	BASIEWICZ, JOHN	PFC
ANDERSON, CLYDE R.	PVT	BATEMAN, LEONARD C.	PFC
ANDERSON, DONALD L.	PVT	BATES, EDWARD C.	CPL
ANDERSON, SAMUEL H.	PFC	BAUGHMAN, RICHARD M.	PVT
ANDERSON, BERLIN P.	PVT	BAUM, ERNEST	PFC

BAUMGARTEN, ARTHUR P.	PFC	BOSSHART, CARL J.	CPL
BAUMMER, ROBERT A.	PFC	BOSWORTH, ELDENE B.	CPL
BAXTER, WILSON R.	PVT	BOUTON, GEORGE R.	SGT
BAYLUS, SAMUEL	PVT	BOWER, JACOB K.	PFC
BEACH, RUSSELL A.	SGT	BOWERS, EDGAR D.	PFC
BEATTY, ROBERT H.	PFC	BOYER, ARTHUR M.	PVT
BECKER, WILLIAM A.	SSG	BOYLIN, JR., HENRY C.	SSG
BEDELL, DALE	PFC	BRABANT, JOHN H.	CPL
BEIRLEIN, FREDERICK J.	PFC	BRADETICH, FRANK.	PVT
BELCHER, OKEY O.	PFC	BRADLEY, JAMES T.	SGT
BELT, JOHN J.	PVT	BRADLEY, WALLACE M.	PFC
BENIDIKTSON, GUNNAR A.	PFC	BRADY, GERALD J.	PFC
BENNETT, HENRY W.	PFC	BREEZE, THOMAS J.	PVT
BENNETT, EARL W.	PFC	BRESETTE, ROBERT W.	SSG
BENNETT, ARNOLD J.	PVT	BRIGANTE, PASQUALE A.	PVT
BENTLEY, MILLARD C.	PFC	BRIODY, FRANCIS P.	PVT
BERKET, MICHAEL	PVT	BRIZZI, VITO A.	CPL
BERNSTEIN, FRANK	PFC	BRODERICK, JOHN J.	PFC
BERTHUME, EDWIN D.	CPL	BRONSTEIN, HYMAN	PVT
BIANCUCCI, AMERICO	PFC	BROOKS, CHARLES W.	PVT
BICKELL, HARRY L.	PFC	BROOKS, WILLIAM H.	PFC
BIGI, VICTOR J.	SGT	BROUNS, EDWIN M.	SGT
BILHARZ, KENNETH O.	PVT	BROWN, ALFRED	PVT
BINN, EDWARD	PFC	BROWN, JAMES K.	CPL
BIRD, WARD B.	PFC	BROWN, JOHN L.	SGT
BISHOP, PAUL O.	PFC	BROWN, HARRY C.	1LT
BISHOW, VERNON Y.	PVT	BROWN, ROBERT A.	PVT
BISSELL, DONALD R.	PVT	BROWN, WILLIE J.	CPL
BLACK, GEORGE W.	PFC	BRUCATO, RICHARD V.	PVT
BLACK, JOHN W.	PVT	BRUMMETT, LOUIE A.	CPL
BLACK, OLIVER J.	PFC	BRUNETTI, ANTHONY	PFC
BLACKMAN, MALCOLM O.	PFC	BRUNO, SAM	PFC
BLAIS, JR., ARTHUR L.	PFC	BRUTKA, JOHN	PVT
BLANKENSHIP, JAMES D.	PVT	BRZEZINSKI, EDWARD J.	PVT
BLANTON, EARNEST E.	SSG	BUCHANAN, ALBERT S.	PFC
BLEVINS, HARLESS L.	PVT	BUDAI, BERTRAM L.	PFC
BLISS, JOHNNY A.	SGT	BUICK, WALTER A.	PVT
BLOCH, ELMER O.	PFC	BUMGARDNER, JAMES W.	PFC
BOEHLKE, LEROY A.	SSG	BUNCH, G. B.	PFC
BOLANOWSKI, JOHN S.	CPL	BUNDA, PAUL	TSG
BOLDEN, JR., EGBERT L.	PVT	BUNJEVAC, PETER T.	PFC
BOND, THOMAS J.	PVT	BURCHFIEL, JAMES O.	CPL
BONNETT, WARREN L.	CPT	BURFORD, WALLACE L.	PFC
BONSER, WILBUR E.	CPL	BURGESS, HERBERT C.	PVT
BORDEN, GEORGE M.	PFC	BURGOS, RAMON L.	SGT

BURLASSI, JOSEPH L.	PVT	CHESTNUT, CLARK W.	PFC
BURNETT, WILLIAM R.	SGT	CHIDICHIMO, HENRY J.	PFC
BURNS, DEWEY	PVT	CHISM, CLAUD	SGT
BURNS, WILLIAM J.	SGT	CHIRUPA, JOHN A.	PVT
BURTON, EVERETT E.	PFC	CHRONISTER, PAUL J.	PVT
BUSCAGLIO, JOHN	PVT	CICCONE, ANGELO F.	PFC
BUSH, WENDALL A.	PVT	CILIANO, MICHAEL E.	TSG
BUSSELL, ELVIN T.	PVT	CLARK, JAMES A.	PVT
BUSZTA, JOSEPH J.	PFC	CLARK, JOHN L.	PVT
BUTTRAY, HAROLD L.	PFC	CLARK, WILLIAM G.	PVT
BUTTS, ABRAM J.	SSG	CLAYTON, MELVIN T.	PFC
BUTTS, JEROME T.	PFC	CLEMENS, BERNARD E.	PFC
BYRD, BILLIE D.	PVT	CLEVELAND, CLIFFORD J.	PFC
BYRD, THOMAS W.	PFC	CLINE, NOLAN L.	PFC
CABRERA, PHILLIP	PVT	CLINTON, WELDON D.	TSG
CAFFEY, ROGER W.	CPL	CLOSNER, CARYL F.	PVT
CAHILL, EDWARD W.	PVT	CLOUTIER, CHARLES E.	1SG
CALDERON, MANUEL M.	SSG	COCHRAN, ALDEN P.	TSG
CALIVA, ANTHONY	PVT	COCHRAN, VICTOR M.	PVT
CAMBRON, JOSEPH W.	1LT	COE, JAMES T.	CPL
CAMERON, ARCHIBALD B.	CPT	COHEN, ISADORE	PVT
CAMPBELL, GARLAND C.	PVT	COHEN, ISRAEL	PVT
CAMPBELL, WILLIAM M.	PVT	COHEN, SIDNEY J.	PVT
CAMPBELL, NOEL	SGT	COLAVITO, LEE A.	PFC
CANO, PHILLIP T.	PFC	COLBY, DONALD J.	PVT
CARBOY, JOHN F.	PFC	COLCLASURE, RUFUS O.	CPL
CARDELLO, FRANK	PVT	COLDREN, WILBERT M.	PVT
CARLSON, KENNETH W.	SGT	COLLIER, JR., ALBERT	PVT
CARLSON, WALLACE B.	PFC	COLLINS, ROBERT H.	PVT
CARPENTER, CHARLES P.	PVT	COLLINS, JR., TRELA D.	1LT
CARPENTER, LESTER R.	PVT	COLON, LEO	PVT
CARRIGAN, GEORGE F.	PVT	COLSON, ANDREW M.	CPL
CARTELL, JERRY	PVT	COLSTON, BEN F.	PVT
CARTER, CHARLES E.	PFC	COMBS, JR., ARTHUR R.	CPL
CARTER, CONWAY G.	PFC	COMFORT, JOHN J.	PVT
CARTER, WILLIAM W	PVT	COMFORT, ROCCO F.	PVT
CARUTA, ALFRED J.	PVT	CONDON, THOMAS J.	SSG
CASTRO, EUTIMIO G.	PVT	CONKLIN, JAMES W.	PVT
CASWELL, JOHN J.	1LT	CONLEY, THURMAN J.	PFC
CAZAYOUX, JR., FRANCIS E.	PFC	CONNELL, WILLIAM F.	1LT
CELLUCCI, ERNEST A.	SSG	CONNELLY, PATRICK F.	PFC
CESARINI, LIBERTY	PFC	CONNER, WILLIAM P.	PFC
CHARLES, JACOB H.	PVT	CONNOR, CYRUS W.	PFC
CHAVEZ, ROMOLO	PFC	CONRAD, PAUL W.	PFC
CHERNISKE, JOSEPH S.	PVT	COOKSIE, CHARLES M.	PVT

COOPER, JOHN W.	1LT	DAVIS, PHILLIP F.	SSG
COPELAND, WILLIAM J.	PVT	DAWSON, LAWRENCE W.	PFC
CORCORAN, JAMES L.	1LT	DAY, KENNETH R.	PFC
CORMIER, FREDERICK A.	PFC	DE CAMP, ERNEST B.	PFC
COSTIGAN, EDWARD F.	PVT	DE FRANZO, ARTHUR F.	SSG
COTA, LELAND F.	PVT	DE JARLAIS, NELS J.	SSG
COUNTRYMAN, RAYMOND M.	PVT	DE JOSEPH, THOMAS	TSG
		DE LA DURANTEY, VIRGI	PVT
COWLES, RICHARD D.	PVT	DE MILIO, DANIEL	PFC
COX, JR., ANTHONY J.	SGT	DE NUCCI, LEONARD N.	1LT
COX, MANUEL G.	PFC	DE RYCKE, OMAR E.	PFC
CRAFT, ROY V.	PFC	DE SEPIO, CARMINE V.	PVT
CRANOR, JR., CHARLES	PVT	DE SILVA, ANTHONY L.	PVT
CRAVER, FRED D.	SGT	DE WITT, BURR	PFC
CRAWFORD, CARL H.	TSG	DE YOUNG, OGDEN E.	1LT
CRAWFORD, LAURISTON	PVT	DEAN, CLAUDE M.	PFC
CRAWFORD, LEON R.	PVT	DEAN, EDWARD J.	PFC
CREEL, MYRON E.	PVT	DEAN, JACK E.	PVT
CRIST, JOHN W.	CPL	DEES, BOBBY	SSG
CROCKER, RAYMOND W.	PVT	DEETER, EARL	PFC
CROMER, WILLIAM M.	PFC	DEMERS, RENE E.	PFC
CROSS, WILLIAM H.	1LT	DEMOS, JR., CHARLIE	PVT
CROWLEY, TROY V.	CPL	DEMPSEY, JOSEPH A.	PVT
CRUDEN, JAMES J.	PVT	DENNY, JOHN M.	PFC
CRUZ, JOSE R.	PVT	DEPIERRO, PASQUALE	SGT
CULVER, DALE J.	PFC	DESMARAIS, ARMAND L.	PFC
CUMBERLEDGE, CHARLES F.	PVT	DETHLEFS, ROWAN J.	PVT
CUNNINGHAM, JARRETT E.	PVT	DEVORE, ROSS S.	PFC
CUNNINGHAM, STREIT W.	2LT	DEWEY, ARTHUR C.	SGT
CURREN, JOSEPH J.	TSG	DI LORENZO, SANTO S.	PVT
CURREN, ROBERT E.	PFC	DI PIETRO, FRANK	PVT
CURRY, ALWIN W.	PVT	DIETL, HENRY J.	PFC
CURTIS, JR., CHARLES E.	PVT	DILLARD, BISHOP H.	PVT
CURTISS, CHARLES W.	PVT	DILLASHAW, A. J.	PFC
CZERNIA, JOSEPH J.	PVT	DINALLO, ANTHONY	PFC
CZYSCON, JOSEPH	PFC	DISHMAN, MILAME E.	SSG
DAHLEN, HENRY O.	SGT	DIXON, HARRY R.	SGT
DALLAIRE, ARTHUR	PVT	DLUGOLENSKI, ANTHONY L.	PFC
DALTON, JOHN J.	PVT	DOBKOWSKI, JOSEPH S.	PVT
DANIEL, JR., HERMAN H.	PVT	DOCKERY, VERNON L.	TSG
DATA, RUDOLPH J.	PFC	DOEL, GORDON T.	PFC
DAUZAT, CURTIS	PFC	DOLES, JAMES A.	PVT
DAVID, JOHN W.	PFC	DORMAN, FRANCIS R.	PVT
DAVIS, GEORGE L.	2LT	DORULLA, JOHN W.	SGT
DAVIS, JAMES E.	PVT	DOSTIE, PAUL E.	PVT

DOTY, JOHN A.	PFC	ESPENSHADE, ROBERT A.	PFC
DOTY, RAYMOND C.	TSG	EVANS, JR., FRED B.	SGT
DOTSERT, PAUL H.	PVT	EVANS, GROVER C.	PVT
DOUGLAS, HOWARD W.	SGT	EVANS, JAMES A.	PVT
DOYLE, JR., EDWARD H.	PFC	EVANS, MICHAEL W.	SGT
DOYLE, JAMES P.	PFC	EVERETT, PAUL A.	PFC
DRAUGHN, NATHAN C.	PVT	EVERETT, WALTER D.	PFC
DREW, KENNETH B.	PVT	EWING, EDWARD	PVT
DROOGAN, PAUL J.	PVT	FACER, JR., JOSEPH E.	PVT
DROZ, JOSEPH L.	1LT	FARGO, III, JAMES C.	PFC
DRZEWIECKI, HENRY L.	PVT	FARKAS, EDWARD D.	SSG
DUCEY, DANIEL D.	PFC	FASSMAN, PETER	SGT
DUGAS, LUCIUS	PVT	FELBER, THEODORE J.	PVT
DUNCAN, JOHN C.	PFC	FELTYCH, CHARLES J.	PFC
DUNCAN, LOREN E.	PFC	FENCIL, WILLIAM L.	PFC
DUNLAP, WILLARD E.	PVT	FENSKE, BRUNO B.	SGT
DURHAM, WILLIAM F.	PFC	FERGUSON, DANIEL R.	PVT
DU RIVAGE, JOSEPH A.	PVT	FERGUSON, JR., WALTER D.	PVT
DURRENCE, WILLIAM	PFC	FERGUSON, WILLIAM S.	PVT
DUVALL, EDWARD J.	PVT	FERLAND, ARMAND L.	PFC
DYKES, JAMES P.	SGT	FERONE, JOE	PFC
DZURY, ANDREW	PFC	FERRARO, RALPH J.	PFC
EARNEST, JAMES E.	PFC	FERRAZZI, LUIGI D.	PFC
EASTER, ELMER E.	SSG	FEY, ROBERT H.	SGT
EASTMAN, VERNON W.	PFC	FIEDLER, HERBERT V.	PVT
EBENHOH, FRANK T.	PFC	FIELD, WARREN E.	PVT
ECKLMEYER, LAWRENCE J.	SGT	FIFIELD, IRA C.	PVT
EDDINGS, ROBERT W.	SGT	FINIK, MARTIN	PVT
EDDINS, HAL	PVT	FINKLEA, FURMAN H.	PFC
EDDY, LYLE A.	PFC	FIORE, NANTI	PFC
EDELINSKY, JOSEPH J.	SSG	FIRTH, JOHN T.	CPL
EDWARDS, ARTHUR W.	PFC	FISHER, DURBIN	PVT
EHART, JR., ALBERT M.	1LT	FISHER, DONALD E.	PVT
EHLERS, ROLAND A.	SGT	FISHER, JOHN F.	CPL
EHRET, SAMUEL D.	PFC	FISHER, KENNETH R.	PFC
ELEWICZ, EDWARD E.	PVT	FITCH, JR., FRANK N.	CPT
ELLIS, CHARLES E.	SGT	FLAD, JAMES H.	PVT
ELLISON, CLARENCE H.	PFC	FLORCAK, JOHN E.	PFC
ELWOOD, JR., CHARLIE	PFC	FLORES, HERMAN L.	PVT
ENGLE, ANSON	PVT	FLOREZ, MANUEL R.	PFC
ERBE, CHESTER	PVT	FLYNN, EDWARD F.	PFC
ERBE, JR., GEORGE	PFC	FLYNN, JOHN W.	PVT
ERICKSON, CARLO A.	PVT	FOGG, DONALD D.	CPT
EROH, CHARLES W.	PFC	FOJARDO, RAY C.	PVT
ERTLE, CHARLES E.	SSG	FOLEY, GEORGE D.	PVT

FORCIER, LEO O.	SGT	GIPPETTI, IGNAZIO	PFC
FORD, JR., GEORGE	PVT	GITLESON, DAVID J.	PVT
FORRESTER, BOBBY B.	PVT	GITZEN, LEO P.	PFC
FORSYTHE, STANLEY V.	1LT	GIUNTOLI, BRUNO P.	PFC
FOSTER, JAMES	PFC	GLANVILLE, WALTER F.	PFC
FOSTER, KENNETH L.	PVT	GLAVAN, LOUIS J.	SGT
FOWLER, DENMAN	CPT	GLIDEWELL, MELVIN J.	PVT
FRANCIOSI, DEL MARZIO J.	PVT	GOAD, HARRY W.	PFC
FRANKLIN, EDD H.	PVT	GOIN, GLEN G.	PVT
FRANTZ, PIERSON A.	PVT	GOLDBERG, BERNARD	PVT
FREVELE, JOHN	SGT	GOLDMAN, EDWARD R.	2LT
FRISCO, SAMUEL A.	PFC	GOLDTHWAITE, MURREY E.	PVT
FRITZ, HOWARD	PVT	GOLDWASSER, LOUIS H.	PVT
FTAK, JOHN	CPL	GOLEMBIEWSKI, THEODORE	PFC
FUNK, JOHN J.	PFC	GONAS, ANDREW A.	PFC
GAITHER, GLENN E.	PVT	GONZALES, MONICO C.	PVT
GALAN, FRANK M.	PFC	GONZALEZ, JESSE	PFC
GALASSO, PAUL C.	SGT	GOODALL, LYLE E.	PFC
GALLOWAY, WILLIAM E.	PVT	GOODRICH, CARLO E.	PFC
GARBETT, RALPH H.	PFC	GORAJ, EDWARD J.	PFC
GARY, WILFRED C.	SGT	GORDON, ALFRED G.	PVT
GARZA, ESTEBAN	PVT	GORDON, KEITH A.	PFC
GASDA, JOHN P.	SGT	GORMAN, JAMES M.	PFC
GASTON, EDWARD H.	SGT	GORMAN, JOHN J.	CPL
GATELY, JOHN J.	CPL	GOSSETT, JR., JAMES Y.	PFC
GATTI, FRANK W.	PVT	GOYNES, HERCHEL F.	PVT
GAUCHER, JR., WALLACE H.	SGT	GRANT, JAMES E.	PVT
GEARS, ARTHUR F.	1LT	GRAVES, WILLIAM E.	SSG
GEERDES, MARVIN L.	SGT	GREATHOUSE, JAMES S.	PFC
GEHRIG, LIONEL L.	PVT	GREEN, JAMES C.	PFC
GELBER, MORRIS	PVT	GREEN, WILLIAM	PFC
GELBER, NATHAN R.	SSG	GREEN, WILLIAM P.	CPL
GENTILINI, ELIO	PFC	GREENE, DONALD R.	PVT
GERDES, LOREN E.	PVT	GREGA, JR., MICHAEL	PFC
GERDIN, WARREN W.	SSG	GREGG, WILLARD B.	PVT
GERLACH, PETER	SGT	GREGORY, JOHN W.	CPL
GIANUNZIO, LOUIE C.	PVT	GREWELL, GERALD M.	PVT
GIBSON, ROBERT I.	PFC	GREY, ROGER A.	PVT
GIDCUMB, JR., ROBERT E.	PVT	GRIFFEY, EDWARD A.	CPL
GILES, HAROLD C.	PVT	GRIFFITH, HARGIS R.	PFC
GILL, EDWARD A.	CPL	GRIFFITH, MERLE	PFC
GILLEN, VINCENT J.	2LT	GRILL, PETER	PVT
GILLILAND, BRUCE A.	PVT	GRIMMER, STEWART W.	1LT
GILMORE, BURRELL G.	PVT	GROSE, JAMES E.	PFC
GIOIA, JOSEPH J.	PVT	GRUNNER, RALPH N.	PVT

GRUNWALD, BENJAMIN	SGT	HAYWARD, FRANKLIN C.	PFC
GRUWELL, JR., ROY A.	TSG	HEBERT, JOSEPH C.	PVT
GUARISCO, CHARLES L.	PVT	HECHT, ROBERT G.	PVT
GUERRA, BENJAMIN	PFC	HEDRICK, GILMER P.	PFC
GUETTES, RAYMOND J.	PVT	HEIMS, LEO D.	PVT
GULICK, LEO I.	PFC	HEINEKE, WARREN J.	CPL
GUMBLE, AUGUST W.	SGT	HEINRICH, OSCAR E.	1LT
GUTHRIE, VERO R.	PVT	HEINZE, HAROLD A.	PVT
GWILT, WILLIAM E.	PFC	HELD, JAMES W.	SGT
HACKETT, CLYDE I.	PVT	HELTON, GEORGE W.	SGT
HADEN, WILLIAM H.	SSG	HENDERSON, DAVIE R.	PVT
HAGAR, RAY W.	PFC	HENDERSON, GERALD M.	TSG
HAGAR, RUDOLPH A. D.	PVT	HENDERSON, JAMES W.	PVT
HAHN, JR., HARRY M.	PVT	HENDERSON, MERLE F.	PVT
HAJDINYAK, STEPHEN G.	PFC	HENDRICKS, AMANA G.	PFC
HALIC, EDWARD F.	SGT	HENNESSEY, LEO	2LT
HALL, BUFORD	PFC	HENNING, WALTER J.	PVT
HALL, WILLIAM	PVT	HENRY, PHILIP L.	SGT
HALMAGY, JACK C.	PFC	HENSLEY, JOHN R	PFC
HALVEY, RICHARD H.	PVT	HERCHICK, MORTIMER H.	PVT
HAMEL, ARTHUR A.	PVT	HERMAN, HENRY J.	PVT
HAMMOND, III, ROBERT C.	PFC	HERRINGTON, CHARLES	SSG
HANES, HARRY J.	PFC	HESS, JR., ROBERT C.	CPT
HANEY, WILLIAM H.	PVT	HESS, WILLIAM E.	PVT
HANGAN, WILLIAM F.	PVT	HETRICK, JESS W.	PVT
HANLON, JAMES A.	PVT	HEUSEL, MYRL D.	PFC
HANNA, WILBERT D.	PVT	HIBBERT, FRANCIS J.	PVT
HANNUM, CRAIG B.	1LT	HICKLEN, CLIFFORD L.	PVT
HANSELL, GEORGE F.	PVT	HICKS, EDGAR E.	PVT
HANSEN, JR., WALTER J.	PVT	HIGGINS, DONALD R.	PFC
HARDING, WILLIAM L.	PVT	HILBERT, RAYMOND A.	PFC
HARMON, JAMES C.	PVT	HILGENDORF, OLIN F.	PVT
HARRINGTON, JR., HERBERT E.	PVT	HILL, II, JOSEPH A.	CPT
		HILL, RAYMOND L.	SGT
HARRINGTON, WILLIAM S.	PVT	HILL, SHIRLEY K.	CPL
HART, KENNETH B.	PVT	HILL, WILLIAM T.	PVT
HARTMAN, RICHARD W.	PVT	HINCH, JEWEL	CPL
HARTMANN, WILLIAM	PVT	HINSON, NORMAN L.	PVT
HARVEY, RALPH Z.	PFC	HIXON, SAMUEL C.	SGT
HASTINGS, HOWARD J.	PFC	HOFF, HARRY H.	PFC
HASTY, WILLIAM A.	PVT	HOFFMAN, HARRY E.	PFC
HATFIELD, J. W.	PVT	HOFLUND, BERNARD A.	PVT
HAYES, JARRELL H.	SGT	HOLDEN, PAUL F.	PVT
HAYNES, HENRY B.	PVT	HOLDER, JONIE F.	PFC
HAYS, LYLE E.	PFC	HOLMES, JR., DWIGHT L.	PVT

HOLMES, JAMES H.	PFC	JEPPSON, JEPPE M.	PVT
HOLSTAD, MAURICE G.	PVT	JEPSON, JR., KENNETH S.	SGT
HOOTEN, TROY D.	TSG	JESSUP, GUY M.	PFC
HOOVER, JR., WILLIAM W.	SGT	JOHANN, ROBERT K.	2LT
HORNER, PAUL P.	SGT	JOHANSON, JAMES E.	CPL
HORTON, ARTHUR C.	PVT	JOHNSON, ALEXANDER E.	2LT
HOTKOWSKI, JOHN J.	SGT	JOHNSON, ALBERT L.	PVT
HOVE, HARRIS M.	PVT	JOHNSON, CLYDE D.	PFC
HOWARD, RUSH R.	PVT	JOHNSON, FRANK R.	SSG
HOWDYSHELL, WILBERT L.	PFC	JOHNSON, GEORGE N.	PVT
HUCKLEBERRY, DALE L.	PVT	JOHNSON, GILBERT W.	PFC
HUFF, JR., COLON J.	PVT	JOHNSON, HAROLD L.	PVT
HUFFER, EMMETT J.	PVT	JOHNSON, KURT R.	CPL
HUGHES, GERARD T.	CPL	JOHNSON, WALTER K.	PVT
HUGHES, ROBERT E.	PVT	JOHNSON, WILLARD R.	PVT
HUMMEL, EDWIN J.	PFC	JOLLEY, WILLIAM P.	PFC
HUMPHREY, FRANCIS A.	PVT	JONES, ALDEWON C.	PFC
HUSKEY, CLELL	PVT	JONES, JAMES B.	PFC
HUSSEY, JAMES C.	PVT	JONES, JAMES R. G.	PFC
HUZAR, JOSEPH A.	PVT	JONES, LYMAN L.	PFC
HYATT, JEWELL A.	PVT	JORDAN, CHARLES M.	PFC
HYDOCK, PAUL	PFC	JOYAL, GEORGE E.	SSG
IANNACONI, MICHAEL	PFC	JUDD, EDWARD M.	PFC
INBODEN, KENNETH L.	PVT	JUSTICE, EARL K.	PVT
INGHAM, BENJAMIN L.	PVT	JUSTUS, JACKSON D.	PVT
INGRAHAM, KENNETH G.	PVT	KABRICH, JOE E.	SSG
IRVIN, KENNETH	PVT	KACPRZYK, EDWARD P.	PVT
IRVINE, LEE T.	PVT	KALLAS, CHRIS	PVT
ISEBRANDS, JOHN S.	PVT	KAMPFER, BEN	PFC
JACK, SIDNEY	PFC	KAPCEWICH, JOHN	PVT
JACKSON, MERVIN A.	PVT	KAPUSHINSKI, WILFRED A.	SGT
JACKSON, ROBERT C.	SGT	KAROLKIEWICZ, FRANK C.	PFC
JACQUINTO, ANTHONY J.	SSG	KARR, EDWARD D.	PVT
JAMES, CLAUDE P.	PVT	KASSEL, ROBERT E.	PFC
JAMES, D. C.	PVT	KASTA, JOHNNIE	PVT
JAMES, HENRY K.	PVT	KAULFUSS, WALTER	SGT
JAMES, JOHN	PVT	KEARNEY, J. C.	PVT
JAMISON, WILLIAM J.	PFC	KEELING, MILO E.	PVT
JANDT, HERBERT H.	CPL	KEEN, JOHN R.	PFC
JASKIEWICZ, CHESTER J.	PVT	KEEN, WILLIAM B.	PVT
JAYNES, HARRY D.	SGT	KELLEY, TERRY A.	PVT
JEANOS, ALFRED R.	PFC	KELLY, THOMAS S.	PVT
JEFFREY, CECIL W.	SGT	KENNEDY, JAMES G.	PVT
JENSEN, CARL C.	PVT	KENNEDY, THOMAS E.	PFC
JENSEN, OSCAR A.	CPL	KENNEY, FRANK	PVT

KENNEY, OLLIE C.	PFC	KRINGLE, GLENN J.	CPL
KENNY, WILLIAM F.	PFC	KRIVE, MICHAEL A.	PVT
KERN, WILLIAM M.	PVT	KUHNA, JR., GEORGE M.	SSG
KERNS, ISAAC	PFC	KUHNS, LLOYD N.	PFC
KERR, EDWARD J.	CPL	KUNTUZOS, JAMES D.	1LT
KETCHERSID, VERNIS E.	PVT	KUPSENEL, ELMER	PVT
KIBBEE, FORREST H.	SSG	KURLAND, JOHN V.	PVT
KIERNAN, KENNETH S.	PFC	KURTZ, JR., CHARLES F.	SGT
KIMBAROW, MORRIS	PFC	KUSHNIR, JOHN	SSG
KIMBLE, CHARLES A.	CPL	KUYKENDALL, GRADY W.	SGT
KIMZEY, EVERETT W.	PVT	LA BELL, JOHN R.	PFC
KING, EDWIN E.	PFC	LA COUR, WALTER J.	PFC
KING, GEORGE W.	CPL	LA GREGA, FRANK J.	PFC
KING, RICHARD I.	SGT	LA MARRE, JAMES G.	SSG
KING, ROY	PVT	LABADEE, ROSCOE H.	PFC
KING, WILSON C.	PVT	LABOWSKY, JOSEPH	SSG
KINNEY, ARTHUR W.	PVT	LABUDA, MITCHELL	PVT
KINNY, DONALD J.	TSG	LACKEY, EARL C.	SSG
KIRK, JOHN T.	PVT	LADD, CHARLES C.	PFC
KIRKLAND, CARROLL E.	PFC	LAFEVER, JOHN W.	PVT
KIRKWOOD, CURTIS A.	TSG	LAKE, EMILE D.	PVT
KLAVERENGA, GEORGE W.	SGT	LAMBERT, ROBERT E.	PVT
KLAY, MICHAEL	SGT	LAMOREAUX, KENNETH	PVT
KLEIN, PETER	PFC	LANDOLFI, ROBERT P.	PFC
KLEVER, JACK M.	PVT	LANDON, GERALD E.	SSG
KLINE, LEWIS E.	PFC	LANGSTONE, JR., ERVIN W.	PVT
KLOP, MENTRO	SSG	LARKIN, EUGENE A.	PFC
KNAPP, DANIEL J.	SGT	LAROSE, JAMES J.	PFC
KNEISEL, JOHN T.	PFC	LARSON, MELVIN A.	PVT
KNIGHT, WALTER B.	PFC	LATHEROW, EARL	PFC
KNOX, ROBERT	PVT	LATHROP, HAROLD V.	PVT
KOBRISH, JOHN	SGT	LATTIMER, PAUL F.	PFC
KOCHOCKI, ALFRED J.	CPL	LAW, JOHNNIE E.	SSG
KOEHLER, JR., GEORGE R.	1LT	LAWES, GEORGE W.	SGT
KOETTING, QUINTIN J.	PVT	LAWRY, MAURICE L.	PVT
KOLASA, HARRY F.	PFC	LAWSON, BERT	PVT
KOONTZ, ORVILLE G.	PFC	LAYNE, HARRY L.	TSG
KORHONEN, WAINO R.	PVT	LAYTON, JAMES R.	PVT
KORNFUHRER, WILLIAM F.	PVT	LEARY, BENJAMIN F.	CPL
KOWALCZYK, JOSEPH J.	PFC	LEATHERWOOD, DOARL W.	PFC
KOWYNIA, MATHEW	PVT	LEE, GORDON M.	PVT
KOZIOL, JOSEPH L.	PVT	LEE, JOHN	PVT
KOZIOL, STEVEN J.	PVT	LEE, MERRILL N.	PVT
KREY, JOSEPH J.	PFC	LEE, ROY	SSG
KRINER, ORVILLE C.	SGT	LEE MASTERS, PAUL F.	PFC

LEEPER, OTIS P.	PFC	MANGES, WILLIAM J.	PVT
LEFKOWITZ, LOUIS	PVT	MANOR, HARVEY R.	PFC
LEHMAN, MICHAEL E.	PVT	MAPES, JOHN A.	1SG
LEONARD, CLARENCE G.	PVT	MARCUM, GEORGE	PVT
LEWELLEN, ALBERT E.	PVT	MARCUS, JEWEL E.	PFC
LEWIN, RALPH	PVT	MAREK, FLORIAN A.	PFC
LEWIS, CLYSON E.	PVT	MARFIONE, ANTHONY N.	PVT
LEWIS, EUGENE C.	SGT	MARKLAND, GEORGE W.	PVT
LEWIS, JAMES D.	PFC	MARKWARDT, VICTOR A.	PFC
LEWIS, LAURIE L.	PVT	MARLETT, WILLIAM M.	PVT
LEWIS, NELSON	PVT	MARTIN, CHARLES W.	SGT
LEWIS, SAMUEL E.	PFC	MARTIN, CARL O.	SGT
LIEDER, MELVIN V.	SGT	MARTIN, CHRISTOPHER	PFC
LIEN, EDWARD A.	PFC	MARTIN, JR., CLEM J.	CPL
LINICO, JR., BATTISTA	PFC	MARTIN, ORIE T.	PVT
LIPSCHUTZ, SIDNEY	PVT	MARTINELLI, JOSEPH	PVT
LIPUMA, FRANK	PVT	MASON, MORGAN D.	PFC
LISTER, WALTER W.	PVT	MASTINE, EMMETT E.	PVT
LLOYD, WALTER T.	PFC	MATHESON, CHARLES R.	SGT
LOHMAN, MICHAEL E.	PVT	MATHEWS, RALPH J.	PVT
LOMBARDO, CHARLES J.	PFC	MATUSZEWSKI, JEROME	PFC
LOMBARDO, ROBERT P.	PVT	MAULUCCI, DONALD P.	PFC
LONG, WALLACE F.	PFC	MAURYCY, CONROY J.	PFC
LORD, JAMES F.	PVT	MAVIS, HOWARD H.	PVT
LUBOWITZ, IRA	PVT	MAXWELL, NOEL J.	PVT
LUCAS, ODIE B.	PVT	MAYER, RICHARD J.	SGT
LUCIANO, CHARLES	TSG	MAYES, FRANK B.	SGT
LUMAN, LONNIE E.	PFC	MAYES, WILLIAM O.	PVT
LUPICA, JOSEPH J.	PFC	MAYKO, ANDREW	PVT
LUSTER, CECIL A.	PVT	MAYTON, DOYLE H.	PVT
LUTZ, JR., FREDERICK P.	PVT	MAZZEO, FERDINAND	PVT
LUTZ, IRVIN	PVT	MC AFFERY, DONALD E.	PVT
LYBARGER, HERBERT W.	CPL	MC BRIDE, CHARLES	TSG
LYTTON, CARL B.	PVT	MC BRIDE, REEDY C.	PVT
MABEE, JAY R.	PVT	MC CALLUM, RICHARD A.	PFC
MAC DONALD, ROBERT A.	PFC	MC CARTHY, EDWARD J.	PFC
MACIAG, VALENTINE J.	SGT	MC CAWLEY, WALTER L.	PFC
MACK, ROLAND C.	CPL	MC CLAIN, THOMAS V.	PVT
MACUCKI, BENNY J.	PVT	MC CLARY, EDWARD E.	SGT
MADDEN, COLVY B.	PVT	MC CLURE, RAYMOND J.	PVT
MAGALHAES, ANTONIO S.	PVT	MC CONKEY, FREDRICK L.	PVT
MALECKI, FRANK T.	TSG	MC CONNALA, RAYMOND F.	PVT
MALLICK, PHILLIP	PVT	MC DANIEL, CLETIS W.	PVT
MALONE, JOHN M.	PFC	MC DONALD, GERARD J.	PFC
MALOTT, CLARENCE	PFC	MC DONALD, PAUL E.	PFC

MC FADDEN, SR, HAROLD E.	PVT	MOLINA, ALFREDO F.	PVT
MC GAHA, HILLIARD	PFC	MOLNAR, JOSEPH J.	PFC
MC GHEE, SHIRLEY	PVT	MOLONEY, GEORGE J.	PVT
MC GIBBONEY, JAMES C.	PFC	MONAGHAN, WALTER A.	PVT
MC GOLDRICK, DENNIS J.	PVT	MONIACK, STANLEY C.	PFC
MC GRUER, JAMES A.	SGT	MONN, JR., SAMUEL D.	PVT
MC GUINESS, VINCENT P.	SGT	MONTGOMERY, ALBERT	PVT
MC HUGH, JAMES E.	PFC	MONTZ, MITCHELL P.	PVT
MC LAMB, GRALLON	PVT	MONZ, ANTHONY J.	2LT
MC LAREN, WILLIAM J.	SSG	MOORE, CLIFFORD B	PVT
MC MEANS, KENNETH	PFC	MOREAU, LEO J.	PVT
MC MULLEN, EDDIE L.	PVT	MORELAND, NOAH E.	PFC
MC NALLY, VINCENT J.	SGT	MORGAN, CLIFFORD P.	PVT
MC PHERSON, GEORGE B.	PFC	MORGAN, DALE L.	CPL
MC QUAIN, CLIDE F.	PFC	MORIARTY, JAMES E.	PFC
MEEHAN, ARTHUR T.	PVT	MORRIS, HAROLD E.	PFC
MEEKS, ROBERT E.	PVT	MORRISON, JAMES L.	PVT
MELLOTT, WILLIAM	PVT	MORROW, WILLIAM H.	PVT
MELTON, EDWARD	SGT	MORSE, JAMES E.	PVT
MELTON, PRENTICE	PVT	MORTELLARO, HENRY	SSG
MELTON, R. D.	PVT	MOSES, TULON L.	PVT
MENCKE, HARVEY L.	SGT	MOSHER, ELZA	PVT
MERKLEIN, PAUL F.	SGT	MOSS, ALBERT	CPL
MEROLD, LAWRENCE E.	WO	MUEHLER, HARVEY E.	PVT
MERRIAM, STEPHEN E.	PVT	MULLEN, ROBERT W.	2LT
MESSER, WILLIAM H.	1LT	MULLIGAN, EMMETT V.	PVT
MICELI, ANTHONY J.	SSG	MULROY, ANTHONY P.	PFC
MICHALEWSKI, WALTER J.	SSG	MUNDY, RAYMOND	PFC
MICKLE, LLOYD H.	PVT	MUNRO, WILLIAM A.	PFC
MIFFLIN, PAUL E.	PVT	MURGA, JOHN	SGT
MIGLIONICO, JOSEPH A.	PVT	MURPHREE, SAMUEL R.	PFC
MIHALKO, JOHN M.	PFC	MURPHY, JOSEPH J.	PVT
MIKOLAJOZYK, TED T.	CPL	MURPHY, PAUL R.	PVT
MILESTONE, LEONARD C.	TSG	MURRAY, ROBERT J.	PVT
MILEWSKI, ROMAN J.	PVT	MURTHA, JAMES J.	PVT
MILLER, BERNARD R.	PVT	MYERS, JAMES E.	SSG
MILLER, JR., JESSE R.	CPT	MYERS, RONALD A.	SGT
MILLER, JOHN S.	PVT	MYERS, WILLIE L.	PVT
MILLER, ROBERT M.	SGT	NATALE, JOSEPH	PFC
MILLER, ROBERT C.	PVT	NEAL, ARVAL E.	SGT
MILLER, ROBERT P.	PVT	NEMETH, JOSEPH	PVT
MILLIKAN, WILLIAM J.	PFC	NERESKI, DOMINIC F.	PFC
MILLING, WILLIAM E.	PVT	NERO, JOHN J.	PFC
MINCH, EVERETT D.	SGT	NETERER, JOSEPH C.	PVT
MODOLO, JAMES A.	PVT	NEUMAN, MARION K.	PVT

NEVERDOUSKY, BERNARD	SGT	PACKWOOD, JR., ALBERT C.	1LT
NEWARK, HAROLD C.	SGT	PADJAN, JR., JOSEPH C.	SGT
NEWCOMB, ROBERT J.	PVT	PAGE, MAURICE A.	PFC
NEWTON, RALPH J.	CPL	PALEY, BEN	PVT
NICCUM, WILLIAM F.	PVT	PALMER, WILLIAM J.	CPL
NIELSEN, ROBERT G.	PFC	PALON, THOMAS F.	PFC
NIELSON, GLENN D.	CPL	PALTRIDGE, DONALD L.	SGT
NIEMAN, JR., ALBERT P.	PVT	PANKO, LLOYD W.	SGT
NIEWIADOMY, EDWARD J.	PVT	PANNELL, FRED M.	PVT
NIX, THOMAS B.	PFC	PARCHINSKI, JOSEPH S.	TSG
NIYORK, CARL E.	CPL	PARISHER, ARTHUR A.	PFC
NOBLE, EDWARD W.	PVT	PARK, FRED	PVT
NOEL, JAMES A.	PVT	PARKER, WILBUR M.	CPL
NOLDER, ROBERT F.	CPL	PARKS, BURNS O.	PVT
NOLLER, LESLIE J.	PVT	PARMELEE, PHILIP W.	SGT
NORESKI, DOMINICK F.	PFC	PARNELL, BUFORD C.	SGT
NOONAN, FREDERICK J.	1SG	PARRISH, RANDOLPH	PFC
NORRIS, WILLIAM	PFC	PARROTT, CLIFFORD G.	PVT
NOVAK, EDWARD	SGT	PASCOE, FRANK R.	SGT
NOVAK, LEONARD J.	PFC	PASINI, GIOVANNI J.	PFC
NUNN, RALPH H.	SGT	PASZEL, MICHAEL J.	PFC
O' BRIEN, JOSEPH W.	SGT	PATENAUDE, KENNETH J	SGT
O' CONNELL, JAMES J.	PFC	PATIRE, NEDDY J.	PFC
O' CONNOR, KENVIN R.	SGT	PATTERSON, CYRUS C.	PVT
O' DONALD, EDWARD W.	SGT	PATTI, GIACOMO V.	SGT
O' KEEFE, PATRICK J.	PFC	PAVLICK, FRANK A.	SSG
O' NEAL, DORSEY J.	PVT	PAYNE, II, FRED W.	SGT
O' NEIL, JOHN M.	PVT	PEARLINGI, MICHAEL W.	PVT
O' NEILL, GEORGE W.	PFC	PEARSON, JR., GRAHAM L	PFC
O' NEILL, JESSE W.	PFC	PECK, GEORGE W.	CPL
O' ROURKE, JAMES J.	CPL	PECORARO, JR., JOSEPH	PFC
OKONOWSKI, CASIMIR S.	PVT	PEDLEY, RAYMOND C.	SSG
OLES, EDWARD K.	PFC	PEDUZZI, BERNARD G.	PVT
OLOUGHLIN, JOSEPH	PFC	PELLEGRINO, FRANK	SGT
OLSON, ARTHUR T.	PVT	PELLETIER, RICHARD F.	PVT
OLSON, ELMER	2LT	PENCAK, HENRY	2LT
OPPENHEIM, IRVING	PFC	PERKINS, WENDELL B.	CPL
ORR, SMILEY A.	PVT	PERRY, FRANK	SGT
ORTIZ, RAMON B.	PVT	PETERS, CLARENCE C.	PVT
OSBURN, HARVEY H.	PVT	PETERSEN, FREDERICK R.	PVT
OSMUN, WARD H.	PVT	PETERSON, CLINTON F.	SSG
OSMUN, WILBUR W.	PVT	PETERSON, GEORGE	SGT
OWCZARCZAK, JOSEPH F.	SSG	PETKIE, RONALD W.	SSG
PACANA, JOHN S.	SGT	PETROSKY, STANLEY I.	PVT
PACHECO, ROBERT M.	PVT	PETROTTA, JOSEPH P.	SGT

PETRUNYAK, ALBERT	CPL	PUMAREJO, EZEQUIEL G.	PVT
PETTIT, CHARLES A.	PFC	PURCELL, CARL M.	PVT
PETTRONE, JOHN J.	CPL	PUSTELNIK, WILLIAM H.	PVT
PEYTON, FRED	PFC	QUALLS, MATHEW H.	SGT
PHILLIPS, DAVE B.	CPL	QUEENER, WILLIAM A.	PVT
PHILLIPS, FRANCIS E.	PFC	QUERY, JESSE Q.	PFC
PHILLIPS, STANLEY	PVT	QUIGLEY, ROBERT L.	PFC
PICKERING, WILLIAM R.	PFC	QUINTERO, JUAN G.	PVT
PIERCE, CHESTER B.	PFC	RABAGO, FERNANDO H.	CPL
PIERCE, FELIX W.	SSG	RADZICKI, ADAM L.	PFC
PIERCE, JACK D.	SSG	RAGLAND, WILLIAM C.	PVT
PIKE, FRANCIS H.	PFC	RAHM, WILLIAM H.	PVT
PINEMI, AUSTIN J.	SSG	RAINES, CHARLES N.	PFC
PINCHEK, STEPHEN J.	PFC	RAINWATER, ROBERT L.	PVT
PINKARD, ANDREW M.	SGT	RALIS, NATHAN	PVT
PINSON, DONALD H.	PVT	RAMER, WILLIAM N.	PFC
PIOTEREK, BRUNO C.	PVT	RANDALL, ABRAHAM R.	PVT
PITRANAS, JOSEPH	PVT	RASCHKE, ERNEST R.	PFC
PITTELKOW, ERIC J.	CPL	RASMUSSEN, HARLEY M.	PVT
PLACK, JOHN D.	PFC	RATCLIFF, WALTER E.	PFC
PLACZCK, EMIL A.	SGT	RAWLEIGH, DAVID G.	SSG
PLANTE, THEODORE	1LT	RAY, GEORGE W.	PFC
PLATIS, EMANUEL G.	PVT	RAY, INNES C.	PVT
POISSANT, CLIFFORD V	PFC	RAYMER, CLIFFORD B.	CPT
POKLEMBA, ANDREW	PVT	RAYMER, DERAY	PFC
POLETTI, PRIMO J	PVT	REA, WILLIAM S.	PVT
POLIZZO, PETER G	PVT	REAGAN, JAMES D.	PFC
POLK, L. W.	PVT	RECK, HAROLD	PVT
PONTZ, WALTER G.	2LT	RECKNAGEL, BENNETT A.	SGT
POOLE, BASSETT S.	PVT	RECTOR, ARTHUR J.	PFC
POOVEY, CARREL F.	1LT	REED, RALPH F.	PVT
POPOVITS, NICHOLAS J.	PVT	REES, LLOYD L.	PVT
PORPIGLIA, MATTHEW L.	PVT	REGALBUTO, SAMUEL	PVT
PORTER, CHARLES W.	PFC	REGISTER, JAMES A.	PFC
PORTER, MORGAN R.	CPL	REID, JAMES A.	PFC
POWELL, HAROLD E.	PVT	REIMER, NORMAND A.	PVT
POWELL, JOSEPH H.	PVT	REINERTSEN, CARL A.	SGT
POWER, ROBERT N.	PVT	REITZ, HENRY	SGT
PRATT, STANLEY R.	PFC	RENTZ, CECIL S.	PFC
PRAWER, JOSEPH J.	CPL	REYES, FRANK S	PVT
PREWITT, ZELBERT T.	PFC	REYES-HUERTAS, RAMON	SGT
PRIVETT, FRED R.	PFC	REYNOLDS, DAVID W.	PFC
PRUITT, DON C.	SGT	REYNOLDS, WILFORD	PFC
PRYNE, JOHN W.	PFC	REYNOLDS, LUKE	SGT
PULEO, PETER	SSG	REYNOLDS, EVERETT	PFC

RHODES, DONALD D.	PFC	RYAN, HAROLD F.	PFC
RHYNE, GLENN G.	PFC	RYAN, JAMES J.	PFC
RICHER, WILLIS H.	PFC	RYCHICK, FRANK R.	PVT
RICHIE, ALBERT W.	PFC	RYON, LOIS E.	SGT
RIFFLE, SCOTTY W.	PVT	SAJDAK, EDWARD A.	PVT
RIGEL, RAYMOND L.	PFC	SALAZAR, JUAN	PFC
RILEY, CLEOPHUS	PVT	SALVA, ELISAO S.	PFC
RINALDI, TONY W.	PFC	SALVAGGIO, PETER A.	PVT
RING, HARRY O.	PFC	SAMS, TROY	SGT
RIVAS, GASPER L.	PVT	SANFORD, MARVIN F.	PVT
RIZZO, VITO, J.	PVT	SANTIMAN, LE ROY W.	PVT
ROBERSON, JAMES C.	PVT	SAUER, HARLAN O.	PVT
ROBERTS, JESSE W.	PFC	SAUL, JAMES R.	PVT
ROBERTS, JR., RALPH C.	PVT	SCALI, ALFRED L.	2LT
ROBERTS, THOMAS V.	PVT	SCHAFFER, DONALD R.	PFC
ROBERTSON, CHARLEY J.	SGT	SCHEAR, ROBERT L.	PFC
ROBINSON, JAMES R.	PVT	SCHERMAN, JOHN D.	PVT
ROBINSON, JAMES L.	PFC	SCHMIDT, JACK	SGT
ROBINSON, LAWRENCE H.	PVT	SCHMIDT, JAMES P.	PVT
ROBINSON, MERLE D.	PFC	SCHMITZ, DONALD H.	CPL
ROBINSON, NATHAN	PVT	SCHOENLEBER, WILLIAM	1LT
ROBITZSCH, JR., FRED M.	PFC	SCHOONAERT, RAYMOND C.	PVT
ROGERS, HILLIARD C.	PVT	SCHREIBER, GEORGE	SGT
ROHR, RAYMOND H.	PVT	SCHUBERT, VIRGIL W.	TSG
ROHRBAUGH, WILLIAM J.	PVT	SCHUEMANN, WILBERT E.	PVT
ROLFING, ALBERT	PFC	SCHULTZ, BENJAMIN L.	SSG
ROSENBERG, MARTIN	PFC	SCHWENKE, JR., GEORGE H.	PVT
ROSS, BARNEY L.	PVT	SCIARILLO, FRANK A.	SSG
ROSS, CLARENCE E.	SGT	SCOTT, HOWARD J	PFC
ROSS, JOHN E.	SSG	SCOTT, RICHARD	SSG
ROSSMILLER, ADOLPH S.	PFC	SCOTT, SAMUEL	CPL
ROSSON, MELVIN V.	PFC	SCOTT, TRAVIS L.	PVT
ROTARIUS, JOSEPH A.	PFC	SEALS, PETER P.	PVT
ROZPAD, JOHN A.	PVT	SEEWALD, MEYER	PVT
RUDYK, STANLEY	PFC	SEGO, JAMES R.	PVT
RUSCZAK, NICHOLAS W.	PFC	SEIDEL, STEVE	PVT
RUSSELL, ROBERT O.	PVT	SELBY, STEVE	SSG
RUSSELL, WILLIAM E.	CPT	SELF, WESLEY S.	PVT
RUSSOM, CHARLIE C.	PFC	SEMPER, VICTOR M.	PVT
RUTIGLIANO, DOMINIK	PVT	SERTINO, FRANK W.	CPL
RYAN, BERNARD R.	PVT	SEUBERLI, RICHARD E.	PVT
RYAN, DEAN A.	PFC	SHADBURNE, CLIFTON M.	PVT
RYAN, EDWARD V.	PVT	SHAFER, JR., LEE K.	PVT
RYAN, FRANCIS C.	PVT	SHANE, RAYMOND L.	PFC
RYAN, GROVER L.	PVT	SHARP, SILAS	PFC

SHAW, JAMES B.	PVT	SNYDER, KENNETH	PVT
SHAW, JAMES C.	PVT	SOBRAK, EDWARD J.	PFC
SHELDON, HUGH C.	PVT	SOLTYSIK, HENRY R.	SSG
SHEPPARD, EDWARD G.	PFC	SOTO, RAMIRO	PFC
SHERBUK, WESLEY J.	PVT	SOUDERS, ARDITH H.	SGT
SHERIFF, HAROLD M.	PFC	SOUSA, REYNOLD J.	PVT
SHERLOCK, JOHN R.	PVT	SOUTH, DELMAS E.	SGT
SHIELDS, FRANK J.	PFC	SOVERNS, CHARLES F.	PVT
SHOCKLEE, ROBERT J.	1LT	SPAIN, JR., WILLIAM A.	PVT
SHREVE, CHARLES W.	PVT	SPARKS, ROBERT L.	PVT
SHULL, DONALD J.	PVT	SPATASSA, DANIEL A.	PFC
SHUMAN, RUDOLPH A.	PFC	SPEARS, BERNARD Q.	PVT
SIBLEY, LEWIS D.	PVT	SPENCE, SAMUEL R.	PFC
SICILIANO, ALEXANDER P.	CPL	SPENCER, CLARENCE F.	PVT
SICKLES, LOUIE L.	PFC	SPINOSE, RALPH J.	PVT
SILBERMAN, BERT	PVT	SPIVEY, HUBERT C.	SSG
SILVAS, ALBERT	PVT	SPOONHOWER, LEONARD R.	PFC
SILVERSTEIN, ERNEST	PFC	SPRADLIN, OLVA	PVT
SIMMONS, GEORGE T.	SSG	SPROULL, EUGENE L.	CPL
SIMMONS, JAMES R.	PVT	SQUAGLIA, FRANCIS A.	PFC
SIPPLE, DONALD E.	2LT	ST ONGE, PAUL E.	SSG
SKOPECK, JOHN G.	TSG	STAHLMAN, ROBERT G.	PFC
SLIWICKI, FRANK J.	PFC	STAMATES, SAM	PVT
SLOCUM, JOSEPH W.	PFC	STANFORD, MALCOLM N.	PVT
SMITH, CLAUD E.	PVT	STANLEY, OSCAR.	2LT
SMITH, DARBY J.	PFC	STEFFENS, CLIFFORD C.	PVT
SMITH, DELNO A.	CPL	STELL, JOHN D.	PVT
SMITH, EDWARD G.	PVT	STEVENS, ERNEST W.	SGT
SMITH, EDMOND J.	PFC	STEWART, CALVIN R.	PVT
SMITH, JR., GEORGE A.	COL	STEWART, ED	PVT
SMITH, GEORGE O.	CPL	STILES, GILBERT R.	SGT
SMITH, HAROLD E.	SGT	STODDARD, DELBERT A	PVT
SMITH, HARRY R.	CPL	STOKES, MARSTON J.	PVT
SMITH, HENRY C.	PFC	STOUTNER, WILLIAM V.	PFC
SMITH, ORVILLE L.	SSG	STRADER, THEODORE V.	PFC
SMITH, R. C.	SGT	STRAB/STREB, JOSEPH M.	SGT
SMITH, RUFUS	PVT	STROUD, WILBUR E.	CPL
SMITH, WAVEL B.	PVT	STULL, RAYMOND	T3
SMITH, WILLIAM W.	SGT	SUHR, BURTELL E.	2LT
SMITH, ZORA	PVT	SULLIVAN, EUGENE C.	SGT
SMITHSON, ALBERT E.	PFC	SULLIVAN, OTIS L.	PVT
SMITHSON, WILLIAM V.	PVT	SUPINA, ANDREW	PVT
SNYDER, CHARLES R.	PFC	SVETECZ, JOHN C.	PVT
SNYDER. JOHN D.	2LT	SWANSON, JOHN F.	CPL
SNYDER, JOHN S.	PVT	SWEENEY, RAYMOND W.	PFC

SWIDERSKI, ZYGMUNT J.	PVT	TROUTT, JERRY A.	PVT
SWOGER, LEONARD	PVT	TROXLER, JOBE	PFC
SYDLIK, STANLEY F.	SSG	TRUE, RUSSEL G.	PFC
SYKES, HARRY E.	2LT	TRUMBULL, JOHN C. W.	PVT
SYKES, JACK W.	1LT	TRUMPOWER, CLAIR E.	PVT
SYKES, JOSEPH F.	2LT	TUCK, MOSES H.	PVT
SYLVINA, ERNEST P.	TSG	TUCKER, KENNETH D.	PVT
SYNOWSKI, GEORGE T.	SGT	TUDOR, ROBERT E.	PFC
SZELUGOSKI, WALTER	CPL	TURNBULL, GLENN W.	PFC
SZORC, PETER C.	PVT	TURNER, RODNEY M.	PVT
SZUMINSKI, MARTIN J.	PVT	TURPIN, JOHN E.	PVT
TADYCH, ROBERT J.	PVT	UGRAN, VASILE	PVT
TAFT, INGWALD P.	2LT	UHLER, EMIL	SGT
TALBERT, GEORGE W.	SSG	ULLMAN, MURRAY	PFC
TANNER, WILLIAM E.	PVT	URBAN, STEVE	PVT
TATE, GARMAN B.	PVT	VANASCO, EDWARD F.	PVT
TAYLOR, JR., AMOS E.	PFC	VANDERBROOK, CLARENCE	PFC
TAYLOR, PAUL	PVT	VARADY, JOHN A.	SSG
TAYLOR, ROY D.	PVT	VARNES, RAYMOND	PFC
TEAL, CLYDE E.	2LT	VARRIEUR, WILFRED A.	PFC
TEAL, JR., HARRY B.	PFC	VASS, LOUIS	PFC
TEISINGER, WAYNE E.	PVT	VATNE, CARSTEN	PFC
TERRITO, SALVATORE C.	PVT	VER DOW, HAROLD L.	PFC
TERRY, THERON C.	CPL	VERMILYES, GERALD P.	PFC
TERRY, WILLIAM E.	PFC	VEST, OSIE W.	PVT
THAYER, ROBERT A.	PVT	VEZZA, LE ROY J.	PVT
THIELE, CARL J.	PVT	VICTOR, EDWARD J.	SGT
THOMAS, JOHN H.	PVT	VIDOUREK, RICHARD E.	PVT
THOMAS, WILLIAM M.	PFC	VITELA, ALFREDO L.	PVT
THOMPSON, GEORGE V.	PVT	VOSS, FREDERICK A.	PVT
THROWER, FRANK A.	PVT	WACLAWCZYK, SYLESTER	PFC
THRUN, ELMER W.	PFC	WAGNER, ANDREW T.	PFC
TILTON, HERBERT	CPL	WALKER, JOHN H.	PFC
TISCHLER, LOUIS	PFC	WALLACE, JAMES F.	PFC
TODD, DAVID B.	PFC	WALTER, SPENCER N.	PFC
TOLLIVER, WILLIE S.	PVT	WALTERS, GEORGE	PVT
TOMKO, JOHN H.	2LT	WALTERS, STANLEY	PFC
TOMLINSON, HERBERT J.	PVT	WALZ, STANLEY W.	PVT
TOUMEY, JOHN J.	PFC	WARBER, DONALD R.	PFC
TOURNAY, HOWARD D.	PFC	WARD, SIMS C.	PFC
TRACY, LELAN E.	SGT	WARFORD, HERMAN M.	PVT
TREADWAY, DAVID W.	PFC	WARGIN, RAYMOND F.	PVT
TRELLA, WILLIAM R.	SGT	WARNER, EARLE W.	PVT
TREVINO, DANIEL A.	PVT	WARNER, JESSE V.	TSG
TROTTER, ANDREW S.	PVT	WARNER, JOSHUA W.	PVT

WASUK, MICHAEL	PFC	WILLS, TILLMAN C.	PFC
WEATHERFORD, WILLIAM R.	PVT	WILSON, ALBERT J.	PVT
WEIGL, ROBERT A.	PFC	WILSON, ALBERT W.	PVT
WEILER, ARTHUR	1LT	WILSON, JAMES C.	PVT
WEINBERG, ISADORE	PFC	WILSON, JAMES W.	PVT
WEINGARD, HERMAN	SGT	WILSON, RAYNOR H.	SSG
WEISENBERG, ROBERT E.	2LT	WILSON, RONALD A.	PVT
WEISS, CHARLES	SGT	WILSON, WALLACE	PFC
WEISSER, JOHN	PFC	WINIANSKI, JOSEPH W.	PVT
WELCH, ALVIN S.	SSG	WINKLER, QUENTIN	SGT
WELCH, JOHN J.	PFC	WINSLOW, EDWIN W.	1LT
WELLS, JR., ARTHUR	PFC	WIRAK, ELMER	SGT
WELLS, JAMES C.	PFC	WISNIEWSKI, THEODORE	PFC
WENTSLER, FREDRICK B.	PFC	WITCHER, SHIRLEY	PFC
WERCHAN, BENNIE O.	SSG	WITT, LAWRENCE W.	PVT
WERNER, JR., JOSEPH F.	SGT	WITTULSKI, KERMIT L.	PVT
WEST, ALVIA R.	SGT	WIYGUL, JOHN G	PVT
WEST, GROVER K.	PVT	WOERMAN, RUSSEL G.	PFC
WESTCOTT, JR., JOHN B.	2LT	WOLF, HAROLD J.	T4
WESTERBERG, CARL B.	PFC	WOLSKY, MICHAEL	PFC
WESTHOFF, FRANK H.	PFC	WOOD, HENRY W.	PFC
WHILDIN, THEODORE R.	PFC	WOODWORTH, WILLIAM M.	PFC
WHITAKER, SR, CLYDE H.	PFC	WORKMAN, JOHN N.	PFC
WHITE, DONALD R.	PFC	WORSLEY, JEAN R.	PVT
WHITE, WILLIAM R.	PVT	WRIGHT, FLOYD	PFC
WHITECOTTON, HOMER M.	PVT	WRIGHT, ISAAC W.	PFC
WHITNEY, IRA T.	PFC	WRIGHT, THOMAS G.	PFC
WHITNEY, HARRY R.	PVT	WUKOVITS, WALTER P.	PVT
WICKENHOFER, PAUL	PVT	YAKOVICH, GEORGE M.	PFC
WIEGAND, CHARLES E.	PVT	YARBOROUGH, THOMAS W.	1LT
WILDE, LEROY E.	SSG	YARROW, JACK	PVT
WILKENS, JESS W.	PVT	YATES, JOSEPH J.	PVT
WILKERSON, EDWIN E.	PFC	YEAMANS, JEROME A.	PFC
WILKINSON, GEORGE W.	PFC	YEMAN, HUGH J.	CPL
WILL, WALTER J.	1LT	YOCUM, JOHN H.	PFC
WILLIAMS, DARELL R.	SSG	YOUNG, JAY A.	PVT
WILLIAMS, JAMES M.	PFC	ZABBIA, VINCENT J.	PFC
WILLIAMS, LAWRENCE C.	PFC	ZAICHICK, SOL G.	PFC
WILLIAMS, RUDOLPH W.	PVT	ZAWATSKI, REGINALD	PVT
WILLIAMS, WILFRED W.	PVT	ZEIDEN, LOUIS	PVT
WILLIAMS, WILLIAM C.	PFC	ZELLNER, MARCUS P.	CPL
WILLIAMSON, WALTER R.	PFC	ZIMMERMAN, JOHN F.	CPT
WILLIS, JAMES H.	PVT	ZIOLKOWSKI, CASIMIR S.	SGT
WILLMAN, HAROLD L.	PFC		

32ND FIELD ARTILLERY BATTALION

ALEXANDER, CLARENCE	CPL
BALCO, ANTHONY J.	PFC
BARBEE, ALVIS E.	PVT
BOLTON, ROBERT J.	SSG
BROOKS, JOHN W.	1SG
BROTHERS, THOMAS R.	
COOKE, JR., CHARLES H.	CPT
COUTURE, HAROLD A.	TSG
DANLEY, JAMES P.	PVT
DONLEY, FRANCIS	SGT
FLEISHER, PAUL R.	PFC
FOGLEMAN, THURSTON D.	TSG
GOUCH, CASIMER	CPL
HALESEY, JR., PETER M.	PVT
HARPER, JR., ROBERT S.	2LT
HOLLO, FRANK	PVT
HUMBLE, NORMAN L.	PFC
INGLE, WILLIAM J.	PVT
KARLICEK, VOLTA	PVT
KLEIN, HERBERT	2LT
LANDA, ALBIN	CPL
LONTIRIE, JOSEPH J.	PFC
LOVE, RICHARD A.	PFC
MADORE, ALBERT	PFC
MARINO, ERCOLE E.	PFC
McCAULEY, HENRY J.	
PYLE, JR., JESSIE	PVT
RAINES, HUBERT L.	TSG
READY, JOHN P.	SGT
ROTH, WALTER F.	SGT
SHIFFER, GEORGE L.	PFC
STEINHOFF, WAYNE R.	PFC
SULLIVAN, DANIEL J.	CPL
WALKER, GEORGE	TSG
WALLACE, CHARLES H.	PVT
WALSH, MICHAEL J.	1LT
WESGAN, WADISLAW F.	SGT
ZUYDHOEK, PAUL B.	1LT

A Guide to Tactical Unit Symbols

Types of Units

⊠	Infantry
⊠ (oval)	Armored Infantry/ *Panzer-Grenadier*
◯	Tank/*Panzer*
⊘	Armored Recon
⊠ with ∧	Parachute Infantry
⊠	Motorized Infantry
TD	Tank Destroyer
△	Antitank
⦿	Armored Field Artillery or *Assault Guns* (*Sturmgeschütze*)
Ⅲ	Engineers

Sizes of Units

•••	Platoon/British Tank or Recce Troop
I	Company/Battery/U.S. Cavalry Troop/ British Tank or Recce Squadron
II	Battalion/U.S. Cavalry Squadron
|II|	Battalion-sized task force or *Combat Group*
III	Regiment
|III|	Regimental-sized task force or *Combat Group*
X	Brigade/Group/ Combat Command
XX	Division
XXX	Corps
XXXX	Army
XXXXX	Army Group

Example

1 ⊠ 18 (with II above)

1st Battalion, 18th Infantry Regiment

☐ Allied Forces

▓ German, Italian or Vichy French Forces

Note. If the specific subelement of a unit is not known, only its size is graphically indicated on the left of the unit box.

Thus, Bn ⊠ 12 would be an unspecified battalion of Panzer-Grenadier Regiment 12.

RANK EQUIVALENCES

US Army	German Army	Waffen-SS
General of the Army	Generalfeldmarschall	
General	Generaloberst	SS-Oberstgruppenführer
Lieutenant General	General (der Infanterie, der Artillerie, etc.)	SS-Obergruppenführer
Major General	Generalleutnant	SS-Gruppenführer
Brigadier General	Generalmajor	SS-Brigadeführer
		SS-Oberführer
Colonel	Oberst	SS-Standartenführer
Lieutenant Colonel	Oberstleutnant	SS-Obersturmbannführer
Major	Major	SS-Sturmbannführer
Captain	Hauptmann	SS-Hauptsturmführer
1st Lieutenant	Oberleutnant	SS-Obersturmführer
2nd Lieutenant	Leutnant	SS-Untersturmführer
Sergeant Major*	Stabsfeldwebel	SS-Sturmscharführer
Master Sergeant/ First Sergeant	Oberfeldwebel	SS-Hauptscharführer
Technical Sergeant	Feldwebel	SS-Oberscharführer
Staff Sergeant	Unterfeldwebel	SS-Scharführer
Sergeant	Unteroffizier	SS-Unterscharführer
Corporal		
Private First Class	Hauptgefreiter Obergefreiter Gefreiter	SS-Rottenführer
	Obersoldat (Obergrenadier, Oberkanonier, etc.)	SS-Sturmmann
Private	Soldat (Grenadier, Kanonier, etc.)	SS-Mann

*Not a rank in the US Army during WWII. NCOs serving as sergeants major during that era were usually Master Sergeants.

NOTES

ORGANIZATION DAY TO WAR

1. Charles H. Cabaniss, "The Eighteenth Regiment of Infantry." The 1st and 2nd Battalions of the 18th Infantry participated in the fighting at Stone's River, TN, during the period 31 December 1862–1 January 1863. The 1st Battalion lost 28 killed and 115 wounded, while the 2nd Battalion suffered 31 killed and 103 wounded.

2. George T. Gentry, Jr., 18th Infantry Regiment Association Historian, Long Beach, CA.

3. Organization Day, 18th Regiment of United States Infantry, Fort Devens, MA, 3 May 1941, 2.

4. Malcolm Marshall, *Proud Americans of WW II: Men of the 32nd Field Artillery Battalion in Action, World War II, as Part of the 18th Regimental Combat Team, 1st U.S. Infantry Division* (New London, NH: self-published, 1994), 4–5.

5. Marshall, *Proud Americans*, 4.

6. Doris Kearns Goodwin, *No Ordinary Time* (New York: Simon & Schuster, 1994), 23.

7. *Boston Herald*, 6 May 1941, 1, 6.

8. Ibid., 6.

9. Maxwell Hamilton, "Junior in Name Only," *The Retired Officer*, June 1981, 30.

10. Later renamed Camp Lejeune.

11. Daily diary entries dated 20 June–16 August 1941, 3rd Battalion, 18th Infantry while attached 1st Marine Division, 301-INF (18)-0.3, June 1941 to March 43, Box 5936, 1st Infantry Division, Record Group (RG) 407, National Archives, College Park, MD (NACP).

12. Daily diary entries dated 13 October–6 December 1941, 3rd Battalion, 18th Infantry, Box 5936, 1st Infantry Division, RG 407, NACP.

13. Irving Yarock, letter to author, 23 July 2001, 3.

OVERSEAS AND THE BATTLE FOR ORAN

1. Daily diary entries dated 10–26 December 1942, 3rd Battalion, 18th Infantry, Box 5936, 1st Infantry Division, RG 407, NACP.

2. Memorandum dated 10 May 1942, "Training Fitness of Divisions for Battle"; and memorandum dated 22 January 1942, subject "Divisions for Force Gymnast," Entry 16A, Box 66, RG 337, Headquarters (HQ) Army Ground Forces, Army Field Forces HQ, General Staff, G-3 Section, Administrative Division, Subject File Correspondence File 1942–49, NACP.

3. Philip Katcher, *US 1st Infantry Division 1939–45* (London: Osprey, 1978), 3.

4. 1st Division General Order #4 dated 13 February 1942, "General Orders II Corps received by 1st Infantry Division 5 . . . 21 February . . . June 1942, Box 5682, 1st Infantry Division, RG 407, NACP.

5. Robert A Baummer, letter to Viola K. Baummer, 19 March 1942.

6. John Downing, "At War with the British," 1980, 7.

7. Official Biography, US Army Military History Institute (USAMHI), Carlisle Barracks, PA.

8. Irving Yarock, letter to author, 23 July 2001, 4.

9. 1st Division General Order #17, 5 June 1942, General Orders II Corps received by 1st Infantry Division 5 . . . 21 February . . . June 1942, Box 5682, 1st Infantry Division, RG 407, NACP.

10. George A. Gentry, 18th Infantry Regiment Association, Long Beach, CA.

11. Memorandum from Colonel Greer to Major General Allen dated 17 September 1942, 1st Infantry Division Operations Plan "TORCH" Vol. V, Combat Team HQ and 1st Armored Division, October 1942, 1st Infantry Division, Box 5668, RG 407, NACP.

12. Samuel E. Morison, *History of the United States Navy in World War II*, Vol. 2: *Operations in North African Waters: October 1942–June 1943* (Urbana: University of Illinois Press, 2001), 33.

13. The special task force, known as "Operation RESERVIST," was virtually wiped out by gunfire from several French destroyers in Oran harbor. The 3rd/6th Armored Infantry lost 180 men killed and 150 wounded (including its commander George F. Marshall) while 113 sailors of the Royal Navy were also killed. George F. Howe, *Northwest Africa: Seizing the Initiative in the West* [Washington, DC: Government Printing Office (GPO), 1993], 47–52.

14. 18th Infantry Regiment Field Order #1, 16 October 1942, Box 5668, 1st Infantry Division, RG 407, NACP.

15. Marshall, *Proud Americans*, 41–43.

16. The landing tables for the 18th CT: the first wave was comprised of 655 men of 3rd/18th Infantry and 332 men of 1st/18th Infantry, each accompanied by approximately 31 supporting personnel such as engineers, forward observers, and naval beach teams. The remaining elements of both battalions (163 and 513 men respectively) landed at H+3. A total of 456 Rangers were also landed at H-hour.

17. Intelligence Annex to Accompany Field Order #1, HQ Combat Command B, 12 October 1942, Box 5668, 1st Infantry Division, RG 407, NACP.

18. Downing, "At War with the British," 69–70.

19. Robert E. Murphy, letter to author, 22 May 2002.

20. Edward Steeg, "Operation TORCH—Anybody Got a Match," 32.

21. H. R. Knickerbocker, et al., Society of the First Division, *Danger Forward: The Story of the First Division in World War II* (Atlanta: Albert Love, 1947), 37.

22. Stanhope Mason, "Reminiscences and Anecdotes of World War II," 24.

23. Steven Ralph, "The Operations of the 2nd Battalion, 16th Infantry (1st Infantry Division) in the Invasion of North Africa (Oran, Algeria) 8–11 November 1942 (The Algeria–French Morocco Campaign), Personal Experiences of a Battalion Adjutant, [Donovan Research Library, Fort Benning, GA: Advanced Infantry Officers' Course, (DRL) 1947–48], 13.

24. Personnel losses found in Appendix 1 (Casualties), After-Action Report, 1st Infantry Division Operations Report, Battle of Oran, Combat Team 18, 18th Infantry Regiment, 8–10 November 1942, Box 5936, 1st Infantry Division, RG 407, NACP.

25. Letter to Herbert Lloyd from Ray Francillo, 12 December 1983, Robert H. York papers, Box 1, USAMHI.

26. Clement C. Van Wagoner, "Military Memoirs," 61.

27. The identity of these units taken from prisoners captured that day in St. Cloud. G-3 Journal entry #134 dated 08 1200 November 1942, Box 5775, 1st Infantry Division, RG 407, NACP.

28. Van Wagoner, "Military Memoirs," 63.

29. Arnold Heidenheimer, *Vanguard to Victory* (Aschaffenburg, Germany: Main Echo Verlag, 1954), 6.

30. Van Wagoner, "Military Memoirs," 64.

31. Marshall, *Proud Americans,* 28.

32. Ben Sternberg, letter to author with comments on draft manuscript, 3 October 2001.

33. Marshall, *Proud Americans,* 31.

34. Ibid., 29.

35. Allen sent a message to II Corps informing them that "shortage of artillery becoming critical. Request your assistance in speeding up unloading process." G-3 Journal Entry, 08 1600 November 1942, Box 5775, RG 407, NACP.

36. Downing, "At War with the British," 78.

37. Robert E. Murphy, letter to author, 9 July 2001.

38. Marshall, *Proud Americans,* 25.

39. Downing, "At War with the British," 80.

40. During the actions involving Cannon Company at St. Cloud on 9 November 1942, Norman H. MacLennan received the Distinguished Service Cross.

41. Marshall, *Proud Americans,* 35.

42. 32nd Field Artillery Battle Report, 8–10 November 1942, Box 5885, 1st Infantry Division, RG 407, NACP.

43. Personnel losses found in Appendix 1 (Casualties), After-Action Report, 1st Infantry Division Operations Report, Battle of Oran, Combat Team 18, 18th Infantry Regiment, 8–10 November 1942, Box 5936, 1st Infantry Division, RG 407, NACP.

44. After-Action Report, 1st Infantry Division Operations Report, Battle of Oran, Combat Team 18, 18th Infantry Regiment, 8–10 November 1942, Box 5936, 1st Infantry Division, RG 407, NACP, 3.

45. 32nd Field Artillery Battle Report, 8–10 November 1942, Box 5885, 1st Infantry Division; and 16th Infantry Regiment After-Action Report, TORCH Operation, 8–12 November 1942, Box 5908, 1st Infantry Division, RG 407, NACP.

46. Marshall, *Proud Americans,* 29.

47. Ibid., 30.

48. 32nd Field Artillery Battle Report, 8–10 November 1942, NACP.

49. Sam Carter, letter to author commenting on draft manuscript, November 2002, 60.

50. Van Wagoner, "Military Memoirs," 65.

51. Marshall, *Proud Americans,* 35.

52. After-Action Report, 1st Infantry Division Operations Report, Battle of Oran, Combat Team 18, 18th Infantry Regiment, 8–10 November 1942, Box 5936, 1st Infantry Division, RG 407, NACP, 2.

53. Mason, "Reminiscences," 29–30.

54. After-Action Report, 1st Infantry Division Operations Report, Battle of Oran, Combat Team 18, 18th Infantry Regiment, 8–10 November 1942, Box 5936, 1st Infantry Division, RG 407, NACP.

55. Field Order #4, After-Action Report, 1st Infantry Division Operations Report, Battle of Oran, Combat Team 18, 18th Infantry Regiment, 8–10 November 1942, Box 5936, 1st Infantry Division, RG 407, NACP.

56. Marshall, *Proud Americans,* 57.

57. 32nd Field Artillery Battle Report, 8–10 November 1942, Box 5885, 1st Infantry Division, RG 407, NACP.

58. Ibid.

59. After-Action Report, 1st Infantry Division Operations Report, Battle of Oran, Combat Team 18, 18th Infantry Regiment, 8–10 November 1942, Box 5936, 1st Infantry Division, RG 407, NACP.

60. Downing, "At War with the British," 94.

61. Personnel losses found in Appendix 1 (Casualties), After-Action Report, 1st Infantry Division Operations Report, Battle of Oran, Combat Team 18, 18th Infantry Regiment, 8–10 November 1942, Box 5936, 1st Infantry Division, RG 407, NACP.

62. S-1 Journal Entry #105, 1st Infantry Division Operations Report, Battle of Oran, Combat Team 18, 18th Infantry Regiment, 8–10 November 1942, Box 5936, 1st Infantry Division, RG 407, NACP.

63. Knickerbocker, *Danger Forward*, 26.

64. Marshall, *Proud Americans*, 109–10.

BATTLE FOR LONGSTOP HILL

1. V Corps War Diary for December 1942, Appendix B to British V Corps Intelligence Summary #24, WO 175/82, Public Records Office (PRO), London.

2. *Joint Forces Quarterly*, "Joint Power Projection: Operation TORCH," Spring 1994, 62–76; and Memorandum, 27 February 1942, "Assignment of Troops to II Corps (GYMNAST)," RG 337, Army Ground Forces, Box 109, NACP.

3. S-1 Journal, Entries #21 and 22, 1st Battalion, 18th Infantry, Box 5951, 1st Infantry Division, RG 407, NACP.

4. References to knobs differed in the Headquarters 18th Combat Team Report of Longstop Hill Engagement from that in the written account of Captain Yarock. In a letter to the author in November 2001, Yarock maintained that he was on the knob that was the furthest to the right, and that "numbers on the knobs were all just blips on the one major crest where all this [his account] took place. All subsequent references to knobs are based on this account. Yarock maintains there were six to seven smaller knobs on this single major crest, the farthest to the east on Longstop Hill. George F. Howe confirms Yarock's location in *Northwest Africa: Seizing the Initiative in the West*, explaining that Company A entered battle from positions near Halte d' el Heri, and were later advancing between the road and Longstop Hill's eastern slopes.

5. 78th Infantry Division Operations Order #4, 21 December 1942, Box 5951, 1st Infantry Division, RG 407, NACP.

6. Franklyn A. Johnson, *One More Hill* (New York: Funk & Wagnalls, 1949), 22.

7. A captured document identified the original defenders as *1st Company, Combat Engineer Battalion 334* and *7th Company, Mountain Infantry Regiment 756*. The latter was also reinforced by a platoon from *3rd Company, Mountain Infantry Regiment 756*. 1st Guards Brigade War Diary for December 1942, 1st Guards Intelligence Summary #14, 30 December 1942, WO 175/186, PRO.

8. 1st Guards Brigade Intelligence Summary for period ending 23 2359 December 1942, WO 175/186, PRO.

9. Marshall, *Proud Americans*, 52.

10. Michael Howard and John Sparrow, *History of the Coldstream Guards, 1920– 1946* (London: Oxford University Press, 1951), 113.

11. *Longstop Hill,* Sergeant Derek Jackson, RJT Internet Services 2000, used by permission, http://www.ean.

co.uk/Bygones/History/Article/WW2/ Derrick_Jackson/ html/body_long_stop_hill.htm.

12. Rudolf Lang, "Battles of Combat Group Lang in Tunisia (10th Panzer Division) December 1942 to 15 April 1943, Part I," MS D-173, US Army Europe (USAREUR) Series, Captured German Documents Section, NACP, 8.

13. S-1 Journal entry dated 22 2045Z December 1942, 1st Battalion, 18th Infantry, Box 5951, 1st Infantry Division, RG 407, NACP.

14. Irving Yarock, Report to General Robert York (US Military Academy, West Point, 1947), 2.

15. Ibid., 3.

16. Irving Yarock, letter to author, 31 July 2001.

17. Yarock, Report to York, 4.

18. Morning report for Company A, 18th Infantry Regiment, National Personnel Records Center, St. Louis, Missouri (NPRC).

19. Donald Parker, letter to author, April 2002.

20. Lieutenant Colonel Stewart-Brown memorandum on Longstop Hill engagement dated 2 January 1943, 1st Guards Brigade War Diary for December 1942, WO 175/186, PRO.

21. Sam Carter, letter to author, July 2002, 16.

22. Ibid., 13–15.

23. Lang, "Battles of CG Lang," 8–9.

24. Marshall, *Proud Americans*, 54.

25. Ibid., 55.

26. Clement Van Wagoner, letter to author, 25 November 2002, 5.

27. Van Wagoner, "Military Memoirs," 3–4.

28. After-Action Report, Headquarters 18th Combat Team, 20 March 1943, 1st Infantry Division, RG 407, NACP, 2.

29. Johnson, *One Last Hill*, 27.

30. Marshall, *Proud Americans*, 52.

31. General Eisenhower was already making plans to send the US II Corps to Sfax in order to prevent Rommel from linking up with von Arnim's *Fifth Panzer Army*. Eisenhower wanted to take some offensive action before the winter rains ended in February 1943. The operation, codenamed SATIN, would have involved the US 1st Armored Division reinforced by the 26th Infantry Regiment. G-3 Journal Entry #20, dated 28 1600 December 1942, Box 5770, 1st Infantry Division, RG 407, NACP.

32. Lang, "Battles of CG Lang," 10.

33. Marshall, *Proud Americans*, 55.

34. Carter, letter to author, July 2002, 17.

35. Marshall, *Proud Americans*, 54.

36. Morning report for Company B, 18th Infantry Regiment, NPRC.

37. The American medium tanks were from the 2nd Armored Division's 67th Armored Regiment, while the light tanks belonged to the 1st Battalion, 13th Armored Regiment of the 1st Armored Division.

38. S-1 Journal entry dated 25 0600Z December 1942, 1st Battalion, 18th Infantry Regiment, Box 5951, 1st Infantry Division, RG 407, NACP.

39. Van Wagoner, "Military Memoirs," 5.

40. S-1 Journal entry dated 23 1300Z December 1942, 1st Battalion, 18th Infantry Regiment, Box 5951, 1st Infantry Division, RG 407, NACP.

41. Stewart-Brown, Longstop Hill Engagement.

42. Terry Allen papers, Box 1, USAMHI.

43. Carter, letter to author, July 2002, 17.

SBIBA AND EL GUETTAR

1. Major General Keightley was described as "another cavalryman, formerly in the 5th Royal Inniskilling Dragoon Guards. He was a commander with an alert and lively personality, a good linguist with a thorough knowledge of the German Army, and had been on the staff of 1st Armoured Division in France in 1940." The 6th Armoured had three division commanders prior to Keightley taking over. R. L. V French Blake, *A History of the 17th/21st Lancers, 1922– 1959* (London: MacMillan, 1962), 111.

2. John Downing, "At War with the British," 150.

3. With the exception of the 6th Commando, Parachutists, and 5th Northamptonshires, all of the British units mentioned were armored units attached to the 18th RCT for counterattack missions during the period 1 January 1943 to 15 February 1943.

4. Downing, "At War with the British," 145.

5. Ibid.

6. Journal of the 18th Infantry, Defense of Medjez el Bab, 28 December 1942 to 15 February 1943, entries dated 12 2250 February 1943 and 13 1500 February 1943, NACP.

7. B. H. Liddell Hart (Ed.), *The Rommel Papers*, translated by Paul Findlay (New York: Harcourt, Brace, 1953), 397.

8. The US tankers suffered 6 killed, 22 wounded, and 136 men missing on 14 February. Operations of the 3rd Battalion, 1st Armored Regiment, from 1 January 1943 to 21 February 1943, Microfilm Collection, Combined Arms Research Library (CARL), Fort Leavenworth, KS, 3–4.

9. A/701st TD losses on 14 February included 3 officers captured or missing in action, 5 enlisted men killed, 6 captured, and 42 missing in action. Operations of Company A, 701st Tank Destroyer Battalion, Period–21 January to 16 February 1943, Microfilm Collection, CARL, 3–6.

10. The 91st AFA lost 2 men killed and 104 officers and men missing in action. On the plus side, however, they recovered one of the 2/17th FA's 12 155mm howitzers from the Sidi Bou Zid battlefield. Report on Tunisian Campaign, S-3, 91st Armored Field Artillery Battalion, 1st Armored Division, Microfilm Collection, CARL, 2–3.

11. 6th Armoured Division War Diary entry dated 17 0700 February 1943. WO 175/146, PRO, London.

12. Johnson, *One Last Hill*, 87.

13. *Panzerarmee Afrika* War Diary (Extracts) 17–22 February 1943, Operations in Northwest Africa, Box 226, RG 319, Records of the Army Staff, Center of Military History, NACP.

14. Frank Beckett, *Prepare to Move: With the 6th Armoured Division in Africa and Italy* (South Humberside, England: Graphic, 1994), 66.

15. Nigel Nicolson and Patrick Forbes, *The Grenadier Guards in the War of 1939 to 1945*, Vol. II: *The Mediterranean Campaigns* (Adershot, UL: Gale & Ploden, 1949), 281.

16. 6th Armoured Division War Diary entry dated 19 1000 February 1943. WO 175/146, PRO. London.

17. 1st Guards Brigade Intelligence Summary No. 60 dated 19 February 1943, WO 175/186, PRO, London.

18. Robert E. Murphy, letter to author, 9 July 2001.

19. 18th Infantry Regiment Journal entries dated 1830 and 2400 hours on

19 February 1943 and 0200 hours on 20 February 1943, S-1 Journal and File, Box 5941, 1st Infantry Division, RG 407, NACP.

20. 6th Armoured Division War Diary entry, 19 1000 February 1943.

21. The 21st Panzer Division had 41 Panzer IIIs and 5 Panzer IVs remaining by the evening of 20 February. Of the 46 tanks, only 30 were fully serviceable. ULTRA Message VM 4753 dated 22 2302Z February 1943. ULTRA Microfilm Collection, CARL.

22. Operations of Combat Team 18 at Sbiba, Tunisia, 16 February 1943 to 9 March 1943, Report of Operations, Box 5936, 1st Infantry Division, RG 407, NACP.

23. 1st Guards Brigade Intelligence Summary No. 62 dated 21 February 1943. WO 175/186, PRO. London.

24. Nicolson and Forbes, *Grenadier Guards*, 283.

25. Journal of the 18th Infantry, Defense of Medjez el Bab, Period 28 December 1942 to 15 February 1943, entry #973 dated 6 March 1943, NACP.

26. Ibid., entry 10 1100 March 1943.

27. John Williamson, "North Africa, Sicily, and England," transcribed in 2003 from the original by family members Kathleen Williamson Barmon, Ward D. Barmon, and Peter Williamson, 28 February 1943 Memo Entry.

28. Alice K. Brayton, letter to author, 25 July 2001. Pfc. Robert E. Kessel's was Brayton's brother. Edwin Blount's letter appeared in the *Huntsville* (Ala.) *Times*, 1 August 1998 and a copy of the original letter was provided to the authors. Kessel was posthumously awarded the Silver Star.

29. Major Ben Sternberg was promoted to lieutenant colonel on 11 January 1943.

30. Louis Neuman, E-mail to author, 18 February 2001.

31. Carlo D'Este, *Patton: A Genius for War* (New York: HarperCollins, 1995), 463.

32. George F. Howe, *Northwest Africa*, 543–45.

33. Michael J. King, "Rangers: Selected Combat Operations in World War II" (Fort Leavenworth, KS: Combat Studies Institute, 1985), 16.

34. 1st Division G-3 Journal entry, 20 1630 March 1943, G-3 Diary, 1st Infantry Division, Box 5771, RG 407, NACP.

35. Sam Carter, "The Operations of the 1st Battalion, 18th Infantry (1st Division) at El Guettar, Tunisia, 17–25 March 1943, Personal Experiences of a Heavy-Weapons Company Commander," (DRL, 1947–48), 9.

36. Robert H. York, letter to Sam Carter, 9 October 1947, 3. York was then teaching at the Department of Tactics, US Military Academy, West Point.

37. Carter, Operations of the 1st Battalion, 11.

38. Herbert A. Smith, Jr., "The Operations of the 3rd Battalion, 18th Infantry at El Guettar 17–23 March (Tunisian Campaign), Personal Experiences of a Executive Officer, Heavy Weapons Company," (DRL, 1949), 10.

39. D'Este, *Patton*, 469. They were probably actually Italian—Author.

40. Carter, "Operations of the 1st Battalion," 12.

41. Ibid., handwritten notation.

42. Journal of the 18th Infantry, Defense of Medjez el Bab, entries dated 1130, 1145, 1350, 1445, 1845, and 2400 hours on 21 March 43, NACP.

43. York, letter to Sam Carter, 5.

44. Ibid., 5–6.

45. Carter, "Operations of the 1st Battalion," 16.

46. Herschel D. Baker, "TD Combat in Tunisia: El Guettar" (Fort Hood, TX: Tank Destroyer School, 1944), 21.
47. York, letter to Sam Carter, 7.
48. Smith, "Operations of the 3rd Battalion," 13.
49. *Stars and Stripes*, "The History of One Day's Battle," 1 May 1943, 9.
50. Ibid.
51. Marshall, *Proud Americans*, 83–84.
52. Baker, "TD Combat in Tunisia," 24–26.
53. Marshall, *Proud Americans*, 78.
54. Journal of the 18th Infantry, Defense of Medjez el Bab, entries dated 1210 and 1230 hours on 23 March 1943, NACP.
55. Ibid., entry dated 23 1340 March 1943.
56. The Division G-3 wrote, "At 1515 hours, II Corps notified G-3 that they had positive information that the 10th Panzer with 1st and 2nd Battalions 86th PGR and 3rd and 4th Battalions 90th Arty Regt, and 1st and 2nd Battalions 7th Panzer Regiment attached will attack at 1600 hours." 1st Division G-3 Journal entry dated 23 1517 March 1943, G-3 Diary, 1st Infantry Division, Box 5771, RG 407, NACP.
57. *Stars and Stripes*, "The History of One Day's Battle," 8.
58. Terry Allen, "A Summary of the El Guettar Offensive (20 March–6 April 1943) During the North African Campaign of World War II," 6.
59. Marshall, *Proud Americans*, 90.
60. Smith, "Operations of the 3rd Battalion," 17.
61. *Stars and Stripes*, "The History of One Day's Battle," 9.
62. Edward Kuehn, letter to author, 4 September 2002, 10.
63. Neuman, E-mail to author.
64. Five 18th Infantry soldiers received the DSC for their courageous actions during the Battle at El Guettar: Lieutenant Colonels Brown, Sternberg and York; Captain Raymer; and Corporal Walter Szelugoski.
65. *Our Battalion: The 899th Tank Destroyer Battalion* (Knorr, Hirth, Sendlinger, 1945), 20.
66. Baker, "TD Combat in Tunisia," 29.
67. The 601st TD Battalion lost 21 75mm SP half-tracks destroyed and 8 more knocked out but repairable. One 37mm SP gun and three personnel half-tracks were also lost. Personnel casualties included 14 killed. The 601st was credited with 30 kills against German panzers. Herschel D. Baker, "TD Combat in Tunisia," 28–30.
68. York, letter to Sam Carter, 8.
69. As of 1200 hours on 25 March, the *10th Panzer Division* possessed 47 operational tanks: 6 Panzer IIs, 26 Panzer IIIs, and 15 Panzer IVs. There were 5 Panzer IIs, 9 Panzer IIIs, and 9 Panzer IVs still in repair shops. This meant that the Germans had recovered no less than 36 damaged tanks from the 23 March battlefield. The Americans destroyed 7 panzers and 2 self-propelled guns that were left behind. ULTRA Message VM 7591 dated 26 1959Z March 1943, HW 1/1520, PRO, London.
70. Smith, "Operations of the 3rd Battalion," 21.
71. ULTRA Message VM 7448 dated 24 0830 March 1943. HW 1/1515, PRO, London.
72. *The New Yorker*, "Profiles: Terry Allen," 1 May 1943, 28.
73. Patton felt Allen positioned the TDs poorly, which led to heavy losses. He believed that neither Allen nor Roosevelt understood how to use TDs.

A total of 29 out of 31 half-tracked TDs were knocked out, as well as 7 M-10s of the 899th. Stanley Hirshson, *General Patton: A Soldier's Life* (New York: HarperCollins, 2002), 324.

74. Henry G. Phillips, *El Guettar: Crucible of Leadership, 9th Infantry Division Against the* Wehrmacht *in Africa, April 1943* (Penn Valley, CA: Henry Phillips, 1991), 13–15.

75. Henry Bowles, letter to author, July 2002.

76. Carter, "Operations of the 1st Battalion," 22.

77. York, letter to Sam Carter, 9.

78. Ibid., 10.

79. Carter, "Operations of the 1st Battalion," 24.

80. Williamson, "North Africa, Sicily, and England," entries for 29–31 March 1943.

81. Smith, "Operations of the 3rd Battalion," 22.

82. Allen, "Summary of the El Guettar Offensive," Terry Allen Papers, USAMHI, 18.

83. Omar N. Bradley and Clay Blair, *A General's Life* (New York: Simon & Schuster), 144.

84. Robert E. Murphy, letter to author, 22 November 2000.

85. George S. Patton, Headquarters II Corps APO 302 US Army, 8 April 1943, Terry Allen Papers, USAMHI.

THE FINAL PUSH

1. A *Leichte* (Light) Division was a scaled-down panzer division with fewer tanks and more motorized infantry.

2. Arthur A. Gottlieb, "The Operations of the 1st Infantry Division at Mateur, 23 April–3 May 1943, Infantry Division Attacking Across Rugged Difficult Terrain," (DRL, 1949–50), 5–6.

3. The *Manteuffel Division: Regiment Barenthin* (three battalions averaging 575 men each); *Parachute Engineer Battalion 11; Marsch Battalion (Panzergrenadier) T-3;* the Italian 10th *Bersaglieri Regiment* (the 16th, 34th, and 63rd *Bersaglieri Battalions* averaging 325 men each); an antitank battalion; 3 artillery batteries; and 2 antiaircraft batteries.

4. The *Barenthin Regiment* was organized with a *Luftwaffe* Infantry Battalion, Parachute Infantry Battalion, and heavy weapons battalion. The 54-year old Walter Barenthin commanded it from 31 October 1942 until 10 March 1943, when he was wounded and evacuated from Tunisia.

5. Mason, "Reminiscences," 146.

6. Johnson, *One More Hill*, 60.

7. Gottlieb, "Operations of the 1st Infantry Division at Mateur," 9.

8. Johnson, *One More Hill*, 61.

9. Kuehn, letter to author, 14.

10. Louis Newman, letter to author, 10 March 2003, 1.

11. Marshall, *Proud Americans*, 96.

12. Johnson, *One More Hill*, 62.

13. Marshall, *Proud Americans*, 100.

14. Alvin L. Newman, "Personal War Diary," Copy to author May 2002, 23–25 April 1943.

15. Johnson, *One More Hill*, 63.

16. "History of the 2nd Battalion, 18th Infantry from 19 April–8 May 1943" [Wheaton, IL: Robert R. McCormick Research Center (RMRC)], 1.

17. Williamson, "North Africa, Sicily and England," entry from 23 April 1943.

18. Ibid, 3.

19. Downing, "At War with the British," 198.

20. Heidenheimer, *Vanguard to Victory*, 12.

21. Downing, "At War with the British," 198.

22. Edward K. Rogers, *Doughboy Chaplain* (Boston: Meador, 1946), 78–79.

23. Headquarters 1st US Infantry Division, APO 1, US Army, Citation of Unit, 11 November 1944, cited in Heidenheimer, *Vanguard to Victory,* 32–33.

24. Williamson, "North Africa, Sicily and England," 26–27 April 1943.

25. Gottlieb, "Operations of the 1st Infantry Division at Mateur," 14–15.

26. Ibid., 17.

27. Robert E. Cullis, "The Operations of the 1st Battalion, 16th Infantry (1st Infantry Division) in the Attack on Hill 523, vicinity of Mateur, Tunisia, North Africa, 30 April–1 May 1943, Personal Experiences of a Battalion Executive Officer," (DRL, 1949–50), 13–17.

28. Operations of 18th Infantry in Mateur Sector, Tunisia, 12 April 1943 to 8 May 1943, NACP.

29. Harold Alexander, "The African Campaign from El Alamein to Tunis: Chapter II, The Conquest of Tunis, 24 January 1943 to 13 May 1943," Copy 10, CMH, 33–35.

30. Terry Allen, "Combat Operations of the 1st Infantry Division during World War II (N. Africa and Sicily)," T. D. Allen Papers, Dwight D. Eisenhower Library, Abilene, Kansas.

31. Record of Events, 1st Battalion, 18th Infantry, 21 April–8 May 1943, Mateur Sector, RG 407, 1st Infantry Division, NACP, 3.

32. Ibid.

33. Van Wagoner, "Military Memoirs," 107–108.

34. Heidenheimer, *Vanguard to Victory,* 56.

35. Journal of the 3rd Battalion 18th Infantry for the Period 19 April–10 May 1943, RG 407, 1st Infantry Division, NACP, 3.

36. Company "H," 1st Armored Division memorandum dated 17 May 1943, 1st Infantry Division North Africa After Action Report (AAR), Microfilm files, CARL, 1–2.

37. Headquarters 2nd Battalion 18th Infantry, 12 April–8 May 1943, NACP.

38. Unpublished history of the 18th Infantry Regiment, RMRC, 56.

39. Williamson, "North Africa, Sicily, and England," 6 May 1943.

40. Bradley/Blair, *A General's Life,* 158.

41. Mason, "Reminiscences," 148.

42. Carlo D'Este, *Bitter Victory, The Battle for Sicily* (New York: Dutton, 1988), 569.

43. Alexander, "The African Campaign from El Alamein to Tunis," 47.

44. J. S. O. Playfair and C. J. C. Molony, *The Mediterranean and Middle East,* Vol. IV: *The Destruction of Axis Forces in Africa,* History of the Second World War United Kingdom Military Series, (London: Her Majesty's Stationary Office, 1966), 460.

45. Downing, "At War with the British," 203.

46. Sam Carter, oral history, tape 2, July 2002.

47. Mason, "Reminiscences," 150–51.

48. Kuehn, letter to author, 16.

49. Remarks by Stanhope B. Mason, at the 57th Annual Dinner of the Officers of the First Division, 24 April 1976, New York, NY, *Mason Memoirs,* 193.

50. Terry Allen papers, USAMHI.

51. Johnson, *One More Hill,* 77.

SICILY

1. Terry Allen and the 1st Division, unpublished account of Allen, written by former members of the 1st Division, Terry Allen papers, USAMHI.

2. D'Este, Carlo, *Bitter Victory.*

3. G-2 Intelligence notes No. 18, 1 August 1943, AFHQ Papers, PRO, Quoted in D'Este, *Bitter Victory*, 195.

4. Samuel W. Mitcham, Jr. and Friedrich Stauffenburg, *The Battle of Sicily: How the Allies Lost Their Chance for Total Victory* (New York: Orion, 1991), 23.

5. Ibid., 35.

6. Albert Kesselring, *A Soldier's Record* (Greenwood: Westport, CT), 1970, 194.

7. Marshall, *Proud Americans*, 110.

8. Ibid., 109.

9. Ibid., 110.

10. Rogers, *Doughboy Chaplain*, 110.

11. John Downing, "No Promotion," (Wheaton, IL: RMRC), 3

12. Albert Garland and Howard McGaw Smyth, *Sicily and the Surrender of Italy*. USAMHI, 1993, 159.

13. 1st Infantry Division G-2 Periodic Report No. 1 dated 11 July 1943, Sicilian Campaign, RG 407, Records of the Adjutant General (RAG), NACP.

14. The Terry Allen papers, "A Factual Situation and Operations Report on the Combat Operations of the 1st Infantry Division during the Campaign in North Africa and Sicily for the period 8 November 1942 to 7 Aug 1943," Part Three: "The Allied Invasion of Sicily," USAMHI.

15. Johnson, *One More Hill*, 88.

16. Record of Events, 1–31 July 1943, Headquarters 1st Battalion, 18th Infantry, 10 August 1943, 2.

17. Marshall, *Proud Americans*, 112.

18. Ibid.

19. Heidenheimer, *Vanguard to Victory*, 63.

20. Rogers, *Doughboy Chaplain*, 111–112.

21. 1st Infantry Division G-2 Periodic Report No. 1, dated 11 July 1943.

22. Clift Andrus, *Amphibious Landings– North Africa, Sicily and Normandy, Infantry-Artillery-Tank Tactical Air Force Elements and Naval Forces*, 1947, 27, Part III, 1.

23. Omar N. Bradley, *A Soldier's Story*, (New York: Henry Holt, 1951), 130.

24. Heidenheimer, *Vanguard to Victory*, 64.

25. Kuehn, letter to author, 20.

26. The Terry Allen papers, "Factual Situation and Operations Report: Sicily," USAMHI.

27. 1st Infantry Division G-2 Periodic Report No. 2 dated 13 July 1943.

28. Ibid.

29. Downing, "No Promotion, 7.

30. Kuehn, letter to author, 23.

31. Battle Report, 32nd Field Artillery Battalion, 23 June 1943 to 8 August 1943 Inclusive, RG 407, RAG, NACP, 3.

32. 1st Infantry Division G-2 Periodic Report No. 6 dated 17 July 1943.

33. Kuehn, letter to author, 25.

34. Ibid., 27.

35. Dwight D. Eisenhower, "Commanders in Chief Dispatch: Sicilian Campaign–1943, 28, GEOG 370.2–Sicily" [U.S. Army Center of Military History (CMH), Fort McNair, DC.]

36. Seventh Army Operations Report– Sicilian Campaign (Operation HUSKY), July–August 1943, RG 407, RAG, NACP.

37. Headquarters Second Battalion, History of 2nd Bn. 18th Inf. from Period July 1 to 31, 1943, 2.

38. D'Este, *Bitter Victory*, 418.

39. Ibid., 445.

40. Marvin Jensen, *Strike Swiftly: The 70th Tank Battalion from North Africa to Normandy to Germany* (Novato, CA, Presidio, 1997), 97.

41. John Williamson, "North Africa, Sicily and England," 29 July 1943.

42. 1st Division G-2 Periodic Report No. 21, dated 1 August 1943, RG 407, RAG, NACP.

43. 1st Division G-2 Periodic Report No, 24 dated 4 August 1943, RG 407, RAG, NACP.

44. Seventh Army Operations Report–Sicilian Campaign (Operation HUSKY), July–August 1943, "The Third Phase," 6, RG 407, RAG, NACP.

45. Williamson, "North Africa, Sicily and England," 3 August 1943.

46. Terry Allen, "A Summary of the Sicilian Campaign during World War II with Special Reference to the Continued Offensive and Night Attacks of the 1st Infantry Division," 1947, 15.

47. History of the 2nd Battalion 18th Infantry Regiment from 1 August to 31 August 1943, 1.

48. Battle Report, 32nd Field Artillery Battalion, 23 June 1943 to 8 August 1943 Inclusive, RG 407, RAG, NACP, 6.

49. Company G Sergeant Arthur J. O'Keefe received the DSC for his gallant actions this day.

50. Terry Allen, The Terry Allen Papers, NACP, 15–16.

51. D'Este, 470.

52. Ibid., 470. General Allen states in his letter to his wife 5 August 1943 that Patton came to his command post to visit him when he was relieved.

53. Bradley, *A Soldier's Story*, 154.

54. Ibid.

55. Ibid., 156.

56. Downing, "No Promotion," 11.

57. Johnson, 119.

58. Bradley, 155.

59. In World War I, each U.S. infantry division included four infantry regiments organized into two infantry brigades; the 1st Division's regiments included the 16th, 18th, 26th, and 28th. In WWII, in the process of "triangularization," the 28th Infantry Regiment was reassigned as part of the 8th Infantry Division.

60. Sean J. Byrne, "Looking for Sam Damon," *Military Review*, Vol. LXXVIII, May–June 1998, No. 3.

61. Downing, "No Promotion," 11.

62. Johnson, *One More Hill*, 116.

63. Ibid., 117.

64. Mason, at the 57th Annual Dinner of the Officers of the First Division, 24 April 1976, New York, NY, "Mason Memoirs," 195–96.

65. Mitcham and von Stauffenberg, *The Battle of Sicily*, 264.

66. Carlo D'Este, *Patton*, 531.

67. Williamson, "North Africa, Sicily and England," 25 August 1943.

68. Johnson, *One More Hill*, 121.

69. D'Este, *Patton*, 541.

70. Sam Carter, oral history, tape 3, July 2002.

71. Downing, "No Promotion," 23.

D-DAY NORMANDY

1. Downing, "No Promotion," 38.

2. Downing, letter from Montgomery to Huebner, in "No Promotion," 39.

3. Downing, "No Promotion," 47.

4. Johnson, *One More Hill*, 136.

5. 29th Infantry Division G-2 Report dated 1 May 1944, RG, RAG, NACP.

6. 1st Infantry Division G-2 Periodic Report.

7. Hein Severloh, *WN 62: Erinnerungen an Omaha Beach, Normandie, 6. Juni 1944* (Hannover, Germany: Creativ Verlag, 2000), i.

8. Pointe du Hoc was defended by 9th Company of the same German battalion. G-2 Journal entry #5 dated 07 1020 June 1944, V Corps, 6–16 Jun 1944, RG 407, RAG, NACP.

9. Downing, "No Promotion," 55.

10. Troop List–CT 18 Force, Final Ship Assignments, CT 18 Assault Group O-3, Headquarters, 1st Infantry Division, 16 May 1944, 5–7.

11. Robert E. Murphy, letter to author, April 2003. Murphy explained to author that his company had practiced these doctrines with Company F during the pre-invasion exercises while in Weymouth and at Slapton Sands.

12. Operations Plan No. 2–44, of the Western Naval Task Force, Allied Naval Expeditionary Force, Short Title "ONWEST TWO," Miscellaneous List, No. 798 to 799, RG 407, RAG, NACP.

13. One report noted that "Gap assault teams and infantry agree that no rockets hit their targets," Operation Report Neptune, Provisional Engineer Special Brigade Group, Omaha Beach, ML Series No. 653 to 660, Miscellaneous Lists, RG 407, RAG, NACP.

14. Lieutenant MacConchie received the DSC for his actions on Omaha Beach that morning, as did Company L's Private First Class Camillus J. Paolini that afternoon. Company C Lieutenant Craig B. "Ben" Hannum received the DSC for actions that cost him his life.

15. Operation Report Neptune, Provisional Engineer Special Brigade Group, Omaha Beach, ML Series No. 653 to 660, Miscellaneous Lists, RG 407, RAG, NACP.

16. History of the 16th Combat Team Invasion of France, S-3 Combat Report, Covering Citation of the 16th Infantry for the Period 6 June 1944, 1st Infantry Division, RG 407, RAG, NACP.

17. The D-Day Experience of E Company, 116th Infantry, 29th Division, G.L. 114 "Colonel Marshall's Notes," 2–3.7 BG American Forces in Action, Omaha Beachhead, U.S. Army Center of Military History, RG 319, Records of the Army Staff, NACP.

18. History of Company G, 16th Infantry, from 6 June–7 June 1944, 1st Infantry Division, RG 407, RAG, NACP.

19. History of the 16th Combat Team Invasion of France, S-3 Combat Report, Covering Citation of the 16th Infantry for the Period 6 June 1944, 10.

20. Ibid, 14.

21. Bradley, *A Soldier's Story*, 270.

22. 18th Infantry S-1 Journal, June 1944. "060910—Orders from General Wyman for 2nd Bn to push up draw as planned and assist CT 16 in overcoming opposition."

23. Robert E. Murphy, letter to author, 12 February 2001, 1.

24. F. C. Progue and J. M. Topete (V Corps), interview with John Spalding 9 February 1945 in Herve, Belgium, about D-Day Landing 6 June 1944–1st Section, Company E, 16th Infantry, 5.

25. Murphy, 1.

26. LCIs 408, 409, 411, 412, and 554 mislanded on Easy Red with members of the 115th Infantry at 1100 hours. 1st Infantry Division G-3 Journal entry 06 1100 June 1944. 1st Infantry Division, RG 407, RAG, NACP.

27. James E. Knight, letter to the crew of the *USS Frankford*, February 1990.

28. William B. Kirkland, Jr., "Destroyers at Normandy–Naval Gunfire Support at Omaha Beach," Naval Historical Foundation, CMH, 1994, 46.

29. Ibid., 50.

30. Ibid., 49–51.

31. Progue and Topete, interview with Spaulding.

32. Gordon Harrison, *Cross-Channel Attack*, CMH, 325.

33. Heidenheimer, *Vanguard to Victory*, 90.

34. Paul Hurst, letter to author, 27 July 2001.

35. Heidenheimer, *Vanguard to Victory*, 91.

36. Raymond J. Klawitzer, Ocean City, NJ, letter to author, May 2002.

37. Sam Carter, Oral history, tape 4, July 2002.
38. Rogers, *Doughboy Chaplain*, 155.
39. Ibid., 157.
40. Heidenheimer, *Vanguard to Victory*, 86.
41. Christopher Cornazzani memoirs, USAMHI.
42. Marshall, *Proud Americans*, Colacicco History, 160.
43. Heidenheimer, *Vanguard to Victory*, 87.
44. Howard J. Johnson, letter to author, 25 January 2002.
45. Marshall, *Proud Americans*, Colacicco history, 160.
46. C. E. Kirkpatrick, V Corps Historian, interview with Walter D. Ehlers, conducted 21 August 1998.
47. Johnson, letter to author.
48. Marshall, *Proud Americans*, Colacicco History, 161.
49. Johnson, *One More Hill*, 142–43.
50. Ibid., 143.
51. Marshall, *Proud Americans*, 154–56.
52. Murphy, Oral history to author, 17 March 2002.
53. Ibid., 3.
54. Downing, "No Promotion," 58.
55. Ibid., 59.
56. Ibid., 66.
57. Ibid., 67.
58. S-1 Journal, 06 1800 June 1944, 18th Infantry, Change of Mission.
59. Headquarters 2nd Battalion, 18th Infantry, Carl O. Randall, Jr., S-3, Record of Events for the Month of June 1944, 2.
60. Omaha Beachhead, American Forces in Action, Historical Division, War Department, CMH, September 1945, 117.
61. 741st Tank Battalion Unit Journal File for June 1944, entry dated 06 2000 June 1944, A/A Rpt–741st Tank Battalion, Jun–Dec 44, RG 407, RAG, NACP.
62. Chester Wilmot, *The Struggle for Europe*, The Reprint Society London, 1954, 286.
63. S-1 Journal, 06 2140 June 1944, 18th Infantry.
64. Edgar A. Wilkerson, et al., "V Corps History," CMH, 64.
65. George A. Smith, Jr., letter to Wife, 21 June 1944, provided to author by Jeffrey G. Smith (Grandson) on 8 November 2001.
66. Citation of Unit, 18th Infantry Regiment St. Laurent-sur-Mer and Colleville-sur-Mer France, for 6 June 1944, dated 17 June 1944.

NORTHERN FRANCE

1. Unit History, 18th Infantry Regiment, for Period of 1–30 June 1944, 2, 1st Infantry Division, RG 407, RAG, NACP.
2. Receiving the DSC on 7 June 1944 were: 1st Lieutenant John Synowsky, Tech 5 Harry Hartman, Pfc. Harry E. Griffin, and Private Fredrick Lutz. Private Lutz received his award posthumously.
3. Battalion Journal, 3rd Battalion, 18th Infantry, for Period 1–30 June 1944, 1st Infantry Division, RG 407, RAG, NACP, 2.
4. Marshall, *Proud Americans*, 160.
5. Johnson, *One More Hill*, 149.
6. Headquarters, Second Battalion, 18th Infantry, Record of Events for the month ending 30 June 1944, 4.
7. Headquarters, First Battalion, 18th Infantry, Record of Events for the Month of June 1944, 1st Infantry Division, RG 407, RAG, NACP, 3.
8. Martin Blumenson, *Breakout and Pursuit* (GPO, 1961), 11.

9. Headquarters, Second Battalion, 18th Infantry, Record of Events for the month ending 30 June 1944, 4.

10. Paul E. Stegall, oral history to author, February 1997. Circumstances of Pfc. Ralph Spinosi's death were confirmed by his nephew, Joseph Spinosi, in February 2002. Pvt. William Uhouse's wounds were confirmed for author by then-Company H commander Robert E. Murphy during returned comments on chapter draft in May 2003.

11. 18th Infantry S-1 Journal, 09 2030 June 1944; CO 18 to 1st and 3rd Battalion.

12. George K. Folk, oral history interview, 3 October 1989, 59.

13. Kirkpatrick, interview with Walter D. Ehlers, 13–14.

14. Battalion Journal, 3rd Battalion, 18th Infantry, for 1–30 June 1944, 4.

15. Headquarters, Second Battalion, 18th Infantry, Record of Events for the month ending 30 June 1944, 4.

16. G-2 Periodic Journal Entry #27 dated 10 1110 June 1944, 1st Infantry Division, RG 407, NACP.

17. Kirkpatrick, interview with Walter D. Ehlers, 14.

18. Medal of Honor Citation, Walter D. Ehlers. President Clinton introduced Ehlers at the D-Day 50th Anniversary in June 1994 on Omaha Beach where he (Ehlers) made the main address, to include the closing statement, "Today, fifty years later, the beaches are quiet. We come back to mourn our losses, and to celebrate our success. Our presence here commemorates our and our comrades' lives, and it validates the sacrifices we all made on D-day."

19. Medal of Honor Citation, Staff Sergeant Arthur F. DeFranzo (Posthumous) 1 December 1944.

20. Battalion Journal, 3rd Battalion, 18th Infantry, for Period 1–30 June 1944, 4.

21. Downing, *No Promotion*, 77.

22. Johnson, *One More Hill*, 153.

23. Marshall, *Proud Americans*, 168.

24. Lieutenant Jesse R. Miller, Jr. received the DSC for his intrepid actions during one of these encounters on 15 June 1944. In July, Tech Sergeant Gerald Henderson received the DSC posthumously.

25. The German units actually opposing the 1st Division consisted of the *3rd Parachute Division* to the west and *2nd Panzer Division* to the east. The *17th SS-Panzer-Grenadier Division*, which had been involved in some skirmishes with the 1st Division, was shifted west to Carentan several days prior to the fall of Caumont.

26. Johnson, *One More Hill*, 158.

27. Heidenheimer, *Vanguard to Victory*, 103.

28. Johnson, *One More Hill*, 159–62.

29. Headquarters 1st Infantry Division APO #1, U.S. Army, Unit History, 18th Infantry Regiment, for Period of 1–30 June 1944, Colonel George A. Smith, Jr., 3.

30. 18th Infantry S-1 Journal, 30 1800 June 1944, Totals Casualties for Month.

31. 18th Infantry Regiment, for Period of 1–30 June 1944, George A. Smith, Jr., 1.

32. Heidenheimer, *Vanguard to Victory*, 102–103. York took command of the 331st Regiment after its commanding officer, Martin Barndollar, was killed in action. York later rose to the rank of lieutenant general.

33. Downing, "No Promotion," 85.

34. The German units that would have been trapped included elements of the *77th* and *353rd Infantry Division*s,

17th SS-Panzer-Grenadier Division, 2nd SS-Panzer Division, and *Parachute Infantry Regiment 6*. Carlos A. Nadal, "The Operations of the 1st Infantry Division in the St. Lô Breakthrough, 25 July–1 August 1944" (DRL, 1949–50), 6–9.

35. Bradley, *A Soldier's Story*, 332.
36. Downing, "No Promotion," 91.
37. Sam Carter, "Breaching the German Defense of the Omaha Beachhead, Normandy, France," 20 July 1994, 1
38. Rogers, *Doughboy Chaplain*, 169; General Huebner quote in Bradley, *A General's Life*, 1983, 280.
39. History of the VII Corps for the period 1–31 July 1944 (Report after action against enemy), VII Corps, RG 407, RAG, NACP, 28–29.
40. Nadal, "The Operations of the 1st Infantry Division in the St. Lô Breakthrough," 18.
41. A. V. Middleworth, S-3, 18th Infantry, 1st Division, interview concerning 1st Division Breakthrough on 25 July 1944, 1.
42. Heidenheimer, *Vanguard to Victory*, 106.
43. Marshall, *Proud Americans*, 175.
44. Ibid., 176. Captain Brown's wounds noted in Heidenheimer, *Vanguard to Victory*, 107. Hiram Shumway, also of Company B, was rendered blind by an explosion of an enemy mine the same day. Over 50 enemy dead were found in the 1st Battalion positions, and 52 were taken prisoner.
45. Middleworth interview, 2.
46. Follow-up of Breakthrough, based on interview with John Williamson and Robert E. Murphy (S-3), 2.
47. Middleworth interview, 2. Interviewer noted this was not substantiated by the "2nd Battalion story." It is unlikely that this command post belonged to the *352nd Infantry Division*, which was much further to the east near St. Lô. In all likelihood, it may have been the *LXXXIV Corps* forward command post.
48. Breakthrough of 25 July, *Action of the 3rd Battalion at Marigny*, based on interviews with Company I Lieutenant D.A. Bramlett (Executive Officer), Lieutenant John C. Comway, Tech Sergeant W. Mille, Staff Sergeant Jack Carter, Tech Sergeant William Buchanan (weapons platoon), and Staff Sergeants Edmund C. Pieler and Eugene Kaltenbrun, 2.
49. Ibid., 2.
50. Carter, "Breaching the German Defense of the Omaha Beachhead," 2. Artilleryman quote is from Marshall, *Proud Americans*, 177.
51. Marshall, *Proud Americans*, 176.
52. Carter, "Breaching the German Defense of the Omaha Beachhead," 2–3.
53. Company I interviews, 3.
54. Carter, "Breaching the German Defense of the Omaha Beachhead," 3.
55. Middleworth interview, 3–4.
56. Nadal, "The Operations of the 1st Infantry Division in the St. Lô Breakthrough," 22.
57. Heidenheimer, *Vanguard to Victory*, 109.
58. Headquarters 1st Infantry Division APO #1, U.S. Army, Unit History, 18th Infantry Regiment, for Period 1–31 August 1944, George A. Smith, Jr., 2.
59. Marshall, *Proud Americans*, 178.
60. Mark J. Reardon, *Victory at Mortain: Defeating Hitler's Panzer Counteroffensive* (Lawrence: University Press of Kansas, 2002), 80–81.
61. Rogers, 172–73.
62. During one of these skirmishes on 11 August, Lieutenant, then Tech

Sergeant, Lawrence Cappoletti received the DSC.

63. Unit History, 18th Infantry Regiment, for Period of 1–31 August 1944, George A. Smith, Jr., 3.

THE WESTWALL

1. Heidenheimer, *Vanguard to Victory*, 116.
2. Robert E. Murphy, "The Operations of the 2nd Battalion 18th Infantry at Sars-la-Bruyère, Belgium, West of Mons, 4–5 September 1944 (Northern France Campaign), Personal Experiences of a Battalion Operations Officer," (DRL, 1949–50), 10.
3. Carmel DeCampo, "Biggest Battle of the War for Company E," 12.1. DeCampo history sent to Ralph "Andy" Andersen, Company E, 7 December 1996.
4. Murphy, "Sars-La-Bruyère," 14.
5. DeCampo, "Biggest Battle of the War for Company E," 12.2.
6. Ibid., 12.3.
7. Murphy, "Sars-La-Bruyère," 15.
8. Ibid., 16.
9. DeCampo, "Biggest Battle of the War for Company E," 12.4.
10. Sam Carter, letter to author, 20 June 2002, sections on Gino Merli.
11. Medal of Honor Citation, Gino J. Merli, 3 May 1945. Captain Murphy drafted the citation.
12. Gino Merli, letter to Sam Carter, 7 July 1995. Merli was then-First Lady Hillary R. Clinton's guest at the 50th Reunion of the Normandy Invasion in June 1994. On 4 September, Sergeant Edward A. Patyniski and Pfc. Roy V. Craft received the DSC (Craft received it posthumously).
13. Murphy, "Sars-La-Bruyère," 19.
14. Ibid., 21.
15. Headquarters 18th Infantry, APO #1, Unit History, 18th Infantry Regiment, for Period 1–30 September 1944, George A. Smith, Jr., 2.
16. Three 18th Infantry soldiers were awarded the DSC during this time: Pfc. Joseph R. Bucci on 11 September, Pfc. Nanti Fiori on 12 September, and Pvt. Albert L. Johnson on 15 September (Fiori and Johnson received them posthumously).
17. Carter, letter to author, 20 June 2002, section on Staff Sergeant Joseph E. Schaefer.
18. Medal of Honor Citation, Staff Sergeant Joseph E. Schaefer, 7 May 1945.
19. Sara J. Gaysek, "One of Many—World War II from My Perspective," written with Frank Gaysek, 1998, 42–45.
20. Quoted in Heidenheimer, *Vanguard to Victory*, 122–23.
21. Edward W. McGregor, "The Operations of the 1st Battalion, 18th Infantry in the Vicinity of Crucifix Hill, Northeast of Aachen, Germany, 8–10 October 1944 (Rhineland Campaign), Personal Experiences of a Battalion Operations Officer," (DRL, 1949–50), 8.
22. Ibid., 8.
23. Ibid., 8–9.
24. "The Rifle Company in Attack, The Attack on Crucifix Hill, 7–9 October 1944, Company C, 18th Infantry" Regimental War-Time History, 18th Infantry Regimental Log for WWII, RMRC, 3.
25. Robert York quoted in "Bobbie Brown, Winner of Medal of Honor, Is Dead," *New York Times*, 11 November 1971.
26. 745th Tank Battalion, Company B, 1st, 2nd, 3rd Platoons, 8–19 October 1944. Interview by Ridgely C. Dorsey,

2d Information & History Service, 1st US Army, 2.

27. "The Rifle Company in Attack, The Attack on Crucifix Hill," 5.

28. Bobbie E. Brown, "The Operations of Company C, 18th Infantry in the Attack on Crucifix Hill, 8 October 1944, Personal Experiences of a Company Commander," (DRL, 1946–47), 8.

29. Ibid., 9–10.

30. "The Rifle Company in Attack, The Attack on Crucifix Hill," 3.

31. Ibid., 6.

32. Phil Krueger, "Sgt. Bobbie Brown, '62 Notch' Sharpshooter Who Captured Crucifix Hill," AGO Microfilm Item No. 3546, DRL, 64.

33. Brown, "The Operations of Company C," 11.

34. Ibid., 12. Lieutenant Joseph W. Cambron was later awarded the DSC posthumously for his courage and bravery that day.

35. Krueger, "Bobbie Brown," 65.

36. McGregor, "Crucifix Hill," 27.

37. Ibid., 35–36.

38. Ibid., 38.

39. Ibid., 40.

40. Brown, "The Operations of Company C," 14–15.

41. "The Rifle Company in Attack, The Attack on Crucifix Hill," 10.

42. Battalion in Attack, Verlautenheide, Germany, 8 October 1944, 2nd Battalion, 18th Infantry, AGO Microfilm Item No. 3546, DRL, 6.

43. McGregor, "Crucifix Hill," 49.

44. Marshall, *Proud Americans*, 221.

45. The Regimental Combat Team in Offensive Action, The Attack on Verlautenheide, Crucifix Hill, and Ravelsberg Hill, 18th Regimental Combat Team, AGO Microfilm Item No. 3546, DRL, 8–9.

46. McGregor, "Crucifix Hill," 14.

47. Robert E. Murphy, letter to author, 14 August 2003, 1.

48. Heinz Günther Guderian, *From Normandy to the Ruhr: With the 116th Panzer Division in World War II* (Bedford, PA: Aberjona, 2001), 222.

49. Sam Carter, "Max Thompson and the Medal of Honor," *Bridgehead Sentinel*, Spring 1997, 7. Carter also drafted Staff Sergeant Max Thompson's Medal of Honor Citation.

50. Heidenheimer, *Vanguard to Victory*, 133.

51. Company B Captain Jesse Miller received his second award of the DSC for his part in the battle, as did Company K's Tech Sergeant Weldon D. Clinton (Posthumous).

52. Heidenheimer, *Vanguard to Victory*, 160–161.

THE HÜRTGEN FOREST AND THE BULGE

1. Marshall, *Proud Americans*, 264.

2. Edward G. Miller, *Dark and Bloody Ground: The Hurtgen Forest and the Roer River Dams, 1944–45* (College Station: Texas A&M Press, 1995), 2.

3. Heidenheimer, *Vanguard to Victory*, 169.

4. Knickerbocker, et al., *Danger Forward*, 302.

5. Sam Carter, "The Hurtgen Forest and the Battle for Langerwehe," *Bridgehead Sentinel*, Summer 2001, 6.

6. Gene Weisenberg, letter to author, 23 September 2003, 1.

7. George E. Moise, 2d Information and History Service (VII Corps), 1st US Army, Interview with Edward W. McGregor about Hill 203, 21–27 November 1944, 2.

8. Marshall, *Proud Americans*, 302.
9. Carter, "The Hurtgen Forest and the Battle for Langerwehe," 6.
10. Heidenheimer, *Vanguard to Victory*, 167.
11. Robert L. Bullard, III, Information taken from personal notebook joined with Roster of Company K, November 1944, at Heistern. Provided to author, June 2003, by Randolf Paulsen.
12. Marshall, *Proud Americans*, 248–49.
13. Carter, "The Hurtgen Forest and the Battle for Langerwehe," 6.
14. Heidenheimer, *Vanguard to Victory*, 173.
15. Marshall, *Proud Americans*, 255.
16. Heidenheimer, *Vanguard to Victory*, 180.
17. Carter, "The Hurtgen Forest and the Battle for Langerwehe," 7.
18. Captain George Folk was awarded the DSC for leading the attack across an open field. Company F's Tech Sergeant Clarance Lackner was also awarded the DSC for his courageous actions in the Hürtgen Forest.
19. Carter, "The Hurtgen Forest and the Battle for Langerwehe," 7.
20. Ibid., 7.
21. Heidenheimer, *Vanguard to Victory*, 181.
22. Ibid., 175.
23. Ibid., 163.
24. Knickerbocker, et al., *Danger Forward*, 299.
25. George A. Smith, Jr., Regimental History for the Month of November 1944, 1.
26. George A. Smith, Jr., Regimental History for the Month of December 1944, 2–3.
27. Ibid., 4.
28. Ibid., 4.
29. Edward M. Soloman, "The Operations of the 18th Infantry in the Counterattack of the 'Bulge' 15–30 January 1945, Personal Experiences of an Anti-Tank Company Commander" (DRL, 1946–47), 10.
30. James Brannen, letter to author, March 2002.
31. Soloman, "Counterattack of the 'Bulge'," 13.
32. Company K Tech Sergeant Osborne F. Sellars received the DSC during his company's advance in the Butgenbacher Heck. Staff Sergeant William E. Graves received the DSC posthumously on 24 January.
33. Operation YUKON, The Infantry Battalion in Offensive Action, 18 January 1945, 1st Battalion 18th Infantry, 5.
34. Ibid., 6.
35. Ibid., 7–8.
36. Ibid., 8.
37. Downing, *No Promotion*, 178.
38. Ibid., 179.
39. Robert E. Murphy, letter to author, 15 September 2003, 2.
40. "The Rifle Company in Attack, The Attack on Moderscheid, 24 January 1945, Company E 18th Infantry," Regimental War-Time History, 18th Infantry Regimental Log for WWII, RMRC, 3.
41. "The Rifle Company in Attack, 'Forty-second and Broadway', 24 January 1945, Company B 18th Infantry, section entitled 'Patrol from Nidrum to Forty-second and Broadway'," Regimental War-Time History, 18th Infantry Regimental Log for WWII, RMRC, 2.
42. Marshall, *Proud Americans*, 259.
43. Ibid., 259.
44. "The Rifle Company in Attack, 'Forty-Second and Broadway'," 7.

45. Soloman, "Counterattack of the 'Bulge'," 22–23.
46. Knickerbocker, et al., *Danger Forward*, 349–50.
47. Downing, "No Promotion," 194–95.
48. Soloman, "Counterattack of the 'Bulge'," 27.
49. Sam Carter, "The Battle of the Bulge, Rounding up the German Paratroopers," *Bridgehead Sentinel*, December 1993, 3.
50. Knickerbocker, et al., *Danger Forward*, 331.
51. "The Rifle Company in Attack, The Attack on Ramscheid, 2 February 1945, Company F 18th Infantry" Regimental War-Time History, 18th Infantry Regimental Log for WWII, RMRC, 3.
52. "The Rifle Company in Attack, The Attack on Ramscheid," 4.
53. Medic Ferdie Schimpf received the DSC for his heroic actions on behalf of the wounded on 2 February 1945.
54. Based on Downing, "No Promotion," 198–99.

THE ROER TO SURRENDER

1. Downing, *No Promotion*, 208–209.
2. Franklin Ferris, interview with Sam Carter, 2nd Information and Historical Service, Headquarters First US Army, APO 230, 22 March 1945, 2.
3. Ferris, interview with Sam Carter, 2–3.
4. Downing, "No Promotion," 225.
5. Heidenheimer, *Vanguard to Victory*, 196. Information on attack on George A. Smith's group provided to author by Peter Branton, Official Historian of the Timberwolf Association, to include unit history, 257–58.
6. "The Rifle Company in Attack, The Attack on Hühnerberg, 'Gravel Pit Operation,' Company A, 18th Infantry, 16 March 1945," Regimental War-Time History, 18th Infantry Regimental Log for WWII, RMRC, 4.
7. Franklin Ferris, 2nd Information and Historical Service, interview with Edward W. McGregor, S-3 18th Infantry, Expansion of the Remagen Bridgehead 17–21 March, Bridgehead Breakout, 24–31 March, Leiberg, Germany, 3 April 1945, 3.
8. Operations Report of the 1st Battalion, 18th Infantry, RG 407, 1st Infantry Division, NACP, unnumbered page.
9. Downing, "No Promotion," 248.
10. Ferris, McGregor interview, 3.
11. Marshall, *Proud Americans*, 260.
12. Heidenheimer, *Vanguard to Victory*, 201.
13. Marshall, *Proud Americans*, 313.
14. Ferris, McGregor interview, 3. During this period of fighting, Tech Sergeant Osborne F. Sellars received his second award of the DSC.
15. Heidenheimer, *Vanguard to Victory*, 192.
16. Ferris, McGregor interview, 4.
17. Staff Sergeant Medal of Honor (Posthumous) George Petersen, 27 July 1945.
18. 1st Lieutenant Medal of Honor (Posthumous) Walter J. Will, 7 August 1945.
19. John H. Lauten, Intelligence Activities, 1 April 1945 to 30 April 1945, Headquarters 1st U.S. Infantry Division, APO 1, U.S. Army, 1–2.
20. Lauten, Intelligence Activities, 1 April 1945 to 30 April 1945, 2.
21. "The Rifle Company in Attack, Battle of Weser River, Company L, 18th Infantry, 8 April 1945," Regimental

War-Time History, 18th Infantry Regimental Log for WWII, RMRC, 2.
22. Ibid., 5.
23. Ibid., 7.
24. Ibid., 7.
25. Lauten, Intelligence Activities, 1 April 1945 to 30 April 1945, 3.
26. "The Rifle Company in Attack, Battle of Weser River," 9.
27. Lauten, Intelligence Activities, 1 April 1945 to 30 April 1945, 4.
28. Kenneth W. Hechler, 2nd Information and Historical Service, interview with Edward W. McGregor, S-3, 18th Infantry, Harz Mountains 11–20 April 1945, Lazne Kynzvart, Czechoslovakia, 1.
29. Hechler interview, McGregor, 1–2.
30. Kenneth W. Hechler, 2nd Information and Historical Service, interview with Henry G. Learnard, Jr., Task Force Y, 11–23 April 1945, 1st Battalion, 18th Infantry, Kladske, Czechoslovakia, 25 May 1945, 1–3.
31. Hechler interview, Learnard, 3.
32. Kenneth W. Hechler, 2nd Information and Historical Service, interview with Clifford Chandler, CO, Company I, 18th Infantry, Harz Mountains 11–20 April 1945, Lazne Kynzvart, Czechoslovakia, 3.
33. "The Rifle Company in Attack, The Attack on Wenderfürth, 19 April 1945, Company G 18th Infantry," Regimental War-Time History, 18th Infantry Regimental Log for WWII, RMRC, 3.
34. Hechler interview, McGregor, 3.
35. Lauten, Intelligence Activities, 1 April 1945 to 30 April 1945, 6–7.

36. Hechler interview, Chandler, 3–4.
37. Hechler interview, Learnard, 4–5.
38. Hechler interview, Learnard, 5.
39. Hechler interview, Learnard, 6.
40. Hechler interview, Learnard, 7.
41. Lauten, Intelligence Activities, 1 April 1945 to 30 April 1945, 8.
42. Knickerbocker, *Danger Forward*, 391.
43. Ibid., 393.
44. Headquarters 1st US Infantry Division APO 1 US Army, 7 May 1945. Copy provided to author by Robert E. Murphy, October 2004.
45. Knickerbocker, *Danger Forward*, 392.
46. Picture captioned "The Most Important Picture of All" notes "All remaining members of the 18th Infantry who sailed on 2 August 1942 from New York at the Third Anniversary of the event in 1945, Germany." The actual number who survived the war is higher, as some officers had returned to the States by this time.
47. Heidenheimer, *Vanguard to Victory*, 210. The 18th Infantry immediate postwar history recorded total killed as 1,498. Painstaking research by 18th Infantry Regiment Association President George Gentry established that there were 1,513 total Regimental Combat Team 18 soldiers killed in action during World War II.
48. Donald Parker, letter to author, July 2003.
49. Irving Yarock, letter to author, August 2003.
50. Downing, "No Promotion," 287.
51. Sam Carter, letter to 18th Infantry Association and author, August 2003.

INDEX

MILITARY UNITS

BRITISH AND COMMONWEALTH FORCES
army groups
  Eighteenth, 85, 108, 130, 168
  Twenty-first, 21st, 175, 260
armies
  First, 44, 46, 48, 66, 72–73, 77–78, 109, 126, 131
  Second, 176, 238, 258
  Eighth, 45, 75, 83, 85, 105, 109, 131, 137–38, 151–53, 155–56
corps
  V Corps, 109, 111, 126
  IX Corps, 109, 126, 131
  X Corps, 107–109
  XXX Corps, 107–108, 225, 236
divisions
infantry divisions
  1st Division, 126
  2nd New Zealand Division, 109
  4th Division, 110
  4th Indian Division, 107–109, 126
  46th Division, 45–46, 75, 126
  50th (Northumbrian) Division, 107, 109, 178, 236
  78th Division, 20, 46, 48, 50–51, 61, 75, 112, 126
armoured divisions
  1st Armoured, 108
  6th Armoured, 46, 50, 72, 74, 77, 79, 82
  7th Armoured, 126, 131, 236, 238
brigades
  1st Guards Brigade, 50, 73, 77, 79–81
  201st Guards Brigade, 126
  1st Parachute Brigade, 50
  11th Infantry Brigade, 75
  22nd Armoured Brigade, 238
  26th Armoured Brigade, 77, 82
battalion-sized units
cavalry
  11th Hussars, 131
  16th/5th The Queen's Royal Lancers, 74
  17th/21st Lancers, 74
  The North Irish Horse, 112
  2nd Lothian and Border Horse Yeomanry, 74
infantry
  3rd Battalion, The Grenadier Guards, 82–83
  2nd Battalion, The Coldstream Guards, 49, 51–52, 54–56, 58, 61, 66, 69–70, 80–82
  5th Battalion, The Buffs (Royal East Kent Regiment), 112
  1st Battalion, The East Surrey Regiment, 112
  5th Battalion, The Northamptonshire Regiment, 49, 65–66
  6th Battalion, The Queen's Own Royal West Kent Regiment, 112
  8th Battalion, The Argyll and Sutherland Highlanders, 112
  2nd Battalion, The Parachute Regiment, 74
  No. 6 Commando, 74

FRANCE
corps
  XIX Corps, 46, 73, 77, 210
  Corps Franc d'Afrique, 109
division
  Oran Division, 24, 28, 43
infantry units
  1st Regiment de la Légion Etrangère, 28
  2nd Algerian Tirailleurs, 21
  2nd Zouave Regiment, 21
  4th Tabor of Moroccan Goums, 157–59
  16th Tunisian Tirailleurs, 28
field artillery units
  68th African Field Artillery, 22, 29, 43

GERMANY
army groups
  Army Group Africa, 131
  Army Group B, 258
armies
  Fifth Panzer Army, 75, 78, 311
  Sixth Panzer Army, 311

404

Index

Seventh Army, 238, 256–58, 311
corps
  XIV Panzer Corps, 170
  LXXXI Corps, 181
  LXXXIV Corps, 181
  XC Corps, 50
divisions
infantry divisions
  Division Hermann Göring, 131, 140
  Division Manteuffel, 111, 131
  Potsdam Division, 354
  12th Infantry Division (later Volks-Grenadier Division), 287–88, 310, 313, 335
  18th Luftwaffe Field Division, 262
  47th Volks-Grenadier Division, 302, 310
  89th Infantry Division (later Volks-Grenadier Division), 299, 320
  246th Volks-Grenadier Division, 272, 295
  275th Infantry Division, 262
  334th Infantry Division, 51, 111, 122–23, 131
  352nd Infantry Division, 181–82, 204, 227
  353rd Infantry Division, 249
  363rd Volks-Grenadier Division, 342
  716th Infantry Division, 181
light divisions
  90th Light Division, 109
  164th Light Division, 108
airborne divisions
  1st Parachute Division, 155
  3rd Parachute Division, 310
  5th Parachute Division, 249
armored infantry divisions
  3rd Panzer-Grenadier Division, 294–95, 310
  15th Panzer-Grenadier Division "Sizilien," 140, 153, 155–58, 163
  17th SS-Panzer-Grenadier Division "Götz von Berlichingen," 234
  29th Panzer-Grenadier Division, 170
armored divisions
  2nd Panzer Division, 357
  9th Panzer Division, 349
  10th Panzer Division, 51, 66, 76, 78, 82, 94, 101–102, 105–108
  11th Panzer Division, 342
  12th SS-Panzer Division "Hitlerjugend," 312–13
  15th Panzer Division, 81, 107–108, 131
  21st Panzer Division, 76, 78, 81, 108–109
  116th Panzer Division, 255, 292–93, 295, 349
  130th Panzer Division (Panzer Lehr), 236, 241
  Panzer Division Hermann Göring, 143–44, 146, 155
regiments
infantry regiments
  Füsilier Regiment 27, 287
  Grenadier Regiment 48, 299, 301
  Grenadier Regiment 104, 302
  Grenadier Regiment 352, 272, 275, 284
  Grenadier Regiment 404, 272
  Infantry Regiment 726, 181–82
  Grenadier Regiment 754, 51, 66
  Grenadier Regiment 755, 123
  Grenadier Regiment 915, 181, 231
  Grenadier Regiment 916, 182, 226–27, 230
  Infantry Regiment 942, 249
  Grenadier Regiment 1055, 320, 323, 325–27
  Grenadier Regiment 1056, 328
  Regiment Barenthin, 111, 127–30
mountain infantry regiments
  Mountain Infantry Regiment 756, 112
parachute infantry regiments
  Parachute Regiment 5, 308, 314, 324, 328
  Parachute Regiment 8, 310, 319, 327
armored infantry regiments
  Panzer-Grenadier Regiment 1, 153, 158–59
  Panzer-Grenadier Regiment 3. See also Combat Group Fullriede, 158
  Panzer-Grenadier Regiment 8, 294
  SS-Panzer-Grenadier Regiment 25, 312
  SS-Panzer-Grenadier Regiment 26, 312–13
  Panzer-Grenadier Regiment 69, 51, 55, 66, 95–96, 105
  Panzer-Grenadier Regiment 86, 95
  Panzer-Grenadier Regiment 104, 81
armored regiments
  Panzer Regiment Hermann Göring, 146
  Panzer Regiment 7, 66–67, 95
  Panzer Regiment 8, 81
  SS-Panzer Regiment 12, 312–13
artillery regiments
  Nebelwerfer Regiment 71, 153, 157
  Artillery Regiment 716, 182

combat groups (*kampfgruppen*)
   Lang, 51
   Fullriede, 157
   Schmalz, 144, 155
   Von der Heydte, 311
battalions
engineer battalions
   Engineer Battalion 12, 287
   Construction Engineer Battalion 17, 227
   Engineer Battalion 334, 51
miscellaneous battalions
   Fortress Battalion XIX, 272
   Füsilier Battalion 275, 256
   Füsilier Battalion 352, 232–33
   Heavy Tank Battalion 501, 51
   Marsch Battalion T-3 (Africa), 119
   Mobile Battalion 517, 231
   Motorcycle (Kradschützen) Battalion 10, 102
   Panzer Battalion 215, 153
   Parachute Tank Destroyer Battalion 3, 317
   Replacement Battalion 352, 233
   Replacement Battalion 453, 272, 275
   SS-Heavy Tank Battalion 101, 230
   SS-Tank Destroyer Battalion 12, 312

ITALY
armies
   First Army, 107–9
   Sixth Army, 139, 150
groups
   Mobile Gruppo E, 143–44
divisions
infantry and coastal divisions
   1st Infantry Division "Superga," 44, 51
   4th Infantry Division "Livorno," 143, 149–50
   16th Infantry Division "Pistoia," 108
   28th Infantry Division "Aosta," 155–57
   136th Infantry "Giovanni Fascisti," 108
   206th Coastal Division, 139, 141, 150
motorized division
   Motorized Division "Trieste," 108
armored division
   131st Armored Division "Centauro," 76, 85–86, 91, 94
battalions
   551st Assault Gun Battalion, 51

UNITED STATES
army groups
   12th Army Group, 260
armies
   First, 2, 238, 241, 254, 260, 269, 299, 313–14, 329, 336
   Third, 257–8, 260, 313
   Seventh, 134, 137–39, 151–3, 155–56, 163, 170–71
corps
   II, 8, 12, 20, 35, 76–77, 83–86, 91, 98, 104, 108–11, 121, 123, 125–26, 130–31, 138, 152–53, 156
   V, 176, 180, 189, 205, 225, 230, 236, 241, 260, 301, 311–14, 326, 332, 358
   VII, 236, 241–42, 246, 254–55, 260–61, 269, 273–74, 299, 313–14, 341, 345
   VIII, 241–42, 254
   XVIII Airborne, 314, 329, 332
   XIX, 241
divisions
infantry divisions
   2nd, 230–31, 235–38, 317–18, 320, 323
   3rd, 20, 45, 83, 132, 139
   4th, 245
   5th, 241
   9th, 20, 45, 98, 103–105, 108–109, 125, 131, 158, 161–62, 241–42, 244–45, 299, 310–11, 335, 351–52
   28th, 299
   29th, 176, 236
   30th, 241, 245, 257, 273, 291–93, 295, 329
   34th, 20, 45, 79, 105, 109, 111, 123, 125–26, 131
   45th, 137–38, 144, 153
   78th, 309, 339
   83rd, 240
   99th, 331
   104th, 297, 300, 310, 333, 336, 351
airborne divisions
   82nd, 138, 144, 328–29, 332
armored divisions
   1st Armored, 8, 20, 41, 48, 76–78, 82, 85, 105, 109, 124–26, 131
   2nd Armored, 20, 45, 54, 139, 144–45, 148, 236, 242, 345
   3rd Armored, 174, 221, 242, 244, 254–55, 257, 261, 299, 312, 341–43, 345–46, 348–49, 351, 355–56

INDEX 407

4th Armored, 254, 359
7th Armored, 323, 329
9th Armored, 335, 357
brigades
  13th FA Brigade, 111
  5th Engineer Special Brigade, 187
regiments
infantry regiments (also Regimental Combat Teams or RCTs)
  6th Armored Infantry, 28, 109–11
  9th Infantry, 230
  10th Infantry, 241
  15th Infantry, 83
  16th Infantry, 5, 11–12, 35–36, 39, 41, 90, 98, 113, 116, 123–24, 146, 149–50, 153, 156–59, 162–63, 176, 178, 186–89, 203–205, 220, 225, 236, 242, 244, 250, 252, 254, 256–57, 273, 277, 300–301, 310–11, 316–17, 341
  23rd Infantry, 317–18, 320, 323
  26th Infantry, 4–6, 46, 85, 105, 111–13, 123–24, 126, 139, 143, 149, 153, 155–57, 161, 205, 225, 228, 236–38, 266, 273, 294, 300, 310, 312–2, 345, 354
  28th Infantry, 167
  30th Infantry, 83
  39th Infantry, 98, 158, 161–62, 245, 299
  41st Armored Infantry, 145
  47th Infantry, 104, 245, 299–300, 311, 356
  115th Infantry, 176, 191, 194–95
  116th Infantry, 204–205
  119th Infantry, 245, 257
  120th Infantry, 245, 257
  133rd Infantry, 79, 125
  135th Infantry, 79
  168th Infantry, 77
  180th Infantry, 144
  393rd Infantry, 331
  413th Infantry, 297
  504th Parachute, 138
  505th Parachute, 138, 144
armored regiments
  1st Armored, 74, 76–77, 126, 128
  13th Armored, 119–20, 125
  67th Armored, 145, 149
group
  14th Cavalry Group, 335

battalion-sized units
cavalry
  4th Cavalry Reconnaissance Squadron, 242
  32nd Cavalry Reconnaissance Squadron, 335
  81st Reconnaissance Battalion, 86, 125
Ranger battalions
  1st Ranger, 19, 20–21, 24–26, 36, 39, 85, 103–104, 139
  2nd Ranger, 176
  3rd Ranger, 139
  4th Ranger, 139
  5th Ranger, 176
tank battalions
  70th Light Tank, 153, 156
  743rd Tank, 226
  745th Tank, 183, 226, 233–34, 244, 249, 262, 272, 278, 281, 307, 315, 320, 328
  753rd Tank, 156–57
tank destroyer battalions
  601st TD, 74, 85, 93–94, 96, 100–102, 105
  634th TD, 244, 292, 312, 314, 320
  701st TD, 76
  899th TD, 98, 100
field artillery battalions
  5th FA Battalion, 36, 39, 111, 183, 205
  7th FA Battalion, 98, 150
  32nd FA Battalion, 4, 8, 21, 29, 31, 33, 34, 36–37, 39, 41–42, 56, 74, 82, 89–91, 93–94, 96–98, 100, 105, 114–16, 119, 140–41, 145, 147–48, 152, 154, 159, 161, 174, 180, 183, 197, 203, 205, 212, 226–27, 231, 238, 244, 247, 249, 252, 261, 273, 327, 346
  33rd FA Battalion, 79, 146, 148, 266
  62nd Armored FA Battalion, 159, 231
  171st FA Battalion, 144
  957th FA Battalion, 273–74, 284
engineer battalions
  1st Engineer Combat Battalion, 8, 74, 180, 183, 188, 273, 291
  37th Engineer Combat Battalion, 274
  146th Engineer Combat Battalion, 185
  237th Engineer Combat Battalion, 274
  299th Engineer Combat Battalion, 191
  1106th Engineer Combat Group, 294

chemical mortar battalions
  86th Chemical Mortar Battalion, 315
  87th Chemical Mortar Battalion, 273, 307
medical battalion
  1st Medical Battalion, 8, 74
task forces
  Task Force Lindo, 320, 322
  Task Force Lovelady, 299
  Task Force Stark, 78
  Task Force X, 255
  Task Force Y, 255, 351, 356
  Task Force Z, 255
air force
  Eighth Air Force, 185
  Ninth Air Force, 268, 273, 276
  IX Tactical Air Command, 292

A–Z

Aachen, Germany, 269–70, 272–75, 277, 285–86, 289–92, 294–99, 310, 336
Aachen State Forest. *See* Aachen, Germany.
Alexander, Sir Harold R., 85, 108–109, 125–26, 130–31, 137, 141, 151–52, 155, 168
Allen, Terry de la Mesa, 12–15, 18–19, 24–25, 28, 46, 48, 70, 83, 85–86, 91, 98, 100, 102, 105–107, 109, 111, 126, 129–30, 134–37, 139, 149–50, 155–59, 161, 163–67, 172, 209–10, 213, 297, 323
Allied Forces Headquarters (AFHQ), 24, 136–7
Amphibious training, 6, 10, 16–17, 138, 212
Anderson, Sir Kenneth A. N., 66, 109, 126, 131
Andrus, Clift, 148
Antwerp, Belgium, 260, 311
Arcole, Algeria, 38–39, 41–42
Ardennes Forest, 260, 311, 349, 352
Argentan-Falaise Pocket, 257–58
Arnim, Juergen von, 63, 75–76, 78, 131
Arzew, Algeria, 20–22, 24–26, 28, 31, 34–35, 39, 41, 132, 138, 213, 240, 297, 358
Aure River, France, 225–26, 230

Bacon, Bradley P., 29–30, 134, 161–62, 208, 236
Baier, Hans, 111

Baker, Hershel D., 94, 96–97, 101
Barrett, Carlton W. 185
Battle of the Bulge, 311–31
Baummer, Robert A., 232
Bavai, France, 261–62, 264–68
Bechtold, Edward S., 145, 147–48, 161
Beja, Tunisia, 75, 109–10
Benedict, Odel G., 92
Bisbee, William H., 2–3
Bizerte, Tunisia, 44–46, 66, 109, 125–26, 131
Bois de Baugy, France, 235–36
BOLERO, Operation, 11
Bonn, Germany, 333, 335–36, 339
Bonnett, Warren L., 32–33, 35, 40
Botsford, Robert, 270
Bou Chebka, Tunisia, 83–84, 100
Bowers, Robert E., 275, 318, 322
Bowles, Henry, 103
Bowles, Thomas, 103
Bradley, Omar N., 106, 109, 111, 125–26, 129–30, 139, 148, 153, 156, 164–68, 176–77, 188, 242, 257, 260, 329
Bramlett, David A., 203
Brannen, James, 316–17
Brécy, France, 255–56
Broadmayne, England, 174
Brown, Bobbie E., 239, 246, 276–77, 280–87, 291, 297
Brown, Courtney P., 19–22, 26, 28, 35, 39–42, 73, 88–90, 93, 95–98, 101, 105, 110–16, 121–12, 126, 128–29, 141, 146, 150–51, 208, 257
Brown, Thomas, 154
Bryant, Carleton F., 191
Bülowius, Karl, 111
Bütgenbach, Belgium, 312–14, 320, 323, 325–26, 329
Bütgenbacher Heck, 313–14, 317, 320, 323–26, 328
Bull, Harold R., 120
Bullard, Robert, III, 194, 305
Burt, Walter, 324–25

Caen, France, 178, 181, 236–38
Caltagirone, Sicily, 140, 143, 150
Cambron, Joseph W., 282–83
Cameron, Archibald, 48, 58–59, 63–64, 66, 68, 89, 94, 122, 127, 161, 196, 226, 232, 246–47

INDEX

Camp Blanding, Florida, 12, 14, 17, 212
Campbell, William K. "Soup," 148, 209
Camprond, France, 242, 244, 248–51, 254
Cantigny, France, 3, 6
Carey, Harry F., 328
Carnes, Paul, 50, 68
Carolina maneuvers, 6, 9
Carrington, Henry B., 2
Carter, Jack, 249
Carter, Sam, 35, 37, 44, 61–63, 68–71, 88–89, 91, 104, 122, 133, 162, 172, 195, 208, 236, 240, 245–46, 252–53, 267, 269–70, 295–96, 301, 304, 306, 308, 329, 333–34, 359
Caruso, Lawrence, 296
Casablanca conference, 137
Caumont, France, 176, 205, 236–38, 241, 253
Cerisy Forest. *See* Forêt de Cerisy, France.
Chandler, Clifford, 346, 352, 354
Chase, William B., 33, 48, 84
Churchill, Sir Winston, 17, 137
Clarke, Gerard, 4
COBRA, Operation, 241–42, 244, 254
Coffman, Hershel T., 227, 278, 293, 304, 306, 323–24, 341
Colacicco, Frank, 31, 34, 38, 43, 144, 177–78, 196–98, 228
Colleville-sur-Mer, France, 178, 193, 200, 203–205, 225–26
Collins, J. Lawton "Lightning Joe," 241, 246, 260–61, 299
Colson, Andrew, 28
Comando Supremo, 139–40
Conrath, Paul, 140, 143–44, 146–49
Conway, John C., 249, 253
Cooke, Charles N., Jr., 147
Corley, John T., 209
Cornazzani, Christopher, 196
Cota, Norman D., 299
Craig, Louis A., 299
Critz, Harry, 77
Cross, William H., 113–14
Crouthamel, Carlton, 264–66
Crucifix Hill, 272–78, 280–81, 283–84, 286–87, 289–92
Cubbison, Donald E., 2, 12

Daniel, Derrill M., 312
Darby, William O. 86, 89, 103, 143–44, 216

Dawson, Joseph T., 186–87, 189, 225
DeCampo, Carmel, 250, 262, 264–67
DeFranzo, Arthur F., 234–35
Denholm, Charles L., 124–25
Denson, Ely P., 1, 3–5, 9, 14, 207
DeNucci, Leonard N., 319
Dessau, Germany, 251–52, 355–56
Djebel (hill). *Also see* Hill.
  Badjar, 111, 123–25
  Berda, 86, 88, 90–5, 98, 102–106
  el Ahmera. *See* Longstop Hill.
  el Ank, 85–86, 90, 104
  el Beida. *See* Hill 407.
  el Guessa, 49–50, 122
  el Mcheltat, 88–90, 95, 101, 106
  el Rhar. *See* Longstop Hill.
  Gare Hadid, 76–77
  Khar, 24, 36, 39
  Lessouda, 76–77
  Murdajadjo, 24
  Rmel. *See* Hill 350.
  Santon, 24
  Sidi Meftah, 123–24
  Tahant. *See* Hill 609.
Dom Bütgenbach. *See* Bütgenbach, Belgium.
Dorchester, England, 174–75
Dorset, England, 174
Downing, John P., 22, 32–34, 40, 42, 74, 120, 132, 145, 151, 166, 168, 176, 183, 200–203, 235, 244, 251, 322, 328, 359
Drewes, Heinrich, 102–103
Drôme River, France, 235, 239
Düren, Germany, 298, 310, 333
Dupree, Frank, Jr., 200

Easter, Elmer E., 253
Easy Red Beach, 178, 180, 182, 186, 188–89, 192–93, 196, 219
Eddy, Manton S., 158, 166
Ehlers, Roland, 197, 233
Ehlers, Walter D., 99, 197, 233–34
Eilendorf, Germany, 273–78, 282, 284–85, 287
Eisenhower, Dwight D., 24–25, 40, 45–46, 66, 73, 84, 131, 137–38, 164–66, 168, 171, 176, 183, 206, 257–58, 260, 339
Eisern, Germany, 343–44

El Guettar, Tunisia, 72, 85–88, 93, 97, 99, 101–102, 104–106, 108, 110, 121, 129, 132, 135, 146, 172, 215
Emerson, Paul J., 92
Engranville, France, 226, 230–31
Enna, Sicily, 151, 153, 155
Erft Canal/River, Germany, 333–36
Ertle, Charles, 29, 32
Etna line, Sicily, 138, 150–51, 153, 156, 170–71
Eudenbach, Germany, 341
Eulenberg, Germany, 342–43
Eupen, Belgium, 222, 311–12

FABIUS, Operation, 176
Falaise, France, 257–58
Fanning, George J., 40
Fitch, Frank, 152, 196–97, 240
Fitzpatrick, Cecil, 185
Flint, Harry A., 158, 209
Fogg, Donald L., 21, 26, 28, 90, 113–14, 119
Folk, George D., 233–34, 248, 250–51, 253, 285, 289, 295, 308, 311, 315, 328
Forêt de Cerisy, France, 180, 182, 234–36
Forêt de Mormal, France, 261–62
Formigny, France, 230–31
Fornier, Maurice G., 115
Forts
  Benning, Georgia, 12, 14
  Bragg, North Carolina, 6, 8
  Canastel, Algeria, 41–42
  Devens, Massachusetts, 1–4, 6, 9–10, 12, 17, 211, 358
  Riley, Kansas, 66, 360
Fowler, Denman, 115
Fox Green Beach, 188
Fredendall, Lloyd R., 12, 20, 35, 40, 47, 84–85, 102
Fricke, George, 48–49, 55–59, 69–70, 73, 84
Frink, Albert W. (Bill), 40, 151
Froncillo, Ray, 28–9, 48, 126–27

Gabes, Tunisia, 70, 85–86, 88, 90–91, 93–94, 96–98, 100–101, 104–105, 108
Gafsa, Tunisia, 76, 85–86, 88, 90–91, 93–94, 96–98, 100–101, 105–106, 108, 110–11, 138
Gangi, Sicily, 156–57
Gaysek, Frank, 270

Gela, Sicily, 137–41, 143–44, 146–51, 171, 216
Gemmenich, Belgium, 310
Gerow, Major General Leonard T., 176, 236, 240
Green, Robert E., 280
Greer, Frank U., 14, 17–18, 22, 26, 30–31, 33, 35–36, 38–41, 44, 46, 48, 50, 54, 62, 65, 69–70, 72–75, 77–78, 81–85, 88, 90–93, 95, 97–98, 104–105, 110, 113–14, 116, 120, 122–27, 129–30, 132–33, 135–36, 207, 213
Grimmer, Stewart, 92
Guth, Gilbert E., 99
Guzzoni, Afredo, 139
GYMNAST, Operation, 11

Haaren, Germany, 272–73, 275, 284–86, 289–92, 294
Hamich, Germany, 300–301, 310
Harmon, Ernest N., 125–26
Harz Mountains, Germany, 224, 345, 348–49, 351–52, 354, 357
Hawkins, Jackson, 95
Heinrich, Lieutenant, 305
Heistern, Germany, 221, 299, 301–302, 304–305, 309–10
Hendrickson, Edward, 115
Hennessy, Leo, 33
Herman, Henry, 30–31
Hess, Robert E., 227, 234–35, 248–51, 269–70, 288–91, 301, 308, 314–17, 352
Hester, Carl L., 191
Highways
  115 (Sicily), 149
  117 (Sicily), 144, 156
  120 (Sicily), 155–58
Hill, Joseph, 29, 33, 43
Hills
  184 (Hürtgen), 307
  192 (Aachen), 273, 285–86, 288
  194 (Hürtgen), 305
  203 (Hürtgen), 302, 304, 306–309
  207 (Hürtgen), 304–305
  231. (Ravels-B), 273, 286, 289–96, 304
  232 (Hürtgen), 301
  232 (Mateur, Tunisia), 126–32, 165
  239. *See* Crucifix Hill.
  242 (Brècy, France), 35, 255

243 (Djebel el Rhar). *See* Longstop Hill.
272. *See* Djebel Berda.
278. *See* Djebel Badjar.
314 (Mortain, France), 256–57
336 (Keddab Ridge), 86, 88–93, 95, 97, 104
341. *See* Djebel Sidi Meftah.
350 (Djebel Rmel), 110, 114, 117, 119–21, 123, 215
407 (Djebel el Beida), 111–16, 119, 121–22, 132, 136
482. *See* Djebel el Mcheltat.
566 (Ardennes), 314–15, 318
570 (Sicily), 162
575 (Kef el Goraa), 111–13
609 (Djebel Tahant), 123–25
Hobratsck, Waldemar J., 213
Hodges, Courtney H., 260–61, 269, 299
Huebner, Clarence R., 165, 167–69, 171–72, 175–76, 205, 209, 225, 230–31, 236, 242, 244–45, 254, 256, 258, 286–87, 289, 301, 305, 326
Hürtgen Forest, Germany, 222, 298–310, 332
Hurst, Paul, 194
Husky, Operation, 138
Hyatt, Harold B., 121

Indiantown Gap Military Reservation, Pennsylvania, 13–14, 151

Jackson, Derek, 52, 61
Jacobsen, Earl R., 278
Jeffrey, Gordon A., 81, 93, 103, 117, 119, 162, 189, 226, 262, 264, 266, 288, 305–306
Johnson, Clark, 315–17, 342–44, 348
Johnson, Franklyn A., 50, 65, 113, 115–16, 136, 146, 167–69, 172, 180–81, 196–98, 228, 235, 239–40
Johnson, Howard J., 197–98
Jones, George R., Jr., 198

Kassel, Robert E., 83–84
Kasserine Pass, Tunisia, 77–79, 82–85, 137, 168
Keeler, Owen F., 191–92
Keightley, Sir Charles F., 72–74, 77, 81
Kemp, John B., 147

Kesselring, Albert, 45, 63, 78, 139–40
Kimbacher, Josef, 302
Klawitzer, Raymond, 195
Knight, James E., 191
Köchstedt, Germany, 351–52, 355
Koehler, George R., Jr. "Dick," 15
Koenig, Alfred E., 262, 288, 293–94, 305, 309, 330–31
Kraiss, Dietrich, 181
Krause, Fritz, 111, 131
Kuehn, Edward, 100, 114, 129, 134–35, 141, 149, 152, 154, 208

Lang, Rudolph, 55, 62–63, 66–68, 70
Langerwehe, Germany, 299, 301, 307–10
Lauten, John H., 344–45, 348, 354, 357
Lauenforde, Germany, 345–48
Leaman, Frank G., 134
Learnard, Henry G., Jr., 208, 247–48, 255–57, 260–61, 269, 274–76, 280–81, 284–87, 289, 291, 297, 300, 302, 306–307, 313–14, 317–20, 322–27, 333, 335, 339, 351–52, 355–57
Lehman, Samuel M., 306
Leonard, John W., 335
Les Andalouses, Algeria, 20, 24
Licata, Sicily, 139, 171
Liége, Belgium, 331
Lindo, Richard, 152, 306, 309, 319–20, 325, 327, 334, 340
London, England, 16–18, 84, 175
Longstop Hill (Djebel el Rhar, Hill 243), 44–74, 83, 110, 112
Lucas, James A., 93, 213, 334

MacQuillan, Raymond E., 76
Madill, Lawrence, 186
Malmédy, Belgium, 311
Mandeville, France, 180, 225, 227–28, 231
Marigny, France, 242, 244, 246, 248–54
Marshall, Malcolm, 4, 33–34, 41–42, 143, 147, 198–99, 227–28, 238, 247, 252, 297–98
Martin, John S., 1
Marvain, Charles, 282–84, 309
Mason, Stanhope P., 24, 39, 111, 129–30, 134–5, 164, 169
Mateur, Tunisia, 46, 109, 120, 123, 125, 131
Mauorga, George, 121
Mayenne, France, 257

MacConchie, Howard P., 185
McGregor, Edward, 30–31, 36–37, 43, 63–64, 67–68, 73, 92–94, 122, 124, 127, 129, 131, 209, 272, 274–77, 284–87, 289–91, 302, 339–42, 349, 351, 354
Medjez-el-Bab, Tunisia, 46, 49–51, 55, 60–61, 65, 72–75, 83, 109
Merli. Gino J., 267
Merrill, Herbert W. "Herbie," 120–21
Messe, Giovanni, 108–109, 131
Michalewski, Walter J., 257
Middleton, Troy A., 138
Middleworth, Henry V., 177, 180, 203, 246–48, 251, 253, 341–42, 345, 353
Miller, Jesse R., Jr., 239, 284–85, 290–92, 302, 304, 306–307, 318, 325, 334–35, 229–40, 352, 355–56
Miller, Michael, 194
Mirakian, Peter, 28, 127–28
Möderscheid, Belgium, 314, 323–24
Monschau, Belgium, 298, 311, 329
Mons, Belgium, 221, 260–62, 268, 354
Monte Bianco (Sicily), 159, 161–62
Monte Etna (Sicily), 138, 150–51, 153, 156, 170–71
Monte Pellegrino (Sicily), 159, 161–62, 167–68
Montgomery, Sir Bernard L., 107–109, 126, 131, 137–38, 151–53, 155–56, 168, 175–76, 257, 260
Monz, Anthony J., 316–17
Moore, Lieutenant, 134
Morgan, George, 31
Morris, Astor A., 95–96, 195
Mortain, France, 255–57
Mosles, France, 180, 225–27, 230–31
Mount Etna. *See* Monte Etna.
Mülde River, Germany, 355–56
Murphy, Robert E., 23, 32–35, 40, 80, 93, 106, 117, 119, 151, 159, 162, 184, 189–91, 200, 203, 208–209, 213, 226, 230, 232, 240, 250, 264–68, 274, 293, 323, 341, 358

New River, North Carolina, 6, 11
Newman, Alvin L., 116
Newman, Louis, 84, 100, 115
Niscemi, Sicily, 143–44, 149–51
Novoteney, Joseph W., 330

Oberkommando der Wehrmacht (*OKW*) 139
Officer Candidate School (OCS), 14
O'Grady, Francis, 200, 202
Ondenval, Belgium, 314, 317–19, 323

Palermo, Sicily, 137–38, 140, 151–53, 155, 158
Park, Nelson, 313, 327, 330, 334, 339, 341–42, 352–53
Parker, Donald, 60, 358
Parker, Richard C., 19–23, 30, 35, 39, 43
Parker, Irving J., 265
Patton, George S., 20, 84–86, 91, 100, 106, 108, 170–72, 257–58, 260
Paulsen, Randolph, 305, 308, 311, 346–48
Peckham, Colonel Elisha O., 159, 201–202, 240, 244, 248, 250–55, 257, 261, 285, 289, 294, 301, 304, 310, 313–16, 323, 333–35, 342
Penick, Charles A., Jr., 32–34, 37, 40, 42, 49, 155, 162, 189, 200, 203, 230, 235, 262, 265
Peterman, Ivan, 300
Petersen, Kenneth, 189
Peterson, George, 343–44
Petralia, Sicily, 156
Piano Lupo, Sicily, 143–44
Piddlehinton, England, 174
"Pimple Hill." *See* Hill 350.
Plante, Theodore "Toot," 10, 30–31
Pointe Canastel, Algeria, 24, 41
Ponte Olivo, Sicily, 149, 151–52
Poovey, Carrel F., 334
Porter, Robert W., 24, 164
Potkay, John C., 57
Powers, John L., 19–20, 22, 31–33, 35, 37, 39, 40–42, 48, 84
Poynter, Robert T., 59
Puddleton, England, 174
Pyle, Ernie, 136

Queen, Operation, 300
Queen Mary, 15–16, 232, 358
Quirrenbach, Germany, 339–42

Ramscheid, Germany, 329–31
Randall, Carl O., 32–33, 40, 42, 93, 103–104, 117, 119, 159, 203, 255, 342, 346, 352

Raymer, Clifford B., 21, 26, 35, 39, 80, 90, 95–96, 99, 100, 114, 129
Reed, William L., 288
Remagen Bridgehead, Germany, 335–36, 338, 341
Requarth, Jack A., 151
Rhine River, Germany, 299–300, 333, 335–36, 338
Rhinehart, Cleveland, 121
Richter, Wilhelm, 181
Ridgway, Matthew B., 329
Ritchie, Robert, 116, 141, 145
Rogers, Edward, 22, 121, 145, 195, 245, 256
Rommel, Erwin, 18, 45, 75–76, 78, 82–83, 85
Roosevelt, Franklin D., 17–18, 25, 137
Roosevelt, Theodore, Jr., 5–6, 9–10, 12, 129–30, 146, 152 154, 163, 165–67, 169, 172, 210
Rose, Maurice, 255, 345
Rosenberg, Orin, 189, 193, 200, 213, 226
Rosinski, Francis J., 21, 26, 90, 95, 113, 128, 141, 154, 157
Rosneath training center, Scotland, 17
Rowland, Henry C., 98
Ruhr area, Germany, 343, 345
Ruquet River, France, 178, 189, 192, 194, 200
Russell, William A., 95, 197, 213, 250–51, 256, 295–96, 301, 304
Ryder, Charles W., 20, 123

Sars-la-Bruyère, Belgium, 262, 264–68
Sawyer, Henry R., 21, 28, 90, 97, 114, 151, 198, 227–28, 274, 308
St. Cloud, Algeria, 20–22, 24, 28–41, 43, 48, 129, 132, 213–14
Sbeitla, Tunisia, 49, 76, 80, 82–83, 85
Schaefer, Joseph E., 269–70
Schevenhütte, Germany, 300–301, 306
Schoenleber, William, 154
Schönthal, Germany, 299, 302, 304, 306
Scott-Smith, Herbert A., Jr. 48, 58–59, 64, 89, 122, 124, 127, 196, 225, 233, 246, 280, 284–85, 287
Seitz, John F. R., 294
Semmes, James L., 191–92
Sherburne, Edward G., 14
Sidi bel Abbes, Algeria, 22

Sidi Bou Zid, Tunisia, 76–79, 85
Sidi Nsir, Tunisia, 111
Siegfried Line. *See Westwall.*
Silva, Frank, 97
Sisson, Joseph W., Jr., 151–52, 154, 162–80, 196, 198–9, 208, 225, 227–28, 230–37, 239–40, 244, 247
Smith, George A., Jr., 72, 90, 95, 99, 101, 105, 146, 148, 151, 156, 159, 161, 163, 168, 171, 174–78, 180, 183, 189, 203–205, 207, 225, 227–28, 230–31, 236–37, 239–41, 244, 248, 250, 252, 254, 256–62, 268, 273–75, 280, 286, 289, 291, 300, 305, 309–15, 323, 326–29, 333, 336
Smith, Herbert A., 72, 90, 95, 99, 101, 105
Smith, P. K., 305, 327
Snyder, Lieutenant, 283–84
Solomon, Edward M., 298, 317
Soissons, France, 3, 259–60
Spalding, John M., 187, 189–90, 193, 200, 225
Spinney, Russell G., 81, 93, 98, 103, 117, 119–20, 129, 202–203, 213
Spinosi, Ralph J., 232
Sproull, Eugene L., 232
Sternberg, Ben, 30, 33, 35, 38, 48, 73–75, 80, 88–91, 93–94, 98, 101–104, 110, 117, 119–21, 123, 128–29, 146, 149, 152–53, 159, 161–62, 171, 203, 209–10, 341
Stewart-Brown, Lieutenant Colonel, 61–62, 65, 69–70
Stockton, Robert F., 84
Stolberg, Germany, 269–70, 297, 300
Stolberg Corridor, 299
Streeter, Jack, 306
Summers, Stanley V., 341–42
Supreme Headquarters Allied Expeditionary Force (SHAEF), 175
Surrain, France, 227, 230

Taft, Ingwald P., 59
Taylor, George A., 143, 146, 159, 163, 187, 340
Tebessa, Algeria, 77–78, 82, 85
Thompson, Max, 295–96
Thompson, Percy W., 21, 31, 39
Three-Power Pact (Tripartite Pact), 10

Tidworth Barracks, England, 16–17
Tilly-sur-Seulles, France, 236, 238
Tine River Valley, Tunisia, 109–11, 117, 121, 123, 125–26, 132
Tolbert, William E., 307
Tomlinson, Herbert J., 28
TORCH, Operation, 18, 20, 26, 45
Tripp, Francis H., 99
Troina, Sicily, 151, 156–59, 161–65, 170
Truscott, Lucian K., 170
Tunis, Tunisia, 44–46, 50, 63, 65–66, 73–74, 108–109, 126, 131

Uckerath, Germany, 341–42
Uhouse, William, 232
Ultra, 181
United States Military Academy (West Point), 12–14, 48, 93, 169, 171, 276

Värst, Gustav von, 131
Van Wagoner, Clement, 28, 30, 37, 64, 69, 127, 280–81, 283, 304, 306, 319–20, 322, 325, 327, 334, 338, 352, 355–56
Vartoni, Sam, 92
Vaubadon, France, 233, 235
Verlautenheide, Germany, 272–73, 275, 277–78, 280–81, 284–89, 291, 293–94
Verviers, Belgium, 333
Vire River, France, 176, 236, 254

Wardner, Captain, 328
Webb, Carl, 128
Wehe Creek. *See* Hürtgen Forest, Germany.
Weir, Robert L., 180, 193
Weisenberg, Robert E., 302
Wenau, Germany, 299, 301
Weser River, Germany, 345–46, 348
West, Bob, 120
Westwall (Siegfried Line), 260–297, 329
Weymouth, England, 174–76, 181–83
Wilck, Gerhard, 273, 292, 296–97
Will, Walter J., 343–44
Williamson, John A., 83, 105, 119, 123, 129, 152, 157, 159, 171, 180, 183–84, 189, 191, 193, 200, 203–204, 207, 209, 226–27, 230, 232, 235–37, 240, 246, 250–51, 255, 257, 262, 264–66, 277–78, 286–88, 300–301, 304–306, 308–10, 313, 323–24, 327, 329, 333, 335, 339–41, 345, 358
"Windmill Farm." *See* Hill 350.
Winterborne St. Martin, England, 174
Wolfbusch, Belgium, 318–20, 322
Worsham, Ben, 121,
Würselen, Germany, 273
Wyman, Willard G., 189, 193, 197, 200, 230

Yarbor, Lieutenant, 287
Yarborough, Thomas, 355
Yarock, Irving, 9, 13, 29–30, 48–49, 51, 55–60, 63–65, 70, 359
York, Robert H. "Bob," 28–29, 33, 36–37, 48, 57, 61, 64, 68, 70–71, 84, 88–96, 101, 103–104, 110, 116, 121–22, 124, 126–27, 134–35, 141, 147, 150–51, 154, 157, 161–63, 180, 194, 196, 206, 209, 226, 230–31, 233, 236–37, 240, 276
YUKON, Operation, 317

ABOUT THE AUTHORS

Robert W. Baumer grew up in rural Connecticut. After graduating from the University of Illinois, he spent 25 years in the computer industry. In the early 1990s, he began writing newspaper and magazine articles about World War II, particularly regarding events related to the 50th Anniversary of Operation OVERLORD. His father's brother, Private First Class Robert A. Baummer, inspired his interest in the 18th Infantry Regiment of World War II. Pfc. Baummer was killed in action in Normandy on 9 June 1944. His mother, Viola K. Baummer, was president of the Gold Star Mothers in the Naugatuck, Connecticut, area, serving until all 92 of that town's World War II dead were brought home for burial.

Bob Baumer knew little about his namesake until his late great aunt, WWII 1st Lieutenant Mark Jane Kamarzel (Army Nurse Corps), brought him to Pfc. Baummer's grave in 1992. Here, he began his journey that resulted in the research and writing of *American Iliad*. Baumer also writes a column for *Armchair General* magazine entitled "Tip of the Spear."

Lieutenant Colonel Mark J. Reardon is a serving US Army officer with extensive experience in a wide variety of tactical assignments in armor and armored cavalry units in Korea, Germany, and the United States. Commissioned through the ROTC and a graduate of Loyola College of Baltimore, Maryland, he is presently assigned as Senior Military Historian at the U.S. Army Center of Military History in Washington, D.C.

His previously book, *Victory At Mortain: Stopping Hitler's Panzer Counteroffensive* (University Press of Kansas, 2002), was voted one of the Top Ten Best Books About World War II on the Stone and Stone annual cyberpoll. *Defending Fortress Europe: The War Diary of the German 7th Army, June–August 1944*, is forthcoming (Aberjona Press, 2004). Mark has also appeared as a guest commentator on Fox News' "War Stories" as well as a History Channel production on the Trojan Wars.

Other Titles by The Aberjona Press . . .

Seven Days in January:
With the 6th SS-Mountain Division in Operation NORDWIND
by Wolf T. Zoepf
312 pages. Maps. Photos. Index.
Hardbound. ISBN: 0-9666389-5-6, $12.95; plus $4.00 U.S. shipping
Paperbound. ISBN: 0-9666389-6-4, $12.95 plus $4.00 U.S. shipping

Into the Mountains Dark:
A WWII Odyssey from Harvard Crimson to Infantry Blue
by Frank Gurley
256 pages. Maps. Photos.
Paperbound. ISBN: 0-9666389-4-8, $14.95 plus $4.00 U.S. shipping

Five Years, Four Fronts:
The War Years of Georg Grossjohann, Major, German Army (Retired)
by Georg Grossjohann
218 pages. Maps. Photos. Index.
Hardbound. ISBN: 0-9666389-2-1, $19.95; plus $4.00 U.S. shipping
Paperbound. ISBN: 0-9666389-3-X, $14.95 plus $4.00 U.S. shipping

Black Edelweiss: A Memoir of Combat and Conscience by a Soldier of the Waffen-SS
by Johann Voss
224 pages. Maps. Photos.
Paperbound. ISBN: 0-9666389-8-0, $19.95 plus $4.00 U.S. shipping

The Final Crisis: Combat in Northern Alsace, January 1945
by Richard Engler
368 pages. Maps. Photos. Index.
Paperbound. ISBN: 0-9666389-1-3, $29.95 plus $4.00 U.S. shipping

From Normandy to the Ruhr: With the 116th Panzer Division in World War II
by Heinz Günther Guderian
648 pages. Maps. Photos. Appendices. Index.
Hardbound. ISBN: 0-9666387-2, $19.95 plus $4.50 U.S. shipping

Vanguard of the Crusade:
The 101st Airborne Division in World War II
by Mark Bando
320 pages. Maps. Photos.
Hardbound. ISBN: 0-9717650-0-6, $29.95 plus $4.00 U.S. shipping

The Good Soldier: From Austrian Social Democracy to Communist Captivity with a Soldier of Panzer-Grenadier Division "Grossdeutschland"
by Alfred Novotny
160 pages. Photos.
Paperbound. ISBN: 0-9666389-9-9, $14.95 plus $4.00 U.S. shipping

Defending Fortress Europe:
The War Diary of the German 7th Army, June–August 1944
by Mark Reardon
Approximately 300 pages. Maps. Photos.
Paperbound. ISBN: 0-9717650-3-0, $19.95 plus $4.00 U.S. shipping

Odyssey of a Philippine Scout
by Arthur K. Whitehead
Approximately 300 pages. Maps. Photos.
Paperbound. ISBN: 0-9717650-4-9, $19.95 plus $4.00 U.S. shipping

Sledgehammers: Strengths and Flaws of Tiger Tank Battalions in World War II
by Christopher Wilbeck
272 pages. Maps. Photos.
Paperbound. ISBN: 0-9717650-2-2, $19.95 plus $4.00 U.S. shipping

---

For much more information, visit our website at:
www.aberjonapress.com